4 INHERITANCE TAX - RATES

Death transfers: *Gross Cumulative Transfers*	Rate
2011/2012:	
Up to £325,000	nil
£325,001	40%
2010/2011:	
Up to £325,000	nil
£325,001	40%

This now means that if the 'nil rate band' is not used in full, a totally and unnecessary payment of up to £130,000 tax will have been paid!

5 NATIONAL INSURANCE

	2011/2012			2010/2011		
	Income £	ee %	er %	Income £	ee %	er %
Class 1 p.w. Contracted in	First 102.00	0	0	First 97.00	NIL	NIL
	102.01 - 136.00	0	0	97.01 - 110.00	0	NIL
	136.01 - 139.00	0	13.8	110.01 - 844.00	11.0	12.8
	139.01 - 817.00	12.0	13.8	Excess over		
	Excess over			844.00	1.0	12.8
	817.00	2.0	13.8			
Class 2 Self-employed	£2.50 p.w.			£2.40 p.w.		
Small earnings exemption	£5,315 p.a.			£5,075 p.a.		
Class 3 Voluntary	£12.60 p.w.			£12.05 p.w.		
Class 4 Self employed profits between "lower" & "upper" limits	£7,225 - £42,475 p.a.			£5,715 - £43,875 p.a.		
Rate up to "upper" limit	9.0%			8.0%		
Rate above "upper" limit	2.0%			1.0%		

(p.w. = per week / p.a. = per annum)

SMITH'S TAXATION

"Providing Tax Information Since 1915"

TAX GUIDE
2011/2012
(115th Edition)

Finance Act 2011

Clive Steward
BA(Hons), FCA

**Other Smith's Taxation products -
Tax Facts, ABC of TAX and Tax Guide Collection
available for download from:**

www.smithstaxation.co.uk

Annual up dates of this book are available by subscription.

COPYRIGHT
© Smith's Taxation Ltd. 2011
Smith's Taxation One hundred &
      fifteenth edition 2011 - V2.0

ISBN:
Book. 978-0-9562226-2-6
Download . . . . ---

For sales contact The Publisher:

Smith's Taxation,
7, Spoonbill Road
Bridgwater,
Somerset,
TA6 5QZ

Tel/Fax no: 44 (0) 1278 427006
e-mail: sales@smithstaxation.co.uk

Produced in the U.K. by

Greenash Systems Ltd.,
9, Capelands,
New Ash Green,
Longfield,
Kent,
DA3 8LG

Tel/Fax no: 44 (0) 1474 871541
e-mail: info@greenash.co.uk

www.smithstaxation.co.uk

PREFACE

Name the taxes or reliefs that apply to the following numbers? 3000; 16,000; 22719; 247,000 & 275,000. No prizes. These numbers just cropped up while I was researching this year's changes.
Governments spend a lot of time and thousands of pages of tax law to, in the great scope of life, 'no' large financial effect. To some political effect 'yes', yet only so that it can be claimed that the tax system is 'progressive'. The more you have the more tax you pay in total, but also the more you keep post tax as well.

The taxes involved are as follows 3,000 new businesses applied for the NIC holiday in the first 6 months of the scheme's operation out of an estimated 132,000 budgeted for in its first year. The number of estates paying Inheritance Tax is around 16,000. The number of protection certificates issued to individuals affected by the £1,500,000 lifetime funding limit (on 'A' day) on their pension funds was 22,719. Capital Gains Tax applies to 247,000 taxpayers and 275,000 people are caught in the additional rate (50%) of income tax.

Dave Hartnett, Permanent Secretary for Tax at HMRC has said that they receive thousands of letters from accountants every year just saying 'thank you' for recent correspondence. It is apparently so widespread that it is significant enough to delay letters with more exciting content. Accordingly we are all requested to stop saying thank you. Just carry on muttering your real thoughts of 'appreciation' in future I suggest.

Clive Steward FCA – Editor

July 2011

LIST OF ABBREVIATIONS

AG	Attorney-General
AP	Accounting period
BTR	British Tax Review
CA	Court of Appeal
CAA 2001	Capital Allowances Act 2001
CAA 1990	Capital Allowances Act 1990
CCA	Chartered Association of Certified Accountants
CGTA 1979	Capital Gains Tax Act 1979
ChD	Chancery Division
CPS	Crown Prosecution Service
CTA 2010	Corporation Tax Act 2010
ESC	Extra Statutory Concession
FA	Finance Act
HL	House of Lords
HMRC	HM Revenue & Customs
ICAEW	Institute of Chartered Accountants in England & Wales
IHT	Inheritance Tax
IHTA 1984	Inheritance Tax Act 1984
IR	Inland Revenue (HMRC from April 05)
ITA 2007	Income Tax Act 2007
ITEPA 2003	Income Tax (Earnings & Pensions) Act 2003
ITTOIA 2005	Income Tax (Trading and Other Income) Act 2005
KBD	King's Bench Division
LLPA 2000	Limited Liability Partnership Act 2000
PC	Privy Council, Judicial Committee
PR IR	Inland Revenue Press Release
QBD	Queen's Bench Division
RMS	Receivables Management Services (from April 2001)
RPI	Retail Prices Index
s	Section
S2P	State Second Pension
Sch	Schedule
SI	Statutory Instrument
SP	Inland Revenue Statement of Practice
TA 1988	Income and Corporation Taxes Act 1988
TIOPA	Taxation (International and Other Provisions) Act 2010
TMA 1970	Taxes Management Act 1970
TCGA 1992	Taxation of Capital Gains Act 1992

CONTENTS

CONTENTS

PART ONE
THE TAX SYSTEM

1 THE RANGE OF TAXES IN THE UK

The UK taxation system basically consists of (a) taxes on income and profits. (b) taxes on capital, and (c) duties on goods and services.

1.1 Taxes on income and profits
These comprise income tax and corporation tax. Income tax is payable by individuals on their income, whether so called 'earned' or 'unearned'. Earned income includes wages or salaries from employment, and profits from unincorporated businesses they own or in which they are partners. Unearned income includes interest and dividends received on savings and investments. Corporation tax is payable on profits made by corporate bodies, of which limited companies are the most numerous.

1.2 Taxes on Capital
These include capital gains tax and inheritance tax. The business rates payable by businesses and the council tax payable by individuals, are also, in effect, taxes on capital since they are based on the value of premises occupied. Capital gains tax is based on the difference between the cost and the sale price or disposal value of assets. It is payable, subject to many exemptions, at income tax rates by individuals and at corporation tax rates by companies.

Inheritance tax is payable, by the executors or administrators, on the death of an individual and, again, there are many reliefs and exemptions.

1.3 Duties on Goods and Services
These include Value Added Tax and various duties on imports, exports and certain home produced goods; also vehicle duties, licences, insurance premium tax, air passenger duty and stamp duties.

1.4 National Insurance Contributions
Regarded by many as a kind of taxation, they produce entitlements to benefits in the form of social security and welfare, especially unemployment and pensions.

Payable at various rates by individuals who are employed (Class 1 - primary), self-employed (Class 2 and 4), or otherwise can be paid voluntarily (Class 3). The employer also pays a rate of Class 1 contributions - secondary, Class 1A on some employee benefits and Class 1B on PAYE Settlement Agreements.

2 WHO IS TAXABLE

2.1 Individuals resident in the UK
Liable for income tax and capital gains on the whole of their income or capital gains whether arising in the UK or abroad, but subject to many reliefs and exemptions.

2.2 Minors
Their income and capital gains are liable to taxation as though they were adults, and the tax is payable by their guardians or trustees, frequently parents or other relatives.

2.3 Non residents
Liable for UK tax on all income arising in the UK except certain government securities. But also subject to a £30,000 p.a. charge after 7 years (see Part 13, p.583).

2.4 Trustees executors and administrators
Trustees, whether for a will trust or other form of trust, are responsible for the tax on the trust income unless the tax is paid by the beneficiaries. Executors (under a will) and administrators (under an intestacy) are responsible for inheritance tax on the value of the deceased's estate, and for income tax and capital gains tax on income and capital gains arising after death and before the assets are distributed.

2.5 Partnerships
Assessed to income tax and capital gains tax on the profits of the partnership and its capital gains. Partners are liable jointly and severally, for the debts of the partnership, but not for the tax liabilities of their partners. The tax is computed for each partner based on their share of the partnership profits, subject to their personal reliefs and allowances.

Corporate partners, such as limited companies, are liable for corporation tax on their shares of the partnership profits.

2.6 Limited Liability Partnerships (LLP)
This alternative structure while registered at Companies House, is, for trading partnerships, taxed in the same way as in 2.5 above. All partners in a LLP usually have their liability limited to an agreed sum. However, in the event of any claim for negligence, a negligent member's personal assets will still be at risk. The LLP is a separate legal entity like Limited Companies.

2.7 Clubs and associations
May be liable to income tax on trading profits, or corporation tax if they are

incorporated bodies, but income from purely charitable activities is not assessable.

2.8 Companies, including limited companies
Liable for corporation tax on their trading profits and capital gains; note that businesses, whether incorporated or not, are liable for value added tax, subject to many exemptions.

3 TAXABLE INCOME

The various categories of income for which a taxpayer is liable to tax are subject to different rules as to the basis of calculating the taxable income, the method of assessment and payment.

The old familiar Schedules (A,C & D) which had been in existence for decades were finally removed, for income tax purposes, from 6 April 2005. The third Tax Law Rewrite Act removed them as part of The Income Tax (Trading and Other Income) Act 2005 (ITTOIA 2005) which came into effect from that date.

Schedule E went on 6 April 2003 as part of the second Act called The Income Tax (Earnings and Pensions) Act 2003. (ITEPA 2003). ITTOIA 2005 is split into the following parts:

(a)   Part 2 (trading income),
(b)   Part 3 (property income),
(c)   Part 4 (savings and investment income), and
(d)   Part 5 (certain miscellaneous income).

The Schedules system remained for corporation tax until the Corporation Tax Act 2009 (CTA 2009) where Schedules A & D were substituted by Parts 4 & 3 respectively.

The final part of the rewrite of income tax known as The Income Tax Act 2007 (ITA 2007) took effect from 6 April 2007.

ITA 2007 covers:
•   basic provisions about the charge to income tax, income tax rates, the calculation of income tax liability, and personal reliefs;

•   various specific reliefs, including relief for losses, the enterprise investment scheme, venture capital trusts, community investment tax relief, interest paid, gift aid and gifts of assets to charities;

- specific rules about trusts, deduction of tax at source, manufactured payments and repos, the accrued income scheme and tax avoidance; and

- general income tax definitions.

4 ORGANISATION OF H.M. REVENUE & CUSTOMS - HMRC

4.1 HMRC
This is a collective term generally referring to the organisation and system of assessing and collecting tax and excise duty in the UK.

4.2 The Board
This board, of which the members are called the Commissioners, has overall responsibility for the taxation system.

4.3 Tribunals (formerly known as "The Commissioners")
Taxation tribunals are incorporated into a simplified two tier tribunals system. The first (non-taxation) parts went live on 3 November 2008 and the new Tax Tribunal went live on 1 April 2009.

4.4 Inspector of Taxes
These officials have offices in local 'HMRC' districts and they generally deal with the taxpayers and businesses in those districts.

For some taxpayers, e.g., civil servants, the Inspectorate is centralised, particularly in the Public Departments offices in Cardiff. Inspectors of Taxes are responsible for examining taxpayers Returns of Income, issuing codes for PAYE, dealing with appeals and, where applicable, authorising repayments of overpaid tax. They have wide powers to enforce the production of relevant documents and can apply to a magistrate to enter and search a taxpayer's premises for those purposes. From 1 April 2009 HMRC has powers to enter the premises of any business to inspect records and assets.

Documents include computer storage media such as hard discs, floppy discs, tapes etc. In "*An Accountant v Inspector of Taxes SpC 258 8.6.00 (2000)* STI Issue 45" an accountant was required to 'produce' a balance sheet which had not previously been prepared. A computer programme allows the Inspector to search for any key words they desire e.g. Ascot, hotels and wine!

In *Neil Martin Ltd v HMRC (2007) EWCA Civ 1041* the Court of Appeal decided in favour of the taxpayer, Neil Martin Ltd, but only on a limited point, whether they have a duty of care. Administrative failings by the HMRC and Mr Martin's own failure to complete and sign the relevant CIS forms caused a three month delay in the issuing of the CIS6 certificate. Mr Martin claimed damages for the loss of business caused by the delay in certification but the claim was rejected by the High Court. The Court of Appeal agreed with the High Court that mere administrative error is not enough to form a duty of care but in this case the HMRC had personally incorrectly completed a CIS form and signed it.

Backdating Offence
Backdating a document, where the date is material, constitutes in law the very serious offence of forgery, as well as a breach of professional conduct and ethical guidelines. In addition, under the new penalty regime, backdating transactions would probably fall into the 'deliberate and concealed' category, which means penalties for the taxpayer could be as high as 100% of any tax loss to the Exchequer.

4.5 Receivables Management Service
They are, in effect, the cashiers of HMRC and have the responsibility for collecting the tax due. They cannot alter an assessment. They may take legal action, including distraint, for non-payment of tax due, and may in suitable cases agree to receive payment by instalments.

In April 2001 the Collector of Taxes was renamed the "Receivables Management Service" and this department of HMRC was tasked with tightening up on late payments of tax. The procedure for the recovery of unpaid tax are summarised as follows:

- Failure to respond as agreed to a single telephone reminder on late payments will lead to the commencement of recovery proceedings;

- Any agreements reached to pay outstanding tax will be critically reviewed and failure to comply with conditions will be strictly followed up; and

- HMRC will want convincing evidence the taxpayer cannot afford to pay their tax liabilities straight away, for example, proof that the taxpayers' bank will not lend the money.

If tax debts are £5,000 and over are not paid on time the local Receivables Managers will make a single phone call to agree recovery. If an agreed payment timetable is not met proceedings will begin and taxpayers may well find the bailiffs knocking at their door. Additionally HMRC are now using private debt collecting firms.

4.6 Telephone numbers for HMRC
Below is a list of the most needed helpline services from HMRC:

a) Agent priority and dedicated helpline
For personal self assessment tax affairs, partnership issues and PAYE for

individuals. The Taxes Contact Centre you need to call will depend on your client's tax office, or a national dedicated number which has just gone live
0845 366 7855

b) Agent priority for tax credits
0845 300 3943

c) Debt Collectors verification of identity
0845 915 5348

d) Pay As You Earn (PAYE) - Employers Employer Helpline
08457 143 143

e) Paying HMRC Payment Enquiry Helpline
0845 366 7816
Payment enquiries for Individuals, Employers and Businesses

f) Self Assessment Helpline (SA) Assessment Helpline
0845 900 0444
General helpline - not specific to agents. For advice completing Self Assessment tax returns and general advice about SA.

g) VAT and EU VAT - Online VAT Online Services
0845 010 8500
Advice on Enrolment, activation and submission enquiries

h) VAT (including EU VAT) VAT Advice Line
0845 010 9000
General VAT queries, European Community Sales Lists, European Union (EU) VAT, Reverse Charge Sales List (RCSL) enquiries

5 THE ADMINISTRATION OF THE TAX SYSTEM

5.1 How taxation is authorised
The statutory authority for the imposition of taxation is contained in many Acts of Parliament:

This legislation is amended by the annual and sometimes more frequent Finance Acts. This enormous volume of legislation has to be interpreted by the Courts in an even greater volume of decided cases. In addition HMRC from time to time publish 'concessions and practice notes', where the strict application of the law would be unjust or unworkable, and to indicate the methods they employ in particular situations.

Some of the proposed amendments and additions to the current law and practice of taxation are presented to Parliament by the Chancellor of the Exchequer in his Budget Speech in the spring of each year. The 'Budget' is strictly a forecast of government income and expenditure for the coming year, and includes a review of the previous year's results.

The Budget proposals and much much more are set out in the Finance Bill which is then debated in Parliament. Some provisions of the Finance Bill have immediate effect under the Provisional Collection of Taxes Act 1968. Amendments made during the debate are incorporated in the Finance Act and which may entail adjustments to the taxation provisionally imposed. With the Budget currently in March or April, the Finance Bill has to be enacted by 5 August.

5.2 The fiscal year and the assessment year

The government accounting year for taxation purposes, or the 'fiscal year', ends on 5 April, and income tax is calculated for each year ending on that date. There is a slight difference in the assessment year for corporation tax on limited companies and other corporate bodies and in these cases the year of assessment is related to the accounting period. The tax is computed by reference to the financial year which ends on 31 March.

For most of an individual's income, for example, income from employment, tax is calculated on the actual amount received in the year of assessment, at the rates of tax applicable to that year. Trading profits are taxed in the tax year which includes the accounts year end.

Corporate bodies, including limited companies, are charged to corporation tax on the profits shown by their accounts. The rate of corporation tax applied is the rate or rates applicable to the period covered by the accounts. If the rate changes, the profits are apportioned, on a daily basis, and a different rate used for each period.

5.3 Self assessment Tax Returns

Every taxpayer has an obligation to make a Tax Return, when required, of income from all sources and capital gains and this return is normally sent to the local Inspector of Taxes. Where the income includes profits from a business accounts may also be submitted.

Tax Returns (SA100) or "notice to complete a tax return" (SA316) are sent, usually in early April, by the Inspector of Taxes to all persons thought to be liable to tax other than those whose only income is from their employment. The failure to receive a form does not, however, absolve the taxpayer from the obligation to make a return of income, whether it has or has not been subject to deduction of tax at source. Return forms are not always sent to taxpayer for completion where all tax is paid on remuneration under PAYE, or by deduction or 'imputation' on interest and dividends.

Nevertheless it is sometimes desirable that Tax Returns shall be submitted in such cases, if only to ensure that applicable personal reliefs and allowances are obtained, and possible overpayments of tax are refunded.

Taxpayers have 6 months after the end of a tax year (i.e. 5 October) to notify HMRC of a new source of income.

For the Self Employed:

- Anyone who ceases or becomes liable for Class 2 or Class 4 contributions must notify HMRC immediately.

- A penalty may be levied (between 30% and 100% of the "lost contributions") if notice is not given by 31 January following the end of the tax year in which you become liable.

- There will be no penalty if you have a reasonable excuse for the late notification.

5.3.1 Self Assessment

Self-assessment means that individuals and trustees can submit with their returns of income and allowances their own computations of their income tax and capital gains tax liability from all sources. The returns need to include details from the accounts of income from self-employment and partnerships. However the accounts themselves do not have to be submitted, unless the business is a very large partnership. The 2011 on-line returns are required to be submitted to HMRC by 31 January 2012. HMRC 2010 original returns (computer generated facsimiles are no longer accepted by HMRC) have to be submitted by 31 October 2011 or, if later, 3 months after the issue of the return.

If they do not wish to calculate their tax liabilities for a tax year, taxpayers must send a return of all income and allowances claimed by the 31 October following the end of the tax year or, if later, 2 months after the issue of the return form.

Companies are required to submit returns within time limits, i.e. within 1 year from the end of their accounting dates or, if later, within 3 months from the issue of the return form. This is under review to align with the new 9 months filing deadline with Companies House and payment of any corporation tax liability.

HMRC naturally have powers to correct mistakes in a self-assessment return and to make further enquiries leading to a determination of the tax due. Such a determination will be made in the absence of a return submitted by the due date. The existing rights of appeal will then apply. If the return is not subject to an enquiry or amendment by the taxpayer within the same period, the return will be final and conclusive.

The enquiry window is 12 months of the date of submission of the tax return, previously an enquiry had to be notified by the Inspector within 1 year of the due date of the return (31 January 2008).

Penalties apply when complete returns are not submitted by the due date, or on failure to satisfy enquiries from the Inspector of Taxes; and provisions apply regarding interest on unpaid tax.

In *BJ Shopfitting Services v HMRC TC 390* the taxpayer argued that the absence of clarity was a good reason for overturning a penalty.

The taxpayer submitted his partnership's paper tax return late. It was due by the end of October 2008 but he sent it in during the following January and paid his tax by the end of that month. He believed this would not give rise to a penalty. The HMRC website stated that: 'If all the tax has been paid by 31 January the penalty notice will be issued in the sum of nil as the penalty cannot exceed the amount of tax outstanding at 31 January.' Of course, this does not apply to partnership returns, but nothing on the website made this distinction from other self-assessment returns.

HMRC accepted that the advice on its website was misleading and the taxpayer had relied on it. Nevertheless, it argued that such ignorance is no defence in law. The tribunal took the view that the taxpayer had not relied on his ignorance but on HMRC guidance. This was a reasonable approach by the taxpayer and the penalty was therefore not due.

Another case where the taxpayer relied on HMRC advice - verbal this time:

Keep records of telephone guidance
(Mr TJ Fisher (trading as The Crispin) v HMRC {2011} UKFTT 235 (TC).)
When Mr Fisher ceased trading as 'The Crispin' he rang HMRC to find out what he should do. He followed the advice he was given, issuing P45s to his employees and writing to HMRC to say that he had ceased trading and that the business had been sold. He also kept a note of the date and time of the call, what he was told and the fact that he spoke to 'Kath'. This record saved him £800.

What he was not told to do, and did not do, was complete a P35 for the final year of trading. HMRC sent the return to the wrong address and the penalty for late submission had reached £800 by the time HMRC notified Mr Fisher that anything was wrong.

Fortunately, the tax tribunal agreed with Mr Fisher that, in view of the details he could produce of his call to the helpline and the advice he had been given, he had a reasonable excuse for failing to complete the P35. It therefore waived the penalty.

The tribunal judge refused to accept HMRC's contention that a reasonable excuse must be based on an exceptional circumstance or event.

Penalties for late filing returns
A new penalty regime for filing returns late has been introduced for Self Assessment Returns 2010/2011 year & onwards. The rules apply to all returns due for income tax, including PAYE and CIS returns, CGT, CT IHT, SDLT, PRT and pension schemes. Penalties will be calculated from the penalty date which will be the day after the filing date for the return.

Returns apart from CIS
Apart from CIS, the basic scheme of penalties will be as follows:

- the basic failure to submit the return will trigger a penalty of £100, even if there is no tax to pay;

- after three months HMRC will impose a daily penalty of up to £10 per day for a maximum of 90 days beginning with the day they specify as the commencement date. This date may be earlier than the date of which the notice is given but cannot be earlier than three months after the filing date;

- after six months the penalty will be the greater of £300 or 5% of the tax shown on the return;

- after 12 months the penalty will again be the greater of £300 or 5% of the liability but, if as a result of the failure to make the return, the taxpayer withholds information which would enable HMRC to assess the liability to tax the penalty can rise to 100% of the tax if the withholding is deliberate and concealed and 70% where it is just deliberate. The 100% or 70% penalty can be reduced by disclosure in the same way as is provided in the new penalty regime for errors in documents.

Penalties for sending your tax return late

Length of delay	Penalty you will be asked to pay
One day	Initial £100.
Three months	£10 each day - up to maximum of £900, starting after 3 months.
Six months	£300 or 5% of the tax due, whichever is the higher.
Twelve months	£300 or 5% of the tax due, whichever is the higher. In serious cases you may be asked to pay up to 100% of the tax due instead.

The penalties are cumulative, and apply to each partner in a partnership.

CIS returns

Late returns under the CIS scheme will trigger penalties as follows:

- a basic penalty of £100 on late monthly returns, including £nil returns;

- where the failure continues after two months a penalty of £200;

- after six months the penalty rises to the greater of 5% of the tax or £300;

- after 12 months the penalty will again be the greater of £300 or 5% of the tax but, where the withholding of information is deliberate and concealed, it will be 100% of the tax (or £3,000 if greater) and where information is withheld deliberately, 70% or tax (or £1,500 if greater).

Payment

Payment of the tax due on all sources of income will normally be due on 31st January following the year of assessment. Payments on account of income tax (not capital gains tax) will be due on 31st January in the year of assessment and on the following 31st July.

The payments on account will normally be based on half each of the total income tax liability for the preceding year, subject to amendment where tax for the current year is likely to be less. No payments on account are due if the total liability for the preceding year (2008/2009) was less than £1,000, (previously £500 to 2008/2009), or more than 80% of the total tax due was made by deduction (PAYE or on CIS25).

Therefore there are three reasons for paying tax on time: -

Penalties for paying late

Length of delay	Penalty you will be asked to pay
Thirty days	5% of the tax unpaid at that date.
Six months	A further 5% of the tax unpaid at that date.
Twelve months	A further 5% of the tax unpaid at that date.

These penalties may be suspended where the taxpayer agrees a time to pay arranged with HMRC.

Interest charges if you pay late

You will have to pay interest on all outstanding amounts, including any unpaid penalties, until payment is received - 3% (July 2011).

2010/2011 Self-assessment payments - The new late payment penalties will first apply to 2010/2011 balancing payments i.e. from 31 January 2012.

CIS returns - It is expected that the new late filing penalties will first apply to returns for the month 6 October to 5 November 2011.

5.3.2 A reasonable excuse?
a) Reliance on accountants

In *Rowland v HMRC (2006) SpC 548* the appellant made a capital gain of £15.6 million in 1999-2000. On the advice of her accountant, to reduce the gain, she became a partner in a film partnership. her accountant advised her that her share of the estimated loss of the film partnership for 2000-01 was to be set against her income and gains for 1999-2000, so that the tax due on 31 January 2001 would be £861,250 instead of £5,592,982. Her return, including an estimated loss relief claim, was filed on 29 January 2001 together with payment. In April, an amended return claiming loss relief was submitted. However, in July 2001, her accountant told there was an issue over the timing of the loss claim, and an amended return was submitted. In October, HMRC imposed a surcharge on underpaid tax.

The appellant appealed claiming reasonable excuse, in that she had relied on her accountant to deal with her tax affairs. The Special Commissioner considered that reliance on a third party could be a reasonable excuse in respect of direct tax. Legislation specifically excluded reliance on a third party as being a reasonable excuse in VAT, but no equivalent provision existed in direct tax. The taxpayer's appeal was allowed.

Three other tribunal decisions where the taxpayer blamed their accountants for their compliance failures:

In the first case *(Huntley Solutions v HMRC TC00272)*, the taxpayer, Huntley Solutions, could not show that reliance on their agent (Marriotts Business Consultants) to supply information to HMRC was a reasonable excuse if the taxpayer could easily have complied with the request itself.

The first case can be contrasted directly with the case of *The Research & Development Partnership Ltd. v HMRC TC00271*. This also concerned Marriotts Business Consulting and the taxpayers reliance on Marriotts to provide information and documents to HMRC following a notice issued under para 27 Sch 18 FA 2008. In this case, the tribunal allowed the taxpayer's appeal and set aside penalties totalling £1,490.

The difference between this case and Huntley Solutions was the complexity of the information that HMRC had given notice that should be provided to them.

In another unrelated case (*G Jeffers A Jeffers and G&A Jeffers v HMRC TC00337*) the tribunal found that a reliance on accountants to submit personal and partnership tax returns for 2006/2007 on time was not a reasonable excuse.

Indeed two later Tribunal decisions are given below:

Example 1
The case of *Browne v HMRC TC 754* related to the failure to deliver a land transaction return for the purposes of SDLT. This case drew heavily on the Special Commissioners decision in *Rowland v HMRC (2006) SpC 548* (see above) where the taxpayer was able to demonstrate that they were let down by their professional advisers and that was sufficient to relieve her from the relevant penalty.

This was a conveyancing matter and it was reasonable for Mrs Browne to rely on her solicitor to submit the SDLT return within the statutory time limit the Tribunal considered that there was no reason for her to think that the solicitors would fail to do so. Their failure was not a fault of hers and she therefore had a reasonable excuse for the failure and no penalty arose.

Example 2
The other case of *Dauti v HMRC TC 786* did not look very promising. Mr Dauti was from Bosnia and worked in the UK as a subcontract labourer. He explained to the Tribunal that many of his friends were working in the UK illegally and therefore needed to stay below the radar. He lent them money and they paid him back. These receipts excited HMRC who claimed that his disclosed earnings were understated and issued discovery assessments.

This was obviously a very difficult challenge to defend - the onus being on him to show that HMRC was wrong - but he clearly impressed the Tribunal. They found his evidence sincere and truthful, sufficient to show that the discovery assessments should be discharged. Mr Dauti represented himself.

b) CIS compliance failure
In 2009 the tribunals saw a number of appeals being brought by subcontractors where HMRC cancelled their 'gross payment status' within the construction industry scheme for failing to fulfil the compliance test set out in FA 2004 Sch 11. Typically, the compliance failings were late payments of tax, in particular late payments of PAYE.

In each case, the appellant argued that there was a 'reasonable excuse' for the compliance failing and so retain registration for gross payment.

Three of the nine reasonable excuse cases were allowed:

Stephen Mutch (S Mutch v HMRC TC00232)
A carpenter's work dried up from his main client, a house building company in Corby. He was forced to make most of his workforce redundant but was still committed to paying high overheads. Tax payments in 2008 were made late citing his shortage of

funds as the reasonable excuse for his compliance failings.

Prior Roofing Ltd. (Prior Roofing Ltd. v HMRC TC00246)
A specialist roofing contractor made eight late payments in 2007/2008, although only one of which was more than 14 days late. The appellant blamed shortage of funds as the result of the significant downturn in the building industry and the difficulty to borrow during this period.

Cormac Construction Ltd. (Cormac Construction Ltd. v HMRC TC00315)
It was decided that a bookkeeper's responsibilities in balancing a full time job, bringing up three children, and arranging childcare during school holidays, provided a reasonable excuse for late payments of PAYE.

Other Cases
In the other six hearings (*Strongwork Construction Ltd. v HMRC TC00236, Darren Munns v HMRC TC00234, Ductaire Fabrications Ltd. v HMRC TC00288, Beard v HMRC TC00228, A Longworth & Sons Ltd. v HMRC TC00230, Grosvenor v HMRC TC00227*), the subcontractors' appeals were dismissed. The excuses that failed to be regarded as reasonable included:

*   suffering bad debts, and personal injury, where these occurred after 'a clear pattern' of late payments;
*   a history of late paying clients and therefore not unexpected or exceptional;
*   the withdrawal of gross payment status would have an adverse impact on the business;
*   downturn in the business;
*   overdraft facility removed
*   delay in sale of property to fund tax payment
*   ignorance of possible impact of late payments
*   compliance failures were not significant;
*   'not sure what had happened' as his girlfriend, who did the paperwork, was having personal problems.

c) Innocent Error

In *Miss MM Anderson (Deceased) v HMRC TC00206* an assessment raised by HMRC under section 29 TMA 1970 was justified as the error made by the appellant, although innocent, was attributable to negligent conduct.

The appellant, Miss Anderson, who died shortly after appealing against the assessment, had included gains of just over £33,000 from investment bonds. In addition she included a figure of £7,306, incorrectly, in respect of 'tax treated as paid' on one of those bonds.

Taxpayers can now submit a 'reasonable excuse' claim in advance of HRMC issuing a late filing penalty notice.

HMRC has outlined a number of situations that they <u>would accept</u> as a reasonable excuse for the late filing of a tax return, as follows:

- fire or flood at the Post Office where the tax return was handled;
- prolonged industrial action within the Post Office;
- loss of records through fire, flood or theft;
- very serious illness such as coma, major heart attack, stroke or any other serious mental or life threatening illness; or
- death of a close relative or (domestic) partner shortly before the deadline.

HMRC <u>does not accept</u> that the following would be a reasonable excuse for late filing of a tax return:

- considering that the tax form was too difficult to complete;
- pressure of work;
- a failure by a tax agent;
- lack of information; or
- absence of reminders by HMRC.

HMRC <u>accepts</u> the following as reasonable excuses for not paying the tax due on time:

- fire or flood at the Post Office where a cheque lost in the post was handled;
- the cheque was dishonoured solely because of an error by the bank;
- very serious illness such as coma, major heart attack, stroke or any other serious mental or life threatening illness but only if it began shortly before the due date for payment and the taxpayer could not have made arrangements to pay; or
- death of a close relative or (domestic) partner; but only if this occurred "at around the due date for payment."

HMRC <u>do not consider</u> the following as reasonable excuses for not paying the tax on time:

- shortage of funds;
- cheque being dishonoured because of lack of funds;
- tax return not having been completed;
- pressure of work;
- failure by tax agents;
- not knowing exactly what to pay (they expect the taxpayer to make a reasonable estimate); or
- absence of reminders from HMRC.

HMRC takes the view that, unless any of the above situations arise, it is very unlikely that a reasonable excuse argument would succeed.

The National Association of Tax Commissioners in their published guidance, make the valid distinction that the above pointers only constitute the views of HMRC and ultimately, it is the role of the General Commissioners to consider what is a reasonable excuse and their decision is based on the specific circumstances of each case.

Appellants are reminded that the onus of proof lies with them. It is for each appellant to demonstrate that a reasonable excuse exists and not for HMRC to prove otherwise.

5.3.3 How to avoid enquiries

HMRC pre-select, at random, a percentage of returns into which to make enquiries. These you cannot avoid, but there are the suggested ways to minimise the likelihood of an enquiry into an actual income tax return.

- disclose reasons for year-on-year changes in business ratios;

- identify private usage clearly, and where this has been netted off in the disclosed figures, use the 'white space' to explain;

- make consistent use of the boxes in the Standard Accounts Information pages from year to year or explain changes;

- analyse items included under the heading 'other expenses';

- consider submitting supporting accounts, computations and analyses where they go beyond the SAI boxes; and use the 'white space' on the tax return for explanations, disclosures and to refer to any supplementary material provided with the return;

- Always, finalise provisional figures.

There is a critical difference between estimated figures (which are unlikely to require revision at a later date) and provisional figures, which, by definition, will need to be finalised later. These are flagged on the income tax return form by ticking box 20, on page TR6 (2008/2009). If these figures are not finalised at a later date, HMRC may open an enquiry to force the issue.

Following an appeal against a late filing penalty, HMRC sought further legal advice about the use of provisional figures. As a result of that advice, HMRC changed their guidance to staff on how to handle ITSA Returns containing provisional figures or CTSA Returns containing estimated figures.

HMRC now accept that a '<u>customer</u>' has made a Return (assuming there are no other problems) where they have used a provisional or estimated figure. HMRC no longer send back a Return that does not have an adequate explanation for why provisional or estimated figures are needed or does not give a date for the supply of final figures. The omission of that information will, however, be a factor HMRC take into account in order to decide whether they need to open an enquiry into the Return.

5.3.4 Payment of tax
<u>Deduction at source</u>
Much of an individual's tax liabilities is satisfied by the payer of the income deducting tax from the payment due, or by the 'imputation' of tax to dividends. Thus payment of wages, salaries and directors' fees is subject to tax deductions in accordance with the recipient's tax code.

The rate imputed to dividends is 10% and the tax deducted from interest is 20%. The payer of the remuneration, interest or dividends then has to pay the total tax deducted to HMRC or otherwise account for it in a tax computation.

In many cases, however, the deduction of tax at source does not satisfy a taxpayer's complete liability for a tax year. This is because the taxpayer may have received income from which no tax has been deducted, such as from self-employment, lettings or interest received gross of tax; the taxpayer may also be liable for higher rate tax. Moreover a person with low income from say, investments, may be entitled to personal allowances which exceed the income or which reduce his or her tax liability so that a refund of tax over-deducted can be obtained. The 10% tax deducted from dividends cannot be reclaimed. For these reasons it is desirable if not essential that an individual should submit to the local Inspector of Taxes a Return of all income showing as appropriate the tax deducted or imputed and including a claim for allowances. It is also desirable that if possible an individual should prepare a calculation of his or her own tax liability each tax year offsetting the tax suffered by deduction or imputation.

5.3.5 Times of payment
<u>Payment by cheque: effective date</u>
HMRC are moving away from deemed payment on 'receipt' of cheque to date it is 'cleared'. Currently only regulations relating to (effective 1 April 2010) VAT and CT (effective 1 April 2011) have been laid.

<u>Payment slip SA361</u>
Payment slip SA361 is available for download from the HMRC website (at www.hmrc.gov.uk/agents/sa361.pdf).

If a taxpayer is paying a self assessment liability by cheque and he chooses to post it, he is asked to use the computer-printed payslip HMRC provides whenever possible. If not, then use form SA361.

The SA361 is not suitable for paying at a bank or post office.

Credit Card. Taxpayers can settle their liabilities with a credit card, but will incur a transaction charge (0.91% if made by telephone, 1.4% online).

If tax returns are filed by 31 December and the tax owing is less than £2,000 the taxpayer can apply to have it encoded in a following year's PAYE code.

5.3.6 Interest on unpaid tax
Interest is normally charged at 3% (if a repayment is due at 0.5%) on tax unpaid from the date when the payment was due.

New penalties for late paid PAYE and NIC
A new regime of penalties was introduced with effect from 6 April 2010. New provisions to charge interest on late payments will be brought in at a later date, probably from April 2012.

The first remittances, of not only PAYE and NIC but also CIS and student loan deductions, affected by the penalties were therefore from May 2010 for in-year payments.

Monthly or quarterly PAYE payments
Employers will not be charged a penalty if only one PAYE amount is late in a tax year - unless that payment is over six months late.

The amount of the penalty will depend on how much is late and how many times your payments are late in a tax year. So if the employer pays part of what is due on time then any penalty will only be charged on the part that is late. The table below shows how the penalties are calculated.

Penalty charges for late monthly and quarterly PAYE payments:

No. of times payments are late in a tax year	Penalty percentage	Amount to which penalty percentages apply
1	No penalty (as long as the payment is less than six months late)	Total amount that is late in the tax year ignoring the first late payment in that tax year)
2-4	1%	
5-7	2%	
8-10	3%	
11 or more	4%	

Additional penalties for monthly and quarterly payments over six months late
If the employer still has not paid a monthly or quarterly amount in full, after six

months he may have to pay a penalty of 5 per cent. A further penalty of 5 per cent may be charged if he has not paid after 12 months. These penalties may be charged in addition to the penalties for monthly and quarterly payments described in the previous section and apply even where only one payment in the tax year is late.

If payments under a PAYE settlement agreement of Class 1A/1B NIC annual payments are late, the penalty is 5% of the amount not paid on time and then further 5% penalties if amounts remain unpaid after five months and eleven months after the due date.

Agreements under a formal Time to Pay arrangement with HMRC will suspend any penalties.

Employers will be informed on any penalty by letter. Although HMRC has the power to charge penalties during the tax year, penalties for 2011/2012 will not be issued until April or May 2012. HMRC must, in any case charge a penalty within two years of the due date for payment.

An appeal against a penalty can be made if you disagree that it is not due, or the amount charged is incorrect, or there is a reasonable excuse.

Rules for interest rates on tax
The number of formulae used by HMRC to calculate its interest rates has been reduced. Interest charged on late payments of tax will be the Bank base rate plus 2.5%. For interest paid on overpayments, the rate will be the Bank base rate minus 1% subject to a minimum of 0.5%.

5.3.7 Arrears of tax through official errors
By concession, where HMRC has failed to make proper and timely use of information supplied by the taxpayer about his or her income or personal circumstances, arrears of tax arising from this failure are wholly or partly waived (ESC A19).

The proportions HMRC will remit are:

Taxpayer's gross income	Tax waived
£15,500 or less	All
£15,501-£18,000	Three-quarters
£18,001-£22,000	One-half
£22,001-£26,000	One-quarter
£26,001-£40,000	One-tenth
£40,001 and over	None

The figures apply to all taxpayers. However where the taxpayer employs an accountant or tax advisor, the taxpayer cannot claim ignorance.

5.3.8 Interest on delayed repayments of taxes

The interest paid on over-paid tax is at the lower rate of 0.5% than charged on tax due (3%), and is payable from 31 January following end of the tax year. The interest, which is tax free to individuals, is known as a repayment supplement.

Provisions apply for corporation tax and income tax on company income taxed at source (including tax credit on franked investment income received), provided the repayment is not less than £100 and is made more than 12 months after the due date of the tax i.e. the material date.

5.3.9 Providing for Payment

It is important to provide in advance for funds to meet taxation liabilities. In particular many small businesses encounter difficulties in paying large demands for tax, especially when current income is low. Likewise many individuals have problems in paying the tax due on income received gross of tax and in paying higher rate tax and capital gains tax after the tax year when the gains were realized.

To avoid these financial difficulties it is first necessary to prepare forecasts of the tax likely to be payable at the due dates, as indicated above. Provision should then be made for having the necessary funds available at the dates when the tax will be payable. A cash flow forecast of all likely receipts and payments, the latter including taxation dues, will be essential. A more certain method is to set aside out of monthly income amounts which will accumulate to the tax payment required at the due date. These monthly provisions should be invested in easily realizable deposits to earn interest.

Even so, the taxpayer might not be able to meet the tax bill in full, due, for instance, to adverse circumstances, such as unemployment. In such situations arrangements can often be made with the Receivables Management Service (RMS) for payment by instalments. It is wise to tell the RMS well in advance that all the funds to meet the liability are not available. The latter will be more amenable to agreeing to take instalments before the bailiff arrives!

Debt collectors are now being used by HMRC. If approached by a firm claiming to be acting for HMRC, their genuineness can be verified on 0845 915 5348.

In 2008 the Inland Revenue introduced a scheme for people suffering problems in paying their tax bills. HMRC introduced a Business Payment Support Service. Their telephone number is 0845 302 1435.

"In the event of genuine cash flow problems and you are experiencing difficulties in meeting any payment to HMRC, PAYE/NIC or other business taxes call them on the above telephone number. If you reach agreement for extended terms late payment surcharges will be waived, but not interest."

As with any 'lender' don't wait for court action to be taken before contacting them. The sooner you get in touch the more likely you are to achieve an agreement to pay the taxes by instalments. But always contact them before the date of payment is due.

6 APPEALS

6.1 General
Due to Self Assessment, assessments to the great extent have been abolished, accordingly appeals have to a great extent also disappeared. Appeals will only be allowed against assessments raised following an enquiry into a self assessment return, an amendment to a partnership statement where tax is 'discovered' or a disallowance of a claim/election included in a return. If any appeal is intended, notice of such intention must be given to the Inspector within 30 days. After the expiration of this period no legal right of appeal remains, unless there have been good grounds for the omission, such as sickness or absence from the country.

The Commissioners' determination need only settle the issues raised in the appeal, without going on to calculate the tax payable in consequence (*Hallamshire Industrial Finance Trust Ltd v CIR* ChD 1978; TMA 1975, S50).

6.2 Appeals against Employment related assessments
The procedure is similar to that stated above in 6.1, and there is the same right of appeal to the Special Commissioners as an alternative to the General Commissioners.

6.3 Appeals under the new Tribunal System
(a) First Tier Tribunal (FTT). A party seeking to appeal to the Upper Tier must first apply for permission from the FTT.

(b) Upper Tier (UT). A party seeking to appeal to the Court of Appeal must first apply for permission from the UT.

(c) The UT takes over the previous route of applying to the High Court.

(d) Taxpayers have the right to apply to UT for Judicial review of a HMRC or FTT decision.

(e) Previous decisions by the General and Special Commissioners are likely to remain persuasive. Accordingly the issues previously ruled upon by the

Commissioners remain in this work as guidance. When new rulings are handed down by FTT and UT these will be included.

If, however, either the appellant or the Inspector considers the decision of the Commissioners wrong on a point of law, he or she may immediately (*R v Freshwell Commrs (ex.p. Clarke)* CA 1971) after the conclusion of the appeal express dissatisfaction with the decision on that point, and within 30 days send the Clerk of the Commissioners a fee of £25, and demand (in writing) a statement of his case for the High Court. The High Court will also hear a stated case where the Commissioners have come to a wrong decision on the facts before them, or where they consider that there was no evidence on which the Commissioners could have come to their conclusion (*Edwards v Bairstow & Harrison* HL 1955).

From the High Court, appeal may be made on a point of law to the Court of Appeal and thence to the Judicial Committee of the House of Lords. Appeal directly from the High Court to the House of Lords may be possible in exceptional cases (Administration of Justice Act 1969, s 12). The Lord Chancellor may provide by order for certain appeals on a case stated by the Special Commissioners to be referred direct to the Court of Appeal rather than to the High Court (TMA 1970, s 56A).

Appeals on cases stated are heard in the Chancery Division of the High Court and applications for one of the prerogative orders (i.e. certiorari, mandamus or prohibition) to remedy a formal defect in proceedings lie to the Queen's Bench Division.

The tax must in the meantime be paid, when due, in accordance with the Commissioners' decision, but when the case has been decided in the High Court, repayment will be ordered if too much has been paid, with suitable interest. Usually the costs of the case would be borne by the unsuccessful side although in certain cases where HMRC wish to clarify legislation, they may agree to pay the costs of both parties.

6.4 Appeals on special matters
Appeals on questions of residence, domicile or settlements are made only to the Special Commissioners (TMA 1970, s 31(3) and Sch 2). The time limit for making an appeal against the Board's decision on residence or domicile is three months (TMA 1970, s 42).

6.5 Production of documents (including computer media)
Inspectors and the Board have wide ranging powers to require the production of documents which they reasonably believe are relevant to tax liability (TMA 1970, ss 20, A to D; FA 1976, s 57 and Sch 6; FA 1994 ss 187 and 225). FA2000 SS149, 145. See 4.4 Inspector of Taxes, p.4 where an accountant had to 'prepare' a balance sheet at the request of the HMIT The power extends over the taxpayer's spouse (including a surviving spouse even after remarriage) and children, over any person

carrying on a business (including a bank) if the enquiry relates to income from another business with which the taxpayer or spouse are or have been concerned, and over any company. In any case an Inspector requires the authority of the Board, and consent from a General or Special Commissioner must be obtained.

The person in question (other than the taxpayer) may elect to make the documents available for inspection. Copies may be taken of any such documents, and the Inspector (or the Board) is obliged to accept proper copies instead of originals, although he or she retains the right to inspect the originals. Documents more than six years old are not (except in cases of suspected fraud, based on reasonable grounds approved by a Commissioner) expected to be produced by a business or company which is not the taxpayer being investigated. Nor do documents to which legal privilege attaches, or which are working papers of a tax accountant (in business as such), have to be produced. In *Morgan Grenfell v SpC(2000)* STC 965 advice by a tax counsel was deemed not covered by professional privilege. The taxpayer's widow or widower, son or daughter cannot be required to produce documents after six years from the taxpayer's death.

If convicted in the UK of any offence in relation to tax or after incurring any penalty for assisting in making false returns, a tax accountant may be required, by an Inspector authorized by the Board, to deliver any documents in his or her possession or power which the Inspector reasonably believes to be relevant to the tax liability of any client. A tax accountant is anyone who assists another with tax returns or accounts. The Inspector must act against such a person within 12 months of the conviction or penalty ceasing to be appealable and only with the consent of a Circuit judge.

A reasonable opportunity to produce the documents voluntarily must be given before any notice is given or consent applied for. Any notice given to a barrister or solicitor must be given by the Board. There is power to enter premises and seize relevant documents under a warrant from a Circuit judge who has been satisfied that the officer has the approval of the Board and that there is reasonable ground for suspecting that fraud relating to tax has been committed and is evidenced in documents to be found there (*Rossminster Ltd.* HL 1979). Documents in the possession of a barrister or solicitor to which privilege attaches are protected from seizure.

The Special or General Commissioners may, prior to the hearing of an appeal, require particulars, including any relevant books, accounts or other documents to be produced. These may be inspected and copied by the Board's officer. They are not bound to accept accounts even when submitted on oath, neither are they compelled to examine books which are produced at an appeal. They may also impose penalties if fraudulent accounts are rendered (though this is extremely rare in practice), and may increase the assessment appealed against.

Fox v McKay (Inspector of Taxes) (2001) SWTI 48. Mr Fox was an accountant and HMRC were investigating one of his clients for tax fraud. HMRC used the procedure in TMA 1970 Section 20 (3) to require the accountant to produce certain files including working papers and link papers concerning the client's tax returns and concerning the preparation of accounts for a company with which the client was linked. The accountant wrote a long letter in reply stating that his records had recently been moved to a depository and that the documents there had been searched but there was no trace of the requested material. The letter did not set out who had conducted the search, the duration of the search or the extent of the search and penalty proceedings were commenced under TMA 1970 Section 100 (c) (1) and HMRC imposed the maximum penalty. HMRC's grounds for doing so were that the accountant was aware of his responsibility to retain papers and that it was not accepted that the requested material could not be traced. The accountant appealed.

It was held that the nature of the documents requested were those that should be held by the accountant. The onus was, therefore, on the accountant to demonstrate that he did not have the requested documents. Had there been evidence of destruction or that a complete search had failed to find the material in question it would have been an end to the matter, however, the Inspector had not accepted that the material requested could not be traced and in the circumstances given the general information provided by the accountant on the search and how it had been conducted the Inspector was correct in levying the maximum amount of penalties under the Act.

6.6 Appeals against assessments
In the case of assessment to corporation tax (except PAYE and company payments taxed without assessment, tax was due and payable as if the assessment was correct unless application had been made to the Inspector for the postponement of payment. The appellant must give notice to the Inspector of his belief that tax was overcharged and of the grounds for this belief, if payment is to be postponed. There was a right to apply for variation of a determination of the amount to be postponed if there is a change in circumstances, and any notice must state the grounds and amount. If necessary, repayment can be obtained.

An application is determined as if it were an appeal, but subject to the possibility of the matter being agreed with the Inspector in or by confirmation in writing. The Commissioners are to determine the amount in respect of which there are reasonable grounds for believing that tax is overcharged and collection of that amount will be postponed, but the balance will become due as if an assessment had been issued at the date of determination (TMA 1970, s 55). If no accounts are submitted in support of an appeal and application, the Commissioners can properly conclude that there are no grounds for believing that tax is overcharged by an estimated assessment (*Parikh v Currie* CA 1978).

The postponed tax becomes payable if found to be due on determination of the appeal, and is due 30 days after an assessment in that amount is issued.

Interest is chargeable from the reckonable date on any additional tax payable if the original assessment was estimated and an appeal made against that assessment.

6.7 Corporation tax appeals settled by agreement

Where a taxpayer has given notice of appeal against an assessment or decision of any kind with respect to corporation tax and the Inspector or other appropriate Crown official on the one hand and the appellant or agent on the other hand, come to an agreement, whether in writing or otherwise, before the appeal is heard before the General or Special Commissioners, the appeal may be treated as determined without the necessity of an appearance before the Commissioners (TMA 1970, s 54).

An appellant or agent may give notice in writing within 30 days of the date on which the agreement was reached, that he or she wishes to repudiate the agreement, and the normal appeal procedure then takes its course.

A verbal agreement must be confirmed in writing, either by the representative of the Crown, or by the appellant or his agent. To constitute an agreement there has to be an offer and acceptance to definite terms, so that 'agreement in principle' that an apportionment was necessary did not preclude a later claim that no apportionment should be made (*Delbourge v Field* CA 1978).

If an appellant or his or her agent notifies the Crown representative that he does not propose to proceed with the appeal or claim, the appeal is then treated as settled, unless the Inspector or other Crown official objects within 30 days of receipt of such notification.

7 PENALTIES

7.0 Finance Act 2007

Clause 96 and Schedule 24 provides a single new penalty regime for incorrect returns for income tax, corporation tax, PAYE, NIC and VAT. The measure repeals penalty provisions for incorrect returns for Income Tax Self Assessment (s95 TMA 1970), Corporation Tax Self Assessment (paras 20(1) and 89(1) sch 18 FA 1998), PAYE and NIC (s98A(4) TMA 1970) and for VAT (ss 60, 61 and 63 VATA 1994).

It replaced these different provisions with a single penalty regime to apply to inaccurate returns, claims, accounts and other documents for each of the taxes. The new provisions provide for penalties based on the amount of tax understated and the behaviour that gives rise to the understatement. There is:

- no penalty where a taxpayer makes a mistake;
- moderate penalties for failures to take reasonable care;
- higher penalties for deliberate action; and

- still higher penalties for deliberate action with concealment.

The measure provides for each penalty to be substantially reduced where the taxpayer makes a disclosure (takes active steps to put right the problem), more so if this is unprompted. So, for an unprompted disclosure of a failure to take reasonable care the penalty could be reduced to nil. Where a taxpayer discloses fully when prompted (by a challenge from MRC) each penalty could be reduced by up to a half.

The measure includes full and explicit provisions for the right of appeal against all penalty decisions.

The provisions applied from 1 April 2008 for return periods commencing after 31 March 2008 where the return is filed after 31 March 2009.

How is the penalty charge calculated?
The penalty is a percentage of the extra tax due. the rate depends on the behaviour that gave rise to the error. The less serious the behaviour, the smaller the penalty will be.

No Penalty Reasonable Care	Max 30% Careless Min 0%	Max 70% Deliberate Min 20%	Max 100% Deliberate & Concealed Min 30%

The main features in the new penalty regime include:-

- A single penalty regime for incorrect returns.
- Penalties based on 'behaviour' with set minimum and maximum penalties being applied depending on the actions of the taxpayer concerned.
- Scope for mitigation but unlike the current situation under Self Assessment, where there is a penalty abatement for Disclosure, Co-operation and Seriousness, **only** the disclosure element remains.
- The introduction of a new concept of suspended penalties, which can reduce or cancel penalties where it can be shown that steps have been taken to prevent errors arising again.
- A right to Appeal.

The penalties are split into categories depending on the type of 'offence' as follows: -

30% of the tax lost for 'careless' behaviour (i.e. failure to take reasonable care).
70% of the tax lost for 'deliberate' (i.e. knowingly making incorrect returns).
100% of the tax lost for 'deliberate and concealed' (i.e. knowingly making incorrect

returns and then covering up the fact).

The mitigation for disclosure in respect of these penalties is then divided into 'prompted' and 'unprompted' disclosures. Where a disclosure has been 'prompted' as a result of HMRC highlighting the issue, the above penalties are halved to 15%, 35% and 50% respectively.

If an 'unprompted' disclosure is made (i.e. before HMRC become aware) then the above penalties can be reduced to 0%, 20% and 30% respectively (these are the minimum penalties in each category).

The new concept of 'suspended' penalties is aimed at giving encouragement to those willing to fully comply with their future obligations. Any penalty imposed can be suspended, (in part or fully) for up to two years if action is taken to correct matters (e.g. new bookkeeping systems and procedures are introduced). The conditions for judging whether sufficient action has been taken will be agreed between HMRC and the taxpayer and/or adviser, as will the level of the penalty to be suspended. It is likely that this 'lifeline' will only be granted to those who fall in the least serious category of 'careless' behaviour.

The new legislation also gives HMRC powers to seek a penalty direct from the directory of a company if it can be shown that any inaccuracy in the return was due to the director's deliberate actions.

7.1 General
A taxpayer is liable to pay various penalties for failure to make returns of income, incorrect returns, false statements and for fraud or negligence. In the case of false statements the penalty can be up to two years imprisonment. Most of the penalties are set out in TMA 1970 as amended by subsequent legislation. Furthermore TMA 1970 s 104 does not exclude criminal proceedings for misdemeanour. Interest will also be payable from the date when the tax was due.

It is therefore essential that a taxpayer shall make correct returns of his income and capital gains for each tax year, whether a return form has been received or not.

7.2 Time limits
Please see Table 8. HMRC - Assessment Time Limits showing new and previous time limits, p.628.

7.3 Criminal proceedings
The Court of Appeal has held that a pecuniary settlement negotiated by HMRC relating to a tax liability does not preclude a prosecution by the Crown Prosecution Service (CPS) in respect of false accounting to evade tax. HMRC's common law power to prosecute was ancillary to, supportive of and limited by its duty to collect taxes.

In contrast, the CPS's statutory duty to conduct criminal proceedings was freestanding, unconfined and reflected much wider public interests, concerns and objectives (see *R v W and Another* (1998) STI 557).

In *Rose v Director of Assets Recovery Agency SpC 543* the police searched the home and garage of Mr Rose (R) and found the following items: Drugs, money, documents relating to drugs, a cash book, bank statements, scales (in a fishing box in the garage).

R accepted that the drugs found in his house belonged to him and that they were for personal use. R claimed that he did not know where the drugs in the garage had come from.

Section 317 of the Proceeds of Crime Act 2002 ('POCA') allows the Assets Recovery Agency ('ARA') to assume the functions of HMRC. The ARA assessed R to tax under Schedule D Case I (trade in the dealing of drugs) and NICs for the years 1997/98 to 2002/03. R appealed against the estimated assessments on the grounds that the drugs were for private use.

The Commissioner found that the drugs in the garage did belong to R but there was no evidence to suggest that he had been undertaking a trade of dealing in drugs. The scales found in the fishing box were consistent with both personal use of drugs and/or fishing. The Commissioner held that the estimated assessments raised under POCA could not be validated as R did have a reliable source of other income.

The taxpayer's appeal was allowed. This case does show a move towards taxation of criminal activities.

8 NEW HMRC POWERS

Across all the main taxes HMRC have a combination of an inspection power (the right to access and inspect business premises, business assets and business documents) and an information power (the power to require the production of information and documents).

For the first time, for corporation, income and capital gains taxes, HMRC have powers to:

*   access records <u>before</u> returns are filed;
*   turn up <u>unannounced</u> to check the records; and
*   routinely have access to business premises and assets and have the right to copy or remove documents.

The records and documents that HMRC will be able to access are very widely defined and there is <u>no</u> right of appeal against an inspection.

On 17 December 2010 HMRC announced their intention to roll out a programme of Business Record Checks in the second half of 2011.

If a business is selected, HMRC staff will visit the premises and ask for access to all the business records. If they feel that there is a significant failure to keep proper records, penalties may be charged and additional tax assessments raised.

HMRC's objectives:

- Use existing powers to check business records in up to 50,000 cases annually.
- Businesses targeted will have 250 employees or less and turnover below 50m Euros. (At present exchange rates just over £40m).
- Checks began in the second half of 2011.
- Impose penalties for significant record keeping failures.

If HMRC are aware that the record keeping is defective this will no doubt trigger visits from a number of their departments. The business may get additional PAYE/ NIC or VAT audit checks for instance.

There are existing guidelines from HMRC on what constitutes satisfactory record keeping that will likely form the basis of their new Record Check processes.

9 COMPANIES

Self assessment for companies and others liable to corporation tax
Unlike Self Assessment for individuals Accounts and Computations <u>still</u> have to be submitted. However brought into the return are

(a)   liabilities under S419 ICTA 1988
(b)   controlled foreign companies
(c)   transfer pricing.

Records have to be kept for six years and the full enquiry regime is applied to companies. Sch 18 FA 1998.
The main features of the system are as follows:

(a)   Companies are expected to make estimates of liability to corporation tax and to pay the tax so estimated by nine months after the accounting date concerned.

(b)   Tax returns, accounts and computations must be sent to HMRC within 12 months after the end of the company's accounting period, and penalties may be charged for failure to do so. (From 1 April 2011 they have to be filed by iXBRL).

(c)   The actual amount of tax due will be settled by payment or refund when the computations have been agreed with the Inspector, and interest will be payable or receivable on the amount outstanding. FA 1993 s 120 and sch 14.

10 OVER PAYMENT RELIEF (FORMERLY ERROR OR MISTAKE RELIEF)

10.1 Overpayment relief
With the replacement of error or mistake claims by overpayment relief claims from 1 April 2010, HMRC have published details of what information must be included in a claim and practice generally prevailing.

Time limits
Claims must be made within 4 years of the end of the tax year or accounting period to which the claim relates.

This time limit does not apply where the claim relates to a mistake in an individual's 2004-2005 or 2005-2006 self-assessment return if they were not given a notice to make the return within 12 months of the end of the tax year. The time limits for claims in these cases are 31 January 2011 and 31 January 2012 respectively.

Form of overpayment relief claims
Claims must be made in writing and:

*   State that the person is making a claim for overpayment relief under Schedule 1AB TMA 1970 (Paragraph 51 Schedule 18 Finance Act 1998 for corporation tax claims).

*   Identify the tax year/accounting period for which the overpayment or excessive assessment has been made.

*   State the grounds on which the person considers that the overpayment or excessive assessment has occurred.

*   State whether the person has previously made an appeal in connection with the payment or the assessment.

- If the claim is for repayment of tax, include documentary proof of the tax deducted or the tax being suffered in some other way.

- Include the declaration signed by the claimant stating that the particulars given in the claim are correct and complete to the best of their knowledge and belief.

Claims cannot be made in self-assessment returns and will not be accepted if they are made on an SA return form (SA100) or equivalent, such as the Trust and Estate Tax Return SA900 or company tax return (CT600).

Both error or mistake relief and overpayment relief have an exception where the tax was calculated in accordance with prevailing practice at the time.

HMRC understand this principle also applies to the new overpayment relief. Therefore, if a claim for error or mistake relief or overpayment relief relates to taxes paid in breach of EU law, HMRC will not seek to disallow it on the basis that the tax liability was calculated in accordance with the prevailing practice.

11 THE CIVIL PARTNERSHIP ACT 2004

From 5 December 2005 the Civil Partnership Act 2004 came into effect. This enables same sex couples to enter into a new legal status of being 'civil partners' and this allows them to obtain the same tax rights as married couples.

HMRC in 2010 published a guide - Pride 1 - for their lesbian, gay, bisexual and transgender customers.

PART TWO

PERSONAL TAXATION

1) Personal Tax Allowance (under 65)

The basic personal allowance rises to £7,475 from April 2011 with a further rise to £8,105 in 2012/13 and further increases towards the promised £10,000 target by the end of the present parliament.

2) Tax bands

The income figure above which higher rate tax becomes payable is reduced from April 2011 to £42,475 from £43,875 (so that higher rate taxpayers do not benefit from the increase in personal allowances).

3) Pension contributions

The annual allowance (the maximum allowable contributions in any year), is reduced from April 2011 to £50,000 (from £255,000) as part of a simplification of the previous proposals intended to limit higher rate tax relief for contributions.

4) Deferring pension annuity decision

The obligation to buy an annuity using your pension fund by the time you reach the age of 75 is changing. As from June 23rd 2010 anyone who had yet to reach age 75 was able to defer a decision to purchase an annuity until age 77. From April 2011 the requirement to take an annuity by any age is removed.

1 THE TAX LIABILITY OF INDIVIDUALS

1.1 The taxes payable

Individuals are liable to pay income tax on their chargeable income, and capital gains tax on their capital profits. In addition they will normally be liable for the council tax and will suffer value added tax on many purchases. Their estate may be liable for inheritance tax on their death.

1.2 Examples of taxable income

The following is a list, which is not exclusive, of the main types of income for which an individual may be liable for tax.

(a) *Remuneration* such as wages, salaries, bonuses, tips and fees payable under a contract of employment. Tax is largely payable by deduction from the earnings under the PAYE system according to the individual's code.

(b) *Taxed interest* from banks, building societies, other corporations, national savings bonds and government securities. Tax is deducted from the interest (except certain national savings) or imputed to the dividends, but higher rate tax, if applicable, will be payable.

(c) *Untaxed interest* from certain national savings, government securities and other sources of income, i.e. where tax has not been deducted, and the payment is made gross. Tax, including possible higher rates, is payable on self-assessment.

(d) *Offshore Accounts.* It is not illegal to hold a bank account outside the UK. The interest however must be declared to HMRC even if not remitted to the UK.

(e) *Rents receivable* from lettings of property, whether furnished or unfurnished and including holiday lettings. The tax due is payable by self assessment.

(f) *Shares of profit* from unincorporated business including partnerships, profits from businesses in sole ownership and part-time businesses, the latter two categories being described as self-employment. The income tax is self-assessed. Tax is normally payable on the business profits, and will be taken into account in calculating the taxpayer's total tax liability.

(g) *Occupational pensions* and retirement annuities from which tax under the PAYE system is normally deducted from the payment, except in the case of the state pension.

(h) *Other sources of taxable income* such as income from abroad; compensation and redundancy pay (subject to certain exemptions); benefits received from employers including those for the private use of company cars; accommodation; loans at below a commercial rate of interest; tips and gratuities from employment.

1.3 Gross income

This is an individual's income from all sources that is subject to tax but is before any tax is deducted. It includes income receivable from all sources, e.g. from lettings, profits from trades and professions, interest, overseas securities and possessions, miscellaneous income, such as dealings in futures and furnished holiday lets, remuneration and benefits from employment and dividends.

1.4 Earned and unearned income

For tax purposes total income falls into the two categories of (a) earned income and (b) unearned income, although the latter description could be misleading. Earned income is that which is derived from the personal efforts of the taxpayer and includes remuneration, compensation (where taxable) and benefits from employment; pensions; profit from unincorporated businesses; and lettings carried out as a business. Unearned income is in effect all other income including, in particular, investment and savings income. The distinction is important for two reasons; first, earned income is the relevant income for limiting allowable pension contributions and for benefits; secondly earned income is normally reduced by charges against income and allowances before unearned income.

1.5 Calculating the tax payable

1.5.1 - The personal allowance is deducted from income for the purpose of calculating the basic tax charge to which the successive bands of tax rates applies.

1.5.2 Paying the tax

Some of the total tax liability may have been paid at source. Thus interest received will normally be subject to deduction of income tax at 20%. Tax under PAYE will be deducted from remuneration; some tax, such as on self-employed business profits, untaxed interest and higher rate tax will be paid by self assessment on the individual. The individual's computation must also take into account tax deducted from certain payments made by the taxpayer (e.g. charges on income) and all pension contributions.

1.5.3 Tax on dividends

In the case of dividends, i.e. shares of profit received from limited companies, the situation is similar to that of taxed interest; the lower rate is said to be 'imputed' to the dividend.

The tax credit on dividends is 10% but *cannot* be reclaimed if the individual's total tax liability is less than the tax imputed. The 10% tax credit satisfies the tax liability at the starting and basic rates. Higher rate taxpayers have an effective rate of 32.5%, (this rose to 42.5% from 6 April 2010 for those effected by the 50% additional tax rate).

1.6 Illustration

2011/2012 - A taxpayer had the following income and allowances:

	£	£
Earned income		
Remuneration from employment	29,475	
Less: personal allowance	7,475	
Net remuneration		22,000
Profit from self-employment		16,000

	£	£
		38,000
Unearned income		
Bank interest net	4,000	
Add: tax deducted	1,000	
		5,000
Dividends net	1,800	
Add: tax credit	200	
		2,000
Chargeable income		£45,000

The payment will be made as follows:

Employment (subject to the PAYE coding)	4,400
Self employment	3,800
	8,200

Higher rate		
On bank interest 40% - 20% = 20% on £5,000	1,000	
On dividends 32.5% - 10% = 22.5% on £2,000	450	
		1,450
		9,650

Tax will be payable as follows:		
On remuneration:		
£0 at 10% *	0	
£22,000 at 20%	4,400	
		4,400
On self-employment:		
£13,000 at 20%	2,600	
£3,000 at 40%	1,200	
		3,800
£16,000		
On bank interest:		
£5,000 at 40%		2,000
On dividends:		
£2,000 at 32.5%		650

	£	£
Total tax liability		10,850
Less: suffered by deduction and tax credits:		
on interest	1,000	
on dividends	200	
	_____	(1,200)
		9,650

* The 10% savings income band is not applicable because taxable earnings / self-employment exceeds £2,560 (maximum of band).

SUMMARY: TOTAL TAX PAYABLE

£0	at 10%	N/A
£35,000	at 20%	7,000
£2,000	at 32.5%	650
£8,000	at 40%	3,200
£45,000		10,850

NB   Please note that, for income tax purposes, dividends are always treated as the top slice of the individual's income.

1.7 The 10% Savings Income Band - £2,560

Prior to 6 April 2008 there was a general band - the starting rate at 10%. This was available to all payers of income tax.

From 6 April 2008, this band was removed for most income taxpayers, but the basic rate was also reduced to 20% (from 22%).

Income Taxes Act (ITA 2007) sets out a strict order in which sources of income will be charged to income tax as follows:

- Firstly, non savings income including earnings, pensions, taxable social security benefits, trading profits and property income, then
- Savings income - including band and building society interest, and lastly
- Dividends.

Accordingly if there is any earned income above the personal allowance level this will eat into the 10% savings band of £2,560. If it exceeds the £2,560 no savings income will be taxed at 10% - probably leading to no refund of tax deducted at source.

Savings rate example #1 2011/2012

Terry - retired teacher aged 60

Income	Total £	Non-savings £	Savings £	Dividends £
Earnings / pension		8,035		
Building Society interest			1,000	
Dividend				100
Statutory total income	9,135	8,035	1,000	100
Less: personal Allowance	7,475			
Taxable Income	£1,660			
Tax Payable				
Non-savings	£560 @ 20%	112		
Savings	£1,000 @ 10%	100		
Dividends	£100 @ 10%	10		
Total	£1,660	£222		

Notes
1. All figures are gross.
2. Tax of £200 will have been deducted at source on the Building Society Interest.
3. Terry will receive a refund of £100 (Building society interest taxed at source @ 20% less 10% due).
4. Tax deducted on Dividends is never repaid.

Savings rate example #2 2011/2012

Terry - retired teacher aged 60

Income	Total £	Non-savings £	Savings £	Dividends £
Earnings / pension		9,035		
Building Society interest			1,200	
Dividend				100
Statutory total income	10,335	9,035	1,200	100
Less: personal Allowance	7,475			
Taxable Income	£2,860			
Tax Payable				
Non-savings	£1,560 @ 20%	312		
Savings	£1,000 @ 10%	100		
Savings	£200 @ 20%	40		
Dividends	£100 @ 10%	10		
Total	£2,860	£462		

Notes
1.   All figures are gross.
2.   Tax of £240 will have been deducted at source on the Building Society Interest.
3.   Terry will only receive a refund of £100 (Building society interest taxed at source @ 20% less 10% due (£240 - £100 - £40 = £100).
4.   Tax deducted on Dividends is never repaid.

Savings rate example #3 2011/2012

Terry - retired teacher aged 60

Income	Total £	Non-savings £	Savings £	Dividends £
Earnings / pension		10,035		
Building Society interest			1,000	
Dividend				100
Statutory total income	11,135	10,035	1,000	100
Less: personal Allowance	7,475			
Taxable Income	£3,660			
Tax Payable				
Non-savings	£2,560 @ 20%	512		
Savings	£0 @ 10%	0		
Savings	£1,000 @ 20%	200		
Dividends	£100 @ 10%	10		
Total	£3,660	£722		

Notes
1. All figures are gross.
2. Tax of £200 will have been deducted at source on the Building Society Interest.
3. Terry will not receive a refund as all the starting rate band for savings income of £2,560 has been utilised.
4. Tax deducted on Dividends is never repaid.

1.8 50% rate of income tax
From 6 April 2010, there are three main rates of income tax, 20% (Basic rate), 40% (Higher rate) and 50% (Additional rate). The 50% rate was introduced for individuals with taxable income over £150,000. Dividend income in excess of this limit is taxed at 42.5%.

Trust income
The majority of trusts pay tax at a special rate applicable to trusts whenever income

exceeds £1,000. Income received by trusts is taxed at 50%. Dividends are taxed at 42.5%.

2 CHARGES AND OTHER DEDUCTIONS

2.1 General

Strictly charges reduce a taxpayer's total income and are applied before tax reliefs and allowances. Charges against income include allowable; Personal Pension Contributions, additional voluntary contributions (AVC), and charitable gifts. Many qualifications apply to this list which is examined below.

2.2 Deduction of tax at source

(a) *Where tax is deductible.* In most cases the payer of an annual charge is bound to deduct tax at the basic rate, from the payment, but there are a number of exceptions. Deduction at source applies, for example, normally to payments of interest on government securities and company debentures; and, in effect, to dividends. The payer then accounts to HMRC for the tax deducted from the payment, and the recipient of the interest suffers tax by deduction. The recipient may also be liable for higher rate tax on their total income. If the recipient is not liable for tax at all, they will be entitled to a refund of all of the tax suffered by deduction (except dividends).

Tax is deductible by the payer of an annual payment, which is one intended to continue from year to year. Tax is also deductible by the payer from gifts to charities.

The payer is liable to tax, at the appropriate rates on their chargeable income after deducting the gross amount of the charge as well as applicable reliefs and allowances. As tax has been retained by the payer by deduction from the payment, that amount of tax must be paid to HMRC, or accounted for as a credit in calculating the final tax liability of the payer.

(b) *Example.* For 2011/2012 a taxpayer's chargeable non-savings income was £11,000 after allowances and has then incurred £1,000 in allowable charges, reducing the chargeable income to £10,000. Tax at 20%, i.e. £200 was deducted from the charges so that the actual payment by the taxpayer was £800. The amount of tax due (some or all of which may have been paid by deduction, e.g. under PAYE) would be:

	£
Chargeable income	10,000
Tax payable:	
£10,000 @ 20%	2,000
Total tax payable on income	
Add: tax retained by deduction from payment	
20% on £1,000	200
Tax due	£2,200
Or, alternatively calculated:	
Income after allowances but before charges	£11,000
tax payable thereon:	
£11,000 @ 20%	£2,200

Of the amount of £2,200 payable to HMRC, the taxpayer has recovered £200 by deduction from the charges, giving a net outgoing of tax of £2,000.

(c)   *Where tax is not deductible.* A different situation arises where an allowable charge reduces the taxpayer's chargeable income but no tax is deducted from the payment. An example is the employee's contribution under an occupational pension scheme established by the employer. in such a case the employee receives the tax benefit through the reduction of his chargeable income.

2.3 Annual Payments

To be allowable charges on income, annual payments must be paid out of profits not capital. To satisfy this rule it is sufficient to demonstrate that there were sufficient taxable profits to make the payments (*CIR v Plummer 1968*). If an annual payment is made out of capital and tax is deducted the payer must account to HMRC for the tax so deducted. Where a company guarantees the dividends of another, and is called upon to implement the guarantee, the payment is an annual payment, provided it is not also a distribution (*Moss Empires v CIR 1937*). The following is not a deduction for computing taxable income: an annual payment (a 'reverse annuity') chargeable on the recipient for a non taxable consideration.

2.4 Maintenance payments

Along with the abolition of married couples allowance (from 6 April 2000), tax relief on most maintenance payments was also abolished.

But tax relief for maintenance payments is retained where one or both of the parties to the marriage is aged 65 or over at 5 April 2000.

2.5 Donations to Charities
2.5.1 Single donations ('gift aid') - individuals

Individuals may obtain tax relief on gifts to approved charities. There is no minimum donation. Basic rate income tax is deemed to have been deducted by the payer and can be reclaimed by the charity. An individual donor is able to deduct the gross payment from his or her taxable income and may thus reduce any higher rate payable, but, of course, must account in his or her tax computation for the basic rate recovered by deduction. Where the donor has paid insufficient Income Tax, or Capital Gains Tax (in total) to cover the donation, i.e. where it is paid out of capital, the donor will be assessed on the tax deducted from the donation. A donating (non close) company obtains relief at the corporation tax rate.

Example:

There are three individuals who donate £900 to the same charity in 2011/2012. A pays tax at the savings rate (10%), B at the basic rate (20%), C at the higher rate (40%) and D at the additional (50%) rate.

A.	Grossing up of donation £900 x 100/90 =	£1,000.00
	Tax deemed deducted at 10% by A =	£100.00
*	Tax reclaimed by charity at 20% £900 x 20/80 =	£225.00
	Tax liability on A to make up short fall =	£125.00
	(In theory this will only be collected if the taxpayer has	
	not suffered £125 tax in total on any of his income.	
	This includes tax deducted on interest and imputed	
	tax on dividends)	
B.	Grossing up of donation £900 x 100/80 =	£1,125.00
	Tax deemed deducted at 20% by B =	£225.00
*	Tax reclaimed by charity £900 x 20/80 =	£225.00
	Further liability on B.	NIL
C.	As in B above, but C is entitled to reclaim	
	an additional 20% of the gross donation	
	(40% - 20%)	
	= £1,125 x 20% =	£225.00

| D. | As in B above, but D is entitled to reclaim an additional 30% of gross donation (50% - 20%) = £1,125 x 30% = | £337.50 |

Note: The reduction in basic rate from 22% to 20% in 2008/2009 would effect Charities income. Previously, a donation of £100 was worth just over £128 to the charity. This reduces to £125 on the reduction to 20%.

However charities benefited from a transitional relief for the tax years 2008/2009 - 2010/2011, following the reduction in the basic rate of income tax. The relief gave them a supplementary payment of 2% in addition to the 20% basic rate tax refunded on qualifying donations.

2.5.2 Payroll deductions
Employees can arrange with their employers to donate to charities through payroll deductions (TA 1988 s 202). The taxation effects are the same as those set out in the previous paragraph.

Employees nominate the charity to which the gifts are payable. The employer's costs in operating the scheme are deductible from profits for tax purposes, but the most effective way of obtaining this relief is to arrange for a charitable agency to distribute the gifts, and to pay that agency's chargeable costs - i.e. CAF (Charities Aid Foundation).

2.5.3 Donations by companies
The taxation rules for gift aid, as set out in paragraph 2.5.1 above do not apply to companies and other bodies subject to corporation tax. The company deducts the donation from its taxable profits and in this way is relieved from corporation tax on the gross donation. No deemed deduction of tax is assessed or imputed. It does not therefore pay over any deemed tax to HMRC and the charity cannot reclaim any tax on donations from companies.

2.5.4 Gifts of shares and securities etc.
Relief is available where a person disposes of listed shares and securities, unit trust units, AIM shares etc. to a charity by way of gift or sale at under value. The amount deductible from total income is the market value of the shares etc. on the date of disposal plus incidental disposal costs less any consideration or value of benefits received by the donor or a connected person.

2.5.5 Gift of real property
The measure provides an income or corporation tax relief for individuals or companies who give land or buildings to a charity. The relief is available for gifts of

freehold or leasehold property, which a charity agrees to accept.

2.5.6 Giving to charity via the SA tax return

Taxpayers, due a tax refund can nominate a charity to receive all or some of it direct by completing the special "Giving your tax repayment to charity" page on the self-assessment return. If the taxpayer pays tax at the higher 40% rate the charity will receive the donation grossed up to and including the 40%. Because the individuals tax repayment is donated after his tax return has been submitted, it is not possible to make a carry-back election under S98 FA 2002. (See below).

2.5.7 Roll back of Gift Aid cash donations to prior year

A qualifying donation can be treated as paid in the previous tax year. An election has to be made by the donor in writing on or <u>before</u> filing the tax return for the previous tax year, and in any event not later than the normal filing deadline for that return of 31 January.

The election does not affect the position of the donee. The donor claims any higher rate tax relief by reference to his income and gains position of that earlier tax year.

Example:
Alan pays tax @ 40% in 2010/2011 but not in 2011/2012. He makes a gift aid donation on 1 May 2011 and can therefore relate it back to 2010/2011. The 2010/2011 return is filed on 1 September 2011 so the election has to be made by that date.

In the case of *Cameron v HMRC.* John Cameron, a farmer, received a substantial sum of money on the sale of his farming assets in 2005/2006. Following the sale, he set up a charitable trust to enable young people to see the world and donated some of the proceeds of the sale to the trust.

Mr Cameron and his advisers calculated the gain on the disposal and submitted the computation with Mr Cameron's tax return for 2005/2006 at the end of August 2006. In January 2007, Mr Cameron made a payment of £936,000 to the charitable trust. Mr Cameron's advisers told him that he could elect for his donation to be treated as made in 2005/2006 and reduce the tax due on the large chargeable gain in that year.

On 29 January 2007, Mr Cameron's advisers submitted an amended 2005/2006 tax return which included an election to carry back the Gift Aid payment made in January 2007 to 2005/2006. HMRC refused to give tax relief in 2005/2006: it argued that an election to treat the Gift Aid payment as having been made in 2005/2006 should have been made on or before the date on which Mr Cameron delivered his tax return and couldn't be made at a later date.

The case was heard by a tax tribunal. Mr Cameron argued that the date on which he delivered his return was the date on which he delivered his amended return and that the election was valid because the amended return was submitted on 29 January 2007 (before the normal self-assessment filing date of 31 January).

The judge found that the date on which Mr Cameron delivered his return could only mean the date of submission of the original return, and not the date of the amended return.

Mr Cameron therefore lost his case and obtained no relief for the Gift Aid payment against his tax bill in 2005/2006.

So what did Mr Cameron do wrong? In essence, he was too efficient in submitting his tax return. He could simply have waited until the Gift Aid payment had been made and then submitted his tax return. The election to carry back the payment of £936,000 would then have been made on his original return for 2005/2006 and HMRC wouldn't have been able to refuse to give tax relief in 2005/2006. Mr Cameron was penalised for submitting his tax return early.

2.5.8 Anti-avoidance provisions

(a) Restrictions apply to the relief from tax obtained by a charity with taxable income (i.e. non-charitable income) exceeding the greater of £5,000 and the lesser of £50,000 and 25 per cent of the charity's income from all sources in a year, including capital gains. The restrictions also apply where funds are used for non-charitable purposes, such as the application of donations for the benefit of the donors, or to an overseas body which will not use the money for charitable purposes (TA 1988 ss 506-507).

(b) Gift Aid cannot be claimed on admission fees. However, if they grant free admission in return for a donation, Gift Aid may be applicable. From 6 April 2006 charities that open to the public for an admission fee may claim Gift Aid if either of the following circumstances apply:

The visitor makes a donation that is at least 10 per cent more than the admission charge for the equivalent right of admission.

or

The donation secures admission rights to the property for a twelve month period whenever the property is open to the public in that period, for example through a season ticket or a membership scheme. Charities may exclude from the right of admission up to 5 days in each 12-month period when the property is otherwise open to the public and still qualify.

2.5.9 Finance Act 2007 Changes (Clause 59)

(a) Chapter 2 part 8 ITA 2007 allows donations by individuals to qualify for Gift Aid tax relief where the value of any benefit that may be received by the donor as a consequence of making the donation does not exceed the proportional limits set out below, subject to an overriding limit of £250.

(b)   Under s418 ITA 2007, the pre FA2007 limits on the value of benefits received relative to donations were:

- 25% of the value of the donation, where the donation is less than £100;

- £25, where the value of the donation is between £100 and £1,000; and

- 2.5% of the value of the donation, where the donation exceeds £1,000.

(c)   For donations of more than £1,000, the limit on the value of benefits received is increased from 2.5% to 5% of the donation. The overriding limit on the value of benefits received by a donor in a tax year as a consequence of donations to a charity will be increased from £250 to £500.

(d)   These new limits came into effect for benefits received as a consequence of donations made on or after 6.04.07.

2.6 Covenants
Separate tax relief abolished from 6 April 2000
See 2.5.1 Single donations ('gift aid') - individuals
A covenant was a 'settlement' in the form of a deed whereby one person undertook to pay an annual or more frequent amount to another person or association.

2.7 Interest payable - general
2.7.1 Allowable loans
In general the only loans on which the interest is allowable for tax purposes are the following:

(a)   For business purposes.

(b)   To acquire shares in an employee controlled company.

(c)   To purchase shares in a partnership or to contribute capital to a partnership or to buy plant for a partnership of which the lender is a partner (TA 1988 ss 359 and 362). The Inspector's Manual at IM 3834 states "It should not normally be contended that a reduction in the credit balance on the current or drawings account amounts to a constructive repayment of capital, even though the account moves temporarily into debit". It is understood that 'temporarily' means made good before the next accounting date. This applies to situations where the partnership balance sheet distinguishes between partners' capital and current accounts.

(d)   To pay inheritance tax or capital transfer tax (TA 1988 s 364).

(e)   To purchase shares in a co-operative by an employee (TA 1988 s 361).

(f)   To purchase an annuity by a person over 65 years of age, where the loan does not exceed £30,000 and is secured on the borrower's principal private residence (TA 1988 s 365). The relief is at the basic rate of 22% and continues if the borrower cannot sell the home after moving out of it.

(g)   To purchase one property but secured upon another.

2.7.2 Deduction of tax

Tax is not deducted from interest payments except for the following loans:

(a)   Annual interest payable to a payee residing outside the UK. The deduction is at the basic rate. HMRC may, however, agree that the interest may be paid gross under a double taxation agreement.

(b)   Loans subject to annual interest payable by companies and local authorities and by partnerships of which a company is a member.

2.8 Mortgage interest (TA1988 ss 369-379)
2.8.1 In general

Tax relief was available up to 5 April 2000 and abolished thereafter except for the following exception:

Individuals over 65 years of age taking out a loan secured on their homes in order to buy a life annuity obtain tax relief at 20% unaffected by the reductions in para. (i). FA 1994 s 81.

There is a cut off date of 9 March 1999. All loans made or offered in writing before this date (budget day) retain the relief for the remaining period of the loan.

2.8.2 Beneficial interest

The benefit of loans at low rates of interest, or interest free, made by employers to their directors or employees is assessable on the latter. The benefit is the difference between an official, e.g., commercial rate (average rate of interest for 2010/2011 is 4%) and the interest actually charged, if any. The employees concerned are those earning over £8,500 a year but the rules apply to all directors.

3 RELIEFS AND ALLOWANCES

3.0 Personal allowances for non residents

Individuals who are not resident in the UK generally have no entitlement to claim personal allowances or reliefs. However, there are a number of conditions, either set out in the Taxes Acts or under Double Taxation Agreements (DTA), which allow people who are not resident and who are subject to UK income tax to claim personal allowances and reliefs.

Previously, there was an entitlement for some individuals to claim purely by virtue of being a Commonwealth citizen but by meeting no other condition. From 2010/2011, non resident Commonwealth citizens no longer qualify for personal allowances, married couple's allowance, blind person's allowance and relief for life assurance premiums by reference to their Commonwealth citizenship status alone. They may, of course, continue to qualify under the other conditions or through DTA provisions if appropriate.

3.1 From 2010/2011 withdrawal of personal allowance for adjusted net income in excess of £100,000

At an "adjusted net income" of £100,000 the personal allowance is reduced by £1 for every £2 of income until the allowance is removed completely, in 2011/2012 this would be £114,950 (£100,000+ 2 x £7,475). The adjusted net income is calculated in the same way as for the abatement of the age allowance, by deducting losses from gross income and deducting the grossed up pension premiums and gift aid payments. Pension contributions made gross are also deducted. The marginal rate of tax in this band is 60% (£100,000 to £114,950).

Therefore this makes the payment of pension contributions particularly tax efficient as follows:

	£	£
Gross income		105,000
Personal allowance		
Maximum amount	7,475	
Abatement		
((105,000 - 100,000) x 1/2)	(2,500)	4,975
Net taxable income		100,025

	£
Tax at basic rate	7,000
Tax at higher rate	26,010
Total tax liability	£33,010
Gross income	105,000
Less pension contribution	(5,000)
Net adjusted income	100,000
Personal allowance	7,475
Net taxable income	92,525
Tax at basic rate	7,000
Tax at higher rate	23,010
Total tax liability	£30,010
Tax saved by pension contribution	£3,000

3.2 The personal allowance

This allowance applies to every taxpayer, of either sex and whether married or not, and the amount depends on age, as shown next:

	2011/2012	2010/2011	2009/2010
	£	£	£
age below 65 years	7,475	6,475	6,475
* age 65-74 years	9,940	9,490	9,490
* age 75 & Over	10,090	9,640	9,640
* Income limits	24,000	22,900	22,900

The income limits apply to persons over 65 years of age and have the effect of reducing the applicable personal allowance by half of the excess of income over these limits until it reaches the basic allowance for a person aged under 65. Thus if in 2011/2012 the total income of a person aged 70 was £24,700, the personal allowance for that person becomes: £9,990 minus 1/2 (24,700 - 24,000) = £9,590.

The income restriction <u>cannot</u> decrease the age allowance to below that for the under 65s. For 2011/2012 the limit for persons aged 65-74 remains unchanged at £28,930 and 75 + £29,230.

3.3 The married couple's & civil partner allowance
Only for couples where either party was born before 6 April 1935.

3.3.1 General
This allowance is available primarily to the husband / higher earner who are living together.

In the year of marriage / civil partnership the allowance is reduced by one twelfth for each complete tax month in the tax year before the ceremony.

3.3.2 The allowance
- where one partner was born before 6 April 1935 (from 2010/2011 this partner will be 75 or over)

The allowance is as follows:

	2011/2012 £	2010/2011 £	2009/2010 £
persons aged 65-74	N/A	N/A	6,865
persons aged 75 & over	7,295	6,965	6,965
Income limits	24,000	22,900	22,900

The above income limits for persons aged 65 and over operate in exactly the same way as for the personal allowances.

This allowance is reduced by £1 for every £2 by which the taxpayer's income exceeds £24,000 (2010/2011 £22,900), until the basic personal allowance (with minimum married couple's allowance, if married of £2,800 (£2,670 2010/2011)) is reached.

For example, a man aged 70 has a wife aged 76. His income is £25,600. His basic allowance is £9,940 plus £7,295 higher married couple's allowance. This equals £17,235. However, because his income of £25,600 is more than £24,000, half the £1,600 excess is deducted. So the allowance is reduced by £800 to £16,435.

The income restrictions cannot decrease the age allowance to below that for the under 65s, the income limits for couples where one is 75+ £38,220. (From 2010/2011 couples aged 65 - 74 do not qualify for married couples allowance).

3.3.3 Transfer of the allowance
An election can be made to transfer to the other partner the proportion of the

allowance which could not be set off, i.e. the chargeable income was reduced to nil by the proportion of the allowance retained. Such an election would reduce the combined tax payable by the two parties only where the second partner's income was sufficient to absorb the allowance transferred.

3.4 Blind person's relief
This allowance applies to all registered blind persons, including each of a married couple who are both blind. The allowance can be transferred to a partner, even though he or she is not blind, if the blind spouse's income is insufficient to use the allowance. The allowance is reduced by any tax free disability pensions provided for the claimant. From 6 April 2011, the relief is £1,980 (previously £1,890).

3.5 Life assurance relief
Relief now only applies to premiums on policies taken out before 14th March 1984, and normally takes the form of the payer deducting tax from the premiums at the applicable rate (see next). Relief is cancelled where benefits or the term of pre 14.3.84 policies are extended. Relief for post 13.3.84 policies continues to apply, to payments to friendly societies for tax-exempt life or endowment policies.

3.5.1 Personal pension term assurance
Clause 67 of FA2007 made changes to deny individuals tax relief for their contributions to fund pension-related personal term assurance. The change does not affect relief for contributions paid by employers.

The change affects all contributions made after 31 July 2007 under occupational registered pension schemes, unless the insurer received the application for the policy before 29 March 2007 and the policy was taken out as part of the pension scheme before 1 August 2007.

3.6 Health Insurance
Taxpayers are entitled to relief of income tax on benefits paid under permanent health insurance policies which provide replacement income where taxpayers suffer loss of earnings due to ill health or disability. The following rules apply: (HMRC LEAFLET - IR 153 - 24.2.97)

(a)   The income received under the policy is exempt from tax (from 6.4.96.) from the date of first entitlement to the benefits for 12 months.

(b)   A lump sum payable as capital under a policy is not regarded as taxable.

(c)   Income received under the policies is taxable if the premiums are paid for by the employer.

(d)   The income is taxable if the premiums are wholly or partly for pensions.

(e)   The provisions apply to qualifying policies taken out by the self-employed and
        the income payable is not chargeable to income tax or corporation tax in the
        business assessment. Insurers do not deduct tax when paying the benefits.

3.7 Superannuation payments -
Please see previous edition for full details

3.8 Pension Contributions - New Rules from 6 April 2011
3.8.1 Pension tax relief
- Tax relief on personal contributions to registered pension schemes continue to
  be available at the individual's highest marginal income tax rate.

- There is no change to the way tax relief is provided on contributions.

- An individual can still contribute 100% of their earnings but only up to the much
  reduced annual allowance.

- If earnings are less than £3,600 individuals can still contribute £3,600 gross of
  tax relief (£2,880 net).

3.8.2 Annual Allowance
- From 2011/2012 reduced to £50,000 (2010/2011, £255,000).

- Fixed until 2015/2016, and may rise by CPI inflation thereafter.

- Where annual contributions exceed £50,000, the excess can be offset against
  any unused allowance carried forward from the previous 3 tax years. There is
  however an assumed maximum annual allowance of £50,000 for each of
  these years.

Accordingly if there had been contributions of £40,000 in the previous tax year there
is £10,000 that can be carried forward. But if there had been £70,000 of
contributions in the previous tax year, there is no unused allowance, when compared
to the new £50,000 limit that can be carried forward. The £255,000 limit is not used
for the carry forward calculation.

- The proposals were announced on 14 October 2010. Provision, for 2011/2012,
  made before this date, even exceeding £50,000 will still be valid. However
  provision made after 14 October 2010 may be caught by anti-avoidance rules.

- The anti-avoidance rules only apply to pension arrangements that:

    - started their 'pension input period' (P.I.P.) before 14 October 2010; and
    - where the 'pension input period' ends in the 2011/2012 tax year; and
    - where pension savings in the total 'pension input period' (i.e. both pre

and post 14 October 2010) exceed £50,000.

Example 1
Alan's marginal tax rate is 50%. His company contributes £20,000 a month into his personal pension, which is paid on the first day of each month. He has no unused allowances to bring forward.

The initial contribution was made on 1 May 2006. The scheme's PIP is 1 May to 30 April; his current PIP began on 1 May 2010 and will finish on 30 April 2011.

If Alan's company continues paying in £20,000 a month, it will make contributions of £120,000 after 13 October 2010 (1 November to 1 April inclusive). This is £70,000 above the £50,000 limit.

Although the overall contribution is below £255,000, he will be taxed at 50% on the excess of £70,000 contributed by his employer after 13 October. This will cost him £35,000.

Tax Years
A pension contribution is deductible from earnings in the tax year of payment (s 188, FA 2004). This hasn't changed. But the interaction with transitional rules can cause some unexpected results, see Examples 2 and 3.

Example 2
Susan's PIP ends on 30 April 2011, in the 2011/2012 tax year. She pays £80,000 into her PIP on 1 December 2010. This is £30,000 more than the maximum allowed under the transitional rules. She has no unused allowances to bring forward.

- In her 2010/2011 tax return she deducts the full £80,000, as she paid it in that tax year.
- In her 2011/2012 tax return she adds the £30,000 excess contribution. Using the 2010/2011 return as a model, this will be entered at Box 9 of the Additional Information Pages.

There is thus a mismatch between the tax relief and the charge on the excess contribution.

Example 3
Simone's PIP ends on 30 September 2011. She pays £5,000 a month into her pension on the first day of each month.

In the pre-announcement period she has paid £5,000 (1 October 2010). In the post-announcement period, but before 6 April 2011, she will pay £30,000 (1 November 2010 to 1 April 2011 inclusive). From 6 April to 30 September 2011 she will pay £25,000.

The £5,000 paid in the pre-announcement period is allowable in full, as it is below £255,000 (old rules).

In the past-announcement period she has paid £55,000 (£30,000 + £25,000), compared to a limit of £50,000, so she will receive no relief on the excess £5,000.

- In the tax year 2010/2011 she claims tax relief on all payments made in that tax year - £35,000.

- In the tax year 2011/2012 she claims further tax relief on the £25,000 paid in that tax year and includes an excess contribution of £5,000 on the Additional Information pages.

Although it would seem logical for her only to claim tax relief on the net £20,000 in her 2011/2012 tax return, both figures need to be entered.

Legislation prevents a double charge where there is an annual allowance and an anti-forestalling charge in the same tax year (para 9, Sch 35, FA 2009). The problem is that the anti-forestalling charge applies for the last time in 2010/2011 and the special annual allowance (using the new £50,000 threshold) begins in 2011/2012. So the relief in FA 2009 doesn't apply.

Example 4
George earns £300,000 in the tax year ended 5 April 2011. His current PIP ends on 30 June 2011, in the 2011/2012 tax year.

On 1 January he pays £120,000 into his personal pension. He has made a similar payment every year for the last four years.

George is allowed £30,000 of his contribution as a 'special annual allowance' (paras 1 and 17, Sch 35, FA 2009). The balance is subject to a special annual allowance charge under the anti-forestalling legislation, so he is only entitled to relief at 20%. This triggers a tax charge of £27,000 (£90,000 x 30%).

However, he has also exceeded the £50,000 cap on contributions for PIPs ending in 2011/2012, by £70,000. This is taxed at his marginal rate of 50%, so there is a further charge of £35,000.

The total tax on George's £120,000 contribution is £62,000, a rate of 51.67%.

3.8.3 Exemptions
- Fewer exemptions are now allowed from the annual allowance.

- Exemptions will continue to apply in year of death, & retirement due to serious ill health (life expectancy to be less than 12 months).

- Exemption from the annual allowance rules in normal year of retirement is removed.

3.8.4 Valuation of Defined Benefit Rights
- The fixed factor for valuing defined benefit accrual to test against the annual allowance was increased to 16:1 (from 10:1) from 14 October 2010.

- The "opening value" of the individual's defined benefits rights is revalued (CPI) for the purposes of the annual allowance test.

- There is no annual allowance test for preserved benefits so long as they increase by no more than CPI or if greater in line with the scheme rules.

3.8.5 Annual Allowance Tax Charge
- The previous flat 40% tax charge has been replaced by a variable tax charge of up to 50% designed to effectively cancel-out ant tax relief on excess provision above the annual allowance.

- To determine if a tax charge is payable, contributions for defined contribution schemes and increases in annual pension for defined benefit schemes over the "pension input period" ending in a tax year is compared against the annual allowance that same year. For example, if the "pension input period" starts in 2009/2010 tax year but ends in 2010/2011 tax year the individual's savings are compared against the annual allowance for the 2010/2011 tax year. For the transitional years of 2010/2011 & 2011/2012 see the anti-avoidance rules under 3.8.2. above.

- This follows similar principles of the previous special allowance tax charge for 2010/2011. It adds the value of any excess provision to an individual's reduced net income for tax purposes.

- Individuals with annual allowance charge above £2,000 are able to elect for the full liability to be met from their pension benefit.

3.8.6 Lifetime Allowance
- From 6 April 2012 the lifetime allowance is reduced to £1.5M (from the previous £1.8M). This limit is to be frozen.

3.9 Pensions reform
3.9.1 The regime
<u>(a) Lifetime allowance</u>
There is a maximum lifetime allowance of pension savings.

The following table gives recent and proposed changes:

Year Beginning	Allowance £	Annual Contribution Limit £
6 April 2006	1,500,000	215,000
6 April 2007	1,600,000	225,000
6 April 2008	1,650,000	235,000
6 April 2009	1,750,000	245,000
6 April 2010	1,800,000	255,000
6 April 2011	1,800,000	50,000
6 April 2012	1,500,000	50,000

The maximum fund applies to 22,719 people as the HMRC were quoted in the Sunday Times (17.05.09).

(b) Recovery charge
If the pension fund exceeds the allowance, there is a recovery charge of 25% of the excess when the money is withdrawn. However if the fund already exceeded the £1,500,000 on 6 April 2006, it can only grow at RPI thereafter.

Excess	£10,000
Recovery charge @ 25%	£2,500
Add: Tax on residual £7,500 (40% x £7,500)	£3,000
Effective tax 55% on excess for higher rate taxpayer	£5,500

(c) Lump sum
All funds can pay a tax free lump sum of 25% of the accumulated fund.

The maximum tax free allowance in 2011/2012 is 25% of £1,800,000 which equates to £450,000.

(d) Retirement age
The minimum age for taking benefits rose from 50 to 55 on 6 April 2010. Existing rights to retire earlier are protected as are the special schemes for different professions e.g. footballers. See Table 17. Pension Contributions & Retirement - Pension Contributions & Limits, p.643.

<u>(e) Retirement not obligatory</u>
You do not have to retire to take an employment pension.

<u>f) Annuity by age 75?</u>
The obligation to buy an annuity using your pension fund by the time you reach the age of 75 is removed.

3.10 Obligations under the Pensions Act 2008
The Act comes into force on 1 October 2012 and all employers will have a duty to enrol eligible workers into a qualifying scheme. Auto-enrolment will be phased in over 4 years, with the largest employers (based on PAYE size) starting first. The smallest firms will not have to implement a scheme until possibly as late as 2016.

Employees will qualify if they are (a) aged between 22 and state pension age and (b) earning above the income tax personal allowance (£7,475 in 2011/2012). Contributions are payable (by both parties) on 'qualifying earnings' i.e. those above the National Insurance contribution threshold (2011/2012 £7,228) and below £33,540.

Two types of scheme will be offered: either a defined contribution scheme (including stakeholder schemes) or NEST (National Employment Savings Trust).

The Government has set up NEST as a straightforward and relatively low-cost scheme. Although not finalised yet, the charges are expected to be 2% on each contribution to cover the start-up costs and an annual management charge of 0.3% of the value of the fund.

Currently transfers in and out of NEST will not be permitted but this will be reviewed in 2017.

There will be an annual contribution limit of £3,600, as with other defined contribution schemes.

When a worker is automatically enrolled into a defined contribution scheme or NEST, there will be a minimum contribution of 8% of qualifying earnings. The employer must pay a minimum of 3% and the employee 4% with a further 1% claimed as tax relief from the Government.

The minimum contribution levels will be phased in between 2012 and 2017 as follows:

* October 2012 to September 2016 - total minimum contribution of 2% with a least 1% from the employer
* October 2016 to September 2017 - total minimum contribution of 5% with at

least 2% from the employer
- October 2017 onwards - minimum 8% contribution as set out above.

Auto-enrolment
Employees will automatically be enrolled in their employer's qualifying pension scheme without any active decision making on their part.

Employees will be automatically enrolled into the default fund (as yet unnamed) but indications are that there will be a choice of funds available. Any worker who joins NEST will be able to continue to contribute even if they leave the workplace or move to an employer who does not use NEST.

Employees will be able to opt out. Those who give notice during the opt-out period will be refunded any contributions made following automatic enrolment and put back in the position they would have been in if they had not been enrolled. There will be a 3 month delay before employers will be required to automatically enrol new employees. So seasonal temporary staff and agency staff are unlikely to be included.

4 OFFICES AND EMPLOYMENTS:
formerly Schedule E - with effect from 6 April 2003

All aspects are covered by the Income Tax (Earnings and Pensions) Act 2003.

4.1 The scope ITEPA
4.1.1 General
ITEPA deals with wages, salaries and other income from offices or employments, pensions, social security benefits, etc. Pay as You Earn comes under its wing and is the method used to collect tax from wages and salaries. There are three types of employment income:

(a)   Persons resident and ordinarily resident in the UK: the total emoluments are assessable, subject to a deduction in respect of duties performed wholly or partly outside the UK.

(b)   Persons not resident, or if resident not ordinarily resident, in the UK, who perform some duties in the UK: all the emoluments for the UK duties are assessable, subject to a deduction for 'foreign emoluments'.

(c)   Persons resident in the UK whether ordinarily resident or not. The liability is on the income not falling within (a) and (b) and is assessable on: (i) the remittances in the tax year of emoluments of that or any previous year in which the taxpayer was a UK resident; and (ii) any remittances in an earlier year of emoluments of the tax year.

This section will confine itself to the UK income of UK residents. For foreign income and persons not resident in the UK See 4.8 Overseas employment, p.105.

The following duties are regarded as being performed in the UK (TA 1988 s 132):

- Crown employments of a public nature, where the emoluments are payable out of the public revenue of the UK or N. Ireland (*Graham v White* ChD 1971; *Caldicott v Varty* ChD 1976). In practice UK tax is not charged on locally engaged (as distinct from UK-based), unestablished staff working abroad who are not resident in the UK, if the maximum rate of pay for their grade is less than that of an executive officer in the UK service working in Inner London (ESC A27);

- Duties on UK coastal vessels, or by a UK resident on a vessel or aircraft which is in the UK for part of its journey.

Duties performed in the UK which are incidental to the employment which is substantially one in which the duties are performed abroad are treated as performed abroad.

4.1.2 Office or employment?
Whether an activity is an office or employment 'employment income' or 'trading income' is a matter of some importance. A distinction is drawn between a contract of service (an office) and a contract for services (an employment). On this distinction may depend the deductibility of expenses incurred or the taxability of sums received on cessation.

A charge to a company by a partnership for management services has been held on particular facts not to be director's remuneration (the partners being directors) (*Redditch Electro-Plating Co Ltd v Ferrebe* ChD 1973). Usually, director's fees taken into a professional partnership as part of the firm's profits are allowed to be assessed as trading income (ESC A40). A person who from time to time acted as an inspector at public enquiries was found to hold a series of appointments and the income assessable as trading income (*Edwards v Clinch* HL 1981).

Workers supplied by an agency, who are subject to supervision, direction or control as to the manner of working, are to be taxed under PAYE on all remuneration (including perquisites) received in consequence. Also excluded are sub-contractors and any worker rendering services wholly at home or at other premises which are neither under the control or management of the contractor nor premises at which the services (by reason of their nature) are required to be rendered (e.g. a window cleaner supplied by an agency would not be excluded but an artisan with his own workshop would be excluded).

For oil exploration, etc., divers or diving supervisors operating off-shore, i.e. within the designated area as designated by s 1(7) of the Continental Shelf Act 1964, are taxed under 'trading income' rules (TA 1988 s 135).

Vision mixing - The Court of Appeal held that a freelance vision mixer was self-employed, because he worked for a considerable number of people on short-term assignments.

In *Hall v Lorrimer* (1993) STI 1382, the taxpayer, a vision mixer, left full-time employment in 1985 and went freelance. He registered for VAT and had an office at his home. Between 1985 and 1989, the taxpayer worked on more than 800 short-term contracts, which each lasted one or two days. It was skilled work, requiring the taxpayer as vision mixer to select which of the television camera shots should be shown on television, subject only to guidance by the programme director.

The equipment used was very expensive and was provided by the studios in which he worked. If he was not available, he would provide a substitute with the studio's consent, but did not hire staff himself. He charged more than union rates, losing money only when a client became insolvent, but did not share in the production company's profit and loss. The taxpayer appealed against employment income assessments raised under 1984/85 to 1988/89 on the grounds that he was assessable under the trading income rules.

The Court of Appeal accepted the taxpayer's contention that he was not employed under a contract of employment in respect of each engagement. Although factors did indicate that each engagement was a contract of service, the overall nature of the taxpayer's activities indicated otherwise, and this outweighed the other factors.

Some more recent status cases include:
Weight Watchers v HMRC TC 367. Weight Watchers holds over 6,000 meetings a week around the country hosted by 'leaders', who are often local people. They provide advice and support, but also closely follow a set formula developed by Weight Watchers. These leaders are self-employed (i.e., no PAYE and national insurance contributions were being paid). HM Revenue & Customs, however, argued they were employees and sought £23m from Weight Watchers based on six years of back payments.

HMRC succeeded at the first-tier tribunal. The contractual arrangements around the holding of meetings were tightly controlled by Weight Watchers and what happened in meetings was very prescribed. The leader could not substitute someone else to do their role and the strength of the brand was maintained by processes that precluded the leader from having much flexibility in what they did. This high level of control meant the leaders were held to be employees.

Sherburn Aero Club Ltd. v HMRC Commissioners (TC6). The flying club engaged flying instructors to provide tuition to its members at its own premises using its own aircraft. The instructors notified the club as to when they were available to take lessons - though this could be changed at very short notice - and they were free to work elsewhere. They had, however, to follow a syllabus laid down by the Civil Aviation Authority (CAA) and were subject to the flying orders set out in the Flying Order Book.

The Club treated the instructors as self-employed, but HMRC issued tax determinations and NIC Notices of Decision that they were employees for 2005/2006 and 2006/2007.

The Club's contentions were broadly upheld in that it was found that there was no mutuality of obligations and that the control test for employment was not met.

4.1.3 Basis of assessment
Emoluments are treated as being received on the earlier occurrence of the following:

(a)   the time of the actual payment of, or on account of emoluments;

(b)   the time of the entitlement to payment of, or on account of emoluments.

In the case of a director of a company who receives emoluments from an office or employment with the company, the date of payment is the earliest occurrence of para.'s (a) or (b), or

(c)   the time when any sums on account of emoluments are credited in the company's accounts or records;

(d)   the end of a period of account where emoluments are determined before the end of that period; or

(e)   the time when the amount of emoluments for a period are determined where the determination is after the end of that period (TA 1988 s 202A; FA 1989 s 38).

Pensions and taxable social security benefits are, however, taxable on an accruals basis.

Benefits in kind are treated as being received when they are provided except where the Taxing Acts or case law set out a time in the case of specific benefits such as vouchers, living accommodation, cars, etc. (TA 1988 s 202A).

4.1.4 Assessable income

Income assessable includes all bonuses, commission, fees, perquisites and profits whatsoever, and it should be especially noted that where the employer pays the employee's share of national insurance or does not deduct PAYE tax from the employee's pay, these items form part of the employee's remuneration and must be taxed.

Generally if benefits are received by reason of the employment and are received in the form of money or money's worth they are assessable. Perquisites, such as free board, which cannot be turned into money, are not regarded as income. It is not always easy to decide what perquisite is an assessable benefit. Thus where an employee accepted a lower wage in return for the use of the employer's car, with an option to give up the car and revert to his former wage, it was held that the use of the car was a perquisite which could be converted into money as the sums payable for the use of the car were an agreed deduction from the gross wages (*Heaton v Bell* HL 1969). Gold sovereigns, given to an employee in discharge of a wages debt equal to their market value, were taxable on that value and not on their face value (*Jenkins v Horn* ChD 1979). If a cash salary is reduced by deducting the value of residence, etc., provided, then the gross salary is assessable. Similarly, an army lodging allowance is assessable though no part of the cost of the lodgings may be deducted as this is a private expense (*Nagley v Spilsbury* ChD 1957). By concession miners are not charged to tax on cash payments received in lieu of coal to which they are entitled under the terms of their employment (ESC No. A6 - now obsolete - enacted in Section 306 ITEPA 2003).

4.1.5 Value of benefits

The case of *Pepper v Hart* (HL 1993) decided that a marginal cost valuation be applied to the benefit obtained by teachers in obtaining places for their children at reduced fees in a private school. Marginal cost means the additional outgoings, not the average cost, incurred by the employer in providing the benefit. The important implications of this case are that the marginal cost principle should be applied in valuing all kinds of benefits received by employees.

A recipient of any gift worth more than £250, be it a crate of wine, theatre tickets, use of car must pay tax on the value of the gift at their marginal rate. This applies to corporate gifts from one company to the staff of another.

4.2 Benefits assessable - housing
4.2.1 Living accommodation

Living accommodation provided by reason of any employment is assessable on the employee except in the following cases (TA 1988 s 145):

(a)   where it is necessary for the proper performance of the employee's duties that he or she should reside in the accommodation (e.g. a caretaker or hostel warden);

(b)   where the accommodation is provided for the better performance of the duties of the employment and it is customary for the employment to involve such provision (e.g. a police officer or farm worker);

(c)   where it is provided because of a special security threat.

In such cases, rates paid or reimbursed by the employer are also not assessable.

If such accommodation is provided by a company and the employee concerned is a director of that or an associated company, the exemptions in para.'s (a) or (b) apply only if:

- he or she has no material interest in the company, and
- he or she is a full-time working director or the company is non-profit making or wholly charitable.

These two conditions must be satisfied for each employment with the company or any associated company.

Accommodation provided for the employee's family or household by reason of the employment is also assessable on the employee. Employees of local authorities are not assessed if the benefit is shown to be no greater than for tenants who are not employees and in similar circumstances. Ancillary services such as cleaning, heating, lighting, and provision of furniture are chargeable only in the case of directors and higher-paid employees. The amount assessable is the annual value of the property as ascertained by s 837 TA 1988 or the rent paid by the employer to provide the accommodation. Any amounts paid by the employee towards the cost of providing the accommodation are deductible from the assessable amount.

An additional charge will be made where the cost of providing the accommodation exceeds £75,000. The cost to be taken into account in determining the amount of £75,000 is the aggregate of the expenditure incurred in acquiring the interest in the property and any expenditure incurred in the improvement of the property before the year of assessment less any amounts paid by the employee towards the total expenditure. If the property was held by the person providing the accommodation throughout the six years preceding the date on which the employee first occupies the property, the additional charge will be based on the market value of the property on that date.

The additional charge will be based on an 'appropriate percentage' of the amount by which the cost of providing the accommodation exceeds £75,000 less any rent paid by the employee. The 'appropriate percentage' is the rate prescribed by the Treasury under Chapter 7 Part 3 ITEPA 2003 as applying at the beginning of the year of assessment for the purposes of calculating the benefit arising from beneficial loan agreements.

Jamie occupies a property which cost his employers £350,000 when it was purchased in April 2010. An amount of £60,000 was spent on improvements to the property and Jamie occupies the property and pays a rent of £12,500 per annum. The official rate of interest for 2010/2011 is 4%. The additional charge to tax on Jamie will be on:

	£
Cost of property (including improvements)	410,000
Less: Statutory exempt amount	75,000
	335,000
4% of £335,000	13,400
Less: Rent payable	12,500
Amount subject to additional charge	£900

Overseas holiday homes

Individuals who have purchased a holiday home through their own company (or equivalent) have been technically liable to a benefit in kind income tax charge as a director (or deemed director). Finance Act 2008 now exempts overseas homes from the employee/director benefit-in-kind rules in defined circumstances.

On 17 March 2011 HMRC published Regulations, The Social Security (Contributions) (Amendment No. 3) Regulations 2011 (SI 2011/797), to align the NIC position with the income tax rules. It is now possible to claim a refund of Class 1A NIC in the same way as it was possible for Income Tax when the rules changed in 2008.

4.2.2 Relocation expenses

The taxpayer is exempt from tax on the following benefits received from the employer:

(a) *Disposal of previous residence*, the expenses concerned including fees for legal, estate agents and auctioneer's costs, advertising, insurance and maintenance whilst unoccupied, disconnection of public utilities, penalty for redeeming a loan on the premises, rent payable whilst unoccupied. The employee, or a member of his or her family or household, must have had an interest in the former residence.

(b) *Acquisition of new residence*, including: legal expenses, procurement fees and insurance on a loan to finance the acquisition, costs of survey, land registry fees, stamp duty, connection of public utilities and abortive expenditure. The new residence must be acquired by the employee or a member of his or her family or household.

(c)   *Costs of transport* of domestic belongings and domestic fittings.

(d)   *Travel and subsistence* of employee, his or her family or household.

(e)   *Bridging loan interest.*

(f)   *Duplicate expenses.* This refers to the net cost of necessary replacement domestic goods and presumably covers such items as curtains and floor covering.

Where any relocation expenses paid for by the employer are not covered by the exemptions indicated above they are treated as benefits chargeable to tax in the hands of the employee.

4.3 Benefits - share schemes
4.3.1 Savings-related share option schemes
A company may establish a scheme linked to an approved saving scheme whereby employees (including directors) may obtain options to acquire shares without any charge to income tax on the receipt of the options and on any increase in the value of the shares between the date of the granting of the option and the date on which it is exercised (TA 1988 s 185, Sch 9). The monthly savings must be between £5 and £250. The minimum number of monthly contributions is 36 and maximum 60.

The shares must be fully paid ordinary shares of the employing company, its parent or a member (or its parent) of a consortium of companies which control the company and which owns at least 15% of the ordinary shares of the company. The shares must be quoted shares or if unquoted must not be of a subsidiary company.

The shares must be paid for out of savings with a certified contractual savings scheme approved under s 326 TA 1970.

The shares must not be offered to the employees at a price less than 80% of the market value when the option is acquired.

The rights to exercise an option must not be exercisable before the bonus date, i.e. the date on which the SAYE repayments fall due except in the following circumstances:

- If the employee dies before the bonus date the rights must be exercised within 12 months after the date of death, and if he or she dies after the bonus date, the rights may be exercised within 12 months after the bonus date.

- If the employee ceases to hold office because of injury disability, redundancy, reaching State pensionable age or retirement age in accordance with the contract of employment the rights must be exercised within six months of the cessation of employment

- If the employment ceases for any other reason and the rights have been held for more than three years, the rights may not be exercised at all or if exercised it must be done within six months of the cessation of employment;

- If the employee ceases to be eligible to participate in the scheme because the particular company or the part of the business employing him or her leaves the control of the company operating the scheme the rights may be exercised within six months of the cessation of his eligibility notwithstanding the fact that he or she may not have held the rights for three years.

- If the employing company has been taken over, the scheme may permit the employee to exchange the options to acquire shares in the employing company for options of a similar value in the acquiring company.

The persons eligible to join the scheme are full-time employees or directors with a minimum service period set by the employer and all eligible employees must be able to participate on similar terms.

4.3.2 All Employee Share Scheme
Three types of shares are available to employees under this scheme:

- Free shares
- Partnership shares
- Matching shares

The scheme operates through an employee trust. Company contributions to the trustees to fund the acquisition of the free and matching shares intended to be transferred to the employees attracts corporation tax relief. The costs of setting up the arrangements are also tax deductible.

The employer is able to give employees free shares up to a value of £3,000 in each year. The receipt of the free shares may be subject to the attainment of performance targets, or made on a "similar terms" basis. The employer may choose. Performance periods could begin from Budget day 2000 and employers are able to recognise individual or team performance by offering free shares on different bases. There are complex rules to ensure that a company cannot award free shares disproportionately to favoured employees.

The employee may allocate up to £1,500 per annum (minimum £5 per month; maximum £250 per month) for 'partnership' shares from his pre-tax salary to purchase shares in his employer company. These shares must be held in the trust and may attract "matching shares".

Matching shares may be awarded by the employer, the maximum ratio being on the basis of 2 for 1. Matching shares must be offered to employees on similar terms and cannot have performance conditions attached to entitlement.

The income tax benefits for the employee will be determined by reference to the time the shares are held within the trust. Shares left in trust for a minimum of five years before ownership is transferred to the employee, will be free of income tax and National Insurance (NI). If shares are left in trust beyond the five year point until they are sold, they will also be free of capital gains tax.

However, if shares are withdrawn from the trust within three years of award/ purchase, an income tax and NI charge will be made based on the market value at the date the shares leave the trust. Withdrawal of shares between the third and fifth years will be taxed at the market value at the date the shares were awarded.

If shares are a "readily convertible asset" and they leave the trust before the five year point, the operation of PAYE/NI is required.

An employee leaving within three years of receiving free or matching shares may be required to forfeit these shares.

Dividends of up to £1,500 per annum on shares held by the trustees will be tax free, providing the dividend is reinvested in shares in the employer company. Extra shares so acquired will be allocated to employees on a pro rata basis.

If the employee acquires the shares from the trust, any future disposal will be subject to the capital gains tax regime. The base cost will be the market value of the shares at the date of exit. Employee shareholdings will qualify for business taper relief.

4.3.3 Enterprise Management Incentive ("EMI")

In the Finance (No.2) Act 2010 an individual who realises a gain on or after 23 June 2010 which would qualify for entrepreneurs' relief will have to choose whether:

- to bank the 10% rate and claim entrepreneurs' relief in respect of the gain; or

- to claim deferral relief and pay tax at the prevailing rate when a chargeable event occurs in respect of the deferred gain, causing it to fall back into charge to capital gains tax.

Previously where a gain qualified for entrepreneurs' relief, the taxpayer could claim deferral relief and then claim the entrepreneurs' relief at the time the deferred gain fell back into charge to capital gains tax, giving an effective rate of capital gains tax of 10%.

Increase in income tax relief

From 6 April 2011, the rate of income tax relief for an investment under the EIS will be 30%, an increase from the current 20%. There are a couple of points to note:

- If an EIS investment made in the 2011/2012 tax year is carried back to 2010/ 2011, the rate of relief will be 20%, not 30%.

- The rate of income tax relief given for EIS investments made through an approved EIS fund will depend on the date on which the fund closes. Funds which closed by 5 April 2011 will receive income tax relief of 20%, but if they close after 5 April 2011 the rate of relief will be 30%.

From 6 April 2012, the maximum amount you can invest in a qualifying EIS company will be doubled from £500,000 to £1m.

Proposed increase in size limits

From 6 April 2012 the following increases in the size limits are proposed:

- The amount that any single company or group can receive under the EIS will be increased from £2m in any 12 month period to £10m.

- The limit on the number of employees will be increased so that investee companies with fewer than 250 employees can qualify.

- The gross assets limit prior to investment will be raised form £7m to £15m.

While this widening of the EIS opportunity obviously benefits the companies seeking funds, it also benefits individual investors, for whom a larger number of eligible companies provides a wider choice of investment.

EMI schemes have now been granted EU Commissions approval for state aid until 2018, legislation is in the Finance (No.3) Act 2010. As is the requirement that companies granting EMI options being required to have a "permanent" establishment rather than operating "wholly or mainly" in the UK.

For options granted after 5 April 2008, the individual employee limit on grants of EMI qualifying options was increased to £120,000 by regulations.

From the date the Finance Act 2008 received Royal Assent (21 July 2008), EMI is limited to qualifying companies with fewer than 250 'full-time equivalent employees'. A new paragraph 12A is inserted in Sch 5 ITEPA 2003 with 'the number of employees requirement' calculation.

Companies involved in shipbuilding and coal and steel production will be excluded.

Another change affecting EMI share option holders is the abolition of business asset taper from 6 April 2008. This previously entitled option holders to taper relief from the date that they were granted the option over their shares. Many EMI option holders will be entitled to the new entrepreneur relief but to be eligible will need to hold 5% or more of the company's shares and retain them for at least 12 months. There are no transitional rules.

EMI schemes are to be targeted at key managers who are needed by small growing businesses to assist their growth. Such businesses are often unable to offer competitive salaries, but are prepared to offer equity as an incentive to attract talented management. Companies which will be eligible to participate in the EMI scheme are those businesses which presently meet the qualifications for Enterprise Investment Scheme relief i.e. their net assets are less than £15 million and they carry on a "qualifying trade".

The EMI scheme permits the company to offer to employees options over shares up to a value of £120,000 each, and the total value of share options is £3m.

The option may permit the acquisition of shares at less than the market value at the date the option is granted and if this is so, there will be an income tax and NI charge to recognise the discount element, but only when the option is exercised. If, under the terms of the option, the employee is required to pay market value (at the date the option is granted) there will be no income tax or NI liability when the option is exercised.

The eventual disposal of the shares acquired under these options arrangements will be liable to capital gains tax, but the shares will qualify for business taper relief, calculated from the date the option was granted.

HMRC approval is not required for an EMI arrangement before it is implemented.

Example:
Collingwood Limited awarded share options over 10,000 ordinary shares under the Enterprise Management Incentives (EMI) share option scheme to its new managing director Mr. Prior on 1 April 2003. The options were exercisable at £2, the market value of the shares at the time of granting. Mr. Prior satisfied the performance conditions attaching to the option on 1 July 2005 and exercised his option when the shares were worth £10 a share.

Collingwood Limited makes up its accounts to 31 December each year and would obtain a corporation tax deduction for £80,000 in year ended 31 December 2005, being 10,000 multiplied by £8 a share (the difference between the market value at exercise and the price paid by the employee). The corporation tax deduction is available despite the fact that there would be no tax or national insurance charge on Mr. Prior.

Mr. Prior is not assessed to income tax as the option price was not less than the market value at grant. His profit will be assessed as a capital gain when the shares are eventually sold, which with the benefit of business asset taper reduces the taxable amount to 25% after two years, i.e. £20,000. The maximum tax payable by him would thus be £8,000.

Had the shares been acquired under an unapproved scheme there would be an IT (EP) A 2003 (formerly Schedule E) charge on Mr. Prior of £8 per share, £80,000. If the shares were readily convertible assets and Mr. Prior and Collingwood Ltd. jointly elected for Mr. Prior to pay the employers NIC due the amount payable would be £9,440. This would reduce the amount charged to IT (EP) A 2003 (formerly Schedule E) on Mr. Prior to £70,560 but nevertheless the corporation tax deduction would still be £80,000.

4.4 Benefits - cars and misc.
4.4.1 Employees' cars used for business purposes

Employees' cars - general rules
If an employee is necessarily obliged to use his or her own car on his employer's business, any reimbursement he receives from the employer normally takes the form of a mileage rate. The option to use actual costs has ended, they have to use the 'Authorised rates'.

The tax and NICs free rates, which have applied since April 2011, are as follows:

Cars and Vans:	
On the first 10,000 miles in the tax year	45p (40p previously) per mile
On each additional mile over 10,000 miles	25p per mile
Passengers	5p per mile
Motor cycles (no limit)	24p per mile
Bicycles (no limit)	20p per mile

If employers pay less than the above authorised rate, employees may claim (using form P87) tax relief up to that level.

The existence of the authorised rates do not prevent employers paying higher rates if they choose to do so, but any amount paid in excess of the statutory rates is liable to tax and NICs. But for NIC purposes the 45p(40p) rate applies to all miles (whether among the first 10,000 or not).

Since any excess is taxable, but goes on the P11D rather than being taxed via PAYE, there is no requirement to payroll payments up to and including 45p per mile just to catch the NIC liability - since there is none.

Amounts paid above 45p per mile attract Class 1 NIC on the excess over that figure (which will therefore need to be payrolled) and the excess (over 45p/25p as applicable) goes on the P11D to be taxed separately.

Employers can, if they wish, to pay up to 5p per mile free of tax and NICs for each passenger carried. The passenger must be a fellow employee making the same business trip. This measure applies only where employers pay extra for carrying passengers. Where there are no payments for carrying business passengers, employees will not be able to claim any tax relief.

In an appeal the special commissioner held that a non-executive director of an NHS trust was not entitled to deduct his travelling expenses from his home to trust sites in computing his tax liability. The commissioner rejected the taxpayer's argument that because papers were delivered to his home to be read, the expenses incurred were in travelling from one place of work, his home, to another, the trust sites. Although the taxpayer might have used an upstairs room in his home to prepare for carrying out his duties by reading the papers, the room was not thereby converted into a trust site. Reading the papers was merely preparation for performing the work the taxpayer was employed to do. The taxpayer did not perform the duties of his employment in travelling from his home to the trust sites. Further, his travelling expenses from home to the trust sites did not fall within the concluding words of S 336 ITEPA 2003 (formerly S198 ICTA 1988). The taxpayer's appeal was therefore dismissed (see *Knapp v Morton* SpC177 (1999) STI 59).

In *Dr Michael Wilkinson v RCC* (TC 00572), a doctor undergoing a six year training contract in urology with Wessex Deanery was unsuccessful in arguing that payments made to him to cover the cost of travelling to hospitals to which he was assigned for periods of less than 24 months should be free of tax. His contract for the period required placements at four hospitals within the region and he was able to nominate one of the hospitals as his base. The tribunal held that none of the hospitals was a temporary workplace. The tribunal reached its decision because the tasks that he carried out in the performance of the duties of his employment were allocated at the hospital to which he was then assigned and which he attended regularly over several months. The decision is difficult to reconcile with the guidance in HMRC's booklet 490 and casts doubt on how a secondment is to be identified if control by the 'home location' is not maintained.

What sort of journeys qualify for relief?
The rules give relief for two types of business journey:

- journeys which employees have to make in the performance of their duties and

- journeys which employees make to or from a place they have to attend in the performance of their duties - but not ordinary commuting journeys.

Relief is available under the rules only where the employee **has to** make the journey or attend a particular workplace. This means the journey or attendance must be a requirement of the employee's duties, not a matter of personal choice.

There is no requirement for the employee to offset any amount saved from their ordinary costs of commuting.

The relief for journeys which employees have to make in the performance of their duties broadly covers the same journeys as the current rules. It gives relief for journeys between two workplaces and business journeys by employees for whom travel is an integral part of their duties.

The relief for journeys to or from a place employees have to attend in the performance of their duties is new. It goes beyond the current rules and for the first time gives relief for many business journeys to or from an employee's home. But employees are not entitled to relief for journeys which are ordinary commuting. But which journeys are "ordinary commuting"?

<u>What is ordinary commuting?</u>
Ordinary commuting is an important concept. No relief is available for a journey which is ordinary commuting except in the unusual circumstances described next where an employee's home is also a workplace for tax purposes.

Ordinary commuting is any journey between an employee's home, (or any other place he or she attends for reasons other than work), and a permanent workplace. For most employees the position is straightforward. Ordinary commuting is the journey they make most days between their home and their permanent workplace.

<u>Teleworkers Travel expenses</u>
The rules on travel for necessary attendance in Sections 338 and 339 ITEPA 2003 assist teleworkers. Relief is available for home to work travel unless that travel is ordinary commuting such as the same day every week - see below. Many teleworkers do not have an ordinary commuting journey and are entitled to tax relief for all of their business travel. Where those costs are met by the employer, they can be covered by a dispensation in the normal way.

In this context the facts of the recent case of *Kirkwood v Evans* (74TC481) are slightly unusual. Mr. Evans worked mainly at home but travelled regularly on one day each week to his employer's office. There was no evidence that he would do so for a limited duration or for a temporary purpose. So his employer's office was a permanent workplace and he was not entitled to tax relief for his travel. This simply shows that a teleworker might still have an ordinary commuting journey.

Many teleworkers no longer use the employer's office as a permanent workplace. Visits to the employer's office become irregular or self-contained, so that the employer's office becomes a temporary workplace. For example, teleworkers may occasionally need to visit the office to attend team meetings or similar events. Irregular visits, or regular but self-contained visits, do not make the office a permanent workplace. Where the employer meets the cost of such visits they can be covered by a dispensation.

Where a teleworker who was previously office based begins to work from home the status of the employer's office as a permanent workplace needs to be reconsidered in the light of the new working pattern. The fact that the employer's office was once a permanent workplace does not mean that it must remain one.

What is a permanent workplace?
A permanent workplace is a place an employee regularly attends in the performance of the duties of the employment but not to perform a task of limited duration or for some other temporary purpose. Broadly speaking a permanent workplace is what is sometimes referred to as a normal place of work - the place an employee normally attends over a long period to carry out the tasks of his or her employment. Where an employee's attendance at a workplace comprises all, or almost all, of the period for which the employee is likely to hold the employment, then it will not be at a temporary workplace for the purposes of Section 198. When someone is sent to work at a particular site for, say, 18 months, it is always necessary to consider whether the secondment is part of the duties of a continuing employment or whether it involves taking up a different employment. Is there an expectation for the employer to return from their secondment?

No permanent workplace
Most employees have a permanent workplace, and most employees have only one permanent workplace. But there are some employees who have nowhere that they attend regularly other than to perform tasks of limited duration or for a temporary purpose. Many site based employees are in this position. They do not have a permanent workplace. This means that they do not have an ordinary commuting journey, so from 6 April 1998 they are entitled to relief for all journeys from home to the temporary workplaces they have to attend to perform the duties of their employment.

Under the rules a place is not a permanent workplace if the employee expects to be working there for 24 months or less. This means the journey from the employee's home to the site is not ordinary commuting and the employee is entitled to relief for the cost of the journey.

In *Phillips v Hamilton: Macken v Hamilton* SpC 366 it was held that a subcontractor was not entitled to claim relief under S 336 ITEPA 2003 (formerly S198 ICTA 1988) for travel expenses as the travel constituted ordinary commuting.

Although each of the contracts was temporary, the location for each employment was permanent and, as the contracts spanned more than 24 months, the travel constituted ordinary commuting and relief was denied.

An employee seeking tax relief for travel between home and a site or other place will always need to consider whether the place is or is not a temporary workplace. The legislation points to the first step in answering this question being to consider whether the attendance is "for the purpose of performing a task of limited duration or for some other temporary purpose". However, the 24 month rule then restricts the situations in which attendance can be regarded as being of limited duration or for other temporary purpose. So, in practice, it will usually be easier to begin by considering whether the 24 month rule applies.

The 24 month rule applies where an employee's attendance at a particular site forms part of a "period of continuous work". It says that a place is not a temporary workplace if the employee's attendance is in the course of period of continuous work at that place lasting more than 24 months or comprising all or almost all of the period for which the employee is likely to hold the employment, or it is reasonable to assume that attendance will be in the course of such a period. A period of continuous work at a place is a period over which the duties of the employment fall to be performed to a significant extent at that place. The practical test is that HMRC will regard duties as performed to a significant extent at a place where an employee spends 40% or more of his or her working time at that place.

Example:
Simon has worked for the same employer for 7 years. He is sent by his employer to work full-time on a site for 26 months. Simon expects to spend more than 40% of his working time at the site, so his attendance there falls in a period of continuous work. He expects to be there for 26 months, so the period of continuous work is <u>expected</u> to be for more than 24 months. This means that the site is not a temporary workplace, it is a permanent workplace. Simon's journey from home to the site is therefore an ordinary commuting journey for which he is not entitled to relief.

However if Simon had only expected to be at the site 22 months, it would have been classified as a temporary workplace up to the end of the 22 months or when he became aware that it would be more than 24 months. It is at the point of him becoming aware that he will be at this new site for more than 24 months that the relief is lost.

<u>More than one permanent workplace</u>
Other employees have more than one place they attend regularly other than to

perform tasks of limited duration or for a temporary purpose and therefore have more than one permanent workplace. But it is unusual for an employee to have more than one permanent workplace in respect of the same employment. In general where an employee has one permanent workplace it is likely that a second place will also be a permanent workplace if the employee spends 40% or more of his or her time there.

Note: Many examples are given in the HMRC publication 490 called "Employee Travel - A Tax and NICs Guide for Employers". January 1998.

4.4.2 Car parking facilities, bikes & motor bikes

Benefits derived from car parking facilities for an employee at or near the employee's place of work is exempt from tax (FA 1988 s 46; TA 1988 s 141). The exemption also applies where the employer reimburses a 'lower-paid' employee for the cost of such a parking space or pays for one by means of a season ticket or voucher.

There is no tax charge on the following commuting benefits provided by employers:

(a)   Works buses with a minimum seating capacity of 9 or more which are used to bring employees to and from work.

(b)   General subsidies to public bus services used by employees to travel to work, provided the employees pay the same fare as other members of the public.

(c)   Bicycles and cycling safety equipment made available for employees to get between home and work.

The Employment Income Manual has been updated to include details of an optional simplified approach to valuing cycles sold to employees after the end of a loan / salary sacrifice period.

The Cycle to Work exemption can only apply if certain conditions are satisfied. These conditions include a requirement for the cycles or equipment to be available generally to all employees of the employer. This does not mean that every employee has to be provided with a cycle or equipment, just that the offer of cycles or equipment is open to all employees if they wish to take it up. However, there has been some confusion amongst employers about what this means in practice where cycles are only offered through salary sacrifice arrangements and some employees are excluded from access to salary sacrifice arrangements. This may happen because of other statutory considerations, such as ensuring that pay is not reduced below the level of the National Minimum Wage or because of legal barriers to under 18 year olds signing up to the type of agreement typically included in a cycle to work salary sacrifice arrangement.

Both HMRC's recently updated guidance (EIM 21664) and the Department for Transport's ('DfT') implementation guidance confirm that even if some employees are excluded from salary sacrifice arrangements, the offer of a cycle must still be open to them in order for the exemption to apply.

However, this does not mean that the cycles exemption cannot be satisfied where an employer uses salary sacrifice arrangements. Both the DfT guidance and HMRC's updated guidance include information about how employers can take action to ensure that the condition about the offer of a cycle being open to all employees is satisfied.

The Cycle valuation table (value when transferred to employee):

Age of cycle	Acceptable disposal value percentage	
	Original price of the cycle less than £500	Original price £500+
1 year	18%	25%
18 months	16%	21%
2 years	13%	17%
3 years	8%	12%
4 years	3%	7%
5 years	Negligible	2%
6 years & over	Negligible	Negligible

(d)   Workplace parking for bicycles (and motorcycles).

(e)   Employees who use their own bicycles for business travel are able to claim capital allowances on a proportion of the cost of the bicycle.

(f)   An authorised tax free mileage rate of 20p per mile for business cycling applies. So employers can pay up to 20p per mile to their employees tax free for using their own cycles on business travel; and employees are able to claim tax relief on 20p per business mile if their employer provides no payment (or be able to claim relief on the balance up to 20p per mile if the employer pays less than this rate).

(g)   Tax free mileage rate of 24p/mile may be paid for motor cycle travel.

(h)   Section 248 ITEPA 2003) helps employers promote car sharing arrangements by their employees. This allows employers to pay tax free for alternative transport to get car sharers home when exceptional circumstances, such as a domestic emergency, mean that the normal car sharing arrangements unavoidably break down.

4.4.3 Cash vouchers and non cash vouchers

Cash vouchers (i.e. any voucher, stamp or similar document exchangeable for a sum of money greater than, equal to, or not substantially less than the cost of providing it) are taxable at the exchange value, when received by, or appropriated (e.g. affixing it to a card) to, an employee, spouse or family by reason of his or her employment (TA 1988 s 143). Exempt savings certificates and vouchers exchangeable for sums not taxable if paid directly, are not charged. The cost of providing any sickness, death or personal injury benefit is deducted from the cost of providing the cash voucher for the purpose of determining whether its exchange value is substantially less than cost. The Board has power to approve schemes under which cash vouchers are taxed when encashed.

Non-cash vouchers are defined as any voucher, stamp or document capable of being exchanged for money, goods or services, but not including cash vouchers (TA 1988 s 141 and FA 1994 s 89).

Any benefits derived from the exchange of vouchers provided by employers are taxable on the amount incurred by the employer in providing the voucher less any amounts paid by the employee towards the benefit derived. A claim under ss 198, 201 or 332(3) TA 1988 could, however, be made if the voucher was used towards expenses incurred wholly, exclusively, and necessarily in connection with the employment.

The liability to tax will arise in the year of assessment in which the employer incurs the expense or if later, the year in which the voucher is received or appropriated to the employee.

4.4.4 Credit tokens

Any employee who uses a credit token provided by the employer to obtain money, goods or services will be treated as having received emoluments equivalent to the cost incurred by the employer in providing the credit token or in connection with the provision of money, goods or services obtained (TA 1988 s 142). The amount chargeable to tax is reduced by any amounts paid by the employee, and any relief claimed under ss 198, 201 or 332(3) TA 1988.

A credit token is defined as a card, token, document or other thing which is given to a third party who agrees to provide the money, goods or services and will in turn receive payment for the items provided. A credit token does not include a cash voucher or non-cash voucher which is already chargeable.

No liability arises if the employer provides the Inspector of Taxes with a statement setting out the cases and circumstances in which the credit tokens are provided for any employees, and the Inspector is satisfied that no additional tax is payable and notifies the employer accordingly. This notification may be revoked retrospectively if the conditions necessary are not complied with by the employer.

4.4.5 Education and training

Payments by employers to a trust fund to meet educational expenses of an employee's child, are income of the child, not the employee (*Barclays Bank Ltd v Naylor* ChD 1960), but income from scholarships provided to children of higher-paid employees are assessable benefits to the employee, subject to qualifications where paid by an employer through a trust fund.

Payments made by an employer for an employee to pursue a course of further education or training in the United Kingdom will not be taxable if the course is of a general education (of a type commonly undertaken at school) and the employee is under 21 years of age when the course starts, or the training leads to the acquisition of knowledge or skills which are necessary for the duties of the employment or directly related to increasing the performance of the employee's present or prospective duties in the employment. The course need not lead to the employee's gaining a qualification. The payments must be made to cover the cost of the course fees, essential books, travelling to and from the course and subsistence whilst on the course and temporarily away from the normal place of employment. An employee cannot be regarded as temporarily away from the normal place of employment unless the period away is less than twelve months and he or she will return to the normal place of work at the end of the temporary period. (PR IR 8 August 1986).

Full-time courses

The existing tax exemption for payments made by employers to employees for periods of attendance at a full-time educational course at a recognised academic establishment (see Statement of Practice 4/86) has been increased. The financial limit on this exemption is £15,480.

Pre-employment training

HMRC have issued an interpretation in the Tax Bulletin (64) concerning the reimbursement of employee's training expenses where the training is undertaken before the employment begins. Section 250 ITEPA 2003 (formerly Section 200B ICTA 1998) provides exemption from tax where an employer pays or reimburses the cost of an employee's "work related training". There has been some inconsistency regarding the application of this provision when an employer reimburses to a new employee the expense of a training or academic course begun or completed before the commencement of the employment. HMRC article explains that such reimbursements will not normally qualify for exemption and sets out some limited circumstances in which the reimbursement of pre-commencement training expenses will qualify.

This clarification has been issued in light of the recent Special Commissioners decision in *Silva v Charnock* (SpC 332).

In order to qualify for exemption under Section 250 ITEPA 2003 the reimbursement must relate to the cost of work related training. Work related training is defined in Section 251 and includes, inter alia, training for a future job with the employer but does not, except in very limited circumstances, cover the reimbursement by a new employer of the training expenses incurred by the employee before the employment began.

HMRC recognise that cases will arise where the link between the employment and the pre-commencement training is so strong that the reimbursement should also qualify for exemption. HMRC quote an example where an individual has accepted an employment offer for a new employer to start work in the reasonably near future and the individual then pays for work related training for that job. Under such circumstances, exemption will not be denied if the employer agrees to reimburse those costs after the employment has begun. If there is no such demonstrable link between the individual undertaking the training and the particular employment that they subsequently obtain, the reimbursement of the pre-employment training costs will continue to be outside the exemption.

Expenditure incurred by an employer in retraining an employee or past employee to acquire new skills is not treated as emoluments under the following circumstances.

- The individual must have been employed by the employer for at least two years prior to the commencement of the course and: he or she is employed by the employer or was employed within the preceding twelve months at the commencement of the course; and

- he or she ceases to be employed by that employer not later than two years after the end of the course;

- he or she is not re-employed by that employer within two years of ceasing the employment with that employer.

The re-training must be designed to enable the individual to acquire new skills which would be applied in gainful employment or self-employment and the training course must take place in the United Kingdom and last for not more than one year (FA 1987 s35 and Sch 5).

Expenses borne by an employee to attend an external training course in the U.K. are allowable where the employee is required or encouraged by the employer to attend the course so as to improve the performance of his or her duties in the employment. The employee must receive full remuneration whilst attending the course full time for four consecutive weeks or more (PR IR 8 August 1986).

But no deduction for training - paid personally.

In *Consultant Psychiatrist v HMRC SpC 557* a consultant psychiatrist undertook a training course with a view to obtaining a further professional qualification. She had to pay for it herself and sought to deduct the cost from her employment income under s336 IT (EP) A 2003.

Her contract of employment stated that it was 'expected' of her to take this course but in any case the Special Commissioner held that as continuing professional education the course was not undertaken 'in the performance of the duties of the employment'. And even if it had been the cost would not have been incurred necessarily, although it would have been incurred wholly and exclusively in the performance of such duties.

The taxpayer's appeal was dismissed.

It is likely that had her employer paid for the cost of the course on her behalf, the employer would have received a deduction for the training costs and there would have been no taxable benefit arising on the employee. Equally, had she been self employed, there is a good chance that she would have received tax relief on the cost of the course. This case further shows the widening gap between the treatment of employees and the self employed.

In *HMRC v Decadt* (2007) EWHC 1659 Ch, a qualified registrar was not allowed to deduct examination fees and associated costs, despite them being required under the terms of his contract. Likewise, in *Consultant Psychiatrist v HMRC* (2006) SpC 557, a deduction was denied for training specified in the contract as 'desirable'. Similarly, in *Perrin v HMRC* (2008) SpC 671, it was held that a trainee accountant could not deduct the cost of training courses that he was obliged to pay for as part of his ACCA training. In each case, it was held that the training in question did not form part of the duties of the employment and as such did not meet the requirements for deductibility laid down in s 336, ITEPA 2003.

However, there are signs that the courts are starting to take a more relaxed view. In *Banerjee v HMRC* the Court of Appeal upheld the decision of the High Court and the Special Commissioner in allowing a deduction for expenses incurred by a consultant dermatologist in attending training courses, attendance at which was a requirement of the contract of employment. Unlike the decisions reached in the cases outlined above, in Banerjee the courts concluded that in undertaking the training the consultant dermatologist was fulfilling her contractual requirements and a failure to fulfil those requirements would lead to the termination of the employment. They also held that if her sole purpose in attending the training course was meeting the requirements of the contract, the costs would be deductible.

4.4.6 Luncheon vouchers
Vouchers provided by the employer to the employees to obtain meals are not

taxable if the vouchers are not transferable, limited to £36 p.a., and restricted to lower-paid staff. The Office for Tax Simplification has recommended that this concession be withdrawn.

4.4.7 Medical insurance
No liability arises on this benefit except where the benefit is provided for directors and higher-paid employees. Payments received from sick pay schemes will, however, be assessable but not payments for cover whilst abroad.

4.4.8 Health screening for employees
Although it was generally accepted that employer-provided health screening did not give rise to a taxable benefit or a national insurance liability.

The Government introduced legislation in Finance Act 2009 which exempts from tax the benefit of health-screening and medical check-ups when they are provided for some of the workforce but not necessarily for everyone (s 55, FA 2009, which introduced new s 320B, ITEPA 2003). This objective is achieved by exempting from tax one health-screening and one medical check-up in any one year but without requiring that these medicals be offered to all employees.

This exemption has now been extended to the provision of such health-screening and medical checks to former employees (the Employer-Financed Retirement Benefits (Excluded Benefits for Tax Purposes (Amendment) Regulations 2009, SI 2009/2886). This is on condition that the individual first received the benefit when they were an employee, and that the benefit would have been exempt under s 320B, ITEPA 2003 if they were still employed.

This exemption is retrospective and applies from the 2006/2007 tax year onwards.

4.4.9 Security assets and services
Any expenditure incurred in providing security assets or security services for an employee or director by reason of his or her employment is allowable as a deduction to the extent that the expenditure is included in the employee's emoluments. Relief will not be given where the employee bears the costs (FA 1989 ss 50-52).

A security asset or service is defined as an asset or service which improves personal physical security, such as a wall or item of equipment but does not include a car, ship or aircraft. The cost of the asset or service must be incurred by the provider with the sole object of meeting the threat to the employee and in the case of a service, it must consist wholly or mainly of an improvement of the employee's personal physical security.

4.4.10 Tax free salaries, pensions, etc.
Income tax paid by a company (or other employer) on behalf of directors or other employees is regarded as an addition to the remuneration, and added thereto for the

purpose of assessment (*N. British Rly Co v Scott* HL 1922; *Hartland v Diggines* HL 1926). The tax so paid should not be added back in calculating the corporation tax liability of the company, as it is part of the remuneration and, as such, an allowable expense.

4.4.11 Late night taxis

If an employer pays for an employee's travel between home and work, the basic rule is that this is a taxable benefit in kind for the employee. But there are exemptions, and one of these is where the employer pays for a taxi home after the employee has been working late. The tax rules are contained in s248, Income Tax (Earnings and Pensions) Act 2003. There are various conditions which must be satisfied before the taxi costs are tax-exempt if:

- all four late night working conditions are satisfied; and
- the number of such journeys for which a taxi has been provided for that employee in the tax year is no more than 60.

For the exemption to apply, these conditions must be satisfied on <u>each</u> occasion that an employee is provided with a taxi for a journey from work to home.

The four late working conditions, all of which must be satisfied are:

(a)   the employee is required to work later than usual and until at least 9pm (EIM21832);
(b)   this occurs irregularly (EIM21833); and
(c)   by the time the employee ceases work
  - either public transport has ceased, or
  - it would not be reasonable to expect the employee to use public transport (EIM21834); and
(d)   the transport is by taxi or similar road transport. This condition is not contentious and is not referred to again in this guidance.

The Office for Tax Simplification has recommended that this concession be cancelled.

4.5 Vehicles supplied by the employer
4.5.1 General

Directors and employees earning £8,500 p.a. or more are chargeable to tax on the benefit arising from the use of company cars. No benefit is chargeable to tax for employees earning less than £8,500 a year. However, the £8,500 includes salary and the car and fuel benefit charges. If the total exceeds £8,500 the benefit charges are operative and the employee is taxed on them.

Cars
A car is defined so as to exclude vehicles not suitable for private use which are not

commonly so used, e.g. invalid carriages. Provided all mileage is business mileage, no taxable benefits arise. Unless private use is both prohibited by the employer and not in fact made, it will be deemed to be available for such use if made available to an employee, his or her family or household, otherwise than in the normal course of business.

A car which forms part of a 'pool' available to employees is not regarded as available for the private use of any of them. A car is part of a pool for the use of employees of one or more employers if for a particular year:

- it was made available to, and actually used by, more than one employee by reason of employment but it was not used ordinarily by any employee to the exclusion of others; and

- any private use by any of them was merely incidental to the business travel; and

- it was not normally kept overnight on or in the vicinity of any residential premises where any such employee was residing (excluding keeping the car overnight on premises occupied by the person making it available) (TA 1988 s 159).

Vans

From April 2007 the nil charge continues to apply to employees where the restricted private use condition is met. Where the condition is not met the scale charge for unrestricted private use is £3,000. Where an employer provides fuel for unrestricted private use an additional fuel charge of £550 applies from 2010/2011 (£500 previously). From 2010 electric vans (propelled solely by electricity) do not lead to a liability for private use.

The 'restricted private use' condition is met if:

- the terms on which the van is made available to the employee prohibit its private use otherwise than for the purposes of ordinary commuting or travel between two places that is for practical purposes substantially ordinary commuting and

- neither the employee nor a member of their family or household makes private use of the van other than for those purposes and

- the van is available to the employee mainly for use for the purposes of the employee's business travel.

The last point means that the van cannot be used for commuting purposes alone. Where there is a taxable benefit under the new regime it may be reduced

- for any periods when the van is unavailable

- in respect of payment by the employee for the private use of the van and

- where the van is shared.

Motor Home
In *County Pharmacy Ltd. v HMRC Comrs; Morris v HMRC* Comrs (2005) SpC 495 it was held that a motor home is a car for benefit in kind purposes, but not for VAT.

The construction of the vehicle did not lend itself to the carriage of goods. It was wholly unsuitable for commercial use. The motor home was of a type commonly used as a private vehicle and suitable to be so used. Thus, the criteria of exception (ii) to s 168(5) was not met. The fact that the vehicle was not a car for VAT and vehicle excise duty was irrelevant. The income tax legislation in ICTA 1988 applied a different test for a car from that applied in the VAT and excise duty legislation.

Thus, the Special Commissioner found that the motor home was a car within the meaning of the benefit in kind legislation. M was liable to pay income tax on the cash equivalent of the benefit of the car and fuel.

4.5.2 Car benefit
Since 6 April 2002, a system which takes account of the pollution caused by the car has been used.

The starting point remains the Manufacturer's List Price (MLP) (the maximum £80,000 is lifted from April 2011) and the charge calculated by reference to a percentage of that price, graduated according to the level of CO_2 exhaust emissions measured in grams per kilometre ("g/km"). From 2012/2013 onwards further changes to the new 2011/2012 rules are planned.

From 2011/2012

- the lower threshold for CO_2 emissions is reduced from 130g/km to 125g/km. A band 1g/km to 75g/km has a 5% benefit charge, the 10% band now covers 7g/km to 120g/km range.

- the £80,000 list price cap abolished, leading to higher tax charges for individuals using more expensive cars;

- rules relating to electronically propelled cars registered before 1998 is repealed, as no such cars now exist; and

- rules relating to electric/petrol hybrid cars, cars propelled by bi-fuels, road fuel gas and bioethanol, and Euro IV standard diesel cars registered before 1 January

1996 will all be abolished, so that the taxable figure will depend on the actual level of CO_2 emissions, rather than the method by which emissions are reduced.

Cars which emit CO_2 at, or below, a specified level are taxed on 10% of the MLP. This specified level will be reduced in gradual stages over the first few years to encourage both fuel and car manufacturers to improve the efficiency of their products. The CO_2 emission level which qualify for the minimum charge is as follows:

2011/2012 - 2008/2009	120g/km CO_2

Thus, a car which emits 168g/km CO_2 when first registered will be taxed at 23% of MLP in 2011/2012. See Table 9. Income Tax - Benefits - Cars - Emission Percentages (2011/2012 & 2010/2011), p.629, for the full table. Except for the 121g/km to 129g/km CO_2 band the actual percentage of the car is rounded DOWN to the band below.

(a)   Diesel Cars

Diesel cars are subject to a supplement of 3% of the MLP subject to a maximum charge of 35% of the MLP. Thus, a diesel powered car which emits 177g/km CO_2 in 2011/2012 is charged at 28% of the MLP (25% plus 3%).

(b)   Electric Cars

From April 2010 electric cars propelled solely by electricity are charged at 0% from 2015/2016 this reverts to 9%.

(c)   Alternative Fuels & Technologies

From April 2010 the discounts for cars that run on alternative fuels and technologies are abolished. See previous edition for detailed information of their work.

(d)   Older and Less Common Cars

Car manufacturers have been required to report the CO_2 emissions for all new cars sold in the EU from January 1998 and, with effect from November 2000, that figure has been recorded in the Vehicle Registration Document. However, there are no accurate figures available for cars first registered before that date.

Furthermore, a car which has been imported from outside the EU (albeit after 1 January 1998) may not have an approved CO_2 emissions figure.

In the case of a car registered prior to 1 January 1998, the tax charge will be based on the engine size, as follows:

Engine Size	Percentage of price charged to tax
up to 1,400cc	15%
1,401cc to 2,000cc	22%
over 2,000cc	32%

In the case of a car registered after 1 January 1998 without an approved CO_2 emissions figure, engine size will again be the benchmark and the figures are:

Engine Size	Percentage of price charged to tax
up to 1,400cc	15%
1,401cc to 2,000cc	25%
over 2,000cc	35%

NB Unlike the CO_2 emission levels these rates will not change for later years.

(e)   Disabled Drivers & automatics

As a rule of thumb automatics tend to have higher emissions than manual cars. If a disabled driver is <u>unable</u> to use a manual car and uses an automatic, the benefit will be based on the emissions of the manual.

They can also use the list price of the manual car - if lower. Class 1A NIC will also be calculated on the lower benefit figure.

(f)   Employee Contributions

Employee contributions made as a condition of the car being made available for private use will continue to reduce the value of the taxable benefit on a pound for pound basis. A contribution of up to £5,000 made by an employee towards the cost of the car or its accessories will continue to reduce the price for tax purposes. A company can also make a tax free loan of up to £5,000 to the employee.

(g) CO_2 emissions data

The Vehicle Certification Agency produces a free, indicative guide to the fuel consumption and emissions figures of all new cars. This guide is available on the internet at http://carfueldata.direct.gov.uk.

Please see Table 9. Income Tax - Benefits - Cars - Emission Percentages (2011/2012 & 2010/2011), p.629.

Notes:

(a)   Where the car is unavailable for 30 days or more all charges are reduced proportionately.

(b)   Pooled cars may be exempt from the above basic charges where private use is incidental and the car is not normally kept at the driver's private residence overnight.

(c)   The benefits will normally be collected under PAYE by adjustments to the individual's coding.

(d)   The employer, not the employee, will be responsible for VAT and for National Insurance contributions on the benefits.

4.5.3 Fuel scale charge

This is also based on exhaust emissions. The aim is to make it easy for employers to implement and employees to understand.

The tax charge is based on the same % as used in calculating the car benefit, which therefore also takes into account any supplements or discounts. The % is then applied to a fixed amount £18,800 for 2011/2012 (previously £18,000). So for a car in the 25% band the tax charge is now £4,700 (25% * £18,800). From April 2009 the fixed amount is increased by, at least, the annual rise in the RPI.

The scale charge is reduced proportionately where private fuel is not provided for the complete tax year.

Each employee will now have to review whether accepting free private fuel is worth having. It may be cheaper to pay for their private fuel as the tax on the benefit may be higher. But some drivers of lowest emission company cars may find it tax efficient to receive fuel for private motoring.

Timely Reimbursement. *Impact Foiling Limited and Others v HMRC SpC 562.* Impact Foiling Limited provided company cars to two employees during 2002/03 and 2003/04. The employees purchased fuel for use in these cars and claimed the cost back through the expenses system. The amount claimed was reduced by 15p per mile of private motoring. The Revenue reviewed this arrangement and determined that the log of private mileage was incorrect and that as a result not all private fuel had been repaid to the company and a benefit in kind charge arose on the provision of private fuel.

In an attempt to clear this liability the company arranged that the employees should repay the full cost of all fuel. In doing this they appear to have relied upon the guidance in HMRC's Employment Income manual (at EIM23782). This guidance states that repayments of the cost of private fuel will be treated as being made within the year of assessment if they are made without unreasonable delay after the end of the year. Alternatively they will also be accepted if they are made within 30 days of discovering an unintentional error.

The special commissioner while regarding the advice at EIM23782 as providing 'extremely sensible administrative concessions' was not able to apply the guidance in arriving at a decision. He said of the instructions in EIM23782 that 'it is perhaps surprising that they are not the law, but they are not, and I can only apply the law'. As a result if a payment is not made to the employer within the tax year in question it cannot be accepted as offsetting the benefit in kind charge on private fuel.

Given that we commonly make adjustments in respect of fuel benefits after the end of the tax year but before the P11Ds are completed this is a worrying development. Hopefully in the normal run of cases the Revenue will continue to apply the pragmatic guidance contained in the employment income manual.

This should not be seen as limited just to reimbursement of petrol costs. Also consider, for example, charging interest on an overdrawn director's loan account. This is usually put through when the accounts are completed but this could be significantly after the tax year has finished and even following completion of P11Ds.

HMRC also publishes guidelines on 'fuel only' mileage rates for company cars, i.e. when the employee is reimbursed for buying fuel for business journeys.

The following rates (VAT inclusive) can be used to calculate the cost of fuel per mile. These rates may be applied to all journeys on or after 1 June 2011 (1 March 2011). These rates are now reviewed every three months.

Engine Size	Petrol	LPG
1400cc or less	15p (14p)	11p (10p)
1401cc to 2000cc	18p (16p)	13p (12p)
Over 2000cc	26p (23p)	18p (17p)
Engine Size	Diesel	
1600cc or less	12p (13p)	
1601cc to 2000cc	15p (13p)	
Over 2000cc	18p (16p)	

Fuel scale charge v mileage rate - 2011/2012 example:

40% Taxpayer

For a Jaguar 2.5 litre petrol engine with a CO_2 emissions level of 33% the tax on the fuel benefit would be £18,800 x 33% = £6,204 x 40% = £2,482 per annum.

Based on 29.5 mpg (6.48 mpl) and £1.35 per litre private petrol for 5,000 miles (772 litres) would cost £1,042 per annum. The break even point would be 11,914 private miles @ £1.35/litre.

20% Taxpayer

Note that for a basic rate taxpayer the break even point would be 5,957 private miles. This calculation needs to be carefully monitored as fuel prices change.

In addition there would be 13.8% Class1A national insurance contributions payable by the employer on the £6,204 fuel benefit = £856 per annum, so both employee and employer are worse off.

Using the HMRC rates above the amount that would have to be reimbursed by the employee, assuming the same private mileage each month for 2011/2012, would be:

5,000 x 2/12 (April/May 2011) =	833 miles x 23 pence =	£192
5,000 x 10/12 (June 2011/March 2012*) =	4,167 miles x 26 pence =	£1,083
	Total =	£1,275

* assumed

This makes the decision very finely balanced for the 20% taxpayer (£1,241) but very favourable for the 40% taxpayer (£2,482).

4.5.4 100% Capital Allowances for low emission cars (≤ 110g/km CO_2)

Cars do not qualify for first-year allowances. Instead expenditure qualifies for allowances at 20% (or 10%) a year on the reducing balance basis (see above, 4.4.1 Employees' cars used for business purposes p.70). The amount a business can deduct when it leases a car may also restricted by reference to emissions.

However, expenditure incurred on a new car can qualify for 100% enhanced capital allowances if:

- It is registered on or after 17 April 2002; and
- either emits not more than 110gm/km CO_2 from 1 March 2008 (previously 120gm/km CO_2); or
- it is wholly electrically propelled.

Please see Table 9. Income Tax - Benefits - Cars - Emission Percentages (2011/2012

& 2010/2011), p.629, which lists some of the cars that now qualify for 100% FYAs.

4.6 Directors and employees with emoluments of £8,500 or more
4.6.1 General
Expenses paid to directors or certain employees with emoluments at the rate of £8,500 or more by reason of their employment are assessable as emoluments, but the person assessed may claim relief for the equivalent expense if it is eligible as an expense of the employment and put at the employee's disposal by reason of the employment and paid away by him or her. Expenses or other sums are deemed to be paid by reason of the employment, if they are paid by the employer to the employee, unless it is shown that they were paid in the normal course of the employer's domestic, family or personal relationships where the employer is an individual (TA 1988 ss 153-168, Sch 6 and 7; FA 1989 s 53).

Director means a member of the board of directors or similar body, a single director or similar person, or a member of the company according to whether the affairs of the company are managed by such a body, or such a person, or by the members respectively. Any person in accordance with whose directions or instructions the directors (as already defined) are accustomed to act (other than a person giving advice in a professional capacity), is a director. A full-time working director, who does not have a material interest in the company, is not charged only by virtue of being a director alone but will probably be caught by the £8,500 rule.

The amount of £8,500 is determined by including all chargeable expenses and benefits but excluding any deduction for allowable expenses in arriving at the £8,500. Emoluments (as above) from two or more employments under the same employer are aggregated and, for this purpose, employees of a partnership, company or any other body over which an individual, partnership, company or any other body has control are to be treated as employed by the controlling persons or body. If any of the employments is within the scope of these provisions, all of them will be treated as within it.

Directors who are not working full-time or who have a material interest in the company are within the charge even though they earn less than £8,500 p.a., unless the company is non-profit making, in which case, a director with emoluments of less than £8,500 is chargeable only if he or she has a material interest in the company (TA 1988 s 167).

Benefits in kind provided, by reason of the employment of such a director or employee, for that person or for members of his family or household are taxable as emoluments on the **cash equivalent**, if the cost of providing them would not otherwise be so taxable (TA 1988 s 154(1)). The person who bears the cost of making the provision is regarded as providing the benefit and any benefit provided by the employer (other than in the normal course of domestic, family or personal relationships) for any of the persons mentioned is deemed to be provided for them by reason of the employment in question. Family and household means the employee's spouse, sons and daughters and their spouses, parents and servants, dependants and guests.

4.6.2 Benefits defined

The provision of accommodation (other than living accommodation), entertainment, domestic or other services and any other benefits and facilities of whatsoever nature are within the charge (TA 1988 s 154) except as follows:

- **Representative residence**: The provision for the employee in premises occupied by the employer or other providing it, of accommodation, supplies or services used by the employee solely in performing the duties of the employment (TA 1988 s 155(2))

- **Structural alterations** or additions to, and repairs to structure, exterior or utility installations of, premises in which living accommodation is provided (TA 1988 s155(3)).

- **Death and retirement benefits**: The provision, by the employer for the employee, or the employee's spouse, children or dependants, of any pension, annuity, lump sum, gratuity or other like benefit to be given on the employee's death or retirement (TA 1988 s 155(4)).

- **Meals** provided by the employer in any canteen in which meals are provided for staff generally (TA 1988 s 155(5)).

    Following the announcement at PBR 2009, HMRC has published draft legislation which will restrict the tax exemption for workplace canteens. It will affect the exemption for free or subsidised meals where an employee has an entitlement in conjunction with salary sacrifice or flexible benefits arrangements.

    The new rules are intended to take effect from 6 April 2011 and affect income tax and NIC.

    In the case of a hotel, catering or similar business, if free or subsidised meals are provided for employees in a restaurant or dining room when meals are being served to the public, part of the dining area must be designated for staff use only and the meals must be taken in that part.

- **Removal expenses**: No assessment is made on removal expenses and subsistence paid for by an employer where the removal arises out of the transfer from one post to another within the organisation, provided the expenses are reasonable in amount and their payment is properly controlled. See under 4.2.2 Relocation expenses, p.64.

- **Overseas holiday homes:** Individuals who have purchased an overseas holiday home through their own company (or equivalent) have been technically liable to a benefit in kind income tax charge as a director (or deemed direct). The Government announced in Budget 2007 that legislation, now included in Finance Bill 2008, exempt overseas homes from the employee/director benefit-in-kind rules in defined circumstances.

- **Medical check-ups:** HMRC has agreed that medical check-ups provided by employers to employees and retired employees can be exempt from tax and NICs even if they are not available on similar terms to all employees. Legislation is in Finance Act 2009, meanwhile a concession continues to apply.

4.6.3 Specific benefits

In addition to liabilities which may arise under other provisions applicable to employees, directors and higher paid employees are liable to tax on benefits in kind as stated next.

<u>Ancillary services in connection with certain residential accommodation</u>
Where the benefit of provision of the accommodation is exempted from charge, a limit is put on the taxable benefit for ancillary services (TA 1988 s 163). The limit is 10% of the net emoluments of the year (or part of a year for which it is provided), less any sum attributable to the services made good to the provider by the employee. Net emoluments are taken after capital allowances, expenses and superannuation or retirement annuity premiums, and emoluments from employments with an associated company are included.

The ancillary services referred to are:

- heating, lighting or cleaning of the premises concerned;

- repairs, maintenance and decoration;

- provisions of furniture or other appurtenances or effects which are normal for domestic occupation (e.g. electrical appliances such as TV, washing machines, etc., would seem to be included).

Where the director or employee pays a full commercial rent, expenditure by the company on rates and insurance, or on repairs which create an asset in the company's hands (restoration of defects) is not assessable as benefits in kind, as the director obtains no benefit to which he was not entitled by paying the rent, or, as regards the repairs, it was an expense in the production of an asset (*CIR v Luke* HL 1963). Any apportionment of the expenses of maintaining a director's residence as between himself and the company must be done on a reasonable basis, no precise formula being possible (*Westcott v Bryan* CA 1969).

Care for children

Benefits provided by way of the provision of care for a child of an employee or director are exempt from tax subject to the following.

- The child is a child for whom the employee has parental responsibility; or is resident with him or her or is a child of the employee and maintained at his or her expense.

Apart from the circumstances where an employer provides a nursery or creche on business premises, employer-supported childcare assistance has hitherto given rise to a benefit in kind charge, based on the cost of such assistance to the employer.

The exemption for workplace nurseries is now found in S318 ITEPA 2003. With effect from 6 April 2005 the exemption requires the provision to be accessible to all employees or, at any rate, all the employees working at the location where the scheme operates.

In addition to the exemption referred to in (b) above, four new sections (Ss318A - 318D ITEPA 2003), together with a new S270A ITEPA 2003, introduce a limited benefit in kind exemption for employer-contracted childcare and employer-provided childcare vouchers. With effect from 6 April 2006, the first £55 per week of such employer-supported childcare will be exempt from income tax and NICs. An employee is only entitled to one exempt amount even if care is provided for more than one child. The definition of qualifying childcare is detailed in S318C ITEPA 2003 - in essence, it must be registered childcare or with an approved home-childcarer.

Summary of Tax and National Insurance contributions, and exemptions on childcare provided by an employer

The table below shows whether you have to pay tax or National Insurance, or both, on the different types of childcare scheme your employer may provide.

Type of childcare	From 6 April 2006*	
	Tax	National Insurance
Vouchers	Nothing on the first £55 a week	Nothing on the first £55 a week
Workplace nurseries	None	None
Other nurseries of childcare	Nothing on the first £55 a week	Nothing on the first £55 a week
Cash allowance	Paid on full value	Paid on full value
Employer pays for childcare or school fees	Paid on full value	Paid on full value

* Every employee is entitled to one £55 a week exemption. The number of children in the family makes no difference.

Except on 19 February 2010 HMRC announced the following changes:

Changes from 2011/2012
- The changes only affect employer contracted childcare and childcare vouchers and not tax and NIC exemptions for workplace nurseries.

- It does not affect anyone in an employer's scheme as at 5 April 2011.

- For employees joining the scheme after 5 April 2011 the amount of exempt income for higher rate and additional rate taxpayers is restricted to £28 per week and £22 per week, respectively, to ensure that the tax relief received is the same as for a basic rate taxpayers (so roughly £11 per week).

- Employees receiving the National Minimum Wage (NMW) cannot legally reduce their earnings, a salary sacrifice, to take part in an Employer Supported Childcare (ESC) arrangement. This prevented some employers offering the scheme as it has to apply to all employees. HMRC have now agreed that employees earning at NMW rates can be withdrawn from the scheme and ESC offered to non NMW workers. This amendment is back dated to apply from 2005/2006 when the scheme was introduced.

- Employers are required at the beginning of the tax year to estimate the level of basic employment earnings that their employee is likely to receive during that year, ignoring potential bonus and overtime payments, but including other known taxable benefits.

Beneficial loan arrangements
A director (other than a full-time working director not having a material interest) or higher-paid employee is taxable on the cash equivalent of the benefit of a loan to the employee (or a relative) which is outstanding during the year (TA 1988 ss 160/1, Sch 8 and FA 1994 s 88). The loan must have been made by the employer (including a prospective employer, or associated company or partnership) other than in the normal course of a domestic, family or personal relationship, or otherwise by reason of the employment. The terms of the loan must be such that either:

- no interest is paid on the loan for the year in question (the loan not having been wholly repaid); or

- the amount of interest so paid is less than interest at the official rate which changes frequently.

The cash equivalent is the difference between interest at the official rate and that actually paid for the year. But aggregate amounts of less than £5,000 are not charged. The official rate is prescribed by the Treasury by Statutory Instrument and the interest is calculated at the official rate on the average balance outstanding at the average rate but can be calculated on a day to day basis at the election of the taxpayer or the Inspector. The average rate for 2010/2011 was 4% (2009/2010 was 4.75%).

Relative means a person's spouse, parent or remoter forebear, child or remoter issue, brother or sister of that person or spouse, or the spouse of any of the foregoing. A loan made to a relative, from which the employee obtains no benefit, is not chargeable on an employee.

Loan includes any form of credit and any loan replacing a loan and making a loan includes arranging, guaranteeing or in any way facilitating a loan.

A loan (or part of a loan), the interest on which is, or would, if payable, be, eligible for relief as a deduction from income, is not affected. No charge is made in respect of a loan outstanding after the employee's death. Interest-free advances to cover employment expenses are not taxed if not in excess of £1,000, spent within six months and properly accounted for. Where the limits are exceeded, and there are good reasons for so doing, e.g. overseas business trips, they will not, in practice be charged to tax (SP7/79 - now obsolete - enacted in the Section 179 ITEPA 2003).

Loans released or written off
The whole or part of any loan which is released or written off is treated as a taxable benefit, if the loan was obtained from the employer (including prospective employer, associated company or partnership or person with a material interest in an employing close company or company associated with it) or otherwise by reason of the employment. The release of a loan made to a relative of an employee is not chargeable if the employee shows that no benefit was derived from the loan. Nor is there a charge if the amount is otherwise taxed as income, unless it is so taxed only by virtue of its arising in connection with termination of the office or employment. Accordingly, except when the release or writing-off takes effect on or after death, the charge is made on the full amount even if the employment has terminated or has ceased to be a director's or higher-paid employee's employment provided that the loan was made to the employee (or to a relative) by reason of employment and was outstanding at some time during its subsistence.

Stop-loss arrangements in share schemes
Employees or directors are often protected against loss under share-purchase schemes by leaving a large proportion of the price unpaid or on loan ensuring that the amounts paid or repaid never exceed the market value of the shares at the date of payment or repayment. The benefit of such arrangements may be taxed in two ways. First, the benefit of a low or nil rate of interest on any loan may be taxable.

Secondly, any loan released or written off may be charged as above. In the case of partly paid shares the difference between the market value of fully paid shares of that class and the amount (if any) paid for them on acquisition is treated as a loan obtained by reason of employment for the purpose both of taxing notional interest and of taxing the benefit of a release or write-off. The shares may be in any company but must have been acquired by a person employed, or about to be employed, in directors or higher-paid employment, or by a person connected with him or her, in pursuance of a right or opportunity available by reason of the employment.

This notional loan (i.e. the difference above) is reduced by any amount otherwise chargeable as an emolument and payments for the shares are treated as repayments of the 'loan'. The 'loan' outstanding is deemed to be released if:

•   any outstanding or contingent obligation to pay for the shares (initially partly paid) is released, transferred or adjusted so as no longer to bind the acquirer; or

•   the shares are disposed of by surrender or otherwise so that the original acquirer no longer has any beneficial interest in them; or

•   the employee dies (but there is no charge on death).

Other beneficial disposals of shares
Shares in the circumstances given previously (whether or not market value exceeds the acquisition price), which are disposed of for more than their market value, will give rise to a taxable benefit on the excess for the year of disposal. The disposal may be by surrender or otherwise but must occur before the death of the employee and must be such that the original acquirer no longer has a beneficial interest in the shares.

These provisions and those on stop-loss arrangements apply, with appropriate apportionments, to cases where less than full beneficial ownership (excluding a share option) is acquired or disposed of. In each case the charge applies also notwithstanding that the employment has ceased.

Scholarships
Income derived from a scholarship provided to a member of a director or higher paid employee's family under arrangements entered into by the employer is taxable as a benefit.

No liability also arises where payments are provided out of a trust fund and 75% or more of the payments from the trust fund are provided to members of lower-paid employee's families.

Entertaining expenses

Sums received for business entertaining will be assessed as employment income, but the expenses incurred will be allowed as a deduction, if disallowed in the employer's tax computation (TA 1988 s 577(3)).

Round sum allowances

From the start of the 2009/2010 tax year, HM Revenue & Customs has agreed that it will not question the amount of round sum allowances paid by employers to employees who are required to buy meals when travelling, as long as those allowances are within HMRC's stated rates and employees do, in fact, incur the costs claimed. The benchmark rates are:

- £5 for breakfast if the employee sets out before 6am;

- £5 for lunch when out for over five hours;

- £10 for both lunch and dinner when out for over 10 hours; and

- an additional £15 if working after 8pm.

The early and late timings rely on this being outside the employee's ordinary working pattern. If the amounts are not to be returned on P11D forms, a dispensation must be obtained. If higher rates are paid without the employee producing receipts, then a sampling exercise must be conducted to demonstrate that the rate does not give rise to a profit for the employees concerned.

In the same announcement (www.hmrc.gov.uk/briefs/income-tax/brief2409.htm) HMRC states that a payment of up to £25 per night to an employee for staying with family or friends, rather than incurring the cost of a hotel, will no longer be accepted as free of tax and national insurance.

In both cases, existing dispensations will continue to apply, but will need to be updated at least every five years.

4.6.4 Tax paid by employer

Tax not deducted under PAYE at the proper time from director's remuneration and not ultimately borne by him or her is treated as an emolument and assessable. If the employment ceased before the tax due is paid by the company, the emolument is treated as having arisen in the year of cessation of the employment. No charge is made if the director dies before the tax due is paid over (TA 1988 s 164).

4.6.5 Dispensations

An employer may give the Inspector of Taxes a statement of cases and circumstances in which payments of a particular nature are made to directors or employees. If satisfied that these payments will not attract liability, the Inspector notifies the employer accordingly and no return of such payments need then be made on form P11D. Such notification may be withdrawn by the Inspector.

4.6.6 Valuation of benefits

The cash equivalent of the benefit (TA 1988 s 156) is the amount of any expense incurred in, or in connection with its provision, less:

- the part (if any) not properly referable to the benefit.
- amounts made good by the employee to those providing the benefit.

If the benefit consists of the transfer of an asset, the market value at the time of the transfer, if less than cost, is taken. An increase in value will be ignored under these provisions, although it would not be so if the transfer of the asset were chargeable as an emolument. A service or facility provided free or on specially favourable terms is valued as its cost of provision.

The use of an asset (the property in which is not transferred), which is put at the disposal of the employee, his or her family or household or used wholly or partly for their purposes, is valued at a proportion, appropriate to the extent that the expense relates to the benefit of:

(a)   the annual value of the use of the asset; plus
(b)   the total of any expense (other than its acquisition or provision) incurred in, or in connection with, the provision of the benefit.

The annual value depends on the type of asset and whether or not the person providing it pays rent or hire charges for it (i.e. because he does not own it). If the rent or hire charge is equal to, or greater than, the annual value that expense is substituted as the amount of the benefit. If that expense is less than the annual value, the benefit is taken as the annual value, plus any expense under para. (b) by excluding therefrom the rent or hire-charge. For land the annual value is the market rent for a yearly tenancy. Special rules apply to cars (see previous para.) and, for any other asset, annual value is 20% of the market value when the asset was first provided as a benefit.

The value of the benefits provided include the value added tax attributable to the expense (whether or not finally borne by the employer). The value of the benefit will be based on marginal cost (*Pepper v Hart* (HL 1993), See 4.1.5 Value of benefits p.62).

4.6.7 Deduction for expenses

Any benefit is reduced by the amount which would have been eligible for relief as an expense if it had in fact been incurred by the employee out of the emoluments.

The cost of travelling by a director to the place where the duties are performed is not allowable as a deduction, and a director is assessable on the amount of the expenses if borne by the company. Reimbursement of expenses, incurred in travelling between home and a place of employment overseas where the whole of the duties of the employment are performed abroad will not be taxed.

The cost of board and lodging for UK-resident directors or employees of foreign subsidiaries of UK-resident companies, incurred when visiting those foreign subsidiaries in the course of their duties, is in practice allowed. If a director carries out duties for a company at more than one place, any necessary expenses in travelling between those places are allowable (*Taylor v Provan* HL 1974). This applies equally to directors of a group of companies (ESC A4).

HMRC has issued an updated (July 2008) list of benchmark rates which employers can use when paying accommodation and subsistence expenses to employees whose duties require them to travel abroad.

Expenses payments at or below the published rates will not be liable for income tax or National Insurance contributions. If covered by a dispensation, employers need not include them on forms P11D.

The detailed list of rates is published by the Foreign and Commonwealth Office and can be found at www.hmrc.gov.uk/employers/wwsr-july08-revisions.pdf. More details about how to use them are in HMRC's Employment Income Manual at EIM05250.

Expenses incurred by a professional person in a directorship held as part of his or her practice are allowable as a deduction from the assessment on the practice. Where these are not claimed, a reasonable amount of expenses is allowed as a deduction ITEPA 2003 (ESC A4).

4.7 Payments on commencement & cessation of employment
4.7.1 Golden Hellos
Generally inducements to sign a contract are taxable, in the following case it was not.

Ms S was paid an £18,000 signing on bonus which was repayable if she left her employment within 1 year. The employer taxed the bonus but Ms S claimed back the tax under Section 200B ICTA 1988 that provides tax relief for work related training provided by employers. Her argument was that the bonus was paid to reimburse her for the cost of an MBA course which she had completed shortly before taking the new job. This had nowhere been specified in writing although the employer wrote to HMRC to confirm that this was the purpose of the payment. The Inspector argued that the bonus paid to the taxpayer was not a reimbursement of training costs, rather it was an inducement for her to join the employer. Furthermore, Section 200B (1) required that the recipient be employed at the time the training was provided.

The Special Commissioner said that the payment was described as a signing on bonus but the amount equated to the cost of the appellants course. Further evidence supplied by the employer showed that such payments were usually only paid to employees joining the company who had recently finished some form of training and concluded that the payment was reimbursement of training costs. As to the Inspector's contention that Section 200B only applied to current employees undertaking training the Commissioner said that the exemption in Section 200B did apply as the employer had committed to reimburse the fees in June 2001 and there was an overlap between the course and the employment. An important practical point stems from the Special Commissioners comment that it would have been helpful if the company had described the payment as reimbursement of training costs rather than a signing on bonus. *Clementina Silva v IRC* (2002) SpC 332.

4.7.2 Cessation of employment
In general all payments made in connection with the cessation of employment or changes in function or remuneration, including payment to the spouse, relative or dependent, valuable consideration other than money and the commutation of annual periodical payments, are assessable as earned income, under s 148 TA 1988 unless otherwise chargeable in full under the normal rules.

Payments taxable under s 148 include the following:
* **Statutory redundancy payments**: These payments are exempt from tax but are chargeable under s 148 thereby making them eligible for reliefs which are not available under the normal rules. Payments to employees under non statutory redundancy schemes are taxable in full.

* **Compensation for loss of office**: This heading includes payments which are made under an order of the Court, in settlement of proceedings or for something which would be actionable.

Exempt payments include:
* the first £30,000 of the payment; but there has to be no contractual obligation or custom and practice to pay - Please see the following:

    A payment in lieu of notice (PILON), made under a contractual provision agreed at the start of the employment, which enabled the employer to terminate the employment on making the payment, was to be regarded as an emolument from that employment. So the Court of Appeal held in *EMI Group Electronics Ltd v Coldicott* (1999) STI 1270.

    Under two senior employees' contracts of employment, the company agreed to give the employee six months' notice of its intention to terminate employment, but reserved the right to make payment of the equivalent of salary in lieu of notice. The company terminated the employments in question and exercised its right in each case to make payment in lieu of giving six months' notice.

But in the case of a contract with no PILON clause

Employees have both a statutory and contractual right to a period of notice, if their employment is to end. An employer may make a PILON if they:

- Want the employee to leave immediately; or
- Do not want them to work their full notice

The payment is to compensate them for the failure to give the proper notice as long as there is no specific reference to a payment in the contract, payments will usually be free of tax (up to £30,000) and national insurance.

- payments where the cessation arises from death, injury or disability;

- payments under retirement and benefit schemes which are already assessable or specifically exempted (payments for loss of office or diminution of emoluments are only exempted if they are due to ill health or the payments are properly regarded as a benefit earned by past services);

- restrictive covenant payments or release of loans which are chargeable;

- terminal grants, gratuities, etc. to HM Forces;

- overseas Commonwealth Public Service Superannuation benefits or compensation for loss of career, interruption of service or disruption due to constitutional changes;

- payments in respect of termination of an office or employment in which foreign service or employment is included;

- a payment which is made as a special contribution to an approved pension scheme under an agreement between the employee and the employer and relates to the termination of employment provided the benefits are within the limits provided by the scheme.

- reimbursement of legal costs incurred in seeking compensation for loss of employment (PR IR 2.9.93).

HMRC updated their guidance on the taxation of PILONs in February 2002.

One of the more important changes in interpretation is that HMRC now accept that an entitlement to pay in lieu of notice cannot be implied. This previously held view was supported by the Court of Appeal in *Thorn EMI v Colicott* 1996 where it was held that there was an implicit entitlement to a PILON in the case of senior management.

The employment law case of *Cerberus Software Ltd v Rowley* (2001) determined that a clause in a contract of employment stating that the employer **may** make a PILON was not the same as an express provision in the contract. In that case the employer was not obliged to give notice nor make a payment in lieu of notice but instead could breach the contact and pay damages. HMRC now confirm that where the contract is not prescriptive in connection with the making of a PILON that conclusion clearly applies and the compensation for breach of contract is not an emolument falling to be subject to income tax under ITEPA 2003. Instead the damages would be charged to income tax under s 148 ICTA 1988 being a payment in connection with the termination of employment to which the £30,000 exemption applies. Furthermore such a payment would not count as earnings for National Insurance Contribution purposes.

HMRC Bulletin article goes on to state that every case will need to be determined on its merits and provides guidance on the factors that need to be taken into consideration in determining whether the payment stems from a breach of contract or a contractual entitlement. In particular HMRC give their interpretation of *Richardson v Delaney* (2002) concerning the timing of the breach where the employee was on "garden leave".

This area continues to be one where specialist advice should be sought both in the drafting of the contract of employment and when an actual payment is being made in connection with termination of employment.

The appellant contended that the "leasing" might be either the leasing by the owner or headlessor or that by the non-resident sublessee. The Court of Appeal held, however, that in a multi-lease case, the relevant lease was the headlease.

Director (Non-Executive) had retired (*Venables v Hornby* (Insp of Taxes)). The House of Lords allowed the taxpayer's appeal in *Venables v Hornby* (Insp of Taxes). Mr Venables had been the controlling director of a company and had retired as chairman in 1994, aged 53. He became a non-executive director and continued to be the company's major shareholder. The company's pension scheme could authorise an immediate award of a pension to a scheme member who retired "in normal health at or after the age of 50". Mr Venables accordingly received a lump sum from the company pension scheme in excess of £500,000.

HMRC contended that the payment was not authorised under the scheme rules and issued assessments in respect of payments made to Mr V. They claimed that as Mr V had continued to be a director, he had not retired. Mr V contended that he had retired in 1994, even though he continued to be a non-executive director.

The House of Lords held that it was not necessary for a member who was an employee and a non-executive director to retire from both positions. The fact that Mr

V remained in his non-pensionable occupation as a non-executive director could not affect his right to benefit on retiring from his only pensionable occupation. Tip: Resign completely, then go back.

HMRC has lost a case (SCA Packaging v HMRC SpC 541) in which it argued that where a company habitually makes compensation payments to departing employees, those payments must be regarded as contractual.

It is commonly assumed that payments in lieu of notice (PILONs) are automatically tax free up to £30,000. The commissioner ruled that although such payments are taxable if they are contractual, habitual payments of this sort should not always be treated as such.

Incorrectly dealing with PILONs can add tax and national insurance contributions on top of the settlement payment creating extra costs for the employer.

During the case, HMRC claimed that SCA's established practice of making PILONs to staff whose employment it terminated meant that the payments had to be treated as if they were made under the contract of employment.

The Special Commissioner found that where SCA offered redundancy with a PILON and the employee agreed, the offer and acceptance meant that the terms of the contract were changed and so the PILON was paid under the contract, and so was taxable.

But if the employer simply went ahead and terminated the employee's contract there was no alteration to the terms of the contract and the payment qualified for the £30,000 exemption.

The appeal was allowed.

Whether compensation payments are taxable

A recent appeal before the First-tier Tribunal held that employee compensation payments can be earnings from the employment instead of compensation subject to the £30,000 taxable limit. The case was *Kuehne & Nagel Drinks Logistics, Mr A Stott, Mr AC Joyce v HMRC TC314*.

The employees were being obliged to move from a defined benefits pension arrangement to a defined contributions scheme and there was concern that the future accrual of pension benefits would be adversely affected. The employees, through their trade union, claimed compensation for the perceived loss they were likely to suffer through the change in pension arrangements.

The tribunal found that the payments made were in compensation for the employees' loss of pension rights but also an inducement for them to work willingly in the future. The tribunal judge said:

As the payments were made 'in reference to the services the employees rendered' they had to be regarded as earnings fully liable to tax (under s 394, ITEPA 2003) and to Class 1 NIC.

The question of whether a payment under a compromise agreement should be taxed as s62 earnings or a s401 payment (up to £30,000 tax free) was the subject of *NJ Wood v RCC* (TC00577). On few reported facts, the individual successfully argued for the latter but the tribunal judge made this statement: 'A prudent employer acting with proper legal advice would therefore always seek clearance from the local Tax Office and DSS (Department of Social Security) office before making a tax free lump sum termination payment.'

Apportioning a termination payment
A Mr Oti-Obihira received a payment of £500,000 from Morgan Stanley pursuant to various claims in connection with the termination of his employment and for racial discrimination and harassment (*Oti-Obihira v HMRC* TC 819).

Unfortunately there was no division of this amount between the taxable and non-taxable elements. There were no payment in lieu of notice issues here so clearly the first £30,000 of the termination payment was exempt under s 403(1), ITEPA 2003. The amount representing damages for racial discrimination or injury to feelings was not taxable; the fact that it was paid on the occasion of the termination of the contract of employment did not make it earnings. The question was how much should be attributable to the injury and discrimination elements and how much should be attributable to the employment element.

HMRC took the view that £28,000 was a reasonable amount of damages for the injury elements and therefore the balance must have been an employment termination payment. The First-tier Tribunal said no: this is the wrong way round. It is necessary to identify whether a payment is received in connection with the termination of the employment rather than looking at what can be attributed to another purpose. Mr Oti-Obihira had a basic salary of £74,000 with a modest expectation of bonus. The Tribunal considered that compensation for the termination of this employment in his circumstances would be a payment representing a loss of earnings for 18 months which they calculated at £165,000. The balance of £335,000 was therefore not related to the employment and therefore not taxable. The Tribunal also considered that such an amount was consistent with the amount which could be regarded as reasonable for the discrimination and harassment claims.

The principle here is clearly important, although it would obviously be possible to have different views on the amount of the termination payment, for example the estimate of future earnings and the 18 month period for which they were lost.

4.8 Overseas employment

The taxation of earnings from employment abroad depends on whether the employee is resident, ordinarily resident or domiciled in the UK or abroad. (A review of the rules was announced in 2002 but still not complete by the 2006 budget).

A person who leaves the UK for a period of less than a tax year normally remains a UK resident for tax purposes and can claim the UK personal and other allowances. Where the stay abroad is for a complete tax year or more residential status is normally lost from the date of leaving the UK, although UK tax allowances continue for the tax year of leaving the UK. However, retention of a place of abode in the UK and visits to the UK for an average of 91 days or more are evidence that UK residence has been retained.

If UK residence is retained the taxpayer remains liable to UK tax on both overseas and UK earnings.

However until March 1998 a 'foreign earnings' deduction of 100% of the overseas earnings, including terminal leave pay, was normally applicable where the stay abroad was at least 365 days, 'the qualifying period'. This qualifying period included visits to the UK for up to 62 consecutive days and no more than one sixth of the total time abroad.

Domicile is where a person has his or her permanent home. If a person is not domiciled in the UK and works abroad for a non-UK resident employer, UK tax is normally payable only on amounts remitted to the UK and the foreign earnings deduction will not apply. However, if some duties are performed in the UK, all the person's earnings will be subject to UK tax, but the foreign earnings deduction will apply.

In *Barrett v HMRC SpC 639* the case deals with whether an individual, Mr Barrett, was resident in the tax year 1998/99 during which he was paid a bonus of £2.8 million by a UK company of which he was a director. Barrett did not declare this on this UK tax return in the belief he was not UK resident because, as his Counsel put it, he had made a 'distinct break' from the UK and had spent more than twelve months abroad.

The evidence was examined in detail by the Special Commissioners but rejected this contention and dismissed Barrett's appeal.

The Commissioner found that although Barrett had spent much of 1998/99 outside the UK, he had visited the UK on at least eleven subsequent occasions during that year, spending a total of at least 45 days in the UK. His partner and sons had continued to live in the UK in a house which he owned, and to which his post was sent. The Commissioner stated that 'there was no evidence of a distinct break in the pattern of Barrett's life' and observed that his employment terms had not changed, he continued to do the same as he had been doing before, no home had been established abroad and there was no overseas business establishment. In addition, Barrett had done nothing to change his banking arrangements, or other matters, such as new driving licence to show any intention to break his residence in the UK.

The case follows the Shepherd and Gaines-Cooper decisions and confirms again the need for a distinct break from the UK and clear evidence of that break.

Payments made by the employer for the employee to travel to and from the place of work, and to travel between different jobs abroad, are not taxable on the employee; nor are payments by the employer to enable the employee to stay near his place of work; nor the cost of visits by spouse and children twice a year whilst the employee is working abroad for at least 60 days continuously. If the employee pays these expenses they are eligible for tax relief by deduction from pay.

The employee is likely to suffer taxation imposed by the country in which he or she works. The effect of overseas taxation can be relieved by a double taxation agreement between the UK and the country of employment. Where there is no such agreement the foreign tax can be set off against the UK tax liability.

Seafarers can, however continue to claim the deduction, but does not include those employed on oil rigs.

4.9 Retiring and other benefits
4.9.1 Social Security (State) pensions
These are taxable, that is they form part of an individual's income for tax purposes. They consist of a basic pension which is dependent upon the payment of national insurance contributions, and a State Earnings Related Pension Scheme (SERPS) which is based on earnings between certain limits.

4.9.2 Occupational pension schemes
These are schemes provided by employers for individuals which must be approved by HMRC for the tax advantages to apply. The pensions, except lump sum payments within certain limits, are taxable in the hands of retiring employees. The contributions by the employee are deducted from remuneration, i.e. provide tax relief, and those of the employer are allowable business expenses. The income of the fund is relieved of income tax and capital gains tax. The maximum final salary on which pensions are calculated (Notional Earnings Cap) is £123,600 in 2010/2011 and 2009/2010 (£117,600 in 2008/2009). From 2011/2012 HMRC will no longer commence a cap. If in future years any schemes still need to know what the earnings cap would have been for tax years after 2010/2011, they may calculate this themselves by using the method shown in s590C Income and Corporation Taxes Act 1998.

Turning commuted lump sums, this has changed in light of the new legislation. Payments can be made on the 'grounds of triviality' when a persons **total** pension arrangements, when they come to take benefits, do not exceed 1% of the life time allowance which stands at £1.80m in 2011/2012 (£18,000). This is easy to calculate when pension plans give current values, however in cases where only maximum benefits are known these need to be multiplied by 20 to give a notional value.

4.9.3 Additional contributions (AVC)
Occupational pensions may be increased (but not lump sums) by the payment of additional contributions to the employer's approved scheme, or to a 'free standing scheme' selected by the employee. The same tax benefits and limitations for the main occupational scheme apply. Controlling directors are not eligible. Contributions must be paid net of basic rate tax and the maximum contribution is either:

(a)   15% of an employee's remuneration in a tax year, i.e. 15% of £123,600 = £18,540 in 2010/2011 or

(b)   The scheme providers have limits on contributions, which are the new limits i.e. 100% of salary up to £50,000 (2010/2011 £255,000).

4.9.4 Special pension arrangements
Employers often provide special pension arrangements to provide extra pensions and other benefits for certain directors and employees. These benefits would be additional to or in place of those provided in the main occupational pension scheme of the business. They are unlikely to be schemes approved by HMRC for tax reliefs. Employee contributions, if any, are not deducted from remuneration for tax purposes, but tax is still payable by the employees on the pensions. Employers' contributions are treated as allowable expenses if a fund is set up to pay the pensions but a trust fund will be liable for tax on income and capital gains.

4.10 Other pensions and allowances
Social security (including armed forces, etc.) pensions are assessable and the full amount must be shown on the return form.

Where a person reduces the scope of his or her business, or the hours of work in order to qualify for a social security pension, he or she may, by concession, treat the business as having ceased and a new one commenced at the date of change.

Wound and disability pensions are exempt from tax. A war widows pension (including allowances for children) payable under UK or foreign law is exempt (TA 1988 s 38).

Disablement pensions under the National Insurance (Industrial Injuries) Acts are exempt from tax.

A special or additional pension paid to a person who has retired because of disability following an injury at work or because of a work related illness is not taxable (PR IR 8 August 1986).

Victoria Cross annuities and additional pensions are exempt from tax (TA 1988 s 317).

A retirement annuity is taxable and so is the income element in a purchased life annuity.

4.11 Gifts and compensation

Gifts of a purely personal nature, made by way of charity or testimonial are not liable to tax (*Cowan v Seymour* CA 1919; *Moore v Griffiths* ChD 1972), but contractual payments that result from the holding of an office are liable. That test has been applied by the Court to the 'benefits' of cricketers and footballers respectively, with the following result.

The benefit of a footballer is provided for in the rules of the Football Association and by the player's contract with his club or as a matter of custom. The same applies to the player's proportion of a transfer fee. Accordingly his receipts from these sources, apart from public subscriptions and collections, are taxable (*Davis v Harrison* KBD 1927; *Corbett v Duff* KBD 1941). Where a cricketer's benefit is a mere retiring testimonial to which there is no right under any agreement it is not assessable (*Reed v Seymour* HL 1927), but if such a benefit were guaranteed by a club, or dependent on length of service, it would be assessable. Ground collections for outstanding performances are assessable if provided for in the service agreement (*Moorhouse v Dooland* CA 1954). A lump sum paid to a professional rugby player on joining a club has been held assessable as a reward for services, but not if it was an inducement to put the player in a position in which he could be employed (*Jarrold v Boustead* CA 1964).

A payment to a rugby player by his club on becoming a professional, and subject to conditions as to the length of service, residence, etc., has been held to be assessable remuneration and not compensation for loss of an amateur status (*Riley v Coglan* Ch.D. 1967). A taxi driver's tips are assessable (*Calvert v Wainwright* KBD 1937), and so are the gifts received by a jockey (*Wing v O'Connell* SC(I) 1926, gifts for song plugging paid by the publisher to a public entertainer (*Radcliffe v CIR* Ch D 1956) and Christmas gifts to a huntsman (*Wright v Boyce* CA 1958).

A bonus, Christmas box or other additional remuneration from the employer is assessable even if there is no contract governing its payment, and it is paid entirely at the discretion of the employer (*H. D. Denny and A. Denny v Reed* KBD 1933).

Christmas presents in kind given to lower-paid employees are not treated as taxable unless their market value is substantial i.e. £50 from 6.4.2001 (previously £10). Christmas gift vouchers for £50 given to all staff other than manual workers and usable at a wide range of shops have been held to be assessable on the employee at the full amount, but it was emphasized (by the House of Lords) that in this case the gifts were made regularly so that the employees came to expect them as part of their remuneration; gifts made exceptionally on special occasions might be regarded differently *(Laidler v Perry* HL 1965).

By concession (ESC No A22 - now obsolete - enacted in the Section 323 ITEPA 2003), awards to directors and employees as testimonials for long service (at least 20 years), in the form of tangible articles which do not cost the employer more than £50 for each year of service, are not taxable (prior to Royal Assent FA03 £20). No similar award must have been made to the recipient within the previous ten years. This concession does not apply to cash payments, which are assessable (*Weston v Hearn* KBD 1943).

By concession an employer's contribution to savings certificates purchased for employees under a savings scheme is not assessed on the employee provided it is in proportion to (and does not exceed) the employee's own contribution, or is allocated by way of ballot. If it is related to the amount of his salary or length of service, or if the contribution seems, in the opinion of HMRC, to be unreasonably large or designed to avoid tax then the employee will be assessed.

Rewards paid to employees for ideas submitted (other than under the terms of the contract of employment) under suggestion schemes, in practice, are not assessed.

Compensation paid by an employer for the loss incurred by an employee on selling his or her residence as the result of a transfer to another area in the course of the employment is not assessable (*Hochstrasser v Mayes* CA 1958; *Jennings v Kinder* HL 1959).

Compensation for loss of rights is not taxable. Where the rights are legally terminated, giving rise to a strike, settled by a payment, this was held to be a form of remuneration substituted for former rights and paid for the main purpose of getting the employees back to work. It was accordingly assessable (*Holland v Geoghegan* ChD 1972).

The value of shares issued to a chartered accountant as a condition of his accepting an appointment as joint managing director, which he contended was compensation to induce him to give up his practice, was held not to be a reward for future services and accordingly not assessable under ITEPA 2003 (*Pritchard v Arundale* ChD 1971).

A substantial gift (£1,000) paid to an engineer by an Electricity Board as a mark of appreciation for specially valuable work done when seconded for this purpose by his employers, has been held to be a gift or testimonial and not his emoluments, and hence not taxable (*CIR v Morris* C of S, 1967). A cash award to a bank clerk paid for passing the Institute of Bankers' exams has been held not assessable as it was paid for the employee's personal success in passing the exam (*Ball v Johnson* ChD 1971).

A loan to enable an employee to take a nine-month training course on condition that if she served for a further 18 months the loan would be irrecoverable was held to be assessable as a reward for past services (*Clayton v Gothorpe* ChD 1971).

4.12 Expenses and deductions

Deductions may be claimed for expenses which are wholly, exclusively and necessarily incurred in the performance of the duties of the office (TA 1988 s 198). The test is not whether the employer imposes the expense but whether the duties do, in the sense that, irrespective of what the employer may prescribe, the duties cannot be performed without incurring the particular outlay (*Brown v Bullock* CA 1961).

In another case Baird was a Clerk, to the General Commissioners and as part of his duties as a clerk was required to maintain an office. while he had emigrated to Malta in about 1980. He had to take out a mortgage for the purchase of these properties. It was accepted that 75% of the running costs of the property were deductible from his emoluments as Clerk to the General Commissioners (chargeable under ITEPA 2003) but his claim to deduct the mortgage interest under Section 198 was refused since it did not appear to be part of the duties imposed to take out a loan at interest and use it to purchase an office.

It was held that whilst it was a requirement of his employment that the taxpayer had an office and the costs of running this were deductible. The borrowing of money and paying of interest could not objectively be viewed as being necessarily incurred in the performance of the duties. Conversely, whilst rent would be deductible, payment of mortgage interest was not. There was an element right the way through of personal choice and it also enabled the Clerk to acquire a capital asset which he sold in due course. Accordingly, the mortgage interest payments could not, therefore, be deductible under Section 198.

With an increasing number people working from home via the internet (and being required so to do), the case sheds an interesting light on deductible expenses. Following the abolition of MIRAS relief is likely to lead to an increase in people arguing that mortgage interest should be deductible to the extent that it relates to part of the property occupied for their employment activities. This case would indicate the dangers involved. (*Baird v Williams* HMIT).

- Homeworking from 6 April 2008, employees can receive up to £156 pa/£3 pw (previously, from 6 April 2003, £104 pa/£2 pw) from their employers towards the additional household costs of working from home (heating, lighting etc) without being chargeable to income tax NI. Amounts over and above this amount can also be paid free of income tax, provided the employee can provide supporting evidence that the payment is wholly in respect of additional household expenses incurred by the employee in carrying out his duties at home.

ITEPA 2003 provides relief for expenses which an employee is obliged to incur wholly exclusively and necessarily in the performance of the duties of employment. An element of personal choice about whether to work from home or at the employer's premises is critical to the employee's eligibility to seek any deduction.

The HMRC article gives four rules which must be complied with in order for additional household expenses to be deductible under s 336 ITEPA 2003.

- the duties that the employee performs at home are substantive duties of the employment. "Substantive duties" are duties that an employee has to carry out and that represent all or part of the central duties of the employment (this condition is unchanged),

- those duties cannot be performed without the use of appropriate facilities,

- no such appropriate facilities are available to the employee on the employer's premises (or the nature of the job requires the employee to live so far from the employer's premises that it is unreasonable to expect him or her to travel to those premises on a daily basis),

- at no time either before or after the contract is drawn up is the employee able to choose between working at the employer's premises or elsewhere.

If one or more of those conditions are not satisfied HMRC officers will contend that he employee is not entitled to relief for the expenses of working at home.

- **Broadband -** For employees, providing the employer foots the bill, s.316 ITEPA 2003 will allow a deduction for broadband in an employee's home, for work purposes, providing private use is not significant. If the employer does not bear the cost, an employee will have the onerous task of trying to persuade HMRC that it is wholly, necessarily and exclusively incurred.

In a press release HMRC say
'Section 316 of the Income Tax (Earnings & Pensions) Act 2003 provides that no income tax will arise on accommodation, supplies and services used in employment duties. This includes computer equipment provided for business purposes where any private use made is not significant. Consequently where employers provide computer equipment to employees solely for them to carry out the duties of the employment at home, HM Revenue and Customs accept it is unlikely that private use of the computer will be significant, when compared with the primary business purpose of providing the computer equipment.'

The Employment manual EIM21613 (as updated) does not define 'insignificant' but gives 4 examples of situations where private use of a computer is treated as incidental.

In the first the employee does not need a computer to do her job, and she does not have any duties of employment outside her employer's premises. There is a taxable benefit in kind purely by virtue of the fact that the employee concerned has an employer provided pc at home.

In the other three examples, the employee cannot work without a computer. As in those circumstances, the primary purpose of providing the employee with a computer is for work, then it stands that any private use is secondary, even if as the examples show private use often exceeds business use.

- Mobile telephones.
The tax exemption for employees who are provided with a mobile telephone has been revised from 6 April 2006. Section 60, FA 2006 restricts the exemption which had allowed employees to be provided with more than one mobile phone tax free. The new rules restrict the exemption so that it applies to one mobile phone per employee. where an employee is provided with more than one phone, there will be a benefit in kind charge for any additional phones, which will usually amount to the cost of private calls together with the line rental.

The change only applies to phones provided on or after 6 April 2006, so employees with more than one from before that date should be advised to consider carefully before accepting a new replacement phone which will trigger a future tax charge.

In future, employees with two phones provided by their employer will need to consider which is to be the 'exempt' phone and which the 'taxable' phone. It seems that there is then nothing to stop the individual from choosing to make most of his personal calls from the exempt one in order to avoid a tax charge.

- Annual tax free limits for staff parties rise to £150 (from 6 April 2003).

- Tax free meals/refreshments can be provided to employees to encourage them to participate on official "cycle to work days". With effect from 6 April 2003 the six day annual limit will be removed from the number of "cycle to work days" on which free meals can be provided.

- Incidental expenses: employees who receive from their employer up to £5 per night in UK (£10 overseas) to cover incidental expenses will not now be liable for a benefit in kind. If employers pay amounts over the limit the whole amount becomes taxable.

- The cost of **machinery or plant** (including books of a professional person) will be eligible for capital allowances if the asset is necessarily provided for use in the performance of the duties.

- A director of a multiple shop company can claim (if defrayed by him or her) the expenses of **railway fares** in visiting branches.

- The cost of **joining London clubs** in order to obtain cheaper accommodation when on business duties, if this is the real purpose of the expenditure, despite any other possible incidental advantages (*Elwood v Utitz* CA N.Ireland 1964) is allowable.

- Medical specialists with **part-time hospital appointments**: The appointments are assessable under ITEPA 2003 and accordingly the ITEPA 2003 rules for expenses apply (*Mitchell & Edom v Ros* HL 1961).

- The **cost of maintaining a room** at home as used as an office, postage and travelling expenses necessary to the employment, is allowable (*Newlin v Woods* CA 1966).

- **Subsistence allowance** - The Special Commissioner confirmed HMRC's decision that a full-time salesman was not entitled to a deduction in his tax assessment for subsistence expenses, because he had not produced any evidence of such expenditure. According to *Bevins v McLeish* SpC 51 (1995) STI 1750, the taxpayer's employer paid his salary and provided a car, but there was no allowance for subsistence expenses. He claimed a deduction for the years 1988/89 to 1991/92, increasing from a daily rate of £5 to £6.50 over the years, on the ground that similar rates had been agreed with HMRC for lorry drivers, stable lads and the civil service, and that all taxpayers should be treated equally. Although he could produce evidence of the journeys undertaken, he had no receipts of any expenditure on meals, and his case failed through lack of evidence.

- **Meals and drinks**: No restriction is made for the saving in living expenses which occurs when meals are consumed in the course of employment.

- **Fixed rates of allowances to manual and other workers** for tools, etc., have been agreed for various trades and occupations. A list of the allowances agreed is set out in Table 10. Income Tax - Flat Rate Deductions by Trade 2008/2009 onwards (previous), p.631. (ESC A1 - now obsolete - enacted in the Section 367 ITEPA 2003).

- **Fees and subscriptions** paid to professional bodies, learned societies, etc., are allowable (TA 1988 s 201).

- **Agents' fees** paid by artistes who perform in live theatre where such artistes are liable to tax under ITEPA 2003. An amount of up to 14½% is allowable as expenses (TA 1988 s 201A; FA 1990 s 77).

Items which have been held to be not allowable include:

- The **cost of travelling from home to place of business** (For full details please see 4.4 Benefits - cars and misc. , p.70).

- Where **car expenses** on business in excess of the allowance given by the employer are incurred, and, although the employer approved the use of the car, the employee was not required to use the car on business and the expenses were not necessarily incurred in the performance of the duties (*Marsden v CIR* ChD 1965; *Perrons v Spackman* ChD 1981).

- The **cost of meals away from home** when required to be on duty in the evening although the taxpayer received a flat rate tea allowance which was assessed (*Sanderson v Durbridge* ChD 1955). Although from the start of the 2009/2010 tax year, HM Revenue & Customs has agreed that it will not question the amount of round sum allowances paid by employers to employees who are required to buy meals when travelling, as long as those allowances are within HMRC's stated rates and employees do, in fact, incur the costs claimed. The benchmark rates are:

  - £5 for breakfast if the employee sets out before 6am;

  - £5 for lunch when out for over five hours;

  - £10 for both lunch and dinner when out for over 10 hours; and

  - an additional £15 if working after 8pm.

The early and late timings rely on this being outside the employee's ordinary working pattern. If the amounts are not to be returned on P11D forms, a dispensation must be obtained. If higher rates are paid without the employee producing receipts, then a sampling exercise must be conducted to demonstrate that the rate does not give rise to a profit for the employees concerned.

In the same announcement (www.hmrc.gov.uk/briefs/income-tax/brief2409.htm) HMRC states that a payment of up to £25 per night to an employee for staying with family or friends, rather than incurring the cost of a hotel, will no longer be accepted as free of tax and national insurance.

In both cases, existing dispensations will continue to apply, but will need to be updated at least every five years.

- The additional cost of living arising as a result of **removal** (*Collis v Hore* KBD 1949; *Bolam v Barlow* KBD 1949) or the cost of a soldier's lodgings, although the army lodging allowance is assessable (*Nagley v Spilsbury* ChD 1957). In practice, subsistence (i.e. reasonable reimbursement of the extra living expenses incurred by employees employed temporarily away from home) at an agreed rate for employees is exempted, if the recipient signs a certificate to the effect that taxation requirements are satisfied.

- **Entertaining expenses**, but if amounts received are assessed then the expenses incurred will be allowed, but disallowed to the employer.

- **Legal expenses** incurred in recovering remuneration (*Eagles v Levy* KBD 1934).

- **Agency fees** paid for obtaining employment (*Shortt v McIlgorm* KBD 1945), but fees paid by artistes who perform in live theatre are allowable (TA 1988 s 201A; FA 1990 s 77).

- The **subscription** of a bank manager to a local club is not allowed, even though paid by the bank and assessed as part of the remuneration (*Brown v Bullock* CA 1961).

- **Trade union subscriptions**, even if membership of the union is a condition of employment, unless part qualifies under TA 1970, s 192. Contributions allocated to superannuation benefits, funeral benefits or life assurance qualify for life assurance relief.

- The cost of attending (on his own initiative and at his own expense) a world road conference (at Tokyo) by a county surveyor to obtain information with regard to a particular road scheme (*Owen v Burden* CA 1971).

- **Reimbursement of Training Costs**. The Special Commissioners' decision in *Hinsley v HMRC, SpC 569* in which an airline pilot was obliged by the terms of his contract of employment with an airline to reimburse training costs if he left their employment within a specified period.

The Special Commissioners went through the traditional analysis confirming that the pilot was required by his employer to take the training; without the training he could not do his job. However, the job itself did not require the expense to be incurred because his job was not going on training courses but flying aircraft. Furthermore, it was not the case that every pilot would have had to have incurred this expense while doing his or her job. A pilot who was already type-rated for the aircraft he or she was to fly before he or she became employed by the airline would not be required to incur this expense. The cost may have been expended as a consequence of the contract pursuant to which the duties were performed, but that was not relevant. The duties were those of a pilot and the expenditure could not be described as being either in the performance of those duties or necessarily expended in such performance.

- **Examination fees** of a solicitor's articled clerk, because not necessarily incurred in the course of the employment (*Lupton v Potts* ChD 1969).

- **Telephone rental charge** at residence has been disallowed as not wholly and exclusively referable to the performance of the duties of a National Health Service official, even though he was required by the council to have the telephone installed for emergency calls. (Private use was 11/12ths and an offer by HMRC to allow 1/4 of the rent as a concession had not been accepted) (*Lucas v Cattell* ChD 1972).

- **Clothing** of an ordinary civilian kind, such as suits worn as required by his employer by a computer engineer, is not an allowable expense (*Hillyer v Leeke* ChD 1976), even if subject to special wear and tear, as in the case of a local authority surveyor required to make site visits (*Ward v Dunn* ChD 1979). Industrial or other special clothing may be claimed (*Hillyer v Leeke* ChD 1976). Please see Table 10. Income Tax - Flat Rate Deductions by Trade 2008/2009 onwards (previous), p.631.

- Schoolmasters and teachers may deduct the **cost of books** used in preparation for classes for lecture, but not the cost of generally improving one's knowledge (*Humbles v Brooks* ChD 1962). The cost of replacement of gowns or hoods was allowed, but not the first cost of such garments.

- A technical instructor employed by a County Council or other body may set against the income the **salary of assistant** if paid by the employee.

- A **commercial traveller** can claim rail fares, porterage, cost of stock rooms, cost of living away from home, tips and similar expenses, but entertaining expenses and gifts may be disallowed. If a motor car is used the costs of running it can be claimed, less any proportion applicable to private use.

- A **colliery manager** may claim an allowance for clothes, boots, etc.

- In two similar cases, the House of Lords held that **newspapers** and periodicals purchased and read by 10 journalists were not acquired and read wholly, exclusively and necessarily in the performance of their duties as journalists, thus, the expenses incurred were not tax deductible (see *Fitz Patrick v IRC* and related appeals (No 2) and *Smith v Abbott* and related appeals (STI) 1994 247).

4.13 HM Forces

Tax-free allowances are restricted to payments made to members of the Forces and certified by the Treasury as being in lieu of food or as a contribution to the expense of a mess (TA 1988 s 316). Lodging allowances are assessable but the cost of lodgings is not allowed (*Nagley v Spilsbury ChD 1957; Evans v Richardson* ChD 1957).

The following allowances to forces overseas are not taxable: disturbance, clothing, ration, travelling and motor mileage.

Mess subscriptions paid by regular and Territorial army officers are not allowable, neither, in the case of the latter, are payments to batmen, expenses of guests in mess, hire of camp furniture, or cost of tickets to sergeants' dances, etc. (*Lomax v Newton* ChD 1953; *Griffiths v Mockler* ChD 1953).

Army bounties payable for voluntary undertaking to serve for a further period are exempted from tax (TA 1988 s 316).

Service gratuities or bounties paid on a re-enlistment and including similar payments to members of the Women's Services are not assessable.

Civil Defence Corps training bounty was held to be assessable, as it was not paid out of the public revenue but from local authority funds (*Lush v Coles* ChD 1967).

Pensions under the Personal Injuries (Civilians) Scheme 1941, are taxable, as there is no statutory exemption.

Compensation for failure to reinstate an employee in civil employment is not assessable.

The cost of uniforms of serving officers is allowable as a deduction as expenses wholly exclusively and necessarily incurred in the performance of their duties. The amounts are fixed by HM Treasury (TA 1988 s 199).

4.14 Clergy
4.14.1 Income assessable

Although certain portions of their income are taxed by deduction, the income of incumbents is treated most conveniently as employment income. There is a special form for the beneficed clergy (No. 12 E.C.), and the headings of official income are set out clearly so as to facilitate returns by those clergymen whose incomes are derived from several sources.

It should be noted that all income received by a minister from his vocation, including income from property or investments, is treated as earned income.

Premises owned by a charity or ecclesiastical corporation and used or held available as a residence for a minister of religion in the performance of the duties, are not charged as a benefit except as a 'higher-paid employee'.

If a vicar farms on Glebe land he is liable on the profits as trading income, otherwise he has no liability to tax on it.

Roman Catholic secular priest
A secular priest is assessed under employment rules if his income exceeds his personal reliefs in respect of the following items:

- salary;
- cost of maintenance, if provided from parish funds;
- Easter and Christmas offerings;
- stole fees, if retained by him, and offerings for Mass intentions.

A priest-in-charge, however, is not assessable in respect of his cost of maintenance (*Daly v CIR* CS 1934).

In the case of Roman Catholic religious communities which are not in law treated as charities, a proportion of the aggregate income of each community, not exceeding £1,018 per monk or nun, is treated as his or her income for the purpose of relief from tax (ESC No. B10).

Nonconformist ministers
A Nonconformist minister should return the amount of any stipend from the Church, including Anniversary or other augmentations of income whether from central funds or collected or subscribed locally annuities, money allowances in respect of children, fees from marriages, burials, etc. in short the whole income that accrues by virtue of the position as minister. The rates paid by the Church Trustees on the minister's house do not fall to be treated as additional remuneration (*Reed v Cattermole* CA 1937).

4.14.2 Expenses and deductions allowable
Ministers of all denominations may set against their income any sums paid by them as expenses incurred wholly, exclusively and necessarily in the performance of their duty, and these may include expenses of attendance at meetings which are 'part of their parochial duties or enjoined upon them by their ecclesiastical superiors'. All expenses of travelling, etc., may be charged when the attendance is within the above rule. Other sums which may be deductible are:

- expenses of visiting distant parishioners (*Charlton v CIR* SC/S 1890);

- cost of entertaining clergy in the course of performance of the duties;

- attending necessary church meetings;

- costs of communion elements (if paid out of stipend);

- stamps and stationery;

- repair or replacement of robes;

- cost of keeping a motor car used for parochial duties. Capital allowances may be claimed in respect of its provision. Where the vehicle is used partly for professional and partly for private purposes, only a proportionate part of these deductions, applicable to professional use, is allowed;

- payments to curates and lay-workers whose services are necessary to the religious work of the parish, so far as these payments are met directly by the clergymen or minister;

- part cost of servant and of telephone;

- Queen Anne's Bounty management expenses;

- cost of locum tenens or pulpit supply during sickness or holidays;

- fees on presentation;

- repairs to chancel, where the incumbent is liable for the outlay;

- pensions paid to retired incumbents;

- sequestration expenses;

- glebe rents: cost of collection;

- expenses of opposing Bill in Parliament for removal of rectory.

The cost of removal between two appointments (*Friedson v Glyn Thomas* KBD 1922), or the expense of claiming an augmentation of stipend (*Jardine v Gillespie* CES 1906) is not allowable.

Expenditure on books is not an allowed deduction, unless necessarily used in the performance of duties (e.g. preparing sermons).

A claim for capital allowances on the cost of a slide projector and an overhead projector used to provide visual sermons was disallowed (*White v Higginbottom* ChD 1982).

A clergyman or minister of religion who uses any part of his or her residence mainly and substantially in connection with the duties (e.g. a room for a study) may claim under the heading of expenses a sum not exceeding a quarter of the rent. An allowance of one quarter of the expenditure on maintenance, repairs, insurance or management of the residence may be claimed. This allowance is not due to Church of Scotland ministers and Nonconformist ministers as they do not pay rent. In practice a claim can also be made for rates, heating, lighting, cleaning, etc., based on such proportion of the residence as is used professionally.

4.15 IR35 Personal Service Companies AND Partnerships
The new Government of 2010 reviewed and re-evaluated the IR35 legislation. Rather than relaxing or abolishing it, it is to remain.

4.15.0 IR35 - is the end in sight?
Recent case law developments have held that individuals engaged through agencies can have employed status with the end-user - that is, the company using the agency staff. In the case of *Franks v Reuters Ltd. and First Employment Ltd,* Mr Franks was held to be an employee of Reuters, even though he had no contract with them and had always worked for them through first Employment, an employment agency. In this case, the implied contract of employment was held to have arisen through the passage of time - Mr Franks had worked for Reuters for five years.

In a similar case, *Dacas v Brook Street Bureau (UK) Ltd. and Wandsworth London Borough Council,* employment was again deemed to be the relationship between the worker and the council, despite the fact that he worked for the council through Brook Street (again, an employment agency).

The outcome of these two cases was that not only did the individuals gain employment rights, but the 'employers' assumed responsibility for payroll taxes and making deductions. However, in both cases, the individuals contracted directly with the agencies rather than through personal service companies.

These decisions were relevant when the Employment Tribunal considered the case of *Cable and Wireless v Muscat*. Here, the case of Dacas could not be distinguished on its facts, and thus although a personal service company was used, it was held that an employment relationship existed between end-user and worker.

In *Novasoft Ltd v HMRC* TC00456. The Tribunal, in hypothesising a notional contract between the worker of the appellant company and its end client, has held that the worker, Mr Brajkovic, would not have been employee of the client. The appeal by Novasoft Ltd against an assessment under the IR35 legislation was therefore allowed.

Between July 1998 and December 2002, Novasoft provided IT services, through an agency to a company in the biotech sector called Avecia. Mr Brajkovic used HMRC's own email service to gain an employment status opinion but this led to an HMRC status enquiry and assessment for PAYE and NIV from April 2000 (when the intermediaries' legislation was introduced) to December 2002.

In the Tribunal, the Judge, Peter Kempster, in forming his conclusion of the notional contract, took into account a large number of factors and reiterated the words of Mummery J in *Hall v Lorimer* who said 'The overall effect can only be appreciated by standing back from the detailed picture which has been painted, by viewing it from a distance'. In Kempster's view, the picture of Mr Brajkovic's notional contract was one of self-employment. Factors forming that view included:

* Although Mr Brajkovic had to undertake his work in accordance with necessary standards and to meet deadlines and budgets, there was no requirement to work specific hours or any necessity to work in any prescriptive manner.

* There was a risk of non-payment.

* There was no entitlement to typical employee benefits or statutory protection.

* He was not 'part and parcel of the client's organisation.

An engineer working on a contract basis for Airbus UK won his appeal against HMRC's determination that he should be taxed as an employee under IR35 rules rather than as self-employed.

In April 2003 Airbus took on Fitzpatrick and his company MBF under a contract via intermediaries at an hourly rate that increased if he worked more than 35 hours in a week. The tribunal noted that the "request for services" to which the contract related included a seven day notice period and a stipulation that substandard service or attendance would give Airbus a legitimate claim to withhold payment.

The tribunal notes that the contract agreed between Morson and Airbus named 53 individuals and appeared to be based on one normally used for the purchase of goods, with Fitzpatrick's "quantity" indicated as 42,500 hours at his usual hourly rate.

The third contract between Morson and Airbus also included a clause setting out the client's right to immediate cancellation of the contract, which was crucial to the tribunal's decision that the terms were inconsistent with the mutuality of obligation that exists between employee and employer.

4.15.1 Outline of the rules

The legislation is designed to increase the NIC revenue from the service industry, which on the whole has found it more tax efficient to distribute income as dividends, usually subject to the payment of a small salary. To this end, it introduces the concept of "Deemed salary" which will be taxed and subject to NIC as if it has been paid as a salary, and will allow the worker to draw this later if he chooses for no further tax charge. Most small service companies will effectively be forced to distribute all of their income as salary to those actually performing the work.

In order to retain some logic to this treatment it is necessary to identify the situations in which these rules are to operate: the acceptable concern is that small limited companies are being used to disguise employment, so this is the test which has been applied. Where the employee is provided by his (or indeed any) company or partnership to an ultimate client on terms which would normally constitute an employment with that client, this is called a "Relevant engagement" and the special rules apply.

As a concession to the objectors, a small list of "deductions" has been prepared to allow the income generated to be applied to certain permitted costs, but over and above this, the company will effectively be required to distribute all of the income to the employee as salary, or otherwise accept unwelcome corporation tax implications. It is important to remember that this rule operates for the purposes of PAYE, but does not affect the actual payments of the company, so the corporation tax computation will be prepared as normal.

These rules have applied from 6 April 2000. Incorrect application will lead to penalties as well as those applicable to submitting false P35 etc.
N.B. It is essential to note that these calculations run for the tax year not the company year. It may be easier to change the company year end to 30 April.

4.15.2 The deemed salary calculation in outline
The precise mechanism of the computation will be dealt with later but to highlight various points of importance, an outline of the deemed Schedule E calculation is set out:

Income from relevant engagements		X
Less: permitted deductions		
Salary and NIC paid	X	
Employer pension contributions	X	
S 336 ITEPA 2003 (formerly S198 ICTA 1988) Claims	X	
Appropriate capital allowance claims	X	
Benefits in kind	X	
Statutory deductions for employees	X	
5% of gross income	X	
		(X)
Deemed Sch E (ITEPA 2003) payment		X

4.15.3 The areas to consider in detail
In order to establish how the rules are likely to affect each individual contractor, and how work may best be planned to minimise the impact of the rules, it will be necessary to consider the following areas in more detail.

- Tests of employment and thus relevant engagements
- Expense available for deduction
- The deemed salary calculation and its impact on tax payment.

4.15.4 Tests of employment
(a) Workers provided by "intermediaries"
Where a worker is provided by an intermediary, the intermediary must identify whether the new rules are triggered, and must therefore identify all "relevant engagements". The rules clearly indicate that an intermediary might be either a company or a partnership, or even a sole trader, although practically this is unusual. For the purposes of this section we will assume it is a company.

(b) Relevant engagements
Where the intermediary provides the services of a member of staff to a client and the terms are such that without the intermediary, the individual would be an employee of that client the new tax treatment is triggered.

Income from such work arises from a relevant engagement, and will be taxed according to the new rules.

(c) Terms of the engagement: contracts
The terms of the engagement will determine whether an individual is employed or self employed.

The Court of Appeal held on 3 September 2008 in the Dragonfly Consultancy Ltd. case that verbal testimony can overrule the substitution clause in the written contract.

However, it would be unwise indeed to pin all hopes on a contract effectively bought "off the shelf" describing a self employed engagement. The parties to the contract must behave in such a way as to make it clear that the contract does indeed summarise their working relationship. A fictional contract will fail the practical test.

4.15.5 Factors pointing to employment or not
If you can answer "yes" to the following questions, you would probably have been an employee of your client for the contract in question and therefore within the new rules:

- Do you work set hours, or a given number of hours a week or a month?

- Do you have to do the work yourself rather than hire someone else to do the work for you?

- Can someone tell you at any time what to do, when to work or how to do the work?

- Are you paid by the hour, week or month?

- Can you get overtime pay?

- Do you work at the premises of the person you work for, or at a place or places he or she decides?

- Do you generally work for one client at a time, rather than having a number of contracts?

If you can answer "yes" to the following questions, you would probably not have been an employee of your client and therefore outside the new rules:

- Do you have the final say in how you do the work for the client?

- Can you make a loss on the contract?

- Do you provide the main items of equipment you need to do the job for the client, not just the small tools many employees provide for themselves?

- Are you free to hire other people on your own terms to do the work you have taken on?

- Do you pay them out of your own pocket?

- Do you have a correct unsatisfactory work in your own time and at your own expense?

- Do you have a number of customers at the same time?

You will have to think about each contract individually. Some people will find that they have some contracts, which would have been employment and so come within the rules, and others which do not.

The number of clients you have may be relevant to the decision whether your work for each as an employee, or as a self-employed person. If you have many different clients this may indicate self-employment, and be a factor that should be considered in addition to the actual details of each contract. If you have a number of different clients, but are unsure whether you are within or outside the rules, you may wish to talk to your HM Revenue & Customs Enquiry Centre.

More information about employment status can be found at Employment-Status http://www.hmrc.gov.uk/employers/tmaemployed_or_self-employed.shtml.

4.15.6 Expenses available for deduction
The expenses available for deduction come under a number of categories. The list is:

- Expenses which can be claimed under Section 198 of TA 1988, dealing with travelling expenses and other claims separately. Travelling expenses are claimed as if the worker is an employee of the Intermediary, and other expenses are claimed as if the worker was the employee of the Client.

- Employer contributions to pension schemes

- Other statutory deductions for employees

- Benefits in kind - the cash equivalent

- Capital allowances claimable by employees.

4.15.7 Examples: tax impact
All examples use a similar basis for deductible expenses. Obviously, to the extent that actual expenses and pension contributions differ from this, the impact of IR35 will vary.

Single Person: Gross income £30,000
Income from relevant engagements for the year £30,000. Salary paid to the employee £8,000 gross. Payments into company approved pension scheme £1,200. Allowable travelling expenses £1,800. Other expenditure: Accountancy fees £800. Sundry office and related expenses £1,000. Balance of profits distributed as dividend.

(a) Non - IR35 tax position (using 2011/2012 rates)

	£	£
Gross pay	8,000	
Personal allowance	(7,475)	
Taxable income	525	
Income tax on salary @ 20%	105	
Employee NIC (£8,000 - £7,228 = £772 x 12%)	93	
Net pay	7,802	

	£	£
Company - y/e 31.03.2012		
Income		30,000
Salary	8,000	
Employer's NIC (£928 x 13.8%)	128	
Travelling expenses	1,800	
Pension contributions	1,200	
Accountancy	800	
Office expenses	1,000	
		12,928
Profit before tax		17,072
Corporation tax 20%		3,414
Net profit (= dividend)		13,658
Total income net of tax (£7,228+ £13,658) =		£20,886

(b) IR35 treatment using 2010/2011 tax rates

	£	£
Gross pay	8,000	
Personal allowance	(7,475)	
Taxable income	525	
Net pay as before	7,802	
Deemed salary reconciliation		
Income		30,000
Salary	8,000	
Employer's NIC	128	
Travelling expenses	1,800	
Pension contributions	1,200	
5% of gross (5% x £30,000)	1,500	

	£	£
		12,628
Deemed Salary including employer's NIC		17,372
PAYE on deemed salary of £15,265	3,053	
Employee's NIC on deemed salary	1,832	
Employer's NIC on deemed salary	2,106	
		6,991
Net deemed salary		10,381

Total income net of tax (£7,802 + £10,381) =   £18,183

Reduction in net income (£20,886 - £18,183) =   £2,703

This is not quite the end, because the company situation will be:

Company
Income		30,000
Expenses as above	12,628	
Deemed salary plus NIC	17,372	
		30,000
Break even		£0

Although relief can be obtained for any loss by carry back against the previous year. the total expenses of the company need to be no more than the 5% allowed for otherwise a loss will be incurred. In this case, the office expenses need to be reduced to avoid incurring losses.

4.15.8 Partnerships as intermediaries
The rules do not apply to partnerships unless one of three triggers is present. Partnerships are only subject to the rules if:

(a)   One partner (or a partner with his connected persons) is entitled to more than 60% of the firm's profits;

(b)   Most of the income of the firm derives from relevant engagements with the same client or client and connected parties; or

(c)   Partnership profits are shared according to the contribution to income of any one partner.

One important point to bear in mind is that the tax treatment of the deemed salary and related (disallowed) expenses in a partnership situation is to exclude the amounts from the partnership income. This is more complex that in a corporate intermediary, and readers should refer to FAQ's on HMRC's website for an excellent worked example.

4.15.9 Managed service company (MSC) schemes
Such structures have proved popular as a way of avoiding IR35 applying to personal service companies. Anti-avoidance measures brought in the FA 2007 bring workers supplying their services through an MSC within the PAYE regime.

Clause 25 and Schedule 3 insert a new Chapter 9 in the Income tax (Earnings and Pensions) Act (ITEPA) 2003. The Chapter defines a 'managed service company' and requires that payments received by persons in respect of services provided through such companies, not already treated as employment income, are treated as employment income and taxed accordingly. Where a company is within the scope of Chapter 9, Chapter 8 ITEPA (rules for IR35) is disapplied.

The clause also inserts a new section 688A within ITEPA relating to the transfer of PAYE debts of managed service companies. Section 688A enables PAYE regulations to provide for the recovery from persons specified within section 688A of an amount of PAYE that an officer of HM Revenue & Customs (HMRC) considers should have been deducted by the managed service company.

What is a 'managed service company'?
Section 61B is inserted into ITEPA setting out the meaning of a managed service company.

Subsection (1) sets out four qualifying criteria. If all four are satisfied, the company is a 'managed service company'.

(a)   That the business of the company consists wholly or mainly of providing, directly or indirectly, the services of an individual (or individuals) to other persons.

(b)   That payments made, directly or indirectly, to the individual providing their services, or their associates, equate to the majority, or all, of the amount the company is paid for the provision of that individual's services.

(c)   That the way the individual, or their associates, is paid, results in them receiving more money than they would have received, after PAYE and NICs had been deducted, if all of the payments had been employment income.

(d)   That a person termed the 'MSC provider', whose business is that of promoting and facilitating the use of companies to provide the services of individuals, is involved with the company. There are three key points in this subsection:

    (i)   the MSC provider's business is that of the promotion or facilitation of companies;

    (ii) the business is not simply that of promoting or facilitating companies, but specifically promoting or facilitating companies to provide the services of individuals; and

    (iii) the MSC provider is involved with the company. 'Involved' is defined in subsection (2). 'Promoting' and 'facilitating' have their normal meaning.

Calculation of deemed employment income

A new Section 61E to ITEPA explains how the managed service company works out the deemed employment payment on which PAYE and NICs is due.

Subsection (1) sets out a three step process to arrive at the sum to be subject to PAYE and NICs (the 'deemed employment payment').

Step 1: the managed service company first takes the payment received by the worker (whether or not it was paid by the managed service company.)

Section 61F provides an explanation of how a payment which is not cash is converted to a cash equivalent for the purposes of calculating the deemed employment payment;

Step 2: the managed service company deducts from the payment received by the worker expenses that are allowable under the Income Taxes Acts. Expenses are deductible:

*   as if the worker had been employed by the client to provide personal services, and
*   they had paid the expenses from their taxable earnings.

Because the expenses to be deducted are calculated on this basis, **the worker is not entitled to expenses for travel to the client's premises, nor to any associated accommodation or subsistence costs.**

If allowable expenses (having regard to the above factors) equal or exceed the payment received by the worker, there is no deemed employment payment to be subject to PAYE and NICs.

Step 3: the amount left after allowable expenses have been deducted from the payment received by the worker represent two amounts:

(a)   The amount of earnings to be subject to PAYE and employees' NICs, and
(b)   Employers' NICs on those earnings.

The managed service company must calculate the employers' NICs due on the payment received by the worker (less allowable expenses) in order to arrive at the two amounts. The sum on which PAYE and employees' NICs is to be deducted is the 'deemed employment payment'.

Note that a worker operating via a managed service company or similar structure is treated less favourably for tax purposes than a worker within the IR35 personal service company regime. Firstly the travelling expenses rules are more favourable under IR35, and secondly there is a cash flow disadvantage as PAYE and NIC would be due monthly as opposed to on 19 April following the end of the tax year under IR35.

4.16 Freelance lecturers
Sometimes genuine freelance lecturers are treated as employees by the university or college to which they are providing services. Sometimes only National Insurance contributions are deducted; sometimes both PAYE and NICs. This situation arises because the university or college is anxious to avoid problems with HMRC. It is still open to the lecturer to regard the fees as being trading income.

4.17 Armed forces
Redundancy schemes
Clause 62 of FA 2007 ensures that recipients of payments under the new Armed Forces Redundancy Scheme operational from 6.04.06 will be in the same tax position as those receiving payments under the Armed Forces Redundancy Scheme 1975.

Operational allowance
The Secretary of State for Defence announced on 10.10.06 the introduction of a new Operational Allowance for UK armed forces serving in specified locations, such as Iraq, Afghanistan and the Balkans. The new Operational Allowance is paid to members of the armed forces for service in specified areas, as designated by the Secretary of State for Defence, where the operational demands are the greatest.

Clause 63 of FA 2007 removes the income tax charge that would otherwise arise where a member of the armed forces is paid the Operational Allowance. it covers all payments made for service after 6.04.06.

4.18 Pay As You Earn (PAYE)
4.18.1 Introduction
PAYE is a method of collecting tax on wages and salaries at the time they are paid. The tax is deducted by the employer and passed on to the Receivables

Management Service. Such amounts of tax are not necessarily the correct tax due for the year. Accordingly, they should only be regarded as payments on account, and any excess will be repaid when the true liability under ITEPA 2003 is ascertained after the end of the tax year. Any underpayment may be recovered by direct assessment, or carried forward and collected by adjustment of the PAYE tax in subsequent years (via a restriction of the Code Allowances). In the latter case a simple form explaining the adjustment will be issued, but this will not affect the taxpayer's right to have a formal assessment (PR IR 22 March 1976). Sums credited to a director's loan account are treated as paid when the director is entitled to the emolument, but, if the credits are not unreservedly at the director's disposal, they do not constitute payment for this purpose (*Garforth v Newsmith Stainless Ltd* (Ch D 1978)).

In addition to income mentioned above, the PAYE scheme applies to annuities paid out of approved superannuation funds and Personal Pension Plans, as well as the deduction of Class I National Insurance Contributions.

The scheme does not apply to certain cases in which deduction of tax is impracticable, such as employees of a foreign government, income from 'tips' where these constitute the main earnings, porters employed by numerous employers, or daily casual workers employed by farmers. From 30.11.93 PAYE includes tax due when remuneration is paid in the form of marketable assets (e.g. gold and commodities), vouchers and credit tokens, and payment to third parties outside the UK. Vouchers and tokens for paying expenses are not included in PAYE. See FA 1994 ss 125-33.

4.18.2 How the scheme works
Every employer must operate PAYE when paying wages, salaries or other emoluments at a rate in excess of the statutory amounts at which PAYE is to be applied. These amounts are adjusted annually to take into account the amount of a single person's allowance.

The procedures for the operation of PAYE are normally set out in Statutory Instruments and are continually being reviewed to reduce the amount of administrative work as well as stationery costs. The up-to-date procedures are set out in the *Employers Guide to PAYE* and *Income Tax - PAYE* which can be obtained at any Tax Office, on-line or Employers CD-ROM. A brief outline of the operation of PAYE is set out below.

When the Inspector of Taxes receives notification of any person who is in receipt of such emoluments, he ascertains the **code** which takes into account the personal allowances and reliefs due, charges on income, underpayment for earlier years, and any subsidiary income on which the liability could be covered by the allowances. A Notice of Coding setting out the allowances and the code number is sent to the employee and a notification of the code number only is sent to the employer. Notice of objection to the code may be made to the Inspector and in the event of disagreement, an appeal may be made to the General Commissioners.

Under the system, where an employee is given a K code the employer will increase his taxable pay by the amount by which his assessable benefits in kind exceed his personal allowances. Tax is then deducted through the PAYE system subject to an overriding limit that the tax deducted cannot exceed 50% of the employee's pay. The 'K' codes replace 'F' codes which were used where personal allowances are less than the state retirement pension. P or V is used for those entitled to the full single or married Age Allowance. T is used for those entitled to marginal Age Allowance. Under D and F codes, tax is deducted on a non-cumulative basis.

When the employer pays the employee the code number is applied to **PAYE Tax Table A** to ascertain the free pay and after deducting the free pay from the gross pay, the total tax to the date of payment is calculated by reference to Tables B-D. The tax payable for the period of payment is the difference between the total tax payable to date and the total tax payable previously. In the event of the total tax payable to date being less than the total tax payable previously, a repayment is due to the employee.

A separate table is used for the deduction of the Class 1 National Insurance contributions, including the employee's share which must be deducted from the gross pay receivable.

Every employer must record the employee's pay, tax deducted and related National Insurance Contributions when the payments are made. HMRC issues **Deduction Working Sheets** (Forms P11) to enable the employer to keep the appropriate record. However, employers may use their own forms if they are approved by HMRC.

The employer must remit all tax and National Insurance contributions deducted as well as the employer's share of National Insurance contributions, less any statutory sick payments made to employees, and student loan repayments, from this payment they deduct any tax credits paid to employees. The payments must be made within 14 days after the end of each tax month or in cases where it is applicable, after the end of the quarter. Employers whose average monthly payments of PAYE and NICs are less than £1,500 in total are allowed to pay the amounts quarterly rather than monthly. Interest will be chargeable on PAYE and N.I. paid after 19 April for the previous tax year. Note is made of late payments and interest will be charged according to a published scale.

At the end of each year the employer must send to the Inspector of Taxes:
- an Annual Return of Pay and Deductions **(Form P14)** for each employee;

- a summary of the total deductions made for each employee. **(Form P35)**; This has to be filed with HMRC by 19 May following the end of the tax year.

- a return of emoluments given to an employee otherwise than in money, payments made on behalf of an employee and not repaid or treated as pay, and any emoluments paid in the year but relating to a different year **(Form P9D)** (a separate return must be made for every employee to whom payments are made); a return **(Form P11D)** for all directors and any employee receiving over £8,500 per annum showing: (i) payments made for expenses; (ii) sums put at employee's disposal; (iii) expenses incurred by the employer in providing the employee with services, benefits in kind, or facilities such as living accommodation, medical insurance, etc. (TMA 1970 s 15; FA 1976 Sch. 9, Pt. I; FA 1977 Sch. 8, para. 1).Under Self Assessment a copy of the P11D has to be given to the employee, and filed by 6 July following the end of the tax year.

At the end of each year the employer must give to each employee a certificate showing the total gross pay, tax deducted therefrom, National Insurance Number and the employer's name and address **(Form P60).**

4.18.3 Employees leaving and new employees
Employee leaving
The employer completes a **Form P45** which is now in four parts and gives Parts 1A, 2 and 3 to the employee and file Part 1 online to HMRC. If it is known that the employee is not going directly to another employment a Form P50 should be provided which enables the employee to reclaim tax refunds during the period of unemployment.

Employee dying
In the event of the death of an employee, Parts 1, 1A, 2 and 3 of the P45 must be filed together with the name and address of the personal representative if known.

Employee retiring
If the employee is in receipt of a pension from the employer, the employer must inform the Inspector of Taxes on Form P46(Pen) of the retirement, and continue operating PAYE by using the existing Code Number on a month 1/week 1 basis.

New employee
If the new employee produces Parts 2 and 3 of the Form P45 from a previous employment, a Deduction Working Sheet must be prepared from the particulars on the Form P45 and PAYE applied on a normal basis. Part 3 of the Form P45 must be completed and filed on line.

If the employee does not have a Form P45 or code authorization, the employer must complete a Form P46, obtain the employee's signature thereon and send it to the tax office. A Deduction Working Sheet must be prepared and tax deducted in accordance with the instructions relating to the particulars on the Form P46. A Coding Claim Form P15 must be given to the employee for completion and submission to the tax office.

Tax refunds exceeding £200 must not be made to a new employee unless authorized by the Inspector of Taxes.

4.18.4 Remuneration earned abroad or by a foreign domiciled person
PAYE procedures apply to all remuneration paid by UK employers, wherever the duties may be performed.

If an employee is entitled to a deduction because some part of the duties is performed abroad, this must be given by adjustment to the coding unless the employer has arranged with the tax office to deduct PAYE from only 75% of gross overseas earnings.

An employee, not domiciled in the UK and entitled to the relief on foreign emoluments, must claim an adjustment to the coding.

Normal PAYE procedures apply in respect of those offshore activities which are treated as carried on in the UK.

Any branch of an overseas employer which employs a person in the UK will be responsible for PAYE whether or not the remuneration is paid by that branch. Similar provision applies to any UK employer who has the benefit of the services of an employee of an overseas employer and who has general control and management of the employee's activities.

4.18.5 Other matters
Expense payments
The onus of deciding what constitutes 'gross pay' rests on the employer and tax must be deducted from such payments unless notified otherwise by the Inspector.

Holiday pay
Tax is deductible from holiday pay at the time that it is paid out. Where the employee receives more than one week's pay at holiday time and no pay for the holiday weeks, the Tax Tables for the respective holiday weeks may be used. However, by arrangement with the employer the holiday pay may be made in full, compensating adjustments being made in the coding or by a system of credits which spreads the tax on holiday pay over the whole year.

Maternity pay
Maternity pay paid after the cessation of employment is assessable as other income.

Superannuation contributions

Employee's superannuation contributions are deducted from gross pay for PAYE purposes, but must be included for the purposes of deducting Class 1 National Insurance Contributions.

Farmers

PAYE is not applicable on payments made to daily casual workers, or contractors or gangmasters who contract for a particular job and are therefore not employees of the farmer. All other workers are subject to PAYE, but the following items are not treated as pay:

- board and lodging provided by the farmer;
- rent free cottage;
- milk or other produce, coal, grazing rights.

Records

All records required to be maintained by the PAYE regulations and which are not required to be sent to HMRC must be retained by the employer for not less than three years after the end of the year to which they relate. PAYE/NIC inspections will also look for compliance with the National Minimum Wage (See Table 16. National Minimum Wage - 1 October 2010 back to 1 April 1999, p.642).

Statutory Sick Pay scheme

Employers are required to pay a statutory amount to employees in respect of sick pay which is subject to PAYE in the normal way. A proportion of the amount paid over to the employee is deducted from the amounts which have to be remitted monthly to the Receivables Management Service in respect of PAYE tax and National Insurance Contributions. There are limits to the amount firms can reclaim based upon the total NI paid.

Information as to fees, commissions, etc.

The Inspector of Taxes can require particulars to be supplied of all payments over £15 where tax is not deducted:

- made in the course of any activity for services rendered by persons who are not employees;

- for services in connection with the formation, acquisition, development or disposal of the business by persons who are not employees;

- in respect of any copyright, whether lump sum or periodical payments.

For this purpose, workers supplied by an agency are treated as employees of any person who remunerates them.

Commission of any kind and payments for expenses are specifically included and any valuable consideration is regarded as such a payment.

There is a penalty of £50 per day for failure to comply.

5 INCOME FROM INVESTMENTS AND SAVINGS

5.1 Summary of the System

Interest and dividends from investment and savings forms part of the taxpayer's total income for tax purposes. The income is subject to income tax, and capital profits on the sale, or other disposal of investments may be subject to capital gains tax. The income is classified as 'unearned income'. Much of the tax payable is borne by deduction of income tax from interest received or by 'imputation' to dividends received. Investment income from overseas sources may, in addition, be subject to a deduction for tax levied in the country of the payer. Investment income may be generally classified as: taxed interest, untaxed interest and taxed dividends, as explained below.

5.2 Taxed Interest

This is interest from which tax has been deducted. It covers most interest paid on company loans and debentures, government securities, local authority loans, other loans and, interest from bank deposits and from shares and deposits in building societies. The taxpayer must enter the gross amount (i.e before deduction of tax) on their return of income. It is the gross amount which forms part of a taxpayer's total income for tax purposes, for instance for calculating any higher rate payable, or for reclaiming tax when there is no liability or when tax is payable at the starting rate only. See 5.4 Taxed Dividends, p.137, for the effect of the system on the overall tax liability of individuals.

Gilt interest

People can receive gilt interest gross rather than after deduction of tax if they want to.

Details:

(a)   Previously gilt interest was generally paid after deduction of income tax.

(b)   There is an exception to this in the case of gilts which are the subject of Treasury directions to the effect that the interest is paid gross. However, holders of such gilts can ask for the interest to be paid net of tax if they prefer, simply by approaching the Bank of England. Holders of such gilts (whether they receive the interest gross or have requested net payment) will not be affected by the change.

5.3 Untaxed Interest

This is interest from which tax is not deducted by the payer and would include interest from national savings accounts, government stock on the national savings and Trustee Savings Bank registers, 3 1/2% War Loan, other government stock held by taxpayers not ordinarily resident in the UK, bank and building society interest for which application (on form R85) has been made for gross payment on the grounds that the investor is not liable to tax, including a charity. Untaxed interest must be included in the taxpayers return of income and tax thereon, possibly at the higher rate, will be directly assessed on the taxpayer or treated as a reduction of allowances for the purpose of coding PAYE on remuneration.

Interest up to £70 on deposits with the **National Savings & Investments (NSI)** (but not investment deposits), or other banks approved by the Treasury, is exempted from tax.

Interest received by **solicitors** on clients' designated deposit accounts is not in practice assessed on the solicitor, who will pay the gross amount to the client. If the client is not resident in the UK the solicitor will deduct tax and account for it to HMRC.

Bank interest retained by an **estate agent** on rents collected is assessable on the estate agent (*Aplin v White* Ch D 1973). Interest on a bank deposit, made as security for a loan from the bank, is 'received' by the depositor and assessable on him as it is credited to the account, even though it cannot be drawn whilst the security subsists (*Dunmore v McGowan* CA 1978). New regulations came into force in April 2007 concerning the remittance to the tenants of this interest.

5.4 Taxed Dividends
5.4.1 General

A dividend is a share of profit received by a shareholder from a company. In strictness tax is not deducted from a dividend but is said to be 'imputed' to the payment. The distinction from the treatment of taxed interest is only a technical distinction, since the shareholder is assumed to have suffered tax on the dividend (plus, possibly) overseas tax if the dividend is from a foreign source). The tax suffered is treated as a 'tax credit' against the taxpayer's overall tax liability, and the credit is shown on the dividend voucher received from the payer:

dividend received (90%)	£900.00
tax credit (10%)	£100.00
gross dividend (100%)	£1,000.00

- The tax credits at 10 per cent are not repayable to shareholders with no tax liability.

• Individual shareholders whose income is within basic rate band will be liable to tax at 20% on their dividend income. The tax credit satisfies their tax liability on UK dividends. The higher rate on dividend income is 32.5%.

	£
Net Dividend	80.00
Tax credit	(10%) 8.89
Gross Dividend	88.89
Higher rate tax	(32.5%) 28.89
After tax income	£60.00

• A quick way of calculating top rate tax on a dividend remains as 25% of the net dividend received (£80 x 25% = £20 top rate tax payable).

5.4.2 Examples - 2011/2012

(a) *Non-taxpayer, i.e. with nil chargeable income after deducting charges and allowances, but including the gross dividends. The taxpayer cannot reclaim the tax credit on the dividend.*

(b) *Taxpayer liable at the basic rate, i.e. with chargeable income up to £35,000. Example:*

	£
gross dividends	1,200
other chargeable income	22,520
total chargeable income	23,720
tax thereon:	
£22,520 @ 20%	4,504
£1,200 (dividend) @ 10%	120
£23,720	4,624
Less: tax credit	120
additional tax payable	£4,504

Note that there is no additional liability on the dividend for tax at the basic rate, for as long as the marginal rate of tax is the basic rate.

(c) Taxpayer liable at the higher rate, i.e. with chargeable income above £35,000 but below £150,000.

Example:

	£
gross dividends	2,000
other chargeable income	40,000
total chargeable income	42,000
tax liability thereon:	
£35,000 @ 20%	7,000
£2,000 @ 32.5%	650 *
£5,000 @ 40%	2,000
£42,000	9,650
Less: tax credit (10%)	200 *
additional tax payable	£9,450

* On these dividends there is an additional payment of tax due. This is because if your marginal rate of tax is at the higher rate you have to account for the extra 22.5% (32.5% - 10%) i.e. £650 - £200 = £450.

(d) Taxpayer liable at the 50% additional rate, i.e. with chargeable income above £150,000.

Example:

	£
gross dividends	2,000
other chargeable income	170,000
total chargeable income	172,000
tax liability thereon:	
£35,000 @ 20%	7,000
£2,000 @ 42.5%	850 *
£115,000 @ 40%	46,000
£20,000 @ 50%	10,000
£172,000	63,850
Less: tax credit (10%)	200 *
additional tax payable	£63,650

* On these dividends there is an additional payment of tax due. This is because if your marginal rate of tax is at the 50% rate you have to account for the extra 32.5% (42.5% - 10%) i.e. £850 - £200 = £650.

5.4.3 Special cases
(a) Stock Dividends
From 5th April 1999 the cash value is treated as having borne tax at 10%.

(b) Foreign dividends
UK shareholders' tax credit relief on foreign dividends
To comply with the EC Treaty the UK has given investors in foreign companies a 10% tax credit relief equivalent to the relief they receive in respect of dividends from UK companies. The relief applied to shareholdings of less than 10% following FA 2008 and has been extended to shareholdings in excess of 10% by FA 2009.

HMRC's Business Brief 76/09 explains how the latest relief works. The relief applies to shareholdings in companies in qualifying territories and over 100 countries which are to be treated as qualifying are listed in the Business Brief.

The relief applies from 22 April 2009 and affects individuals who hold share in:

• foreign companies with a holding that is 10% or more of the issued share capital of the company.

• foreign companies with a holding that is 10% or more of a specific class of share in the company.

• offshore funds.

The tax credit is not available where the distribution is one of a series of distributions made as part of a tax avoidance scheme, and the company must not be an 'excluded company'. The excluded companies are set out in regulations and cover particular corporate regimes in Barbados, Cyprus, Jamaica, Luxembourg, Malaysia and Malta.

The Business Brief contains an example of how the relief will work in practice. Basic rate taxpayers will be exempted from any further tax on these foreign dividends but any withholding tax suffered on the dividend will be 'wasted'. However, higher rate taxpayers who are liable at the rate of 32.5% or 42.5% on the dividend, including withholding tax, plus the tax credit will have any withholding tax set off against the further 32.5% / 42.5% liability.

(c) Non-resident shareholders
Double taxation agreements often provide for payment of partial tax credits on

dividends from UK companies.

(d) Trustees

Dividends paid to beneficiaries with an interest in possession have a tax credit of 10%. Payments to beneficiaries of discretionary trusts have a tax credit of 34%. Trustees will be liable for tax at 34% on dividends received by the trust but can set off the tax credit of 10% against this liability.

(e) Deceased estates

The income of the estate is subject to income tax at 20% except that, dividend income is chargeable at 10% which matches the tax credit.

5.5 Accrued Interest Bond Washing, etc.

5.5.1 Accrued interest - general

Accrued interest arises for tax purposes on interest bearing securities and stock such as government securities, local authority loans and company loans or debentures. It consists of the proportion of unpaid interest added to the price when the securities are sold close to the date when interest is payable.

If a seller transfers 'securities' with accrued interest, so that the purchaser receives the next interest payment, the seller is taxed on a proportion of that interest. The proportion is A/B. 'B' is the total days in the period for which the interest is paid and 'A' is the part of the period during which the seller held the securities. When the purchaser receives their first interest payment the taxable amount is reduced by A/B.

Example:
If X sells a long held bond on 30 November for £1,110. Y receives £120 interest on 31 December. A is 335 days and B is 365 days.

$$A/B = 335/365 \times £120 = £110.$$
$$X \text{ is taxable on } £110, \text{ and } Y £10.$$

In the other case if the seller disposes of the security but still receives the next interest payment the taxable amount is reduced by (B-A)/B. The purchase is taxed on the same proportion which actually corresponds to their period of ownership.

Using the above example where X receives the interest.

$$(B-A)/B = (365 - 335)/365 \times £120 = £10.$$

The rules do not apply to dealers in securities, non residents and all persons owning securities with a total nominal value of no more than £5,000 in the year of assessment or the previous year. Securities are normally quoted 'cum div' so that the buyer receives the full interest payment, i.e covering a period before the date of purchase. The price will take account of the interest payable, which will normally be taxable in the hands of the buyer, unless the rules as to accrued interest apply. The seller may then carry out what is called 'bond washing' by buying back the securities immediately they have gone 'ex div'. Thus the seller will not be liable for income tax on the interest which has in effect been received in the original sale price. The higher sale price cum div will however tend to increase the seller's capital gain on the original sale but this gain may be covered by the personal exemption of £8,800 in 2006/2007. Market dealers are exempt from the bond washing rules (TA 1988 s.732; see also FA 1993 s 63).

5.5.2 Manufactured dividends and interest
Manufactured dividends are payments made to compensate recipients for dividends or interest not received on purchases of securities 'cum div' but acquired after the securities have become ex div; or where the securities have been lent. The recipient of the manufactured dividend or interest is taxable thereon (FA1991 s.58 and Sch 13; TA1988 s.737 and Sch 23A).

FA 2002 introduced a restriction on the circumstances in which individuals are able to obtain a tax deduction for manufactured payments, made on or after 17 April 2002.

This highly technical area relates typically to stock loans and repos, where a person holding the security receives an interest or dividend payment but has agreed as part and parcel of a contrived arrangement to pay an equivalent amount to the original owner.

Individuals have been able to deduct such payments from total income but this regime, originally intended for traders in financial markets, has been extended to schemes where individuals, not connected with the financial market, generate tax relief in circumstances where it would not have been available for actual payments of interest.

The new measure will limit relief on such payments, to circumstances where an equivalent amount is brought into charge, to tax in respect of the same securities.

5.5.3 New Securities - extra return
Sch 12 of the FA1991 (amending TA1988 s.587) refers to the 'extra return' which may be received when new securities are issued to replace old securities of the same kind. The extra return is the amount included in the issue price of the new securities to cover interest unpaid on the old securities. This extra return is taxable in the hands of the recipient but is not relieved of tax payable by the issuer of the securities.

5.5.4 Deep discount or deep gain securities
A deep discount arises where a returnable security is issued at a discount which represents more than 15% of the amount payable on redemption; or is 15% or less,

but more than 1/2% per annum between the date of issue and redemption. This does not apply to shares in a company or any form of distribution of profits or assets. The discount is chargeable to tax on the person acquiring the security at the end of each income period of ownership; and the income element is a charge against the profits of the issuing company. Many detailed provisions apply, (TA s.57 and Sch 4, FA1991 Sch 12) and see FA 1993 s 64-65.

5.6 Investment in unquoted companies
5.6.0 Industries now excluded
From 6 April 2008 investment in ship building, coal and steel production are excluded from these schemes.

5.6.1 EIS and VCTs: The "gross assets test"
From April 2006 the relevant assets of the company (or group of companies) raising money under the venture capital schemes could not exceed £7 million immediately before the investment and £8 million immediately afterwards.

For VCTs the limits apply to investment of funds raised after 6 April 2006. For EIS the limits apply to shares issued on or after 6 April 2006. EIS investments made by Approved Investment Funds (AIFs) are similarly subject to the new limits from 6 April 2006.

5.6.2 Enterprise Investment Scheme (EIS)
A number of changes are made to the venture capital schemes in the 2009 Finance Act.

Changes are made to the EIS to:

- remove the limitation that only the costs of shares purchased before 6 October can be carried back, and remove the £50,000 limit on the amount that may be carried back, and the rule restricting carry-back to half of shares issued for 2009/2010 onwards. The only remaining restriction on carrying back relief is the overriding investment limit for any year, currently £500,000;

- remove the link to other shares of the same class issued at the same time as the qualifying shares for shares issued on or after 22 April 2009;

- correct an anomaly regarding the capital gains position for investors in the event of a share for share exchange for new holdings issued on or after 22 April 2009.

In addition, currently 80% of money raised by a share issue has to be employed by the company in a qualifying activity within 12 months of the issue of shares (or the time the trade commences, whichever is later) and the balance within a further 12 months. This rule is replaced with a simple condition that all the money must be employed within two years of the date of the issue (or commencement of trade if this is later) for shares issued on/after 22 April 2009.

- Income tax relief is available at 20% on new subscriptions by individuals for eligible ordinary shares in qualifying unlisted trading companies (including shares traded on the alternative investment market (AIM)) satisfying the conditions of the EIS scheme. The maximum amount qualifying for relief in a single tax year from 2008/2009 is £500,000 (2007/2008 £400,000).

- Unlimited capital gains arising from the disposal of other assets can be deferred by investment into the EIS, provided the EIS investment is made in the period starting 12 months before the date of disposal and ending 36 months after.

- A capital gain on disposal of the shares after the minimum holding period (see below) will be exempt from CGT. Capital losses may generally be relieved against either capital gains or taxable income.

- EIS investments may qualify for inheritance tax (IHT) business property relief.

Notes:
- For shares issued between 6 April and 5 October in any year, up to half may be treated for EIS purposes as if issued in the previous tax year (see above).

- The reliefs are withdrawn if various conditions are not met or cease to be met. For EIS investments made since 6 April 2000, these include a minimum holding period of three years, where relevant starting only from when the company begins trading (five years for earlier investments).

EIS and connected parties
The case of *RJ Taylor v HMRC* TC 426 provides guidance about whether an individual is connected with a company for the purposes of the Enterprise Investment Scheme (EIS).

It is well known that if you have more than 30% of the shares in the company, you are connected with the company and disqualified from EIS relief. Actually, the test is rather more complicated than that. The individual must not possess more than 30% of:

(a)   the issued ordinary share capital.
(b)   the loan capital and issued share capital of the company; or
(c)   the voting power in the company.

Mr Taylor had an interest in Wrapit Plc, and although he held less than 30% of the issued share capital, he held more than 30% of the loan capital of the company. He obviously did not breach condition (a) or (c), and he claimed that he did not breach condition (b) because he did not hold more than 30% of the loan capital and more than 30% of the issued share capital.

HMRC said this was not the right interpretation. He possessed more than 30% of the aggregate of the loan capital and the issued share capital, and therefore he was connected with the company.

The Tribunal concluded that the taxpayers' interpretation was clear and easy to apply and did not trap the bona fide investor.

The Tribunal concluded that condition (b) was not breached.

5.6.3 Venture capital trusts (VCTs)

In the 2009 Finance Act legislation is introduced to make improvements to the scheme to relax the time limits concerning the employment of money raised by companies to two years or if later two years from the commencement of the qualifying activity, for shares issued on or after 22 April 2009.

- VCTs are quoted companies similar in concept to investment trusts. At least 70% of the VCT's underlying investments must be invested in a spread of small unquoted trading companies within three years.

- Income tax relief is available at 30% on new subscriptions for ordinary shares in VCTs by individuals aged 18 or over.

- The maximum amount qualifying for relief is £200,000.

- Dividends received from VCTs are exempt from income tax, provided the shares acquired (by subscription or purchase) are within the annual limits.

- Shares in VCTs which attract income tax relief are also exempt from CGT on disposal at any time, but losses on disposal are not allowable as capital losses.

- Qualifying holding period.
  The period that individuals must hold VCT shares to qualify for income tax relief is five years.

5.7 Bonus shares and scrip issues
5.7.1 Bonus share

Bonus shares which represent a capitalization of profits or reserves, if issued other than for full consideration, are not normally taxable on the shareholder. Nor are rights issues or share exchanges normally taxable, but these issues may affect the shareholder's capital gains computation.

5.7.2 Share in lieu of dividend
Where an option is exercised to take shares in lieu of dividend, the shareholder is liable to tax or the grossed up cash equivalent. HMRC may however substitute the market value of the shares issued where the cash dividend is 15% less than the market value at the first dealing date or, for unquoted shares, the date of the issue.

5.8 Individual Savings Accounts ("ISAs")
From 6 April 2011:

• The annual ISA investment allowance was raised to £10,680 (£10,200). Up to £5,340 of that allowance can be saved in cash with one provider. The remainder can be invested in stocks and shares with either the same or a different provider.

• ISA savers can invest in two separate ISAs each tax year; a cash ISA and a stocks and shares ISA.

• ISA savers are able to transfer money saved in their cash ISA to their stocks and shares ISA but not visa versa.

For example, you can chose to save £1,000 in a cash ISA with one provider and £9,680 in a stocks and shares ISA with a different provider.

• Only those aged 18 and over can invest in a full ISA, but it is possible for those aged 16 and 17 to invest in a cash based mini ISA.

Junior ISA
From November 2011 a "Junior ISA" will be available for under 16 year olds.

Until the child who owns a Junior ISA reaches the age of 16, his or her accounts will be managed by the person with parental responsibility for them. Eligible children over the age of 16 will be able to open Junior ISAS for themselves.

No withdrawals from Junior ISAS by account holders will be permitted until the child reaches 18. It will also not be possible to transfer Child Trust Funds into Junior ISAS, or vice versa. The government will impose no limit on minimum contributions to Junior ISAS.

Children will be able to hold up to one cash and one stocks and shares Junior ISA at a time. The limit for annual contributions is £3,000, which will operate across both accounts if they have both a cash and stocks and shares ISA.

Any cash put into Junior ISAS will be 'locked in' until the child is 18, and the ISA will then, by default, become an adult one.

5.9 Life Policy - Partial Disposal

At the end of each policy year, the policy attracts a 'notional allowance' of 5 per cent of the total premium then paid under the policy. This allowance is then set against the value of any partial surrenders made up to that date. If the value of those partial surrenders exceeds the current cumulative allowance, a 'chargeable event' occurs; if the cumulative allowance is equal to or exceeds cumulative withdrawals, no chargeable event occurs. Allowances are given up to 100 per cent of the total premiums paid so that, for a single premium investment bond, the allowances are given at the rate of 5 per cent for 20 years.

Example: Cumulation of allowances and withdrawals

X invests £10,000 in a single premium investment bond; £1,200 is withdrawn after four policy years, a further £4,500 after six policy years and £1,000 after eight policy years.

Policy Years	A Cumulative Allowances	B Partial Surrender chargeable events	C Cumulative surrender	D Taxable Gain between (C-A)
	£	£	£	£
1	500 (1 x 500)	0	0	0
2	1,000 (2 x 500)	0	0	0
3	1,500 (3 x 500)	0	0	0
4	2,000 (4 x 500)	1,200	1,200	0
5	2,500 (5 x 500)	0	1,200	0
6	3,000 (6 x 500)	4,500	5,700	2,700
7	500 (1 x 500)	0	0	0
8	1,000 (2 x 500)	1,000	1,000	0
9	1,500 (3 x 500)	0	1,000	0
10	2,000 (4 x 500)	0	1,000	0
etc				

Note: (1) A chargeable event occurs only when C exceeds A.
(2) The value of the policy is irrelevant to these calculations so that it is possible to have a taxable gain under a policy at a time when the policy itself is worth less than the premiums paid.

When the final chargeable event occurs under the policy (i.e. death, maturity, final surrender or assignment for value) the total profit on the policy is brought into account. The profit is the final proceeds (excluding any mortality profit where the event is death), plus previous partial surrenders, less premiums paid and any taxable gains from previous partial withdrawals.

Example - Total surrender after partial surrenders

Using the example immediately above, if the policy were totally surrendered at the end of the tenth policy year for £10,400, the taxable gain on that final encashment would be as follows:

£10,400 + £1,200 + £4,500 + £1,000 - (£10,000 + £2,700) = £4,400

Top Slicing:

Legislation recognises that the gain will have accrued over a number of years and the concept of 'top slicing' is applied.

The slice is calculated by reference to the size of the gain divided by the number of complete years the policy has been in force.

This slice is added to the taxpayers income and the average rate of tax (minus basic rate tax) is computated. This rate is applied to the total gain (all the slices) and the liability calculated.

Examples follow:

Example - no tax on the gain

Y invests £20,000 in a single premium investment bond in May 200X and cashes it in after five years for £27,500. The gain is therefore £7,500 and the 'slice' is £1,500 (£7,500 divided by five).

	£
Taxable income (excluding policy gain)	15,000
'Slice'	1,500
Taxable income	£16,500

The tax rate applicable to the 'slice is therefore 20 per cent less 20 per cent = 0 per cent.

Example - slice falling into basic and higher rate bands

Z invests £12,000 in a single premium investment bond in May 200X. After five years he cashes it in for £17,000. The gain is £5,000 and the slice is £1,000 (£5,000 divided by five). In that year his other taxable income after reliefs is £31,000.

Tax calculation on gain:

Taxable income + 'slice' (£31,000 + £1,000) =	£32,000
Tax Applicable to slice	
On £400 (i.e. £31,000 to £31,400) at 0% (20%-20%) =	Nil
On £600 (i.e. £31,400 to £32,000) at 20% (40%-20%) =	£120
Total tax on slice =	£120
Average rate on slice	
$\dfrac{120}{1,000} \times 100$	12%

The tax payable is £5,000 x 12% = £600

To illustrate the effect of top-slicing, if it had not been available the calculations would have been:

Tax applicable to the gain on £400 at 0% (20%-20%) =	Nil
On £4,600 at 20% (40% - 20%) =	£920
Tax payable =	£920

Notes:
1) The whole gain (without top-slicing) is counted as income in determining whether any age allowance should be reduced.
2) There is no top-slicing where the taxpayer is a company.

Taxing gains on chargeable events (TA 1988, ss 547 and 550)

In the majority of cases where the policyholder owns the policy for his own absolute benefit, the gain is treated as the top-slice of his income and is taxed appropriately.

However, because the income and gains attributable to the underlying assets of the policy have already been taxed in the hands of the life company, life policy gains are not chargeable to income tax at the basic rate. Despite the fact that, in effect, the gain is treated as having already suffered basic rate tax, there is no grossing up of the gain for the purposes of higher rate tax.

Accordingly, for an individual paying tax at the higher rate, the maximum rate of tax payable on life policy gains will be 20 per cent (40 per cent less 20 per cent). An individual whose income (including the gain) is taxable at the basic rate only will have no further income tax liability on the policy gain. Non-taxpayers or those paying tax at the lower rate of 20 per cent will not be able to make any reclaim in respect of tax notionally paid by the life company.

Gains on life insurance policies
The rate of tax treated as paid is the lower rate of 20%, (FA 2003 Cl 172 & Sch 35).

6 DEATH OF TAXPAYER

6.1 Executors' liability for tax
The executors or administrators of a deceased taxpayer are liable to pay out of the estate funds all income tax and capital gains tax on the deceased's income due to the date of death. This liability includes not only tax for the tax year in which the death occurs but also outstanding tax for prior years. The tax due for prior years may or may not have been assessed at the date of death, but if not HMRC may make assessments thereon within three years from the date of death. The assessments can be made in respect of up to six years before the date of death in the case of fraud, wilful default or neglect. (TMA ss 74 and 77).

For the tax year in which the death occurs the income will be reduced by charges incurred in that period, the full personal and, if applicable, the full married couple's allowance.

Capital gains tax will, if relevant, also be payable for capital profits realized in the period. Unless covered by the exemptions available, Inheritance Tax will be payable on the value of the estate at the date of death.

6.2 The administration period
The administration period is the time after the death until the debts of the estate have been paid and the assets have been distributed to the beneficiaries; or until, in accordance with the will or the rules of intestacy, a trust has been established to take over the residue of the estate. Special regulations apply to the taxation of trust income - see below:-

6.3 Deeds of family arrangement
Some mitigation of tax may be effected by means of a 'deed of family arrangement' drawn up after probate of a will and varying the legacies. Such arrangements can reduce inheritance tax and income and capital gains tax for certain beneficiaries. The use of an 'excluded property trust' has now been accepted by the Capital Taxes Office.

6.4 Payment of tax
During the administration period the executors are liable to pay income tax at the

basic rate on the income from the estate. The liability to basic rate tax will be satisfied by deduction at source from much of the income, e.g., taxed interest and taxed dividends. The beneficiaries must make returns to HMRC of the income they receive from the estate, grossed up at the basic rate if paid net to them, and may be liable to the higher rate thereon. They must also make returns of capital in the form of specific assets, e.g., securities, chattels, land and buildings, received from the estate. These specific assets will be valued at probate values for the purpose of capital gains tax if and when they are disposed of, e.g., sold; but the death of the taxpayer does not represent a 'disposal' for the purpose of that tax.

7 TRUSTS AND SETTLEMENTS
(TA 1988 ss 660-685 FA1991 ss 83-92 and Sch 16-18)

7.0 June 2010 Budget
The Budget on 22 June 2010 raised the rate of tax on gains accruing to the trustees of a settlement or the personal representatives of a deceased person, with effect from 23 June 2010, to 28% from 18% previously.

7.1 S660 Settlements
This topic is still not finally settled as the effects of the 'Arctic Systems' case await the views of the new Government.

Income Shifting
The leading case remains *Jones v Garnett*, but the first tier tribunal has just considered a variant on this theme in the case of *Patmore* (TC00619). Mr and Mrs Patmore purchased the shares in a company in which Mr Patmore had previously worked. They paid partly in cash (by means of taking out a mortgage on their jointly held property) and the rest was to be paid in instalments. The husband owned 98% of the 'A' shares and his wife had the remaining 2%.

The company then issued some non-voting 'B' shares to Mrs Patmore and a significant dividend was paid out on these shares. She then passed the money to her husband to pay for the shares. The issue was whether the dividend received by Mrs Patmore should be reallocated to Mr Patmore and he should be taxed upon it.

The first tier tribunal found that when the shares were purchased, the consideration was from both the spouses equally but Mrs Patmore only got 2% of the shares. There was therefore a constructive trust in her favour. She had put up half the capital to buy the shares and was jointly liable on the loans and mortgage and therefore she was entitled to a half share in the 'A' and 'B' shares.

There was no bounty in the issue of the 'B' shares to Mrs Patmore and consequently no settlement under the rules that are now found in s619 onwards in the Income Tax (Trading and Other Income) Act 2005.

7.2 The nature of trusts

Trusts, otherwise known as 'settlements' are created when an individual, 'the settlor', transfers assets to specified trustees for the benefit of named beneficiaries. Trusts may be created by declaration of the settlor. They may be established while the settlor is still living, or by provision in a will, after his death - a 'Will Trust'; or they may be set up on an intestacy (where there is no will). The following categories of trusts are relevant for tax purposes:-

7.3 Categories of trusts
7.3.1 Revocable and Irrevocable

A revocable trust is one which the settlor has power to cancel the settlement at any time, and an irrevocable settlement is one where the settlor has no such power.

7.3.2 Discretionary trusts

These are trusts under which the trustees have discretion as to the application of the income or the capital.

7.3.3 Accumulation trusts

These give the trustees power to accumulate the income until a certain event, such as a child beneficiary attaining a certain age (normally 18).

7.3.4 Foreign trusts

A trust has a 'residence' in much the same way as an individual. In general a foreign residence applies where a majority of the trustees are resident abroad and the trust is managed abroad, but certain qualifications to this general statement were brought into effect by the FA 1991 ss 83-92 and Sch 16-18, particularly as regards capital gains of trusts.

7.4 Taxation of trusts
7.4.1 Liability of trustees

Trustees must make returns to HMRC of the trust income for each tax year. They are liable for basic rate tax on that income plus the additional rate of 12% on the income and capital gains of discretionary and accumulating trusts after deducting expenses. Much of the liability to basic rate tax will be satisfied by deduction at source but the trustees will be assessed to tax on untaxed income. They will also be assessed to the additional rate where applicable. The additional rate, if payable, will be calculated on the grossed up amount of taxed interest and dividends.

7.4.2 Taxation of income

The main changes introduced by the new measures are:
- a basic rate band of £1,000

- a common meaning of "settled property", leading to a common meaning of "settlement"

- a common meaning of "settlor"

- provision for the trustees of a settlement to be treated as a single person

- a common test to determine whether the trustees of a settlement are resident in the United Kingdom

- provision for the trustees of a settlement to elect that a sub-fund of the settlement be treated as a separate settlement in certain circumstances.

All the above changes, with the exception of the increase in the standard rate band, are to apply for the purposes of the Income Tax Acts and the TCGA.

In addition, the following changes have been introduced:

- the income of settlor-interested settlements is treated as though it had arisen directly to the settlor

- a measure to legislate the existing practice of not taxing beneficiaries who receive discretionary income payments from the trustees of settlor-interest trusts.

Tax is charged at the basic rate on the income of trusts, except that the additional rate of 12% is also charged on 'income' (after deducting trust expenses and income vested in a beneficiary) which:

- is to be accumulated, or

- is payable at the discretion of the trustees or any other person (whether or not there is a power of accumulation).

Income includes stock dividends and the gross equivalent of building society or bank interest, close company apportionments and income passed on by the personal representatives of a deceased person (TA 1988 s 686). Interest received is subject to tax being deducted at 20% at source.

Income below £1,000 is taxed at source at either 10% (dividends) or 20% (interest). Above £1,000 dividend income is additionally taxed at 42.5% and interest at 50%.

Income distributions
Where income is distributed, the trustees should give a tax voucher showing that tax has been deducted at 50% (as the trustees will have paid tax on the income).

For example:
A cash distribution of £3,000 per individual in June 2010 would be shown as follows on the tax voucher provided:

Gross distribution:	£6,000
Tax:	£3,000
Net distribution:	£3,000

If the gross distribution from the trust is lower than the available personal allowance (£7,475 for 2011/2012) and they have no other income during the tax year, they will be able to reclaim the tax credit (i.e. £3,000 in the example above).

If the individual does have other income, but this amounts to less than £150,000 in total, then they will be able to reclaim a proportion of the tax credit.

Capital distributions
A capital distribution is more likely to be a one-off, larger distribution from the trustees. As the distribution does not represent income, there is no tax credit attached to it and the recipients would not be able to reclaim any tax on the distribution.

Income tax adjustments between settlors and trustees
From 6 April 2010, settlors who receive repayments of tax on trust income because their personal tax rate is lower than the trustees' rate will be required to pass such repayments to the trustees. These payments to trustees will be disregarded for IHT purposes. The measures are contained Clause 7 of the F(No2)B 2010.

The condoc published after the June Budget 2010 explains the provisions as follows:- "Section 646 of ITTOIA provides for adjustments between the settlor and trustees where the amount of tax paid by the trustees is different to the settlor's own liability on that income. Sections 646(1) to (3) of ITTOIA provide for the situation where the settlor has additional tax to pay on the trust income. In recognition that he may not have the money to pay the tax he is entitled to recover the additional amount from the trustees. Sections 646(4) to (8) of ITTOIA provide for the situation where the settlor obtains a repayment of tax on trust income because his liability is lower than the tax funded by the trustees. Where the repayment is in respect of an allowance or relief he is required to pay it over to the trustees. The clause extends this requirement to all repayments, such as where the settlor is liable to income tax at a rate lower than that of the trustees. Inheritance tax (IHT) is charged on the value transferred by a chargeable disposition that diminishes the value of the transferor's estate. Repayments of tax on trust income paid over by the settlor to the trustees under a statutory obligation, as provided by the clause, will not diminish the value of the settlor's estate and so will not be liable to IHT (where they might otherwise have been)."

Tax is chargeable at the basic and, in some cases, the additional rate, on profits from a business carried on for the benefit of an estate in trust (*McDougall v Smith* CS 1919; *Fry v Shiel's Trustees* CS 1915). However, where a trustee is also a beneficiary as regards the whole or a share of the profits of the business and further takes an active and responsible part in its management or conduct, his profits are treated as earned income.

7.4.3 Taxation of payments

As the income in their hands has borne tax, either by deduction or by direct assessment, the trustees are deemed to have deducted income tax when paying out annuities (but not when distributing capital monies). Where the income of a trust estate is insufficient to pay annuities, and part of such annuities are paid out of capital, the trustees are assessable on the part paid out of capital, but it does not follow that a payment must be capital in the hands of a beneficiary merely because it is paid out of trustee's capital. The trustee and the beneficiary are quite separate persons and the nature of the payment in the hands of the beneficiary must alone be considered in deciding whether it is capital or income, the source from which the trustee obtained it being normally irrelevant (*Brodie's Trustees v CIR* KBD 1933; *Lindus & Horton v CIR* KBD 1933; *Postlethwaite v CIR* Ch D 1963; TA 1970 s 53). However, in exceptional cases the nature of the receipt (e.g. a bonus issue) may be dictated by its nature when it arises in the original source (e.g. a company) (*Lawson v Rolfe* Ch D 1969). Whether the amount paid out of capital should be grossed up in arriving at the income of the beneficiaries depends upon the circumstances in which it is paid (*Morant Settlement Trustees v CIR* CA 1948), but the trustee will be accountable for income tax at the basic rate where the income benefit is not paid out of profits kept in charge to tax. The trustees will be accountable for tax at the sum of the basic and additional rates in respect of the grossed-up payments to beneficiaries in exercise of their or another's discretion. From that amount the trustees may, however, deduct the following amounts of tax suffered (or deemed to be suffered) by them:

*   income tax charged at the basic and additional rates on 'income' (other than apportionments) accumulated or subject to discretion.

*   income tax charged at the additional rate on apportionments and stock dividends, and at the basic rate on distributions not treated as income on account of prior appointments.

*   income tax equal to two-thirds of the net income available for distribution at the end of 1972-1973 (TA 1988 s 687).

Discretionary payments by charitable trusts which are received as income will be liable to tax, at the basic and additional rates, by a deduction at source (HM Treasury Press Release, 25 October 1974).

7.5 Anti-avoidance

Higher-rate taxpayers have sought to reduce their liabilities by transferring income or capital to third parties. At the same time, many persons do not wish to part entirely with the income and capital, but to retain some degree of control over it and anti-avoidance legislation has been introduced to counteract such schemes.

The settlor, i.e. the person by whom the settlement is made or who has directly or indirectly provided the funds, is taxed on the income arising under dispositions (including any trust, deed of covenant, agreement or arrangement), as follows.

7.5.1 Short disposition

Income from dispositions made other than a deed of covenant in favour of a charity (TA 1988 ss 660-662). Income from deeds of covenant made prior to 15 March 1988 in favour of individuals for full consideration was treated as income of the beneficiary if the period of payment exceeds six years.

In examining the deeds of covenant for validity and repayment of tax, HMRC considers the following:

- evidence as to payment and deduction of tax. (this is normally satisfied by a Certificate of Tax Deducted on Form R185AP);

- non-reciprocity (a declaration is required from the covenantor and covenantee that there are no arrangements for a return to the covenantor of any part of the benefit of the deed);

- evidence of sealing.

A 'reverse annuity' scheme had been held not to be caught by this provision because there was sufficient consideration for the annuity (*CIR v Plummer* HL 1979). However, this decision has been reversed by *Moodie v CIR,* February 1993.

7.5.2 Settlement by a parent in favour of own child

The settlor will be charged tax:

(a)   where the settlor or spouse retains interest in the settlement; OR

(b)   settlement is in favour of minor or unmarried children and the trust income is greater than £100 p.a.; OR

(c)   on annual value (by reference to the official rate of interest and actual interest paid) of any loans received or made by the settlor.

From 9 March 1999 a loophole was closed in the settlements legislation which had been used to avoid the rule that income from investments made by parents on behalf of their minor children was taxed as income of the parent (subject to a £100 de minimis limit).

The idea was to create a *"bare trust"* in which the child had an indefeasibly vested interest in the income and capital of the trust. Any income arising to the trust which was not distributed was treated as the child's even if the funds in the trust came from the parent.

Any trusts of this type created on or after 9 March 1999 is not be effective and income arising will be taxed as that of the parent, subject to the £100 limit. The changes will also apply to any income arising on funds added on or after 9 March 1999 to existing trusts.

7.5.3 Settlements of annual payment revocable within six years
The power of revocation must be found in the settlement itself (TA 1988 ss 671-672; *CIR v Payne* CA 1940; *CIR v Wolfson* HL 1949) but any person may have it, not merely the settlor (TA 1988 s 681).

The six years run from the date of the first payment. The wording of the deed should be extremely careful and clear to avoid any possibility of revocation within six years (*CIR v Verdon-Roe* CA 1962).

A supplemental deed extending the payment period is a new settlement (*CIR v Nicholson & Bartlett* Ch D 1953).

If the revocation cannot take place within six years, the income remains that of the beneficiary until such time as the power of revocation can be exercised.

Revocation includes a power to diminish the capital in, or annual payments to, the settlement, unless made in connection with separation or divorce.

7.5.4 Discretionary power
Where under the settlement any person can at his discretion apply any part of the capital or income for the benefit of the settlor or his wife, the income is regarded as the settlor's. If the power cannot be exercised within six years after the income or property first arises, this ruling will not operate until the power can be exercised, nor does it apply when the benefit arises in the circumstances stated in the following paragraph, i.e. bankruptcy or assignment or charge by him (TA 1988 s 674).

7.5.5 Undistributed income of a settlement in which the settlor (or wife) has an interest
The mere possibility of an interest, present or future, in any undistributed income will be sufficient for such income to be treated as the income of the settler (if living). The settlor, however, is not deemed to have an interest if this is as a result of the

bankruptcy of a person who may become beneficially entitled to the property or income, or an assignment or charge by him, or his prior death if his title would not arise until he attained age 25 (or less), or the death of both parties and all or any of the children in the case of a marriage settlement.

Nor is he deemed to have an interest so long as there is a person under 25 during whose life the settlor cannot receive any benefit except on that person's bankruptcy or an assignment or charge by him (TA 1988 s 673).

7.5.6 Capital sums paid to the settlor by the trustees or connected body corporate

Any capital sums paid to the settlor by a company connected with the settlement shall be treated as income of the settlor only if there has been an **associated payment** to the company from the settlement. An associated payment means any capital payment or transfer of asset at less than the full value by the trustees to the connected company, within five years ending or beginning with the date on which the capital sum is paid to the settlor (TA 1988 s 677-678).

A capital sum will be matched against income of the settlement in the year of payment and treated as income of the settlor in that year. If the trust income of the year is insufficient to cover the capital sum, then any excess of the capital sum will be carried forward and set against the trust income in the next and subsequent years up to a maximum of 11 later years, i.e. a total of 12 years including the year of payment. Where income of the settlement has already been treated as income of the settlor, these amounts are excluded to avoid a double charge to income tax. Any tax or additional tax paid on the income will be set off against the tax chargeable on any income treated as income of the settlor.

Where the capital sum treated as income of the settlor is a loan which is repaid in a later year, no part of that sum will be treated as settlor's income for any year after the year of repayment.

Where a capital sum is paid by the trustees and is in respect of a loan previously made by the settlor, and the amount of any part of it is subsequently lent back to the trustees, no part of the original capital repayment by the trustees is to be treated as income of the settlor in any year after the year of the further loan.

7.5.7 Minor as settlor

A minor who signed an exclusive service agreement with a company and provided the funds thereby, on account of her services being saleable for much more than she was paid, has been held to be a settlor and, accordingly, dividends paid by the company to trustees were regarded as her income. The argument that she had not reached the legal age of discretion and was thus too young to understand the documents, was rejected by the House of Lords where it was also held that funds must be taken to have been provided for the purpose of the settlement in the absence of evidence of any other purpose (*Mills v CIR* HL 1974).

7.5.8 Maintenance funds for historic buildings

Trustees of such funds, which have qualified for the relief from Inheritance Tax may elect that certain sums should not be charged to excess liability. These sums comprise any income arising which would be aggregated with the settlor's income under any of the previous provisions, or any sums applied out of accumulated income or capital towards maintenance and which benefit either a person interested in or occupying the land or the settlor. The latter sums are exempted, even if no election is made, to the extent that they exceed income arising which is aggregated with the settlor (FA 1988 s 691).

PART THREE

NATIONAL INSURANCE CONTRIBUTIONS

1 INTRODUCTION

Despite what Governments claim this <u>is</u> a tax on earned income. The National Insurance Contributions (NICs) do not go into your own personal pension pot, they pay today's pensioners.

Employees' contributions are 'very' loosely calculated on the same band of income that applies to the basic rate of Income Tax. These contributions are calculated at 12% (previously 11%), and if added to the Income Tax basic rate of 20% would mean that tax is 32p in the pound.

The self-employed pay £2.50 per week. This gives entitlement to most state benefits. The profits related rate of 9% does not entitle the payer to any more benefits such as SERPS - the income related element of the state pension.

The amount payable is calculated on the amount received in a particular pay cycle – either per week or month. What was calculated and deducted the previous week or month is ignored. (Directors' contributions are however, to avoid manipulation, calculated on an annual basis.)

To obtain the benefit of your contributions to sick pay or state pension you must pay contributions every week or month within a tax year. Otherwise the whole year's contributions will not count.

Credits to your record may be received if you do not work for certain specific reasons – such as looking after your children at home. You may have to apply for these. See 2.3.2 Carers' credits replace HRP, p.171 below.

Tax relief on the contributions?

- Employers paying Class1 – Secondary, Class1A & Class 1B obtain tax relief on the contributions.

- Employers deduct Class 1 – Primary on behalf of their employees. As gross pay, include these deductions, employers receive tax relief on the total cost of employing staff.

- Employees paying Class 1 – Primary. Employees do not save any tax by paying Class 1 contributions.

- Paying Class 2, 3 or 4 - also does not affect the payer's personal tax liability.

Age limits on payment of contributions.

- Employers - there is no upper age limit for Class 1 Secondary, Class 1A or Class 1B.

- Employees - Class 1 Primary. None payable once retirement age has passed.

- Class 2 - self employed. None once retirement age has passed.

- Class 3 - voluntary. If state pension not yet taken.

- Class 4 - none payable if over retirement age at the end of the previous tax year.

2 THE DIFFERENT CLASSES

2.0 Retirement age
Contributions are payable by employees and the self employed until they reach state retirement age. Until 5 April 2010 this was 60 for women and 65 for men. Accordingly as the state retirement age for women increases (from 6 April 2010) the date of payment of Class 1, 2 or 4 also increases. For Class 4 please see p.172.

2.1 Class 1 - The Employed
It is paid both by employees and the employer. It is deducted from the employee's pay packet and paid over monthly direct to HM Revenue and Customs with the income tax also deducted. This class is divided further.

Class 1 – Primary. This is paid by employees, and is calculated using a percentage on a certain band of income. Each pay period is used in isolation to calculate in either per week or per month. If you have two jobs, with unassociated employers, each job is looked at in isolation.

If their employer has opted out of the State Second Pension (S2P) and has its own company pension scheme contributions are at a lower percentage.

The rates are given in the table below:

Effective from 6 April 2009 the Upper Accrual Point is a new threshold for the calculation of both State Second Pension and contracted-out rebates. It replaces the Upper Earnings Limit in both the State Second Pension and rebate calculations.

The weekly limit has been set at £770.

Class 1 – Secondary. This is a tax paid by employers, and is calculated using a percentage on a certain band of income. No benefit accrues to the employer or employee. Each pay period is used in isolation to calculate - either per week or per month.

If the employer has opted out of S2P and has its own company pension scheme contributions are at a lower percentage - note the descent for COMPS is scheduled to cease after 5 April 2012 (See Table 15. National Insurance - Weekly Rates - 2011/ 2012 Class 1 - Class 4, p.640).

	2011/2012			2010/2011		
	Income £	Employee %	Employer %	Income £	Employee %	Employer %
Class 1 p.w. Contracted in	First 102.00	0	0	First 97.00	NIL	NIL
	102.01 - 136.00	0	0	97.01 - 110.00	0	NIL
	136.01 - 139.00	0	13.8	110.01 - 844.00	11.0	12.8
	139.01 - 817.00	12.0	13.8	Excess over 844.00	1.0	12.8
	Excess over 817.00	2.0	13.8			

2.1.1 Employers Contribution Holiday Scheme
The Scheme will last from the date of the 22 June 2010 until 5 September 2013. The Holiday targets help on certain 'new businesses' who are also employers and who start up outside Greater London, the South East and the Eastern regions of the UK.

New businesses are able to make National Insurance contributions (NICs) savings under the Holiday from earnings paid to employees.

For the first ten qualifying employees that a new business employs in its first year of business, following start up, it will be entitled to an individual Holiday for each of those employees. the Holiday period for each employee will last for the shorter of the employee's first year of employment or the time left until the Holiday scheme ends on 5 September 2013.

The Holiday will apply to all relevant earnings paid to a qualifying employee during the first year of the employee's employment but there will be a maximum saving of £5,000 in employer NICs in respect of each employee.

Statistics published in May 2011 state that only 3,000 employers in six months have taken up this scheme out of the 132,000 estimated per year.

2.1.2 NIC free car user allowance
In the case of *Total People Limited* (TC00661) the first tier tribunal held that a flat rate, annual allowance paid to employees who provided a car for business journeys was not a payment of earnings on which Class 1 NICs were due. What distinguished this situation from many others was that the employees who received the allowance were only reimbursed at 12p and 13p per mile, while their colleagues without the allowance were paid 40p per mile. HMRC may appeal, if only to prevent it having to handle thousands of refund claims from employers who have followed the previously established guidance.

2.1.3 Female employees entitled to reduced rate NICs
Up until 11 May 1977 some married women or widows could opt to pay Class 1 National insurance contributions (NICs) at a reduced rate and not to pay Class 2 NICs if self-employed.

Eligible women who applied at the time may still be able to pay Class 1 NICs at this reduced rate. See Table 15. National Insurance - Weekly Rates - 2011/2012 Class 1 - Class 4 for current rates, p.640.

If an employee tells you that she now wishes to pay NICs at the full rate you should:

- return the certificate of election to her after completing part 2
- calculate full rate NICs on your subsequent payments to her

The employee must return the certificate to NICO after completing part 1. If appropriate, she must also send a completed form CF9 (for married women) or CF9A (for widows).

A woman loses the right to pay reduced rate NICs if she:

- gets divorced
- has her marriage annulled
- becomes a widow but is not entitled to certain bereavement benefits after an initial period
- has not in any two consecutive years since 6 April 1978 had any earnings on which Class 1 NICs were payable or treated as paid and has not been self-employed.

2.1.4 Changes to NI rules for workers moving within EU
With effect from 1 May 2010, new rules mean that:

* A temporary secondment to another EEA state can last up to 24 months before Social Security Contributions have to be paid in the country in which the duties are performed. (Previously it was 12 months).

* If duties are performed in more than EEA state, and less than 25% of the working time and remuneration is in the country where the worker lives, then contributions must be paid in the country where the employer has its place of business. (Previously, contributions are paid where the employee lives provided that some of the duties are performed there).

* Special rules of international transport workers are repealed.

* Liability for and recovery of social security contributions is extended across EEA borders.

Class 1A
– are paid by employers on taxable benefits provided to their employees.

Car & fuel benefits are therefore taxable as these create a tax liability for the employee but mileage paid at the approved rates do not.

These Class 1A NICs are payable at 13.8% in 2011/2012 (2010/2010 12.8%) and have to be paid to HMRC by 19 July following the end of the previous tax year.

To be liable the employee must either be a director or be paid at a rate of £8,500 or more annually, including the cash value of any benefits.

Reclaim Class 1A NIC on holiday homes
On 17 March 2011 HMRC published Regulations The Social Security (Contributions) (Amendment No. 3) Regulations 2011 (SI 2011/797), to align the NIC position with the income tax rules. It is now possible to claim a refund of Class 1A NIC in the same way as it was possible for Income Tax when the rules changed in 2008.

Many people buy foreign holiday homes through a limited company. Often this is driven by foreign property law rather than tax considerations but before 2008 this could sometimes give rise to a tax charge where HMRC saw the owner/director of such a company benefiting from using the accommodation.

Finance Act 2008 introduced new provisions to ITEPA 2003, effectively providing an exemption from the living accommodation benefit in kind tax charge, where such accommodation outside the UK is provided by a company for a director or their family and certain conditions apply.

At that time HMRC advised that refunds of tax could be claimed on the basis that the living accommodation tax charge was never intended to apply in these circumstances and the new legislation was treated as always having had effect. The same was not true of employers class 1A NIC which had been paid.

Any individual who can show that they have paid Class 1A National Insurance contributions for any year before 2008/2009 on the benefit of living accommodation which qualifies for exemption in accordance with sections 100A and 100B of ITEPA, will need to submit a claim in writing, with evidence, as explained on the HMRC website.

There are some special circumstances that affect Class 1A.

Disabled employees
(Blue badge holders) who drive automatic cars will be able to calculate the taxable benefit using the lower list price of the equivalent manual car. They can already base the benefit on the CO_2 emissions of an equivalent manual car. The change will also apply to the calculation of Class 1A NICs on the taxable benefit.

In the motor trade there are special arrangements that exist for dealing with car benefits to employees, who may take home many different vehicles over the course of a tax year. However, prior to 5 April 2009, it operated in ways that varied from one area of the country to another.

HMRC introduced a standard method of calculation for the trade with effect from 6 April 2009. Details are included in the Employment Income Manual at EIM23650.

Class 1B
– paid by employers. Employers may enter into a PAYE settlement agreement (PSA) with HMRC.

This allows employers to account for tax on certain expense payments and benefits in a lump sum after the end of a tax year. If the employer enters such an agreement they will be liable to pay Class 1B contributions on the items covered by the PSA which would normally give rise to a Class 1/Class 1A liability and the employees liability for tax paid on the PSA.

2.2 Class 2 – Self employed - flat rate
This was the last remaining 'stamp'. The newly self-employed must register with HM Revenue and Customs (HMRC) immediately.

2.2.1 Post 5 April 2009
The key features of the new rules are:

- Anyone who becomes or ceases to be liable to pay Class 2 must notify HMRC 'immediately'.

- A person will be liable to a penalty if they do not notify their liability for Class 2 NICs by 31 January after the end of the tax year in which they become liable.

- The penalty will be a percentage of the 'lost contributions', the percentage varying depending on whether the failure is deliberate and/or concealed. For a deliberate and concealed failure the penalty is 100% of the lost contributions, for a deliberate but not concealed failure it is 70%, and for any other case it is 30%. The penalty can be mitigated if the person makes a disclosure. This structure mirrors the new penalty rules for incorrect returns in FA2007 and FA2008.

- There will be no penalty if there is a reasonable excuse for the failure to notify.

Example:
If you start to trade on 2 January 2010 you have until 31 January 2011 to notify, free of penalty, of commencement to trade. However as you have to submit your tax and pay any tax return by this date it is unwise to wait that long.

As the Class 2 payment for 2011/2012 is only £2.50 per week (2010/2011 £2.40) the penalty is more an incentive to tell HMRC in advance of your plans.

Class 2 contributions give rights to almost all state benefits apart from Job Seekers Allowance and the S2P the income related element of the state pension.

If taxable profits are below £5,315 (£5,075) you can reclaim, by the following 31 January, your Class 2 contributions. Although for what the £2.50 gives back in relation to state pension this may be only a short term benefit.

Changes to Class 2 payment dates
The statutory payment dates for Class 2 National Insurance contributions (NICs) have changed to 31 January and 31 July. This is so that they match self assessment due dates. The change applies from 2011/2012.

Previously Class 2 NICs were paid either quarterly, or monthly by direct debit. HMRC published the following guidance about the change to the new payment dates:

Payments made by internet/telephone banking, CHAPS, Bank Giro, Post Office or post: Those liable will receive just two payment requests from HMRC during the year (instead of four). These will be sent out in October and April, showing payments due by 31 January and 31 July respectively. There is no need to wait until the due date to make payment.

Payment made by direct debit: To meet the new due by dates, HMRC will delay collection of monthly direct debit payments to bring the payment dates into line.

This means that:

- for the first year only, monthly direct debits will stop for a short period and then start again

- Class 2 contributions due for April 2011 will be requested from the payer's bank in August 2011

- payments thereafter will be monthly unless the payer chooses to pay six monthly.

A new option to pay by six monthly direct debit, collected in January and July each year, is available from April 2011 for those who do not wish to spread their payments.

Those affected by the changes should have received further detailed information in the post from HMRC.

2.2.2 Self-employed females entitled to reduced rate NICs

A self-employed female and holding a valid 'certificate of election' - form CA4139, form CF383 or form CF380A - does not need to pay any Class 2 National Insurance contributions. But may have to pay Class 4 contributions if annual taxable profits fall within the Class 4 limits.

This only applies to some married woman who opted before 11 May 1977 to pay reduced NICs at a reduced rate. This election applied to both Class 1 & Class 2. Some eligible women may still be able to pay reduced Class 2.

A married woman who now wishes to pay Class 2 NICs should return the certificate to NICO after completing part 1. If appropriate, she must also send a completed form CF9 (for married women) or CF9A (for widows).

A woman loses the right not to pay Class 2 NICs if she:

- gets divorced
- has her marriage annulled
- becomes a widow but is not entitled to certain bereavement benefits after an initial period
- has not in any two consecutive years since 6 April 1978 had any earnings on which Class 1 NICs were payable or treated as paid and has not been self-employed.

2.2.3 Special Case #1: Share fishermen:

Since April 1975, share fishermen have been treated as self-employed because their conditions of service are more like self-employment. However, because share fishermen had previously been treated as employed earners, with entitlement to Unemployment Benefit, they are allowed to pay a special higher rate of Class 2 NIC to retain entitlement to this benefit. This concession also recognises the arduous and hazardous nature of their occupation.

The Class 2 contribution for 2011/2012 is £3.15 pw (2010/2011 £3.05).

2.2.4 Special Case #2: Volunteer development workers:

In June 1985, the European Communities Council recommended that Member States take steps to encourage young people to take part in projects organised by the Community beyond its borders.

A volunteer development worker does not pay the "standard" rate of Class 2 NIC they pay a special rate.

The weekly rate is calculated as 5% of the weekly lower earnings limit for the week for which the NIC is being paid. For example, the rate of NIC for the 2011/2012 tax year is £5.10 pw (2010/2011 £4.85). This amount is 5% of £102.00 (£97.00), the weekly lower earnings limit.

The special rate of Class 2 NIC counts towards the following benefits:

- basic retirement pension
- bereavement benefit
- contributions-based jobseeker's allowance
- incapacity benefit

A volunteer development worker may also be entitled to industrial injuries benefit. Providing:

- the accident arises out of, or in the course of, the employment; or
- the disease is contracted as a result of the employment,

Any benefit will be payable from the date of their return to Great Britain, even though;

- the accident happened abroad; or
- the disease was contracted abroad.

2.2.5 Small earnings - self-employment

It was possible for an employed person with a small, separate self-employment to not pay Class 2 NIC without the need for a small earnings exception (SEE) application. This was provided the self-employed profits were £1,300 or less for the year in question.

As a result of the HMRC review of concessions following *R v IRC, ex parte Wilkinson (2005) UKHL 30* this easement has now ceased (HMRC National Insurance Manual NIM20011). Thus, now any person who is self-employed must register as such and if they have low income from self-employment they should claim SEE if they do not want to pay class 2 contributions.

2.2.6 Paying voluntary Class 2 NIC while abroad

There has been concern in some cases where persons are working abroad and wish to pay voluntary contributions. Class 2, although normally only for the self-employed, can be paid by some employees in that circumstance - and this is to be preferred to Class 3, as Class 2 is both cheaper and provides coverage for more benefits. In order to be eligible to pay Class 2 it is necessary to have been employed or self-employed 'immediately' before leaving the UK.

HMRC now states that having reviewed the legislation it has changed the way that such applications are processed.

2.3 Class 3 – Voluntary

As stated above, contributions for a full year need to be made for that year to count for benefits. If there gaps in your contribution record you can pay voluntary contributions of £12.60 per week in 2011/2012 (2010/2011 £12.05).

The large rise in weekly contributions from 2008/2009 to 2009/2010 was due to the decrease in the number of years required to achieve a full basic state pension. This fell from 39/44 years to 30 years from 6 April 2009.

2.3.1 Late payment of Class 3 NIC

In *HMRC v Kearney (2008) EWHC 842 (Ch)* Mr Kearney, who appeared in person, made 10 contributions after the introduction of the National Insurance scheme in July 1948 before leaving for Kenya in October that year to join the Kenyan police.

In 1971 he notified the National Insurance authorities that he was living in Kenya, having found out that his assumption that contributions would be made on his behalf as a Government servant was incorrect. He immediately made voluntary contributions for the previous six years.

However, he later applied to make payments in respect of the period from 1948 to 1965. While failure to pay had been due to ignorance or error, there was a failure to exercise due care and diligence as required. It was also held that there was no obligation on the National Insurance authorities to chase up a former contributor where there was not any obligation to pay.

Tribunal agrees Class 3 NICs can be paid late

In a reversal of the usual outcome in this kind of case, a Mr Goldsack (G) was successful at the First-tier Tribunal in establishing his right to pay Class 3 (voluntary) contributions for 1955-1964 (*John Redman Goldsack v HMRC* TC 784).

Soon after leaving school G had two periods of work abroad in quick succession. Although he paid six (different) years' arrears of Class 3 contributions in 1970, he still had a substantial gap in his record (and therefore stood to suffer a 15% reduction in basic state pension for life). HMRC accepted that non-payment was due to ignorance or error, but asserted that this was due to 'failure to exercise due care and diligence'. G said that his only failing had been to not ask questions that no reasonable person could anticipate should be asked.

The Tribunal noted that G had registered for NIC at the age of 18 and had been given a contribution card that referred to 'Special Contribution Provisions' affecting six categories of people, one of which was 'men who go abroad'. In the context of G being in the flush of youth and also for a while paying into the East African Widows and Orphan Pension Fund, and the view formed as to his honest, careful and diligent nature, the Tribunal found that G had not failed to exercise due care and diligence and decided that he was entitled to pay arrears late.

Class 3 extension Allan v HMRC

In *George William McDonald Allan v HMRC* (TC 991), Mr Allan had retired and had spent some time abroad soon after leaving school. He had not made voluntary contributions at the time he could have and now sought to pay beyond the normal six year time limit. HMRC contended that Mr Allan had not exercised due care and diligence so that the potential extension was not available.

In the case of Mr Allan, some of the time abroad was with HM Overseas Colonial Service serving in the Kenya Police Force during the Mau Mau uprising - he said 'it was a bloody and barbarous campaign ... suffice to say the last thing on my mind was the UK National Insurance Scheme'.

Taking on board the Goldsack finding as well as that in Kearney the Tribunal held in the circumstances of this case that the arrears that Mr Allan wished to pay could indeed be paid.

Change of mind, No refund!

Mr Fenton had paid voluntary Class 3 NI contributions after his redundancy in 2002 on the strength of 'deficiency notices' from HMRC. In May 2006 the Government announced that the number of qualifying years needed for a full rate state pension would be reduced to 30 and thus the payments made were supposedly redundant. Mr Fenton claimed repayment of the Class 3 contributions made, which HMRC refused. That action was confirmed as correct in *HMRC v Fenton* (2010) ALL ER (D) 130. A refund is only due if there was an error or if no benefit entitlement could accrue as a result of the payment ('precluded contributions').

The General Commissioners had decided that there was no error, but allowed Mr Fenton's appeal as HMRC could not show that any bereavement benefit entitlement had been enhanced.

On HMRC's appeal, it was held that the contributions were not refundable and the General Commissioners had been wrong to find otherwise.

2.3.2 Carers' credits replace HRP

Home Responsibilities Protection (HRP) was replaced from 6 April 2010 by new carers' credits. These are actual Class 3 credits and governed by the Social Security (Contributions Credits for Parents and Carers) Regulations 2010, SI 2010/19.

The main group of recipients of these credits are those in receipt of child benefit for a child under the age of 12. As with HRP, the new credit is given automatically to those receiving child benefit in their own name. Partners and foster carers wishing to receive the credit must make an actual claim to HMRC. In the case of other carers an actual claim must be made to the Department for Work and Pensions. In either case the time limit to claim is generally the end of the tax year following that in which the week or weeks subject to the claim fell.

2.4 Class 4 – Self employed - profits related

These are a tax on profits; they do not benefit the payer.

Profits are calculated using the same rules as for income tax, disallowed expenses and depreciation added back, and capital allowances deducted.

The first £7,225, for 2011/2012 (2010/2011 £5,715), of profits are ignored and the excess charged at 9% (2010/2011 8%). There is an upper limit of £42,475 (£43,875) for the 9% rate, however profits in excess of £42,475 are taxed at 2% (2010/2011 1%) with no upper limit.

These Class 4 contributions are paid at the same time and same way as the income tax on the profits. That is - by balancing payment on 31 January following the end of the tax year and by estimated payment on account on 31 January in the tax year and the following 31 July.

2.4.1 Class 4 and losses

Where trading losses have been set against other income for tax purposes, these losses remain available for relief from Class 4 contributions. It is unlikely that this has been monitored automatically by tax software, and therefore should be checked regularly and repayments sought where appropriate. There is a six year time limit for reclaiming contributions overpaid, so this should be reviewed to ensure that no repayments are missed.

2.4.2 A sleeping partner

is not liable for Class 4 NICs because they cannot be held to have profits which are 'immediately derived from the carrying on or exercise of one or more trades, professions or vocations'. (HMRC - NIM24520).

2.4.3 Class 4 relief and annuities

Following the Income Tax Act 2007 (ITA 2007) and consequential provisions it made, there has been no Class 4 relief in the case of annuities and other annual payments since 5 April 2007 i.e., those amounts that fell within the previous ss 349 and 349(1), ICTA 1988. This was merely an oversight and replacement relief tied to ITA 2007 provisions is restored, effective from 6 April 2007, by the Income Tax Act 2007 (Amendment) Order 2010, SI 2010/588.

2.4.4 Proposed changes affecting people born between 6 April 1953 and 5 April 1960

The proposed changes to the State Pension age timetable, announced in November 2010, affect those born between 6 April 1953 and 5 April 1960.

Under the new proposals, from December 2018 the State Pension age for both men and women will start to increase to reach 66 by April 2020. This would mean that women's State Pension age will increase more quickly to 65 between April 2016 and November 2018.

These proposed changes to the timetable are not yet law and still require the approval of Parliament. It has also been indicated that these proposals may be changed.

The 'current' legislation for self-employed women reaching retirement age and their liability for Class 4 is given in 2.4.5 following.

2.4.5 Cessation of Class 4 NIC liability for women

Date of birth	Pension age (years.months)	Final Class 4 liability
6 April 1950 to 5 October 1950	60.0 - 60.5	2010/11
6 October 1950 to 5 April 1951	60.6 - 60.11	2011/12
6 April 1951 to 5 October 1951	61.0 - 61.5	2012/13
6 October 1951 to 5 April 1952	61.6 - 61.11	2013/14
6 April 1952 to 5 October 1952	62.0 - 62.5	2014/15
6 October 1952 to 5 April 1953	62.6 - 62.11	2015/16
6 April 1953 to 5 October 1953	63.0 - 63.5	2016/17
6 October 1953 to 5 April 1954	63.6 - 63.11	2017/18
6 April 1954 to 5 October 1954	64.0 - 64.5	2018/19
6 October 1954 to 5 April 1955	64.6 - 64.11	2019/20

PART FOUR

"IS THIS TAXABLE OR ALLOWABLE?"

1 WHAT IS TAXED?

The income assessable, is the annual profits or gains. 'Annual profits' is interpreted very broadly and means profits earned within a year; they do not have to recur year by year (*Martin v Lowry* HL 1926).

But not every profit or gain is taxed. It must come from a trade or profession or vocation to be caught. A person may possess a picture, a private car or some personal article which he or she sells at a profit but pays no income tax on this; nor on a residence for more than it cost. A person may win a large sum by betting, on a football pool, or draw a prize with a Premium Bond or The National Lottery; or may sell some stocks and shares at a profit; or may make valuable articles for his or her own use and thereby save a great deal of expense. These are profits and gains, but HMRC does not tax them as profits or gains under this section, though some (e.g. sale of stocks and shares) may well be subject to Capital Gains Tax.

It has been left to the Courts in a long succession of cases to try to decide just what 'annual profits or gains' means.

Two clear principles emerge: one very limited, though important enough, the other of very widespread application.

When anything is in the nature of a trade, chiefly a purchase and sale transaction, it is only assessed as trading income. To get the profit as trading income some sort of organized activity (however slight) showing that there was a concern or adventure in the nature of trade, must be established. This is not always present where the transactions are isolated or few in number and it is on these grounds that the profits made on the sale of a picture, private car, residence or an investment mentioned above are not taxed (unless as capital gains): where the existence of a trade or organization in the nature of trade cannot be established. On the other hand, the granting, for royalties, of licences to use a copyright fictitious character has been regarded as a trade because it involved 'skill and labour of a continuous and variegated kind' (*Noddy Subsidiary Rights Co. Ltd v CIR* Ch D 1966).

A **trade** is defined as a 'trade, manufacture, adventure or concern in the nature of trade' (TA 1988 s 831) and this has the effect of widening the meaning of 'trade'. It need not be carried on with a view to profit (*Harrison (JP) (Watford) Ltd v Griffiths* HL 1962). However, there must be commercial operations such as the provision to customers for reward of some kind of goods or services, and procuring others to trade is not the same as trading.

Capital gains are not taxed as trading income unless expressly deemed to be income, but come within the rules of capital gains tax see PART 11 - CAPITAL GAINS TAX, p.423. The distinction between capital and income must still be made as the rules for taxing capital gains are very different from those for taxing profits. The distinction between capital and income is one of the most difficult points in the taxation system. By **capital** is meant the fixed capital: the permanent equipment which a manufacturer or trader uses over and over again in the course of making or selling goods or providing services. If, owing to some change in circumstances or intention, a trader should decide to sell such an asset, and makes a profit on the sale, no tax is payable (except as a capital gain): it is a capital profit.

There are many borderline cases where it is most difficult to decide whether the profit relates to the permanent structure of the business and is hence capital, or whether it is part of the day-to-day activities and hence income. The case most frequently used in deciding this issue is *Atherton v British Insulated and Helsby Cables Ltd* HL 1925.

John Lewis Properties plc (JLP) was the property holding company for the John Lewis retail group and rented various properties to the trading companies for use within the group's retail trade.

JLP entered into a transaction with the UK branch of a Dutch bank to assign the right to receive rent for a five year period in return for a lump sum. The John Lewis retail companies then paid rent to the bank's UK agent.

The lump sum was treated by JLP as a part disposal of its interests in the properties and claimed rollover relief in respect of expenditure on new stores and the upgrading of existing premises.

HMRC contended that the lump sum should be chargeable to corporation tax under Schedule A (became Part 4 of Corporation Tax Act 2009), or alternatively Schedule D Case VI (became Part 3 of Corporation Tax Act 2009).

The Special commissioner followed the decision in *Paget v IRC (1937)* 21 TC 677 that the proceeds of sale of a right to receive income in the future was not income but capital. He also found that rollover relief was available for the lump sum received. *John Lewis Properties plc v IRC* SpC 255 (2000).

Annual profits or gains not in the way of trading, are caught by the old Case VI. This was the residual Case of the old Schedule D taxing structure. The profits which did not fit in anywhere else were brought into it, and here again it was left to the Courts to decide what was proper to be taxed and what is not.

We, thus, have a very varied assortment of profits covering wide fields of activity. They are set out alphabetically and a good impression of the nature of taxable profits will be gained by glancing down these lists of what the Courts have decided so far. It must be emphasized that, often, much depends on the circumstances of any case.

Accordingly, some types of profit have, in different circumstances, been held to be assessable or not assessable. Both the following lists should be consulted.

2(a) PROFITS ASSESSABLE

Please see text for full details

Advances
Under the Sugar Subsidies Scheme of 1931 (*Smart v Lincolnshire Sugar Co. Ltd* HL 1937).

Advances
On account of royalties (*Taylor v Dawson* KBD 1938).

Advertisement hoardings
If not attached to property, otherwise rental income.

Annual payment

To cover trading loss, received from an associated company (*British Commonwealth International Newsfilm Agency Ltd v Mahony* HL 1962).

Author

Casual profit.

Cessation of business

Trading receipts generally.

Charity

Profits from the sale of periodicals paid to a charity (*Hutchinson & Co. (Publishers) Ltd v Turner* Ch D 1950).

Compensation

For:

- cancellation of agency (*Kelsall Parsons & Co. v CIR* CS 1938; *CIR v Fleming & Co. (Machinery) Ltd* CS 1951; *Elson v James G. Johnston Ltd* Ch D 1965), or other trading contract (*Shove v Dura Manufacturing Co. Ltd.* KBD 1941; *Blackburn v Close Bros. Ltd* Ch D 1960), if this does not affect the structure of the company's profit-making apparatus (*John Mills Productions v Mathias* Ch D 1964);

- death of employee (under insurance policy) (*Gray & Co. Ltd v Murphy* KBD 1940);

- delay in implementing agreement (*Renfrew Town Council v CIR* CS 1934);

- loss (temporary) of profits arising from compulsory acquisition of property (*Stoke-on-Trent City Council v Wood Mitchell & Co. Ltd* CA 1978: see also SP 8/79) (permanent loss of profits (i.e. damage to goodwill) is a disposal for capital gains tax);

- surrender of licence for use of property (*Greyhound Racing Association (Liverpool) Ltd v Cooper* KBD 1936);

- alleged damage to company's goodwill, paid by directors to a company, by engaging in activities not known to the company (no permanent damage to the company's structure resulted) (*Roberts v W. S. Electronics Ltd* Ch D 1967).

Damages

- For: breach of contract (*Vaughan v Archie Parnell & Alfred Zeitlin Ltd* KBD 1940);

- breach of agency agreement, if really equivalent to the future profit lost (*CIR v*

David Macdonald & Co. CS 1955; *Wiseburgh v Donville* CA 1956).

Debt
Remitted by creditor, even after cessation of trading (TA 1988 ss 89, 103).

Debts
Unclaimed (*Lambert Bros. Ltd v CIR* CA 1927) unless credit balances unclaimed (*Morley v Tattersall* CA 1938).

Deposits unclaimed
By customers ordering made-to-measure garments. They became the company's property on payment and were only returned if requested by the customer and then only voluntarily and as a matter of policy (*Elson v Prices Tailors Ltd* Ch D 1962).

Discount
On purchase price of goods as a consideration for not manufacturing them (*Thompson v Magnesium Elektron Ltd* CA 1943).

First sale in a series
A person started driving schools and then converted them into separate limited companies. He agreed this constituted a trade except for the first one, which was formed to obtain a capital asset. The Court held, however, that the Commissioners were entitled to look at the later transactions in order to consider the nature of the first one and were entitled to conclude that all the transactions were of a trading nature and the profit taxable (*Leach v Pogson* Ch D 1962).

Foreign ambassadors
Consuls, etc. and members of staff: all profits earned by them (although exempt from paying tax on earned income) (TA 1988 ss 320, 321, Sch 29).

Foreign currency
Profit on sale of dollars bought to purchase tobacco and resold (*CIR v Imperial Tobacco Co. (GB & Ireland) Ltd* KBD 1940).

Foreign partnerships
The profits of a UK resident partner derived from a foreign partnership are assessable to UK tax.

Gifts
If received as payment for work done or goods or services supplied, e.g. gifts received by a jockey (*Wing v O'Connell* SC(I) 1926), gift for song plugging paid by publishers to public entertainers (*Radcliffe v CIR* Ch D 1956). A voluntary contribution by a club towards the excess of the cost of providing sports facilities over revenue therefrom was held taxable on the recipient, because the taxpayer received the sum as a supplement to its revenue and in order that it might be used in

its business (*CIR v Falkirk Ice Rink Ltd* CS 1975). Estate agents were taxed on gratuitous compensation for loss of opportunity to earn fees on development of a site, it being admitted that they were inadequately remunerated for acting in relation to the purchase of that site (*McGowan v Brown & Cousins t/a Stuart Edwards* Ch D 1977). See also Part 2 - 4.11 Gifts and compensation, p.108.

Grants under Industry Act 1972

Grants other than those designated as made towards the cost of specified capital expenditure or as made by way of compensation for the loss of capital assets are treated as trading receipts. If the grant was receivable by an investment company, the income is assessable under Schedule D Case VI (Schedule D became Part 3 of Corporation Tax Act 2009).

Guarantee of bank overdraft

Commission received (*Ryall v Hoare* KBD 1923; *Sherwin v Barnes* KBD 1931), but not where a capital sum, or shares, is given in return for the guarantee (*Trenchard v Bennet* KBD 1933).

Hire-purchase payments

Received after sale of business (*Parker v Batty* KBD 1941). But a payment for hire-purchase debts at book value may be partly for trading stock and partly for the right to receive future payments from the hirers which is not trading stock (*Lions Ltd v Gosford Furnishing Co. Ltd* CIR CS 1961).

Illegal profits

If taxable apart from the illegality (*Mann v Nash* KBD 1932; *Southern v AB* KBD 1933).

Journalism

Casual, e.g. racing articles (*Graham (A) v Arnott* KBD 1941; *Housden v Marshall* Ch D 1958; *Alloway v Phillips* CA 1980).

Know-how and technical knowledge

A disposal by a vendor who continues to trade and had previously used the 'know-how' in a trade is a trading receipt. If the vendor had not used the 'know-how' in a trade, it is assessable under the old Schedule D Case VI: if the 'know-how' is disposed of at the same time as the trade, it is treated as goodwill and subject to the capital gains tax provisions. See Part 7 - 10 INTANGIBLES, p.312 for goodwill, intellectual property and other intangibles acquired after 1 April 2002.

Lease premium

Lynch v Edmondson SpC 164 (1998) STI 968, see Part 9 - 3.3 Capital allowances for flats and shops, p.347.

Life assurance policies

* Profits from dealing in them (*Smith Berry v Cordy* CA 1946;

* surrender value when given to honorary medical staff member on nationalization of hospitals (*Temperley v Smith* Ch D 1956);

* capital sum received on death of expert adviser whose life was assured by the company (*Keir & Cawder Ltd v CIR* CS 1958).

Mutual business

By companies (TA 1988 s 491). A receipt on winding up or dissolution of a corporate body which has at any time carried on a mutual business is taxable if payments have been allowed as an expense, but not receipts of loans or other capital subscribed, income derived from the investment of capital, taxed profit from a business or any taxed investment income. This does not apply to a registered industrial or provident society or other trade where the profits are fully taxed.

Own use of trading stock

Profit on goods taken from a business for use in a hobby (horses transferred from a stud farm business to a hobby of racing and training. Transfer to be at market price) (*Sharkey v Wernher 1955 36TC 275*). See Trading Stock below.

Purchase and sale of property

There are very many cases on this subject and the individual circumstances are all-important. A builder is in a very weak position as the natural assumption is that he or she builds (or converts) for resale, and the use of nominees will not help disprove trading (*Smart v Lowndes* Ch D 1978). Where the intention changes from a non-trading to a trading purpose, the value of the property at the date of change must be ascertained and the taxable profit calculated from that date. Such a change of intention ought not to be inferred merely from the fact of steps being taken to enhance the value of the property (e.g. by applying for planning permission) (*Taylor v Good* CA 1974). Where a right of pre-emption held as an investment is exercised with a view to trading in the land acquired, the cost of the land is the value of the right of pre-emption plus the price payable on its exercise (*Bath & West Counties Property Trust Ltd v Thomas* Ch D 1978). A building company which acquired land, formerly held as an investment by its principal shareholder, was held to have acquired it as stock-in-trade (*Bowie & Reg. Dunn (Builders) Ltd* Ch D 1974).

Purchase and sale transactions

An isolated transaction gives rise to tax on the profits if it is in the nature of trading (*Rutledge v CIR* CS 1929), or if it was part of the trade or business to sell for profit, even though particular things sold were not acquired principally with a view to resale (*Gloucester Railway Carriage & Wagon Ltd v CIR* HL 1925; *CIR v Livingston & others* CS 1926), or where the sole intention of the purchase was to re-sell at a profit (*Johnston v Heath* Ch D 1970).

Profits from purchase and sale of equipment by an amusement caterer (*Cole v Lloyd* KBD 1950).

Racehorses
Sale of nominations to services of racehorses (*Benson v Counsell* KBD 1942). Race winnings from horses leased to other persons to be raced by them (regarded as arising from a businesslike transaction, not from any recreational activity of the recipient) (*Norman v Evans* Ch D 1964).

Research scholarship
Granted by a company to a medical practitioner (*Duff v Williamson* Ch D 1973).

Royalties
Received by an author or trade mark owner.

Sale of practice
A payment to a retiring partner of a share of profit for 15 years in return for nominal services was held to be assessable as other income as being consideration for transfer of the partner's share in the assets (*Hale v Shea* Ch D 1964).

Sale of sub-agency
If this does not amount to selling the essential framework of the trade (*Fleming v Bellow Machine Co. Ltd* Ch D 1965).

Sales
Payment received by a company, based on the quarterly sales of the purchaser of shares in that company (*CIR v 36/49 Holdings Ltd* CA 1943).

Shares
Profits on shares received in exchange for concessions as and when the shares are allocated (*Gold Coast Selection Trust Ltd v Humphrey* HL 1948).

Exchanges or conversions may qualify for roll-over relief.

Profit on shares taken over from a dealing company by a non-dealing company and vice versa (TA 1970 s 486).

Shares sold by a bank to reduce its overdraft. Investments by a bank are part of its ordinary trading operations and not to be confused with investments held by ordinary trading and commercial businesses as part of their capital (*Frasers (Glasgow Bank) v CIR* HL 1963).

Shares sold at far below market value by a share-dealing company to its principal company. This was held to be not a normal trading transaction and the assets transferred should be valued at market price, following *Sharkey v Wernher.* (*Petrotim Securities Ltd v Ayres* CA 1963).

Sickness and disablement benefits
Where paid for more than a year assessable as annual payments (*Forsyth v Thompson* KBD 1940).

Stud farm profits
Excluding the cost of breeding racehorses for recreational purposes (*Wernher (Lady Zia) v CIR* KBD 1942).

Subsidiary company
Profits of UK subsidiary to a foreign company (*Firestone Tyre & Rubber Co. Ltd v Lewellin* HL 1957).

Technical Knowledge
(Please see Know-how and Technical Knowledge, p.178).

Trading by executors
Even if only for a short period to realize the estate to the best advantage (*Wood v Black's Exors.* Ch D 1952).

Trading stock
FA2008 replaced the long established case law in (*Sharkey v Wernher 1955 36TC 275*) that business profits for tax purposes will be adjusted where goods are added to or removed from trading stock other than by way of trade; and that in these circumstances, the cost of, or proceeds from, the stock is replaced by the market value.

FA2008 puts this established principle on a statutory footing.

Turf
Right to cut and take (*Lowe v A J W Ashmore Ltd* ChD 1970).

Underwriting shares
Commission received (*Lyons v Cowcher* KBD 1926).

2(b) PROFITS NOT ASSESSABLE

Please see text for full details

Betting profits
(Except in the case of a bookmaker) (*Partridge v Mallandaine* QB 1886) including bets on matches made by a professional golfer (*Down v Compston* KBD 1937), but monies merely alleged to be betting winnings without proof may be regarded as business profits (*Roberts v McGregor* Ch D 1959; *Chuwen v Sabine* Ch D 1959). And card winnings of a club proprietor have been held taxable as cardplaying was part of an organized activity, i.e. the club (*Burdge v Pyne* Ch D 1968).

Compensation
For:
* loss of agency through liquidation of company (*Barr Crombie & Co. Ltd v CIR* CS 1945);

* agreement by actor not to act (*Higgs v Olivier* CA 1952);

* reconditioned ship, in excess of amount expended (*CIR v West (Francis) and others* CS 1950);

* change in terms of annual agreements by motor manufacturers with main distributors (*Sabine v Lookers Ltd* Ch D 1958);

* relinquishing possible rights in a property development scheme (*Scott v Ricketts* CA 1967);

Debts
Unclaimed balances in hands of auctioneers (*Morley v Tattersall* CA 1938).

Exchanges or conversions
Of securities by a dealer may qualify for roll-over relief.

Exclusive use of plant
Annual sum received for exclusive use within a prescribed area (*Margerison v Tyresoles Ltd* KBD 1942).

Flooding
Coastal flooding rehabilitation payments (these payments to restore to productivity being a capital asset) (*Watson v Samson Bros.* ChD 1959).

Foreign exchange
Exchange profits on repayment of agents' deposits in China (*Davies v Shell & Co. of China Ltd* CA 1951).

Garage costs (contribution)
- McClymont and anor v Jarman (Insp of Taxes) SpC 387
M and his brother purchased the filling station in which they traded in partnership using funding in part provided by S Ltd, whose fuel they agreed to sell at the filling station.

S Ltd provided the funding in two instalments, the first just before completion of the purchase and the second a year later when a deferred payment of part of the purchase price was due.

The agreement between the taxpayers and S Ltd described the payments as "contributions to the operating costs of the business" and the payments were shown in the taxpayers' accounts as revenue receipts. After reading HMRC guidance on payments made under exclusivity agreements, the taxpayers submitted a claim for error or mistake relief on the basis that they should have been treated as capital receipts.

HMRC refused the claim, relying on the description of the payments in the agreement and the absence of any restriction on the manner in which the payments were spent. The taxpayers appealed, contending that while there was no documentary evidence that S Ltd had required them to use the money for capital purposes, all the available evidence pointed clearly to the conclusion that S Ltd must not only have known but must also have intended that the money would be used in that fashion as S Ltd had known that the taxpayers could not fund the purchase without the security of the payments from S Ltd.

The Commissioner stated that it was necessary to consider not what the taxpayers intended, or even did, but what S Ltd intended. All the evidence showed that the purchase could not have proceeded without S Ltd's money. It was not merely a strong inference, but inescapable, that S Ltd was well aware of that fact. It paid the money in advance of the completion of the purchase and that fact was consistent only with an intention that the money should be used in part payment of the price, i.e. capital.

The only possible inference was that S Ltd, as well as the taxpayers, intended that it be used for the purposes of acquiring the business. The Commissioner therefore determined that the first payment was **of a capital nature**. The second payment, which was earmarked with S Ltd's knowledge and agreement to be used in paying one of the deferred instalments of the purchase price was also to be treated as a **capital receipt**.

Gifts or voluntary allowances

Even if regularly received. An introduction fee received by a solicitor as an intermediary in bringing two companies together has been held not assessable as the work was done as a personal friend and not in a professional capacity and there was no obligation to make the payment (*Bloom v Kinder* Ch D 1958).

Similarly, with regard to a payment for recommending a purchaser to a vendor of property: there was no contractual obligation (*Dickinson v Abel* Ch D 1968). An unsolicited solatium received by a firm of accountants for the loss of office of auditors for a company is not taxable if a proper charge has been made for professional work done (*Walker v Carnaby Harrower, Barham & Pykett* Ch D 1969; *Ellis v Lucas* Ch D 1966). A voluntary payment by a brewer to a tenant on the withdrawal of certain tenancies (others continued) was not a trading profit in view of the payer's motive (reference to long, friendly relations and desire of brewer to maintain its goodwill generally) (*Murray v Goodhews* CA 1977).

Gifts for employees

Employers may find the following Revenue concession useful - we have copied the note directly from the HMRC handbook:

"An employer may provide employees with a seasonal gift, such as a turkey, an ordinary bottle of wine or a box of chocolates at Christmas. All of these gifts are considered to be trivial and as such are not taxable. For an employer with a large number of employees the total cost of providing a gift to each employee may be considerable, but where the gift to each employee is a trivial benefit, this principle applies regardless of the total cost to the employer and the number of employees concerned."

One final caution regarding VAT and staff gifts. VAT is chargeable by the employer when an employee receives gifts totalling more than £50 in a year. Turkeys however are zero rated for VAT purposes!

Grants

From Unemployment Grants Committee (*Seaham Harbour Dock Co. v Crook* HL 1931).

Hobby
Proceeds from a hobby are not taxable, neither would any loss be allowed. But what begins as a hobby may develop and turn into a trade. The distinction is a question of fact and there could well be differences of opinion. In one case a trade in selling puppies was established from activities which began with a hobby of coursing greyhounds (*Hawes v Gardiner* Ch D 1957).

Housing grant
A statutory grant towards expenses of providing, maintaining or improving housing accommodation, unless the expense is deductible in computing taxable profits (TA 1988 s 376).

Injury to feelings
The employment case of *Vento v Chief Constable of West Yorkshire Police (2002) EWCA 1871* gave guidance to Employment Tribunals concerning the appropriate level of damages for injury to feelings.

In early 2009, the Special Commissioner held, in the case of *A v HMRC (SpC 734)*, that a payment made to compromise the taxpayer's Employment Tribunal claim for compensation for losses arising 'by reason of his dismissal' was chargeable to income tax as a termination payment. But added that £10,000 of the taxpayer's claim was fairly attributable to injury to feelings. That element was not part of his employment income and therefore not taxable.

The decision of the Employment Appeals Tribunal in the recent case of *Da'Bell v NSPCC UKEAT/0227/09* confirms an inflationary increase to the 'Vento' guidelines on injury to feelings compensation. The following now apply:

* Lower band: up to £6,000 (formerly £5,000).
* Middle band: £6,000 to £18,000 (formerly up to £15,000).
* Higher band: £18,000 to £30,000 (formerly up to £25,000).

Insurance
Money received by shipowners for delay in delivering new ships (*Crabb v Blue Star Line Ltd* Ch D 1961). Sums received on liquidation of mutual insurance company (*Brogan v Stafford Coal & Iron Co. Ltd* HL 1963).

Strictly, insurance commissions surrendered by an agent to the insured may be taxed on the agent (*Way v Underdown (No. 2)* CA 1975), but in practice this is not done in bona fide cases.

Introduction fees
Please see Gifts, p.177. A payment to a theatrical producer for an opportunity of acquiring a share in the profits of a show belonging to a company wholly owned by

the producer was held to be a capital receipt and not taxable. The introduction to the company and procuring it to assign a share in the profits did not constitute an undertaking to provide services (*Bradbury v Arnold* Ch D 1957).

Life assurance policies
Sums received on death, maturity or surrender.

Loans
Premiums on repayment of advances to a foreign company (*Lomax v Peter Dixon & Son Ltd* CA 1943).

Lottery
Winnings on the National Lottery are free of all tax. But gifts thereafter to members of the family potentially fall within Inheritance Tax. All profits, interest earned from investing the monies will be taxable.

Lump sum payments
For:

• termination of agreement (*Van den Berghs Ltd v Clark* HL 1935)

• setting up pharmaceutical industry in a foreign country (*Evans Medical Supplies Ltd v Moriarty* HL 1957).

• sale of film rights (*Shiner v Lindblom* Ch D 1960)

• covenants not to compete, as part of an agreement to grant manufacturing licences (*Murray v I.C.I. Ltd* CA 1967).

Mutual profits
E.g. a mutual assurance association (*Ayrshire Employers Mutual Insurance Association Ltd v CIR* HL 1946), members' clubs. But receipts on dissolution of a mutual body may be taxable.

Personal injury damages
A new measure will enable the victim of a personal injury to receive damages in the form of a tax-free annuity payable for his or her life. Under the existing rules, the injured person who is entitled to receive a lump sum payment free of tax is unable to receive those payments directly from an annuity without tax being deducted. Instead, the payments must go through the defendant's insurer, who is responsible for grossing up the payment to take account of tax, before passing it to the injured person and then reclaiming the grossed-up tax from HMRC. The new provision removes this administrative burden so that annuity and lump sum payments are treated in the same way.

Premium Bonds
Prizes drawn.

Prizes
In newspaper competitions.

Realization of assets
Executors may either be carrying on the business, in which case they will be assessable on the profits; or merely disposing of the assets, in which case the profit will not be taxable. When executors carried on farming activities it was held on the facts that they were merely disposing of the assets in a reasonable manner at the earliest possible date. The purpose of the activity is the dominant consideration. Here the object of the executors was to occupy the land, not for the purpose of husbandry, but for the termination of husbandry (*CIR v Donaldson's Trustees* CS 1963). Activities in improving and developing land which has been inherited amount to the carrying on of a trade (*Pilkington v Randall* CA 1966).

Regional development grants
On certain capital expenditure are ignored for all income tax purposes, including capital allowances.

Shares or debentures
Premium on issue. Profit on sale where acquired by moneylenders as an investment (*Dunn Trust Ltd. v Williams* Ch D 1950).

Exchanges or conversions may qualify for 'roll-over' relief.

Sidings
Payments toward cost of sidings, based on amount of traffic done (*Legge v Flettons Ltd* KBD 1939).

Tolls
Exempted under a Public Act (*Ancholme Drainage Commissioners v Welden* KBD 1936).

Voluntary allowances
Please see Gifts, p.177.

3(a) EXPENSES ALLOWED

Please see text for full details

The profits chargeable to tax are computed under the provision of Sections 74-99 TA 1988; and the general rules setting out the items which are not deductible are set out in s 74 TA 1988. In considering s 74, the most important 'disallowing' provisions are those which disallow 'any expenses not wholly and exclusively expended for the purposes of the trade' and 'any capital withdrawn from, or any sum employed or intended to be employed as capital in, the trade'. A few expenses are expressly allowed.

Many years ago the fundamental principle was laid down that 'where a deduction is proper and necessary to be made in order to ascertain the balance of profits and gains, it ought to be allowed . . . provided there is no (statutory) prohibition against such an allowance (Lord Parker in *Usher's Wiltshire Brewery Ltd v Bruce* HL 1914).

What is 'proper and necessary' has to be decided in accordance with general commercial principles: there is no other guide. This is the only basis on which the Courts have to work in dealing with the exceedingly varied kinds of circumstances and a considerable body of authority has been built up piecemeal as one disputed expense after another has come before the Courts for decisions.

It will be seen that many of these payments are disallowed because they are capital expenditure. As a guide, and no more, it may be said that expenditure made with a view to bringing into existence an asset or advantage of a capital nature for the enduring (i.e. permanent not transitory) benefit of the trade, or to rid the trader by a once and for all payment of an obligation of a capital nature, is capital.

Where, following the ordinary principles of commercial accountancy, the expenditure is properly charged to revenue, as may be the case with delayed repairs (*Odeon Associated Theatres Ltd v Jones* CA 1971) or payments to an employee's share incentive scheme (*Heather v P.E. Consulting Group Ltd* CA 1972), it is not capital expenditure and is allowable if expended wholly and exclusively for the purposes of the trade.

In *Duple Motor Bodies Ltd v CIR* HL 1961, it was held that actual expenditure properly incurred and referable to the trade was chargeable for the year in which it fell due, even though such expenditure was spread forward in the business accounts. However, this decision was overturned in the Court of Appeal in *Threlfall v Jones* (Inspector of Taxes) CA 1993.

Some typical items of allowable and non-allowable expenses are listed next.

Accountancy
Normal expenses of preparing accounts and agreeing taxation liabilities are allowed.

HMRC is considering queries regarding the application of SP 16/91 concerning accountancy expenses incurred in connection with self-assessment enquiries. However, it has said that additional expenses arising out of an accounts investigation will be disallowed only where an enquiry reveals discrepancies and additional liabilities for the year of enquiry, or any earlier year, which arise from negligent or fraudulent conduct. If the discrepancies and additional liabilities are not the result of such conduct, then additional accountancy expenses incurred in dealing with the enquiry will be allowed.

Advertising
If not of a capital nature (signboards, etc.) advertising costs are allowable if not considered excessive, having regard to the character of the business; but in a new business, part, at least, of the cost of advertising it might be treated as a capital expense of setting up. The cost of advertising against the nationalization of an industry is allowable (*Morgan v Tate & Lyle Ltd* HL 1954), but not a pamphlet

criticizing the Government's Acts and policy (*Boarland v Kramat Pulai Ltd* Ch D 1953).

Bad debts

In general bad debts are allowable charges against income, but general provisions for possible doubtful debts, e.g. calculated as a percentage of debtors, are not so allowable.

The legislation is contained in TA 1988 s. 74(j) and FA 1994. This legislation provides that the following are allowable:

(a)   Debts proved to be bad.

(b)   Debts released by creditors for trading purposes as part of a voluntary arrangement under the Insolvency Act 1986. Such arrangements are formal agreements between creditors and debtors for the purpose of allowing the latter's trade to continue, and avoiding liquidation or bankruptcy. From 30.3.93 the amount of the debt given up is not added to the debtor's trading profit. Otherwise when recoveries are made of bad and doubtful debts which have been treated as allowable charges, the amounts recovered are taxable.

Bonus payments

Based on members' purchases even though directors had power to apply the bonuses to the purchase of shares in the company so that they never reached the hands of the members (*Staffordshire Egg Producers Ltd v Spencer* CA 1963).

Business purchase

Please see Goodwill, p.195.

Canteen meals

HMRC has published draft legislation which will restrict the tax exemption for workplace canteens. It will affect the exemption for free or subsidised meals where an employee has an entitlement in conjunction with salary sacrifice or flexible benefits arrangements.

The new rules are intended to take effect from 6 April 2011 and affect income tax and NIC.

Usually, meals provided for employees, including directors, in a canteen or on the employer's premises are not taxable benefits provided the following conditions are met:

•   the meal is on a reasonable scale;

•   all employees, or all employees at a particular work location, may obtain a free or subsidised meal (or a voucher for one); and

- in the case of a hotel, catering or similar business, if free or subsidised meals are provided for employees in a restaurant or dining room when meals are being served to the public, part of the dining area must be designated for staff use only and the meals must be taken in that part.

The change will remove the tax exemption in circumstances where employees are in effect using a designated amount of their gross remuneration to fund the purchase of food and drink at work. It will apply to arrangements such as salary sacrifice and flexible benefits packages.

Car hire
From April 2009 - New leases are treated as follows:

- Abolition of lease rental restrictions for cars with CO_2 emissions up to and including 160g/km, thereby allowing a full deduction for lease rentals.

- Application of a uniform fixed percentage disallowance of 15% on leasing payments for cars with emissions in excess of 160g/km (i.e. the new 10% special rate capital allowances pool w.e.f. April 2009).

  Using the above example post 5 April 2009 the restriction is 15% and allowable proportion 85%.

Car purchase
From April 2009 business cars attracted 20% Writing Down allowance (WDA), which only applies to cars with CO_2 emissions of 160g/km or less. Expenditure on cars with CO_2 emissions above 160g/km only attracts 10% WDA. (See Part 7 - for full details, p.292).

Charities
Expenditure incurred and attributable to the employment (salary and related costs) of an employee who has been seconded to a charity on a temporary basis is allowable (TA 1988 s 86).

Child care
All expenditure incurred by employers for the care of the children of their employees whilst the latter are at work is allowable for tax purposes. The facilities provided include nurseries or payments direct to nurseries or carers. Employees are exempt from tax on the cost except where they receive actual money payments or vouchers. Directors and employees earning £8,500 or more a year are, however, not exempt for payments made by employers directly to nurseries or carers.

Christmas Party
The cost of a staff party or other annual entertainment is allowed as a deduction for tax purposes. Also as long as the criteria below are followed, there will be no taxable benefit charged to employees:

(a)   The event must be open to all employees at a particular location.

(b)   The cost is only tax deductible for employees and their partners (which would include directors in the case of a company) but not sole traders and business partners in the case of unincorporated organisations.

(c)   An annual Christmas party or other annual event offered to staff generally is not taxable on those attending provided that the average cost per head of the function does not exceed £150. Partners and spouses of staff attending are included in the head count when computing the cost per head attending.

(d)   All costs must be taken into account, including the costs of transport to and from the event or accommodation provided, and VAT. The total cost of the event is merely divided by the number attending to find the average cost. If the limit is exceeded then individual members of staff will be taxable on their average cost, plus the cost for any guests they were permitted to bring. No deduction will be allowed for the £150 exemption.

(e)   VAT input tax can be recovered on staff entertaining expenditure. If staff partners/spouses are also invited to the event the input tax has to be apportioned, as the VAT applicable to non-staff is not recoverable. However, if non-staff attendees pay a reasonable contribution to the event, all the VAT can be reclaimed and of course output tax should be accounted for on the amount of the contribution.

Commission
Paid for guarantee of floating debt.

Compensation for loss of office
Incurred during the currency of a business (*Mitchell v Noble* CA 1927).
When considering whether compensation and damages are deductible it is necessary to consider whether they have been incurred wholly and exclusively for trade purposes. IM660A concerning the trade purpose test has been amended. The section states that the test is unlikely to be met in four circumstances:

(a)   Payment to facilitate business winding up.
(b)   Compensation for loss of office connected with a change of control.
(c)   Payment on termination of employment to connected person.
(d)   Payment to compensate for illegal actions.

As a result of the decision in *CIR v Cosmotron Manufacturing* (1997) STC1134 - a Privy Council case from Hong Kong - payments made to employees under pre-existing contractual or statutory obligations for the purpose of winding up or disposing of a business, should not be disallowed. However ex-gratia payments and other payments in excess of an employee's pre-existing contractual or statutory entitlement will not be allowable.

Co-partnership schemes
Where under arrangement a share of profits is paid to employees as additional remuneration, such share is deductible from the profits on the business and assessable upon the recipients, if liable to tax just as any other addition to wages would be.

Debts
Outstanding of vendor paid for voluntarily by purchaser of business to conserve goodwill (*Cooke v Quick Shoe Repair Service* KBD 1949).

Directors' fees
And other remuneration: allowed as expenses. They will be assessed on the individual if liable. Tax paid by a company on directors' fees and other remuneration of employees, is an admissible debit in the accounts of the company. The fees must bear a reasonable relationship to the services rendered. If a fee was paid without anything at all being done by the directors it would not be allowed as an expense (though it would still be assessable on the recipient). Similarly, if the whole of the rents received by a property investment company were taken out as directors' fees, only a part would be allowed equivalent to the services rendered (though the whole amount would still be assessable unless waived) (*Berry (L.G.) Investments Ltd v Attwool* Ch D 1964).

Directors & National Minimum Wage
In common law, company directors are classed as office holders and can do work and be paid for it in that capacity. This is true no matter what sort of work they do and how it is rewarded.

The National Minimum Wage does not apply to office holders, unless they **also** have contracts which make them workers. It is unlikely that a company director will have an implied contract which makes him a worker. The rights and duties of an office are defined by that office, and it exists independently of the person who fills it. Directors can be removed from their office by a simple majority of the votes cast at a general meeting of the company. This contrasts with the rights and duties of an employee which are defined in a contract of employment.

Donations
To charitable bodies (TA 1988 s 660, FA 1990 ss 25, 26).

Effluent disposal
Expenses (and capital allowances for any capital expenditure).

EURO Conversion costs
HMRC considers that purely conversion-driven costs required in adapting computer systems for the euro are unlikely to be capital costs. But if changes of this nature are overtaken by, or form part of, the development of new business systems that could, for example, exploit changes in the financial markets accompanying EMU, such expenditure may be capital.

Exclusivity agreements - garages
(also see Garage costs - contributions, p.183)
Petrol companies commonly agree with garage proprietors to pay a certain sum of money for decoration, new frontage, pump maintenance, i.e. in return for which the garage proprietor purchases his petrol exclusively from that company for a number of years. The payment is usually calculated directly by reference to petrol sales. The agreements vary considerably in their terms, but in one case it has been held that the payments by the petrol company were allowable as they were recurring payments made to preserve goodwill and did not create a capital asset (*Bolam v Regent Oil Co. Ltd* Ch D 1956).

In another case, where there was a lease to the oil company and a leasing back to the retailer, it was held that the premium was paid for acquisition of an interest in land and was hence disallowed as capital expenditure (*Strick v Regent Oil Co. Ltd* HL 1965).

The garage proprietor may find that the amount received is capital or it may be income. The particular conditions of the agreement must be considered and these vary widely. If the proprietor is effectively getting nothing more than a discount on purchases of petrol then it is clearly an income receipt and taxable. If, however, as will commonly be the case there are other obligations, it may well be a capital receipt and not taxable.

Thus, where the payment was really a contribution towards sales promotion, advertising and other revenue expenses, and varied amount according to the gallonage purchased, it was held to be a revenue receipt, despite the fact that there had been a restriction of future trading rights (i.e. the obligation to buy only from one company for a number of years) (*Evans v Wheatley* Ch D 1958). But where it could be shown that the amount was a contribution towards the cost of buying additional land and buildings for the garage, or of improvements to the premises, it was held to be a capital receipt, especially as there was a restriction of future trading rights (*CIR v Coia* CS 1959; *McClaren v Needham* Ch D 1960; *Saunders v Dixon* Ch D 1962).

Films and audio products
Expenditure on the production or acquisition of the original master version of a film,

tape or disc, but not reproductions, is treated as revenue and not capital expenditure. Likewise receipts from exploitation of the master negatives are treated as revenue incomings. The amount of the expenditure which is allowable in a particular tax year may be calculated either by the 'income matching method' or by the 'cost recovery method'. By the income matching method the expenditure is spread over the period during which it is expected to earn income, in a fair and reasonable manner. This generally means apportioning the expenditure in relation to the actual and estimated future income of each year and involves frequent adjustments as actual and estimated income varies. The cost recovery method means charging expenditure each year equal to income of that year so that no profit arises until all costs have been recovered.

Foreign tax
A 1% tax payable on capital of all companies trading in Argentina (*Harrods (Buenos Aires) v Taylor-Gooby* CA 1964).

Gifts
Business gifts of a promotional nature i.e. incorporating a conspicuous advertisement for the donor costing not more than £50 - from 1 April 2001 (previously £10) other than food, drink, tobacco or a token or voucher exchangeable for goods (TA 1988 s 577).

Gifts: educational establishments
Relief is granted for gifts made to designated educational establishments on or after 19 March 1991, where the gifts are articles of plant and machinery. The gifts must either be made or sold by the donor or be used in the course of business and capital allowances may be claimed on the items gifted (TA 1988 s 84; FA 1991 s 68).

Relief is granted for any payments in cash or kind made prior to 19 March 1991 to a university, technical college or other institution approved by the Secretary of State for Education and Science, for the technical education of persons employed in the class of trade carried on by the donor (TA 1988 s 84). This relief was superseded by the relief given for gifts of plant and machinery to educational establishments (FA 1991 s 68) and cash donations to charities (FA 1990 s 25; TA 1988 s 339).

Goodwill
Yearly payments have been held admissible (*Ogden v Medway Cinemas Ltd* KBD 1934), if they are not instalments of a capital sum (*CIR v Pattison & Others* CS 1959). Payments intended to preserve a business connection or reputation are deductible even if the payment effects a change in the nature of a capital asset (e.g. release of option over shares) provided that the value of the asset is unaffected (*Walker v Cater Securities Ltd* Ch D 1974). However, if the payment creates a valuable asset, it is not deductible even although an asset of equal value was surrendered at the same time and there is no element of improvement (*Pitt v Castle Hill Warehousing Co. Ltd* Ch D 1974).

Health checks for employees

The Government introduced legislation in Finance Act 2009 which exempts from tax the benefit of health-screening and medical check-ups when they are provided for some of the workforce but not necessarily for everyone (s 55, FA 2009, which introduced new s 320B, ITEPA 2003). This objective is achieved by exempting from tax one health-screening and one medical check-up in any one year but without requiring that these medicals be offered to all employees.

This exemption has now been extended to the provision of such health-screening and medical checks to former employees (the Employer-Financed Retirement Benefits (Excluded Benefits for Tax Purposes) (Amendment) Regulations 2009, SI 2009/2886). This is on condition that the individual first received the benefit when they were an employee, and that the benefit would have been exempt under s 320B, ITEPA 2003 if they were still employed.

This exemption is retrospective and applies from the 2006/07 tax year onwards.

Hire costs & Hire purchase

Simple hire costs are allowed in full. In the case of hire purchase, the interest payable is allowed as an expense proportionately to the payments made in each accounting period i.e. the interest is allocated over the 'hire' period (*Darngavil Coal Co. Ltd v Francis* CS 1913). Capital allowances can be claimed on the cash price of the asset.

Homeworkers

Revenue & Customs has increased from £2 to £3 per week the amount employers of homeworkers can pay them, without receipts or questions, and without PAYE or national insurance liability, towards the extra costs of working from home. The guidance on who may be paid is set out in the Employment Income Manual at EIMO1476, and the rate increase applies from 6 April 2008.

The rules on deducting expenses are notoriously strict: most expenses other than travel costs may only be deducted if they are incurred wholly, exclusively and necessarily in the performance of the duties.

Insurance

Against deprivation of an employee's services provided that such insurance is intended to meet loss of profits due to the loss of the employee's services and that the policy is an annual or short term policy. Any sums recovered under the policy are assessable (*Keir & Cawder Ltd v CIR* CS 1958).

Fire, burglary, accident, glass, fidelity, etc. Workmen's compensation, etc. Brewers contributions to compensation fund. Fire and licence (tied houses) may be charged by brewers. Loss of profits. (Any sum recovered fall to be included in the profits as at the date the liability was determined) (*R v British Columbia Fir & Cedar Lumber Co. Ltd* PC 1932).

Interest
See Part 2 - 2.7 Interest payable - general, p.46.

Interest on loans paid in advance
New rules, effective immediately, (PBR October 2007) have been introduced to prevent individuals skirting existing anti-avoidance provisions on 'sideways loss relief' and accelerating their tax relief by paying all the interest in advance on certain business loans (for investing in partnerships or small companies for example).

The change will deny tax relief for interest that relates to a later year than the year in which the interest is paid.

Lease renewals - property
Where the renewal is for a period of less than 50 years, the cost thereof is in practice allowed.

Leased plant & machinery
A HMRC press release (21.07.05) announced that changes have been made to the way in which some leases of plant and machinery are taxed with effect from 1 April 2006.

The reform applies to finance leases and some operating leases. With the exception of some hire purchase transactions, leases of less than 5 years are not be affected by the reform.

Where leases of plant or machinery function essentially as financing transactions the new regime taxes them as such. In particular:

- the lessor brings in only the finance element of the rentals arising under the lease as income, and is not entitled to capital allowances.

- the lessee deducts only the finance element of the rentals payable over the life of the lease, and is entitled to capital allowances.

Legal expenses and fines
A stockbroker's legal expenses in defending disciplinary proceedings the Stock Exchange Council brought were deductible in computing his profits, since his purpose in defending the action was to preserve his trade. The fines imposed were not deductible, however. So the House of Lords held in *McKnight v Sheppard* (1999) STI 1077.

Legal fees

Costs of recovering book debts, disputes with customers and damages and costs arising in course of trade. Costs in connection with brewers' tied houses, except when in respect of new houses or licences. Costs incurred in protecting title to business property (*Southern v Borax Consolidated Ltd* KBD 1940). Costs of amending charter in order to remove obstacles to proper management such as restrictions on borrowing powers, shares issues, voting rights, etc. (*CIR v Carron Co. Ltd* HL 1968). Costs of generally maintaining existing rights.

Loan finance costs

Incidental costs incurred in obtaining finance raising a loan or loan stock which has rights of conversion to shares or other securities within three years will qualify for the relief if the right is not exercised or wholly exercised within the three year period (TA 1988 s 77).

Local business rates

Of all kinds.

Local Enterprise Agencies and Companies

Contributions to a Local Enterprise Agency or Company made prior to 1 April 1995. A Local Enterprise Agency is a body approved by the Secretary of State which has been set up to promote industrial or commercial enterprise. A Local Enterprise Company is the equivalent body in Scotland and acts under an agreement made with the Scottish Development Agency, the Highlands and Islands Development Board, Scottish Enterprise or Highlands and Islands Enterprise. Contributions may be made in cash or in kind and the contributor or a connected person must not be entitled to receive any benefit in return for the contribution (TA 1988 ss 79, 79A; FA 1990 ss 75,76).

Locum tenens: insurance policies

Some professional people who practise alone or in partnership, medical professionals in particular, take out insurance policies to indemnify themselves against the cost of engaging a locum, or against other practice expenses, in the event of the policyholder's illness or other incapacity.

Premiums on indemnification policies of this nature are deductible in computing profits. Equally, benefits payable under the policies should be regarded as trading receipts.

Loss from burglary, theft, embezzlement, etc.

Loss of stock

By fire, water, etc. in excess of compensation recovered from insurance; but not loss of buildings, plant or similar 'capital' assets.

Lump sum payment
To obtain relief from an onerous contract relating to trade (as distinct from capital) matters (*Anglo-Persian Oil v Dale* 16 TC 253), or to end trading relationship with another company (*Scammell (G) & Nephew Ltd v Rowles* CA 1939).

Marketing meetings
In Netlogic Consulting Ltd. v HMRC N Ltd. organised a function for 250 of its potential customers or clients. It spent £1,800 on catering and £681 on room hire. N Ltd. argued that the £2,481 was an allowable trading deduction as expenses on advertising or promotion rather than hospitality or entertainment. The Inspector disallowed the deduction on the basis that it was "business entertainment".

The Special Commissioners found that the £1,800 was an expense incurred in providing business entertainment and was therefore disallowed as a trading deduction. However, the room hire charge of £681 was a charge for the provision of the room so that the meeting of N Ltd.'s potential clients or customers could take place. The purpose of the meeting was to attract business to N Ltd. and not entertainment. Accordingly, the room hire was incidental to the provision of the entertainment and should be allowed.

Mining concerns
Expenditure on abortive exploration is allowable as a trade expense if capital allowance has not been given (CAA 1968 s 62).

Miscellaneous expenses
Such as postage, carriage, and the ordinary expense of business.

Mortgage interest relief
A loan may be taken out to acquire a house or flat which is used partly for residential purposes and partly for business (whether property letting or a trade or profession).

In response to the problem, HMRC allow such a loan to be treated as two separate loans, so that a deduction is obtained in computing profits for that part relating to business use.

National Insurance contributions
The employer's contribution for employees of the business is allowed as a trade expense in the normal way. The self employed contributions under Class 2 and 4 are not allowable.

Outplacement counselling
Before 16 March 1993 the cost of outplacement counselling services for redundant employees was allowable to employers and tax free to employees as part of a redundancy package, of which the limit is £30,000. The expenditure can include help in adjusting to the loss of the job, writing CVs, interview skills, job searches and the

provision of applicable office equipment. On and after 16 March 1993 the expenditure was removed from the redundancy package; will apply irrespective of when the services are provided; but qualifies for tax exemption only where the employees concerned have been employed for at least two years; is available to all employees of a particular class; and is provided in the UK.

Patents, designs, trade marks and copyrights
Costs of successful or abortive applicants for the grant renewal of such franchises (TA 1988 s 83).

Post-cessation business expenses
Under the provisions introduced in s 90, FA 1995, individuals may claim relief for certain post-cessation expenses against income and gains generally of the year in which the expense is regarded as arising. The relief is given for payments made wholly and exclusively: in remedying defective work done, goods supplied or services rendered while the business was continuing, or damages in respect of such work, goods or services; legal and other professional expenses connected with such costs; in insuring against such costs; and for collecting the discontinued business's trade debts. To qualify for relief, the payment must have been made on or after 29 November 1994 and within seven years from the discontinuance. A claim for relief must also be made within two years of the end of the year of assessment in which the payment was made.

Premiums, assignments of leases granted at undervalue
Where tax has become chargeable in these cases in relation to land used for a business, the amount may be spread over the duration of the lease, etc. and allowed accordingly. No allowance is made if mineral depletion allowance has been given for the same expenditure (TA 1988 s 87).

Pretrading expenditure
Subject to the following qualifications and explanations relief from tax is available for pretrading expenditure, i.e. expenditure incurred before the commencement of trading (TA 1988 s 401).

(a)   The expenditure must be such as would be allowable if the trade had actually started. Capital allowances would normally be available for pretrading capital expenditure as though it had been incurred on the day when trading began.

(b)   The period before trading in which the expenditure is allowable, seven years.

(c)   Interest on short term debts, such as payable to a UK bank is included in the relief as are other charges, such as royalty payments, provided such charges are trade related.

(d)   Relief applies to expenditure on the preparation of a site for waste disposal.

Provisions for contingent liability
If of a revenue character and estimated on a reasonable basis (*CIR v Titaghur Jute Factory Ltd* CS 1977).

Redundancy
Payments up to £30,000 made under the Employment Protection (Consolidation) Act 1978 and other statutory redundancy schemes are allowable. Rebates recoverable are taxable as receipts (TA 1988 ss 569/71). Payments under non-statutory schemes are also allowable with qualifications.

Removal expenses
The whole of the expenses of dismantling and re-erecting plant and machinery and of removal of goods is in practice allowed whether the removal is voluntary or compulsory. Exception might, however, be taken where the removal is due to expansion of business. The difference between the cost of new fittings and the selling price of the old ones is not allowable (*Hyam v CIR* CS 1929). But removal expenses are not allowed when they are reimbursed as part of the disturbance element in compensation for compulsory acquisition.

Renewals
Of plant and machinery, loose tools, furniture, typewriters, etc. where a capital allowance has not been claimed. Loose tools are generally dealt with by allowing the whole expenditure, valuing the commencing and ending stocks and adjusting for any increase or decrease in value.

The replacement of a building is not allowable, but the replacement of a part of a building, e.g. a chimney, is allowable (*Samuel Jones & Co. (Devondale) Ltd v CIR* CS 1951).

Rent
Rent payments will be allowed.

Repairs
Except for any element of improvement over the condition of the asset when it was purchased. Structural alterations in a rather different form to the original are allowable if the result is to repair something and not to produce something new (*Conn v Robbins Bros. Ltd* Ch D 1966).

Repairs or improvements?
Where single windows are replaced by double-glazed ones, HMRC's immediate reaction is to claim that there is an element of improvement and to disallow relief for part of the cost. However, in *Conn v Robbins Bros. Ltd Ch D 1966*, it was held that structural alterations may, in some cases, be the most efficient and effective way to restore a building to its original condition. In such circumstances the whole of the

cost is regarded as repairs.

It has been reported that HMRC has accepted that the full cost of replacing single windows with double-glazed units should be allowed, where it was evident that this was the cheapest method of 'repair' (i.e. new single-glazed windows would have been more expensive than the double-glazed units used).

Security
Expenditure incurred by an individual or partnership of individuals on providing security assets or services for the individual or partner to meet a special threat arising wholly or mainly by virtue of the particular trade, profession or vocation. The expenditure will be allowed as revenue expenditure or will be eligible for capital allowances if it is capital expenditure (FA 1989 ss 112, 113, 117, 118). Assets excluded are cars, ships, aircraft and living accommodation.

Share of profits
Paid under agreement for services rendered (*British Sugar Manufacturers Ltd v Harris* CA 1937).

Share scheme for employees
Contributions by the employer will, normally, be allowable as tending to promote employee goodwill (*Heather v P. E. Consulting Group* CA 1972). However, contributions in the form of loan to trustees for the scheme are not allowable since the employer retains an asset, i.e., the loan (*Rutter v Charles Sharpe & Co. Ltd* Ch D 1979); contributions to approved profit sharing schemes are allowable.

Ships
Repairs, renewals, costs of surveys, are allowable.

Subscriptions
To trade associations which have entered into an arrangement with HMRC and other subscriptions if the expenditure is for the purpose of the business, e.g. maintaining contracts and goodwill, and not merely personal or charitable. A substantial payment to a trade association in order to obtain restoration of old rights (in this case Sunday opening of public houses in Wales) and to combat competition has been allowed as one of the incidents of carrying on the company's business: it was not regarded as capital expenditure (*Cooper v Rhymney Breweries Ltd* Ch D 1965).

Superannuation fund contributions
Contributions of both employers and employees to these funds are admissible deductions from profits of the employer and remuneration of the employee, subject to Regulations of the Board of HMRC. A lump sum payment to commute additional premiums for certain employees is allowable (*Green v Craven's Railway Wagon Co.* Ch D 1951), but a lump sum paid to set up a pension scheme has been held to be

capital expenditure (*Atherton v British Insulated and Helsby Cables Ltd* HL 1925). However, in the case of an exempt approved scheme such special contributions may be allowed as deductions spread over such period as the Board thinks. The Board has published guidance notes as to its usual practice (HMRC Pamphlet IR12). Widows' and Orphans' Annuity funds are entitled to similar treatment.

Telephone costs

For many years it was the case that when determining adjusted trading profits, the proportion of the proprietor's home telephone bill which related to business calls was an allowable deduction. The cost of the line rental was historically always disallowed in full because it was not incurred 'wholly and exclusively for the purposes of the trade' and the dual purpose of the expense prevented a deduction.

For 2005/06 onwards, this rule does not prohibit a deduction for any identifiable part or identifiable proportion of an expense which is incurred wholly and exclusively for the purposes of the trade, s 34(2), ITTOIA 2005. consequently, a proportion of the line rental may also now be deducted. This change will in due course be reflected in the Business Income Manual (at MBIM 47800).

This rule may have changed just in time since most bills for household tele-communications can now cover so many other related services; internet access, television and even mobile telephone often being combined. A more pragmatic approach is clearly needed.

Training

Expenditure incurred on retraining an employee or past employee to acquire new skills is allowable. The retraining should enable the employee to apply the acquired skills in a new job or self-employment. The costs of the training provided is not to be treated as emoluments in the hands of the employee (TA 1988 s 588/9; FA 1991 s 32; FA 1994 s 84).

HMRC takes the view that a course which is designed to provide business proprietors with new expertise or knowledge or to equip them with skills that they lack creates an intangible asset that is of enduring value to the business. As a result, the expenditure incurred in relation to the training is regarded as capital expenditure and is not deductible in computing profits. For example, a course that leads to a recognised qualification will generally be regarded as capital rather than as revenue.

By contrast, expenditure on attending a course which updates the proprietor's existing knowledge or expertise is regarded as revenue expenditure. Consequently, a deduction is allowed as long as the expenditure is incurred wholly and exclusively for the purposes of the trade or profession.

The tax-free amount employers may pay to employees for periods of attendance on full-time educational courses (including sandwich courses) is £7,000 a year.

Travelling & subsistence expenses

The cost of meals and other travelling expenses, where it can be shown that this is an additional expense arising in the course of carrying on the trade. In practice no restriction is made for the cost of meals saved at home.

If you make yourself a pack-up lunch using your domestic supplies, the cost of the food cannot be reimbursed tax free by your employer nor can you make a claim on your tax return if you are not reimbursed. If however you purchase a ready made sandwich this cost can be reimbursed or a claim made on your tax return!

Where home is the only place of business, travelling expenses between home and the various places where the work is being done, as in the case of a building sub-contractor, are allowed (*Horton v Young* CA 1971). But not the cost of travel between home and the main place of business.

Waste disposal: restoration payments

Expenditure incurred by a person holding a disposal licence under the Control of Pollution Act 1974 or a waste management licence under the Environmental Protection Act 1990, where the expenditure is incurred in connection with the preparation or making good a landfill waste disposal site.

Relief is given either by way of a revenue deduction where the expenditure does not qualify for capital allowances, or by way of capital allowances where the expenditure is eligible for such relief (TA 1988 s 91A; FA 1990 s 78).

Websites

Many small and medium-sized businesses have now constructed their own websites. According to HMRC building a website is capital expenditure which creates a fixed asset. Updating the website is revenue expenditure that can be set against profits.

The consequence of this approach is that building a website becomes a tax 'nothing', apart from the hardware and software involved. It is significant that some inspectors are using the cases of *Anglo-Persian Oil v Dale* 16 TC 253 and *Strick v Regent Oil Co. Ltd.* HL 1965 in order to support their views. Both of these cases were decided before the Internet was invented, and are clearly out of date.

This approach also ignores the fact that all businesses in accordance with s 42, FA 1998, must calculate their profits in accordance with GAAP. This means adopting the accounting standards issued by the ASB.

One of the latest instructions issued by the ASB is Urgent Issues Task Force Abstract 29 concerning website development costs. The abstract requires that planning costs for a website should be charged against profits when they are incurred. The website development and design costs should only be capitalised if it can be shown that this expenditure will create an asset which has long-term benefit to the business. The website must generate sales or other revenues directly if the costs are to be capitalised. This restricts capitalisation to websites that include on-line sales or booking facilities. Otherwise the expenditure should be charged against current profits.

If HMRC challenge the inclusion of website development expenditure in revenue expenditure in the year when incurred, then UITF Abstract 29 should be quoted in defence.

Welfare of employees
Expenditure which is not of a capital nature including subscriptions to youth centres and similar bodies.

Wives (inc. husband & civil partner) & National Minimum Wage (NMW)
National Minimum Wage and family businesses.

There is an exemption for family members working in the family business, the NMW regulations specifically refer to the employer's family. If the family business (i.e. the employer) is a limited company, then it does not have a family. Even if the family business operates as a sole trade or partnership, the only family members exempted are those who actually live at home.

Wife's (inc. husband & civil partner) wages
Where the wife (or, the husband or civil partner) of a self-employed person has no other taxable income, claiming a deduction for 'wife's wages' is a simple and effective tax-planning device. It is usual to pay such wives a salary that falls just short of the National Insurance lower earnings limit. Typically, the wife spends a few hours a week answering the telephone, making appointments, dealing with correspondence and possibly keeping the business's books. Clearly, few people these days can expect to get much done for such a pittance, but the Inspector of Taxes does not always agree. There can be no deduction unless the wages are actually paid to her own bank account not joint. Payments to family (including 'wives') do not fall within the National Minimum Wage regulations if they live in the family home.

Working from home (Self-employed)
These are the expenses claimable by the self employed when they work from home - without then becoming liable to Capital Gains Tax on sale.

The new (2008) guidance is in the HMRC manuals. These are published on their website: http://www.hmrc.gov.uk/manuals/bimmanual/bim47820.htm contain examples of the level and nature of home expenses that can be claimed.

A new element is termed 'fixed costs' and includes mortgage interest, council tax and home insurance. This is in addition to the previously allowed claim for a fair proportion of variable running costs.

HMRC are content to allow a proportion of these costs to be claimed against the income of the business if certain criteria are met, such as:

•   The area of the home is used 'exclusively' for business purposes for a prescribed amount of time - say, 9am to 5pm - if you only work at the kitchen table you won't qualify for the new deductions. HMRC are looking for an area that has the appearance of an office - so it will contain a desk, chair, storage etc.

•   The amount claimed has to reasonable in relation to the business in relation to time spent and proportion of the whole house.

•   Apart from these two provisos, a claim for a percentage of the total cost of running the home can be made.

HMRC have given a number of example of how the system operates in their http:// www.hmrc.gov.uk/manuals/bimmanual/BIM47825.htm.

Working from home (Limited Company)
If you run your business through a limited company and your base of operations is your home office, it is possible to charge your company rent. Of course if you do this the company will be able to deduct the rents from its profits and you will need to declare the rents on your self-assessment return. On the face of it there would seem to be no advantage.

But what if you also have buy to let properties and are making losses? Very often buy to let property owners have more costs (loan interest etc.) than they have rents receivable. Unfortunately it is not possible to set off these rental losses against other income. The losses have to be carried forward to be set against rental profits in future years.

If on the other hand you do charge your company rents for the use of a Home Office it would be possible to set off any buy to let losses against this income. The rents from your company and your buy to let rents are taxable as property income. Effectively you would be getting tax relief through your company for the rental losses you personally suffer on your buy to let property. A number of considerations need to be taken into account;

(a)   If you charge your company rents you must have a proper rental agreement between you and your company, otherwise the revenue could seek to treat the rental payments as part of your salary from the company.

(b)   The rents that you charge for your home office must be charged on a commercial basis. It may be sensible to have a formal valuation undertaken.

(c)   The rental agreement should state that the office space at home is only available for fixed periods each day. This is necessary to observe the non-exclusive principle. Without this you could jeopardise your principal private residence exemption for capital gains tax purposes.

(d)   If you have a mortgage, you may need to check with your lender before entering into such an arrangement.

3(b) EXPENSES NOT ALLOWED IN COMPUTING PROFITS

Please refer to text for full details

The following have been held not to be allowable, and for income tax purposes must be 'written back', or added to net profits shown in the accounts.

Advertising
If of a capital nature (i.e. signboards).
See also sponsorship below, p.219.

Annual payments
Annuities, patent royalties for example, where income tax is deducted by the payer.

Bad debts
Not incurred in trading (e.g. a loan) (*Curtis v Oldfield (J. & G.) Ltd KBD 1925*). But specific debts incurred in trading are allowable where proved to be bad, released by the creditor or estimated to be irrecoverable in insolvency. FA 1994 s 144. A general provision is not allowable.

But in this extreme case a supplier of processed meats to supermarkets initially made a provision of £180,000 and then increased it to £850,000, representing the difference between the credit limit allowed to supermarkets and the limit advised by a credit rating agency. HMRC refused to allow a deduction of £670,000 of the provision. The company was only owed £180,000, the extra £670,000 was the unutilised credit limit! In the decision (SpC), the directors of M had anticipated future losses in dealing with supermarkets but that had not entitled them to make a deduction in the accounts. Even though their actions had been judged to be permissible by M's auditors, their action had not been compatible with the requirements of tax law. The appeal was dismissed. (*Meat Traders Ltd. v Cushing* (1997) STI 1034).

Brewers
Rehabilitation costs and increased cost of keeping public houses open during rehabilitation (*Mann Crossman & Paulin Ltd v Compton* KBD 1947). Costs of transferring brewery licences on redevelopment scheme for an area, even though increased trade unlikely (but they were incurred in the hope of improving the trade) (*Pendleton v Mitchells & Butlers Ltd* Ch D 1968).

Brokerage on issue of shares and debentures
This is an expense of obtaining capital.

Clothing
The cost of providing clothing predominantly associated with a trade or profession if it could also be used for normal everyday use (*Mallalieu v Drummond* HL 1983).

If you are an employee, can you make a deduction for what you wear to work? The test is the famous 'wholly, exclusively and necessarily' rule. The first-tier tribunal decision saw *Sian Williams v HMRC TC 397*, the BBC1 Breakfast Presenter, arguing that she should be able to claim a deduction for the clothes and hair-styling costs required to be on national TV. This amounted to an annual cost of about £4,500. The tribunal dismissed her claim on the basis that she wore clothes that, although smart, were not that dissimilar to those that you would wear 'off duty'.

Capturing the headlines, it was noted that 'she does not need the clothes for warmth as it is warm inside the studios', and that she 'would be prepared to read the news without clothes and only wears the clothes because her employer requires it'. The tribunal remained unconvinced and her claim failed. Of course, if you have a 'costume' or 'uniform', the chances of success are far higher.

Commission paid for guarantee of debenture
(*Ascot Gas Water Heaters Ltd v Duff* KBD 1942).

Company and partnership formation expenses

Compensation paid
*   By brewers to tenant on transfer of licence to new house (*Morse v Stedeford* KBD 1934);

*   for loss of office to officials in connection with share purchase transactions (*Overy v Ashford Dunn & Co. Ltd* KBD 1938; *Bassett Enterprise Ltd v Petty* KBD 1938) or for period after cessation of trading (*Godden v A. Wilson's Stores Holdings Ltd* CA 1962).

*   by monthly instalments for closing down competitor's works for a period of years (*United Steel Co. Ltd v Cullington (No 1)* HL 1940);

*   for refraining from working a coal seam under a factory which would possibly have caused subsidence (*Bradbury v United Glass Bottle Mnfg. Ltd* Ch D 1958);

*   to redundant directors and employees on take-over of a business and paid out of the consideration (*Peters & Co. Ltd v Smith* Ch D 1963).

Contributions to a joint drainage scheme for improvement
(*Bean v Doncaster Amalgamation Collieries Ltd* HL 1946).

Conversion of works
For manufacture of a different product (*Lothian Chemical Co. Ltd. v Rogers* CS 1926).

Cost of acquiring property rights
(*CIR v Land Securities Investment Trust Ltd* HL 1969).

Cost of sea wall to prevent erosion
(*Avon Beach & Cafe Ltd v Stewart* Ch D 1950).

Demurrage
Claim provided for and subsequently released by railway company (*CIR v Niddrie & Benhar Coal Co. Ltd* CS 1951).

Depreciation
The writing off of the cost of a capital asset over its useful life is not allowed, but is replaced by Capital Allowances - See PART 7 - CAPITAL ALLOWANCES, p.292

Discount
On issue of shares or debentures.

Distribution of profits
Sometimes seemingly allowable expenses are shown to be not expenses incurred in earning profits, but ways of disposing of them, and hence not deductible. On such grounds expenditure out of a racecourse totalisator's profits on augmenting prize money and contributions towards the cost of horse transport and runners allowances was not allowed. The profits were first made, and then expenses were incurred under a government-approved scheme. More narrowly, they were not incurred in connection with the operation of the totalisers, but 'to attract more horses' (*Young v Racecourse Betting Control Board* HL 1959).

Entertaining
No deduction is allowed for business entertaining expenses in computing profits or income, nor are any capital allowances to be given for machinery or plant used to provide business entertainment (TA 1988 ss 77).

Business entertaining expenses include those incurred by an employee (including directors of a company) which are recouped from the proprietor.

Entertainment includes 'hospitality of any kind' but not 'anything provided for bona fide members of staff unless its provision for them is incidental to its provision also for others' (members of staff include directors of a company).

It includes gifts (including Christmas gifts) except small advertising gifts not worth more than £50, and not being tobacco or a goods voucher.

In Netlogic Consulting Ltd. v HMRC N Ltd. organised a function for 250 of its potential customers or clients. It spent £1,800 on catering and £681 on room hire. N Ltd. argued that the £2,481 was an allowable trading deduction as expenses on advertising or promotion rather than hospitality or entertainment. The Inspector disallowed the deduction on the basis that it was "business entertainment".

The Special Commissioners found that the £1,800 was an expense incurred in providing business entertainment and was therefore disallowed as a trading deduction. However, the room hire charge of £681 was a charge for the provision of the room so that the meeting of N Ltd.'s potential clients or customers could take place. The purpose of the meeting was to attract business to N Ltd. and not entertainment. Accordingly, entertainment was incidental to the provision of the entertainment and should be allowed.

Exhaustion of capital
In money or kind. Capital withdrawn. Depreciation or loss on sale of investments (conversely appreciation or profit on sale of investments is not assessable) (*Coltness Iron Co. v Black* HL 1881).

Fines
Incurred by employees in the course of the business are customarily allowed, but not those incurred by the directors or proprietors.

A stockbroker's legal expenses in defending disciplinary proceedings the Stock Exchange Council brought were deductible in computing his profits, since his purpose in defending the action was to preserve his trade. The fines imposed were not deductible, however. So the House of Lords held in *McKnight v Sheppard* (1999) STI 1077.

Franchises
The purchase of a franchise, excluding goods and capital items for which other reliefs may be available.

Gifts
Please see Entertaining, p.210.

Goods for proprietor's use
Please see Maintenance of Trader's Family or Establishment, p.215.

Goodwill
Payment by instalments (*CIR v Pattison & Others* CS 1959).

Guarantee payments
Made by development company for builders (*Homelands (Handforth) Ltd v Margerison* KBD 1943) or made by a parent company for its subsidiary (*Milnes v J. Beam Group Ltd* Ch D 1975).

A partnership could not deduct a payment made under a contract of guarantee, because there was a right of indemnity against the personal estate of one of the partners (TA 1970 s 130(k); *Bolton v Halpern & Wood 9* Ch D 1979).

Hospital facilities
To enable patient to carry on his business whilst receiving treatment disallowed as the expenditure was not exclusively for business purposes (*Murgatroyd v Evans-Jackson* Ch D 1966).

Illegal payments
Illegal payments are not allowable. From 30.9.93 payments made in response to threats, menaces, blackmail and other forms of extortion are specifically disallowed.

Improvements
Cost of improvements paid by landlord and repaid by tenants by half-yearly instalments (*Ainley v Edens* KBD 1935). The repayments by the tenants are not allowable.

Improvements and additions to machinery, plant fittings, furniture, in order to make them more suitable; do more business; increase convenience; render more attractive (beyond reasonable repairs) - these are really additions to the capital assets, and their cost is not an allowable deduction from profits (but capital allowances will be available in respect of plant, machinery and trade fixtures).

Income tax (British)
On the business property or profits. Income tax paid as employment income on behalf of the employees is an admissible expense, being tantamount to additional remuneration.

Interest and overdrawn capital accounts
If the proprietor withdraws money from the business in excess of the amount he is owed, and this withdrawal has to be funded by borrowed money, it is only right that the interest attributable to that withdrawal should be disallowed, it being for a private purpose and not for the purposes of the trade.

HMRC has traditionally taken a simple approach. If the bank overdraft is £10,000 and the capital of the account is overdrawn by £4,000 they disallow 40% of the interest. However, this is completely wrong as it misunderstands the argument. It assumes that the whole of the excess drawings increased the overdraft. That could be right but it is equally likely that the excess drawings would have taken place when the bank account was in credit and the overdraft was caused by the subsequent payment of trade creditors. What needs to be identified is the extent to which every withdrawal caused an increase in the business borrowings, because only then will the interest be able to be attributable to a business or a private purpose.

It is also necessary to identify why the proprietor's account is overdrawn in the first place. It is not enough to say that it will be overdrawn because the drawings exceed the profits; you need to look at the make-up of the profit to see whether they contain any <u>non-cash items</u>. For example, depreciation will be charged in arriving at the profits and this would have the effect of reducing the profit and increasing the overdrawn proprietor's capital account. However it would not affect the business borrowings and should not effect any interest disallowance. Furthermore, because depreciation is charged year by year and the accumulated depreciation diminishes the profits over a period, in considering whether the proprietor's drawings have caused the overdraft, it is necessary to add back the accumulated depreciation. One must also look to see how much of the business funding is provided by the creditors. Accordingly movements in debtors and creditors from one year to the next will also be relevant.

The case of *Silk v HMIT (SpC 201) 2000* dealt with this point and HMRC accepted that the cumulative depreciation should be added back and that the movements of debtors and creditors ought to be taken into account. However, to do the full analysis and identify the position with each withdrawal would be extremely time consuming and the Special Commissioner agreed that a broader brush approach could be accepted.

Interest on late payment of PAYE & NIC
Interest paid by businesses on overdue tax (for example, PAYE, NIC) is not usually deductible for corporation tax purposes. Legislation has been introduced to formalise current practice into statute and will apply for accounting periods ending on or after 9 April 2003.

Interest on loans paid in advance
New rules, effective immediately, (PBR October 2007) have been introduced to prevent individuals skirting existing anti-avoidance provisions on 'sideways loss relief' and accelerating their tax relief by paying all the interest in advance on certain business loans (for investing in partnerships or small companies for example).

The change will deny tax relief for interest that relates to a later year than the year in which the interest is paid.

Land bought and resold
By an opencast mining company, even though only done in order to obtain coal (*Knight v Calder Grove Estate* Ch D 1954).

Legal charges out of ordinary course of trading
Conveyancing, etc. in connection with purchases of property, Partnership deeds, cost of promoting company or of altering its Articles of Association. Costs of mortgages and lease, misconduct (successful) and breach of employment contract (unsuccessful) (*Knight v Parry* Ch D 1972). The general principle is that legal expenses are allowable only when incurred in the ordinary course of earning profits or in defending rights.

Legal damages

Only such losses can be deducted as are actually incidental to the trade itself. They cannot be deducted if they fall on the trader in some other character than that of a trader. Thus, where an indemnity was granted to employees who were also shareholders, but after the threat posed to the company by the plaintiff (a former director-controlling shareholder) had passed, it was held reasonable to conclude that business motives were not the only motives (*Hammond Engineering Co. Ltd v CIR* Ch D 1975). Nor is it enough that the damages be payable in the course of the trade; they must be incurred in respect of some act done for the purpose of earning profits. Cost of application by brewers for new licence on removal, or by hauliers for additional road licences (*Pyrah v Annis & Co. Ltd* CA 1956). Cost of pursuing an unsuccessful planning application for development of minerals by a mining company, despite accountancy evidence to the effect that the expense was properly chargeable to revenue (*EEC Quarries Ltd v Watkins* Ch D 1975).

Cost of claiming an allowance for the expenses of PAYE work on staff wages (*Meredith v Roberts* Ch D 1968). A fine for contravention of the USA anti-trust laws is not allowable (*Cattermole v Borax Chemicals Ltd* KBD 1949).

A sum paid by a company to settle actions for fraud is allowable (*Golder v Great Boulder Proprietary Gold Mines Ltd* Ch D 1952).

Life assurance premiums

Paid as pension provision in respect of two controlling directors (*Dracup (Samuel) & Sons Ltd v Dakin* Ch D 1957).

Losses

(a)   Incurred in connection with loan transactions (*Henderson v Meade-King Robinson & Co. Ltd* KBD 1938).

(b)   On transactions where the loss was contemplated from the outset, and accordingly the transaction was not considered to be in the nature of trading (*Johnson v Jewitt* CA 1961).

(c)   Incurred by subsidiary company (*Odhams Press Ltd v Cook* HL 1940).

Lump sum payment

•   in release of liability to pay annuity to widow of a director (*Howard Co. Ltd v Bentley* KBD 1948);

•   in release of future liability to minimum payment for electric current, where the particular activity (a quarry) was closed down (*CIR v Sharp & Sons* CS 1959);

•   for surrender of lease (*Mallett v Staveley Coal & Iron Co. Ltd* CA 1928);

- by open-cast mining company for right to enter land and mine the coal (*Rorke Ltd v CIR* Ch D 1960).

Maintenance of trader's family or establishment
Personal expenses of a trader for his convenience, comfort or necessity are not allowed; they are expenses after profit is earned and not 'necessary to earning the profits'.

Where goods are taken out of the business for personal use by the trader or his or her family a credit must be made in the accounts of the cost of these goods. The principle of valuing goods at market value set out in *Sharkey v Wernher* HL 1955 are not considered to be applicable in such cases; nor is it applied to services rendered to the trader personally or to his household, nor to the construction of fixed assets to be used in the business.

Medical expenses
Incurred as a result of working conditions (*Norman v Golder* CA 1944). For instance, the cost of an operation to a finger to restore its flexibility was not allowed to a spare-time guitar player as he also played the guitar as a hobby as well as for financial gain (*Prince v Mapp* Ch D 1969).

Misappropriation by director
(*Bamford v ATA Advertising Ltd* Ch D 1972).

Money spent as capital
E.g. pit sinking, cost of restoring a pit that has become neglected (*United Collieries Ltd v CIR* CS 1929) (Please see Repairs p.217). Replacing old machinery by new. New fittings in rebuilt or new premises (*Hyam v CIR* CS 1929).

Monopoly value
Instalments in respect of monopoly value attaching to a public house (*Kneeshaw v Albertolli* KBD 1940).

Patents
Cost of acquiring but capital allowances may apply.

PAYE tax
Not recovered from a director (*Bamford v ATA Advertising Ltd* Ch D 1972). If reimbursement of tax which should have been deducted is not made, the amount of tax which should have been deducted is treated as a benefit received by the director and chargeable as an emolument (FA 1983 s 22).

Payments in consideration of being allowed to cancel contracts in respect of capital expenditure
(*Devon Mutual Steamship Association v Ogg* KBD 1927).

Payments to directors to refrain from carrying on certain activities
(*Associated Portland Cement Mnfg. Ltd v Kerr* CA 1945).

Payment to retiring director for 'assets' in a business
(*Deverall, Gibson & Hoare Ltd v Rees* KBD 1943).

Planning application
Please see Legal Charges out of Ordinary Course of Trading, p.213.

Premium
On shares or debentures, or on repayment of loan (*Bridgewater & Bridgewater v King* KBD 1943).

Private expenses
Such as rents, rates, etc. of dwelling-house, cost of a season ticket to residence (not necessary to earning the profits). Cost of meals 'in the city' or meals taken daily by the trader alone at cafes, etc. near to the various sites at which he worked (*Caillebotte v Quinn* Ch D 1975). The need to eat out was dictated by personal rather than business reasons, as the regularity evidenced. It is suggested that occasional business trips which compel a person to eat out are not covered by the case (and travelling expenses on business are allowed).

Where the expenditure is incurred for the dual purpose of the business and private or personal advantage it will not be allowed (*Mallalieu v Drummond* HL 1983).

Private use of business cars
The private proportion is usually calculated on a mileage basis and deducting this proportion from both the running expenses and capital allowances. A further restriction may be made to the extent that there is an element of personal choice in purchasing the cars (*G. H. Chambers (Northian Farmers) Ltd v Watmough* Ch D 1956). Travelling from residence to place of business is private use (*Newsom v Robertson* CA 1952) including unnecessary calls for business being made *en route* (*Sargent v Barnes* Ch D 1978).

Proprietors' or partners' withdrawals and sums drawn as own remuneration are not allowed

Quarry
Fixed rent and lordship on stone (TA 1970 s 156; *Craigenlow Quarries Ltd v CIR* CS 1952).

Remuneration to children
The question as to whether such remuneration is allowable as an expense of earning profits is one of fact. Remuneration is not allowable if it is not wholly and

exclusively laid out for the purpose of the business (*Copeman v Flood & Sons Ltd* KBD 1940).

Rent
An increase in rent under an arrangement whereby the period of the lease was shortened and the freehold sold to a subsidiary company of the lessee, so that a capital asset was being acquired by the subsidiary company (*CIR v Land Securities Investment Trust Ltd* HL 1969). A payment of £122,000 to obtain a reduction in the rent chargeable under a 50-year lease was held to be capital (since it improved a fixed capital asset, i.e. the lease) and was not deductible (*Tucker v Granada Motorway Services Ltd* HL 1979).

The partners moved from four locations to one new office. They prudently assumed it would be impossible to sublet all of the old premises and that there would be an ongoing expense in respect of outgoings even after receiving some rent. They made a provision against current profits for future rents of the old premises and sought to charge against receipts for the basis period the whole of the provision relating to rents payable by the firm in subsequent years. HMRC disallowed the provision. The partners appealed the decision to SpC. They held that the accounts were drawn up within commercially acceptable principles. It was accepted that excess rentals were a proper subject for a provision from the point of view of prudence, but that concept should be disregarded in the computation of profits for tax purposes even though the application of the prudence concept is required by established accountancy principles. The provision for excess rentals was therefore disallowed and was not an 'essential charge' against the receipts for that accounting period. The excess rentals should be charged as they fell due against the firms receipts relating to the periods in which they fell. The appeal was dismissed. (*Herbert Smith v Honour (Spc 138)*). However at a subsequent appeal the partners won and HMRC did not appeal this finding.

Repairs
The estimated cost of repairs to an old roof where extensions to buildings are carried out (*Lawrie v CIR* CS 1952). Repair expenditure on an asset recently purchased to the extent this improved it over the condition it was in when purchased, was regarded as the equivalent of an addition to the purchase price and hence not allowable (*Law Shipping Co. Ltd v CIR* CS 1923). Where an existing business had been taken over the point of change of ownership was considered, so that expenditure by the purchaser on repair work in the first year of trading was not allowed (*Bidwell v Gardiner* Ch D 1960).

The *Odeon Theatre* case (*Odeon Associated Theatres Ltd v Jones* CA 1971) has severely restricted the interpretation of the *Law Shipping* decision. In the Odeon case the company acquired some theatres which were in a poor state of repair as a result of wartime and post-war stringency, but quite usable. It put right this deterioration and it was clear that if the expenditure had been incurred by the vendors it would have been regarded as revenue expenditure and allowable for tax purposes. In accordance with sound commercial principles the expenditure was properly charged to revenue by the purchaser. HMRC's contention that this was capital expenditure was not accepted. The 'ordinary principles of commercial accountancy' were held to be the criterion and the *Law Shipping* case was distinguished as the ship was virtually unusable until the repairs required by a Lloyds survey had been carried out, and there was no evidence that charging the expenditure to revenue was in accordance with the ordinary principles of commercial accountancy.

This decision does not affect the disallowance against rents of expenditure on dilapidations which occurred before a lease commenced (except by concession, where the property passes to the surviving spouse, or to or from trustees of the spouses, on death) (HMRC Pamphlet IR 23), as this is a statutory prohibition (TA 1988 s 72).

But in *C Wills v HMRC* TC00479 the Tribunal has agreed with a landlord's submissions that expenditure on repairing the outbuilding of a let property should be an allowable expense of the rental business.

The appellant incurred over £100,000 on work to an outbuilding of a rental property. The outbuilding was listed, in a poor state of repair and becoming dangerous. Of the amount spent, £63,000 was regarded by the appellant to be capital expenditure but £43,665 was claimed as a repair cost. HMRC had disagreed and raised an assessment on the basis that all the expenditure was wholly capital and not an allowable deduction.

the taxpayer successfully argued that, following the decision in *Lurcott v Wakely and Others*, the expenditure was a repair to only part of the entire property (the house and the outbuilding) and not a renewal of the entity itself (the outbuilding). In addition, the Tribunal accepted that the case of *Willliam P Lawrie v CIR* did not apply because in that matter the taxpayer had claimed for notional repairs rather than repairs which had actually been carried out.

The Tribunal also decided that their decision was supported by HMRC manuals at PIM 2020 which states under the subtitle 'Extensive alterations to a property' that the actual cost of normal revenue repairs to a part of an old building which is preserved in the rebuilt structure is allowable as an ordinary revenue business expense. Moreover, HMRC's manual was supported by the case of *Conn v Robins Bros Ltd.*

Not only did the Tribunal agree that the claim for repair expenditure should be allowed but that the cost of structural works to ensure the outbuilding did not collapse should also be allowed.

For a recent case concerning the provision for future repairs please see Provisions and accruals, p.223.

Replacement
Of plant on which a wear and tear allowance is claimed. Neither is the cost of replacing buildings, or a barrier to protect a factory from canal water (*Phillips v Whieldon Sanitary Potteries Ltd* Ch D 1952), or the replacement of furniture which represents an improvement over the condition when taken over from the previous proprietor of the business (*Bidwell v Gardiner* Ch D 1960).

Reserve for cost of replacing assets, e.g. hired canteen equipment (*Peter Marchant Ltd v Stedeford* CA 1948).

Reserves and provisions
For doubtful debts, sinking funds, general reserves (provisions for specific bad or doubtful debts are allowable). Reserve made by money-lending company for collection expenses attributable to the capital element in outstanding loans (*Monthly Salaries Loan Co. Ltd v Furlong* Ch D 1962). Please see Rent, p.217 & Bad debts, p.190.

Royalties on minerals, patents, etc.
From which tax has been deducted at source. Where under an agreement an annual sum paid includes benefits other than for the use of a patent, the amount to be treated as in respect of patent royalties is one of fact to be decided if necessary by the Commissioners on appeal (*Paterson Engineering Co. Ltd v Duff* KBD 1943).

Service charge
Where an exceptionally heavy charge was made to a professional firm by a service company formed to provide staff, accommodation, etc. on the understanding that a correspondingly lighter charge would be made in later years, only a reasonable amount was allowed (the ordinary principles of commercial accountancy must be adopted) (*Stephenson v Payne, Stone, Fraser & Co.* Ch D 1967).

Shares allotted to employees
Excess of market over par value (*Lowry v Consolidated African Selection Trust Ltd* HL 1940).

Sponsorship
In *Interfish Ltd v HMRC* TC00520 sponsorship payments of £45 million to a rugby club were held not to be wholly and exclusively for the purposes of the trade as they had a dual purpose of financially supporting the club and promoting Interfish's business.

The Tribunal dismissed the taxpayer's argument that the purpose of financial support was incidental to the business exposure gained by Interfish. It was also decided that there was not an identifiable part of the expenditure that was incurred solely on promoting Interfish's business.

Structural alterations
And alterations generally, unless they are not very different from the original and their result is to repair something not to produce something new (*Conn v Robbins Bros. Ltd* Ch D 1966).

Subsidiary company's expenses
Even if expressed to be on account of agency commission, and under an agreement to pay a minimum annual sum (*Marshall Richards Machine Co. Ltd v Jewitt* Ch D 1956) (Please see Guarantee Payments, p.211).

Surrender of lease
(*Mallett v Staveley Coal & Iron Co. Ltd* CA 1928).

Tax avoidance scheme
Expenses incurred partly with a view to facilitating a tax avoidance scheme are not wholly and exclusively for the purposes of the trade, and so not allowable (*Kilmorie (Aldridge) Ltd v Dickenson* HL 1974).

Timber
A payment by timber merchants for the right to enter woodlands and get the timber is not allowable (*Hood Barrs v CIR (No. 2)* HL 1957), although a payment for standing timber would be. A purchase of woodland could be regarded either as a purchase of timber, and hence an allowable expense, or as capital expenditure and hence not allowable (*Hopwood v C. N. Spencer Ltd* Ch D 1964).

Trade association contributions
These are usually allowed only if an arrangement has been entered into by the association in consequence of which tax is paid by the association on the balance of its income over expenditure. Premiums for insurance against strikes are disallowed. If, however, the trade association is for mutual insurance only, the payments are allowable (*Thomas v Evans & Co.* HL 1927). The question whether a company is a mutual insurance company is one of fact (*Faulconbridge v National Employers Mutual General Insurance Association Ltd* Ch D 1952). Sums paid to a trade protection association towards the cost of acquisition of a business or of shares in a business are not allowable (*Collins v Joseph Adamson & Co.* KBD 1937), nor is that part of a subscription by shipbuilders to a trade protection association which is paid by the association to the Economic League (purposes of the League not the same as purpose of the shipping company's trade)(*Thompson & Sons Ltd v Chamberlain* Ch D 1962).

Travelling expenses
Of a barrister between home, where the profession is exercised, and the London chambers, are not deductible (*Newsom v Robertson* CA 1952). The cost of a

dentist's daily travel between a laboratory and surgery, being part of the dentist's daily journeys between home and surgery, were not allowed (*Sargent v Barnes* Ch D 1978). Expenses of attending a professional association conference abroad have been disallowed because there was a dual purpose of business and holiday (*Bowden v Russell & Russell* Ch D 1965). Expenses of travelling abroad with the object of emigrating and farming there are not allowable, farming abroad being a separate trade (*Sargeant v Earyrs* Ch D 1972).

Ultra vires payments
A company paid debenture interest at an extremely high rate. It had no need to do so and no power to agree to such a payment. The payment was held to be disallowable as it was not lawful for the company to make it (*Ridge Securities Ltd v CIR* Ch D 1963).

Underwriting commission
And expenses of raising capital.

War injuries: payments to employees
No payment to employees or their personal representatives or dependants on account of incapacity, retirement or death owing to war injuries is allowable as a deduction from profits unless made under any policy or arrangement made before 3 September, 1939, or under any established practice which was such that the same or a greater payment would have been made if the incapacity, etc. had not been due to war injuries. Where larger payments are made under the above heads owing to war injuries, the excess only is disallowed (TA 1988 s 571).

4 IN WHICH YEAR?

4.1 General

Difficulty often arises as to the particular year in which an item of income or expenditure should be credited or charged. It is not correct to take the date on which the cash was received or paid. (FRS 5 (application Note G) came into effect for accounting periods ending on or after 21 June 2005. This effectively means that businesses which were in a position to bill but failed to do so should have the total invoice value included as accrued income. However partially completed contracts are brought in at a value reflecting the part completed of the final invoice e.g. A half completed contract worth in total £2,000 is brought in at £1,000, see 4.2 Earlier recognition of revenue in accounts, p.226. Delaying the profit, by billing after a year end, to a subsequent period is no longer an option.

The correct date is that on which the right to the income arose, or when the expenditure was incurred (i.e. date on which the amount becomes payable). On a sale of goods this is at the time of delivery, subject to contrary express terms in any contract, which often makes it invoice date. When, subsequently, further amounts are received in respect of goods or services supplied at some earlier date, these may be related back and the accounts for the earlier period re-opened.

Estimated amounts for an expenditure which has not yet been made cannot be included, even if the damage has in fact happened (*Naval Colliery Co. Ltd v CIR* HL 1928). However, if a right or liability has actually arisen, an estimated amount is often included where the final figure has not been ascertained, but this is regarded as only provisional, and when the matter is finally agreed the final figure must be substituted for it, even if this means re-opening the earlier accounts. Where accounts have to be re-opened because a liability has not been included and had not been finally established, an estimate of the liability should be made according to all known circumstances and not merely those which existed at the date of the accounts (*Simpson v Jones* Ch D 1968). The following examples illustrate this point of principle.

Bill of exchange dishonoured
On failure of drawer to honour a bill, a party to it estimated his liability. In the next accounting period this was settled at a lower amount. The lower amount was carried back to the earlier period in place of the estimate (*Bernhard v Gahan* CA 1928).

Contingent right
A builder received compensation from a county council for refusal to allow building on certain ground. He contended that this should be related back to some earlier period, e.g. when he purchased the land, or when development was refused. It was held that his right to receive the compensation did not arise until it was paid (*Johnson v Try (W. S.) Ltd* CA 1946).

Delay in delivery
Where a contract is for manufacture and delivery, and there is a delay in delivery, the sale price becomes a debt only on delivery and the profit is credited then (*J. P. Hill & Co v CIR* CS 1924).

Discount on money bills
Discount on money bills receivable by a bank is not assessable as profits until the bills are sold or mature, even though brought in for accounting purposes (*Willingale*

v *International Commercial Bank Ltd* HL 1978).

Forward contracts

Anticipated losses on forward contracts, e.g. where the current market price has fallen below the contracted price cannot be allowed (*Collins & Sons v CIR* CS 1924).

Lloyd's underwriters

The profits from underwriting are based on a three-year period covering the year in which the policies are underwritten and the two following years. Nevertheless, when the profit is computed it must be credited in the year in which the policy was underwritten (*CIR v Gardner Mountain & D'Ambrumenil Ltd* HL 1947).

Option

The value of an option to take up shares at par value instead of market value is income arising on the date the option was obtained, not when it was exercised (*Abbott v Philbin* HL 1960). When a finance company made a loan in return for an option to buy shares, it was held that no trading profit arose until the shares were sold (*Varty v British South Africa Co. Ltd* HL 1965).

Pawnbroker's unredeemed pledges

When a pledge is not redeemed by the borrower the goods may be sold. The surplus of sale money over the loan must be claimed by the borrower and on failure to do so within a certain time limit by law the right to the money is lost. These unclaimed surpluses should be credited in the pawnbrokers' accounts on the date the time limit for claiming them expired (*Jays the Jewellers Ltd v CIR* KBD 1947).

Provisions and accruals

Two cases demonstrates the thinking applicable

(a)   Whether or not the accruals method of providing for aircraft engine overhauls every three or four years gave a full and fair picture of a company's profits, was a question of fact and degree for the Commissioners, according to the Chancery Division in Johnston v Britannia Airways Ltd (1994) STI 791.

Britannia operated an airline. Every three or four years each aircraft engine had a major overhaul, to meet the Civil Aviation authority's requirements.

Britannia accrued the costs of the overhaul in the accounts. The average cost of an overhaul per hours flown was calculated and multiplied by the number of hours flown by the engine in the accounting period. The inspector believed that the accruals method of accounting for the overhaul costs was inappropriate and that, instead, the costs should have been capitalised when incurred and amortised over the subsequent hours flown. For the accounting periods ended 31 December 1978 to 1987, he raised assessments on a capitalisation and amortisation approach. Britannia appealed.

The Special Commissioners allowed the appeal. Having considered all the accountancy evidence, they could see no reason for holding that the correct principles were any different from those Britannia applied in accounting for the overhaul costs. Furthermore, nothing in statute or case law precluded the sums provided from being deducted. The accruals method gave the most accurate picture of Britannia's profits and complied with the concept of prudence in SSAP 2.

(b)   The Special Commissioners held that a provision for the cost of a major refurbishment of a retail premises, that was carried out and paid for over the following two years, was an allowable deduction for corporation tax purposes (see *Jenners Princes Street Edinburgh Ltd v IRC* SpC 166 STI (1998) 1119).

The taxpayer company carried on a retail trade from a listed building in Princes Street, Edinburgh. In 1994, the escalating costs of repair work prompted the company to carry out a feasibility study on the possibility of a major refurbishment of the building. In the year ended 31 January 1995, the company decided to proceed with the refurbishment at an estimated cost of £2.25m, including the costs of the feasibility study of £190,000, and made a provision in its accounts of £2.06m. The p&l account showed a deduction of £2.17m, being £2.25m less a provision of £80,000 made in earlier years. The work was carried out and paid for over the next two years.

The inspector refused the company's claim to deduct the provision of £2.17m in computing its tax liability for the year ended 31 January 1995 on the grounds that the phrase 'actually expended' in s 74 (I) (d), TA 1988 restricted deductions for repairs to the amount physically spent in the period.

The commissioners said that the adverb 'actually' qualified the verb 'expended' by adding a degree of precision, and the phrase meant no more than what was truly expended in the accountancy sense. This simply required an accurate assessment as opposed to a broad notional figure. The accruals method as recorded in SSAP 2 and used by the company was based on a similar approach. The commissioners therefore found that the provision was properly deductible in computing the assessable profits in the year ended 31 January 1995. In reaching their conclusion, the commissioners made a detailed analysis of both the legislation and case law.

Provisions, contingent liabilities and contingent assets

FRS12 was published in September 1998. It addresses the problem that large provisions were being made for future restructuring or reorganisation where, in many cases, all that had happened by the balance sheet date was that the directors had made a decision. FRS12 permits provisions only where there is an obligation on the part of the business to transfer economic benefits as a result of past transactions or events. Mere anticipation of future expenditure is not enough.

The most important tax consequences of FRS12 are:
- Provisions for future repairs and overhauls are not permitted, except where there is an operating lease containing a repairing obligation; see Britannia Airways.

- A provision for future restructuring or reorganisation is permitted only where, at the balance sheet date, the business has a detailed formal plan for the reconstruction and has raised a valid expectation among those affected that it will take place.

- A provision cannot be made for future expenditure required by legislation where the business could avoid its obligation by changing its method of operation.

<u>HMRC's view</u>
HMRC accepts that provisions correctly made under FRS12 are tax deductible except where specific tax rules remain to the contrary. For example, provisions for capital expenditure are not tax deductible. Provisions for employee or director remuneration are subject to the rule in FA1989, s43, that is deductible remuneration must be paid within nine months after an accounting period.

HMRC's revised approach applies in settling open years.

In cases where businesses may have disallowed provisions in the past on the basis of HMRC's previous view, deductions may be made for expenditure incurred when computing tax profits for the period in which the next view is first applied. In addition, any closing provision correctly computed in accordance with FRS12 may be allowed. Of course, no expenditure can be relieved more than once.

Illustration:
A construction company enters into a long term contract in 1995. In preparing the 1996 accounts it is clear that the contract will make a loss. The directors make a provision of £100,000 in the 1996 accounts which, on HMRC's current view of the law, should have been allowed. However, at that time, negotiation with HMRC results in an allowance of only £15,000 for tax, the balance of £85,000 being disallowed as an anticipation of a loss. The 1996 tax position was settled in 1998.

A further provision of £50,000 is made in the 1997 accounts and again £20,000 in the 1998 accounts, both for which should be allowed on HMRC's current view of the law. The tax position for both years is still open.

Assuming all provisions are estimated with sufficient accuracy, for 1997 the company can claim both the £50,000 provision and also the £85,000 previously disallowed for 1996. For 1998 the company can claim the £20,000 provision.

Provisional payment
Payments made by the government during periods of government control are often on a provisional basis. Where the remuneration is finally agreed, the final payments must be dated back to the period in which the work was done (*Isaac Holden & Sons Ltd v CIR* KBD 1924). This applies similarly to payments to doctors under the Dankwerts award (*North v Spencer's Exors. & C. H. Spencer* Ch D 1956).

Shares instead of cash
When shares are received and are not immediately realizable, they must be credited at their commercial value at the date of receipt (*Gold Coast Selection Trust Ltd v Humphrey* HL 1948).

Spreading forward and new business
Where a partnership is formed into a limited company and the cessation and new business provisions are applied, an agreement with the partnership to spread forward a lump sum superannuation fund payment does not apply to the company (*Clarke (J. M.) & Co Ltd. v Musker* Ch D 1956).

Stock requisitioned
Stock was requisitioned by the government and payment made, but this payment was not accepted as final by the recipients. New legislation followed, as a result of which a further payment became due. This was related back to the date of requisitioning (*CIR v Newcastle Breweries Ltd* HL 1927).

4.2 Earlier recognition of revenue in accounts
- UITF 40 & spreading of the initial uplift
4.2.1 Background
This issue affects people who supply services.

The service is supplied over a period of time, and invoiced irregularly. Therefore this matter does not apply to hairdressers who may take 10 minutes or 2 hours to perform their service and then immediately ask (invoice) for payment.

The only aspect of concern is the level of unbilled work at a businesses' year end and how to value it. Traditionally this 'work in progress' has been valued at cost – staff wages plus an aspect of overheads. The profit being taken in the accounting period in which the client is finally invoiced. The new rules state that the profit element should also be calculated and debited to 'accrued income'. Income is effectively recognised earlier than was previously the case.

Please see Smith's Taxation 111th Edition 2007/2008 for full details.

PART FIVE
SELF-EMPLOYED / PARTNERSHIPS

1 KINDS OF ORGANISATION

It is important to distinguish, for tax purposes, what may be called a 'company' and an unincorporated business operated by individuals either in partnership or as sole owners. A particular reason is that the profits of a limited company are chargeable to corporation tax and those of an unincorporated business to income tax, subject to certain exceptions. For these purposes the term 'company' includes bodies incorporated under the Companies Acts and special Acts, chartered bodies, as well as some associations, such as clubs which carry out trading. Incorporated companies are called 'legal persons' which means they have an identity distinct from the identity of the shareholders or subscribers of the capital. Persons owning and operating unincorporated businesses are usually described as 'self employed' and embrace not only members of large partnerships but also those carrying on spare time activities for profit.

An alternative business structure known as a 'Limited Liability Partnership' (LLP) is also available. LLPs are registered at Companies House and are available for trading and professional partnerships. They are taxed in the same way as ordinary partnerships.

Whether a business is incorporated or not much the same rules apply to the assessment of profits, that is what income or expenditure is allowed or disallowed for tax purposes. However, certain special rules apply to assessments to corporation tax on companies. In particular salaries, wages and directors' fees payable to the owners of the business are allowable in the tax computations of companies (although assessable to income tax on the recipients) but not allowable for owners of unincorporated businesses, being in effect allocation of profit. Dividends paid by companies, and shares of profit paid to self-employed persons, are in both cases not allowable charges. The basis of assessment for unincorporated businesses are the profits shown by the accounts (as adjusted for tax purposes) drawn up to a date in the tax year, which ends on 5 April. This is known as the current year basis.

In the case of companies the basis of assessment for corporation tax is the profit shown by the accounts drawn up to a date which determines the company's accounting period.

2 NEW NAMES FOR SCHEDULES

From 6 April 2005, for the self employed and partnerships, the Schedule D Cases have been replaced by parts of the ITTOIA 2005. The full text can be found on the website: www.legislation.hmso.gov.uk/acts/acts2005/2005005.htm.

The Act is split into 10 Parts and 4 Schedules. The Parts relevant to business taxation are as follows:

(a) Part 2 (trading income),
(b) Part 3 (property income),
(c) Part 4 (savings and investment income), and
(d) Part 5 (certain miscellaneous income).

3 BADGES OF TRADE

The decision whether a transaction is a trading or a capital receipt can be significant especially with the highest rate of income tax being 50% versus 18%/28% for capital gains.

The badges of trade have evolved over a period of time from the element of doubt which exists whether a transaction or series of transactions fall within the statutory definition of 'trade'. ICTA 1988 s832 widely defines a trade as including "every trade, manufacture, adventure or concern in the nature of a trade".

The question of what precisely constitutes a trade has been considered in the courts over many cases.

In Marson v Morton (1986) 59TC381 the profit on a single transaction in land was held to be capital. The judge (Sir Nicholas Browne-Wilkinson V-C) stated that whether there had been an adventure in the nature of a trade is a question of fact that depends on all the facts and circumstances of each particular case. He specified nine factors that had to be considered in determining the nature of a trade.

3.1 "Frequency or number of similar transactions by the same person".
Although a single transaction is capable of being seen as a trade, a lack of repetition tends to point away from a trade. See Marson v Morton above. See also Lynch v Edmondson SpC 164, Salt v Chamberlain (1979) 53TC143 & Leach v Pogson (1962) 40TC585.

3.2 "The subject matter of the realisation".

In the above mentioned Lynch case a bricklayer built 2 flats on a piece of land and then sold a 99 year lease on one of them. He claimed the sale of the lease was capital, it was held to be part of his trade. Sale of land can therefore be either capital or a trade depending on all the circumstances. In Rutledge v CIR (1929) 14TC490 the purchase and sale of 1 million toilet rolls was an adventure in the nature of a trade because of the nature of the asset involved.

3.3 "Was the transaction carried through in a manner typical of the trade in a commodity of that nature?"

In Lynch the fact that the lease was sold immediately after the building was completed was held to be a pointer to a trade. In Murray v IRC (1951) 32TC238 the sale of rights to cut timber on land owned for some years was also held to be a trade.

3.4 "What was the source of the finance of the transaction?"

If money is borrowed to finance the transaction this is held to be a pointer to a trade. In Lynch the bricklayer had borrowed to finance the building of the flats and intended to repay the loan from the sale proceeds.

3.5 "Was the transaction in some way related to the trade which the taxpayer otherwise carries on?"

Again as in Lynch his main trade of bricklaying was closely related to the sale of newly built flats.

3.6 "Supplementary work on or in connection with property realised".

Work carried out on an asset prior to sale is a factor in point to a trade. As was the land on which Lynch has constructed the flats.

3.7 "Was the item purchased resold in one lot, or was it broken down into several lots?"

The sale of the flats individually was thought to be another factor in Lynch.

3.8 "Motive".

An intention to sell in the short term could be a factor pointing towards a trade. In Lynch his bank loan agreement included a commitment to sell one of the flats on completion.

3.9 "Did the item purchased either provide enjoyment for the purchaser, or produce income pending resale?"

Where one or both of the above factors are involved the usually points away from a trade towards an investment.

4 SELF ASSESSMENT

4.1 Introduction
By using standardized formats for tax returns, schedules and the accounts therein HMRC are able to use computer analysis to review returns, and also a percentage are selected at random for more detailed review or enquiry.

Tax on a particular tax year is paid on the profits of the business ending in that same tax year, e.g. Brenda who makes up her annual accounts to 30 June 2011 (in tax year 2011/2012) will be taxed on those profits in 2011/2012.

Capital allowances for 2011/2012 will be based on the same period as the profits (1 July 2010 - 30 June 2011).

4.2 Total profits = total taxable profits
If the accounting year ends on 5 April for the whole life of a business, profits will always be taxed in the year they arise. If a different year end is chosen some profits will be taxed twice at the beginning of the businesses's life and carried forward possibly 50 years and deducted from the final period's taxable profits. There is no indexation on these profits carried forward.

4.3 Opening years
Special rules operate in the first tax year of a business as there will normally be no accounts which end in that year, viz. People normally prepare accounts for 12 months and very few businesses start life on 6 April.

Accordingly these special rules have to:-

(a)   Adjust or pro rata the profits for 12 months which overlap the 5 April to obtain a figure for X/365 of profits which fall into the tax year in which the business started (if a leap year X/366 is used).

(b)   The second tax year's assessment is normally the unprorated profits for the lst 12 months.

(c)   The third tax year's assessment will be based on the profits on the accounts ending in the tax year (i.e. the second year's accounts).

Example: Shaun started in business on 1 May 2007 and he makes profits to 30 April 2008 of £72,000. Profits to 30 April 2009 are £96,000. Note 2008 was a leap year.

He will be assessed as follows:

	£
2007/2008 'actual' basis	
341/366 x £72,000 (1.5.07 - 5.4.08)	67,082
2008/2009 1st 12 months (1.5.07 - 30.4.08)	72,000
2009/2010 Current year basis (yr. to 30.4.09)	96,000

It will be noted that the profits for the period 1 May 2007 to 5 April 2008 are taxed twice. These are £67,082 and known as 'overlap profits'. The sum must be noted in the 'permanent file' and also disclosed on the Tax Return, and ready for the cessation of the business, possibly decades ahead.

4.4 Final year
When an individual ceases trading he will be taxed for the period running from his last set of accounts (if in the previous tax year) to the date of cessation.

Continuing the above example. Shaun makes profits of £78,000 in the year to 30 April 2010 and stopped trading on 31 October 2010. The profits in the final six months are £30,000.

	£
2010/2011 Untaxed profits (1.5.09 - 31.10.10)	
(£78,000 + £30,000) =	108,000
But less overlap profits	(67,082)
Taxable profits	40,918

Please note if Shaun had ceased trading on 3l March 2011, 23 months of profits would have been taxed in 2010/2011. A nasty surprise! There are arguments both ways on the cash flow advantages of a year end early in the tax year and the avoidance of a nasty surprise at the end of a business by having a year end late in the tax year, on say 31 March or 5 April.

You will note that the total profits of business were as follows:

	£
Year to 30 April 2008	72,000
" " " " 2009	96,000
" " " " 2010	78,000
Six months to 31 October 2010	30,000
	£276,000

and were taxed as:-

	£
2007/2008	67,082
2008/2009	72,000
2009/2010	96,000
2010/2011	40,918
	£276,000

The total of profits achieved and taxed are the same but if Shaun had not ceased trading for another 40 years the effects of inflation may have made the profits made in the final 18 months period 1.5.2047 - 31.10.2048 not £108,000 but £608,000. The same, unindexed, overlap relief of £67,082 would still be deducted but not have as much effect on taxable profits.

As stated, previously, the advantage of a year end late in the tax year reduces the proportion of a year's profit carried forward as 'overlap profits' and subject to the effects of inflation.

4.5 Partnerships
4.5.1 Current year basis
Partners are assessed individually. They are responsible for only their own individual tax liability and no longer jointly and severally liable for their partner's tax liabilities.

4.5.2 Changes of ownership
The same opening year rules apply as for new individual businesses.

When a new partner joins individual opening year rules (i.e. actual basis) apply to that partner alone. The other partners continue on their current year basis.

Individual overlap rules apply to each partner and will be 'cashed in' when an individual partner retires or leaves the partnership.

4.5.3 Wife as sleeping partner
The extent of loss of earnings of a partner in a business was examined in (*Ward v Newalls Insulation Co Ltd* TAXline April 1998 p2).

Two men worked together. Their wives were partners in the business. Each partner received one-quarter of the profits. The arrangement was not challenged by HMRC. One man fell ill and sued his former employer on the basis that his illness was attributable to an industrial disease contracted whilst working for the employer. The defendant in those proceedings argued that the earnings of the plaintiff were his one-quarter share of partnership profits.

It was found that the earnings of the partner who fell ill were in truth half the partnership profits. The two wives were partners only for tax purposes and not in substance.

A sleeping partner is not liable for Class 4 NICs because they cannot be held to have profits which are 'immediately derived from the carrying on or exercise of one or more trades, professions or vocations'. (HMRC - NIM24520).

4.6 Limited Liability Partnerships (LLP)
LLPs are in law regarded as 'bodies corporate' and subject to aspects of company law. But for tax they are generally treated as 'partnerships' and treated for the purposes of income tax, corporation tax and capital gains tax as if they were partners carrying on business in partnership (each member will be assessed to tax on their share of the LLPs income or gains).

4.6.1 Income tax
(a) Work in progress
Partners time should be included in work-in-progress as their work now equates to that of directors.

(b) Capital Allowances
Where a LLP succeeds to a business previously carried on by an old partnership this will not of itself give rise to a balancing event for the purposes of the Capital Allowance provisions.

(c) Interest Relief
Members of a LLP, who are individuals, will be entitled to claim interest relief on the loans applied in the circumstances set out in Section 362(1) ICTA 1988. (Part 2 - 2.7.1(c), p.46).

(d) Loss Relief
Unlike Section 117 ICTA, the undrawn profits of a member of a LLP cannot normally be added to their subscribed capital in order to calculate the limit of their entitlement to sideways loss relief. This is because, subject to any agreement between them, a member's undrawn profits will normally be regarded as a debt of the LLP. This means that the member ranks, for that sum, alongside the other creditors in the event of liquidation. If however the terms of the agreement between the members specifically provide that the undrawn profit stands as part of a member's capital contribution and that agreement is unconditional then that amount can be taken into account in calculating the limit.

Example:
Mr Stevens becomes a member of a LLP on 6 April 2008. He introduced capital of

£10,000 into the partnership. The LLP carries on a trade. During the year ended 5 April 2011 he makes a further capital contribution of £6,000.

His share of the LLP's trading loss is as follows and he claims relief under Section 64 ITA07 for those losses against his other income.

Y/E 5 April 2009	£6,000
Y/E 5 April 2010	£6,000
Y/E 5 April 2011	£3,000

Mr Stevens is entitled to Section 64 relief as follows:

2008/2009	£6,000	(Unrelieved capital contribution £4,000)
2009/2010	£4,000 (1)	(Unrelieved loss £2,000)
2010/2011	£5,000 (2)	(Unrelieved capital contribution £1,000)

(i)   Sideways (S64) loss relief is restricted to the unrelieved capital contribution brought forward of £4,000. The balance of the loss of £2,000 (£6,000 - £4,000) is carried forward.

(ii)   Sideways (S64) loss relief of £5,000 available i.e. loss of year £3,000 + unrelieved loss brought forward £2,000. Unrelieved capital contribution carried forward is £1,000 i.e. total contributions £16,000 less total Sideways (S64) loss relief given £15,000).

(e) Overlap relief
Where a partnership carries on a trade or profession each partner is deemed to carry on a personal trade or profession. The basis period rules are applied to that deemed trade or profession and any overlap profit is personal to each partner.

If, on conversion, a LLP succeeds to the business previously carried by an old partnership then a partner's personal trade or profession will be regarded as continuing.

(f) Demergers
Where a LLP takes over only part of the old partnership's trade, such an event constitutes a 'demerger'. Unless it can be shown that on the demerger the part of the business carried on by the LLP is recognisably 'the business' previously carried on by the old partnership then the cessation provisions will apply. In that event each member of the old partnership will be entitled to their personal overlap relief. Equally the commencement provisions will apply to all the members of the LLP. This would

be the case where an accounting firm transferred just its audit practice to an LLP but retained the taxation practice within the old partnership.

If it can be shown that the LLP does carry on 'the business' previously carried on by the old partnership then, as it will have succeeded to the old partnership's business, the cessation provisions will not be applied to the old partnership and any overlap relief will be carried forward. Equally the commencement provisions will not be applied to the members of the LLP. But the old partnership will be assumed to have commenced a new business in relation to the part of the trade it retains.

Whether or not the business carried on by the LLP is recognisably 'the business' previously carried on by the old partnership is a question of fact.

(g) Cash basis - catching up charge
If on conversion the LLP succeeds to the business previously carried on by an old partnership then the spreading rules for the catching up charge will continue to apply as if the conversion had not occurred.

(h) Cessation
Where a LLP succeeds to a business previously carried on by an old partnership this will not of itself involve the cessation of the old partnership's trade or profession.

(i) Tax returns
Where an old partnership incorporates as a LLP during an accounting period then if the partners so wish a single partnership return need only be made for the one tax year. They may do this even if the partnership changes its accounting date. single PAYE returns may also be made for the tax year in which an old partnership incorporates as a LLP.

4.6.2 Capital Gains
(a) Partners capital interests
So long as the LLP carries on a trade or profession with a view to profit a partner's capital interest as a member of a LLP will not be regarded as a chargeable asset in its own right. In these circumstances the members of the LLP will be directly taxable on their share of the chargeable gains arising on the disposal of the LLP's assets.

(b) Transfer of a business to a LLP
Where a business, previously carried on by an old partnership, is transferred to a LLP then, for the purposes of the Capital Gains legislation, this will not of itself constitute a disposal by the partners in their interests in the old partnership's assets. This applies equally to the members of partnerships in Scotland as it does to those in England and Wales. Furthermore such a transfer will not affect:

(i)   the availability of indexation allowance,
(ii)   the ownership period for retirement relief,

(iii)   the holding period for taper relief.

(c) Liquidation/Winding up
Where a LLP ceases to carry on a trade or profession then it will no longer be regarded as a 'partnership' for the purposes of the taxation provisions and will instead be regarded as a 'body corporate'. The LLP will thus cease to be transparent.

Where a LLP goes into liquidation, chargeable gains on the disposal of the LLP's assets by the liquidator will be computed by reference to the date on which they were first acquired by the LLP and their cost at that date. In the liquidation period, the LLP's capital gains will be treated in precisely the same way for tax purposes as those for any other body corporate. LLP members will be taxed on any gain (or given relief for any loss) that arises on the disposal of their capital interests in the LLP. The base cost of a partner's capital interest is not equal to the market value of that interest at the time when transparency is lost. The allowable acquisition cost of each partner's interest will be determined according to the historical capital contributions made as if the LLP had never been transparent. This treatment does not affect preliquidation asset disposals, which remain undisturbed.

Where the members of a LLP proceed to wind up its affairs in an orderly way, without the formal appointment of a liquidator, by settling outstanding liabilities and realising the assets following or in the course of a cessation of commercial activity, then it will be accepted that the transparency of the LLP will be preserved during the period in which the assets are being disposed of provided certain conditions are met.

Accordingly it is advisable to avoid a 'members voluntary winding up' by writing into the partnership agreement that one is not allowed.

4.6.3 Inheritance tax
(a) Business property relief and agricultural property relief
Where an old partnership incorporates as a LLP a partner's period of ownership for both reliefs will not be regarded as being interrupted.

(b) Deemed transfers by close companies
Because Section 267A(d) IHTA 1984, inserted by Section 11 of the LLP Act, deems transfers of value to be made by the members of the LLP and not by the LLP itself, liability under Section 94 IHTA 1984 cannot arise even if the LLP might otherwise be a close company.

(c) Availability of reliefs
The normal reliefs and exemptions available to partners in an old partnership will equally be available to members of a LLP.

4.6.4 Stamp duty

(a) Transfer of property to a LLP

Section 12 of the LLP Act requires that for the stamp duty exemption to apply the proportions of property conveyed or transferred into a LLP must either be unchanged 'before' and 'after' the transfer, or the proportions must not have been changed for tax avoidance reasons. Strictly under property law the partners' interest in the LLP will replace their interests in the old partnership's assets. In determining whether the stamp duty exemption applies HMRC will not, however take this point.

HMRC will accept that any property transferred to the LLP within one year of its incorporation will qualify for relief from stamp duty under Section 12 of the LLP Act, provided that the conditions for that relief are met.

Section 12(2) of the LLP Act prevents stamp duty exemption being available if property is transferred at the time of the LLP's incorporation and also there are retirements of former partners and/or admission of new partners to the LLP.

(b) Transfers of interests in a LLP

An interest in a LLP is not a chargeable security for Stamp Duty purposes. So if stamp duty is due on the transfer of such an interest it will be payable at the 1%, 3% or 4% rate, as appropriate, rather than the 0.5% rate applicable to shares. This is in line with the intention behind the LLP Act that the treatment of LLPs should be the same as for partnerships. Since the sale of an interest in any other type of partnership bears duty at the property rates, the sale of an interest in a LLP will be charged in the same way. There is no stamp duty on conversion if the same partners are as before. If the partnership membership is to change do this some time (say 6 months) in advance.

(c) National Insurance Contributions

The National Insurance Contributions (NICs) position of members of a LLP is the same as that of partners in an ordinary partnership. Thus the members of a LLP will be liable to Class2 and Class 4 NICs as appropriate.

5 CHANGE OF ACCOUNTING DATE

With the move to taxing total profits a change in accounting date is not so difficult. A move forward i.e. to later in the tax year is usually accepted without question. Overlap profits can be deducted from the larger profits on the new longer period.

Unless there are commercial reasons HMRC will not accept more than one change any five year period. Notice has to be given by 31 January following the tax year of change.

6 RELIEF FOR LOSSES AND FOR INTEREST PAID

6.1 Set-off against statutory income of year or prior year (S64 ITA2007)
If an actual loss is made 'in any trade, manufacture, adventure, or concern or in any profession, employment or vocation', carried on by a taxpayer, either as an individual or in partnership an election may be made, within one year from 31 January following the year of assessment, for the loss to be set off against the statutory income for that year (ITA07 - S64).

Losses can be set against other income for the year of loss or the preceding year. The taxpayer can elect which has priority.

Example:
Becky, a 21 year old, starts in business on 1 January 2009 and makes a loss of £20,000 in her business for the year to 31 December 2010 having made a profit of £6,000 for 2009. The 2011 profits are £22,000. Her only other income are dividends including tax credits of £5,000 in 2009/2010 and £6,000 in 2010/2011. What loss relief can Becky obtain?

Becky's loss of £20,000 (31.12.10) relate to tax year 2010/2011.

	£
2009/2010 Loss Relief	
Against 2009/2010	6,000
Against 2009/2010 Dividends	5,000
2010/2011	
Against 2010/2011 Dividends	6,000
2011/2012 *	
Balance against 2011/2012	
(20,000 - 6,000 - 5,000 - 6,000) =	3,000
	£20,000

* Assessment is £19,000 (£22,000 - £3,000)

The trade must be conducted on a commercial basis and with a view to the realization of profits, i.e. 'so as to afford a reasonable expectation of profit' if it is not a local authority or a public undertaking (TA 1988 s 384). This rules out the allowance of hobby farming losses.

Where a partner's liability to third parties is limited to the amount of the capital contribution to the partnership and the partner bears losses under the terms of the partnership agreement in excess of this liability, relief is only available up to the amount of the liability.

The loss is computed in the same way. A loss under these provisions must be set off firstly against other earned income of the claimant, then against unearned income.

Losses on backing horses, on capital transactions, on stock exchange speculations, or on other matters unconnected with trading, cannot normally be the subject of loss claims.

Banks and investment businesses which show a profit by including taxed income in their accounts are entitled to relief if a loss is shown after deducting such taxed income.

In the case of a share-dealing business operating on contango account, any dividend declared in the period a contango account is open cannot be treated as a taxed receipt of the company for the purpose of a loss claim, and the net so-called dividend received is part of the profit of the company (*Multipar Syndicate Ltd v Devitt* KBD 1945).

Where, however, 'capital redemption' business is carried on in conjunction with any other business, the profits arising therefrom are treated as those of a separate concern, and in ascertaining whether a loss has been made, the investment income of the business falls to be treated as part of the profits (TA 1988 s 210).

Where the loss can be proved before payment of tax is due, the Inspector will not insist on payment and repayment as the Act requires, but will adopt the more convenient course of discharging or reducing the assessment. In cases of dispute an appeal may be made to the General or to the Special Commissioners, and in an appeal on a point of law a case may be stated for the opinion of the High Court.

Capital allowances as part of loss
Capital allowances in respect of plant and machinery and motor vehicles, etc. (which are deductions from the assessment and not a deduction in arriving at profits or losses), may be allowed in arriving at a loss for relief purposes. There are special provisions dealing with a claim involving capital allowances on cessation of a business CAA2001 - S64 (TA 1988 s 383).

Balancing charges are included for the year of loss, but they may be reduced by capital allowances brought forward from previous years which cannot otherwise be allowed in the year of loss.

Where there would otherwise be a loss of relief, the profits of the final year of a closing business may be reduced by the amount of unused capital allowances brought forward.

6.2 Restriction on individual's loss relief

Individuals who spend on average less than ten hours a week on the commercial activities of their trade will be treated as non-active traders. They will not be able to set their trading losses against their other income if the loss arises as a result of tax avoidance arrangements made after 11 March 2008. There will also be an annual limit of £25,000 on the total amount of trading loss relief that a non-active trader may claim against other income.

6.3 Restrictions on partnership loss relief

FA2007 enacted additional restrictions on amounts that a 'relevant partner' may claim as relief for trading losses under ITA2007 S64, S103(B) (ICTA 1988 ss 380, 381, and FA1991 s 72). It was effective from 2 March 2007.

Previously, the amount of trading losses for a tax year for which a non-active partner can claim sideways loss relief is restricted broadly to the amount of capital that the partner has contributed to the partnership. The new legislation excludes certain capital contributions from this amount. The capital contributions excluded are those paid by non-active partners on or after 2 March 2007 where the main purpose, or one of the main purposes, for contributing the capital to the partnership is for the partner to have access to losses for which sideways loss relief can be claimed.

The Government introduced an annual limit of £25,000 on the amount of trading losses for a tax year for which an individual who is a non-active partner in a partnership can claim sideways loss reliefs. The new limit applies to trading losses sustained as a non-active partner on or after 2 March 2007.

A non-active partner for these purposes is a limited partner or any other partner who spends an average of less than ten hours a week personally engaged in carrying on the partnership's trading activities.

A trading loss for which sideways loss relief is not available can be carried forward and set against the individual's share of the partnership's trading profits for future tax years.

The new limit will not apply to losses from carrying on a profession or a Lloyd's underwriting business.

All references in this note to a partnership include a limited liability partnership (LLP), and all references to a partner include a member of a LLP.

Partners affected

A 'relevant partner' for this purpose will be an individual who, on or after 2 March 2007:

- carries on a trade as a partner in a partnership at any time during the tax year; and
- is a limited partner, or any other partner who does not devote a significant amount of time to the trade in the relevant period for the tax year.

These are referred to in this note as "non-active partners".

A relevant partner's contribution of capital to the partnership for the purpose of applying restrictions will exclude any amount of capital paid by the partner to the partnership where the main purpose, or one of the main purposes, for contributing the capital to the partnership is to obtain a reduction in tax liability by means of sideways loss relief.

The "purpose" test will apply to all contributions of capital paid by a relevant partner to a partnership on or after 2 March 2007, except those paid under a relevant pre-existing obligation. A relevant pre-existing obligation for this purpose is an obligation in a contract made before 2 March 2007 where the obligation cannot be varied or extinguished by the exercise of a right conferred on the individual (whether or not under the contract).

Example: Mrs Anderson starts a small business from home. She has no other income and she expects that the business will be loss-making for the first year or two. Her husband Mr Anderson is a higher-rate taxpayer with a full-time job and he is happy to fund the start-up losses. They form a partnership where losses are shared 90% Mr A 10% Mrs A. First-year losses are £50,000 and Mr Anderson subscribes capital of that amount. Under the previous rules he would have obtained tax relief on £45,000. Under the new rules relief is restricted to £25,000.

6.4 Set-off against capital gain
Where a claim has been made under ITA2007 S64 (TA 1988 s 380) for trading losses to be set off against the statutory income of that year, it would be possible to extend the claim for any utilized losses to be set off against capital gains made in that year. The relief will be given before deducting the annual capital gains exemptions and the claim for relief must be made when the claim for relief under ITA2007 S64 (TA 1988 s 380) is made and not later than two years after the end of the year in which the losses arose.

If there are unutilised losses carried forward to the following year and there is sufficient income to offset the losses, any further excess of the loss brought forward may be set against the capital gains of that later year.

6.5 Relief for losses on unquoted shares in trading companies
Where shares in certain companies are sold at a loss, the allowable loss may be set against income for income tax purposes S131 ITA2007 (FA 1988 s 574).

The main conditions are that:
* the disposal is made by an individual;
* the shares were acquired by subscription;
* the company is, or was, a trading company;
* the company was not quoted;
* the disposal was either for valuable consideration at arms length, in winding up or subject to a negligible value claim;
* a claim is made within two years.

6.6 Annual payments and interest treated as a loss

Any person who makes an annual payment which is not wholly paid out of profits brought into charge to tax, must account for tax at the basic rate on such payments by assessment and must deduct tax of that amount on making such payments ITA2007, S24 & S25 (TA 1988 s 387, 390). These payments cannot be deducted in computing business profits (TA 1988 s 74), but, with minor exceptions, provided the cost is borne by the payer and not charged to capital, the payment so assessed may be treated as a business loss available for carry forward (see following), if the payment was wholly and exclusively for the purposes of the business.

Interest paid wholly and exclusively for the purposes of a business may be treated as losses available for carry forward or as terminal losses (see following). Building Society interest is included ITA2007 S24 (TA 1988 s 390).

6.7 Carry-forward of losses

Losses may be carried forward indefinitely, if they have not been allowed otherwise, e.g. in being set off against other income in order to compute the total income of a basis period for assessment ITA2007 SS 20-26 (TA 1978 s 385).

Taxed interest or dividends on investments which are trading stock of investment dealing or similar financial concerns are treated as part of the profits for the purpose of the carry forward provisions.

The loss can only be set off against subsequent profits of the same business. This is important where two or more businesses are carried on by the same person. It is often not easy to decide whether two activities are separate businesses or parts of one business. The kind of activity, degree of common control and interdependence must be considered carefully. In an extreme case, the relative scales of activities were a material factor, the trade being said not to be the same after distinct activities (principally aero engineering) amounting to at least 75% of the business had been sold (leaving automobile engineering) (*Rolls Royce Motors Ltd v Bamford* Ch D 1976).

Lloyds underwriting and ship and insurance broking have been held to be separate trades (*Scales v Thompson (George) & Co. Ltd* KBD 1927), but boiler-making and shells (armaments) have been held to be one business (*Howden Boiler & Armaments Co. Ltd v Stewart* CS 1924). Brewers, who ceased to brew, but continued to bottle and sell beer brewed by another company to their own specification, were held to have ceased one business and started another (*Gordon & Blair Ltd v CIR* CS 1962). So was a confectionery company which ceased to manufacture and closed down its retail shops but continued to deal in sugar and cellophane (*Seaman v Tucketts Ltd* Ch D 1963). However, where a company was about to be taken over and sold off its stock and plant, dismissed many of its employees and ceased production with the intention of taking on the similar operations of the acquiring company as its works, the trade was held not to have been discontinued and the losses could be carried forward against profits from the new activities (*Tobroyston Brickworks Ltd v CIR* CS 1976).

A definite claim to carry forward a loss should be made when such a loss is ascertained. A partner in a business can carry forward his or her share of loss. Where a trade ceases and the owner is in receipt of an annual payment only, no allowance can be claimed for previous trading losses (*Morning Post Ltd v George* KBD 1940). This would apply in the case of the coal-mining industry after nationalization, when the sole income of a company might be derived from interim income or from Government securities. When persons or firms have converted their business into companies they may, in certain circumstances, carry forward losses and payments against any income receivable from the company ITA2007 S23 (TA 1988 s 386).

Losses incurred in a trade which has been dormant for several years are not available for carry forward purposes (*Goff v Osborne & Co. (Sheffield) Ltd* Ch D 1953).

Strictly speaking, an allowance or carry forward of capital allowance takes precedence over a carry-forward of losses.

6.8 Carry-backward of terminal losses
Where a trade, profession or vocation is permanently discontinued and a loss is incurred in the last 12 months of trading, and relief cannot be given in any other way, it may be set against the profits of the three years of assessment preceding the year of cessation ITA2007 SS 27-31 (TA 1988 s 388).

The loss may include capital allowances for the same period apportioned on a time basis and excluding amounts brought forward from previous years.

The relief is given in the year of cessation and the three previous years taking the latest year first of the three available, taking each year in turn.

If the profits of these three years are insufficient to cover the loss then the loss can be set against any interest or dividends receivable on investments which are trading stock of a dealing or similar financial concern.

Before giving the relief the profit must be reduced by the amount of annual payments, etc. retained in charge. The loss is also reduced, but only by retainable charges of a kind which could not rank for assessment under s 349 and carry forward as a loss under ITA2007 S 25 & 26 (s 387) (Please see Annual Payments and Interest Treated as a Loss, p.242).

Example:
Ian trades as a car dealer

		£
Profit - Year ended 31 March 2007		500
Profit - Year ended 31 March 2008		400
Profit - Year ended 31 March 2009		400
Profit - Year ended 31 March 2010		300
Loss - Year ended 31 March 2011		2,000

The business ceased on 31 March 2011
Ian paid each year, £50 copyright royalties abroad and £100 annual payments wholly and exclusively incurred for the business.

Adjustment of profits:	2007/08	2008/09	2009/10
	£	£	£
Agreed profit	400	400	300
Retainable charges	150	150	150
Profit ranking for relief	250	250	150

Adjustment of loss:	
Agreed loss	2,000
Less: retainable charges of a kind which could be assessed and	
treated as a loss - copyright royalties	50
Loss available	1,950

Application of loss:	
Total available	1,950
Firstly allowed against the 2009/10 profit	150
	1,800
Then allowed against the 2008/09 profit	250
	1,550
Then allowed against the 2007/08 profit	250
Not available for any further relief	1,300

6.9 Set-off of losses in opening years

A claim may be made by an individual to set business losses of any of the first four years of assessment against income of any of the three years of assessment preceding the year of the loss. The earliest year's income is relieved first, and so on.

Example:

Judith is made **redundant on 30 September 2009**, and with the compensation sets up business as manufacturer. The income and trading results are as follows:

	£	£
Salary from employer:		
2006/2007		20,000
2007/2008		11,000
2008/2009		22,000
Losses from trading activities:		
Year ended 30 September 2010		15,000
Year ended 30 September 2011		12,000
Year ended 30 September 2012		1,000

The losses will be allocated as follows:
The loss relief to be claimed under S72 ITA 2007 will be:

2006/2007		
Salary		20,000
less loss		15,000
Taxable		5,000

2007/2008		
Salary		11,000
less loss		12,000
loss carried forward		(1,000)

2008/2009		
Salary		22,000
loss for 2011/2012	1,000	
loss brought forward	1,000	
		2,000
Taxable		20,000

The time limit for claims is two years after the year of assessment in which the loss is sustained. The activity must have been carried on on a commercial basis with a reasonable expectation of profit in the year or within a reasonable time thereafter. The relief cannot be obtained artificially for an established business by transferring it to one's spouse or by introducing a partner.

The relief may be limited by excluding income of the spouse and is to be given against earned income before unearned income (except for a sleeping partner).

A loss augmented (or created) by excess capital allowances of the year qualifies for the relief.

6.10 Losses in casual transactions (other income)

Where a loss is made in any transaction which, if a profit had been made would have involved liability to tax, then such loss may be set off against any other assessment on casual profits in the same year, and any part of the loss not covered in this way may be carried forward to the same extent as in the case of trading losses, but only against profits assessed as other income ITA2007 S46 (TA 1988 s 392).

PART SIX

CORPORATION TAX

BUDGET MARCH 2011

Change in rates from 2011
The March Budget announced an acceleration of the reduction in Corporation Tax main rate.

The 28% corporation tax rate for larger companies was reduced by 2% from 1 April 2011 as follows:

1 April 2011 - 26%
1 April 2012 - 25%
1 April 2013 - 24%
1 April 2014 - 23%

For smaller profits, those of taxable profits below £300,000, the small profits rate of corporation tax reduced from 21% to 20% on 1 April 2011.

(Note: Corporation Tax Act 2010 (CTA 2010) now refers to "Small Profits Rate" instead of "Small Companies Rate".)

1 CHANGES

1.1 iXBRL is now underway
Online filing for all corporation tax (CT) returns and electronic payment of corporation tax became compulsory on 1 April 2011.

Companies under a winding-up order, in administration or in administrative receivership are excluded from the new rules about returns. A company may also be excluded if the directors and secretary are practising members of certain religious societies.

The way is also paved for the two-year 'soft landing' which is being discussed by HMRC and the professional bodies through Working Together.

HMRC has confirmed that amended corporation tax returns do not have to be submitted using iXBRL. They may be submitted either:

*   online using iXBRL' or
*   online using PDF format; or
*   on paper.

1.2 Schedules A & D replaced
The 2009 Corporation Tax Act substituted Schedules A & D with Parts 4 & 3 respectively.

2 GENERAL NATURE AND APPLICATION OF CORPORATION TAX

A 'company' is liable for corporation tax, not income tax on its taxable profits. For this purpose the word 'company' has a wide meaning including incorporated bodies, such as limited companies, other corporate bodies, such as building societies, and certain unincorporated associations engaged in trading, The Taxes Act 1988 refers to the word 'company' in this context and, for simplicity, this following description will be used in relation to bodies subject to corporation tax.

The taxable profits on which a company is assessed for corporation tax are those for the company's accounting year. However the rate of tax to be applied to the profits is fixed in the Budget and subsequent Finance Act for the 'financial year', to the 31 March. In the legislation the financial year is referred to as a single year, e.g. FY2011, the year to 31 March 2012, and not, as with income tax, 2011/2012. For FY2011 the rates of corporation tax are 26% for large companies and 20% respectively for small profits (companies), these descriptions being defined later. Where an accounting year overlaps two financial years which have different rates of corporation tax, the profit shown in the accounting year will need to be apportioned for calculating the charge.

The computation of profit for corporation tax follows the same principles as apply to income tax. The calculation of the tax payable is, however, subject to certain modifications in the case of companies. For instance, the chargeable profits of a company include its capital gains made in the accounting period.

3 CORPORATION TAX PAYMENTS

Corporation tax is due nine months after the end of the accounting period.

- A large company is one whose annual profits exceed £1,500,000. The limit of £1,500,000 is shared between group companies where appropriate.

- Large companies pay their corporation tax in four equal quarterly instalments on the basis of anticipated current year liabilities. quarterly instalments started in month 7, so two of them will be in-year. Medium-sized and small companies do not have to pay any of their corporation tax by instalments.

- For example, a large company with an accounting period ending on 31 December 2011 will pay 25% of its estimated tax on each of 14 July 2011, 14 October 2011, 14 January 2012 and 14 April 2012.

- If the amounts paid prove to be inadequate, interest will be payable in much the same way as is currently the case when insufficient tax is paid 9 months after the end of the accounting period. Similarly, interest will be paid to companies which have paid too much tax. The spread between the interest rates on underpaid and overpaid tax is reduced, but only for the period between the due date for the first instalment payment and the present payment date, 9 months after the end of the accounting period. The interest will be deductible or taxable.

- Growing companies will not have to pay their corporation tax by instalments if their taxable profits do not exceed £10m and they were small or medium-sized in the previous year.

Unlike self assessment for individuals where payments on account are based on the previous year's liability companies have to estimate the current year's results and make four equal payments. The problem of how seasonal businesses estimate their Christmas rush or summer ice cream sales in advance has not been resolved.

Paying corporation tax electronically
From 1 April 2011, all payments of corporation tax (including related interest and penalties) must be made electronically. HM Revenue & Customs has set out the different methods of paying electronically on its website (see www.hmrc.gov.uk/payinghmrc/corporationtax.htm).

It is worth noting that some forms of payment will take longer to set up or to clear HMRC's account than others, and that payments can still be made by cheque at the company's bank or at the Post Office.

3.1 Rate of corporation tax on winding-up

In order to prevent delay in winding up a company the rate in a company's last year is to be the same as for the penultimate year. The rate proposed in the latest Budget resolution is to be taken as final where the winding-up is completed after that resolution in the final year but before the passing of the Finance Act. If the winding-up commenced before the final year, the same Budget resolution rate is taken as final for the penultimate year also.

3.2 Recovery of tax from members

Corporation tax on chargeable gains may be recovered from persons receiving capital distributions, if it is not paid by the company. This is to prevent avoidance by winding up without providing for tax.

3.3 Tax on qualifying distributions

The company must, on request, issue a statement to the recipient showing the amount of value of the distribution and the tax credit relating to it.

3.4 Charities

Charities receiving dividends from UK companies can no longer reclaim refunds of the tax credit on such dividends.

3.5 Stock dividends

The cash value of the shares received will bear the appropriate tax credit.

3.6 Foreign dividends

Taxation of foreign profits: dividends

Foreign dividends are generally exempt for all companies where received on or after 1 July 2009. This applies regardless of the level of shareholding in the foreign company.

The legislation establishes that, in principle, UK and foreign distributions and subject to corporation tax, unless they are specifically exempted according to given rules.

The rules for distributions received by small companies are distinct from the rules for medium and large companies but, in each case, the result is that the majority of distributions are exempt from corporation tax. The Schedule contains anti-avoidance rules to prevent abuse of distribution exemption.

<u>What is a small company?</u>

The definition follows the 2003 European Commission recommendation except that certain financial companies (e.g. unit trusts and insurance companies) are not treated as small companies.

Small company exemptions
A distribution received by a small company is exempt subject to the following conditions:

- the company paying the distribution must be resident of the UK or a 'qualifying territory';

- the distribution must not be an amount of interest that is treated as a distribution in accordance with s209(2)(d)(e) ICTA 1988 (e.g. interest paid at more than a commercial rate);

- the distribution must not be a dividend that qualifies for a tax deduction in the payer's jurisdiction;

- the distribution must not be made as part of a 'tax advantage scheme'.

A 'qualifying territory' is a territory with which the UK has a double taxation treaty that includes a non-discrimination provision in a standard form.

Exemptions for medium and large companies
There are two non-qualifying types of distributions which correspond to the second and third bullet points above. Much more detailed anti-avoidance rules are, however, applied than in the fourth bullet point to each of the exempt classes of distributions below.

Distributions will be exempt if they fall into any of five exempt classes. Distributions will frequently fall into more than one of these classes but it is sufficient to fall into any one of them for a distribution to be exempt.

The most important exemptions are:

- Distributions paid to a parent company that controls the company making the distribution. Control for this purpose is defined by reference to the Controlled Foreign Company (CFC) control rules, including the extension to certain joint ventures.

- Distributions paid in respect of non-redeemable ordinary shares. A share is an ordinary share provided it carries no preferential rights to income or capital.

- Portfolio holdings, which are defined as holdings that represent less than 10% of their class of share. (From 1 July 2010 10% limit removed).

Other matters
A company can make an election that a particular distribution that would otherwise be an exempt distribution shall instead be taxable. Two reasons why a company

might wish to make such an election are:

- dividends can only be taken into account for the purposes of the CFC 'acceptable distribution policy' exemption if they are subject to tax;

- it is possible that exemption could lead to an increased rate of withholding tax.

An exempt foreign distribution is included within the Franked Investment Income definition for the purpose of calculating entitlement to small companies' relief, consistent with UK distributions.

4 SELF ASSESSMENT FOR COMPANIES AND OTHERS LIABLE TO CORPORATION TAX

4.0 HMRC enquiry window in CT returns

For accounting periods ending after 31 March 2008, the enquiry window for most returns delivered by the filing date will close 12 months after the day on which HMRC receives the return. For example, if a return for an accounting period ended 30 April 2011 is received by HMRC on 26 November 2011 notice of enquiry will not be given after 26 November 2012, 12 months after delivery. Previously the statutory filing date was 12 months after the company year end of 30 April 2012 and the 12 month enquiry window closed on 30 April 2013.

Linking the end of the enquiry window to the date on which a particular return is submitted provides certainty sooner for companies that file early, bringing forward the date at which they can be sure their return will not be subject to enquiry.

The change applies to the majority of companies, including those in small groups as defined in sections 383(2) and 474(1) of the companies Act 2006. There is no change for companies in groups that are not 'small' and the enquiry window for such companies is still linked to the statutory filing deadline.

Companies in groups that are not 'small' have to identify themselves on their company tax return. HMRC have provided a new box on the front page of the CT600 return form and a similar option for returns delivered electronically.

For all companies that file late, there is no change. The enquiry window still closes on 31 January, 30 April, 31 July or 31 October next following the first anniversary of the day on which the return is delivered.

4.1 Self assessment for companies

The rules apply both to limited companies and all other concerns within the charge to

Corporation Tax. Clubs and societies are therefore affected.

The records required are those which enable the organisation to make a correct and complete company tax return. The company will need, in the event of an enquiry, to be able to explain and substantiate the information in a return.

It is not the purpose of the legislation to require companies to retain greater quantities of prime records than they do now. It must also be able to demonstrate, in reply to enquiries, that it has kept sufficient records. The precise nature and extent of records needed to discharge that obligation will depend on the type and size of the business.

Any company satisfying the requirements of the Companies Act will have satisfied the requirement to keep and preserve records for tax purposes, subject to keeping adequate records for arm's length pricing purposes.

Transfer pricing (Arm's length pricing records)
Small and medium-sized enterprises are exempt from the transfer pricing and thin capitalisation rules in most circumstances. From 1 April 2004 for other companies the transfer pricing rules were extended to transactions within the UK. Where a company is taxed under the transfer pricing rules, the connected company will be able to make a corresponding adjustment in calculating its own taxable income.

The transfer pricing legislation requires taxpayers to apply an arm's length standard to certain arrangements and transactions. The legislation relates primarily to dealings between a UK taxpayer and an associate operating outside the UK. It will rarely be relevant where the parties are not connected. The requirements of para 21 sch 18 FA 1998 are in some aspects more stringent than those of s221 Companies Act 1985.

Record keeping period
The Companies Act requires records to be kept for three years. Para 21 sch 18 FA 1998 requires records to be kept for six years. Records will need to be kept longer if an enquiry into a return remains open at the six year point. Further, rarely, where no enquiry has been started, but the statutory period for starting an enquiry has not expired at the six year point, because the return is late, the records for that Accounting Period must be kept until the latest date for starting an enquiry has passed or, if later, the date on which such an enquiry is completed.

Also rarely, there may be circumstances in which the date on which a company is requested to complete a tax return is itself more than six years after the end of an accounting period.

Records kept in an alternative form
Optical imaging systems may now be used, provided that what is contained

represents a complete and unaltered image of the underlying paper document. Other record keeping methods are acceptable so long as all the information is captured which is needed to demonstrate that a complete and correct tax return has been made. When using computerised packages, taxpayers must make sure they have the software to access old data.

Penalties
There can be only one penalty of a maximum £3,000 in relation to all the offences relating to a particular year of assessment or accounting period. Penalties under s12B(5) TMA 1970 will be sought only in the more serious cases such as where records have been deliberately destroyed to obstruct an enquiry etc.

PAYE records
These must be kept like other business costs records. Under Reg 55(120 Income Tax (Employments) Regulations 1993, additional PAYE records must be kept for three years after the end of the tax year to which they relate. Any paper PAYE records may now be preserved by the use of optical imaging systems.

4.2 Industrial and provident societies and co-operative associations (TA 1988 ss 486-489)
These bodies are liable to corporation tax on trading activities subject to the following qualifications:

(a)   Dividends, interest, bonuses and rebates paid to members (to be paid without deduction of tax) are allowable as expenses against taxable income, but not such payments to overseas residents or those made by credit unions.

(b)   No tax on capital gains is payable on the transfer of assets between one society and another in the course of an amalgamation or union of the bodies.

(c)   Rent received from members of housing associations is not taxable, nor are sales of property to tenants liable to tax on capital gains. The same provisions apply to self build societies.

4.3 Registered friendly societies; tax-exempt societies
Where there are no restrictions as to the limits for life assurance or annuity contracts, exemption was granted from corporation tax, subject to certain other conditions being satisfied, on the profits from life and endowment business for contracts of assurance not exceeding £750 and annuity contracts not exceeding £156 per annum. These limits were removed in respect of contracts made after 31 August 1987 provided the annual premium payable does not exceed £200. (See F (No 2) A 1992 s 56 and Sch 9).

4.4 Mutual business by companies; non-trading companies
Distributions paid out of profits brought into charge to corporation tax or out of

franked investment income, are treated as such notwithstanding that they are made to persons participating in the mutual activities, except in the case of mutual life insurance (TA 1988 s 490).

4.5 Company partnerships

A company's share of profits is regarded being earned in a separate trade and is computed as if the partnership was a company. Similarly, an individual's share is computed as if the partnership was an individual. Distributions, charges, capital allowances and losses are separately computed and the full profit arising to the individuals is assessed on them. Their share for a year of assessment is to be not less than the profits of the basis period less the company's share, despite any change in the sharing of profits (TA 1988 s 114).

Where other partners (or connected persons) receive a payment of benefit in respect of the company's share of partnership profits, or where the company receives a payment or benefit (other than group relief) in respect of its share of partnership losses, the company's share of partnership profits or losses (including capital allowances) cannot be set off against other income of the company, nor can ACT be set against the corporation tax on the company's share of the partnership profits.

4.6 Loan and money societies

Dividends to members are not treated as distributions for corporation tax purposes.

4.7 Clubs, voluntary organisations and self assessment

HMRC is reviewing its treatment of member's clubs and organisations.

The Financial Secretary to the Treasury made the following statement:

'For many years the Inland Revenue and, latterly, HMRC have not sought corporation tax returns from clubs and unincorporated associations with very small tax liabilities. That practice was established before the introduction of the starting rate of corporation tax, and it will not be affected by the changes in clause 26. Any club or society that is unclear about its tax position should ask its local HMRC office for advice'.

HM Revenue & customs (HMRC) is now putting the practice into the public domain to assist its customers. In the following text 'club' means 'club and unincorporated association'.

Where:

• the annual corporation tax liability of a club is not expected to exceed £100;
• the club is run exclusively for the benefit of its own members,

the HMRC will

- prevent the issue of a notices to file returns, and
- treat the club as dormant, subject to review at least every 5 years.

To be within the scope of this practice the body must not be a:

- holiday club;
- privately owned club run by its members as a commercial enterprise for personal profit
- housing association or registered social landlord as designated in the Housing Act 1986
- trade association
- thrift fund
- friendly society; or
- company which is a subsidiary of, or wholly owned by, a charity and for each year of dormancy the body must have no:

  - anticipated allowable trading losses
  - chargeable assets likely to be disposed of; or
  - anticipated payments from which tax is deductible and payable to HMRC.

This practice is also extended to certain property management companies that meet certain additional criteria. However, where a property management company receives service charges which it is obliged to hold on trust for the tenants under the Landlord and Tenant Act, the company will be liable to income tax on any interest arising on that fund. The company, in its capacity as trustee, will be within Income Tax Self Assessment and may be required to make a return to the relevant Trust Office. income is chargeable at the special trust rates (40% for bank interest) except for the first £1,000 which remains chargeable at basic rates (20% for bank interest). Generally, where the income is below £1,000 and taxed at source, a return will not be required every year.

Most existing clubs and property management companies that meet the conditions are already likely to be treated as dormant by HMRC. Any body that makes a return every year but considers it meets the conditions for dormancy treatment, should contact the HMRC office responsible for its corporation tax liabilities.

A body which has received a letter from HMRC to say it is being treated as dormant need not contact HMRC until the end of the dormancy period, unless it breaches any of the conditions set out in the letter, or is subject to some other significant change affecting its tax position. The IR46 leaflet relating to clubs, societies and voluntary associations is being discontinued. Updated guidance will be available shortly on HMRC website.

4.8 Authorized unit and investment trusts

These are treated as investment companies and liable to corporation tax. Relief is given for management expenses and chargeable capital gains are exempt from tax.

4.9 Controlled foreign company

Controlled foreign companies rules amended to comply with EU Law.

The Cadbury Schweppes case

On 12 September 2006, in the Cadbury Schweppes case, the European Court of Justice (ECJ) held that the UK CFC regime is prima facie contrary to the freedom of establishment provisions of the EC Treaty; but that the breach may be justified provided the regime applies only to "wholly artificial arrangements" which do not reflect economic reality. In other words, companies which are carrying on genuine economic activities in the EEA should not be caught by the UK CFC rules. The case has now been referred back to the UK Special Commissioners.

Summary of proposed changes

The CFC rules were initially amended with effect from 6 December 2006 with a view to making them compliant with the ECJ's judgment in Cadbury Schweppes. In particular:

- Companies may apply to HMRC to exclude from an apportionment of the CFC's chargeable profits an amount which represents the net economic value created by work carried out by individuals working for the CFC in business establishments within the EEA.

- The exempt activities exemption is to be amended such that a CFC resident in an EEA territory will only be regarded as effectively managed in that territory if there are sufficient individuals working for the company in the territory who have the competence and authority to undertake the company's business.

HMRC published draft legislation and guidance notes and invited comments.

The Finance Act 2009 introduced new legislation because some of the rules are no longer necessary due to the new exempt distribution rules.

The legislation:
- repeals the exemption from the CFC rules for overseas companies which pay most of their profits back to shareholders in the UK (the acceptable distribution policy exemption);

- amends the exempt activities exemption to remove the special rules applying to holding companies apart from those applicable to local holding companies.

- The changes apply to accounting periods beginning on or after 1 July 2009.

Provision is made to split accounting periods which straddle this date.

4.10 Close investment-holding companies

The apportionment of undistributed income of close companies was abolished in respect of accounting periods beginning after 31 March 1989, and in order to ensure that non-trading companies are not used by higher-rate taxpayers to avoid tax, legislation was introduced in the 1989 Finance Act to counteract this potential avenue of tax avoidance. The legislation introduced a new category of company known as a close investment-holding company which will be liable to corporation tax at the normal rate. A close investment company is a close company as defined by s 414(2) TA 1988 and exists throughout any accounting period commencing after 31 March 1989 wholly or mainly for purposes other than carrying on a trade or trades on a commercial basis or making investments in land or property which is let to unconnected persons (TA 1988 s 13A; FA 1988 s 105).

5 WHO IS CHARGEABLE?

Any company is chargeable, including any body corporate or unincorporated association (except a partnership and Limited Liability Partnership), which is resident in the UK, and also companies not so resident which carry on a trade in the UK through a branch or agency (TA 1988 s 6(2)). Certain corporate bodies are either exempt or chargeable under special rules.

5.1 Local authorities

These are specially exempted from corporation tax (TA 1988 s 519 (1)(2)).

5.2 Insurance companies

Special rules apply, which are outside the scope of a general work such as this. The legislation for the taxing of insurance companies is contained in TA 1988 ss 431-458, FA 1993 and FA 1994.

5.3 Building societies

Building societies are liable to corporation tax at the full rate.

A company receiving building society interest or dividend must gross up the amount received at the basic rate of income tax, and the gross amount is chargeable to corporation tax. Tax credit equivalent to the tax deemed to have been deducted is allowed as a set-off against the corporation tax payable and may be repaid if the corporation tax payable is less than the income tax deemed to have been deducted.

Section 47 of the Building Societies Act 1988 allows building societies to become public limited companies which would then become subject to corporation tax in the normal way. Special provisions were introduced by s 145 and Sch 12 of the Finance Act 1988 to avoid substantial potential tax liabilities which may arise on the changeover.

6 CORPORATION TAX RATES

For the Financial Year 2011 (2010) (the year ending 31 March 2012 (31 March 2011)) profits up to £300,000 are taxed at 20% (21%).

The Small Profits rate fell to 20% from 1 April 2011 (intended rise from 1 April 2011 reversed), and the Large Company rate reduced from 28% by 2% from 1 April 2011 (also by 1% every year until 1 April 2014 where it will be 23%).

The full chart of rates is thus:

	FY 2011		FY 2010	
Corporation Tax	01.04.11 - 31.03.12		01.04.10 - 31.03.11	
	£	%	£	%
Small Profits Rate	1 - 300,000	20	1 - 300,000	21
Intermediate Profits	300,001-1,500,000	27.50	300,001-1,500,000	29.75
Large Companies	1,500,000 +	26	1,500,000 +	28

Example:
A small trading company, with no associates has annual profit of £20,000 in the 3 year to 31 March 2012.

	FY 2011 (y/e 31.03.12) £
Tax payable - (20%)	£4,000

Where profits exceed £300,000 a company is basically liable at the full or large company rate of 26%(28%). However, where profits are between £300,000 and £1,500,000 marginal relief applies. This means that the full rate is applied to the profits subject to corporation tax less 3/200(7/400th) of the amount by which the profits fall below £1,500,000.

Assume a simple case where there was no franked investment income and the profits were £600,000 in FY 2011 (y/e 31.03.12). Corporation tax would be calculated as follows:

	FY 2011 (y/e 31.03.12) £
26% of £600,000	156,000
Less: marginal relief	
£1,500,000 - £600,000 times (3/200)	13,500
Corporation tax payable	£142,500

In this case the effective rate on the profits is 23.75% and the marginal rate on the additional £300,000 of profits is always 27.5%.

Where the accounting period is less than 12 months the profit limits and the marginal relief are reduced pro rata. Where an accounting period overlaps the end of the financial year, each period before and after the end of the financial year is treated as a separate accounting period.

The calculation is qualified where the company has franked investment income and where it has associated companies, as shown next.

The effect of franked investment income (dividends from other UK companies)
The basic profit is that on which corporation tax falls finally to be borne; this is the profit exclusive of franked investment income. For the purpose of marginal relief, however, the shortfall on the limit of £1,500,000 is based on the basic profit plus franked investment income. Thus, if the basic profit was £600,000 and franked investment income was an additional £100,000, the shortfall would be: £1,500,000 - (£600,000 + £100,000) = £800,000. The full rate of 26% is charged on the basic profit less marginal relief. Marginal relief is reduced by the proportion which the basic profit bears to total profit.

Example 1:

The formula in the TA 1988 s 13 (2) is: $(M - P) \times \dfrac{I}{P}$ the solution being multiplied by 3/200

where: M   is the upper profit limit.
         P   is the full profit including franked investment income.
         I   is the basic profit excluding franked investment income

Using the previous figures marginal relief becomes:

3/200th of (£1,500,000 - £700,000) x $\dfrac{600,000}{700,000}$ = <u>10,286</u>

Corporation tax is:

26% of £600,000	= £156,000
Less: marginal relief	<u>10,286</u>
	<u>£145,714</u>

If a company has **associated companies** the limits referred to above are divided by the number of such companies plus one.

Example 2:

Company A is a member of ABC group of companies and has three trading associated companies. The profits for the year ended 31 March 2012 are £30,000.

The limit for small companies rate applicable to A is:
£300,000 ÷ 4 (associated companies plus one) = £75,000
Tax is chargeable on £30,000 at 20%.

Example 3:

Company X is a member of the XYZ group of companies and has three associated companies. The profits for the year ended 31 March 2012 are £80,000 and this includes franked investment income of £4,000. The tax payable and marginal relief is computed as follows:

		£
Tax on trading income: £80,000 at 26%	=	20,800
Marginal relief:		

$\left(\dfrac{1,500,000}{4} - 80,000\right) \times \dfrac{76,000}{80,000} \times \dfrac{3}{200}$ = <u>4,204</u>

Corporation tax payable	=	<u>£16,596</u>

From 1 April 2008 for the purpose of a claim for the small profits corporation tax rate, companies are normally no longer treated as associated just because their shareholders are members of the same business partnership. Companies may be treated as associated if there have been 'tax planning arrangements'. SI8 of CTA 2010 as well as changing the term "Small Companies Rate" to "Small Profits Rate" also removes the need to make a "claim".

Section 13(4) ICTA 1988 allows an associated company to be disregarded if it has not carried on a trade or business at any time during the relevant accounting period.

The High Court upheld the Special Commissioners decision in *Salaried Persons Postal Loans Limited v HMRC* to allow the taxpayer's appeal in connection with a claim for small profits relief. Both sides agreed that the company was not carrying on a trade. The question was how much, or little, constitutes carrying on a business. There is existing case law precedent in *Jowett (Inspector of Taxes) v O'Neill and Brennan Construction Ltd. (1998)* where the issue was whether or not £100,000 cash on deposit was being actively managed.

In this more recent case, a company owned a property which it had occupied for the purposes of its trade until it ceased trading. It then let the property to the same tenant for many years, with limited activity being required by the company to earn the rents. Was the company putting its assets to gainful use by letting for rent, and was this prima facie the carrying on of a business, as was contended by HMRC?

The facts are that company had:

- Not had its own bank account but had maintained an inter-company balance with the group's banker;
- Two directors but no other employees;
- Not paid any directors' fees or salaries;
- Not paid any dividends nor made any distributions;
- Not purchased any assets or disposed of any assets;
- Neither received nor paid any interest on its inter-company balance;
- Not negotiated any rent reviews. Rent reviews had taken place automatically by reference to a pre-existing formula;
- Not sought to let the premises nor any part of them to a new tenant.

The High Court has upheld the opinion of John Avery Jones, the Commissioner, who, having looked at what the company had actually done during the period, had decided that it had not been carrying on a business. In his concluding remarks, Mr Justice Lawrence Collins said:

'The Special Commissioner came to the view on the facts that MML did not carry on an investment (or any other) business, especially in the light of the following matters: MML did not purchase the West Regent Street premises as an investment; it did nothing in the relevant years except receive the rents from its agent, and authorise a rent review; and the premises were a small part of its assets. This was a case of a company left with former trading premises which it let out without any active participation or management. It is not in any sense an artificial arrangement to take advantage of small companies' rate, and nothing in this judgment (nor, it is plain, in the Decision of the Special Commissioner) is intended to deal with, or encourage, any artificial scheme so designed.'

7 WHAT IS CHARGEABLE?

7.1 Profits chargeable

Companies resident in the UK are chargeable on all profits wherever arising, including profits accruing for their benefit under a trust or arising under a partnership, or in winding up the company (TA 1988 s 8).

Companies not resident in the UK, but carrying on a trade here through a branch or agency, are chargeable on all their trading profits arising directly or indirectly through or from the branch or agency, on any income from property or rights of the branch or agency, and on any gains which would be chargeable to capital gains tax if made by an individual not resident or ordinarily resident in the UK (TA 1988 s 11). If any amount is received in the UK from which tax is deducted and is chargeable to corporation tax, the income tax deducted can be set off against the corporation tax payable. Exceptionally, income arising in the UK but not connected with a branch or agency here will, subject to any double tax agreement, be liable to UK income tax as a non-resident company, and not to corporation tax. In such a case income tax deducted at source is not repayable.

7.2 Basis period

This is usually the company's period of account, but it must not exceed twelve months. If it does, the period of account is divided into twelve months' accounting periods plus an accounting period for the balance if less than twelve months. When a company is being wound up, periods of twelve months are taken from the commencement of the winding-up (TA 1988 s 12).

7.3 Computation of income

The income is to be computed according to income tax principles as laid down and then all sources of income (computed on a current-year basis) are aggregated and assessed in one sum (TA 1988 s 70). Capital allowances are deductible as an item of expense and balancing charges are included as part of the company's income (CAA 1968 ss 73-74). In the case of other income, if capital allowances cannot be given because the income is insufficient, they can be carried forward against income of subsequent periods, or backward against an immediately preceding period of the same length (apportioned on a time basis if necessary) as the loss period. Business management expenditure is similarly treated but not estate management expenditure. Foreign tax is allowed as a deduction in computing income where no credit is allowed for it (TA 1988 s 811). In computing income from any source, no deduction may be made for dividends or other distribution, yearly interest (other than bank interest), annuities or annual payments (TA 1988 s 337) paid by the company.

7.4 Chargeable gains

These are, in the first instance, computed in accordance with the rules for capital gains tax (TA 1988 s 345). The net chargeable gains, so computed, are then charged to corporation tax at the appropriate rate applicable to the basic profits of the company: i.e., basic profits means income and capital profits.

Losses arising during the accounting year are carried forward and set off against profits arising in the later year. The major changes to Capital Gains Tax made in the 1998 Finance Act do not apply to companies.

7.5 Exemption from corporation tax on gains on substantial shareholdings

The Finance Act 2002 includes an exemption from corporation tax on gains arising on the disposal of substantial shareholdings.

The new relief forms part of the Government's stated objective to modernise the system of company taxation and is intended to provide stability for business in the longer term. The main exemption applies where a single trading company or a company which is a member of a trading group disposes of all or part of a substantial shareholding in another company which is itself a trading company or the holding company of a trading group.

A substantial shareholding is defined as 10% or more of the ordinary shares of the company invested in for a period of at least twelve months in the two years before the share sale. A higher threshold of 30% applies for life insurance companies disposing of assets in their long-term insurance funds. Special rules apply for aggregating holdings by members of groups of companies. A group consists of the principal company and its 51% subsidiaries on a world-wide basis.

In most cases it is suggested that it will be straightforward to determine whether companies or groups satisfy the trading requirements. Activities of joint ventures in which the company or group holds 10% or more of the shares can be taken into account for these purposes. Where the exemption applies (relief is available without a formal claim), any gain on the disposal of the shares will not be chargeable to tax. It should however be noted that any loss arising on the disposal of a substantial shareholding will not give rise to an allowable loss and will not be available to set against any gains on non-exempt assets.

Where a company satisfies the conditions for the main exemption but also owns an asset related to shares in the company forming the substantial shareholding (for example options over, or securities convertible into or exchangeable for, such shares), any gain on a disposal of that asset is not chargeable and any loss not allowable. This extension of the exemption applies only where the company making the disposal, or another member of its group, also owns shares in the company invested in immediately before the disposal.

If, at a time when the substantial shareholding requirement is met, a disposal of shares or a related asset in the company invested in does not qualify for either of the exemptions outlined above, but a disposal at any time in the previous two years would have qualified, any gain on the disposal is not chargeable and any loss will not be allowable.

A wide anti-avoidance provision is also to be introduced to disallow the exemption under a "main purpose" test or if a disposal largely represents untaxed accrued profits.

In the course of the consultation the qualifying holding was reduced from 20% to 10% and this represents a welcome change. The ability of groups or other companies with significant investments to realise tax free gains will potentially boost the opportunity for reinvestment. Similarly groups of companies will have greater freedom to reorganise without the constraints of other tax-free routes. It is to be hoped that the overall benefits of exempt gains will outweigh those companies who now lose the ability to crystallise capital losses on shares to offset gains on other taxable assets.

The use of overseas holdings companies for tax planning was significantly reduced by the double taxation relief changes which took effect in 2001. The exemption of gains on substantial shareholdings now limits further the benefit of ownership of subsidiaries outside of the UK.

It should however be noted that it is not yet apparent how use of the anti-avoidance provision will be applied and some indication from HMRC of circumstances in which they might expect to use the provision would no doubt be welcomed by many large groups.

7.6 Charges on income
In computing the profits chargeable to tax there may be deducted the following charges (TA 1988 ss 338-340):

- yearly interest, annuity or other annual payments (other than amounts chargeable under Schedule A, (Schedule A became Part 4 of Corporation Tax Act 2009));

- interest paid to a bank, member of a stock exchange or discount house.

Reliefs (other than group relief) must first be deducted from profits.

The payments must be made under a liability incurred for consideration which, at the time the charge is created, is in a real commercial sense valuable and sufficient. The removal of possible discontent among staff does not qualify as such an event (*Ball v National & Grindlay's Bank Ltd.* C of A 1971).

Interest will not be deductible, unless either:

(a)   the company exists wholly or mainly for the purpose of carrying on a trade, or

(b)   the interest is laid out wholly and exclusively for a trade carried on by the company, or

(c)   the company is an investment company or authorized unit trust, or

(d)   the interest is in respect of land or buildings and would be eligible for relief if paid by an individual. If the land is occupied by the company (see *Tennant v Smith* HL 1982 for 'representative occupation') all necessary conditions are treated as satisfied if the land is not used as a residence, or is used as an individual's main or only residence, and, in the latter case, the £30,000 limit applies (TA 1988 s 338(6)).

Covenanted donations to charities under covenants for more than three years are allowed as charges. They are not treated as distributions (TA 1988 s 339).

A donation made to a charity by a company will qualify for relief as a charge on income. The company must be resident in the UK and must deduct tax at the basic rate from the payment. The company making the gift must provide a certificate to the charity stating that it has or will account for income tax on the grossed-up amount of the donation. In the case of a close company, the certificate should also state that the donation satisfies the statutory anti-avoidances legislation.

Interest paid and charged to capital is allowable as a charge on income.

Annuities, not granted in the ordinary course of business of granting annuities (*Stevenson Securities Ltd v CIR*, C. of S.S. 1959), are not deductible as charges on income if made under a liability incurred for non-taxable consideration (TA 1988 s 125). This catches the 'reverse annuity' schemes whereby a commercial company 'sells' an annuity to a gross fund, such as a charity, for non-taxable consideration.

Dividends or other distributions are not charges on income.

Tax is deducted from charges paid to a non-resident unless otherwise permitted under a double taxation agreement and accounted for to HMRC. The charges paid are allowable as a deduction. If the interest is payable out of income charged under Case IV or V of Schedule D (Schedule D became Part 3 of Corporation Tax Act 2009) it will be allowed, as will be any payment outside the UK either incurred for a foreign trade or payable in foreign currency for a trade carried on anywhere (75%, resident groups being treated as one trade) (TA 1988 s 340).

Interest on a foreign currency loan, which is paid by purchasing investment currency, may be taken at the actual sterling cost of purchasing the required currency including any premium payable.

Subject to what has been said before concerning non-resident companies, income received under deduction of income tax is liable in full (i.e. the gross amount) to corporation tax, and the income tax is set against the final liability to corporation tax, or, to the extent that it exceeds it, is repaid (TA 1988 s 7).

Distributions received from a UK resident company are not chargeable to corporation tax (TA 1988 s 208).

	£	£
Example of corporation tax computation C Ltd. has made net profits for the year ended 31 March 2012 of		150,000
after crediting:		
Franked investment income	1,000	
Capital gains	2,800	
Bank interest (inc. net accrual £100)	500	
Debenture interest	1,000	
	5,300	
and after charging		
Depreciation	13,000	
Bank interest		
on fixed loan	2,000	
on overdraft (inc. net accrual £50)	500	
	15,500	
Capital allowances are	22,000	

	£	£
The computation will be:		
Net profits per accounts		150,000
Less: Non-trading credits	5,300	
Capital allowances	22,000	
		27,300
		122,700
Add: Depreciation	13,000	
Overdraft interest	500	
		13,500
Trading income		136,200
Case III (bank interest)		400
Taxed investment income (excluding F.I.I)		1,000
Chargeable gains		2,800
Total profits		140,400
Less: Charges on income paid		
(overdraft interest)		450
Chargeable to corporation tax		£139,950

Notes:

(a) Only unfranked investment income receivable is charged.

(b) The interest on the fixed loan may be deducted in arriving at trading income (TA 1988 s 338(3)) but that on the overdraft probably must be claimed as a charge on income (TA 1988 s 338(3)). In practice, all bank interest is normally allowed as a trade expense.

(c) Income tax will have been suffered at source on debenture interest received, but this may be set off against corporation tax due.

7.7 Release of trade debts S302 CTA 2009

S74(1)(j) ICTA 1988, which previously gave relief where trade debts had become bad or doubtful, was repealed by Finance Act 2005. Where a company writes off a money debt that has arisen in the course of a trade, or a UK or overseas property business, the debit in the company's accounts is now brought into the ambit of the loan relationships rules.

The result is that where the creditor company is unconnected with the debtor, the creditor will get relief for the impairment, either as a trading expense or as part of a non-trading loan relationships deficit. HMRC would also regard relief as being available if the debit arises from the creditor having formally released the debt.

If, however, the creditor is connected with the debtor company (for example, they are companies within the same group) the loan relationship legislation means that no relief for impairment losses is available. This also applies to debt releases.

7.8 Interest relief on loans - CTA 2009 S375
Under the loan relationship rules, interest is relieved when it accrues, not when it is paid. This could lead to a mismatch if:

- the borrower gets relief when the interest accrues; and

- the interest is not paid for some time; and

- the lender, not being within the loan relationship rules, is taxed on the interest only when it is received, rather than when it accrues; or

- is outside the UK tax net entirely.

Connected parties could arrange their affairs to take advantage of this mismatch. For this reason, there are provisions to postpone relief for the borrower, in certain circumstances, when interest is paid later.

Where the following three conditions are satisfied, the borrower can only bring the debit into account when it actually pays the interest:

- the borrower and lender are connected in one of the four ways summarised below; and

- the interest is not paid within 12 months of the end of the AP in which it accrues. Finance Act 2009 changes the 12-month rule in one situation. Where the interest is payable to a company, interest will be deductible as it accrues in the accounts, not when it is paid; and

- the lender does not account for the whole amount of the interest under the loan relationship rules.

The four ways of connecting the borrower and lender are (in summary):

- Connection through control e.g. companies in the same group.

- Connection through participation in a close company e.g. associated companies, or companies and individuals that are participators, may be connected in this way.

- Connection through having a major interest. A company on its own may not have control of a company but it may have a 'major interest' and be able to control a company together with one other person.

- Connection through a pension scheme. Where a pension scheme lends money, there are various ways for the scheme to be connected to the borrowing company.

8 DISTRIBUTIONS

Distributions made are not deductible in computing profits chargeable to corporation tax, nor are distributions received chargeable as part of total profits. A distinction is made between distributions which are **qualifying distributions** and those which are not, as the former attract a tax credit when charged to tax on the recipient, but non-qualifying distributions are only charged to excess liability on the recipient.

Distributions by a company comprise the following kinds of payment:

(a)   Dividend, including capital dividend.

(b)   Any other distribution out of assets in respect of shares except a repayment of capital, or for new consideration received (not applicable to transfers between UK companies unless there is common control).

(c)   Redeemable share capital or any security issued in respect of shares or securities unless for new consideration received.

(d)   Interest or other distribution in respect of securities except repayment of the capital sum, if the securities are

   (i)   as para. (c);

   (ii)   securities convertible directly or indirectly into shares in, or securities carrying any right to receive shares in or securities of the company, not being securities quoted on a stock exchange or issued on similar terms to such securities;

   (iii) securities where the payment for the use of the capital is to any extent dependent upon the results of the company's business, or is more than a reasonable commercial return (only the excess over the reasonable amount is treated as a distribution);

   (iv)   securities issued by a company to a non-resident company of which it is a 75% subsidiary, or where both are 75% subsidiaries of another non-resident company (or of a UK company unless 90% or more of the share capital of the issuing company is directly owned by a UK company);

(v) securities connected with shares (e.g. debentures) in such a way that it is necessary or advantageous for a person who acquires or disposes of them to do so similarly with a proportionate holding of the shares.

Securities includes money advanced even though the loan is not secured on the assets.

(vi) On transfer of assets or liabilities to or from members not at market value, the benefit received by the member. This does not include a transfer by a 51% subsidiary company to a parent company or fellow 51% subsidiary. Nor does it apply to transfers of assets other than cash between UK companies unless there is common control.

Repayment of paid-up share capital issued without consideration, up to the amount of the share capital (except fully paid preference shares issued before 7 April 1965, or after then if the consideration was not derived from ordinary shares) (TA 1988 s 210).

(vii) Repayment of bonus shares (TA 1988 s 211). If the issue has not been treated as a qualifying distribution, the repayment is not treated as a repayment of capital.

Except as regards closely controlled companies this rule does not apply if the repayment is made more than 10 years after the issue of the bonus shares, unless they are redeemable shares.

(viii) Stock dividend options. The allotment of bonus shares except by a close company is not a distribution (*CIR v Blott* HL 1921), even where there is an option to take cash, if that option has not been exercised; but the recipient may nevertheless be liable to tax thereon.

(ix) Reciprocal arrangements (TA 1988 s 254(8)). Where two or more companies enter into reciprocal arrangements to make distributions to each other's members, anything done by one company may be treated as if done by the other.

(x) For close companies only, provisions of living or other accommodation, entertainment, domestic or other services or other benefits or facilities of whatever nature for a participator (or his associate) in that company or any controlled by it. This does not include benefits on death or retirement to dependants in the way of pension, annuity, lump-sum, etc., and does not include benefits on cessation of employment to a director or other employee if the payment was at arm's length and the amount reasonable and allowable for corporation tax purposes (TA 1988 s 418).

Stock dividends are treated as distributions equivalent to the appropriate amount of cash (TA 1988 s 249). Payments by two or more companies acting in concert to participators are treated as payments to their own participators. Material interest means beneficial ownership of, or liability to control, directly or indirectly, more than 5% of the ordinary share capital or entitled to more than 5% of the total income apportionable for income tax. Associates are regarded as one.

(xi)   Payments to members of registered friendly societies (TA 1988 s 461). Payments to a member in respect of his or her interest, so far as they exceed their contributions or deposits, are to be treated as qualifying distributions, liable to ACT on the society and income tax on the recipient.

(xii)   Purchase of own shares by a company (TA 1988 s 219). Where a company which is an unquoted trading company or the holding company of a trading company purchases its own shares, the transactions will not be treated as a distribution if the following conditions are satisfied.

The purchase or other transaction must be (i) made wholly or mainly for the purpose of a trade carried on by the company or by a 75% subsidiary, and (ii) not part of a scheme to avoid tax, and (iii) the vendor must satisfy the condition in ss 220 and 223; or the proceeds from the purchase or other, transaction must be used to pay capital transfer tax on deaths and the CTT must be paid within a period of two years following death.

9 DISSOLUTION OF COMPANIES AND ESC C16

HMRC is proposing a statutory provision to replace ESC C16.

ESC C16 provides a simple and straightforward way for companies to be struck off the company assets returned to the shareholders. In essence, where HMRC agrees that C16 can apply, the company can be dissolved and the lawful distributions it makes prior to the dissolution are only liable to CGT not income tax. There is no limit to the amount of the lawful distributions that qualify.

What is proposed under the new legislation is that in future the amount that can be paid out will be limited to £4,000.

The effect of the proposal, would be that companies would be forced to put them into formal liquidation, with the attendant costs of an insolvency practitioner, if they want to benefit from the CGT treatment.

10 TAXATION OF DISTRIBUTIONS

10.1 Tax credit

A UK-resident company receiving a qualifying distribution is entitled to a tax credit corresponding to the rate in force for the financial year in which the distribution is made (TA 1988 s 231).

A person other than a UK resident company can claim to have the credit set against the tax chargeable on him. No tax credits are refundable.

Where a distribution is deemed to be income of a person other than the recipient, that other person stands in the place of the recipient as regards tax credit. Trustees are entitled to the tax credit if no other person falls to be regarded as the recipient.

10.2 Schedule F - now renamed

Schedule F became Chapter 5 of Income Tax (Trading and Other Income) Act 2005
This schedule, under which income tax on distribution is charged, provides as follows.

- The charge is made on all dividends and other distributions from a UK resident company not specially excluded from income tax.

- Any distribution in respect of which a person is entitled to a tax credit, is treated as representing income amounting to the distribution plus the credit, and Schedule F (Schedule F became Chapter 5 of ITTOIA 2005) tax is charged on that aggregate. The tax credit is set against the liability.

- No distribution chargeable under Schedule F (Schedule F became Chapter 5 of ITTOIA 2005) is to be charged elsewhere.

- When a person (other than a UK resident company) has as part of his income a distribution not ranking for tax credit and is assessed to excess liability, the distribution is regarded as not brought into charge to income tax (i.e. not available for set-off against charges). Where any such payment of a non-qualifying distribution is followed by a repayment of the share capital or security, the tax liability arising on the repayment is reduced by the excess liability already suffered (TA 1988 s 233).

10.3 Franked investment income
Franked investment income represents qualifying distributions received plus the tax credits thereon.

10.4 Distributions to exempt funds
Where a person holds at least 10% of a class of shares, and is exempt from tax, the exemption does not apply to a qualifying distribution (except as regards certain bonus issues). It is treated as income not brought in to charge to tax and is not available for set-off against interest paid.

10.5 Disallowance of relief for bonus issues
Certain receipts treated as distribution (i.e. bonus issues following repayment of capital, certain payments in respect of shares not issued for new consideration, certain premiums on redemption of share capital, and distributions in excess of new consideration) do not rank for relief by way of exemption from tax or setting off losses against profits or income. A company cannot treat the distribution as franked investment income. The tax credit cannot be set against tax on annual payments and interest paid cannot be set against the bonus issue (TA 1988 s 237).

11 LOSSES

11.1 Trading losses
A loss is computed in the same way as a profit, except that interest or dividends received may be included in Case I or Case V computations if they are trading receipts of a financial concern (TA 1988 s 393; *Bank Line Ltd v CIR*, CS 1974). Charges on income made wholly and exclusively for the company's trade which exceed the profits against which they are deductible may be treated as trading expenses in computing a loss to be carried forward. A trading loss may be set against:

(a)   income of the same trade in succeeding accounting periods; or
(b)   profits, of whatever description, of the same accounting period; or
(c)   The general carry back of trading losses will be only against the profits of the preceding year. (See 11.2 below for extension 24 November 2008 - 23 November 2010, p.275).

A three year carry back is available for trading losses arising in the twelve months before a trade comes to an end, and for losses due to the special 100 per cent allowance on the costs of decommissioning North Sea oil and gas installations.

Para.'s (b) and (c) do not apply to trades falling under Case V of Sch D (Schedule D became Part 3 of CTA 2009) or to a trade not carried on a commercial basis other than by public authorities. Special restrictions also apply to certain losses of oil companies (TA 1988 Sch 30). A claim under Para. (a) must be made within six years, and a claim under Para.'s (b) and (c) within two years of the end of the accounting period. See also FA 1994 ss 159, 160, 209, 210.

Carry Back of Trade Losses and First Year Allowances
A company made a loss in the year ended 31 March 1998 and sought to apportion it on a time basis based on 2 July 1997 when the loss carry back rules changed from 3 years to 1 year. All but a minimal amount of the loss was caused by FYAs on some assets acquired via hire purchase agreements entered into after 2 July 1997. However, HMRC said that an apportionment on a time basis would be unjust or unreasonable in this case since, broadly, the loss itself was almost wholly due to first year allowances which by definition meant that the expenditure had occurred after 2 July 1997. The Special Commissioner held in favour of HMRC and excluded the first year allowances from the apportionment. *Camcrown v McDonald* (1999) STC (SCD) 255.

11.2 Losses - extended carry back
Prior to 24 November 2008 (PBR) losses, in normal situations, could only be carried back one year - see 11.1 Trading losses above. There is no limit to the size of the trading losses that could be carried back – save for the size of the total taxable profits to be relieved.

Following the PBR and 2009 Budget any losses unused in the above carry back could be carried back a further two years. There was a limit of £50,000, per year, the losses must relate to accounting periods ending in the two year period 24 November 2008 – 23 November 2010. If there was more than one accounting period in 12 calendar months, there was no additional £50,000. If the accounting period was less than 12 months the £50,000 was reduced proportionately.

For companies the relief was given against total taxable profits, therefore allowing relief against rental income and capital gains.

Example of losses - extended carry back
Darling Limited made a loss of £150,000 in the accounting period ending 31 December 2008. In the three previous accounting periods the profits had been 2007 £75,000, 2006 £40,000 & 2005 £30,000.

The losses were relieved as follows:

		Profits	Losses Relieved
		£	£
AP ending 31 December 2007		75,000	
	Losses utilised	-75,000	75,000
	Profits assessable	0	
AP ending 31 December 2006		40,000	
	Losses utilised	-40,000	40,000
	Profits assessable	0	
AP ending 31 December 2005		30,000	
	Losses utilised *	-10,000	10,000
	Profits assessable	20,000	
			125,000

* Carry back three years limited to £50,000 (£40,000 + £10,000)

N.B. Balance of unrelieved losses of £25,000 (£150,000 - £125,000) carried forward.

11.3 Losses on shares

An investment company may claim relief against income in respect of capital losses arising on unquoted ordinary shares if they are in a qualifying trading company for which it has subscribed and subsequently disposed of after 31 March 1981 (TA 1988 s 573). The company making the loss must have been an investment company throughout the six years prior to the sale or have been such for a shorter continuous period and not previously been a trading company or an excluded company. In addition to this, it must not have been with or be members of the same group as the qualifying trading company.

A qualifying company is a company whose shares have never been quoted on a recognized stock exchange and which satisfies the following criteria:

(a)   is a trading company (as defined by TA 1988 Sch 19 para 7) at the date of disposal or, has ceased to be a trading company within the previous three years and has not since then been an investment company nor an excluded company; and

(b)   has been a trading company for a continuous period for at least six years up to the date of disposal (or when it ceased to be a trading company, if earlier) or, alternatively, for a shorter continuous period provided it was not previously an investment company nor an excluded company.

The claim must be made within two years of the end of the accounting period in which the loss arose.

In September 2009 the Tax First-tier Tribunal published its decision in the case of *Philips Electronics UK Limited*. This is a loss relief case and it has been found in favour of the taxpayer. The case concerns a UK company's claims to offset losses of a UK branch (of a Dutch company) against its profits. The claims were made on the basis that the UK group and consortium relief rules are contrary to European law.

The Philips case is very different from the *Marks & Spencer case (Case C-446/03)*, although both concern claims made by UK companies for losses and both were argued on EU grounds. However, this is where the similarity ends. The M&S case was concerned with group relief claims made by a UK company for EU losses incurred by companies resident outside of the UK. The Philips case, however, concerns claims to offset UK trading losses (incurred by a UK branch of a Dutch company) against UK profits. It is highly likely that the case will be appealed on by HM Revenue & Customs.

11.4 Change of ownership
Losses cannot be carried forward from the old ownership to the new if:

* in any period of three years there is both a change in the ownership of a company and a major change in the nature or conduct of its trade; or

* the trade had become small or negligible and there is a change of ownership before any considerable revival occurs.

A major change in the nature or conduct of the trade includes a major change in the type of property dealt in or services, etc., provided, or in customers, outlets or markets, even if this is the result of a gradual process which began outside the three-year period (TA 1988 s 768). This does not apply to company reconstructions where the change of proprietorship is ignored (i.e. under TA 1988 s 343 - See 11.6 Company reconstructions, p.280).

The accounting period in which the change of ownership occurs is divided on a time basis (unless this would be unjust or unreasonable), and treated as two separate accounting periods.

Detailed rules are described as follows:

A **change of ownership** occurs if a single person (or two or more persons, ignoring an acquisition by any person which still leaves his total holding under 5%) acquires more than half the ordinary share capital. There are detailed provisions for applying this rule.

The **holdings** of connected persons are aggregated, but inherited shares (subject to safeguards) are ignored.

Other kinds of share capital, voting and other powers may be taken into account instead of ordinary share capital, in considering change of ownership, if ordinary shareholdings are not an appropriate test of ownership.

Circumstances occurring prior to a change of ownership giving rise to a **restriction of carry-forward of loss** are not to be taken into account in considering any subsequent change of ownership.

Provision is made for the application of these rules to principal and subsidiary companies in **groups.**

Various expressions are defined.

Date of change of ownership is the date of the contract, or the date an option to purchase the shares was acquired.

In computing a balancing charge after a change of ownership where this section has been applied, **capital allowances** before the change, which could not be given effect to owing to insufficiency of profits, are not deducted in computing the written-down value.

The **time limit** for making assessments is six years after the latest relevant event.

The Inspector has powers to obtain **information** as to beneficial ownership from the registered owner of the shares.

Trading losses and transfer of trade
The case of *Barkers of Malton Limited v HMRC SpC 689* was concerned with the ability of a company to transfer its trade to another company under s 343, Taxes Act 1988 and for the successor company to continue to benefit from the accumulated trading losses.

Section 343 allows the successor company to be treated as continuing to carry on the trade and to obtain relief for losses brought forward providing that there is at least 75% common ownership before and after the trade, and that the successor company carries on the relevant trade.

In this case, the only question for consideration was whether or not the successor company continued to carry on the trade in question.

11.5 Terminal loss

A loss in the last 12 months of a ceasing trade may be set against the trading profits of the three preceding years, taking a later year first. Any trading charges paid in the accounting period in which trading ceased should be included in computing the amount of terminal losses available to be carried back against profits (TA 1988 s 393A (7)).

Terminal loss relief is not to disturb any relief for earlier losses or charges on income eligible for carry-forward as trading expenses. Capital allowances in respect of the trade but which are given by discharge or repayment of tax (e.g. agricultural buildings allowances) can be added so as to create or augment a terminal loss.

A claim must be made within six years of cessation.

		£	£
Austin Limited has trading results as follows:			
12 months ended 30 September 2008	Profit	10,000	
12 months ended 30 September 2009	Profit	4,000	
12 months ended 30 September 2010	Profit	3,000	
12 months ended 30 September 2011	Loss	9,000	
The assessments and terminal loss relief will be as follows:			
12 months ended 30 September 2011			Nil
12 months ended 30 September 2010	Profit		3,000
Less: Loss carried back			3,000
			Nil
12 months ended 30 September 2009			4,000
Less: Loss carried back			4,000
			Nil
12 months ended 30 September 2008			10,000
Less: Loss carried back			2,000
			£8,000

A loss arising under Case VI can only be set against Case VI profits of the same or later years. This does not apply to a loss arising out of premiums of leases, assignment of lease at undervalue, or sale of land with right to reconvey (TA 1988 s 396).

11.6 Company reconstructions

Where a company (the predecessor) ceases to trade and another company (the successor) carries it on, and at any time within two years after the change three-quarters of the interest in the trade belongs to the same persons as within a year before the change, and the trade is throughout the period carried on by a company chargeable to tax in respect of it, then the change of proprietorship is ignored and losses and allowances are given to the successor as if the predecessor had continued the business (TA 1988 s 343).

However, the losses available for carrying forward are restricted if the transferor company is insolvent. The losses are restricted to the amount by which the relevant liabilities of the transferor company exceed the relevant assets. **Relevant assets** are assets which are vested in the transferor company immediately before the change which were not transferred to the successor nor were apportioned to the successor on a previous change. The assets are valued at open-market valuation immediately before the date of the change. **Relevant liabilities** are liabilities which were not transferred to the successor nor were apportioned to the successor on a previous change, and remain as liabilities of the transferor company. Relevant liabilities do not, however, include:

- share capital;
- share premium account;
- reserves; or
- relevant loan stock.

Accordingly, if the successor ceases to trade within four years of its commencement, any terminal loss can be allowed to the predecessor if necessary until the preceding three years are exhausted. If the successor ceases within one year, relief may be given to the predecessor.

The trade carried on by the successor must be the same trade as that carried on by the predecessor but if the trade is carried on by the successor as part of its trade, or if a company ceases to carry on part of its trade, the part in both cases is treated as a separate trade and appropriate apportionments made.

Any securities treated as trading stock are regarded as having been sold and purchased at market value at the date of cessation.

If a company contracts to sell its subsidiary company's shares, it ceases to be the beneficial owner of those shares when the contract becomes binding and enforceable and it cannot then transfer an undertaking to the subsidiary with the benefit of losses (*Wood Preservation Ltd v Prior* CA 1968). A contract may be made by negotiations preceding a formal agreement (*J. H. & S. (Timber) Ltd. v Quirk* Ch D 1973), but will not be binding if a fundamental term remains to be agreed (*Blower v Langworthy Bros Ltd* Ch D 1968). On commencement of winding-up a company ceases to be beneficial owner of its assets (*Olive Mill Ltd v CIR* Ch D 1963) and cannot thereafter successfully carry out a reconstruction.

In computing the profits of the successor, repairs to machinery, or replacement cost where the renewals basis operates, are not in practice restricted on account of the assets having been taken over in a used condition.

11.7 Losses allowable against surplus franked investment income

Where a company has a surplus of franked investment income, i.e. an excess of franked investment income over franked payments during an accounting period, it may treat it, or any necessary part of it, as being profit for the period, and may set against it losses which cannot be allowed against profits in the ways described before.

The losses which can be set off in the manner described before are:

(a)   charges on income under TA 1988 s 238;
(b)   management expenses under TA 1988 s 75 or 76;
(c)   excess capital allowances (not taken into trading account) under CAA 1968 s 74(3);
(d)   trading losses under TA 1988 s 393;
(e)   losses of investment companies on disposal of unquoted shares subscribed for in certain trading companies under TA 1988 s 573.

Where relief has been claimed for a set-off against para.'s (c), (d) or (e) against surplus franked investment income of an earlier accounting period, the relief is restricted to the surplus franked investment income proportionate to the part of the earlier accounting period whose profits may be relieved under the carry-back provisions (TA 1988 s 242(4)).

The relief is given by the repayment to the company of the amount of the tax credit on the surplus franked investment income set off (TA 1988 s 242(1)) and the claim must be made within time limits as follows:

•   claims under para.'s (a) or (b) - within six years of the end of the accounting period in which the charges were paid or the management expenses incurred;

•   claims under para.'s (c), (d) or (e) - within two years of the end of the accounting period in which the loss was incurred or for which the capital allowances were due.

11.8 Leasing contracts

Where the lessor company makes a loss on the contract (i.e. by way of heavy capital allowances) and there is a company reconstruction arrangement for a successor company to take over the lessor company's business, the loss can only be allowed against subsequent profits from the same contract (TA 1988 s 395).

12 CLOSE COMPANIES
(TA 1988, Chapters I, II and III; 12.10 FA 1989 ss 103-107 and Sch 12)

12.1 The provisions summarised

The purpose of the close company legislation is to prevent shareholders in control of certain companies from restricting dividends and thus avoiding higher rates of tax.

The basic rules are as follows:

A close company is one which is:

(a)   Resident in the U.K.

(b)   Controlled by 5 or fewer 'participators' or 'associates' (e.g., husbands, wives, close relatives and partners); or by directors who are participators; and participators who would be entitled to more than half of the assets on a notional winding up of the company.

(c)   Not quoted on a recognised stock exchange except where less than 35% of the shares are held by the public.

The FA 1989 provided that the legislation is confined to close investment holding companies (CIC), i.e., not trading companies, members of a trading group nor those investing in property for letting. Probably most family companies holding investments are close investment holding companies.

The essential effect of the current legislation is as follows:

(a)   Apportionment no longer applies.

(b)   The small profits rate does not apply to close investment holding companies which are liable for the full rate of corporation tax at 28%.

(c)   The tax credit may be restricted where a shareholder waives a dividend in favour of someone else.

(d)   Profits on the realisation of life assurance policies will be taxed.

12.2 Control
A person **controls** a company (TA 1988 s 416) if:

- he or she 'exercises, or is able to exercise, or is entitled to acquire, control, whether direct or indirect, over the company's affairs'; or

- he or she possesses or is entitled to acquire:

    (a)   the greater part of the share capital or voting power; or

    (b)   the greater part of the company's income if it were distributed to the participators; or

    (c)   such rights as, in the event of winding-up or in any other circumstances, would entitle him to the greater part of the assets available for distribution among members.

A participator in para. (b) excludes a loan creditor.

Two or more persons who together satisfy the these conditions are treated as controlling the company.

Nominee holdings are treated as those of beneficial owners, and rights and powers of associates or of companies controlled by a participator or his associates are attributed to the participator.

12.3 Participator
A participator (TA 1988 s 417) is defined as any person who has a share or interest in the capital or income of a company and in particular any person who:

(a)   possesses or is entitled to acquire share capital or voting rights;
(b)   is a loan creditor (this in turn is defined and excludes bank loans);
(c)   has a right to distributions or a premium on redemption of loan;
(d)   can have the company's assets or income applied directly or indirectly for his or her benefit.

12.4 Associate
An associate (TA 1988 s 417) means:

(a)   relative (husband or wife, lineal ancestor and descendant, brother, sister);

(b)   partner;

(c)   trustee of settlement made by the person or relative;

(d)   any person interested with the participator in shares or obligations of the company which are subject to any trusts (except, in certain circumstances, superannuation funds and retirement schemes and trusts for the benefit of the employees) or are part of the estate of the deceased person.

With regard to para.'s (c) and (d) it has been held that:

•   a deceased person's estate is not a settlement within para. (c);

•   'trustees of any settlement' (see para. (c)) cannot refer to executors as such;

•   'interested in' (see para. (d)) means interested in a fiduciary or a beneficial capacity;

•   beneficiaries under a will are not 'interested in' the estate of a deceased person during the course of administration.

Accordingly, it was held that, where interest was paid to the executors of a deceased person, one of whom was a director and participator, the executors were all associates of a participator and the interest was a distribution (*Willingale v Islington Green Investment Co.* CA 1972).

12.5 Director
A **director** (TA 1988 s 417) includes any person occupying the position of director by whatever name called, and any person in accordance with whose directions or instructions the directors are accustomed to act; and any person who:

•   is concerned in the management of the business, and

•   alone or with his associates can control directly or indirectly 20% of the ordinary share capital (i.e. all capital except that with a fixed dividend rate). The director need not himself own or control any shares.

12.6 Exceptions
(a)   A non-resident company is not a close company.
       A company is not a close company if shares carrying not less than 35% of the voting power and not entitled to a fixed rate of dividend were acquired unconditionally and held beneficially by the public and have been quoted and dealt in on a stock exchange in the previous 12 months. 'Public' does not include directors or their associates or a company controlled by them, but includes all shareholders other than the five largest, and shares held by open companies being regarded as held by the public and not as part of the five largest holdings (TA 1988 s 415(3)).

(b)   A company is not a close company, if companies which are not close companies control it by way of beneficial ownership of its shares and it can be treated as close only by taking a non-close company as one of the five participators. Nor is a company to be treated as close if it can only be treated as close by reference to the control within para. (See 12.2 Control, p.283), or participators (other than loan creditors who are non-close companies). In these cases the other company need not be resident in the UK, to rank as a close company (TA 1988 s 418(4)(5)).

(c)   In certain circumstances the trustees of superannuation fund investments (TA 1988 s 417(7)) are regarded as beneficial owners of the shares and are treated as a company which is not a close company.

(d)   Industrial and provident societies and building societies subject to the special arrangements are not close companies.

(e)   A Crown-controlled company is not a close company unless it can be treated as a close company under the control of persons acting independently of the Crown.

For more information please refer to previous editions of this work.

13 INVESTMENT COMPANIES

An investment company is 'any company whose business consists wholly or mainly in the making of investments and the principal part of whose income is derived therefrom' (TA 1988 s 75). The nature of the company's business is to be ascertained over a reasonable period of time. It does not cease to be an investment company merely because the principal part of its income in a particular year is not derived from investments, unless there has been a definite change in the nature of the business (*FPH Finance Trust v CIR* HL 1944). It also includes savings banks other than trustee savings banks. Very little activity is necessary to constitute a 'business' of an investment company (*CIR v Westleigh Estates Co.* CA 1924).

Management expenses of such companies if resident in the UK are allowed as a deduction from total profits unless:

- they are deductible in computing Schedule A income (Schedule A became Part 4 of Corporation Tax Act 2009);

- there is income, other than franked investment income or group income, which is derived from sources not charged to tax. The management expenses are restricted by the amount of this income.

Expenses of advertising unlet properties are deductible for Schedule A (Schedule A became Part 4 of CTA 2009) and these are not 'management expenses' (*Southern v Aldwych Property Trust Ltd* KBD 1940), but brokerage and stamp duties on changes of investments (*Sun Life Ass. Soc. v Davidson* HL 1957) and entertaining expenses (TA 1988 s 577(1)) are not deductible. Reasonable directors' remuneration can be included (*LG Berry Investments v Attwooll* Ch. D. 1964), but a claim for a management charge paid to a parent company was disallowed because no services were provided (*Fragmap Developments Ltd v Cooper* Ch. D. 1967). Valuation costs incurred to comply with the disclosure requirements of companies legislation are in practice allowed.

Any expenses which cannot be allowed may be carried forward and set against future profits.

Charges on income are allowable in the same way as management expenses and can be carried forward if wholly and exclusively incurred for the purposes of the business.

Capital allowances are given for machinery and plant used for management, and also maintenance, etc. of property if these cannot be allowed against Schedule A Income (Schedule A became Part 4 of CTA 2009).

I Ltd has the following income and expenses:	£	£
Case III (bank interest)		500
Taxed investment income (inc. FII £10,000)		12,000
Part 4 of CTA 2009 (less expenses)		3,000
		15,500
Expenses of management	2,000	
Charges on income	500	
		(2,500)
		13,000
Less: Franked investment income		10,000
Profits chargeable to corporation tax		3,000

14 GROUPS OF COMPANIES

14.1 General
There are special provisions relating to groups of companies which:

- enable income to be transferred within the group without deduction of income tax;

- enable losses, charges on income and other reliefs or deductions to be so transferred;

- exempt from tax on chargeable gains transfers of assets within the group.

Groups can present very complex tax-planning problems, the solution of which are necessary merely to utilize all available reliefs.

14.2 Group income
Group income consists of dividends received by a company in relation to which the payer is:

(a)   a 51% subsidiary or a 51% subsidiary of the company of which the recipient is also a 51% subsidiary:

(b)   a trading or holding company owned by a consortium of which the recipient is a member. (TA 1988 ss 246-247).

A **51% subsidiary** is a company in which another owns directly or indirectly more than 50% of the ordinary share capital (see *Burman v Hedges & Butler Ltd* Ch D 1978) or is entitled to more than 50% of the profits available for distribution and assets on a winding-up. A **trading company** is one whose business consists wholly or mainly of the carrying on of a trade or trades. A **holding company** means one whose business consists wholly or mainly in the holding of shares or securities of trading companies which are its 90% subsidiaries (TA 1988 s 247(9)). A **consortium** owns a company if it owns 75% or more of the ordinary share capital of the company and consists of 20 or fewer companies which are resident in the UK each of which must hold at least 5% of the ordinary share capital of the company making the payment or is entitled to not less than 5% of the profits available for distribution or not less than 5% of the assets available for distribution on a winding-up.

Companies may receive charges on income from the companies within para.'s (a) or (b), or from a company of which the recipient is a 51% subsidiary (i.e. from the parent company) without deduction of income tax. A Joint election is necessary.

All companies concerned must be resident in the UK and provision is made to prevent certain forms of dividend-stripping.

14.3 Group relief
Finance Act 2000 - Section 97 Modernisation of group relief
The changes to the group relief rules in Finance Act 2000 allow groups and consortia to be established for group relief purposes through companies resident anywhere in the world. Group relief has also been extended to UK branches of non-resident companies, and the rules for the surrender of losses attributable to overseas branches of UK-resident companies have been brought into line.

The new rules apply for accounting periods ending on or after 1 April 2000. But periods straddling 1 April will be apportioned so that the changes take effect only in respect of losses arising from that date.

Companies and their advisers may find it helpful, in submitting claims for group relief, to have some guidance on the operation of the new Sections 403D and 403E Income and Corporation Taxes Act (ICTA) 1988, which contain the rules for branch losses.

Certain tax reliefs may be transferred within a group of UK resident companies or may be surrendered by certain companies owned by a consortium (TA 1988 ss 402-413) where either the surrendering company or the claimant company is a member of a consortium and the other company is:

(a)   a trading company which is owned by the consortium and which is not a 75% subsidiary of a company, or

(b)   a trading company which is a 90% subsidiary of a holding company which is owned by the consortium, and is not a 75% subsidiary of another company, or

(c)   a holding company which is owned by the consortium and which is not a 75% subsidiary of any company.

The reliefs which are available against total profits are:

(a)   trading losses computed under s 393;

(b)   capital allowances (excluding amounts brought forward) available by discharge or repayment so far as they exceed income against which they are primarily available in the surrendering company;

(c)   management expenses (excluding amounts brought forward, so far as they exceed the profits of the surrendering company;

(d)   charges on income so far as they exceed the profits of the surrendering company;

Relief is available to members of a group either by way of group relief or by way of consortium relief where the companies are members of a consortium.

The income or profits of the surrendering company for the purposes of para.'s (b) - (d) are not to be reduced by reliefs carried forward or backward from other periods.

The income or profits of the claimant company are not to be reduced by any other reliefs (except those carried back from a later accounting period) before group relief is set off, and the claimant will be assumed to have made all the claims it could to offset losses and capital allowances against total profits.

Group relief is available in respect of a trading company that was a subsidiary of a holding company owned by a consortium even though the holding company owned shares in companies not resident in the UK (*ICI v Colmer* Ch.D 1991).

Where accounting periods do not coincide or where a company joins or leaves a group or consortium, the relief is apportioned according to the respective lengths of the accounting periods involved. These provisions are widely drawn but, briefly, they prevent group relief for trading losses being transferred for any accounting period during which arrangements are in existence under which the surrendering company might cease to be a member of the group and become a member of another group or might cease to carry on all or part of the trade concerned. They apply with apportionate modifications to consortia.

Claims must be made within two years of the surrendering company's accounting period and require the consent of that company or, in the case of a consortium, of all the members (TA 1988 s 412). A provisional claim will be accepted if the surrendering company's loss is not agreed within the two year time limit. A claimant may pay for its group relief and, provided it does not exceed the amount of the relief, such a payment is ignored for tax purposes (TA 1988 s 402(6)). There are provisions to counteract stripping operations by dealing companies (TA 1988 S 402(3)).

Relief may be divided amongst any number of companies and the full amount available need not be claimed.

In this context, a **group** consists of a parent company and all its 75% subsidiaries and an industrial or provident society may be included as such (TA 1988 s 413(3)).

A company is a **75% subsidiary** if another company directly or indirectly owns that proportion of its ordinary share capital. For 90% subsidiaries that proportion must be owned directly.

P Ltd, and its 75% subsidiaries, S Ltd and T Ltd, have the following total
profits (£000):

	P Ltd	S Ltd	T Ltd
Trading income (loss)	-	130	(150)
Unfranked investment income	20	20	-
Chargeable gains (as reduced)	30	-	10
Total profit	50	150	(140)
Charges on income paid	(5)	(5)	-
Management expenses	(60)	-	-
Net profits (reliefs)	(15)	145	(140)
P Ltd may surrender its excess			
management expenses to S Ltd	15	(15)	-
T Ltd may surrender £130 of its losses to			
S Ltd (it may not surrender £135 so			
as to enable S to carry forward its			
charges on income)	-	(130)	130
profits chargeable (losses forward)	Nil	Nil	(10)

Notes:
(i)   If the management expenses included £12 brought forward, the
      amount available for relief would be £48, less the net profits of (50 -
      5) = 45, i.e. £3.
(ii) If this were a 'close' group, T Ltd could surrender £130 to S Ltd (as
      above) but carry forward the whole of the balance (£20) to its next
      AP. This would be advantageous if there was then income liable to
      apportionment, for the £10 left in charge above would not be subject
      to apportionment, because it is chargeable gains.

14.4 Chargeable gains

In effect, a company and all its 75% subsidiaries are treated as one person (a
'group') for the purposes of tax on chargeable gains. Accordingly, transfers of assets
within the group do not give rise to a tax liability (except on deemed disposals and
re-acquisitions) and the transferor's acquisition cost and time is deemed to be the
transferee's.

However, the satisfaction of any debt (or part thereof), the redemption of any shares
and the receipt of any capital distribution from a company are not so exempted.
Disposals arising from the receipt of compensation for loss of or injury to assets are
regarded as made to the person ultimately bearing the burden of the compensation
and so, usually, will not be exempt.

Transfers of assets which were trading stock before the transfer but which are acquired by the transferee as other than trading stock are treated as appropriated from trading stock by the transferor immediately before transfer. In the converse case, the transferee is deemed to appropriate the asset to trading stock immediately after the transfer.

Tax on chargeable gains can be recovered from other or former members of the group in certain circumstances and there will then be a right of indemnity.

There is no 'group relief' for capital losses, so that appropriate inter-group transfers must be made before disposal outside the group to ensure that loss relief is obtained.

From 17.3.98 it has been prohibited to transfer into a group a company with realised gains to take advantage of capital losses already in the group.

Where share exchanges are made within the same group, the shares are to be treated in the hands of the transferee as being acquired at the market value at the date of the transfer. (TA 1988 s 115; TA 1970 s 273(2A)).

Capital gains indexation allowances are not granted where a company disposes of, or receives payment in respect of a debt on a security owned by a linked company, or on the disposal of redeemable preference shares of a linked company. The restriction also applies on the disposal of other shares in a linked company where the finance for the original purpose was provided from within the group for the sole or main purpose of obtaining an indexation allowance. Companies are regarded as linked if they are within the same group, or under common control, or if one controls the other (TA 1988 s 114, Sch 11).

Where assets are transferred within a group the recipient company has dual residence and there is a double taxation treaty between the UK and the other country of residence which gives that country sole taxing rights over the new assets, no relief will be given under the nil gain/nil loss provisions and a liability to tax on the chargeable gains on the disposal will arise (TA 1988 s 276; FA 1990 s 67).

Where a non-resident company transfers assets of its branch or agency in the UK to a UK company, and the transfer is made in accordance with a scheme for the transfer of all or part of the branch or agency's trade, the transfer will be deemed to have been made at a consideration giving rise to a nil gain/nil loss position. Both the non-resident company and the UK-resident company must be members of the same group and the claim for the relief must be made by both companies within two years of the end of the UK's company's accounting period in which the transfer arose (TA 1988 s 273A, FA 1990 s 70).

PART SEVEN

CAPITAL ALLOWANCES

1 BUDGET MARCH 2011

1.1 Change in rates from 2012
Most rates of capital allowances are to be reduced - from 1 April 2012 (for limited companies) and from 6 April 2012 (for unincorporated businesses).

The proposed reductions are:
(a) Writing down allowances will be reduced from 20% to 18% on the cost of qualifying plant and machinery. This will also affect any unrelieved expenditure in the main rate pool;
(b) Writing down allowances on long life assets, integral features and specified cars will be reduced from 10% to 8%. This will also affect any unrelieved expenditure in the special rate pool;
(c) The annual 100% investment allowance (AIA) available for qualifying capital expenditure up to £100,000 will be reduced to £25,000.

1.2 Short-life assets - extension to 8 years
Legislation in Finance Act 2011 increases the period over which expenditure on plant or machinery can be given "short life assets" (SLA) treatment.

If a business "elects" for plant or machinery to be treated as a short life asset, capital allowances are calculated individually on the asset until a "cut-off" point. This ensures that, if the asset is sold or scrapped before the cut-off point, the total allowances given over the period of ownership equal the actual net cost of the asset to the business.

This measure applies to expenditure from 1/6 April 2011. It increases the cut-off period for expenditure to eight years from the end of the chargeable period in which this expenditure is incurred.

2 GENERAL NATURE OF THE ALLOWANCES

Depreciation on fixed assets as charged in business accounts is not allowed for tax purposes. Instead, relief of tax for most types of depreciating assets is given by capital allowances under the Capital Allowances Act 2001 (as amended). These allowances are percentages of the cost of newly acquired assets, and of the written down value after the year of acquisition. The written down value is the remaining value at the beginning of the tax year after deducting the allowances of previous years.

For plant and machinery, in particular, the written down values of all the relevant assets are consolidated into a 'pool', to which the cost of newly acquired assets is added to the existing written down balance and the proceeds from the sale of an asset are deducted. The allowance for the year concerned is then calculated on the resultant balance, from which it is deducted. Separate pools are set up for industrial buildings, short life assets (see following), plant and machinery used overseas. Assets which also have an element of private use are also given separate pools.

2.1 Capital allowances - general
For a summary of all current rates please see Table 1, p.615.

Expenditure, up to £100,000 p.a., can be claimed on the date it is incurred on plant or machinery, by all businesses that qualify for an Annual Investment Allowance (AIA) at a rate of 100% from the above dates. This decreases to £25,000 from 1/6 April 2012. Where the accounting period straddles 1 April 2012, a prorated rate will apply. See Table 2, p.616.

Expenditure on any excess of the AIA on plant or machinery, can claim a writing down allowance @ 20% (decreasing to 18% from April 2012) on the excess in the year of purchase.

The rate will apply to the first year for which allowances are due. If the full AIA allowances are not claimed in the first year, in subsequent years, only writing down allowances (WDA) will be due on the balance remaining at 20% (18% from April 2012) (or 10% (8% from April 2012) if in the special pool) after the deduction of allowances claimed in prior years.

Hybrid rates of WDA will apply to accounting periods spanning April 2012's decrease in WDA from 20% to 18% and 10% to 8%. See Table 4, p.621 & Table 5, p.623.

Small or medium sized defined:
The rate will apply to businesses which are small or medium-sized using the following definitions. These are broadly that it satisfies two of the following conditions:

'Related' companies and businesses
Where a person or persons control(s) one or more unincorporated businesses or companies, (but not a combination of the two, as the entitlement to an AIA for

companies is considered totally separately from that for unincorporated businesses, and vice versa) then the entitlement to one or more AIA will depend on whether either 'the shared premises' or 'similar activities' condition is met.

If either of these conditions is met then the companies or unincorporated businesses will be 'related' and so only entitled to a single AIA between them.

For businesses under common control, the two conditions are considered on a financial year basis for companies and on a tax year basis for unincorporated businesses:

	Turnover	Balance sheet total	No. of employees
Small	£5.6m	£2.8m	50
Medium	£22.8m	£11.4m	250
or was small or medium-sized for the previous year			

Annual Investment Allowance (AIA)

A business will be able to claim the AIA on the first £100,000 (£25,000 from April 2012) spent on plant or machinery, long-life assets or integral features, but not cars, see Table 2, p.616. Where businesses spend more than £100,000 in any chargeable period, any additional expenditure will be dealt with as usual in either the special rate of 10% (8% from April 2012) or main pool of 20% (18% form April 2012), where it will attract WDAs at the appropriate rate.

Hybrid rates of WDA will apply to accounting periods spanning the April 2012 decrease in WDA from 20% to 18% and 10% to 8%. See Table 4, p.621 and Table 5, p.623.

The AIA is available to:

- any individual carrying on a qualifying activity (this includes trades, professions, vocations, ordinary property businesses and individuals having an employment or office);

- any partnership consisting only of individuals; and

- any company (subject to limitations).

A point to note is that although a company can only ever have one AIA at most, no matter how many qualifying activities it carries on. In fact individuals and partnerships are entitled to a different AIA for each separate qualifying business they carry on as long as the activities are carried on from different premises.

Shorter or long periods

Where a business has a chargeable period which is more or less than a year, the maximum allowance is proportionately increased or reduced.

Periods spanning change in AIA

However, where a business has a chargeable period that spans 1 April 2012 (corporation tax) or 6 April 2012 (income tax) the maximum allowance is calculated as when the chargeable period began and ended. See Table 2, p.616 for different year ends.

Example of period spanning change in AIA (2010):

Clegg Ltd prepared accounts for the year to 28 February 2011. It bought a new computer costing £5,000 on 20 March 2010.

Section 5, FA Act 2010 gives its maximum AIA for the year ended 28 February 2011 as:

31/365 x £50,000 + 334/365 x £100,000
=4,246 + 91,507 = £95,753

However, in accordance with s 5(5), FA 2010, the maximum AIA for expenditure incurred before the 1 April 2010 is calculated as if the rate had not been amended, and so is £50,000.

In this example, the maximum AIA which Clegg Ltd could claim for its computer was £5,000.

Periods spanning change in AIA (2012)

The 100% annual investment allowance for expenditure incurred each year on most types of plant, was increased to £100,000 by Finance Act 2010 (FA 2010), will be reduced to £25,000 from April 2012.

The increase to £100,000 has effect for expenditure incurred on or after 1 April 2010 for businesses within the charge to corporation tax, and on or after 6 April 2010 for businesses within the charge to income tax (s 5, FA 2010).

The decrease to £25,000 has effect for expenditure incurred on or after 1 April 2012 for businesses within the charge to corporation tax, and on or after 6 April 2012 for businesses within the charge to income tax.

Clauses giving effect to this reduction are contained in Clause 11, Finance Act 2011.

Although the impact of the decrease in Clause 11, Finance Act 2011 is very similar to the impact of the increase in s 5, FA 2010, it is not quite the same. The problem relates to accounting periods which span the two expenditure limits before and after

31 March 2012 or 5 April 2012.

Example:
Hulme Ltd prepares accounts for the year to 30 April 2012. It buys a new computer costing £5,000 on 20 April 2012.

Clause 11(6), Finance Act 2011 gives its maximum AIA for the year ended 30 April 2012 as:

341/366 x £100,000 + 25/366 x £25,000
= 93,169 + 1,708 = £94,877

However, Clause 11(7) limits the AIA for expenditure incurred by a company after 31 March 2012 to the maximum allowance calculated for the part of the period after 31 March 2012. In this example, the maximum AIA is £1,708. Therefore the £5,000 computer qualifies for AIA of only £1,708 - even if the potential for a further AIA on £93,169 from before April 2012 has not been used in full. The balance of the £5,000 will qualify for WDA at a hybrid rate because the accounting period spans 1 April 2012. For the year to 30 April 2012, the applicable rate of WDA is:

341/366 x 20% + 25/366 x 18% = 19.86%

If we compare this legislation to s 5(5), FA 2010, the maximum AIA for expenditure incurred before 1 April 2010 (for companies) was calculated 'as if the amendment ... had not been made'. In most cases, the maximum AIA which can be used to cover expenditure before the change was £50,000.

The current straddling rule prevents the benefit of the increased allowance being taken for expenditure incurred after it ceases to have effect. To achieve an exact mirroring of what happened in 2010, it should be capped at £25,000. People planning even modest expenditure in the period post March 2012 will need to take care.

The only other advice which can be given in cases such as Hulme Ltd is to consider a short life assets election see 1.2 above, p.292 using s 85, Capital Allowances Act 2001. At least if the computer is scrapped after a few years, a balancing allowance will be available for any expenditure which remains unrelieved.

Example showing period not spanning the change in AIA:
Year end 31.03.2012

		£
Year 1a	Cost of asset (not a car)	120,000
	AIA @ 100%	100,000
Year 1b	Balance	20,000
	writing down allowance at 20%	4,000
Year 2	written down value b/f	16,000
	writing down allowance at 20%	3,200
Year 3	written down value b/f	12,800

Claw-back and restriction of AIA

All purchases of plant and machinery made after 1 April 2008, must be added to the main pool (the 20% pool), even where the cost is fully covered by the Annual Investment Allowance (AIA). When one of those items is sold, the disposal proceeds must be deducted from that pool. This can result in a charge (a negative capital allowance) where the balance in the main pool is very small or zero before the sale. This is effectively a clawback of the AIA given.

Example:
Karen opens a shop on 6 April 2011 and spends a total of £30,000 on a van, shelving and a till. All these assets qualify as plant and machinery and the full cost is covered by the AIA for her business of £100,000. In her second year Karen decides she doesn't need the van so sells it for £3,000. Although the balance in her main pool is zero the £3,000 proceeds must be deducted from that pool leading to a balancing charge of £3,000.

2011/2012		£
Purchases		30,000
AIA		(30,000)
WDA c/f		0
2012/2013	Disposals	(3,000)
	Balancing charge	3,000
WDA c/f		0

This clawback of AIA rule also applies to the 10% pool

<u>Leased plant and machinery - rules</u>
The rules are designed to align the tax treatment of lease and loan finance. Capital Allowances on plant and machinery which is subject to a 'long funding lease' is available to the lessee (rather than the lessor as under rules). A long funding lease is very broadly a finance lease with a term of more than five years.

AIA practical points and issues

*   Driving school cars. Driving school cars are not treated as cars for capital allowance purposes. Therefore are available for AIA. (Capital Allowances Manual 6A 23510).

*   HMRC have sought to disallow a claim for AIA (FYA) on a van owing to an element of private use. the inspector claimed that the private use element made it a 'car'.

    The legislation in ITEPA 2003 and CAA 2001 are very similar on the point but not identical. The Chartered Institute of Taxation has requested guidance and clarification.

<u>AIA and Tax credits</u>
The allowance can result in a large reduction in taxable income where a taxpayer has made a significant capital purchase. This reduction could make a taxpayer eligible for tax credits, but by the time you have the information to realise this, your client may have missed the chance to claim from the beginning of the relevant tax year, and maybe lost several thousand pounds. This is because tax credits are based on income for the year as a whole.

Take the example of a self-employed plumber who has two children at school and is earning about £35,000 p.a. he buys a van costing £20,000. Let's assume that he had not claimed tax credits before because it was 'too much hassle for £500'. In the year in which he buys the van (2008/2009) he would be entitled to tax credits of over £5,600. Provided that his income in the following year is not more than £25,000 higher, he will be entitled to a further £5,600.

As tax credits can only be backdated by three months from the date of the claim, the client will lose out unless his claim is in place at the beginning of the year. To avoid a risk of professional negligence claims, it may be prudent to suggest that all clients who are eligible make protective claims for tax credits. These may initially show £nil but may result in much higher claims when adjusted for the lower income after claiming AIA.

<u>AIA and mortgage applications</u>
When assessing mortgage finance, many mortgage providers now ask for details of

net taxable profits of a sole trader or partner, rather than accounts profits. Now that we have the annual investment allowance (AIA), these taxable profits may be very low in some years where there has been significant capital expenditure.

Practitioners may wish to discuss the effect of a large AIA on their clients' ability to secure appropriate finance, as the client may prefer to defer the allowance if they are likely to need finance in the near future.

2.2 Other 100% first year allowances

(a)   Capital R&D expenditure on scientific research related to the trade is eligible for an allowance of 100% in the year when the expenditure was incurred. Likewise revenue expenditure, including contributions to approved bodies for scientific research is allowable as a charge against profits when incurred. (Please see Scientific Research, p.330).

(b)   Converting flats over shops, see Part 9 - 3.3 Capital allowances for flats and shops, p.347.

(c)   Investments in designated energy-efficient plant and water saving equipment will be able to claim 100% first year allowance.

Under the scheme, businesses that invest in qualifying energy-saving technologies will be able to write off immediately the whole cost against their taxable profits.

Qualifying technologies
100% capital allowances can be obtained on environmentally beneficial technology in three categories:

(i)   Energy saving plant and machinery.
(ii)   Low carbon dioxide cars.
(iii)   Water conservation plant and machinery.

From 1 August 2011 a new website gives further details: http://etl.decc.gov.uk/etl.

First year tax credits - for companies only
Originally proposed as 'payable enhanced capital allowances' in HMRCs technical note of 17 December 2007, Finance Act 2008 renames the proposed relief as 'first-year tax credits' in a new Schedule A1 to CAA 2001.

The rules for first year tax credits follow a similar mechanism that applies to R&D and, in broad terms, allows a company to claim a payable tax credit if it has a 'surrenderable loss' attributable to 100% first year allowances on relevant first year expenditure.

Relevant first year expenditure is expenditure on energy saving plant and machinery (section 45A CAA 2001) or environmentally beneficial plant and machinery (section 45H) incurred in between 1 April 2008 and 31 March 2013.

The surrenderable loss is the 'unrelieved loss' in carrying on a qualifying activity (being a trade, ordinary property business, overseas property business, a furnished holiday lettings business or from managing investments) but limited to the amount of the 100% FYAs.

Detailed provisions are included in Schedule A1 for calculating the unrelieved loss. Essentially, where the loss could be used to set-off the company's own other taxable profits in the same period or surrendered as group relief then it may not be surrendered for a first year tax credit. Any losses available to carry forward are reduced by the amount of the loss surrendered.

The first year tax credit is 19% of the surrenderable loss but capped by an upper limit, being the higher of the company's PAYE and NICs liabilities and £250,000.

For example, a company incurs £200,000 on expenditure qualifying for 100% ECAs and claims £200,000. The company makes a loss of £300,000 after deducting ECAs and therefore may surrender up to £200,000 of that loss. The payable ECA will be £38,000 (19% of £200,000).

ECA payments will however be clawed back by HMRC where a relevant asset is sold or disposed of within four years of the end of the chargeable period for which the tax credit was paid, except to the extent that the company makes a net loss on disposal.

For example, a company spends £5m on qualifying expenditure, makes a loss of £10m and surrenders £5m to receive an ECA payment of £950,000 (19% of £5m). Two years later it sells the asset for £4m. HMRC would recoup £760,000 (19% of £4m). the company effectively benefits by £190,000 overall being 19% on the net loss of £1m.

The quid pro quo of the clawback is that losses previously surrendered are restored. These may be relieved under another provision if still within statutory time limits.

(d)   FA2003 CL 166 and Sch 30 added investment in designated water efficient technologies. The qualifying technology categories are meters, flow controllers, leakage detection equipment, efficient taps and efficient toilets.

The government has also announced that it will introduce further categories to the list.

Details of the criteria that must be met by qualifying technologies and products can be found on the internet at www.eca.gov.uk.

(e) Business premises renovation allowance
It has been confirmed that business premises renovation allowances will be extended for a further five years from April 2012. These were due to expire on 11 April 2012, and had been recommended for abolition by the Office of Tax Simplification in its final report on the review of reliefs.

FA2005 introduced a scheme enabling people or companies who own or lease property that has been vacant for a year or more in designated disadvantaged areas of the UK to claim full tax relief on their capital spending on the conversion or renovation of the property, in order to bring it back into business use. The scheme came into effect from 11.4.07.

Business Premises Renovation Allowance (BPRA) provides 100% initial allowance for capital expenditure on the renovation or conversion of business properties that have been vacant for a year or longer in designated disadvantaged areas of the UK. It provides an enhanced rate of allowance for expenditure that currently qualifies for capital allowances, and new relief for renovation expenditure on commercial buildings (such as offices and shops), which does not currently qualify for any capital allowances.

Since the scheme was first announced two changes have been made. Disadvantaged areas are now defined as Northern ireland and the areas specified as development areas by the Assisted Areas Order 2007. All EU Member States are required to define a new set of Assisted Areas for the period 2007 to 2013, in accordance with the European Commission's Regional Aid Guidelines, published on 21.12.05. The previous Assisted Areas expired on 31.12.06. The EC granted approval of the UK's new Assisted Areas on 20.12.06 (State Aid N673/2006).

A postcode database, derived from The 2007 Assisted Area Map can be found online at www.dtistats.net/regional-aa/aa2007.asp.

Secondly, excluded from scheme are any premises that are refurbished by, or used by, businesses engaged in the following trades:

- fisheries and aquaculture;
- shipbuilding;
- the coal industry;
- the steel industry;
- synthetic fibres;
- the primary production of certain agricultural products; and

- the manufacture of products which imitate or substitute for milk or milk products.

(f)   Low emission cars
Cars with CO_2 emissions equal to or below 110gm/km receive capital allowances of 100% until 1 April 2013.

2.3 Writing down allowances (WDA)
These are annual allowances which may be claimed in the year in which the cost of the asset was incurred (if not covered by AIA) and for each year thereafter until sale or disposal otherwise of the asset.

20% Pool (becomes 18% pool from April 2012)
For most plant and machinery the allowance is calculated at 20% on the pool value, on cost in the first year and on the written down balance in subsequent years, i.e. on a reducing balance basis. From 1 April 2009 cars purchased with emissions ≤160 gm/km on cost price are included.

10% Pool (becomes 8% pool from April 2012) Integral features and thermal insulation
A new asset classification of 'integral features' is added to 'List C' in section 23 CAA 2001 that will be allocated to the new 'special rate' pool and attracts a writing down allowance of 10%. The lower rate of 10%, HMRC argue, reflects more closely their economic depreciation.

The list of assets (incurred on or after 1 April 2008 for companies and 6 April 2008 for businesses within the charge to income tax) are in a new section 33A CAA 2001:

- Electrical systems (including lighting systems);

- Cold water systems;

- Space or water heating systems, powered systems of ventilation, air cooling or air purification, and any floor or ceiling comprised in such systems;

- Lifts, escalators and moving walkways;

- External solar shading (brise soleil).

The inclusion of electrical and cold water systems is notable not only as they were previously excluded (in most cases) from 'plant and machinery' but their inclusion going forward means that enhanced capital allowances can be claimed on specific items in these systems that are on the 'green technology' ECA list.

The Government proposes to allow environmentally beneficial features incorporated in modern buildings to qualify for the integral features allowance. The revised list included brise soleil and active facades, but further technologies to add to the list are being considered. Active facades were then removed from the list published in the Finance Bill.

Section 33A also provides that where either the whole or more than 50% of the integral feature is replaced in a 12-month period then a revenue deduction is not allowed and the expenditure instead qualifies for 10% WDAs. The 'more than 50%' test is determined by reference to the replacement cost of the asset when expenditure is first incurred within the 12-month period in question.

Thermal insulation, which previously only qualified when incorporated in an industrial building, now qualifies (effective from 1 April / 6 April) for 10% WDAs in the 'special rate' pool when added to any existing buildings, used for any qualifying business purpose, other than residential property businesses.

Expenditure in the main pool incurred prior to April 2008, which would fall to be integral features, will effectively be grandfathered and continue to receive the higher rate of plant and machinery allowances (20%). Integral features (and long-life assets) incurred after April 2008 will receive 10% even if the accounting period straddles the date of the rule change.

For accounting periods straddling 1 April 2012
The hybrid rate is arrived at by calculating the proportion of a chargeable period falling before the change date and the corresponding proportion falling after the change date.

For example, if a company's chargeable period began on 1 January 2012 and ends on 31 December 2012, roughly one quarter of that period would fall before the date of the change (on 1 April 2012) and roughly three-quarters would fall after that date. The calculation, using days, of the hybrid rate on the main rate of WDAs would therefore be as follows, (See Table 4, p.621 and Table 5, p.623 for different year ends):

For the 'main' pool	For the 'special' pool
91/366 x 20%= 4.973%	91/366 x 10% = 2.49%
Plus 275/366 x 18% = 13.525%	275/366 x 8% = 6.01%
Therefore, the hybrid rate for the transitional period = 18.498%	Therefore, the hybrid rate for the transitional period = 8.5%

Cars purchased after April 2009 have their WDA split according to emissions equal to or below 160 gm/k 20% and above 10%. The limit on cars costing more than £12,000 was lifted for new purchases but remains for cars owned prior to April 2009.

Small pools - write off

Finance Act 2008 enables businesses to claim a WDA of up to £1,000 in the case of each pool, once the unrelieved expenditure in either the main rate pool and/or the integral fixtures pool is £1,000 or less. This will write off small historic pool balances immediately so that small claims of ever decreasing amounts will no longer be needed going forward.

The measure had effect for chargeable periods beginning on or after 1 April 2008 for businesses within the charge to corporation tax and on or after 6 April 2008 for businesses within the charge to income tax.

Businesses investing in plant and machinery, particularly small and micro businesses, may find that their expenditure will be fully relieved by the annual investment allowance (AIA). If however, they are left with a small pool balance, this will also be written off immediately.

Example:
Writing off small pools

Mr Singh's 2006/2007 tax computations show the carried forward TWDV of his main pool to be £2,000. He prepares his accounts to 5 April each year. In 2007/2008 he incurs expenditure of £500 on office equipment, and £750 on a heating system. In 2008/2009 he incurs further expenditure of £1,100 on additions to the heating system.

For the purposes of this example, the impact of the AIA is ignored (one may assume, for example, that it has been used in another business controlled by Mr Singh).

	Main pool £	Special rate pool £
2007/2008		
Brought forward	2,000	
Additions	1,250	
	3,250	
WDA @ 25%	(813)	
	2,437	
2008/2009		
Additions		1,100
WDA @ 20%/10%	(487)	(110)
	1,950	990

	£	£
2009/2010		
WDA @ 20%	(390)	
Write off pool		
(<£1,000)		(990)
	1,560	Nil
2010/2011		
WDA @ 20%	(312)	
	1,248	
2011/2012		
WDA @ 20%	(250)	
	998	
2012/2013		
Write off pool		
(<£1,000)	(998)	
	Nil	

10% Pool

For a <u>Long Life Assets</u> 10% rate applies to businesses spending more than £100,000 p.a. on plant and machinery with an expected working life of at least 25 years. It does not apply to plant and machinery which is (i) second-hand where the 25% rate applied to the vendor; (ii) in a building used wholly or mainly as, or for purposes ancillary to, a dwelling-house, retail shop, showroom, hotel or office; (iii) motor cars; or (iv) sea-going ships and railway assets purchased before 31 December 2010. For companies, the £100,000 de minimis limit is divided by one plus the number of associated companies (if any).

2.4 Balancing allowances

A balancing allowance may be claimed where the proceeds of selling an asset (not included in the plant and machinery pool) are less than the written down value, in the case of non-pool assets.

Thus in Maxime Ltd.

			£
2007/2008	Cost of asset		16,000
	writing down allowance at 25%		4,000
2008/2009	written down value		12,000
	writing down allowance at 20%		2,400
2009/2010	written down value		9,600
	sale proceeds		7,000
	balancing allowance		2,600
Net cost of asset: £16,000 - £7,000 =			9,000
(Cost less sale proceeds)			
Allowances claimed: £4,000 + £2,400 + £2,600 =			9,000
(Assuming a year end of 31 March)			

2.5 Balancing charge

A balancing charge arises where the proceeds of selling an asset (not included in a pool) are greater than the written down value, thus:

			£
2007/2008	Cost of asset		16,000
	writing down allowance at 25%		4,000
2008/2009	written down balance		12,000
	writing down allowance at 20%		2,400
2009/2010	written down balance		9,600
	sale proceeds		12,000
	balancing charge		2,400
Net cost of asset: £16,000 - £12,000 =			4,000
(Cost less sale proceeds)			
Allowances claimed: £4,000 + £2,400 - £2,400 =			4,000

For plant and machinery consolidated into a pool a balancing charge (or allowance) or in a 10% long life pool arises only on the cessation of the business, because in a continuing business the proceeds of selling one of the assets is deducted from the written down balance in the pool, and subsequent writing down allowances can be claimed on that balance. A balancing charge or allowance may, however, arise when individual assets, such as motor cars with private use, are allocated to separate pools.

2.6 Sale of asset at profit on cost

Where the sale proceeds of selling an asset exceed the original cost the amount to be deducted from the written down value is the cost, not the sale proceeds. This treatment applies to the plant and machinery pool, as well as other pools or individual assets subject to capital allowances. For this reason it is necessary to maintain records of the cost of each asset. The excess of the price obtained over the cost plus expenses is likely to be subject to a charge for capital gains. The following example illustrates the treatment.

		£
2010/2011	Cost of original asset	250,000
	AIA *	100,000
2011/2012	written down balance	150,000
	allowance at 20%	30,000
2012/2013	written down balance	120,000
	sold for 270,000, deduct cost only	250,000
	balancing charge	130,000

£100,000 + £30,000 - £130,000 = £0

* Note - this simplified example ignors that WDA @ 20% on £150,000 could also have been claimed in 2010/2011.

In the case of the sale of an asset included in the plant and machinery pool, and assuming the sale proceeds exceed the cost of the asset, the deduction of the cost of the asset sold has the following effect: the written down balance on the pool is now reduced so that the lower level of writing down allowances will mean that the excess allowances on the asset sold will be recovered. If the sale proceeds exceed the balance in the pool the difference represents a balancing charge.

2.7 Renewals basis for plant and machinery

Instead of capital allowances relief for capital expenditure on plant and machinery may be claimed on a renewals basis. This means that in the year of the expenditure the amount which may be claimed is the cost of the new asset less the sale price of the old asset and any improvements made to the old asset. The renewals basis may be changed to writing down allowances at any time provided the change covers all assets subject to the renewals basis. The written down value for this purpose will be calculated by assuming that writing down allowances had applied each year to the assets concerned.

Capital allowances - repairs to integral features

Revenue & Customs Brief 66/08 includes very helpful draft guidance and related matters in respect of the Capital Allowances Finance Act 2008 changes, including draft revisions to the Capital Allowances Manual. this can be found at http://www.hmrc.gov.uk/briefs/company-tax/brief6608.htm.

CA22340 deals specifically with the replacement of integral features, rather than the repair. If it is replacement, the expenditure will attract WDAs at 10% in the special rate pool.

Expenditure >50% of replacement cost
Where expenditure on an integral feature amounts to the whole or more than 50% of its replacement cost, either at once or within any rolling period of 12 months, such expenditure is treated as capital expenditure for capital allowance purposes, and cannot be deducted as a revenue expense.

The manual states that HMRC intend to adopt a "light touch" approach in respect of these provisions, and do not expect the need for running totals of expenditure of special or precise valuations. They believe that, in most cases, taxpayers will know whether an integral feature has worn out and whether they would plan to replace the bulk of it within the next year.

There are a few examples are given in the tax brief to clarify how the legislation is intended to work:

Here is one example:

Jack decides to replace the electrical system in his factory. The cost of replacing the whole system is around £100,000. Jack's business's chargeable period ends on 31 December each year. He pays £40,000 towards the new system on 31/12/08 and pays the balance of £60,000 on 30/06/09 after the work is completed. Although Jack's initial expenditure in the 2008 chargeable period on beginning to replace the integral feature represented only 40% of the replacement cost, that initial expenditure plus the further expenditure incurred within 12 months represented more than 50% of the replacement cost and so the total expenditure is deemed to be capital expenditure and should be allocated to the special (10%) rate pool.

3 BASIS PERIOD: YEAR IN WHICH ALLOWANCE MADE

If the expenditure is incurred before trading commences then it is regarded as having been incurred on the day trading commenced.

Under the current year basis of assessment capital allowances are given for accounting periods and treated as trading expenditure or receipts (as appropriate).

4 SUBSIDIES AND GRANTS

Subsidies or grants towards the expenditure which are made by the Crown or any public or local authority, or by any other person for the purpose of a trade carried on by the recipient or his or her tenant, must be deducted from the expenditure before capital allowances are computed unless it is granted under Part I of the Industry Act 1972 (or corresponding N. Ireland enactment) or Part II of the Industrial Development Act 1982. The other person referred to (or the tenant) can, of course, claim capital allowances in respect of the subsidy or grant so paid.

5 CONTRIBUTIONS TOWARDS CAPITAL EXPENDITURE

Where a person (who is not a connected person) contributes towards capital expenditure by another person in respect of an asset for that person's or a tenant's trade the contribution will rank for capital allowance. It applies to a contribution towards the provision of trade effluent treatment assets by a sewerage authority, but not an extension pipe to connect up with the sewerage system, as this in a particular case was held to be for the conveyance of the effluent, not the treatment of it, and furthermore was not machinery or plant in relation to the company's business (Bridge House Ltd v Hinder CA 1971).

Where the contributions are received from a connected person, the capital allowances are granted to the recipient and not the contributor. FA 1993 s 114.

Where a lessee of a building or land incurs capital expenditure on assets which form part of the fabric of the building or land and which become landlord's fixtures he or she will be entitled to claim capital allowances on the expenditure.

6 SUCCESSIONS TO TRADES

Where a person succeeds to a trade including its plant without it being sold there is deemed to be a sale at market value on the date of succession, subject to the right of a beneficiary of a will or intestacy to elect to adopt the lower of that value or written-down value. Following such an election, any balancing charge will be computed as if the allowances given to the predecessor were given to the successor. The successor will not be entitled to initial allowance nor first year allowance.

Where a succession to a trade is by a person connected with the previous trader and both parties are chargeable to UK tax on the profits, they can make an election for the capital allowances to be granted as if the trade had continued in the same ownership, i.e. the purchaser takes the assets at their tax written down value. The election has to be made within two years of the succession. Connected persons are as defined in TA 1988 s 840 and in addition to those covered by that definition the following are treated as being connected:

* one party is a partnership and the other has the right to a share in that partnership;

* one party is a company and the other controls it;

* both parties are partnerships and some other person has the right to a share in both of them; or

* both parties are companies, or one of them is a partnership and the other is a company and in either case, some other person has control over both parties.

In *Parmar & others (t/a Ace Knitwear) v Woods* Spc 291 (2001), the taxpayers traded in partnership as Ace Knitwear between 1979 and 1994. Unfortunately, there was a fire at the premises in April 1988 and a further fire at the taxpayers premises in October 1991, both involving significant insurance claims for loss of machinery, plant, stock and profits. From the receipt of insurance proceeds replacement machinery and plant was purchased in order to recommence trading. Towards the end of 1994 two of the partners retired from business and the two remaining partners wished to carry on the business and formed a limited company, Ace Knitwear Limited. The assets of the partnership including stock and machinery were transferred to the company but no payments were made by the company for the transfer. The company commenced trading on 1 January 1995 but in 1998 went into voluntary liquidation and was wound up with debts of £444,000.

HMRC commenced an investigation into the taxpayers affairs and raised assessments for 1992/93 through to 1994/95. The taxpayers appealed against the assessments contending, among other things, that the disposal value of the machinery destroyed by fire in 1991 exceeded the original amounts paid on the provision of that machinery and that on the discontinuance of the trade and transfer to Ace Knitwear Limited in 1994 there was not disposal of the machinery to the company as no payment was received for it by the taxpayers. The Special Commissioner considered a number of areas but on the questions as to whether the discontinuance of the trade in 1994 a nil value should be used for capital allowances purposes, the Commissioner did not accept that there was no disposal for the purpose of the capital allowances legislation if no money was received. The scheme of the legislation was that any disposal which was less than the market price was treated as a disposal at market value and this value should also be used where there is a succession to the trade.

7 OTHER SALES AND TRANSFERS

The open-market price will also be adopted instead of the actual price (or insurance, salvage or compensation monies) where:

- the trade is discontinued or transferred to another person and not treated as discontinued but the asset continues to be owned by the trader;

- the asset is given away or sold at less than market price;

- the plant is transferred to use other than in the trade.

These provisions have been extended to include, not only industrial buildings, but also qualifying hotels, commercial buildings in enterprise zones and scientific research assets.

Where the purchaser of such plant can claim capital allowance and both parties elect the asset may be treated as having been sold at market value or written down value, whichever is the lower. Balancing charges arising after the transfer are computed as if allowances given to the transferor were given to the transferee.

8 COMPOSITE SALES

If assets ranking for capital allowance are sold together with any other assets, the total price must be apportioned reasonably. A valuation of separate assets which is not reasonable will not be adopted even if the separate amounts are set out in the sale agreement.

9 DEMOLITION OF PLANT OR MACHINERY

Where any machinery or plant used for the purpose of a trade is demolished the net cost of the demolition (i.e. cost less any relevant receipts) is treated as follows:

(a)   If the plant or machinery is replaced. The net costs of the demolition are added to the cost of the replacement asset for the purpose of capital allowances thereon.

(b)   If the asset is not replaced. The capital expenditure on the asset is increased by the net cost of demolition for the purpose of calculating a balancing allowance or balancing charge on the disposal of the asset.

10 INTANGIBLES

A regime was introduced for the treatment of intellectual property goodwill and other intangible assets acquired by companies after 1 April 2002.

What originally began as a review of the taxation of intellectual property has now been widened to extend to most non-financial intangible assets, following the accounting definition in FRS 10. In addition to intellectual property this covers know-how, secret information, goodwill, quotas and franchises.

The new rules treat all expenditure on such assets as being of a revenue rather than a capital nature with the tax treatment following the accounting treatment. Thus the rate of amortisation in the accounts will also be applied for tax purposes. The downside is that the sale of intangibles such as goodwill will not be treated as a chargeable gain but as a trading receipt. Nevertheless, a form of rollover relief is available to the extent that the excess of the proceeds on sale over cost may be deducted from the cost of reinvestment in intangible assets. There is no deduction for internally generated goodwill nor for goodwill arising on consolidation or incorporation.

The new rules only apply to companies and only in respect of expenditure on intangible assets incurred on or after 1 April 2002. In exceptional cases, where the intangible assets are not amortised, a 4% per annum straight line amortisation may be claimed purely for tax purposes. A revaluation surplus is taxable but only to the extent of recovering amortisation previously written off. There are a number of anti-avoidance provisions to prevent the artificial utilisation of non-trading credits or where there has been a change in ownership and an increase in capital or a major change in the conduct or nature of the business.

Group treatment of intangible assets broadly follows the capital gains tax rules and allows tax neutral intra-group transfers. There are degrouping charges on subsidiaries owning intangibles leaving a group, where intra-group transfers have previously taken place, subject to rollover relief. Certain assets such as rights in or over land, oil licenses, financial assets and rights in companies, trusts or partnerships are generally excluded from the new rules relating to intangibles. Films and sound recordings and computer software may be dealt with under existing rules.

Related party transactions are deemed to take place at market value.

The hold-over relief on the incorporation of a business cannot be used to bring existing goodwill etc. into the new regime, as it would be a tax neutral transfer, whereby the tax history is taken over by the acquirer. In other words, in these cases goodwill will continue to be treated under the old regime.

There is a deemed disposal and reacquisition at market value where companies cease to be within the charge to corporation tax, but there is no corresponding step-up in value on a company, for example, becoming resident in the UK. Interestingly, it is possible to treat the acquisition of shares in the company owning intangibles acquired from a third party as if it was an acquisition of the underlying intangible property, on making the appropriate claim.

The new rules are highly complex but have been subject to extensive consultation. The old rules continue to apply for intellectual property acquired prior to 1 April 2002 by companies and for unincorporated businesses, including partnerships. There are now effectively two regimes for intellectual property. Because acquisitions by companies from 1 April 2002 of goodwill and quotas are brought under the new rules it is no longer possible to rollover chargeable gains into the acquisition of such assets, even where the original disposal took place prior to 1 April 2002.

Example: Peter Ltd. disposed of goodwill at a gain before 1 April 2002. After 1 April 2002 but before 1 April 2005 it reinvested the proceeds into buying further goodwill. Peter Ltd. will, broadly speaking, be entitled to roll-over the capital gain under the Intangible Asset rules at Sch 29.

Peter Ltd. will not be entitled to claim old-style capital gains roll-over relief; nor (except in some unusual circumstances) will it be entitled to claim deferral relief under FA2002. But Peter Ltd. can still claim old-style CG roll-over if it reinvests into tangible assets.

11 ANTI-AVOIDANCE PROVISIONS

11.0 Anti-avoidance law

Finance Act 2010 (FA 2010) introduced targeted anti-avoidance legislation that applies where there is a change in ownership of a trade carried on by a company at a point where the tax written down value (TWDV) of its plant and machinery exceeds the balance sheet value of those assets. The legislation only affects instances where the main purpose, or one of the main purposes of the change in ownership, was the obtaining of a tax advantage.

Where the legislation has affect, the amount by which the TWDV of a pool exceeds the balance sheet value is transferred to a new pool and future losses generated by allowances on that new pool are restricted. These provisions generally have affect from 21 July 2009, although certain elements only apply where the change in ownership occurred on or after 9 December 2009.

If a company has excess trading losses, it has been an established planning method to disclaim capital allowances in order to reduce the amount of any unutilised current year trading loss carried forward. By doing this, the company is able to claim higher capital allowances in a future period, which in turn can lead to the creation of, or increase in, a current year trading loss at that time. This can give the company a tax advantage, as the current year trading loss can be set against other profits of the company in that year or could be group relieved, whereas a brought forward loss would only be able to be set against future profits of that same trade. HM Revenue & Customs' concern was that this well known idea was then developed into various planning devices to create a pool of unclaimed capital allowances that were then sold to a profitable company in order to reduce their tax liability.

Section 26 and Sch 4 of FA 2010 inserts a new chapter 16A (made up of s212A through to s212S) into the Capital Allowances Act 2001. This new chapter contains provisions that target these types of schemes where there is a change of ownership of a company and the main, or one of the main, purposes of the change in ownership was the obtaining of a tax advantage. HMRC issued a technical note on this area on 9 December 2009, which can be viewed on its website - www.hmrc.gov.uk/pbr2009/capital-allowance-5405.pdf.

11.1 Artificial sales, common control, connected persons lease back

Where an asset is sold with the main object of obtaining capital allowance, and where there is common control of buyer and seller, HMRC may ignore the actual sale price for the purpose of capital allowances and adopt in its place the open market value (or, if lower, the cost price in the case of machinery and plant).

If it is simply a case of common control without the object of tax avoidance, and the parties are both resident in the UK, they may elect to have the written down value at the date of sale adopted instead. In this event, no balancing allowance or charge will arise on that sale, but when the asset is ultimately sold to a third party, a balancing allowance (or charge) will be given to the first buyer just as if there had been no change of ownership at the first sale, i.e. the seller's computation is continued.

The election has to be made within two years of the date of the sale.

Common control occurs where the buyer is a body of persons controlled by the seller, or vice versa, or where both buyer and seller are bodies of persons and some other person has control (i.e. the power to secure the affairs are conducted in accordance with his or her wishes) over both of them. Shares held as a trustee are not regarded as being available to establish control of a company as the trustee must vote in accordance with the terms of the trust and not his own wishes (*CIR v Lithgows Ltd* CS 1960). FA 1993 s 117, FA 1994 s 119.

11.2 Time when capital expenditure is incurred

Capital expenditure is deemed to be incurred on the date when the obligation to pay becomes unconditional, whether or not there is a later date by which the payment has to be made. However, where the credit period has been extended to an unreasonable delay or the obligation has been brought forward to an artificially early date, the date on which the expenditure is deemed to be incurred will be as follows.

- Where the obligation to pay becomes unconditional more than four months before the amount in question has to be paid, the date is the date on or before which it is required to be paid.

- Where the obligation to pay becomes unconditional on a date earlier than that which accords with normal commercial usage and the sole or main benefits arising would be to bring forward the expenditure into an earlier accounting or basis period, the date is the date on or before which it is required to be paid whether or not that date is more than four months after the obligation to pay becomes unconditional.

11.3 Winding up of businesses to create balancing allowances

Under the old rules, expenditure on cars costing over £12,000 was allocated to a single asset pool and the WDAs were restricted. When the car was disposed of, the pool ceased and there was a balancing adjustment, often a balancing allowance.

Under the new rules, when cars are disposed of, the disposal proceeds will be deducted from the appropriate pool and there will be no balancing adjustment unless it is the final chargeable period of the business. The final chargeable period for the main pool or the special rate pool is the chargeable period in which the qualifying activity is permanently discontinued.

CAA2001 - new s104F applies if a company:

- incurs expenditure on cars which is allocated to the special rate pool;

- the qualifying activity carried on by the company is permanently discontinued; and

- three further conditions are met.

The three conditions are:

- the qualifying activity consisted of or included (other than incidentally) making cars available to other persons;

- at any time in the six months after the qualifying activity is permanently discontinued, the qualifying activity of a company in the same group consists of or includes making cars available to other persons; and

- the balancing allowance to which the taxpayer would be entitled (but for s104F) in respect of the special rate pool is greater than the total of the balancing charges (if any) to which the taxpayer is liable for the final chargeable period in respect of any pool less the total of the balancing allowances to which they are entitled to for that period in respect of any pool other than the special rate pool.

The new s104F restricts the balancing allowance due to the company that permanently discontinues the activity to an amount equal to any balancing charges it might have. Any surplus balancing allowance is treated as notional expenditure incurred by the other company with a qualifying activity which consists of or includes making cars available to other persons, regardless of whether or not they own any cars previously owned by the company that ceased the qualifying activity.

The taxpayer can nominate, not more than six months after the end of their final chargeable period, which company is to be treated as having incurred the notional expenditure. In the absence of such a nomination by the taxpayer, HMRC can nominate the relevant company. The other company is treated as having incurred the expenditure on the day after the end of the taxpayer's final chargeable period.

12 INDUSTRIAL BUILDINGS ALLOWANCE (IBA)

Abolished with effect from 1 April 2011 for companies (6 April for income taxpayers) (Please see previous edition for details).

13 POINTS OF NOTE & TRIBUNAL RULINGS

13.0 Who may claim
The allowance is given to traders, market gardeners, farmers, occupiers of woodlands, professional persons, employees and lessors of the machinery or plant, and against rental income.

13.1 Part private use
The asset must be used for the purposes of the business. Where there is part private use (e.g. a motor car) a proportionate reduction in the allowance is made even where the allowance is already restricted on account of the fact that the particular type of asset was chosen for reasons other than the necessities of the trade (e.g. personal fancy as regards a motor car).

A van may be claimed against the AIA and receive 100% Capital Allowance. However any claims for private use may disqualify the van for any AIA as it becomes akin to a car. Accordingly only a WDA of 20%, before adjustment for private use, becomes claimable.

13.2 Prior usage and gifts
If the machinery or plant has been used by the owner prior to use in the business, and no capital allowance has been given, or has been received by way of gift from a person who has claimed allowances, it is treated as capital expenditure equal to the open market value when it was brought into the business. This is not applicable to exploration, etc. expenditure in connection with mines, oil wells, etc.

13.3 Meaning of machinery and plant
The FA 1994 s 117 attempts to clarify the distinction between structures which do not qualify for capital allowances and those which are plant and machinery. In principle, and subject to a number of exceptions, it is provided that land, buildings and structures are not plant. From 2008/2009, the rate of writing-down allowances on certain fixtures integral to a building is set at 10%. The detailed design and scope of the integral fixtures provisions will be the subject of consultation. Furthermore, the expenditure on plant must be notified to the Inspector of Taxes within 12 months from the filing date of the return.

Assets excluded from plant and machinery for the purpose of capital allowances include assets incorporated in a building or of a kind normally incorporated in a building. Comprehensive examples of assets treated or not treated as plant and machinery are set out in the 1994 Finance Act, to which reference should be made. There will, however, be no change to the treatment of assets which the Courts have held to be plant. In brief, the assets included in the expression 'buildings' are as follows: parts of the building such as walls, floors, ceilings, doors, gates, windows, stairs; shafts for lifts, hoists and escalators; systems of water, electricity, gas, sewerage, drainage, waste disposal, security and fire safety.

Assets which the Courts have held to be plant include: ships; rails of a railway or tramway; knives and lasts with a shoe-making machine (*Hinton v Maden & Ireland Ltd* HL 1959); partitioning which was intended, at the time the building was fitted out, to be moveable (*Jarrold v John Good & Sons* CA 1963); electric wiring, electric light fittings and decor (pictures, plaques, tapestries, etc.) in hotels and public houses (*CIR v Scottish and Newcastle Breweries Ltd* HL 1982); wash basins and lavatories; central heating systems; farmers' milking parlours and grain dryers; designs as part of the cost of blocks, screens, etc., as used in wallpaper and fabric printing (*McVeigh v Arthur Sanderson & Sons Ltd* Ch D 1968); the complete cost of a dry dock, including extensive excavation and concreting (*CIR v Barclay Curle & Co Ltd* HL 1969); water towers (*Margrett v Lowestoft Water & Gas Co* KBD 1935); books used by practising members of any learned professions, e.g. accountants, doctors and lawyers (*Munby v Furlong* CA 1976, see also *Daphne v Shaw* KBD 1926) and storage platforms installed by wholesalers (*Hunt v Henry Quick Ltd* Ch D 1992).

Items held not to be plant and machinery include: stallions at stud (*Earl of Derby v Aylmer* KBD 1915); wallpaper retailers' pattern books (*Rose & Co Ltd v Campbell* Ch D 1967); a canopy over a petrol station (*Dixon v Fitch's Garage Ltd* Ch D 1975); a boat converted into a floating restaurant (*Benson v Yard Arm Club Ltd* CA 1979); false ceilings (*Hampton v Forte Autogrill Ltd* Ch D 1979); a football stand (*Brown v Burnley Football Co Ltd* Ch D 1980); and prefabricated school buildings (*St John's School v Ward* CA 1974). Expenditure on an underground electricity substation was not eligible for capital allowances as a single entity, because the structure as a whole did not perform a plant-like function. So held Chancery Division in *Bradley v London Electricity plc* (1996) STI 1294. The site and building containing a car-wash, although designed specifically for that purpose, were the premises in which the trade was carried on and thus were not plant for the purposes of capital allowances. So held the Court of Appeal in *Attwood v Anduff Car Wash Ltd* (1997) STI 1026, confirming the High Court's decision. The company hiring out items of street furniture was not entitled to capital allowances on the cost of acquiring them (see SpC 84, *J C Decaux (UK) Ltd v Francis* (1996) STI 1041). Capital allowances were not available to an equipment lessor in respect of expenditure incurred prior to 12 July 1984, where the leased equipment became a fixture on the lessee's land and, accordingly, belonged to him. The equipment lessor could claim capital allowances in respect of expenditure incurred after 11 July 1984 under Sch 17, FA 1985, even though the lessee was exempt from tax. So held the House of Lords in *Melluish v BMI* (No 3) and Related Appeals (1995) STI 1607.

Where an asset might be regarded either as part of a building or as plant, the general rule is that where it is part of the setting in which the business is carried on it is not plant, but where it is something with which the business is carried on it is plant. Thus, a school laboratory and gymnasium, made of prefabricated panels not fixed to the ground, were held to be buildings not plant, and the benches and sinks attached to the walls were held to be an integral part of the building (*St John's School v Ward* CA 1974). Whether an asset is part of the setting or not depends, not merely on its physical appearance, but on the function which it serves in relation to the business (*Leeds Permanent Building Society v Proctor* Ch D 1982).

The Special Commissioner held that the construction of **three new greens and holes on a golf course** did not qualify as 'plant' for the purposes of capital allowances. The appellant company owned a golf club that ran a nine-hole course. In the year ended 31 December 1994, it discarded three of the holes and constructed new ones, including the greens. On the evidence presented, the commissioner found that the greens were part of the company's business premises. (see *Family Golf Centres Ltd v Thorne*, SpC 150 (1998) STI 613).

Glasshouses. HMRC has confirmed that its views about features that would need to be present to make a sophisticated glasshouse eligible for capital allowances, as expressed in its Tax Bulletin, Issue 5 (p 46), are still relevant, notwithstanding para 8, 5(2), Sch AA1, CAA 1990. This paragraph does not automatically classify them as plant, but merely prevents their exclusion because they are fixed structures. Each case will, however, continue to be considered on its own merits.

In addition, HMRC has agreed with the National Farmers Union that **sophisticated greenhouses** that qualify for allowances as machinery and plant are not long-life assets for the purposes of ss 38A to 38H, CAA 1990. In view of advances in technology, HMRC proposes that this agreement should include only expenditure incurred up to 31 December 2005 and that, if in the interim glasshouses are developed that have a life exceeding 25 years, they will be outside the agreement. Taxpayers, for their part, are not bound by this agreement and are free to argue individual cases.

A **swimming pool** on a camp site, though physically part of the setting, in relation to the business carried on had the function of plant and the whole expenditure thereon was eligible (*Cooke v Beach Station Caravans Ltd* Ch D 1974). Similarly, a **'purpose-built' dye-house** incorporating many structural features necessitated by the manufacturing carried on within, was regarded as 'in the nature of a tool' (except as regards external walls and the roof) and not merely a special factory (*Wangaratta Woollen Mills Ltd v Comm. of Taxation* HC Australia 1969). Further, the **whole of a**

grain silo of an importer including its external walls and roof, has been held to be plant (*Schofield v R & H Hall Ltd* CA(NI) 1974), the external structure not being capable of rational existence independently of the plant within it. Ceilings and tilings and wall coverings which have a special function in relation to the trade are plant.

An item does not need to be mechanically active at all, provided it performs a function in relation to that trade (*Hinton v Maden & Ireland Ltd* HL 1959) which goes beyond keeping out the elements and providing shelter for people or equipment. These principles are applicable with slight modification to retailing as well as to manufacturing, repairing or wholesaling.

13.4 Synthetic football pitch qualifies as plant

Anchor International Ltd v IRC (2003) SpC 354 case provides an excellent analysis of the requirements for expenditure to qualify as plant and concerns the availability of capital allowances for plant and machinery in respect of expenditure on synthetic football pitches.

A Limited's trading activity was the provision of leisure facilities, it incurred capital expenditure on the construction of five-a-side football pitches which included excavation, infilling, draining, geo-textile material and sand filled synthetic grass carpet. The carpet had an expected life of between 5 and 9 years depending on use. A limited claimed capital allowances in respect of expenditure on machinery and plant but HMRC considered that the expenditure was excluded by what was Capital Allowances Act 1990 Schedule AA1 para 2 which provided that expenditure on the provision of machinery or plant did not include expenditure on any structure or any other asset which fell within Table 2 Column 1. HMRC further contended that the foundation works and the carpet were to be treated as a whole (the pitch) since it was constructed as an entity and the carpet on its own was of no use for playing football without the works underneath. "Structure" was defined in paragraph 5 as a fixed structure of any kind other than a building. HMRC further contended that the pitch and the carpet were the premises at which A Limited carried on its business not with which it carried it on, in other words it was part of the setting rather than performing a function within the trade.

The Special Commissioner considered that the carpet and the foundations were not an entirety and that the relevant item for consideration was the carpet alone not the pitch as a whole. The carpet had a separate identity, it would wear out and when completely worn out the works underneath would be retained. He considered that this was analogous to a heavy machine standing on a concrete base, the machine could not be used without the base but the machine could be replaced and a new one put on the same base. In that case, the relevant item of plant was the machine which retained its separate identity, here it was the carpet not the pitch even though the carpet could not be used without the preparatory works to the ground on which the carpet was laid. Having determined that the relevant expenditure was the carpet, the Special Commissioner then went on to consider whether the expenditure was on the provision of plant. He said that the carpet could be regarded as both the setting for the business and the means by which the business was carried on. The trade was the provision of synthetic football pitches which generated 70% of the turnover of the business and so in one sense the trade was the provision of the setting but in another sense the pitch and the carpet were the plant with which the trade was carried on. He concluded that the carpet was the means by which A Limited generated profits rather than merely the setting and was accordingly plant on which capital allowances are available.

However in *Shove v Lingfield Park* 1991 - The High Court has ruled that an artificial all weather race track surface was the setting for the trade and did not therefore qualify for capital allowances. This overturned the decision of the Special Commissioners.

These cases remind us of the need to be wary of relying on a Commissioners decision in deciding whether items qualify for allowances.

13.5 Computers
Any additional VAT payable under the VAT Capital Goods Scheme in any accounting period on computers or items of computer equipment worth £50,000 or more (or is computer software) qualifies for capital allowances as plant and machinery. The allowance will be granted for the year of assessment for which the year in which the payment is made forms the basis period. Where a repayment is received under the VAT Capital Goods Scheme, the amount of repayment will be deducted from the residual value of the pool (FA 1991 s 59 and Sch 14 and F (No 2) A 1992 s 68).

13.6 Security assets
Capital expenditure incurred by an individual or partnership of individuals to provide a security asset to meet a special threat to the individual's personal physical security arising wholly or mainly from the particular trade, profession or vocation is to be treated as plant and machinery and eligible for writing down allowances of 25% on a reducing basis. Expenditure incurred on a car, ship, aircraft or dwelling will not rank for capital allowances. When the asset ceases to be used, the disposal value is to be taken as nil thereby giving rise to a nil balancing allowance/nil balancing charge position.

13.7 Fire precautions
The following expenditure on buildings is treated as expenditure on plant and machinery and eligible for capital allowances as such, unless other allowances may be claimed. When the assets are disposed of, the disposal value is regarded as nil.

- Expenditure incurred in respect of premises used for the purposes of trade either in compliance with s 5(4), Fire Precautions Act 1971 or pursuant to instructions from a fire authority not contained in a statutory notice under s 5(4) but which could have been so contained.

Other examples:

*   Expenditure incurred in respect of premises used for the purposes of the trade, and required by an order under s 10 Fire Precautions Act 1971.

*   Expenditure incurred in adding any insulation against loss of heat to an industrial building or structure.

*   Expenditure incurred on any sports stadium used for the purposes of trade where the expenditure was carried out to comply with a safety certificate issued under the Safety of Grounds Act 1975 or certified by the Local Authority as falling within the requirements if a safety certificate had been applied for. Expenditure incurred after 31 December 1987 on any sports ground will also qualify as plant and machinery.

*   Expenditure incurred after 31 December 1988 on stands at undesignated sports ground in order to comply with the safety certificate requirements of a local authority under the Fire Safety and Safety of Places of Sports Act 1987.

*   Expenditure incurred prior to 16 March 1988 to replace or alter authorized quarantine premises (as defined under the Diseases of Animals Act 1950) and to comply with legal requirements. Relief will also be granted on expenditure incurred prior to 1 April 1989 if it was under a contract entered into prior to 16 March 1988 (FA 1988 s 94).

13.8 Installation and erection costs
Such costs (including incidental building alterations) are part of the eligible expenditure on plant and machinery.

13.9 Interest
Interest (and commitment fees on finance used to provide the price of plant) is not eligible for allowances, even if capitalized (*Ben-Odeco Ltd v Powlson* HL 1978), but an exchange loss on repayment of a loan linked with the purchase of plant was held to be eligible for allowances (*Van Arkadie v Sterling Coated Materials Ltd* Ch D 1982) as was the payment to cancel an option to purchase plant (*Bolton v International Drilling Co. Ltd* Ch D 1982).

13.10 Pig industry
HMRC has published Revenue and Customs Brief 03/10, Guidance on plant and machinery capital allowances for the pig industry, giving guidance to illustrate the range of assets on which the pig industry might claim plant and machinery capital allowances, including the availability of the AIA allowance.

13.11 Silage & slurry

The ICAEW's Farming Special Interest Group has agreed with HMRC that both 'silage clamps' and 'slurry handling facilities' (pits) qualify for capital allowances. These items are included in List C at s 23, Capital Allowances Act 2001.

Therefore, any farmers proposing purchasing and installing new silage clamps and slurry handling facilities can obtain capital allowances and may currently qualify for the 100% annual investment allowance (AIA) tax relief on expenditure. With the complexities of the AIA and capital allowances generally, tax planning in advance is going to be important, particularly as there is likely to be further investment in slurry storage for a large number of farmers due to the Nitrate Vulnerable Zones (NVZ) rules.

13.12 Pubs and capital allowances

Wetherspoons and HMRC at the Special Commissioners (*J D Wetherspoon plc v HMRC TC00312*) in 2008 were in a dispute over capital allowances on fitting out costs on two pubs, chosen as a representative sample of larger claim involving nearly 300 establishments.

The parties came back to the Tribunal where further arguments were heard to deal with items of expenditure where neither side could agree the application of the previous decision. Much of the debate centred on the meaning of section 66 CAA 1990 (now section 25 CAA 2001) which treats as plant or machinery any expenditure on 'alterations to an existing building incidental to the installation of plant or machinery'.

The Tribunal decided on its application to the following expenditure:

- Only tiling functioning as splash-backs immediately around sinks and toilets fell within section 66. Allowances for wipe-clean tiling generally to wall and floors would not be allowed.

- The cost of altering flooring to a cold store, inclined to allow proper drainage, should be allowed in full, including the cost of removing the existing floor and not just the incremental cost of installing a sloping floor compared to the cost of a level floor.

The Tribunal also considered the eligibility of 'trade-specific' lighting and found that uplighting in toilets which had been installed to create an attractive ambience should be allowed.

13.13 Gazebo = plant?

In the case of *Andrew v HM Revenue & Customs* (2010) UKFTT 546 (TC), the first-tier tribunal considered whether a freestanding gazebo in a pub garden qualified as plant for capital allowances. Mrs Andrew purchased the gazebo in order to provide outside cover for customers who, as a result of new legislation, could not smoke inside the pub. She then claimed first year capital allowances.

The tribunal considered whether the gazebo was:

(a)   plant, being apparatus used in a business in order to carry on the business;
(b)   a fixed structure or building; or
(c)   a decorative asset within item 14 of list C in s23, Capital Allowances Act 2011.

In the context of a pub, it was concluded, the provision of an environment in which people may sit and talk and consume food and drink is a fundamental part of the business.

The tribunal found that the gazebo was merely a piece of apparatus used as a function of the business and that it was not a fixed structure or part of a building. As it had a function to provide seating and shelter, any visual amenity was secondary and therefore it was not classified as a decorative asset. It was therefore held that the gazebo qualified as plant and first year allowances were available.

13.14 Secure control room qualifies for capital allowances
In *B&E Security Systems v HMRC* TC00452 the Tribunal has accepted that expenditure on adapting a room within an existing building to be secure control room qualified for capital allowances, under S25 CAA 2001, as building alterations incidental to the installation of plant and machinery.

The company carried out the installation, maintenance and monitoring of alarm and surveillance systems. To coordinate that activity, the control room was needed to house security equipment and constructed the room to a certain industry standard. Walls, floors and ceilings were strengthened. The room was also adapted to ensure that it was capable of operating independently from the rest of the building (such as own power supply, own kitchen, toilets, etc).

The Tribunal held that the expenditure was incidental to the installation of the IT equipment and was required in order for the equipment to serve its intended purpose.

13.15 Dwelling-house update
HM Revenue & Customs has issued Brief 45/10 on its interpretation of the meaning of 'dwelling-house' for the purpose of s35, Capital Allowances Act 2001. This follows a period of consultation following HMRC's previous Brief 66/08 and confirms that its interpretation of the term dwelling-house now includes communal areas of student accommodation. This will mean that any fixtures and fittings in shared spaces, such as kitchens and TV rooms, will no longer qualify for capital allowances.

14 MOTOR CARS AND ROAD VEHICLES

Regime for cars from April 2009

Under the changes, the entire regime of capital allowances on cars was replaced by a system based on emissions.

*   The 100% system of first year allowances on car emitting no more than 110g/km provides relief for the lowest emission cars.

*   To allow cars emitting from 111g/km to 160g/km to be included in the main plant and machinery pool, attracting writing down allowance of 20%. Pooling, will however, ensure that there are no balancing allowances on the disposal of more expensive cars.

*   To have a separate pooling arrangement for cars emitting more than 160g/km, with rate of WDA of 10%. Once again, the loss of balancing allowance will be the key issue for business.

*   The limit of £12,000 for cars (WDA = £3,000 max) is removed.

*   Where there is some private use, a separate pool, for each affected car remains.

Existing cars

The rules will not apply to cars purchased before 1 April 2009 (5 April for income tax businesses) and these will remain in the expensive car regime until sold. However, at the fifth anniversary of the change, any remaining cars will be brought into the new regime by pooling them in the appropriate pool at tax written down value.

Other changes

An amended definition of a car to exclude motorcycles, means they therefore become part of plant and machinery. Motorcycles attract AIA from April 2009.

For motor cars owned prior to April 2009 the following qualifications apply:

*   Where the expenditure exceeds £12,000 (this rule ended 1 April 2009) it is not taken into the pool and the writing-down allowance is limited to £3,000, (reduced proportionately if only part of a year is applicable, or where a subsidy or grant towards the cost is received from the Crown or any public or local authority). A balancing allowance or charge arises on disposal or disuse, but there is no restriction of the balancing allowance by reference to the period of use.

- Where the car is sold to a connected person, with the obtaining of a capital allowance as the main benefit, and continues to be used in the seller's trade, open market value is to be taken as the disposal value (up to the amount of the cost) and as the cost to the buyer.

- Where there is only partial use for trade or a contribution is received towards wear and tear, restrictions of the allowance are made as may be 'just and reasonable.'

- Where the cost of a car exceeded £12,000 a contribution towards it is treated as being towards the purchase of a car by the contributor, but only a proportion of the writing down allowance is given, being the proportion which the contribution bears to total cost.

These rules compared pre & post April 2009

Assume John's company purchases a new BMW 520 car for £25,000 and uses it for four years before it is sold for £12,000. The table below shows the differences that may arise during the ownership period.

	Old rules (pre-April 2009)		More than 160g/km CO_2 - relief at 10%	Up to 160g/km CO_2 - relief at 20%
	£		£	£
Year 1 - cost	25,000		25,000	25,000
Allowance	3,000	(max)	2,500	5,000
Amount to carry forward	22,000		22,500	20,000
Year 2 - allowance	3,000	(max)	2,250	4,000
Amount to carry forward	19,000		20,250	16,000
Year 3 - allowance	3,000	(max)	2,025	3,200
Amount to carry forward	16,000		18,225	12,800
Year 4 - sale	(12,000)		(12,000)	(12,000)
Balancing allowance	4,000		None	None
Year 4 - allowance	-		623 (6,225 x 10%)*	160 (800 x 20%)*

* Further WDA @ 10%/20% will continue in subsequent years following the period of disposal on the same reducing balance principle.

Of course, if John ran a self-employed business and used the car privately, the situation would be rather different. It would be kept in a separate pool and although there would be a reduction in the WDA each year to reflect any private usage, there would be a balancing allowance when the car was sold. This applies to pre & post April 2009 purchases.

The definition of a 'motor car' is highly relevant to business seeking to take advantage of the temporary availability of first year allowances. A 'motor car' is: 'any mechanically propelled road vehicle other than:

- a vehicle of a construction primarily suited for the conveyance of goods or burden of any description, or

- a vehicle of a type not commonly used as a private vehicle and unsuitable to be so used.'

The Capital Allowances Manual CA23510 gives a list of car derived vans. Mini vans and 600 cwt vans were held in *Roberts v Granada TV Rental Limited* (1970) 46 TC 295 not to be 'suitable for private use'. In the light of the cases there is probably a question mark over any van smaller than a transit.

A van may be claimed against the AIA and receive 100% Capital Allowance. However any claims for private use may disqualify the van for any AIA as it becomes akin to a car. Accordingly only a WDA of 20%, before adjustment for private use, becomes claimable.

It has been held that a car converted for trade use, by having its own rear seats etc. removed can be treated as a van if it cannot be re-converted in an evening prior to a family outing. This applies for Car and Van benefit purposes but could be argued as applying to capital allowances as well. (See Part 2 - 4.4 Benefits - cars and misc. p.70).

Double cab pick-ups have been designated as cars for VAT purposes if their pay load is less than 1000 kg (this status is under review). Similar claims for converted cars may be possible.

15 SHIPS

Expenditure incurred on ships is eligible for writing-down allowances in any amount specified by the taxpayer, i.e. the allowances can be rolled up and used at will, known as 'free depreciation'.

16 HIRE PURCHASE

Any expenditure incurred before the asset is brought into use (e.g. the deposit) is eligible for allowances when incurred and any expenditure still to fall due when the asset is brought into use is deemed to be incurred at the latter time, so that if the contract is made and the asset brought into use in the same basis period, the whole capital amount to be paid under the contract is regarded as incurred in the basis period. When this is cancelled or assigned without the trader becoming the owner and he has used the machinery, etc. in the meantime, the disposal value is the compensation, insurance or other consideration received plus any capital expenditure not incurred, limited to the whole capital expenditure under the contract. On the other hand, if the asset has not been brought into use, any writing-down allowances and the excess (if any) of the expenditure incurred (including, on assignment, but not cancellation, the expenditure to be incurred on due performance of the contract) over disposal value may be added to the pool of qualifying expenditure. The expenditure eligible for capital allowances is the capital cost, not the interest which is, however, deductible against profits as it is incurred.

17 CONTRIBUTIONS TOWARDS WEAR AND TEAR

It may happen that a person uses an asset whilst working for someone else, and the latter may make a payment to cover the depreciation of the asset. This frequently occurs when an employee uses a private car and is reimbursed by the employer. Where the employee receives such a payment and uses the asset for business or employment purposes, he or she can claim the usual capital allowances if he or she is assessed on the amount received, but not if not so assessed. Reimbursement for partial use is dealt with on a proportionate basis.

18 PARTNERSHIPS

A partner may act in an individual capacity in relation to the firm, e.g. he or she may sell to the firm some machinery which he or she owned privately, or may lease some such machinery to the partnership. If so the partner is treated in his or her private capacity as a separate person just as if he or she were a stranger.

19 AGRICULTURAL BUILDINGS ALLOWANCE (ABA)

Please see Section 12 Industrial Buildings Allowance (IBA) above, p.317.

20 PATENTS

20.1 The expenditure

The allowance is given in respect of capital expenditure on the acquisition of patent rights by outright purchase or licence, but only if the income from the patent rights is liable to tax (TA 1988 ss 520-524).

The capital expenditure which ranks for the allowance is the sum of the expenditure incurred on the purchase of patent rights during the period or previously but excludes expenditure which, or any part of which, has formed part of the qualifying expenditure for a previous period plus the balance of the qualifying expenditure for the previous period less the writing down allowances for that period. It also includes expenditure incurred in obtaining a right to acquire future patent rights, and payments for exclusive use during the whole area or a term of years. Where payments are made for past user or a future limited use other than just mentioned, they are royalty payments, on which the payer deducts tax when making the payment; they do not rank for capital allowance.

A person who deals in patents claims the 'capital' expenditure as an item of expense but as a capital allowance.

20.2 The allowance

The annual allowance is given at 25% on a reducing-balance basis.

If the patent rights are wholly or partly sold, the net disposal proceeds must be brought into account in the accounting or basis period in which the disposal is made. The net disposal proceeds to be brought into account must not exceed the total capital expenditure incurred.

20.3 Balancing allowance or charge

Where the expenditure was incurred prior to 1 April 1986 and the purchaser of the patent rights sell them or allows them to lapse, a balancing allowance is given of an amount equal to the price paid, less the sale price received, and less the annual allowances already given. If the annual allowances already given exceed the cost less sale price, then a balancing charge is made to recoup the excess, but the balancing charge is never permitted to exceed the allowances already given. However, there are special provisions for the taxation of capital gains tax on sales of patent rights.

Where only a part of the patent rights is sold, the amount from the sale is deducted from the written-down value, and future annual allowances are given only on the net remainder, spread over the term of years, which remain before the patent rights expire. If the sale price of the part sold exceeds the written-down value of the whole, a balancing charge is made equal to the excess. No further annual allowances will then be given and the whole proceeds of any subsequent sales of remaining parts will be assessed as further balancing charges.

21 SCIENTIFIC RESEARCH

21.1 Small or medium sized companies (excludes unincorporated businesses)
A definition of small or medium-sized enterprises for the purposes of R&D credits, vaccines research relief and community investment tax relief is given below. The definition of a SME for these purposes is given below. These reliefs are 'notified state aids' which means the schemes may only be operated with prior approval from the European Commission, which requires that relief is only given to SMEs within its own definition.

	Employees	Annual turnover	Balance sheet total
New limits	500	€100 million	€86 million

Research and development for SMEs
The rate of relief for large companies is 130% of qualifying R&D expenditure. In the case of the SME R&D tax credit scheme, the rate of relief is 175% for companies claiming enhanced deductions against profits.

How much R&D relief SMEs can claim
Amount of expenditure
Tax relief is only available if a company or organisations spends at a rate of at least £10,000 a year on qualifying R&D costs in an accounting period. There's an upper limit of €7.5 million on the total amount of aid if received on any one R&D project.

Rate of tax relief or credit
The tax relief on allowable R&D costs incurred after 1 August 2008 is 175 per cent - that is, for each £100 of qualifying costs, a company or organisation could have its Corporation Tax bill reduced by an additional £75 on top of the £100 spent.

If instead there is an allowable trading loss for the period, this can be increased by 75 per cent of the qualifying R&D costs - so that's £75 for each £100 spent. This loss can be carried forward in the normal way, but only if it chooses not to convert it to tax credits.

Example - R&D Relief for expenditure of £20,000 where the company has made a profit of £20,000

Calculation step	Amount
R&D expenditure	£20,000
R&D Relief	£20,000 x 75% = £15,000
Normal taxable profit	£20,000
Taxable profit less R&D Relief	£20,000 - £15,000 = £5,000
Revised taxable profit	£5,000

Example - R&D Relief for expenditure of £20,000 where the company has made a loss of £10,000

Calculation step	Amount
R&D expenditure	£20,000
R&D enhancement	£20,000 x 75% = £15,000
Normal trading loss	£10,000
Trading loss less R&D Relief	£10,000 - £15,000 = £25,000
Loss available to carry forward or back for Corporation Tax purposes	£25,000

If a company makes a loss, it can choose to receive it's tax relief by way of tax credits - a cash sum paid to it by HMRC - if the company or organisation has PAYE and National Insurance contributions (NIC) liabilities for that period. The amount of tax credit it can receive is limited to the total of PAYE and NIC liabilities for that period. But it includes liabilities for all directly employed staff - not simply those working on the R&D project.

Example - Converting R&D Relief on expenditure of £20,000 to a tax credit payment

Calculation step	Amount
R&D expenditure	£20,000
R&D enhancement	£20,000 x 75% = £15,000
Normal taxable profit	£5,000

Calculation step	Amount
Trading loss (after R&D Relief)	£10,000
R&D expenditure qualifying for conversion to credits	£10,000
Potential tax credit	£10,000 x 14% = £1,400
PAYE and NICs liabilities (say)	£5,000
Payable tax credit	£1,400
Losses available to carry forward or back	Nil

Sch 13 FA2002 provides for tax relief for companies of all sizes carrying out vaccine research. The relief is in the form of a 50% enhancement of qualifying expenditure and in the case of small and medium companies can result in a payable tax credit.

Definition of R&D
(a)   Definition of research and development (R&D) for tax purposes was introduced in Finance Act 2000. The definition is based on two tests:

- first, the activity in question must be one that is treated as R&D under generally accepted accountancy practice for companies in the UK, as set out in Accounting Standard SSAP13; and

- second, the activity must also fall within Guidelines issued by the Secretary of State for Trade and Industry. Some extracts are shown below.

(b)   "The boundaries of R&D are illustrated by the following examples. They are not intended to be exhaustive.

- in <u>medicine</u>, routine testing (such as body scanning, autopsies or blood tests) is not R&D. But a special investigation to determine the effectiveness of a certain type of cancer treatment that requires, for example, certain tests to generate a data set for the programme of research would be R&D.

- For <u>physical phenomena</u>, routine monitoring such as daily records of temperature and pressure variation or quality control on material composition and properties is not R&D. But a programme of work to investigate the effects of climate change, to devise new or substantially improved methods or instruments for measuring temperature and pressure, or for developing new materials and evaluating their properties all of which require the collation and analysis of data would be R&D.

- In <u>engineering disciplines</u>, R&D generally includes the development of a piece of fundamental research up to the start of the production stage. This may include incremental developments where they arise from a programme of research designed to result in substantial improvement. For example design, drawing and operating instructions for the setting up and operation of pilot plant and prototypes primarily to test R&D hypotheses would constitute R&D. However, design and drawing work for the preparation, execution and maintenance of production standardisation (e.g. jigs and tools), or to promote the sale of products <u>would not</u> constitute R&D ...

(c) <u>Software</u> may qualify in two respects (i) as the object of the R&D and (ii) as the means to achieve the R&D. Software should be given equal treatment to other forms of technological activity. That is to say, for a project to be classified under case (i) as 'a software R&D project' it must seek to achieve a scientific and/or technological advance, and the whole or part of a project to resolve scientific and/or technological uncertainty on a systematic basis.

(d) Software R&D might include investigations in such areas as theoretical computer science, new operating systems, new programming languages, significant technical advances in algorithms, new or enhanced query languages, or object representations, software engineering methodologies for improved computer programmes and artificial intelligence. In this context, artificial intelligence might cover technical advances in such areas as machine vision, robotics, expert systems, neural networks, the understanding of natural language and automatic language translation. The development of, say, a new natural language interface for a computer game could qualify as R&D, although the game may be a mature product and represent non-R&D activity in most other respects.

(e) Software-related activities of a routine nature are not considered to be R&D."

21.2 Qualifying bodies for R&D purposes

A company can obtain tax relief in respect of qualifying expenditure incurred on research and development (R&D) (Part 13 of the Corporation Tax Act 2009). Qualifying expenditure includes expenditure on research and development undertaken on the company's behalf by 'qualifying bodies' as defined in s 1142, CTA 2009. In addition to the categories of qualifying body listed in s 1142, specific bodies can be prescribed as qualifying by Treasury Order.

A recent Order (the Research and Development (Qualifying Bodies) (Tax) Order 2009, SI 2009/1343) lists a range of institutions located outside the UK which are qualifying bodies. It has effect in respect of expenditure incurred on or after 1 April 2002.

PART EIGHT

INCOME FROM FARMING

1 THE SCOPE OF THIS PART

A separate Part has been allocated to the subject owing to its special nature, although much of the income concerned represents a business profit. Where the income is received by individuals it is subject to income tax, and where the income is received by companies it forms part of the corporation tax assessment. Both individuals (subject to many exemptions) and companies are liable for capital gains tax on disposals of farm land and buildings at a capital profit. The assessments to corporation tax are, made under the rules of Sch D Case I (note: Schedule D became Part 3 of Corporation Tax Act 2009). For income tax purposes (i.e. individuals), all sources are combined into one pool and is covered by Part 3 of ITTOIA 2005.

The profits of farming (including market gardening) are assessable as trading income and are calculated in the same way as other businesses.

1.1 Farming with a view to a profit?
Walsh and anor v Taylor (Insp of Taxes) (SpC) 386
A married couple carried on a partnership farming livestock, an activity which commenced in 1994. In 1994/95 their accounts disclosed no trading income. Various professional projections in 1997 and 1998 were made, none of which projected profits until 2000. The partners intended to make a profit and put substantial effort into following the professional advice which they had been given.

HMRC refused the loss relief claimed for the tax years 1994/95 to 1997/98 under ITA 2007/S66 on the basis of sub-s (4) which provided that relief should not be given unless the trade was carried on throughout the relevant period on a commercial basis and in such a way that profits in the trade could reasonably be expected to be realised in that period or within a reasonable time thereafter; and (ii) on the basis that trade had not commenced for 1994/95.

The Commissioner held that there was insufficient evidence that a farming trade had actually started in 1994/95 and accordingly, the losses for that year were not allowable against other income. In the later years, although the Commissioner accepted that the taxpayers wanted to make a profit, he held that a commercial profit could not reasonably have been expected in any of the years up to and including 1999/00.

The best predictions had not suggested a commercial profit before that time even on the assumption of further purchases of land and consequent increase in the size of the herd. No profits could have been reasonably expected therefore in any of the periods under appeal.

Farm contracting & 'Farming'
As a result of the farming decline many farming families are forced to contract hire their services and/or their equipment to other farmers. The tax office says categorically that the trade of 'the contractor' is not farming. It should be taxed separately. However, if this is occasional and the amounts are small it can be included in the farming accounts, rather than treating it as a separate trade.

In practice many small farms can only survive with the contracting income. The structure of these trading activities can make it very difficult to extract the details from the farm profits. Many contracts take the form of share farming arrangements which are included in the farm accounts. In many circumstances it is the contracting income which secures profitability for the original farming unit and without which the farmer would have a loss which could question the five year profitability rules, i.e. there must be a profit in year six. The decision as to the tax treatment of farm contracting can therefore be critical.

1.2 Averaging profits
The profits of any two consecutive years of assessment may be averaged if the profits of either year are 70% or less of the profits of the other year. Marginal relief applies where the variation in profits is between 25% and 30%. The variation is multiplied by 3 and reduced by 75% of the higher of the two years' profits and the difference is transferred from the higher to the lower profits. For this purpose, profits mean the profits chargeable to income tax for that year after taking into account losses, capital allowances and balancing charges (TA 1988 s 96).

Adjustments for averaging do not preclude a claim being made for loss relief for any year, nor when HMRC adjusts the basis of assessment to an actual year basis when trading ceases. If assessments are revised after making a claim the averaging is cancelled but may be reclaimed if desired, before the end of the year of assessment following that in which the adjustment is made (TA 1988 s 96).

Giles started farming on 6 April 2010 he has the following assessable profits from farming in the UK (before capital allowances).

2010/2011	£10,000
2011/2012	£6,100
2012/2013	£11,000

He may initially claim to adjust his assessable profits as follows:

2010/2011	£8,000
2011/2012	£8,000

He may further claim to adjust his assessable profits as follows:

2011/2012	£8,750
2012/2013	£10,250

Marginal relief only may be claimed for these two years because the initially adjusted 2011/2012 assessment is greater than £7,700 (i.e. 70% of £11,000) but is less than £8,250 (i.e. 75% of £11,000). The relief is 3 x (£11,000 - £8,000) - 75% of £11,000 = £750, which is added to 2011/2012 and deducted from 2012/2013.

The time limit for claims is two years after the end of the second year of assessment. No claim can, however, be made for any year before one for which a claim has already been made (e.g. if Giles above claimed for 2011/2012 and 2012/2013 before making a claim for 2010/2011 and 2011/2012 he could not then make a claim for 2010/2011 and 2011/2012). Nor can any claim be made for the year of commencement or of cessation. Consequential claims may be made, revoked or amended within the time limit for the average claim, but not later than the determination of the averaging claim.

Only individuals (not companies) can claim. Partnerships can claim on a joint election by all members concerned (other than companies) or their personal representatives.

1.3 Cessation and new businesses

The normal provisions apply. The farming carried on in the UK by one farmer is treated as one business, i.e. when a farmer has several farms they are not regarded as being separate businesses (TA 1988 s 53(2)). Accordingly, if a second or third farm is taken over by a farmer the commencing provisions are not applied to the new farm(s); and similarly, if one is given up, the cessation provisions are not applied to its profits (*Bispham v Eardiston Farming Co. (1919) Ltd* ChD 1962). The reason for this is that farming is considered to be an activity personal to each particular farmer, so that when he or she takes over another farm he or she does not succeed to an established and continuing business but merely buys stock, plant and machinery and acquires the right to occupy the land.

1.4(a) Maintenance expenditure on a farmhouse

The practice is to restrict the allowance of such expenditure (rent, rates, repairs, insurances) to the extent that the farmhouse is used for domestic purposes, i.e. the living quarters.

Owner-occupiers of farms who do not farm on a commercial basis, but are still able to claim relief for maintenance repairs and insurance against other income, now have the proportion of allowable expenditure on farmhouses determined by reference to all the facts and circumstances of their particular case.

1.4(b) Agricultural building allowance - ceased April 2011

For full details please see previous editions.

1.5 Valuation of livestock

Livestock is valued on the same basis as trading stock except where an election has been made for the herd basis. If accurate records are not available for home-bred animals, HMRC will accept a valuation at 75% of the market value for livestock other than cattle, and a valuation at 60% of the market value for cattle.

1.6 Farming stock: herd basis

1.6.1 Normal treatment

Farming animals are normally treated as stock in trade and valued as <u>1.5 Valuation of livestock</u>. However, a farmer may elect to have the animals forming part of a production herd or flock kept mainly for the sale of products of living animals, or of their young, to be dealt with on a herd basis. This means essentially that the cost of the herd is capitalized and not treated as trading stock. Such an election must normally be made within two years of the end of the year of assessment (or the year for which a loss is claimed) in the basis period for which a production herd of the same class is kept. Once an election is made it is irrevocable, and a new election must be made when there is a change in proprietorship, i.e. the admittance or departure of a partner even though an election for the continuation basis of assessment may have been made (TA 1988 s 97). An election for the herd basis may be made outside the normal two-year time limit where compulsory slaughter of the whole or a substantial part of a production herd takes place by an order made under the animal disease laws and compensation is payable for the animals destroyed. An election for the herd basis may be made within two years after the end of the first year of assessment for which the profits assessed include the compensation payable for the animals destroyed. Where it is a new farming business and a claim has been made for the profits for the second and third year to be assessed on an actual-year basis and the compensation is relevant to the second year, notice of the election may be given not later than the date on which the claim for revision of the second and third years is made. The election applies to the year of assessment to which the compensation relates and subsequent years, and for corporation tax to the accounting period to which the compensation relates and subsequent years. If, however, a claim for loss relief is made and compensation was receivable for that year, the herd basis may be adopted for that year.

The method of dealing with a herd to which the herd basis applies is as follows.

The initial cost of the herd and of any additions is treated as capital. Transfers from trading stock are made at the initial cost or cost of breeding, together with the cost of rearing to maturity. Where an animal dies or is sold, the proceeds are credited to the revenue account, and the cost of the animal replacing it (excluding any element of improvement) debited to revenue. In the case of an animal slaughtered by Government order, which is replaced by an inferior animal, the amount to be included as a trading receipt must not exceed the amount allowed as a deduction. Where a herd is sold and another herd of the same class is acquired, the transaction is treated as a replacement of a similar number of animals either in the old or the new herd, whichever is the less. Cases of compulsory sale receive special treatment.

If during a period of a year the whole or a substantial part of the herd is sold and not replaced, any profit or loss on the transactions is excluded from the trading account (20% is normally regarded as a substantial part of the herd). The acquisition of another herd within five years of sale is treated on replacement lines.

If a herd is sold and replaced by a herd of a similar class and the number of animals in the new herd is not substantially less than the number in the original herd, any profit or loss on the difference in the numbers is credited or charged to revenue. Insurance and compensation money received on death or destruction of an animal are treated as proceeds of sale.

The scheme does not apply to working animals nor to racing stables. Immature animals are excluded except to the extent that they are necessary for replacement purposes. It is understood that Inspectors of Taxes will accept as the initial cost of the herd the figures at which mature animals stood in the accounts for the year prior to that in which the herd is capitalized even though such values are much below present costs.

If any of the herd animals are sold for less than market price to a person who controls, or is controlled by, the vendor (or when a third party controls both vendor and purchaser), and one of the main benefits which might be expected to follow from the sale is the right to adopt, relinquish or affect the herd basis, then the animals must be valued at open market price for all tax purposes.

The Herd basis as discussed previously had operated under an ESC, Clause 75 in FA 2000 has put this on a firm legal basis. There are no changes to previous practice.

1.6.2 Herd Basis: Minor Disposals without Replacement (Tax Bulletin 64)

The profit arising from minor disposals from a herd without replacement is chargeable by virtue of ITCA 1988 Schedule 5 paragraph 3(10). HMRC have recently reconsidered their interpretation of this legislation and issued revised guidance in the April 2003 Tax Bulletin.

HMRC no longer consider it necessary or appropriate to compute the profit on a minor disposal from a herd without replacement using what they have previously described as the herd basis cost. In the previous interpretation of the herd basis provisions the herd basis cost consisted of initial cost of the herd and the cost of any improvement or increase in the herd size. There costs were not and still are no deductible in the farm trading account. When an animal replaced another of the same quality it took on the herd basis cost of its predecessor.

HMRC consider a disposal amounting to less than 20% of the herd to be minor. Profits on these disposals are taxable and in the past HMRC computed this profit by reference to "herd basis cost". In old established herds the original animals would have been replaced, perhaps several times and this brought into charge a profit largely due to inflation. Following HMRCs' revised view of the situation where a farmers sells, without replacement, a small part of the herd, HMRC now accept that profit should be computed by reference to the actual cost of the animal or animals disposed of. The fact that an animal taken from the herd replaced an earlier one is no longer relevant.

HMRC included a worked example in the Bulletin article.

1.7 Single farm payments - Special Tax Bulletin June 2005

The Bulletin deals with the income tax, CGT, IHT and VAT aspects of the scheme.

A Single Payment (SP) is not based upon production a 'farmer' may receive SP without doing any actual farming. Cross compliance conditions, have to be adhered to. These cover good farming and environmental practice as well as a range of statutory management requirements. There was a one-off opportunity to claim 'payment entitlement' (PE) in 2005. After that PE has to be bought, leased or otherwise acquired (like milk quota etc.).

Income tax - SP is liable to income tax as trade receipts where the farmer still carries on a farming business. Where there is no actual production then the land is not occupied for the purpose of husbandry and therefore no farming trade. For unincorporated businesses, SP will be taxable under Chapter 8, Part 5, ITTOIA 2005 (Income not otherwise charged). Companies will be assessable under Schedule D Case VI. (Note: Schedule D became Part 3 of Corporation Tax Act 2009).

CGT - PE held by a company is an intangible asset. Otherwise PE is a (non-wasting) chargeable asset for CGT purposes, which is separate from the land to which it relates (like milk quota etc.). Therefore the receipt of PE in 2005 has no CGT base cost. PE will be a business asset if an actual farming trade is still carried on and will thus qualify for Business Asset Taper Relief and roll-over relief. (again, similar to milk quota etc.).

IHT - PE, being an asset separate from the land does not qualify for Agricultural Property Relief (APR) Land taken out of production may still qualify for APR but if production ceases entitlement to APR will cease as for this purpose land must be occupied for agricultural purposes. PE should however qualify for Business Property Relief (BPR) where actual farming is carried on or if the farm is put to other (non farming) business use. Where actual farming (or any other business) ceases to be carried on on a commercial basis, neither PE nor the land will qualify for BPR.
For full details of APR please see Part 12 1.3.1, p.502.

VAT - A sale of PE separate from land will be standard-rated and this may be the case even where PE and land are sold in one transaction. The Transfer of Going Concern (TOGC) rules may apply where a farming business is sold, including PE included in the sale. Where SP is the only income and no actual farming or other business is carried on VAT registration will be cancelled.

It will be seen from the above that the complete cessation of farming will cause loss of BATR and APR/BPR and therefore these factors need careful consideration before taking that route. It may be possible to continue a level of activity sufficient to preserve entitlement to these valuable reliefs.

1.8 Herd conversion grant
A grant receivable under an EEC scheme aimed to induce farmers to change from dairy to beef cattle was held to be assessable as trading income (*White v G. M. Davies* ChD 1979).

1.9 Cereals deficiency payments
These should strictly be credited on the dates when the crops were harvested (or as regards wheat or rye, the date of sale and delivery). By concession, however, final deficiency payments for cereals other than wheat may be credited on the dates the payments are notified, except where the 'commencing' or 'ceasing' business provisions apply.

1.10 Ploughing grant
A ploughing grant received under the Agricultural Development Act 1939 is a revenue receipt (*Higgs v Wrightson* KB 1944).

1.11 Growing crop on trees
Where farm land, including a cherry orchard, is purchased for an inclusive sum, and the cherry crop is sold, no part of the purchase price can be treated as applicable to stock in trade (*CIR v Pilcher* CA 1949).

1.12 Sale of turf
Receipts by a farmer for the right to cut and take turf are taxable farming receipts (they are not for the disposal of part of the freehold) (*Lowe v A J W Ashmore Ltd* ChD 1970). In a barely distinguishable case, it was held that receipts from the grant to another farmer of grass-keeping were not receipts of the trade of the grantor farmer (*Bennion v Roper* CA 1970).

1.13 Coastal flooding: rehabilitation payments
Payments by the government to promote the rehabilitation of land damaged by sea flooding are capital receipts and not taxable (*Watson v Samson Bros* ChD 1959). Expenditure on rehabilitation would similarly not be admissible as an expense.

1.14 Compulsory slaughter compensation
Any profits attributable to the compensation may be spread evenly over the three following accounting years instead of the year of receipt. This is modified where commencement or cessation adjustments are involved, or where the accounting date is changed, or where the herd basis operates (See 7.5 for treatment in herd basis cases, p.337) (ESC B 11).

1.15 Stud farms
An agreement has been entered into between the Commissioners of HMRC and the Thoroughbred Breeder's Association, as to the valuation for taxation purposes of stallions and mares. Particulars may be obtained from the Association.

1.16 Losses: restriction of relief
Relief by setting off a farming loss against other income of the same or following year under (ITA 2007/S64) is restricted to trading conducted on a commercial basis and so as to afford a reasonable expectation of profit (ITA 2007/S66). A more precise restriction operates as regards farming and market gardening losses. Such losses cannot be allowed under ITA 2007/S64 if a loss was incurred in each of the previous five years unless it can be shown that the activities were carried on (for the year of claim) in such a way as to have justified a reasonable expectation of profits in the future if they had been undertaken by a competent farmer or market gardener who, if he or she had carried on the business for the previous five years (or longer if the losses went back continuously further), could not reasonably have expected the business to become profitable until after the year of claim (ITA 2007/S67).

This restriction does not apply to farming (or market gardening) which is ancillary to a larger trade.

The loss is computed before capital allowances, but if it is disallowed, capital allowances are also excluded from the ITA/S64 relief.

Changes in proprietorship as between husband and wife or companies controlled by them are disregarded, as are company reconstructions without change of ownership.

1.17 Short Rotation Coppice
Short rotation coppice is a way of producing a renewable fuel for 'green' biomass-fed power stations. Willow or poplar cuttings are planted on farmland at a rate of around 3000 to 4000 per acre. They are cut back to ground level after a year. This causes them to throw up stocks which are harvested every three years or so and made into chips which are used as fuel. From 29th November 1994 the related income is to be treated as taxable trading income.

1.18 Pig industry (Capital Allowances)
HMRC has published Revenue and Customs Brief 03/10, Guidance on plant and machinery capital allowances for the pig industry, giving guidance to illustrate the range of assets on which the pig industry might claim plant and machinery capital allowances, including the availability of the £100,000 annual investment allowance.

The Brief discusses the implications of the new regime for the pig industry, which is a particularly heavy investor in buildings and structures with very short economic lives.

1.19 Silage & slurry (Capital Allowances)
Both 'silage clamps' and 'slurry handling facilities' (pits) qualify for capital allowances. These items are included in List C at s 23, Capital Allowances Act 2001.

Farmers can obtain capital allowances and may currently qualify for the 100% annual investment allowance (AIA) tax relief on expenditure of up to £100,000. With the complexities of the AIA and capital allowances generally, tax planning in advance is going to be important, particularly as there is likely to be further investment in slurry storage for a large number of farmers due to the Nitrate Vulnerable Zones (NVZ) rules.

What are the NVZ rules?
The new NVZ rules implement the EU Nitrates Directive in the UK, and came into effect on 1 January 2009. By 1 January 2010 a risk map must have been produced for all holdings that spread organic manures. From 1 January 2012 livestock farmers must have sufficient storage capacity to store all slurry and poultry manure produced on the holding between 1 October and 1 March (1 October and 1 April for pigs and poultry). Storage facilities are not required for slurry sent off the holding. Slurry stores must have, in addition to the slurry capacity, the capacity to store all the rainwater, washing or any other liquid that enters the store. More details are on the Environment Agency website.

2 WOODLANDS

2.1 Generally

There is no change to income tax on woodlands.

No relief is given when planting and profits when they arise are not taxed.

Short rotation coppice, a way of producing green fuel for power stations from willow or poplar cuttings is treated as farming for income tax, corporation tax and capital gains tax and as agricultural land for inheritance tax.

2.2 Christmas Trees

In *Jaggers (T/A Shide Trees) v Ellis* (1996) STI 1550 the contention whether land was occupied for forestry purposes within s53(4) TA 1988, when it was used to grow Christmas trees.

T owned nine acres, closely planted. Some trees had been dug up, others removed by cutting at ground level. Many had been pruned to achieve a bushy pyramidal appearance. T did not apply for government assistance for woodland. She sold trees direct to the public as Christmas trees, advertising in the local newspaper. Buyers could cut down or dig up the trees. T bought in extra trees to cope with demand and sold Christmas tree stands and Christmas wreaths. She was assessed as a farmer but appealed, claiming, by s53(4) TA 1988, to be outside the charge to tax.

The decision of the Special Commissioners was that S53(4) required either "occupation of land which comprises woodland" or that the land "is being prepared for use for forestry purposes". The land was not being prepared for forestry purposes; it was already in use. The Commissioner inspected the site. It was not woodlands. Timber was not going to be produced: even the oldest and largest trees looked like big Christmas trees. The spacing was for Christmas trees, not timber production. It was a Christmas tree plantation, not woodland. The appeal was dismissed.

PART NINE
RENTAL INCOME

1 THE SCOPE OF THIS PART

For the purposes of this Part income from land includes rents from furnished and unfurnished lettings and furnished holiday lettings. Other sources of income from land are mentioned below.

A separate Part has been allocated to the subject owing to its special nature, although much of the income concerned represents a form of business profit. Where the income is received by individuals it is subject to income tax, and where the income is received by companies it forms part of the corporation tax assessment. Both individuals (subject to many exemptions) and companies are liable for capital gains tax on disposals of land and buildings at a capital profit. The assessments to corporation tax are, made under the rules of Sch D Case I (note: Schedule D became Part 3 of Corporation Tax Act 2009). For income tax purposes (i.e. individuals), all sources are combined into one pool and is covered by Part 3 of ITTOIA 2005.

1.1 Budget March 2011 - Furnished Holiday Lettings (FHL)
The Finance Act 2011 revises the tax rules for furnished holiday lettings (FHL) and to extend the regime to the European Economic Area (EEA).

- From April 2011 loss relief may only be offset against income from the same FHL business.
- UK losses can relieve UK FHL income only and similarly with the EEA losses.
- From April 2012 to qualify in a year, a property must be available to let for at least 210 days and actually let for 105 days.
- Businesses meeting the actually let threshold in one year may elect to be treated as having met it in the two following years ("period of grace"), providing certain criteria are met.

Periods of grace provisions apply from 2010-2011.

2 INCOME GENERATED

2.1 Individuals (changed under Part 3 of ITTOIA 2005)
Are charged as follows:
- rents and other receipts from land (including buildings) in the UK;

- rent charges, ground annuals and feu duties, and any other annual payments in respect of such land;

- premiums for leases not exceeding 50 years.

any other receipts arising from an estate or interest in or right over such land. This would include payments to the landlord for maintaining property, and payments for easements or sporting rights. Exceptions are:
- yearly interest (e.g. mortgage interest);

- rents, royalties, etc. paid by mines, quarries and other concerns as explained in

Please see Mines, Quarries, Sand and Gravel Pits, Ironworks, Gasworks, p.351.

2.2 Companies (changed under Part 4 of CTA 2009)
- All profits and losses from UK rental activities are treated as representing a single source, and computed broadly in the same way as trading profits Part 2 ITTOIA 2003.

- The profits or losses can be decreased or increased (as appropriate) by capital allowances.

- Relief for the management expenses of an investment company and for interest continue to be available.

- Rental losses can be set against other income or gains of the company or surrendered by way of group relief or carried forward to set against future income (of all descriptions), in the same way as management expenses.

2.3 Real Estate Investment Trust (REITS)
The 2006 Finance Act set up a special regime, and started on 1 January 2007, it shifts the burden of taxation of property rental business from the company that carries on the business to the shareholders that invest in the company. The special regime is available to companies whose business is at least 75% property rental and this includes overseas as well as Uk property.

The rental income from the properties is exempt from corporation tax, as are capital gains on disposal of rental properties. The REIT must distribute 90% of the rental profits from its tax-exempt property rental business and pay these distributions under deduction of basic rate income tax. For UK tax purposes, these property income distributions are treated in the same way as UK property income in the hands of the investors. However, losses from other UK property income cannot be set against UK-REIT income.

There are six basic conditions that a REIT must satisfy:
• the company must be UK resident;

• its shares must be listed on a recognised stock exchange;

• the company is not an open-ended investment company

• it is not a 'close' company (that is, controlled by five or fewer participators);

• the company can issue only one class of ordinary shares and fixed rate non-voting preference shares.

• it cannot borrow money on terms that effectively entitle the lender to a share of the profits.

The four conditions relating to the property rental business are as follows:
• the business must have at least three rental properties;

• no one property can represent more than 40% by value of the rental portfolio;

• properties occupied by the company are excluded from the property rental business;

• the company must distribute 90% of rental profits (calculated on a tax basis) as dividends.

FA2007 (Clause 51 and Schedule 17) brings in the following changes to:-

• make it easier for newly established companies to become UK-REITS, by relaxing the conditions which must be met before giving notice to join the regime;

• clarify the definitions of various terms used in the UK-REIT legislation;

• extend the UK-REIT takeover rules to cover de-merger;

• ensure that charities are exempt from tax on distributions from UK-REITS.

3 PARTICULAR KINDS OF INCOME

3.1 Subletting by trader
Rents from subletting are assessed.

3.2 Furnished lettings not holiday lets
Companies are charged under Sch D I (note: Schedule D became Part 3 of Corporation Tax Act 2009) and individuals under Part 3 ITTOIA 2005.

3.3 Capital allowances for flats and shops
The allowances for capital expenditure on flats over shops is open to all property owners and occupiers who have an interest in the property in which the flats are to be provided. More specifically, the property must have been built before 1980 and must not have more than five floors in total. The floors above the ground floor must have been originally constructed primarily for residential use and the ground floor can have either been originally used for commercial or residential purposes or a mix of both. The upper floors must have been unoccupied or used for storage for at least one year before being converted into flats in order for full relief to be obtained.

There are limitations on the size of a new flat. For example, the conversion must take place within the existing boundaries of the building and extensions will qualify only if they are required to provide access to the flats. In certain circumstances, high value flats will not qualify.

Broadly, the rules governing industrial buildings allowances will apply to the new allowance. The allowance will be clawed back if, within seven years of completion, the relevant interest in the flat is transferred to another person, or a long lease is granted over the flat for a capital sum or the flat ceases to be let, or to be available for letting. The allowance cannot be transferred to a purchaser.

The claimant should be aware of a possible pitfall here. If storage space, which has previously qualified as a business asset, is converted into a residential flat it will almost certainly cease to be a business asset for the purposes of capital gains tax taper relief. It would from then only qualify for non-business asset taper relief, which could significantly increase the capital gains tax payable on a disposal.

3.4 Letting of furnished bedsits not a trade
Business asset taper relief could not be claimed on the disposal of furnished bedsits as the property disposed of was not in use for the purposes of a trade.

In *Mervyn Jones & Annette Southam v HMRC TC00256*, a brother and sister in partnership, owned the bedsits in Rhyl and prior to disposal of the property in 2005, both before and after self assessment, had always shown the profits as deriving from a trade. (It should be added that the property did not qualify as furnished holiday lettings). On its disposal, they therefore claimed business asset taper relief on the understanding that the property had been used in a trade and it was therefore a 'business asset' as defined by para 5(1A) Schedule A1 1992.

HMRC rejected the claim for taper relief. They argued that 'no evidence had been provided to suggest that services had been rendered beyond those which a landlord would normally be expected to undertake in the normal course of conducting a rental business. A letting activity would only constitute a trade where the owner remained in occupation of the property and provided services over the above those usually provided by a landlord'.

The Tribunal found in favour of HMRC. They also considered whether HMRC were estopped from arguing that there had been no trade in view of the position they had taken prior to 2005. The Tribunal said: 'Whilst HMRC accepted self assessments submitted by the appellants for a number of years, mere inaction on the part of the Revenue is not sufficient for the purposes of establishing stoppel.

3.5 Rent a room scheme - Part 7 ITTOIA 2005
The basic rule, introduced by F(No2)A 1992 s 59, is that the gross annual rents up to £4,250 from letting furnished rooms by owner occupiers or tenants in their only or main home is altogether exempt from income tax. The limit of £4,250 applies to the income tax year. The following qualifications apply:

(a)   Where separate lettings are made in the same house by two individuals the tax free limit applicable to each individual is £2,125. This limit also applies where the rental income is shared by husband and wife but otherwise the exemption of £4,250 applies to the spouse who receives the income.

(b)   Losses from furnished letting available from earlier years will be carried forward to be set against profits of later years.

(c)   No capital allowances are available under the 'Rent a Room' scheme, but balancing charges from earlier years will be added to the gross rents in order to determine whether the landlord is exempt.

(d)   Where a loss is incurred on furnished letting of rooms an election may be made for the exemption not to apply.

(e)   Where annual receipts from the lettings exceed £4,250 election can be made either:

       (i)   For paying tax on the gross letting income above £4,250, or
       (ii)   For paying tax on the total gross receipts less expenses.

No capital allowances will be available under option para. (i), for which the election must be made within one year from the end of the relevant tax year.

3.6 Furnished holiday lettings (FHL) - Part 3 ITTOIA 2005 (C.T. - Part 4 of CTA 2009) From 6 April 2011

Details of the changes announced in the March 2011 Budget are given in 1.1 above. The following summary table shows the current situation.

	2012/2013	2011/2012	2010/2011	2009/2010
Available for	210+ days pa	140+ days pa	140+ days pa	140+ days pa
Let for	105+ days pa	70+ days pa	70+ days pa	70+ days pa
Period of grace - if conditions met in one year applies to next two years	Yes	Yes	Yes	n/a
UK FHL losses relieved against	UK FHL income	UK FHL income	Total income	Total income
EEA FHL losses relieved against	EEA FHL income	EEA FHL income	Total income	Total income

Prior to 6 April 2011 the lettings of furnished holiday accommodation were treated as profits derived from a trade. All qualifying lettings by the taxpayer were treated as a single trade. Relief was available as shown below.

* The profits were regarded as earned income.

* The tax was payable in two instalments on a similar basis to trading profits.

* Relief is available on pre-trading expenditure.

* The profits were treated as relevant earnings for the purposes of retirement annuity relief.

* Capital allowances were available for expenditure incurred on plant and machinery acquired for the purposes of the lettings.

* Roll-over and retirement reliefs for the purposes of capital gains tax could be claimed.

In order to qualify as furnished letting accommodation, the property must be let on a commercial basis with a view to profit and must satisfy the following conditions.

* It must be purchased with an intention to generate income, and therefore not primarily as a personal holiday home, and accordingly only letting it out when not being used for personal purposes.

* A large mortgage or loan may jeopardise the commercial credibility of the

project. It has to be able to make a profit (after interest) in the early years, say by the second to fifth years, depending on location in the country.

- A written business plan made 'before' the purchase, possibly by a professional would underline its commercial nature, as would full details being made available to the mortgage provider as to its commercial use.

- It must have been available for letting for at least 140 days in the 12-month qualifying period and actually let for at least 70 of the available days; and

- for a period of at least seven months (which need not be continuous but includes any months in which it is actually let) it is not normally occupied continuously by the same persons for more than 31 days.

A qualifying period applicable to a person other than a company will normally be the year of assessment. However, where the property was not let as furnished accommodation in the preceding year of assessment but continued to be so let in the following year, the 12-month period begins on the day it was first let in the current year. Correspondingly, where the property was let in the preceding year but not in the following year, the 12-month period ends on the date which it ceased to be let in the current year.

In the case of the accommodation being let by a company, the 12- month period will normally be the accounting period. Where commencement or cessation occurs, the 12-month period will commence from the date of commencement or end on the date of cessation as applicable. Where the taxpayer has more than one property and one fails to qualify because it has been let for less than 70 days, he or she could average out the total number of letting days between the properties and if the average is at least 70 days, all properties specified in the claim will qualify as eligible properties. A claim for averaging has to be made within two years after the end of the year of assessment or accounting period for which it is to apply.

What the law does not specify is where the furnished holiday accommodation has to be. There is nothing to prevent a city centre apartment from being let to businessmen or visitors to the city on short lets in order to meet the qualification. The tax inspector may not like the concept, but should be reminded that holiday accommodation is not defined in the legislation.

3.7 Letting with services
Where the services constitute a trade, the income will be divided, the rental part being assessed under Part 3 and the services part under Part 2 of ITTOIA 2005. If there is no separate payment for the services, the whole income may be assessed under Part 3.

3.8 Hotels, boarding houses, theatres etc. - Part 2 ITTOIA 2005
In cases like these, where a charge for admission is made but no tenancy is created, the income is in practice assessed as trading profit.

3.9 Tied premises - Part 2 ITTOIA 2005 (C.T. Part 4 of CTA 2009)

3.10 Assignment of leases granted at undervalue
The assessment is under Part 3 ITTOIA 2005 (C.T. Part 4 of CTA 2009).

3.11 Right to reconveyance
The assessment is under Part 3 ITTOIA 2005 (C.T. Part 4 of CTA 2009).

3.12 Mines, quarries, sand and gravel pits, ironworks, gasworks, canals, fishing, market rights, tolls, railways, etc. - Part 3 ITTOIA 2005 (C.T. Part 4 of CTA 2009)
Rents and royalties in connection with land used by any of these kinds of concerns must be paid under deduction of tax (TA 1988 s 119) and such payments will neither be allowed as an expense to the payer (but they are a charge on income) nor assessed on the recipient. A lessor can claim expenses incurred (TA 1988 s 121).

As regards mineral rents, tolls and royalties, relief from income tax and corporation tax is given by taxing only half of the royalties (after deduction of management, etc. expenses). The other half is, however, subject to capital gains tax. Expenses are not deductible in computing the capital gains tax. There is provision for allowance of a loss for capital gains tax purposes on termination of the lease. The relief applies also on disposal of the land and allows recoupment of tax charged on amounts exceeding actual net profits.

3.13 Lost rent (bad debts) - Part 3 ITTOIA 2005 (C.T. Part 4 of CTA 2009)
Tax is not payable on rents not received if reasonable steps have been taken to enforce payment, or if the rent has been waived without consideration and reasonably in order to avoid hardship. Subsequent recoveries are assessable.

3.14 Property dealers
The rents will be separately assessed under Part 3 (C.T. Part 4 of CTA 2009) and not included in the Part 2 (C.T. Part 3 of CTA 2009) computation. If the expenses exceed the rents, the excess will be allowed against the Part 2 (C.T. Part 3 of CTA 2009) income and, if still not absorbed against the Part 3 (C.T. Part 4 of CTA 2009) income, for subsequent years until the property is sold. Premiums paid are treated as part of the cost of the property and hence allowed as expenditure under Part 2 (C.T. Part 3 of CTA 2009).

Property dealers may make deductions in computing trading profits so as to avoid being double taxed on the same income (TA 1988 s 99).

3.15 Wayleaves and easements
Income from easements or rights over land received by the occupier is assessed under Part 2 ITTOIA 2005.

3.16 Cutting turf - Part 3 ITTOIA 2005 (C.T. Part 4 of CTA 2009)

The sale of a right to cut and take turf is assessable as income from the property (*Lowe v A J W Ashmore Ltd* ChD 1970).

3.17 Grass-keeping

The sale of a right of grass-keeping for two years gave rise to income assessable under Part 3 ITTOIA 2005 (*Bennion v Roper* CA 1970).

3.18 Sale of minerals or surface deposits - Part 3 ITTOIA 2005 (C.T. Part 4 of CTA 2009)

In appropriate circumstances, the grant of a licence to enter and take away deposits which have been sold *in situ* will be assessable, so far as the consideration for the grant is concerned, but not so far as the consideration for the sale of the minerals is concerned (which normally will be a capital transaction).

3.19 Compensation - Part 3 ITTOIA 2005 (C.T. Part 4 of CTA 2009)

Compensation for rent not received owing to a trespasser having been in occupation of the property is income.

3.20 Trading in land

The Special Commissioner held that a self-employed bricklayer was liable to tax under Sch D, Case I (now Part 2 ITTOIA 2005) on the lease premium of a flat that was one of two he had built (see *Lynch v Edmondson* SpC 164 (1998) STI 968).

The taxpayer was a self-employed bricklayer. In 1991, he obtained planning permission to build two flats. He did bricklaying himself and employed contractors for the other parts. The building was financed by a bank loan, which was increased on the basis that he would sell both flats. In August 1992, he leased both flats to the local authority for three years and later in the same month he leased one of the flats for 99 years to his girlfriend, W, for a premium of £41,500 and a peppercorn rent. W borrowed £39,500 to pay the premium and did not pay the balance. The taxpayer used the premium to repay his bank loan. In 1996, the taxpayer and W sold both flats.

The taxpayer appealed against an assessment under Sch D, Case I (now Part 2 ITTOIA 2005) on the premium and against Sch A assessments on the rent from the council, claiming a deduction for the mortgage interest W had paid. The taxpayer contended that he had built the flats with the intention of living in one of them, but had been unable to sell his existing house. He also submitted that W had given him a tenancy at will so that he could let her flat for his own account and pay the outgoings, including W's mortgage interest.

The commissioner found that the following facts suggested that the taxpayer was trading: the building was related to the taxpayer's trade; the immediate grant of the lease on the completion of the building; the source of finance and the manner in which it was to be repaid; and the fact that the first flat to be completed would have to be sold to repay the loan.

Although the taxpayer had not originally intended to lease the flat to W, a sale would still have been necessary to meet his obligations to the bank. It was no less a trading transaction if the taxpayer intended to live in the flat with W. The commissioner concluded that the grant of the lease was a trading transaction and that the premium was an arm's length value, since it was based on a professional valuation required for the purpose of W's mortgage. The commissioner also dismissed the taxpayer's claim to deduct W's mortgage interest from the rent he received from the council.

3.21 Reverse premiums and rent free periods - Part 3 ITTOIA 2005 (C.T. Part 4 of CTA 2009)

The sums landlords pay to induce potential tenants to take out a lease - often called reverse premiums - will be subject to tax. This also includes fitting out and rent free periods. Such sums were often considered taxable before a recent adverse decision of the Privy Council (*CIR v Wattle and another*). The legislation will have effect for reverse premiums payable under agreements made on or after Budget day (9 March 1999). Under the legislation F.A. 1999 reverse premiums will be chargeable to income or corporation tax in the hands of the recipient. Very broadly, the timing of the charge will follow accepted accountancy practice. It will be spread over the period in which the reverse premium is recognised in the accounts, i.e. spread over the life of the lease. Where the person receiving the premium is a trader occupying the building for which he gets the reverse premium for the purposes of his trade, the sum received will be treated as income of the trade. In most other cases, such as a receipt by an intermediate landlord for a lease which they are to sublet, the sum received will be taxed as income of a letting business. Special rules will apply to life assurance companies which receive reverse premiums. That where receipts are taken into account to reduce the amount qualifying for capital allowances they should not also be charged to tax as reverse premiums.

In Tax Bulletin - December 1999 (Section 54 & Sch 6 FA 99) HMRC gave guidance on the taxation of reverse premiums enacted in Finance Act 1999 as follow.

The new rules charge benefits procured by actually laying out money and not inducements representing amounts forgone or deferred by the provider. Other than straight forward cash, the other inducements that will be taxable include:

(a)   Contributions towards tenants costs, e.g. fitting out;

(b)   Sums paid to third parties to meet the tenant's obligations, e.g. rent to a landlord under an old lease;

(c)   Effective payments of cash, e.g. the landlord writing off a sum which a tenant owes.

The type of inducements which are not caught include:

(a)   Rent free period;

(b)   Replacement of an existing lease at a rent which is lower because of a change in market conditions;

(c)   Replacement by agreement of an existing lease where certain provisions have become onerous.

"Fitting out costs" in HMRC's view is expenditure on equipping a building with tenant's or trade fixtures or chattels. The cost of these items is usually the responsibility of the tenant. Where the landlord incurs the cost, directly or indirectly, then it is caught. However, if reimbursed to the landlord by, say, charging a higher rent then there is no charge.

HMRC also state that a contribution towards the cost of completing the building is not chargeable under the new provisions. For example, where the parties agreed that the tenant should be responsible for completing the building and the landlord reimburses all or part of the costs.

3.22 Simplification for Companies' Large Land Portfolios at 31 March 1982
An article in the January 2002 Tax Bulletin aims to consolidate previously published information about two schemes, the Multiple Land Valuation Scheme and the Pre-disposal Portfolio Valuation Scheme, which are available to reduce the compliance burden for those taxpayers who make large numbers of property disposals in any one accounting period. Both schemes offer the benefit of a full monitoring service and a single contact point. There is no charge for either of these services.

The first of these schemes, the Multiple Land Valuation Scheme, was introduced in 1990 and is open to taxpayers who dispose of 30 or more interests in land in a year of assessment or in an accounting period. A group of companies is considered together to decide if the disposal threshold has been reached.

Sampling is carried out by the Land Portfolio Valuation Unit of the Valuation Office Agency (LPVU) whereby only a proportion of the total number of valuations referred, usually between 25% and 50% of valuations may be selected for valuation review.

The second scheme, the Pre-disposal Portfolio Valuation Scheme, was announced on 21 March 2000 to run for an initial trial period. The scheme enables participants to agree the value of land and buildings owned on 31 March 1982 in advance of a statutory need for such valuations. The portfolio valuation service helps companies and groups of companies to meet their obligations under Corporation Tax Self-Assessment by avoiding the need to agree individual 31 March 1982 valuations as and when properties are sold. Participation is conditional on holding a property portfolio that meets the minimum size requirement of:

- 30 or more properties owned at 31 March 1982; or

- a lesser number of properties, also owned at 31 March 1982, with a current aggregate value of more than £30 million.

4 DEDUCTIONS ALLOWED

4.1 General

The following payments made by the lessor are allowed as deductions from rent (TA 1988 s 25):

- maintenance, decoration, repairs, insurance and management;

- services provided;

- council tax and water rates;

- rent, rent charge, ground annual, interest paid to purchase property, if wholly and exclusively incurred;

- accountancy fees;

- wear and tear allowance. Where the property is let furnished (carpets, curtains, some furniture) instead of claiming capital allowances on these a wear allowance may be claimed. This is 10% of the result of deducting the cost of council tax and water rates from the rents received.

- repairs not covered by the wear and tear allowance.

	£	£
e.g.		
Rent received		7,000
Council tax paid	1,000	
Water rates paid	500	1,500
	———	———
		£5,500

A wear and tear allowance of £550 may be claimed (£7,000 - £1,500) x 10%.

The payment must be reduced by any insurance recovery or contribution by another person towards the expenditure.

No deduction is allowable for rents misappropriated by an agent (*Pyne v Stallard-Penoyre* ChD 1964).

In the case of an estate which includes agricultural land, if the expenditure exceeds the rents, etc., an amount not exceeding the excess of husbandry expenditure over husbandry income can be allowed against other agricultural income (TA 1988 s 33).

Capital allowances are given on machinery or plant used for the maintenance and repairs, etc., of the property rented.

Where expenditure is incurred by the lessee of a building and the machinery or plant becomes a landlord fixture, capital allowances will be available on such expenditure.

In *C Wills v HMRC* TC00479 the Tribunal has agreed with a landlord's submissions that expenditure on repairing the outbuilding of a let property should be an allowable expense of the rental business.

The appellant incurred over £100,000 on work to an outbuilding of a rental property. The outbuilding was listed, in a poor state of repair and becoming dangerous. Of the amount spent, £63,000 was regarded by the appellant to be capital expenditure but £43,665 was claimed as a repair cost. HMRC had disagreed and raised an assessment on the basis that all the expenditure was wholly capital and not an allowable deduction.

The taxpayer successfully argued that, following the decision in *Lurcott v Wakely and Others*, the expenditure was a repair to only part of the entire property (the house and the outbuilding) and not a renewal of the entity itself (the outbuilding). In addition, the Tribunal accepted that the case of *William P Lawrie v CIR* did not apply because in that matter the taxpayer had claimed for notional repairs rather than repairs which had actually been carried out.

The Tribunal also decided that their decision was supported by HMRC manuals at PIM 2020 which states under the subtitle 'Extensive alterations to a property' that the actual cost of normal revenue repairs to a part of an old building which is preserved in the rebuilt structure is allowable as an ordinary revenue business expense. Moreover, HMRC's manual was supported by the case of *Conn v Robins Bros Ltd.*

Not only did the Tribunal agree that the claim for repair expenditure should be allowed but that the cost of structural works to ensure the outbuilding did not collapse should also be allowed.

Rented property: professional fees
"The normal legal and professional fees incurred on the renewal of a lease are also

allowable if the lease is for less than 50 years." Thus HMRC booklet IR 150 "Taxation of Rents" widens the scope of allowance of the deduction of the costs of a lease renewal. As a general rule the costs of setting up a new lease have not hitherto been allowed but it would seem, in the light of the booklet, that such fees will be allowed in the future.

Landlord's energy saving allowance (non corporate landlords)
(a)   Private landlords who install cavity wall and loft insulation in residential property which they let out are now able to claim a special deduction for such expenditure against their rental income (in the past, expenditure of this nature did not qualify for relief). The rules are set out in new Ss31A and 31B ICTA 1988. This was extended in 2005 to include expenditure on solid wall insulation. From 6 April 2006, the scope of the Landlord's Energy Saving Allowance (LESA) is extended further to include draught proofing and insulation for hot water systems.

(b)   The main conditions which must be satisfied are as follows:

   (i)   The expenditure must be incurred between 6 April 2004 and 5 April 2015 (inclusive).

   (ii)   The expenditure must be incurred wholly and exclusively for the purposes of the landlord's business.

   (iii)   The expenditure must be capital expenditure which does not otherwise qualify for relief.

   (iv)   No deduction can be given for expenditure on a property:

-    which is in the course of construction or which is in the process of being acquired;
-    which is let as furnished holiday accommodation; or
-    which qualifies for rent a room relief.

   (v)   The maximum deduction is limited to £1,500 per property (not per building as pre 6 April 2007.

   (vi)   When a taxpayer incurs qualifying insulation costs prior to the commencement of a rental business, the pre-trading expenditure relief rules of S401 ICTA 1988 apply, subject to a time limit of six months rather than seven years.

4.2 Deductions for income other than rent
Where the amount received is not a rent payable under a lease, payments for maintenance, repairs, insurance or management, rent or other periodical payment or

other expense (not of a capital nature) may be deducted. All like transactions may be lumped together, and any unallowed expenditure may be carried forward to future years (TA 1988 s 28).

4.3 Sporting rights
Where these are not granted in any year the amounts which would have been deductible are allowed. An appropriate restriction is made for personal use of the sporting, or user by a company director or employee not taxed as a benefit in kind (TA 1988 s 29).

4.4 Sea walls
Expenditure on making sea walls or embankments is spread evenly over the year of expenditure and the following 20 years. Capital allowance is not also given (TA 1988 s 26).

4.5 Agricultural land and buildings
4.5.1 Maintenance & repairs
In the case of agricultural land and buildings, where the expenditure exceeds the income, the excess can be set against other income of the same or the following year, or it can be carried forward and set against income of subsequent years from farming or ownership of agricultural land and buildings (TA 1988 s 33). See also FA 1993 ss 113 and 114 and sch 12. See Part 8 - 1.4(a) Maintenance expenditure on a farmhouse, p.337.

4.5.2 Agricultural Buildings Allowance (ABA) - ceased April 2011
For full details please see previous editions of this work.

4.6 Land sold and leased back
Where a lease has not more than 50 years to run, part of the lump sum receivable for its assignment or surrender, will be charged as a trading receipt (or as other income, if not in the course of trade), if not in the course of trade) (TA 1988 s 780). This applies where the new lease is for a term not exceeding 15 years. Where the rent decreases after a certain time or the lessee can vary the terms to his advantage, the lease is regarded as ending at the time of the decrease or variation. Rent payable includes any rent charge. The proportion to be charged (and consequently not regarded as a capital receipt) is $(16-N) \div 15$, N being the number of years of the new lease (fractions are counted as whole years). There is provision for apportionment where the property under the old and new lease is not identical, and for top-slicing relief to be applied by spreading the charge over the period of the lease.

A variation of the lease so that a lump sum is received for an increased rent for a period of up to 15 years, is treated as a new lease.

Where the lessee had, before 22 June 1971, a legal or equitable right to a new lease, the above provisions do not apply. However, where the new lease is so excluded, it is provided that the principle in the Austin Reed case should not apply, i.e. that no part of the rent should be disallowed as capital.

The following kinds of sale and leaseback are normally outside any of the above counteracting measures, and any rent will be fully allowable and any capital receipt taxable as a chargeable gain:

- sale of freehold with lease-back at a rent not exceeding the 'commercial rent';

- sale (or grant) of a long leasehold with a lease-back at a rent not exceeding the 'commercial rent';

- sale of a short (less than 50 years) leasehold with a leaseback for more than 15 years not exceeding the 'commercial rent'.

5 COLLECTING THE TAX

Where the owner defaults, tax may be collected from the tenant up to the amount of the rent. The tenant can then deduct this tax from any subsequent rent payment. A sub-lessee is similarly taxable (TA 1988 ss 21,23).

An agent in receipt of rents may be required to pay the tax out of the rents where the principal has not paid.

Non-resident landlords

If the principal is not resident in the UK, the rents are treated as payments not made out of profits or gains brought into charge to tax, and tax must be deducted at the basic rate and paid to HMRC under s 53, TA 1970. But a tenant has no right to deduct tax that should have been deducted from earlier payments of rent to a non-resident landlord from later payments of rent to the same landlord. The High Court so held in *Tenbry Investments Limited v Peugeot Talbot Motor Co Ltd* (1992) STI 873.

HMRC Centre for Non-residents (CNR) is the department responsible for administering the non-resident landlord scheme under which rents may be received without deduction of tax. It also oversees the operation of self-assessment for non-residents. CNR is presently reviewing non-resident individual landlords who have no net UK income with the intention of not issuing future self-assessment returns to those individuals. This is being done to minimise the time, effort and expense involved for these non-resident individuals in meeting their UK obligations. CNR will still be responsible for their tax affairs and will ask them to complete a self-assessment return occasionally to keep their records up to date and check their liability to tax. If there are special circumstances that mean that the non-resident individual landlord still wishes to complete a return, perhaps because of the requirements of an overseas tax authority, CNR will consider such a request. In every case where CNR propose to stop asking for returns to be completed they will write to tell the non-resident individual landlord and will send a copy of the letter to any agent acting on their behalf. The letter explains that the individual must contact CNR if their circumstances change.

6 PREMIUMS

Premiums received in respect of leases are, in part, assessable (TA 1988 ss 34-38).

Where a lease does not exceed 50 years, any premium is treated as a rent arising when the lease is granted. A deduction of 1/50 is allowed for each year of the lease but the first year is ignored. Thus, a premium of £1,000 given for a 21-year lease would give rise to an assessment on the premiums of 30/50 of £1,000 = £600. Rules are laid down for ascertaining the duration of a lease (TA 1988 s 38).

The value of any work which a tenant is obliged to do is treated as a premium unless it is work of the kind deductible (maintenance, repairs, etc.).

A payment in lieu of rent or for surrender of the lease is treated as a premium if provided for by the terms subject to which the lease was granted. The period of the lease is then taken to be the period in relation to which the sum is payable and the sum is treated as a rent arising on the date it becomes payable.

Consideration for variation or waiver of any terms of a lease is treated as a premium. The period of the lease is then taken to be that during which the variation or waiver has effect, and the consideration is treated as a rent arising on the date the contract for variation, etc. was entered into.

It has been held that for this purpose there is no distinction between the waiver of the breach of a term in the lease and the waiver of the term itself, for the operation of the term is waived on the occasion of the breach, although the term remains operable as regards the future (*Banning v Wright* HL 1972).

The tax on premiums, etc. may, if the taxpayer satisfies the Board that he or she would otherwise suffer undue hardship, be paid by such instalments as the Board allows over a period not exceeding eight years ending not later than the date the last instalment is payable.

Provision is made for the deduction of an appropriate proportion of a premium on the head lease from premium receivable and taxable on the grant of a sub-lease.

Note that liability arises in connection with the granting of leases and does not occur on the assignment of a lease, unless that lease was granted at an undervalue. Premiums receivable on grants or assignments are taxable consideration which may give rise to a chargeable gain.

7 LOSSES

The computation and use of losses varies according to whether or not the business is conducted through a company.

7.1 Individuals (incl. partnerships & LLPs) ITA 2007, S117 et seq.
Interest on borrowings to buy or repair the property is an allowable expense.

Losses can only be set against other income to the extent that they arise from capital allowances.

April 2011 - changes implemented
Losses arising from furnished holiday lettings are no longer treated in the same way as losses from a trade. Losses, cannot be set off against other income for the year of loss or of the previous year (S64 ITA 2007), they can only now be set off against UK FHL or EEA FHL income as appropriate.

Unrelieved losses can only be carried forward for set off against any future property profits from the same source.

Therefore for individuals and partnerships the opportunities to use losses are rather restricted.

7.2 Companies - (Note: Schedule A became Part 4 of Corporation Tax Act 2009)
A loss under Schedule A can be set off against the company's total profits for that period. These profits would include capital gains and any other income.

This gives a company a major advantage compared with individuals.

Also any surplus Schedule A (note: Schedule A became Part 4 of CTA 2009) losses can be carried forward and set against any profits in the future. In addition Schedule A (note: Schedule A became Part 4 of CTA 2009) losses do not disappear when the rental business comes to an end. For as long as the company continues to have an investment business the losses can be carried forward for set off against any profits.

Schedule A (note: Schedule A became Part 4 of CTA 2009) losses of a company cannot be carried back for set off against past profits.

But, unlike the position for income tax, interest is not an expense in computing a company's rental business profits.

S83 FA 1996 contains the provisions. The interest will create or contribute to a "non-trading deficit on loan relationships" ("NTDLR"). Such a deficit can first be set off against any profits, for the deficit period; and any deficit not used can be carried forward but it can only be set off against any future 'non-trading profits'. This means that the deficit carried forward can only be relieved against future Schedule A (note: Schedule A became Part 4 of CTA 2009) profits or capital gains, but not against any future trading profits.

If you run a company from home

If you run your business through a limited company and your base of operations is your home office, it is possible to charge your company rent. Of course if you do this the company will be able to deduct the rents from its profits and you will need to declare the rents on your self-assessment return. On the face of it there would seem to be no advantage.

But what if you also have buy to let properties and are making losses? Very often buy to let property owners have more costs (loan interest etc.) than they have rents receivable. Unfortunately it is not possible to set off these rental losses against other income. The losses have to be carried forward to be set against rental profits in future years.

If on the other hand you do charge your company rents for the use of a Home Office it would be possible to set off any buy to let losses against this income. The rents from your company and your buy to let rents are taxable as property income. Effectively you would be getting tax relief through your company for the rental losses you personally suffer on your buy to let property. A number of considerations need to be taken into account;

If you charge your company rents you must have a proper rental agreement between you and your company, otherwise the revenue could seek to treat the rental payments as part of your salary from the company.

The rents that you charge for your home office must be charged on a commercial basis. It may be sensible to have a formal valuation undertaken.

The rental agreement should state that the office space at home is only available for fixed periods each day. This is necessary to observe the non-exclusive principle. Without this you could jeopardise your principal private residence exemption for capital gains tax purposes.

If you have a mortgage, you may need to check with your lender before entering into such an arrangement.

PART TEN

VALUE ADDED TAX (VAT)

BUDGET MARCH 2011

1) VAT - Increase in registration limits from 1 April 2011
Registration and deregistration limits increased from 1 April to £73,000 and £71,000.

2) VAT - Fuel Benefit - Charges effective 1 May 2011

1 THE GENERAL NATURE OF THE TAX

VAT came into effect for transactions made on and after 1 April 1973. The legislation is now contained in the Value Added Tax Act 1994, as amended by subsequent Finance Acts, and detailed provisions set out in numerous statutory orders issued from time to time.

The standard rate for all taxable goods and services not zero rated is 20%. The reduced rate of 5% applies to supplies of (see Section 9 - Reduced Rate, p.396):

- fuel and power for domestic or charity use;
- energy saving materials;
- contraceptives and women's sanitary products;
- repairs on listed buildings used as churches (see 10.14 Grants under the listed place of worship grants scheme, p.404);
- children's car seats;
- ground source heat pumps (from 1 June 2004);
- certain house alterations for elderly people - ramps, stair lifts etc;
- smoking cessation products (from 1 July 2007 - 30 June 2008);
- basis for children's car seats (from 1 July 2009).

The Government have powers to alter the rate by 25% either way.

VAT is a common method of indirect taxation in the Common Market and, subject to variations of treatment amongst the member States, is made obligatory by a Directive of the Council of the EEC. In the UK it takes the form of a charge on the invoiced value of applicable goods and services made by traders who are not exempt. The amount so charged to customers may be reduced by the VAT suffered by the trader on his purchases; in some cases this calculation may lead to a repayment of tax to the trader. The tax suffered by a business on its purchases is called 'input tax' and that which it charges its customers is called the 'output tax'.

The system operates right through the chain of importation or production of goods, through the distribution via wholesalers, until the final sale from the retailer to the consumer. It is thus the ultimate consumer who bears the tax on the sale price of purchases. As will be seen from the example that follows, the tax eventually takes the form of a tax on value added to basic raw materials.

Some goods and services are 'exempt' from the tax, and this means that the trader will not be able to charge the tax on sales to customers nor obtain a credit for 'input tax' on relevant purchases. Exemption from all goods sold may also apply to traders with an annual turnover of no more than £73,000 from 1 April 2011 (£70,000 from 1 April 2010), but exemption may not be an advantage since, although they cannot charge their customers with the tax, they are unable to claim credit for input tax suffered.

Many categories of goods and services are 'zero rated'. This also means that the trader dealing in such goods cannot charge customers with the tax but can claim credit for relevant input tax.

2 THE SYSTEM ILLUSTRATED

Assuming that the goods are taxable and not zero rated, and that the traders concerned are not exempt but are 'registered' with HMRC, the system, in its simplest form may be illustrated as follows:

		£	£
(a)	A manufacturer buys raw materials at a basic price of on which his supplier charges VAT at 20%, i.e.	1,000 200	
	giving a cost to the manufacturer of	1,200	
(b)	The manufacturer sells to a wholesaler goods produced from the raw materials at a basic price of to which he adds VAT of	2,000 400	
	the wholesaler paying	2,400	

	£	£
(c) The manufacturer pays to HMRC:		
VAT on his invoice	400	
Less: VAT on his purchase	200	
a net payment of		200
(a) The wholesaler sells the goods to a retailer at	2,800	
plus VAT	560	
the retailer paying	3,360	
(b) The wholesaler pays to HMRC:		
VAT on his invoice	560	
Less: VAT on his purchase	400	
a net payment of		£160
(a) The retailer sells to the consumer at	4,200	
plus VAT	840	
the consumer paying	5,040	
(b) The retailer pays to HMRC:		
VAT on his sale	840	
Less: VAT on his purchase	560	
a net payment of		280
The total tax to HMRC is		£640
This represents 20% on the value added to the raw material, i.e. 20% (4,200-1,000) =		£640

3 TAXABLE SUPPLIES

VAT is payable only where there is a taxable supply, i.e. the goods or services are those covered by the tax and are not exempt. VAT is payable on imports of taxable goods as though it were a customs duty, and it may be payable by a UK agent who is working on commission for an overseas principal. There are different rules for imports from other EC countries and those outside.

Goods produced by a business or acquired by a business and used for the purposes of that business, e.g. stationery printed in the business, are taxable at market value. This is the process known for VAT purposes as 'self supply'. Where, however, goods are produced by a business or acquired by a business and applied by the owner for personal use, the cost of those goods is taxable. Cost is not defined for this purpose but, in the case of manufactured articles, it is thought to mean direct cost, e.g. materials and labour, plus manufacturing overheads.

Samples and promotional gifts are taxable at the cost to the supplier but if that cost is no more than £50. VAT can be recovered on the cost of gifts over £50 if they are accompanied by a certificate indicating that output tax will be accounted for. Industrial samples for testing and market research are also tax free, whatever their cost or value, provided they are not of the kind obtainable in the market place. However, only the first of a number of identical samples (supplied as gifts) will be tax free (FA 1993 s 47). But see the following EU case:

Treatment of samples and business gifts
The European Court of Justice (ECJ) has given its decision in the very long-running case of *EMI Group Ltd C-581/08.*

EMI gave samples of its CDs to various producers, businesses and others in the industry to promote its musical sales, and accounted for VAT in accordance with the current UK VAT rules. The ECJ decided that UK VAT law in relation to the treatment of samples and business gifts is not in line with the EU legislation. The opinion is as follows:

- UK law should not apply VAT where more than one sample is given to the same person;

- UK VAT is currently due on business gifts exceeding a £50 value, with this £50 limit being calculated as the cumulative value of a series of gifts given to the same person, rather than their individual value. This 'cumulative value' assessment is incorrect; and

- UK law should allow exceptional circumstances for business gifts over £50 to be considered not subject to VAT.

The ECJ went on to define a 'sample' as being any supply by a taxable person for the purpose of promoting future sales, to an actual or potential customer or person able to influence the market for the product, of several items of goods that are examples of the products to be sold.

Goods supplied on hire purchase are taxable on their cash price, i.e. excluding interest or hire purchase charges, which are not subject to VAT.

Goods and services will be taxed net of any credit charge and net of cash discount, provided the rate is shown on the invoice and whether or not the discount is taken by the customer.

For retailers using the standard basis, VAT is paid on cash received, so that bad debts are automatically relieved of the tax. With the alternative basis, VAT is paid on credit sales invoiced, plus cash sales less cash received from credit customers.

Where the consideration for the supply of goods or services is wholly or partly non-monetary VAT is payable on the equivalent monetary value of the consideration.

4 THE TAX POINT

This is the point when liability to the tax arises, although the actual payment or repayment of tax may not be due until some months later. Basically the tax point is when the goods are despatched or made available to the customer, but the tax point may be extended to the date when the invoice is issued within 14 days of the despatch of the goods. The Commissioners are authorised to agree special arrangements as to the tax point with particular traders.

In the case of goods on sale or return, the tax point is when the goods have finally been accepted by the customer, but this date must not be more than 12 months after despatch to the customer.

In the case of goods on hire (not hire purchase or credit sale) the tax point is when each successive payment becomes due, and such point may be expressed in the agreement, or when an invoice is issued, if earlier.

For goods on hire purchase the tax point is when the goods are supplied.

5 ADMINISTRATION

5.1 Registration
A trader is obliged to register for VAT with HMRC if his turnover in a rolling 12 month period exceeds £73,000. On registration the trader must show on the invoices issued the tax added, except in the case of retailers making cash sales; and must make normally quarterly returns, paying or reclaiming the difference between his input and output tax. Registration is obligatory where the annual turnover of the past

12 months exceeds the limit, or if the turnover in the next 30 days is likely to exceed this threshold. It could, however, be advantageous to register, even though turnover is expected to be below the limit, where input tax was likely to be less than output tax and the difference could be reclaimed. Registration may now be done on-line and by agents acting on behalf of the trader.

Example:
John became VAT registered on 1 July 2010 - he is a carpenter. His first VAT return will be completed for the quarter ended 30 September 2010.

On his first VAT return, he can claim input tax on any tools, vans, materials and other assets he purchased after 1 July 2006 i.e. four years before VAT registration. He can also claim input tax on any services he paid for after 1 January 2010 (six months before registration) as long as the service was not consumed before he became VAT registered. So there would be no problem, for example, claiming input tax on the cost of designing a website because a website is an ongoing cost to the business.

Waiver of VAT registration
Businesses that exceed the VAT registration can apply to HMRC for a waiver of that registration requirement, which will be granted if the business can demonstrate that the input tax it would have claimed would have exceeded the output tax due on a regular basis. The purposes of this is to give the business an administrative saving, while relieving HMRC of a net repayment to the taxpayer.

From the case of *Llanfyloin Group Practice* (16156) advisers and businesses should be aware that, in requesting a waiver of VAT registration, they do not have any right to change their minds retrospectively. They can, if they wish, apply for registration from any current date, thus concluding a period of waiver.

5.2 Records
All traders who are registered are obliged to keep records of their purchases and sales including records of the VAT applicable on those transactions. They are also obliged to keep what is called a 'tax account' in which their total liabilities or claims in respect of VAT are recorded. No particular form or record or account is specified. The authorities have the right to inspect records (including computer operations) and tax invoices, and may obtain the power to enter premises for this purpose, special regulations apply to the records of retailers.

It is a common assumption that HMRC has the power to disallow input tax claimed where, at the time it carries out an inspection, the evidence of the purchase (the purchase invoice) is not present in the records. Such a view leaves open the ultimate potential nightmare, namely that records are destroyed in a fire, for example, and that HMRC would therefore have the power to disallow all input tax where replacement invoices could not be obtained from suppliers. It is true that HMRC has powers to allow an inferior form of evidence, but this is a discretionary power that it can exercise to the taxpayer's detriment.

It has been established in a VAT tribunal (MS Vaughan/14050) that the above is not the correct interpretation of the law. In fact, both UK and superior EU law states that the right to deduct tax depends on the taxpayer holding the relevant documentary evidence at the time that the deduction is made. As long as there is reason to accept that the documents existed at that time, the right to deduct remains unimpaired and is not subject to HMRC' discretion. In practical terms, an honest businessman who suffers the calamity of losing purchase records can retain the right to recover tax on the basis that he held the required evidence at the time the deduction was made.

The special commissioner found that, in the particular circumstances of the appeal, the taxpayers' order book was an adequate record of their partnership sales, despite the inspector's arguments to the contrary. The taxpayers used their order book as the basis for completing the business' VAT quarterly return, adjusting for cancelled orders and credit notes. The fact that the VAT officer had not found anything amiss was significant in the commissioner's opinion. The inspector's revised assessments, made on the basis that sales were understated, were therefore excessive, and the commissioner found that there was no neglect on the taxpayers' part. (See *G S & F Marsden (trading as Seddon Investments) v Eadie* SpC 217 (1999) STI 1766.

TOGCs and business records
With effect from 1 September 2007, the transfer of a going concern (TOGC) rules changed such that the vendor is not required to transfer the records of the business to the purchaser, nor to obtain Revenue & Customs' permission to retain those records except where the buyer takes over the seller's VAT number. This is replaced by a requirement on the seller to provide all relevant information to the purchaser to enable the purchaser to fulfil his VAT obligations.

5.3 VAT Invoice
5.3.1 EU Invoicing directive
Lack of standardised VAT invoicing rules within the EU led to the introduction of European invoicing directives which aim to simplify and harmonise requirements across Europe and to remove barriers to electronic invoicing.

The key changes for UK businesses were as follows;
* A requirement to show the unit price of goods and services on the invoice;

* An increase in the upper limit for retailers' simplified invoices to £250;

* There is no requirement to get HMRC's approval to self bill; and

* The right to send invoices electronically without authorisation (subject to meeting certain conditions).

5.3.2 Invoicing format

Most issues required by the new EU legislation were already in place in the UK.

However, four specific changes are required to the current invoicing format:

(a) The type of supply is not required;
(b) VAT does not have to be shown at each rate;
(c) The unit price must be shown for supplies of both goods and services;
(d) There is no requirement to show a sterling equivalent of the **total** invoice amount - but remains for the individual supplies and for the total amount of VAT.

HMRC is reasonably relaxed about the items which need to be removed (a, b and d above) and will allow businesses to continue to include these on UK VAT invoices for the immediate future. However, they are required to ensure that the additional item, number c above, referring to unit price, is included on future UK VAT sales invoices in order to comply with the European Legislation. See 5.3.5 VAT invoices: Details to be included on a VAT invoice, p. 371 for a list of items now required on an invoice.

Whilst the "unit price" requirement for goods is straightforward, it is causing considerable concern for service industries where it is difficult to determine the unit price. For example, is a solicitor now required to quote the hourly rates for each individual involved in the job? In most people's view, the hourly rate is an internal charging mechanism and the unit price would be the VAT exclusive charge for the advice given. However, where a consultant charges for his time at a daily rate, the unit price has effectively been agreed and is countable at the rate and should be shown on the invoice.

5.3.3 Electronic invoicing

HMRC has said that it does not want to introduce restrictions to electronic invoicing and storage and are seeking to ensure that all the methods that are currently approved in the UK will continue to be available. HMRC has also expressed a desire to facilitate the future developments of invoicing by electronic means.

The new rules allow for electronic invoicing using either:
• An advanced electronic signature; or
• Electronic Data Interchange (EDI).

HMRC has also agreed that UK businesses may use the following systems to transmit VAT invoices:

• Internet based systems such as XML/XSL;
• EDI files sent under FTP or as e-mail attachments;
• Using an intermediary service provider to receive messages; and
• Presenting invoices on web sites which are hosted by suppliers or their agents.

The key to using other electronic invoicing systems is that there must be a satisfactory level of control over the authenticity and integrity of the invoice data. If you already have approval to invoice electronically there is no need to notify HMRC. Otherwise new electronic invoice users must notify HMRC in writing within 30 days of starting to invoice electronically. This is a welcome development of most businesses.

5.3.4 Self billing

Businesses can operate self-billing without HMRC approval. It is necessary to ensure that:

- There is a written agreement between the customer and the supplier which can be produced to HMRC on request,

- The supplier must be VAT registered throughout the agreed period;

- The self-biller must keep an up to date list of suppliers who have agreed to self-billing; and

- The self billed invoices must state "The VAT shown is your output tax due to HMRC".

5.3.5 VAT invoices: Details to be included on a VAT invoice

(a) An identifying number (that is unique and sequential from 1 October 2007);
(b) The time of supply;
(c) The date of issue of the document;
(d) The name, address and registration number of the supplier;
(e) The name and address of the person to whom the goods or services are supplied;
(f) A description sufficient to identify the goods or services supplied;
(g) The quantity of goods or the extent of the services, and the net and VAT amount payable, expressed in sterling;
(h) The gross total amount payable, excluding VAT;
(i) The rate of any cash discount offered;
(j) The total amount of VAT chargeable, expressed in sterling;
(k) The unit price.

5.3.6 Second-hand scheme

It is required to include one of three references on an invoice - a reference to the relevant article in the EC Directive, a reference to the relevant UK legislation, or any other reference indicating that a second-hand margin scheme has been applied.

The way in which margin scheme treatment is referenced on an invoice is a matter for business and not for HMRC. The legend detailed in Notice 718, paragraph 3.7 is no longer acceptable to reference the fact that the supply is a margin scheme supply. Businesses may, if they wish, use this legend until they migrate to a new form of acceptable reference over time as they reprint invoices or upgrade software.

- 'This is a second-hand margin scheme supply'.
- 'This invoice is for a second-hand margin scheme supply'.

5.4 Returns and payments
5.4.1 New penalty regime
The HMRC penalty regime (effective from 1 April 2009) applies to all VAT issues. Full details are given in Part 1, 5.3.5 Times of payment, p.17.

5.4.2 Cheque payments
From April 2010, when paying by cheque, it must have cleared before the due date (last business day of the month).

Payment by cheque in the post or by hand does not count as an electronic method. However, businesses that want to pay by cheque can meet the electronic payment requirement by paying in their cheque at a bank or building society, using a Bank Giro Credit pre-ordered from HMRC (this will have pre-printed on it the customer details, and will ensure it reaches the right account). Bank Giro payments are treated as electronic payments. This means that businesses paying by Giro will get up to an extra seven calendar days for the payment to reach HMRC's account (unless the business uses the annual accounting scheme or is required to make payments on account).

5.4.3 VAT returns online
From April 2012, businesses must submit their VAT returns online and pay VAT electronically. Currently compulsion only affects those whose:

- turnover is £100,000 (exclusive of VAT) or more - based on returns filed in the 12 months before 2010; or

- newly registers for VAT on or after 1 April 2010 (regardless of turnover).

Once returns have been submitted online, businesses cannot return to paper filing even if turnover falls below £100,000.

Agents must first register and enrol to use 'VAT for Agents' service to be able to file client's returns online. An existing user of HMRC's Online Services can simply add the service to their existing services. Otherwise, new users must register first for HMRC Online Services. Online Service users can also, optionally, sign up for VAT EU Refunds for Agents service.

Since 23 November 2009, there has been no requirement for the agent to be VAT registered themselves for an agent to use VAT for Agents.

Businesses or their agents registering for online filing must provide the following information:

- VAT registration number

- Post code of principle place of business (from last VAT return)

- Date of VAT registration (which should also be in the February letter)

- Final month when last VAT return was submitted

- Box 5 figure (tax payable / repayable) on the last return (no minuses!)

Where an agent registers, an activation PIN is sent to the client. The client must then forward the PIN to the agent, and within 28 days to ensure the PIN remains valid.

HMRC have confirmed that no penalties for non-compliance will be issued until periods ending after 31 March 2011.

5.4.4 Online access to VAT returns
VAT returns are only retained on the HMRC website for 15 months.

5.4.5 A reasonable excuse?
The appellant, *Lee Patterson Limited (TC00023)*, was concerned that he might be late paying his VAT, so he phoned directory enquiries to be put through to 'Customs & Excise', whereupon he was transferred erroneously to the Isle of Man enquiries desk. He was assured there would be no problem. HM Revenue & Customs took a different view, recorded a default surcharge, and refused to accept that the advice given by the Isle of Man desk constituted a reasonable excuse. The tribunal was more forgiving. It heard evidence that directory enquiries commonly routed calls to the Isle of Man when asked to contact 'Customs & Excise', and that the Isle of Man enquiries people usually spotted the mistake. They had not done so this time, and it was reasonable for the appellant to assume he was talking to the right person.

The tax tribunal result in the case of *Team Brand Communication Consultants Ltd* (TC00884) will cause widespread interest in times of frequent redundancies.

The company argued that the reason for late submission of its VAT return was that the responsible person had been allocated to a redundancy pool and feared losing his job. HM Revenue & Customs argued that, as redundancy was a common feature of business, this could not be a reasonable excuse for a lapse in concentration or poor performance. There were particular facts that made this person fear (wrongly as it turned out) that he was almost certain to be made redundant, and the general tenor of the decision is that, if a person is put under short-term stress from fear of redundancy, this should be treated as a reasonable excuse.

A harsh decision has been handed down by the tax tribunal in the case of *Russell Francis Interiors* (TC00983) relating to a penalty for a careless error.

The business purchased a property to use for its taxable activities and reclaimed VAT on the full price even though it held an invoice only for the deposit initially paid for the purchase. The invoice for the remainder of the price fell into the following quarter.

There was no real prospect that HM Revenue & Customs would lose tax overall. Nonetheless, it imposed a carelessness penalty of 15%. The tribunal decided that this was too high in the circumstances and halved the penalty. It decided that the business ought to have obtained advice on the correct timing of its claim and failure to do so should not go completely unpunished.

The error created a short-term timing problem alone, and is harsh for the tribunal to impose any penalty at all, and almost inexplicable that HMRC should regard these as circumstances in which to seek to allege carelessness in the first place. A penalty can arise by claiming a valid sum only three months early.

5.5 Penalties
Penalties, interest and surcharges are payable for failure to comply with VAT legislation. These penalties, etc., relate primarily to misdeclarations of tax, i.e. understatements of tax due or overstatements of tax receivable. They also apply to failure to make returns or pay at the due dates.

From a date yet to be announced a new penalty regime will come into force. It will apply separately to:

(a) late returns; and
(b) late payments.

Time based penalty systems will run independently of each other.

5.5.1 What happens if a VAT Return or VAT payment deadline is missed?
Turnover is £150,000 or more - what happens if you miss a VAT deadline.

If your turnover is £150,000 or more you will be 'in default' if by the due date:

•   HMRC has not received your VAT Return
•   payment of the VAT due has not cleared to HMRC's account

HMRC will send you a 'Surcharge Liability Notice' explaining what will happen if you miss another deadline during the following 12 months, this is called your 'surcharge period'.

If you default again during this 12 month surcharge period, you may also have to pay a 'default surcharge' on top of your unpaid VAT. This is a percentage of your unpaid VAT. Each additional time you send another late VAT Return or payment, your surcharge percentage will increase and your surcharge period will be extended for a further 12 months. The table below explains this further.

Defaults	Surcharge to pay (calculated as a percentage of your unpaid VAT)	Surcharge period
First default	No surcharge. Surcharge Liability Notice issued.	12 months
Second default in a surcharge period	2% (unless it is less than £400, in which case you won't be charged a surcharge at this rate)	12 months from the date of the most recent default
Third default in a surcharge period	5% (unless it is less than £400, in which case you won't be charged a surcharge at this rate)	12 months from the date of the most recent default
Fourth default in a surcharge period	10%	12 months from the date of the most recent default
Fifth and subsequent defaults in a surcharge period	15%	12 months from the date of the most recent default

5.5.2 Your turnover is less than £150,000 - what happens if you miss a VAT deadline
If your turnover is less than £150,000 you will be 'in default' if by the due date:

- HMRC has not received your VAT Return
- payment of the VAT due has not cleared to HMRC's account

HMRC will then send you a letter offering help and support. If you default again within 12 months HMRC will send you a 'Surcharge Liability Notice' explaining what will happen if you miss another deadline during the following 12 months, this is called your surcharge period.

If you default again during this 12 months surcharge period, you may also have to pay a 'default surcharge' on top of your unpaid VAT. This is a percentage of your unpaid VAT. Each additional time you send another late VAT Return or payment, your surcharge percentage will increase and your surcharge period will be extended for a further 12 months. The table below explains this further.

Defaults	Surcharge to pay (calculated as a percentage of your unpaid VAT)	Surcharge period
First default	No surcharge. Help letter issued	None, but if you miss another VAT deadline within 12 months of the issue of a help letter you will formally enter the surcharge system
Second default	No surcharge. Surcharge Liability Notice issued	12 months
Third default in a surcharge period	2% (unless it is less than £400, in which case you won't be charged a surcharge at this rate)	12 months from the date of the most recent default
Fourth default in a surcharge period	5% (unless it is less than £400, in which case you won't be charged a surcharge at this rate)	12 months from the date of the most recent default
Fifth default in a surcharge period	10%	12 months from the date of the most recent default
Six and subsequent defaults in a surcharge period	15%	12 months from the date of the most recent default

What happens if you don't submit a VAT Return at all
If you don't submit a VAT Return at all, HMRC will estimate the amount of VAT you owe and base the amount of the surcharge on this amount. This is known as an assessment. If after an assessment you still don't send a correct return, HMRC may increase the estimated amount of VAT you owe and base the increased surcharge on that amount.

Where a corporate body is involved in dishonest tax evasion the penalty may be recoverable from directors or other 'managing officers' to whom the dishonesty was attributable. Any person knowingly concerned in the fraudulent evasion of tax may be liable to criminal proceedings involving monetary penalties or imprisonment (VATA 1983 s 39 and FA 1985 s 12 and Sch 6). Where evasion of the tax does not give rise to criminal liability penalties apply in cases of misdeclarations of the tax liability, whether involving understatements of the liability or over claims for tax refunds.

The misdeclaration limit is the greater of £10,000 or 1% of turnover, subject to a £50,000 upper limit. However by adjusting under paid VAT as indicated by the new limits may not absolve taxpayers from the new unified penalty regime - Part 1 - Section 7, p25. Adjustment, by itself, does not notify HMRC of the error.

Example:
Sugar Ltd incorrectly reclaimed input tax of £35,000 on its March 2008 return, an error it discovered on 1 April 2010. The company is now completing its quarterly return for June 2010, which includes sales of £4m in Box 6.

The company can adjust the error on the VAT return because the value is less than £50,000 and less than 1% of sales (£4m x 1% = £40,000). If the error had been for £45,000, then a disclosure to HMRC would have been necessary.

What is classed as disclosure?
The key point is that an error is not classed as 'disclosed' simply by including it on the next VAT return. Although many errors can be adjusted on the next VAT return under the error correction procedures (if the net value of the error or errors is less than £10,000 or less than 1% of the outputs figure in Box 6 of the return up to a ceiling of £50,000), this does not automatically avoid a penalty. This is because an adjustment on a VAT return does not count as a full and unprompted disclosure under the new penalty regime. An 'unprompted disclosure' is only made by meeting the 'telling', 'allowing' and 'helping' conditions below:

- TELLING HMRC about the error
- HELPING HMRC work out what extra tax is due
- ALLOWING HMRC access to their records to check the figures

5.6 Cash accounting
Application may be made to HMRC for VAT to be based on the amounts paid and received during a quarterly or monthly accounting period. This system can simplify the accounting requirements for many of the smaller businesses and, where substantial credit is given to customers, improve the cash flow. Bad debts are automatically accounted for by failure to receive the amount due. It could be a disadvantage in terms of cash flow when tax receivable on purchases is higher than tax payable on sales and where long terms of credit are taken on supplies.

Cash accounting, subject to conditions, is available where turnover is not expected to exceed £1.35 million in the next 12 months, but once it is in effect the system can be used until turnover reaches £1.6 million. It operates from the beginning of the normal tax period for the business and must be continued for at least 2 years. Transactions excluded from a cash accounting system are: imports, exports, hire purchase, conditional and credit sales. An application is no longer required to be made in writing.

Tax invoices must continue to be kept and, for cash (not cheque) payments they need to be receipted. Receipts and payments by credit card are entered at the date of the invoice, but giro transactions, standing orders and direct debits at the date of entry in the bank account. Part payments or receipts should be related to specific invoices.

Businesses are no longer able to use the scheme for sales of goods and services invoiced in advance of the supply being made, or for sales where payment is not due for more than six months after the date of the invoice. Businesses which incur a VAT penalty, other than for fraud, or have claimed back their input tax before they have paid for their purchases, will no longer be automatically withdrawn from the scheme.

Measures allow businesses to continue to apply the scheme for a further six months after leaving the scheme to payments outstanding on that date. This option will only be available to businesses that either leave the scheme voluntarily or who must do so because their annual taxable turnover exceeds the de-registration (£1.6m) limit. Any VAT that is still outstanding at the end of the six-month period must be brought to account on the VAT return then ending.

5.7 Annual Accounting Scheme
Businesses, with a turnover below £1.35 million p.a. can opt for the Annual Accounting Scheme subject to nine estimated payments in advance of a return with a tenth adjusting payment. If in one year the turnover exceeds the £1.35 million but not £1.6 million the trader may be allowed to stay in the scheme if HMRC can be convinced that the turnover will return below £1.35 million in year 2.

5.8 Deregistration
Traders may deregister if turnover falls below, and is projected to stay below, certain limits. The limit from 1 April 2011 is £71,000 (1 April 2010 £68,000).

5.9 Flat rate scheme
Table 20. VAT - Flat Rate Percentages - by Trade Sectors - from 4 January 2011 (20%), p.650 shows the flat rate percentages applying to the 20% rate of VAT for different businesses.

The limits on the flat rate scheme are for businesses with taxable supplies (standard rated plus zero rated but excludes exempt) of less than £150,000 (excluding VAT) and can stay in the scheme until year total income (flat rate income including VAT) exceeds £230,000. Applications to HMRC have to be made in advance of applying the scheme.

However, beware of the effects on other currently exempt or zero rated income. EU

Law Directive 2006/112/EC, Art9(i) refers to "economic activity" which clearly includes for example rental income and investment property sales.

Bank interest received - not in flat rate scheme
HMRC's view that flat rate scheme (FRS) users should apply their relevant flat rate percentage to bank interest received from a business account (either current or deposit) has been successfully challenged at a VAT tribunal.

The joined case of *Fanfield Ltd and Thexton Training Ltd* TC 919 confirmed that bank interest received is classed as non-business income and is therefore excluded from the scheme calculations.

However, the case outcome still means that if bank interest or investment income is earned by a business as a core part of its trading operation, eg a money-lending business, then it is in the scheme calculations because it is then both business and exempt income. But for most business it is now excluded, assuming HMRC does not appeal the case.

Note that if taxpayers have paid FRS tax on bank interest received on past VAT returns, there is now scope to go back four years and correct this error. The amount of tax involved will almost certainly be less than £10,000 (the standard error correction limit) so can be adjusted on the next VAT return submitted by the business rather than separately notified to HMRC.

The basics are, however, quite simple. Rather than calculate both input tax and output tax on every transaction an eligible business will merely apply a predetermined percentage to the turnover on a quarterly basis. This becomes the tax due to HMRC.

This measure is intended as a business simplification. The intention is that businesses that qualify will not be required to account for VAT by reference to invoices. Nevertheless, where supplies are made to other VAT registered businesses it will be necessary to issue the appropriate VAT invoices. Thus, the simplification and or cost saving is purely in relation to the requirement to compile VAT returns. In many cases the requirement to make VAT returns is a discipline on small businesses which might be lost in these circumstances.

Example:
A photographer undertakes portraits for unregistered private customers and also does commercial photography work. In a VAT period, the commercial work amounts to £10,000 and the photographer will issue invoices for £12,000 (£10,000 plus VAT at 20%). The portrait work undertaken raises £7,500 including VAT.

During the course of the VAT period the photographer will not have to record any purchases or expenses relating to the work done. At the end of the period, to work out the net VAT due, he adds the gross sales in the period, which in this case comes to £19,500, (£12,000 commercial + £7,500 private). He multiplies that figure by the flat rate percentage for photography businesses of 10%. The resulting amount of £1,950.00 will be the figure the photographer will have to pay HMRC.

This will only be beneficial if the 'real' outputs £3,250 (0.2/1.2 x £19,500) less the real inputs produced a figure greater than £1,950.00.

When and where to send the forms
The VAT Flat Rate Office at Grimsby advise that when applying for VAT Registration and wanting to use the Flat Rate Scheme from the date of registration, the VAT 600FRS form should NOT be submitted with the VAT 1. Instead it is recommended that one waits for the VAT registration number to be issued and then send the VAT 600FRS directly to HMRC at the Flat Rate Office:

Grimsby National Registration Service
HM Revenue & Customs
Imperial House
77 Victoria Street
Grimsby
DN31 1DB

This is apparently because the VAT 600FRS cannot be processed without the VAT Registration Number and the forms were then being overlooked after the VAT number was issued.

But if the VAT 600FRS has been overlooked in these circumstances, there seems to be no problem having the effective date of the FRS being back-dated to the date of the VAT Registration.

The VAT tribunal case of *Morgan (The Harrow Inn)* (VTD 19671) highlights quite how rough and ready is the flat rate scheme for small traders.

Mr and Mrs Morgan got it wrong. They ran a pub at which they also sold meals. The food sales marginally exceeded the drink sales, though following a refurbishment of the bar they expected that to reverse. But it didn't. And the tribunal upheld HMRC's view that VAT should have been paid at the restaurant rate of 12 per cent instead of the pub rate of 5.5 per cent.

There are 3 points to bear in mind here.

The first is that HMRC do not accept that a pub is a pub is a pub. In the Morgan case there appears to have been no separate restaurant area; the sale of food was ancillary to that of bar sales; for planning and rating purposes the premises were classed as a public house; they had an on-licence; and the lease of the premises described them as a public house. The Morgans understandably but erroneously thought that that made the business a pub and that 5.5 per cent was the applicable rate.

Second, a flat rate trader needs to be alert to the possibility that the category of trade (and hence the VAT rate) may change with time.

Third, even where it is obvious that a business straddles two categories there is no scope for apportioning turnover between them. For a 'gastro-pub', if the turnover is expected to be split 50.1 per cent drink; 49.9 per cent food, the applicable rate is 5.5 per cent. If it is expected to be 49.9 per cent drink: 50.1 per cent food, it is 12 per cent. The logical and sensible option of using an average rate of 8.75 per cent is not available.

Nor are these the only problems that lie beneath the surface of the flat-rate scheme. For example, the flat rate percentage may give a distorted result if the business would otherwise have any substantial zero-rated sales, perhaps through doing business with non-UK customers. Generally, the scheme works well only for simple fully-taxable cash businesses; and (as the Morgan case shows) even they can fall foul of it.

Clarification (Tax Bulletin 64)
In tax Bulletin Issue 61 HMRC published an article on the implications of a VAT flat rate scheme for the computation of profits. Following comments on that article HMRC have now revised their guidance on the interaction of the VAT flat rate scheme and calculation of trading profits.

An important point here is that where capital assets are purchased with a VAT inclusive value of £2,000 or more that VAT can be recovered in the normal way. This concession, however, cannot be used where the assets were:

- Acquired for resale or for incorporation in goods to be sold;
- Acquired to be hired out, leased or let;
- For consumption within one year; or
- Covered by the capital goods scheme.

The flat rate scheme removes the necessity to calculate VAT on each individual input and output for the VAT account. Instead, only the flat rate VAT will need to be posted to the VAT account. Where the concession for capital assets is adopted the VAT reclaimed will also be posted to the VAT account. Expenses will probably be shown inclusive of VAT as it is irrecoverable (similar to a business not registered for VAT) and it is likely that turnover will be shown net of the flat rate VAT payment. You may, however, find that the flat rate VAT payment is shown as a P&L account expense rather than deducted from total turnover. Where there is irrecoverable VAT on capital items it will form part of the cost of the asset on the balance sheet and the cost for capital allowances purposes. HMRC provides the following example:

Example:
The business has gross sales of £96,000 (including output VAT at 20% £16,000) and expenses of £60,000 (including irrecoverable VAT). The flat rate VAT for this business is 6% i.e. £5,760. A new machine is purchased (qualifying for capital allowances) at cost of £2,400 including VAT of £400.

The accounts will show:

	£	
Turnover	90,240	(96,000 less 5,760 flat rate VAT)
Expenses	60,000	
Profit	30,240	

If VAT is not reclaimed on the asset the cost for capital allowance purposes will be £2,400. If VAT is reclaimed the cost will be £2,000.

Disclosure of VAT avoidance schemes
*   Finance Act 2004 imposed new requirements on businesses to disclose certain transactions to HMRC. for example, any business which is involved in sale and leaseback arrangements, arrangements with confidentiality clauses, certain business promotions (including those using vouchers) or pre-payments between connected parties may have a requirement to disclose.

*   In addition to those listed above, there are also many other types of transaction which are caught. Because the legislation is so widely drawn, many businesses are likely to be affected. In addition, disclosure is subject to strict time limits and there can be severe penalties for failure to disclose (up to 15% of the tax involved). It is essential that a business knows whether it is required to disclose a particular transaction or series of transactions and the manner and time in which this is required to be done.

Choosing the correct rate
When a business moves onto the flat rate accounting scheme for VAT they are responsible for choosing an appropriate trade classification and flat rate percentage for their supplies. In the case of *Archibald and Co* the appellant intended to provide bookkeeping services and used the trade classification for accountants. However, she actually provided tax services to investment management businesses. She applied for a retrospective change to 'business services not listed elsewhere' which has a lower flat rate percentage. Unfortunately, the Tribunal found that choice of sectors made by the appellant was not unreasonable and there is no obligation in legislation for HMRC to retrospectively change a category or for a business to insist

that it be changed.

5.10 Transfer of a going concern (TOGC)
This covers the transfer of a business to another person or legal entity. The special rules only apply if the business transfers some or all of its assets.

These assets can include stock in trade, machinery, goodwill, premises and fixtures & fittings.

There are many conditions but if satisfied, then the transfer does not attract output VAT (there is no taxable supply) thus aiding the cash flow of the purchaser.

The TOGC rules are 'compulsory', people cannot opt out. So if operated incorrectly and output VAT is charged the new owner cannot reclaim this VAT as input VAT.

In FA2007 (Clause 99) where a business is transferred as a going concern after 31 August 2007, the seller will retain the VAT records except in cases where the buyer takes over the seller's VAT number.

In *Sam's Bistro Ltd VTD 19973* hearing it was established that Taylor's Coffee Shop was owned by Gillian Taylor and Susan Grant. They sold the premises and business to Neil Barker, who leased the premises to Sam's Bistro Ltd. (owned by Mr Barker), which carried on a licensed bistro and coffee shop business therein.

The question was whether there had been a transfer of a going concern for VAT purposes. the Tribunal held that the fact that the premises were now licensed did not mean a different business was being carried on after the transfer. The question therefore remained whether it made a difference that the premises and business had been sold to Mr Barker, who was not himself carrying on that business.

The Tribunal said that there was a distinction between the transfer of a business for VAT purposes, which had happened between Ms Taylor and Ms Grant, on the one hand, and the appellant on the other, and the transfer of legal and equitable interests. This was a TOGC for VAT purposes, despite the intervention of Mr Barker as landlord.

The appeal was therefore dismissed.

5.11 Distance selling
Distance selling occurs when a taxable person in one EC Member State (Member State of origin) supplies and delivers goods to a non-taxable person in another EC Member State (member State of destination). The most common type of distance selling occurs through mail order transactions. A non-taxable customer may be a private individual, public body, charity or any business which is too small to register or whose activities are totally exempt. It is important to note that distance selling can

only occur between Member States, so that mail order sales to the UK from outside the VAT territory, for instance from the Channel Islands, are not distance sales.

When a business established in another Member State exceeds the distance-selling threshold (£73,000) in the UK, they become liable to be registered here. Once registration is effected, all distance sales to the UK are taxed here.

The threshold limit is based on sales made during a calendar year from 1 January to 31 December. Taxable persons must keep records showing the value of their distance sales to each Member State, and must notify the fiscal authorities in the relevant State one their particular threshold has been reached. Under UK law, a liability to register for UK VAT arises from the day that sales exceed our threshold.

You may have already opted to make the place of supply the UK therefore you do not need to register for distance selling.

Distance sales are usually taxed in the member state of origin until you exceed the distance selling threshold of the destination member state, you will then be required to register with the member state in question.

5.12 EU & Services 1 January 2011
Some additional rules are introduced on 1 January 2011 that were not covered by the changes on 1 January 2010.

Here is a summary of the changes to be introduced with effect from 1 January 2011 (the relevant legislation to confirm the changes is contained in paras 15 and 16, Sch 36, Finance Act 2009);

- For business customers, the place of supply in respect of the following services is where the events actually take place: services in respect of admission to cultural, artistic, sporting, scientific, educational, entertainment or similar events (including fairs and exhibitions) and ancillary services relating to admission to such events.

- For non-business customers, the place of supply of the following services is where the activities concerned actually take place: services relating to cultural, artistic, sporting, scientific, educational, entertainment or similar activities (including fairs and exhibitions) and ancillary services relating to such activities, including services or organisers of such activities.

- For other services linked to these categories, the place of supply will revert to the default position, ie location of the customer for B2B sales. It is only the admission to cultural, artistic events, etc that will have a place of supply based on where the event takes place in the case of B2B sales.

Example 1:
Jane is VAT registered in the UK and has been asked to give computer training to a group of Italian employees who work for a company in Rome. The employees in question will travel to the UK and will be trained at Jane's office in London. Jane will invoice the Italian company for her services.

Until 31 December 2010, Jane must charge UK VAT to the Italian company. This is because the place of supply for such services (which are classed as educational) is based on where the work is performed until this date. The Italian company will then seek to reclaim this VAT by making an Eighth Directive claim to get a refund from the UK tax authorities (assuming they have no partial exemption issues that restrict input tax claims).

With effect from 1 January 2011, the place of supply will become the default position, ie based on the location of the customer in Italy, because this is a B2B sale. The work will now avoid a charge of UK VAT and the Italian company will deal with the VAT on its own return instead, using the reverse charge system. Jane will declare the sale on both her VAT return (Box 6) and on an EU Sales List.

Example 2:
Jane from Example 1 was so pleased with the interest shown in her services by the Italian company that she has decided to hire a room in a London hotel and present a course called 'Computer Services for Italians', charging a fee of £100 per head for Italian business customers to come and learn about computer issues.

In this situation, Jane is charging an admission fee for an educational event and the place of supply will continue to be where the service is physically performed (where the event takes place), ie the UK. The Italian delegates will all be charged UK VAT on their course fees, even though some or all of them will be 'in business', which they may be able to reclaim through the overseas refund system.

Example 3:
Jane is VAT registered in the UK as a freelance tax lecturer, working for a UK business, and does a number of lectures each year in Jersey. The place of supply until 31 December 2010 is Jersey (where the service is performed) so no UK VAT is charged on her sales invoices to her UK based client. However, VAT will be charged after 1 January 2011 because the place of supply is now where the customer is based, ie UK rather than Jersey.

- This applies to both professional services (architects, surveyors, estate agents) and construction services (plumber, bricklayer, carpenter).

- The rules could mean a UK business having to register for VAT in another country if that is where the land is based (See Example 4).

Example 4:
Mike trades as an architect in the UK and is VAT registered. He is working on a project for a wealthy individual who lives in Spain, concerning a property being built by the Spaniard in Ireland. In this situation, the place of supply in relation to Mike's services is Ireland, and Mike will need to register for VAT in Ireland if the value of his services (and the value of other services he supplies in Ireland) exceeds the Irish VAT registration threshold.

Many EU countries have zero VAT registration threshold. Our UK threshold (£73,000 of taxable sales in any previous 12 month period, or £73,000 of taxable sales in the next 30 days) is one of the highest in the EU.

Note that the place of supply rules for land related supplies are different.

The changes to international services rules from 1 January 2010 introduced new reporting requirements, based on the requirements for despatches of goods across the European Union. They allow member states whose taxpayers receive such services to ensure that the reverse charge is applied.

The above changes refer to services performed in the UK for a EU VAT registered business customer. If the EU customer is not VAT registered as a business UK VAT is charged at the usual rate. If the services are carried out in the EU country, the local VAT rules and regulation limits apply.

There is a list (EC Sales List (ESL)) which has to be submitted to HM Revenue & Customs, giving the identity of each customer (via its VAT registration number) and the value of the relevant services provided to it during the reporting period. Relevant businesses introduced a new reporting requirement into their systems to gather such data. Organisations which already despatch goods within the EU will be familiar with the appropriate system changes.

The reporting period is quarterly, although monthly submissions will be allowed. The EU requires that these details be disseminated across the EU within one month at the end of each reporting period. This means that taxpayers and HMRC together cannot take more than one month from the end of the reporting period to have fully processed and provided the information. Currently, HMRC proposes to give only two weeks for submission of the data by paper means, and three weeks for such submission by electronic means. It may be that the option to submit by paper is quickly abandoned. The reporting requirements for movement of goods are currently a much more generous six weeks.

If a service is exported under these rules and therefore not charged to UK VAT it will automatically go on the ESL. However, that will not always be so. First, if a customer is a business but not registered for VAT in its own member state, it cannot be included on the ESL and will simply drop out. Second, is that the ESL is designed to report those cases where a reverse charge applies in the member state of the customer, which can sometimes be a different situation in cases where no VAT is chargeable in the UK.

Freight transport services

HM Revenue & Customs brief 13/2010 deals with an anomaly in the new place of supply rules, which became effective from 1 January 2010.

Under the new rules, where there is a supply of freight transport that goes on outside the EU entirely, but is made between a UK-based freight supplier and a UK customer, VAT is chargeable as though it were a UK supply. Under the previous rules, it had been treated as supplied where performed, which was outside the EU altogether. The new rules have the potential effect of disadvantaging caryatides in particular - they may buy their freight supplies from a UK supplier, and have no means of reclaiming VAT charged to them. By concession, HMRC will agree that such a supply will be treated as 'used and enjoyed' outside the EU and therefore not subject to VAT. This is a temporary measure, since it contradicts EU legislation, and will therefore be adopted until such time as a more permanent solution can be found. Unhelpfully, the treatment is said to be applicable from 15 March, rather than 1 January, thus leaving a period of some 11 weeks in which the supplies in question are subject to VAT despite the obvious unfairness and illogicality of the position.

5.13 Option to tax

On 1 June 2008, changes to the 'option to tax' regime were introduced following lengthy consultation. The purpose of the changes is to introduce new flexibility to the regime but also to rewrite the provisions in Schedule 10 VATA 1994 to clarify its scope. It is also to prepare for the first revocations on 1 August 2009 after 20 years since the first properties opted to tax.

These changes deal with:

- new rules for relevant associates;

- introduction of certificates to disapply an option to tax for buildings to be converted into dwellings and land supplied to housing associations.;

- introduction of disapplication of the option to tax for intermediaries supplying buildings to be converted into dwellings etc.;

- revised definition of occupation including new exclusion for automatic teller machines;

- introduction of a new way to opt to tax (a real estate election) which does not require individual notifications of each option;

- extension and changes to the cooling off period;

- automatic revocation of an option to tax after six years if no property interest has been held during that time;

- introduction of rules governing the revocation of an option to tax after 20 years;

- provision that in future, an option to tax applies to land and buildings on the same site - with a special transitional rule for existing options;

- a new ability to exclude a new building and land within its curtilage from an option to tax;

- new appeal rights.

A revised Schedule 10 VATA 1994 is brought in by statutory instrument. Guidance is contained in a new HMRC Notice 742A which in turn refers to new forms that must be used for notification of an option, etc.

National option to tax unit - new contact details
From 4 February 2009, all postal correspondence relating to options to tax, should be sent to:

Option to Tax National Unit
Cotton House
7 Cochrane Street
Glasgow
G1 1GY

Tel: 0141 285 4174/4175
Fax: 0141 285 4454

Forgot to notify HMRC about your decision to opt to tax?
The important reference point on the late notification issue is HMRC's Business Brief 13/05, which clearly clarifies HMRC's policy on belated notifications.

The key point to identify is whether the business has <u>acted as though it had made the option to tax election</u> (e.g. accounting for output tax on rental income and reclaiming input tax on related costs) <u>or whether it is now trying to retrospectively go back and adjust its records to gain a VAT advantage</u>. In simple terms, is there an attempt to "backdate an option" or is it simply a case of making a "belated notification."

HMRC have the power to accept a belated notification if a trader "provides evidence, such as the minutes of a Board or management meeting, or correspondence referring to the decision." However, alternative evidence or confirmation that VAT has been accounted for as though the option had been made can also be provided.

5.14 Appeals

The case of *NVM Private Equity Ltd (TC00418)* provides a salutary lesson concerning the tactic of refraining from appealing. It appears that the taxpayer received an appealable ruling from HMRC on an issue and took the view that it would antagonise HMRC unnecessarily to lodge a formal appeal. Instead, it continued 'discussions' and followed advice to the effect that a change of HMRC policy on the issue was imminent. That, as it turned out, was correct in its case, but it did not lead HMRC to withdraw the original negative ruling. HMRC argued that an appeal against that ruling was out of time by the time the taxpayer realised that HMRC would not relent. The fact that HMRC's policy was now inconsistent with that ruling was irrelevant. The tribunal agreed, and dismissed the appeal. This may seem contrary to natural justice, but it makes the point that lodging appeals to protect one's position cannot be regarded as confrontational or provocative. HMRC sees it as a natural part of the process between the taxpayer and itself, and fears that HMRC may be offended are almost always misguided.

6 EXEMPT TRADERS

These are (a) small traders with a turnover of no more than £73,000 from 1 April 2011, and (b) traders who deal only with exempt supplies. The first category need not register, do not have to charge VAT on their sales, and are not liable to account for VAT, but they cannot recover from HMRC the VAT charged on their purchases. They can register voluntarily and if they do so they are no longer exempt. The second category of trader cannot obtain refunds of input tax, but where there are both taxable and exempt supplies a proportion of the input tax is refundable. The Partial Exemption De Minimis scheme allows certain predominately exempt businesses with only minor taxable income to register voluntarily for VAT and achieve full import tax recovery up to a maximum of £7,500 p.a.

HMRC has announced changes to the partial exemption de minimis rules for VAT. They take effect for VAT periods commencing on or after 1 April 2010 and are designed to make it easier and less time-consuming for businesses (especially smaller ones) to confirm their de minimis status.

The April 2010 changes introduce an optional simplified test to establish whether or not a business falls below the de minimis threshold and a further option of applying the test annually instead of in each VAT period. The new rules can be used without prior approval from HMRC.

The de minimis limit remains the same, i.e. input tax relating to exempt supplies must be no more than £625 per month on average and no more than 50% of total input tax.

Simplified tests

The simplified tests can be used instead of a making a full partial exemption calculation. If, in a VAT period, a business passes Test 1 or Test 2, it may treat itself as de minimis and can provisionally recover input tax relating to exempt supplies.

Test 1: Total input tax is no more than £625 per month on average and the value of exempt supplies is no more than 50% of the value of all supplies.

Test 2: Total input tax less input tax directly attributable to taxable supplies is no more than £625 per month on average, and the value of exempt supplies is no more than 50% of the value of all supplies.

Annual adjustment

At the end of its partial exemption year a business must apply the de minimis test to the year as a whole. If it passes either Test 1 or Test 2 for the year, it can recover all of its input tax relating to exempt supplies and is not required to carry out any further partial exemption calculations.

If Test 1 and Test 2 are both failed for the year, the business must carry out a full partial exemption calculation to see if it passes the normal de minimis test. Any under/over recovery of input tax must then be accounted for as part of the annual adjustment.

Annual test

The current rules require a business to apply the de minimis test in each VAT period. The new annual test gives the option of applying the de minimis test once a year instead. It allows a business to treat itself as de minimis in its current year if it qualified the year before. This means it can provisionally recover input tax on exempt supplies in each VAT period with no need for in-year partial exemption calculations.

There are three conditions for using the annual test.
The business must:

(a) Pass the de minimis test for its previous partial exemption year.

(b) consistently apply the annual test throughout any given partial exemption year.

(c) Have reasonable grounds for not expecting to incur more than £1m input tax in its current partial exemption year.

If any of these conditions are not met then the business must apply the de minimis test in each VAT period.

A business that qualifies for the annual test must still review its de minimis status at the year-end. If it fails the test for the year, it must repay the input tax relating to exempt supplies that was provisionally recovered.

7 EXEMPT GOODS AND SERVICES

A large number of kinds of goods and services are exempt from VAT, that is to say VAT cannot be charged when such goods are sold, even by a registered trader. These categories are summarised below.

Group 1   The grant of any interest in or right over land but not the construction of buildings for industrial or commercial use, the letting of accommodation, parking or camping facilities or fishing or taking game. Bedroom accommodation in hotels is taxable but not other accommodation in hotels, or elsewhere. From 1 August 1989 an election (subject to many qualifications) can be made to waive this exemption, and thus recover input tax. Non residential buildings and civil engineering works are standard rated from 1 April 1989.

Group 2   Insurance, covering also services provided by brokers and agents: most marine, aviation and transport insurance is zero rated, but not for merely providing a list of clients to a financial consultant and sharing commission.

Group 3   Postal services, but not cable services, telephone or telex. From 31 January 2011 some postal services are standard rated. See 10.32 below, p.410:

Group 4   Betting, gaming and lotteries, but admission charges, club subscriptions and takings from gaming machines are taxable. Partial exemption and bookies (Business Brief 17/06). HMRC have decided not to appeal a decision at Tribunal that bookmakers who add content to specialist racing TV to advertise their taxable services, may now treat the VAT as residual. HMRC remain of the view that, where no such content is added, the VAT incurred is wholly related to exempt betting and in not recoverable.

HMRC accept that bookmakers may treat VAT incurred on Sky Sports as residual because the broadcasts are not exclusively related to exempt betting. VAT incurred on TV equipment is also residual provided it is used for broadcasts that relate to both taxable and exempt supplies. If the equipment is used wholly for specialist racing TV, then the VAT incurred id irrecoverable.

Group 5   Finance, i.e. dealing in money or credit, banking and the sale of securities, but stockbrokers' commissions and unit trust management fees are taxable. The charge made by credit card companies on retailers is exempt.

Group 6   Education, including the supply of incidental services and covering the facilities provided by universities, colleges, schools, non profit-making education bodies, youth clubs and similar organisations.

Group 7   Health, covering goods and services provided by medical practitioners, (dentists are not wholly exempt), opticians, nurses, pharmaceutical chemists, hearing aid dispensers, hospitals, osteopathy, chiropractors, practitioner psychologists (from 1 July 2009) and health services generally. Protective boots and helmets purchased by businesses are chargeable.

Group 8   Burial and cremation services.

Group 9   Trade unions and professional bodies.

Group 10   Sport, sports competitions and physical education.

Group 11   Works of art etc. Disposals exempt from capital gains tax.

Group 12   Fund raising by charities.

Group 13   Cultural services etc.

Group 14   Supplies of goods where input tax cannot be recovered.

Group 15   Investment gold.

The salary foregone is exempt from VAT when employees opt to use a company car instead of salary.

8 ZERO RATED GOODS AND SERVICES

Zero rating means that, although the goods are theoretically taxable, the rate of tax is nil. Because zero rated goods are taxable, suppliers of these goods can recover tax they have suffered on relevant purchases; they do not, however, charge tax on their sales of zero rated goods. All goods exported by a registered trader are zero rated, but not goods exported or imported for processing and re-exported. Other zero rated supplies are set out in Schedule 8 VAT Act 1994, subsequent statutory orders, and these groups are summarised below.

Group 1   Food for human consumption, including many packaged goods; animal feeding stuffs but not soft drinks (it has now been held that freshly-pressed citrus fruits are zero rated), alcoholic drinks, confectionery, ice cream, pet foods, seeds, and animals yielding food for human consumption. There are many exemptions to this group.

Group 2   Water, other than distilled water, and sewerage services except when supplied to businesses.

Group 3   Publications such as books, newspapers, periodicals, music, maps, etc., but not stationery.

Group 4   Talking books, radio sets, boats, maintenance of 'talking books', recorders and magnetic tape and radio sets for use by the blind and handicapped, much other equipment for handicapped persons or charities, including lifts, alarms and welfare vehicles; medical sterilising equipment for charities, and toilet facilities in charitable buildings.

Group 5   Construction of dwellings, residential accommodation and charitable purposes and the grant of a major interest in the property, including sale of the freehold or grant of lease for over 21 years, but only when the trader is the person constructing the building. Residential accommodation includes homes for children, the aged and infirm, students, the armed forces, monasteries and nunneries. In accordance with EC law the construction of new industrial and commercial buildings will be subject to VAT. The letting for one or two weeks in a year of time-share holiday homes by a long lease is not zero rated (*Cottage Holiday Assoc. Ltd. v Customs and Excise,* 1982). Note that land is exempt and that the maintenance of buildings is chargeable at the VAT rate. VAT applies to structural alterations, sheds and greenhouses in private gardens, and fixtures in new buildings, but not to substantial conversion, alteration and enlargement of ancient monuments and listed buildings, zero rating applied to building alterations for the benefit of a resident handicapped person.Landlords can opt to charge VAT on non-residential rents. In this case tenants pay tax on half the rents in the first year, or for five years where they are charities.

Group 6   Protected buildings.

Group 7   Services to overseas traders or for overseas purposes.

Group 8   Transport, covering the supply, services and maintenance of ships above 15 tons and not used for recreational purposes, and aircraft above 18,000 pounds and not used for recreation; and the transport of passengers in vehicles carrying 10 or more passengers from 1 April 2001 (previously 12) passengers (i.e. excluding taxis). Airline meals are not taxable. Cycle helmets from 1 April 2001.

Group 9   Caravans above the limits for use as trailers (i.e. 7 metres in length or 2.3 metres in width) and houseboats.

               With effect from 20 April 2010, the minimum width of caravan that will be eligible to be zero-rated will rise from 2.3 metres to 2.55 metres. The minimum length will remain unchanged at 7 metres. All caravans less than 2.55 metres wide (and less than 7 metres long) will be subject to VAT at the standard rate.

               This change means that, from 20 April 2010, the zero rate will cease to apply to the sale of second-hand caravans that are up to 2.55 metres wide and that were originally supplied zero-rated.

Group 10   Gold bullion and gold coins, when supplied by a Central Bank to another Central Bank or to and from a Central Bank to a member of the London Gold Market. The Finance Act 1993 s 45 provides that on and after 1 April 1993 where any person makes a supply of gold for business purposes that supply is a taxable supply, but not a zero-rated supply. Where the supplier is a taxable person and the supplies are made in connection with the business of the customer, the latter (i.e. the purchaser) must account for and pay tax on the supply on the supplier's behalf. The supplies may consist of gold, gold coins and goods containing gold, taxable at the open market value of the gold contained in the goods.

Group 11   Bank notes.

Group 12   Drugs, medicines and appliances supplied on prescription, whether under the National Health Service or otherwise including, ambulances and wheelchairs supplied to hospitals and car adaptations for the disabled; also cars leased to disabled persons under mobility schemes, medical and scientific equipment, including computers, donated to hospitals, bathroom equipment for the handicapped in charitable residential homes, and equipment for charitable first aid (including certain resuscitation models) and rescue services. A recent tribunal (*GB Searle & Co Ltd.* 13439) has decided that an aerosol spray used to kill asthma- causing dust mites cannot qualify for the relief, because asthma sufferers are not to be regarded as being handicapped. This follows an earlier tribunal decision in which it was held that dyslexia is not a disability.

Group 13   Imports and exports subject to qualifications.

Group 14   Tax free shops.

Group 15   Charities. Much equipment used or supplied by charities is zero rated (See under Group 4) and zero rating applied to medicinal products supplied to a charity for medical research both for humans and animals - see Value Added Tax (Handicapped Persons and Charities Order) 1986; also television, radio and cinema advertising, donated goods, and equipment for veterinary research. Fundamental alterations to the zero-rating reliefs enjoyed by charities (and organisations that covenant profits to charities) came into effect from 1 April 2000.

In addition to the existing relief on the sale of donated goods to charities (and other organisations covenanting profits to charities), zero-rating will now also be available in respect of goods that are made available to disabled people or those in receipt of means tested benefits. At the same time, the hire of donated goods will also be zero-rated, provided that the sale would have so qualified.

The number of charity events increased to up to 15 of each type or kind of event in any one location in a 12 month period. For small-scale events the exemption will apply to any number of events, provided the gross weekly income does not exceed £1,000.

Click through services on websites also fall within this group.

Group 16   Clothing for young children, industrial protective clothing (other than boots and helmets supplied to employees) and motor cycle crash helmets.

Group 17   HMRC has issued Revenue & Customs Brief 46/09 confirming that the zero rate will apply to any transaction in EU emissions allowances and transferable units issued pursuant to the Kyoto Protocol. This will include over the counter spot trades, transactions for future delivery and options. Cross-border transactions are not affected.

The tax point for these supplies will be the earliest of either the transfer of title or payment. Therefore any amount purporting to be VAT on tax invoices dated from 31 July 2009 will not be recoverable as input tax.

9 REDUCED RATE GOODS AND SERVICES

The reduced rate band was initially introduced on 1st January 1995 with the first step of VAT on domestic fuel or power. It was initially planned to raise it to the full standard rate then 20%. Once a higher band has been imposed on a particular group of services or goods it cannot then be totally removed or reduced to below 5%.

As with any VAT issue there are many exclusions and special rules that apply. As a result the following can only be taken as a brief outline. "For more information please see Notice 701/39 Schedule 7a - Reduced Rate".

Group 1   Domestic fuel or power.
> (a)   coal, coke or other solid substances held out for sale solely as fuel. Includes kindling but not matches.
> (b)   coal gas, water gas, producer gases or similar gases. Excludes any road fuel subject to excise duty.
> (c)   petroleum gases, or other gaseous hydrocarbons, whether in a gaseous or liquid state. Excludes any road fuel subject to excise duty.
> (d)   fuel oil, gas oil or kerosene. Excludes any hydrocarbon oil on which excise duty is payable.
> (e)   electricity, heat or air-conditioning.

Group 2   Energy - saving materials: Insulation.
Includes the supply of, and installation services of, energy-saving materials in residential accommodation and a building intended for use solely for a relevant charitable purpose. For the purposes of this Group "energy-saving materials" means any of the following -
> (a)   insulation for walls, floors, ceilings, roofs or lofts or for water tanks, pipes or other plumbing fittings;
> (b)   draught stripping for windows and doors;
> (c)   central heating system controls (including thermostatic radiator valves);

    (d)   hot water system controls;
    (e)   solar panels;
    (f)   wind turbines;
    (g)   water turbines.

Group 3 Heating equipment, security goods and gas supplies: grant funded installation or connection.

1.   Supplies to a qualifying person of any services of installing heating appliances in the qualifying person's sole or main residence.
2.   Supplies of heating appliances made to a qualifying person by a person who installs those appliances in the qualifying person's sole or main residence.
3.   Supplies to a qualifying person of services of connecting, or reconnecting, a mains gas supply to the qualifying person's sole or main residence.
4.   Supplies to a qualifying person of services of installing, maintaining or repairing a central heating system in the qualifying person's sole or main residence.

For the purposes of this Group, a person to whom a supply is made is "a qualifying person" if at the time of the supply he -

    (a)   is aged 60 or over; or
    (b)   is in receipt of one or more of the following benefits: Council tax benefit, disability living allowance, any element of child credit other than the family element, working tax credit, housing benefit or income support, an income-based jobseeker's allowance, disablement pension or war disablement pension.

Group 4 Women's sanitary products.
These mean women's sanitary products of any of the following descriptions.

    (a)   Products that are designed, and marketed, as being solely for use for absorbing, or otherwise collecting, lochia or menstrual flow.
    (b)   panty liners, other than panty liners that are designed as being primarily for use as incontinence products;
    (c)   sanitary belts.

Group 5 Children's car seats.
For the purposes of this Group, the following are "children's car seats" -

    (a)   a safety seat;
    (b)   the combination of a safety seat and a related wheeled framework;
    (c)   a booster seat;
    (d)   a booster cushion,
    (e)   bases for the above (with effect from 1 July 2009).

In this Group "child" means a person aged under 14 years.

Group 6   Residential conversions.
1.   The supply, in the course of a qualifying conversion, of qualifying services related to the conversion.
2.   The supply of building materials if –
     (a)   the materials are supplied by a person who, in the course of a qualifying conversion, is supplying qualifying services related to the conversion, and
     (b)   those services include the incorporation of the materials in the building concerned or its immediate site.

A "qualifying conversion" means –
     (a)   a changed number of dwellings conversion (as defined);
     (b)   a house in multiple occupation conversion (as defined); or
     (c)   a special residential conversion (as defined).

Group 7   Residential renovations and alterations.
1.   The supply, in the course of the renovation or alteration of qualifying residential premises, of qualifying services related to the renovation or alteration.
2.   The supply of building materials if -
     (a)   the materials are supplied by a person who, in the course of the renovation or alteration of qualifying residential premises, is supplying qualifying services related to the renovation or alteration, and
     (b)   those services include the incorporation of the materials in the premises concerned or their immediate site.

Meaning of "alteration" and "qualifying residential premises"
1.   For the purposes of this Group -
     "alteration" includes extension;
     "qualifying residential premises" means –
     (a)   a single household dwelling,
     (b)   a multiple occupancy dwelling, or
     (c)   a building, or part of a building, which, when it was last lived in, was used for a relevant residential purpose.
2.   Where a building, when it was last lived in, formed part of a relevant residential unit then, to the extent that it would not be so regarded otherwise, the building shall be treated as having been used for a relevant residential purpose.
3.   A building forms part of a relevant residential unit at any time when -
     (a)   it is one of a number of buildings on the same site, and
     (b)   the buildings are used together as a unit for a relevant residential purpose.

10 MISCELLANEOUS

10.1 Local authorities
(And similar bodies) are entitled to refunds of VAT suffered on purchases in relation to non-business activities.

10.2 Entertainment
10.2.1 VAT on entertaining overseas customers
In 2010 HMRC announced a change in policy on the treatment of business entertainment provided to overseas customers. This followed a decision in the European Court of Justice.

Essentially the change is that the UK's block on recovering input tax for entertaining overseas customers is contrary to EU law, and businesses can now recover input tax and make claims for earlier years.

However, the block on recovering input tax on entertainment provided to anyone other than an overseas customer, for example, UK customers and non-UK business contacts who are not customers, remains effective and any VAT incurred on the costs of such entertainment cannot be recovered.

10.2.2 Business entertainment
Tax suffered on business entertaining cannot be deducted from output tax. Tax on allowable subsistence for business purposes is, however, deductible from output tax.

Certain recent VAT tribunal decisions have dealt with entertainment and the VAT position where staff, partners and guests may be present. Where staff and partners are present and the entertainment provided is to maintain or improve staff relations, it is done wholly for business purposes and any VAT incurred was input tax and is recoverable despite the presence of partners. If, however, it was mainly a partner function at which employees were in attendance then that expenditure would not be for business purposes and the VAT incurred would not be input tax.

Where, however, employees and guests are present (including guests of employees (by definition this should include spouses and partners of employees)) that expenditure is non deductible under the business entertainment provisions. Such expenditure requires apportionment between employees and guests so that the VAT attributable to the entertainment of employees only is recovered.

HMRC make the point that as this is a result of the clarification of the law by the VAT tribunals, retrospective claims can be made subject to the four year capping provisions. However, HMRC do make the point that the entire area is under review as they do not agree. HMRC position is that staff entertainment inherently involves private consumption which, as VAT is a tax on private consumption, in principle ought to be taxed.

10.3 Hotel, B&B etc. accommodation (& conferences)

(a) Up to four weeks accommodation, including board and service, is taxable at the current full 20% rate. After four weeks the charge for the rent of the room or rooms is not taxable. The charge for the use of services will be assumed to be not less than 20% of the accommodation charge excluding meals. The charge for meals also bears the current rate. Gross profits by tour operators on tours in the European Community are taxable.

In Business Brief 15/06 HMRC announced a change in their interpretation of the law regarding the application of the reduced value rule for long stay guests in hotels.

VAT registered businesses that are involved in providing accommodation, such as hotels, guest houses and B&B's etc. may be able to take advantage of the Afro Caribbean HA VAT Tribunal Decision. This case overturned the long held HMRC view that continuous long term stays (over 28 days) could only be VAT free or subject to a reduced amount of VAT on ancillary services where the supply was direct to the individual and not an organisation that was responsible for placing the individual.

HMRC have accepted the decision and are inviting claims for overpaid VAT from organisations that may have incorrectly declared and paid VAT on such long term stays.

(b) Where a room is provided for a meeting, conference or similar function organised by a third party (but not where the primary purpose is for a supply of catering), HMRC now accepts that the provision of conference/function room hire, meals and sleeping accommodation under the 24 hour delegate rate, even where made in return for an inclusive charge, should be treated as separate supplies. These will be taxable supplies, with the exception of the conference/ function room hire, which will be an exempt supply, unless the hotel has opted to tax its supplies. In cases where a single consideration is paid for supplies having different liabilities, for example where a charge for room hire is made under the 24-hour delegate rate by a hotel which has not opted to tax its room hire, a fair and reasonable apportionment of the consideration must be made.

There is no change to the treatment of eight hour delegate charges.

Where hotels organise and run conferences or similar events themselves and charge for entry to delegates, their supplies are always taxable supplies.

10.4 Farming and fishing

Farmers and fishing businesses need not register for VAT unless they choose to do so. Non-registration means that they will not charge VAT on their sales but they will not recover VAT on their expenditure, and not have to make VAT returns. They are, however, able to charge VAT registered customers with a flat percentage of 4% on their sales, and this amount will be credited to the customers on the latter's returns. This flat rate percentage is viewed as compensation for the input tax not reclaimed and is retained by the farmer.

10.5 Second-hand goods

From 1 January 1995 the second-hand scheme previously only used by antique and second-hand car and boat dealers was extended to all other second-hand goods (except precious metals and gems). The output VAT is calculated on the gross profit, i.e. difference between the purchase and selling prices, and not on the selling price alone.

With effect from 17 March 1998 purchases of businesses whose assets include goods within the second-hand margin scheme can no longer use the 'transfer of going concern' purchase price to calculate the margin - instead they must use the price paid by the transferors for the goods in question.

10.6 VAT on Business Gifts

No output tax will be due if the total value of gifts to the same person does not exceed £50 in any 12 month period. If this limit is breached, VAT is due in full.

10.7 Credit card charges - additional & included

HMRC has issued a Business Brief on the VAT treatment of the extra charges made in return for accepting a credit card in payment for goods.

Where the vendor of the goods charges the extra sum. HMRC views this as further consideration for the goods themselves, which therefore follows the liability of these goods. Where an agent, such as a travel agent, makes the charge, it is an exempt financial commission.

It should be remembered that this is only HMRC view, but it is a policy that has attracted considerable opposition. It is by no means clear that a charge made specifically for allowing the purchase to be made by credit card attaches to the goods themselves, rather than to the means of payment. It should also be noted that any future court decision ruling that HMRC was incorrect in applying this policy would not automatically oblige HMRC to make a refund to disadvantaged retailers, since it would apply the 'unjust enrichment rules' as it clearly states in the Business Brief.

Businesses should consider their position carefully before deciding whether to follow HMRC' policy, and if not, should also consider informing it of their decision.

Reclaiming VAT on purchases made using credit/debit cards

The docket signed by the purchaser includes a section stating that a 2.5 per cent charge has been made by the store's finance company for processing the transaction, and that the total price paid by the purchaser has remained the same. This creates a non-VATable supply on the 2.5 per cent element of the total, leaving only the 97.5 per cent element as being VAT-inclusive, enabling the store group to retain a larger amount of the proceeds than they would otherwise have done had the 2.5 per cent not been charged. Consequently, on a purchase costing, say, £235, if settled by credit card, VAT of only £34.13 will be included in the purchase price, not £35. This benefits the store, but not the consumer.

HMRC won their appeal against the ruling made in the High Courts in favour of Debenhams. The House of Lords refused Debenhams right to appeal to them.

10.8 Mobile phones

HMRC has published its revised policy concerning mobile phones, following a change to the income tax arrangements for these devices. With immediate effect, those businesses that provide mobile phones free-of-charge to employees may (subject to partial exemption) reclaim VAT on the cost of the mobile phone and its connection charge. This is the case even if the mobile phone would be used partly privately and partly for business.

The VAT on the phone calls will be apportionable as between private and business use, but businesses that only reimburse business use phone calls, or recharge the private use element to the employee, will be able to recover VAT in full on the telephone charges. In the last case, the recharge to the employees must carry VAT, even if it is simply deducted from the monthly payslip.

10.9 Tour operator's margin scheme

First *Choice Holidays plc* (16379) discovered during the course of 1998 that, in its view, it had over-declared VAT on its tour operators' margin scheme calculations. It had treated all of its holidays as being sold at catalogue price. Under its commission arrangement with the travel agents, it received 90% of the catalogue value, with the remaining 10% being kept by agents. But the agents had sole discretion whether to discount the holidays in order to attract customers, with the full financial consequences of such a discount falling on themselves and not on First Choice.

The tribunal reasoned that, if there had been no agent in place, then there could have been no debate that the selling price to the customer was the discounted price. It could not see that the agent was providing third party consideration in any meaningful way, and therefore the tribunal was happy to overlook the valuations in the documentation that First Choice had issued.

10.10 Delivery charges - Plantiflor

The *Plantiflor* case hinged on whether charges Parcel Force made for delivering products to customers could be regarded as the provision of an exempt postal service directly as between Parcel Force and the customer, or whether Parcel Force was providing that service to Plantiflor, which then had to sell the service on to the customer as a standard-rated supply of commercial delivery.

In this case, the tribunal had decided that Plantiflor's collection of the Parcel Force charges was in essence an agency arrangement and that the exemption should flow through to the customer. The High Court disagreed, and now the Court of Appeal has had the opportunity to consider the matter and has reinstated the tribunal's view.

This is a decision that will perturb HMRC and which it is likely to appeal to the House of Lords. It is not a decision whose scope would be restricted solely to postal charges relating to mail order. It potentially strikes at the very root of the VAT supply chain's integrity. It raises the question about whether any activity that is not transformed as it is sold on need be regarded as a supply through that chain, as opposed to being supplied directly to the end user.

10.11 Holiday assessment

The Edinburgh VAT tribunal has foiled HMRC' attempt to obtain VAT from the wrong taxpayer for a period during which he was on holiday.

Franco and Maria Cortellessa (16333), who ran a fish and chip shop, took a six week holiday in Italy. For that six week period alone they rented their shop to another operator, who used it to carry on a fish and chip trade.

It seems that the tenant did not register for or account for VAT on its six weeks' worth of takings. This came to light while the appellants were on holiday, when a HMRC officer visited the shop and became aware that the tenant was failing to declare VAT. But instead of pursuing the tenant, the officer pursued the owners for VAT on the turnover that belonged to the tenant. In order to back up this argument, HMRC argued that the owners should have deregistered for VAT because they had ceased trading, despite the fact that they had a clear intention to trade after the six week holiday.

10.12 Professional fees in connection with exempt supplies

In *RAP Group Plc v C & E Commissioners* (2000) STC 980 it was held that KPMG's services were in connection with the issue of shares, an exempt supply and accordingly input VAT could not be reclaimed.

10.13 Composite and multiple supplies

In *Card Protection Plan Ltd. v C & E Commissioners* (2001) UCHL/4, it was held that the supply was essentially insurance (exempt) and that the other supplies were 'ancillary' so they were exempt also. HMRC have issued a business brief (2/01) following this and states that "supply which comprises a single supply from an economic point of view should not be artificially split so as to distort the VAT system".

The first group to fall foul of this are opticians who previously split the supply of glasses from the supply of the lens prescription are to charge VAT at 20% on the total supply.

10.14 Improved grants under the listed place of worship grants scheme
The existing listed place of worship grants scheme provides grants which in effect reduce the irrecoverable VAT on certain church repairs from 20% to 0%. From 4 January 2011 the scheme will no longer include works on clocks, pews, bells, organs and professional services such as architect fees. As of 1 April 2011 the scheme has quarterly budgets and claims paid pro rate per total claims received in any one quarter.

10.15 Labour only suppliers and the VAT threshold
Labour only suppliers of services are sometimes able to stay below the VAT registration turnover threshold by arranging for their customer to buy the materials directly. As a result, the materials do not form part of the labour only supplier's turnover. Another way to do this is to arrange for the labour only supplier to act as the customer's buying agent. However, there is a trap for the unwary. If the goods are acquired in the agent's name and the customer's name is not disclosed the agent is treated as supplying the goods as principal. Accordingly, the materials form part of his turnover. This can be avoided by disclosing the customer's name and obtaining an invoice for the materials in the name of the customer.

10.16 Care homes
By a quirk of the VAT legislation it is only possible to zero rate the construction of a new building which will become a care home if the new building makes up the entirety of the institution. Therefore, if a new freestanding building, which creates additional capacity for an existing care home institution, is constructed, the services are subject to VAT.

A taxpayer, *St Andrew's Property management Limited (20499)*, was informed by Revenue & Customs that its construction services would be standard rated because, although the new building would constitute the entirety of the actual car home, the care home was part of a wider institution which carried out wide-ranging services of a care and health nature.

The tribunal disagreed. The home should be regarded as an institution in its own right. The new building, which comprised all of the care home, could be zero rated.

10.17 Care home lift
The VAT tribunal decision in the case of *Friends of the Elderly (20597)* provides

welcome clarification concerning the scope of the zero rate for a qualifying installation of a lift in a care home. The appellants argued that the architect's services could also be zero rated as a necessary part of the installation of the lift. Although it is a general rule of thumb that the legislation precludes any zero rate applying to professional services associated with such construction work, that is not the case with regard to the zero rate for these lifts. The tribunal accepted that the legislation was broader in this case, and that the professional services in question were zero rated.

10.18 Weight Watchers fees
Slimming group Weight Watchers was told that it must pay VAT on the full weekly fee it receives from slimming members. At London's High Court, Mr Justice Morgan backed Revenue & Customs in its claim that the £4.95 weekly fees - which constitute the majority of Weight Watchers' members' payments - should all be subject to VAT at the standard rate.

10.19 Animal Charities
Animal refuge charities may be able to recover hundreds of thousands of pounds following a recent VAT tribunal ruling that the sale of donated cats and dogs is zero-rated.

The sale by a charity of donated goods is currently zero-rated for VAT. However, prior to this decision, animals were considered donations only if they were directly handed over by their owners. This meant that the sale of strays and other abandoned animals handed over by the Police, RSPCA, wardens and general members of the public resulted in a charge of VAT at the standard rate of 17.5%.

Gables Farm Dogs' and Cats' Home were successful in their argument at the tribunal that all animals given to the charity qualified as donated and therefore zero-rated when sold. HMRC have confirmed that they will not be appealing against the decision.

Charities that have accounted for and paid VAT on sales of animals which are now considered to be zero-rated should submit claims for overpaid output tax.

10.20 Excess charges in non-local authority car parks
HMRC has issued Revenue & Customs Brief 57/08 to explain its revised policy on the VAT treatment of excess charges and other penalties levied in non-local authority car parks. It includes information about what to do if VAT has been incorrectly accounted for on such charges.

The effect of the change is that certain excess charges which have previously been treated as a taxable supply of parking are now regarded as outside the scope of VAT. The most common situations affected are:

- no parking ticket on display;
- underpayment;
- overstaying purchased parking time;
- returning within a specified time;
- parking outside marked bays;
- parking in bays set aside for disabled drivers or parents with children.

However, where the parking terms and conditions make it clear that the driver can continue to use the facilities after a set period upon payment of a further amount without being in breach of the contract, then the payment will be consideration for use of the facilities and subject to VAT.

In cases where parking site owners contract out the management and operation of their parking sites and allow the contractor to retain all or part of the penalties collected, any such payments retained by the contractor will be subject to VAT. HMRC is accepting claims from businesses that have previously overpaid VAT due to the former policy. any such claims are subject to normal VAT rules and capping, as appropriate.

10.21 Pool accoutrements
HMRC has long accepted that swimming pools can be fitted to new houses on a zero-rated basis as being items 'ordinarily installed' in homes. It is less happy with

various accoutrements of pools.

In the case of *Rainbow Pools London (20800)*, the Revenue had partial success. A false floor to the pool, which could be raised or lowered to change the depth or create a floor over the pool, was adjudged too advanced in design to have yet become a normal aspect of a domestic pool. But the electronically-wound pool cover, used to reduce humidity, heat loss and danger of drowning, was held to be sufficiently ordinary to be zero rated.

10.22 VAT on canteen food may be reclaimable, says court
A recent European Court ruling means that businesses with canteens may now be able to claim back the VAT incurred on the catering.

The case centred on the attempts of two businesses, engineering group Danfoss and pharmaceuticals giant AstraZeneca, to reclaim VAT on catering expenditure where they had provided food free of charge during meetings attended by both clients and staff. The food had been prepared in the canteen and eaten on the premises.

The decision means that VAT is recoverable where meals are provided free in company canteens to business contacts during meetings. Similarly, VAT incurred on catering provided to employees, to ensure uninterrupted work meetings, is also recoverable.

VAT should, in principle, also be reclaimable where food is delivered to businesses or indeed off-site, provided the cost was incurred for business purposes.

10.23 Redrow principles re-affirmed

In *Airtours Holiday Transport Ltd v HMRC TC201* input tax incurred on accountancy services, aimed at rescuing the business from closure, was deductible by the company.

In this case, Airtours paid for accountancy services provided to both itself and the company's creditors. The Tribunal applied the reasoning of the Lords in the case of Redrow Group plc (1999) STC 161 and allowed Airtours entitlement to an input tax credit.

The case highlights the importance of getting the relevant documentation right including letters of engagement, and in particular insuring that contracts must not restrict the supply of services to one party.

But the upper tribunal has decided that the first tier tribunal was wrong. In its view the engagement was substantively between the advisors and the financial institutions. The fact that the financial institutions forced Airtours to pay the cost was merely an arrangement, and did not mean that Airtours had commissioned the services. The benefit to Airtours was too tangential to create a direct and immediate link between the costs and the Airtours business. The main benefit was in securing the finance, and it was not a separate benefit.

This decision is very disappointing, since it appears to have the effect of partly reducing the scope or impact of the Redrow decision. It was also based on a particular view of the facts that differed from the first tier tribunal's view. It seems likely to go to further appeal.

10.24 VAT on entertaining expenses may not be blocked

In *X Holding BV and Oracle Nederland BV* heard by the ECJ, concerning the validity of Dutch 'blocking' legislation, the Advocate General has opined that national input VAT 'blocking' provisions (such as the UK's blocking of VAT recovery on entertainment expenses) must clearly define the nature of goods and services which are blocked for them to be valid.

The AG considers that blocking of 'gifts' or 'entertainment' could be too wide in their scope to be valid from an EU law perspective. And if the opinion is followed by the ECJ, there could therefore be significant implications for UK businesses. Businesses should consider protecting their position by submitting claims in respect of any input tax which has not been recovered. After 1 april 2010, the time limit for claims is four years.

10.25 Share acquisition costs

The tribunal has held that the company set up to acquire the BAA group (*BAA Ltd v HMRC TC00357*) was able to recover input tax on costs incurred.

The Spanish group, Ferrovial, set up a company, Airport Development and Investments Ltd (ADIL) as the acquisition vehicle to acquire the target, BAA plc. The takeover was completed in July 2006 and ADIL joined BAA's VAT group in September 2006. ADIL had already incurred significant sums on legal, investment banker's and other professional fees. BAA Limited, the representative member of the BAA VAT group reclaimed the input tax suffered by ADIL, attributable to the group's general overheads.

HMRC rejected the claim on the basis that the costs related to the acquisition and were therefore investment costs with no direct and immediate link with any taxable supplies. The assessment on BAA was for £7.6 million. BAA appealed.

The tribunal held that ADIL carried on an economic activity from its inception. It did more than merely acquire and hold shares. ADIL was involved in the management of the companies in the BAA group including negotiating group finance facilities. And while ADIL did not itself demonstrate any intention to make taxable supplies, it had joined BAA's VAT group and could therefore regard itself as part of a single entity with other group members in making taxable supplies. As a result ADIL carried on an economic activity.

10.26 Share sales by holding companies

In *Skatteverket v AB SKF Case C-29/08* ECJ has held that input tax attributable to the sale of shares in a subsidiary company can be recovered.

The case concerned a large Swedish industrial group, SKF, and the sale by the holding company of shares in two subsidiary companies.

10.27 Potatoes and crisps

The Court of Appeal has reinstated the tribunal's decision in *Procter & Gamble's* case concerning Pringles crisps. These are usually 40% potato as opposed to normal crisps, which have a potato content of around 70%. The Court of Appeal nonetheless opined that they were potato crisps and standard rated.

10.28 Pay-per-click charity advertisements

HMRC has issued Revenue & customs Brief 25/10 to explain its revised policy on the VAT treatment of pay-per-click (PPC) charity advertising on sponsored links and other associated services.

PPC is used by organisations on internet search engines to encourage searchers to click on the organisation's link in priority to any other links on the results page following a search.

PPC arises where an organisation pays a search engine provider each time its website is accessed through a sponsored link. HMRC had previously taken the view that a PPC-sponsored link is not in itself an advertisement, but merely a means of access to the organisation's website. However, it now accepts that PPC-sponsored links appearing on search engine websites are advertisements, which qualify for zero-rating when supplied to a charity. It follows that the supply of copyright and design services associated with such sponsored links fall within the zero-rating. However, HMRC still maintains that services supplied by copywriters and designers for the purpose of search engine optimisation (structuring a website so that it contains as many keywords as possible) do not qualify for relief.

Businesses that have accounted for the paid VAT on supplies of charity advertisements that are now considered to be zero-rated my submit claims for overpaid VAT, subject to the normal four year cap and unjust enrichment provisions.

10.29 Single or multiple supply of services?
In *Diana Bryce t/a The Barn v HMRC TC242* this concerned premises hired out for weekends for children's parties, it was found that the provision of those parties comprised two separate supplies of catering and hall hire.

The tribunal rejected the taxpayer's contention that there was a principal supply of the licence to occupy and two ancillary supplies of use of play equipment and the provision of catering.

The tribunal found that the use of the hall and provision of refreshments were the main or principal components of the supply. The supply of the use of equipment and the use of chairs and tables were ancillary to those two main supplies. Moreover the two main supplies were not so closely linked they formed a whole supply. One element could be enjoyed without the other evidenced by the fact that a 75 minute booking of the hall was made up of first stage of use of the hall and second stage of refreshments.

This was reversed by the upper tribunal in Diana Bryce t/a The Barn UKUT26 by deciding that the supply was a standard rated composite supply of a 'children's party'.

10.30 Abuse of VAT system
The lower tribunal decision in the case of *Lower Mill* (UKUTB25) resulted in a decision that Lower Mill had carried out an 'abuse' of the VAT system by arranging to sell plots of land on which holiday accommodation could be built, where a company in common ownership to the vendor offered construction services to create the finished product. The lower tribunal decided that this was a contrived situation, which led to a result inconsistent with the purposes of the VAT Directive. Its motivation was purely to create a tax saving. It was an abuse.

The upper tribunal has reversed that decision. It took the view that the lower tribunal's analysis was faulty. It decided that a structure involving the sale of a plot by one company and the separate provision of construction services by another is not uncommercial or unusual. The only aspect that could make it seem that way was the connectedness of the two providers. But that in itself was not enough to make the arrangement artificial.

10.31 VAT on temporary staff

In *Reed Employment v Commissioners* LON/2004/0130 the First Tier Tax Tribunal decided that employment bureaux may have incorrectly charged VAT on supplies of temporary staff following the withdrawal of the staff hire concession on 1 April 2009.

The decision suggests that an employment bureau should only charge VAT on the commission element of the fee that it charges to clients.

Affected persons should consider the implications of this decision with the view to either making protective claims, or entering into discussions with their service providers to request refunds of VAT overcharged.

10.32 VAT on certain postal services from 31 January 2011

Although the First and Second Class postal rates are unaffected, as are franked mail and standard parcels, there are a number of postal services that will include VAT from 31 January 2011. These include:

Express and tracked services

* Special delivery 9am, stamp, franking and account customers
* Special delivery next day, account customers only
* Royal Mail tracked and tracked next day
* Royal Mail Same Day

International Services (EU destinations only)

* International contract services
* International Airsure
* International Admail and Admail Packets
* International redirections

Advertising, Catalogues and Magazine services

* Big Book
* Royal Mail heavyweight
* Mail Media

Unaddressed Mail

* Door to Door

If you are a business user of these services you should be able to reclaim the VAT. However businesses that use these postal services who are not VAT registered or have Exempt Services may have to absorb the 20% VAT increase.

10.33 Charge to pay by a certain method
The European Court of Justice (ECJ) has given a decision in the case of Everything Everywhere Ltd (C-276/09), formerly T-Mobile Ltd.

The telephone company charges its mobile phone users who wish to pay by certain means a further tariff that is not included within the general mobile phone tariff. It argued that this charge represented separate payment for processing services, and was therefore exempt from VAT under the financial exemptions, and was not a charge for the telephone supplies made to customers. In no case, however, were charges made by the company in respect of payment for transactions that it had not made with customers.

The ECJ decided that the further charge was simply further consideration for the original supply. The purchasers themselves really wanted one service, namely 'telecommunications'. If they chose to pay a high tariff because of the means of payment, that was incidental to the fact that only telecommunications were provided.

10.34 Zero-rating for printed matter
Printed materials such as books and newspapers are generally zero-rated for VAT. Many services such as training include printed course materials bundled into the price. In such cases the service provider may charge separately for the printed items to preserve the zero-rating on those materials.

The law is going to be changed in Finance Act 2011 to ensure that such combinations of services and printed materials cannot be artificially divided.

10.35 Debt collection services subject to VAT
In January 2011 HMRC announced it was changing its view on what should be defined as 'debt collection services' following the judgment in the case *AXA UK Plc* (C-175/09). If a business involves collecting money on behalf of another organisation, even if the money is never overdue as such.

Financial services are generally exempt from VAT, with the exception of debt collection services which are subject to standard rate VAT. AXA UK Plc was the VAT representative company of a group that includes Denplan Ltd. Denplan collects monthly fees from dentist patients and pays them to their dentists. The ECJ concluded that this action amounted to debt collection services, even though the money was collected at exactly the date it became due so that the amounts paid were not outstanding debts.

The result is that from 12 January 2011 any service that collects payments from one person, to pay them on to another person to which the money is owed, will be subject to standard rate VAT. This applies even where the business concerned has previously received a ruling from HMRC that its fees collection service was exempt from VAT. If this applies to your businesses you may have to review their partial exemption de minimis calculations.

10.36 Salary sacrifice

Changes to HM Revenue & Customs policy on 'salary sacrifice', and related concepts, could result from the European Court of Justice decision in the case of *AstraZeneca* (C-40/09). This involved employees exchanging salary for retail vouchers. AstraZeneca had reclaimed input tax (assuming it to be a business expense), but followed HMRC policy to the effect that 'salary sacrifice' need not be consideration for a supply. HMRC argued either that it was indeed a taxable supply, or that input tax was irrecoverable.

the ECJ opted for the analysis that there was a taxable supply for the value of the salary foregone.

11 MOTOR CARS

11.1 Cars and VAT

VAT is charged by the seller on the price charged to the buyer and is only reclaimable by a dealer whose business it is to sell cars.

11.2 Reclaiming VAT

An individual buying a car for private use, cannot reclaim the tax which it has paid to the dealer or on importing the car. But from 1.8.92 the VAT can be reclaimed by taxi firms, self-drive hire firms and driving schools, subject to adjustment for personal use. From 1 August 1995 a car used wholly for business purposes will entitle the input VAT to be reclaimable. This will be very beneficial to car leasing companies. When the car is sold, output VAT will need to be charged. However, cars being leased from a leasing company which have a proportion of private use will have a restriction on the amount of input VAT able for reclaim. This restriction is 50% of the input VAT.

Car derived vans and combi vans

HMRC has updated guidance referring to a list of 'car-derived vans' or 'combi vans' on which input VAT may be deducted (subject to the normal rules) as they are not seen as cars for VAT purposes. Businesses which are considering whether input VAT can be recovered in respect of purchases of such vehicles, and whether VAT must be charged in respect of sales of used vehicles of these types, should refer to HMRC's guidance. The list has been compiled by HMRC and is based on information supplied by manufacturers. At any one time it may not be complete or up to date where models change or information has not been provided and taxpayers need to ensure the correct position is clear.

Motor car delivery charges - VAT can be reclaimed
HMRC has issued a Business Brief outlining its policy concerning car delivery charges arising from the Court of Appeal's decision in the case of British Telecommunications plc. The court found in favour of BT's policy of reclaiming VAT on charges made for the delivery of cars to its fleet. HMRC intends to appeal this decision to the House of Lords. Meanwhile, it will entertain claims from businesses whose car delivery arrangements are identical to BT's.

In this case it was found that the contract for delivery was quite separate from any contact for the purchase of the car. This would not apply where dealers pass on a manufacturer's delivery charge when selling the car, or if there is no difference in the price of a car whether delivered or not.

Those who wish to make such claims would have to prove that the arrangements are identical to BT's, and must be prepared to repay the claim, plus interest, should HMRC win the House of Lords.

Cars used exclusively for business
A farmer bought two BMW X5 vehicles. (*Philip James Robert Shaw VTD 19594*). One was used as a normal car (petrol), the other (diesel) for use on the farm. He reclaimed input tax on the purchase of the latter vehicle. The commissioners issued an assessment to recover the tax, and he appealed, contending that he had purchased the diesel X5 solely for use on his farm, 'to provide the high torque necessary for towing'. The tribunal accepted his evidence and allowed his appeal, finding that 'he had no intention of driving the vehicle himself for private use as he had purchased a second and almost identical vehicle for himself'.

In another tribunal case involving cars a company carried on a business of 'the supply and laying of conducting media for the utilities industry'. It reclaimed input tax on the purchase of two rally cars, which the company's managing director drove in races and which displayed the company's name. The Commissioners issued an assessment to recover the tax, on the basis that the expenditure had been incurred for the personal pleasure of the director, rather than for the purposes of the company's business. The company appealed, contending that it had purchased the cars for the purpose of advertising its business. The tribunal accepted the company's evidence and allowed the appeal.

11.3 Vehicles chargeable to VAT
These are essentially private type cars for use on public roads and constructed or

adapted for carrying passengers. Vehicles not chargeable are those accommodating only one, or more than twelve, passengers; of above 3 tonnes unladen weight; caravans, ambulances, prison vans, approved taxi cabs, and special vehicles not for carrying passengers, such as ice cream vans, mobile shops and offices, hearses and bullion vans. VAT is payable when an exempt vehicle is converted to carry passengers. Cars used by manufacturers for research and development are relieved from VAT from 1 April 1989. From 29 July 1989 exemption was extended to cars leased to handicapped persons, and to members of visiting forces and to individuals with diplomatic privileges.

11.4 Leasing and hire purchase
VAT must be paid on the sale price when a car is acquired by hire purchase and can be reclaimed by a dealer. If a car is leased VAT must be charged on the rentals and can be reclaimed by the lessor if in business and registered for VAT. However, if there is any private use of the car a restriction on the amount of VAT reclaimable has been introduced: this has been set at 50%. Vehicles purchased for leasing to the disabled are relieved from car tax.

VAT rules prevent businesses that lease their cars avoiding the 50 per cent restriction on VAT recovery.

The change, following the judgement of the Court of Appeal in *C & E Commissioners v BRS*, ensures that the 50 per cent restriction on input tax recovery will apply as Parliament intended to all leased business cars also used for private motoring.

11.5 Repairs and maintenance
VAT is chargeable on the cost and can be reclaimed by a business in total even if there is some private use.

11.6 Sale of used cars
Basically VAT must be charged on the sale price of used cars, only sold by a dealer of motor cars. However, the special scheme applicable to such sales enables the VAT to be charged only on the excess of the selling price over the purchase price of the car. No tax invoice is issued and the input tax cannot be reclaimed. Other businesses should not charge output VAT on the sale of a car, neither can they recover input VAT on the purchase of a car, for leasing companies who have reclaimed the input VAT when the car was purchased must charge VAT on its disposal.

Second-hand cars
Following the Italian case, the resale of goods on which a taxable person has not been entitled to recover VAT on purchase is exempt from VAT, and the classic example of this is the resale of goods that have been bought for a business entertainment purpose. HMRC has interpreted the Italian case as not including an exemption for goods that have been purchased without VAT being charged, such as

the sale of second-hand cars. *Stafford Landrover* (16388) has been to the tribunal in an attempt to extend the exemption principle to cover second-hand cars. The tribunal decided clearly that exemption only related to goods on which VAT had been charged, but which had proved non-recoverable.

11.7 Fuel benefit
The scale charge is based upon the emissions of the vehicle concerned.

This is the scale charge for income tax on fuel provided free or below cost to employees for their private mileage. The benefit is subject to VAT from 6 April 1987, and is calculated on the tax inclusive charge. This is only payable if input VAT is reclaimed on fuel. Depending on mileage it may be beneficial not to reclaim the input VAT if this is less than the fuel benefit, and accordingly not have to pay the fuel benefit. (see Table 19. VAT - Car Fuel Scale add back rates from 1 May 2011, p.646).

11.8 Demonstrator cars
The main issue relates to both the motor manufacturers' and dealers' ability to reclaim VAT on stock in trade cars. This would allow the VAT on demonstrator models, for example, to be recovered in the VAT return. However, the dealer must also account for VAT on the value of any private use such a car is put to. HMRC has established an agreement with the Retail Motor Industry Federation (RMI) over the calculation of deemed output tax on the private use of dealer demonstrator cars. Second-hand cars are unaffected by this change.

11.9 Car derived vans and combi vans
HMRC has updated guidance referring to a list of 'car-derived vans' or 'combi vans' on which input VAT may be deducted (subject to the normal rules) as they are not seen as cars for VAT purposes. Businesses which are considering whether input VAT can be recovered in respect of purchases of such vehicles, and whether VAT must be charged in respect of sales of used vehicles of these types, should refer to HMRC's guidance. The list has been compiled by HMRC and is based on information supplied by manufacturers. At any one time it may not be complete or up to date where models change or information has not been provided and taxpayers need to ensure the correct position is clear.

In addition, there has been some tightening up of the definition of a motor car. Any vehicle with a payload of one ton or more will not be regarded as being a car (including double cab pickups), while London taxis and 12-seater vehicles that do not meet road safety regulations are reclassified as motor cars for these purposes.

11.10 VAT and car fuel reimbursed to employees
In 2005 the European Court of Justice (ECJ) decided that the UK VAT recovery rules were not compatible with EC VAT rules and took action against the UK Government. It held that VAT recovery could not be claimed by businesses because (a) the fuel

was being purchased by the employee not the business, and (b), the business did not hold a VAT invoice.

Under new rules, businesses are still be able to reclaim VAT on the petrol element of mileage claims paid to employees; however, to do so, the business must hold an appropriate 'full' or 'less detailed' VAT invoice.

In practical terms if businesses want to reclaim VAT, employee's mileage claims must be supported by an appropriate VAT invoice. In most circumstances, (for purchases below £250) a 'less detailed VAT invoice', i.e. a petrol station till receipt, will suffice.

The following rates (VAT inclusive) can be used to calculate the cost of fuel per mile. These rates apply to all journeys on or after 1 June 2011 (1 March 2011).

Engine Size	Petrol	LPG
1400cc or less	15p (14p)	11p (10p)
1401cc to 2000cc	18p (16p)	13p (12p)
Over 2000cc	26p (23p)	18p (17p)

Engine Size	Diesel
1600cc or less	12p (13p)
1601cc to 2000cc	15p (13p)
Over 2000cc	18p (16p)

11.11 Free motor insurance
Ford Motor Company has followed in the footsteps of Peugeot in appealing against an assessment for VAT on the ostensible value of 'free insurance' provided to car purchasers. The tribunal (19750) held that, even where this was to be regarded as a separate supply (based on the nuances of fact), it would be regarded as ancillary to the taxable supply of the car, and therefore, following Card Protection Plan, a single supply at the standard rate.

12 RETAILERS

Retailers are not obliged to prepare tax invoices unless they are demanded by customers, and hence a number of special schemes for accounting for VAT are available for retailers and are set out in Notice 727 issued by HMRC.

13 BAD DEBTS

Repayment of input tax by customers

For supplies made on or after 1 January 2003 customers are required to repay to HMRC any input tax which they have previously claimed in respect of supplies for which they have not paid within 6 months of the due date not the invoice date.

The repayment to HMRC should be made by means of a negative entry in the VAT allowable portion of the customer's VAT account for the prescribed accounting period in which bad debt relief was claimed by the supplier.

Customers who subsequently pay all or part of their debt can reclaim the input tax by means of a positive entry in the VAT allowable portion of the VAT account for the prescribed accounting period in which the payment is made. The amount adjusted will be the VAT fraction of the payment made.

Revised time for claims

Bad debt relief cannot be claimed until six months after the time payment is due and payable on if later, six months after the time of supply.

Previously, where a supplier had suffered a bad debt incurred by an insolvent customer, the supplier could reclaim VAT he has already paid on the supplies concerned. The sale must have been at open market value and the property in the goods must have passed.

(a) The supplier must have proved in the bankruptcy, or liquidation in the case of a limited company, for the debt less the VAT.

(b) By the exercise of an option for cash accounting, where turnover is below £1.3 million, bad debts will be automatically relieved from VAT.

HMRC acknowledges in HMRC Brief 18/09, following a Tribunal decision, that VAT bad debt relief (BDR) is available for output VAT declared on a VAT return even if the net amount of VAT due on that return to HMRC has not been paid in full to HMRC. Deductible input VAT included in the return constitutes payment or part payment of the output VAT. Businesses which have VAT debts due to HMRC over an extended period and businesses trading in receivership should review their position to ensure that all available BDR is claimed.

The Tribunal in Times Right Marketing Limited (In Liquidation) (20611) accepted that the Appellant was entitled to VAT bad debt relief (BDR) in respect of output VAT declared on a VAT return even though the net amount of VAT which it had been due to pay to HMRC for that period remained unpaid due to the liquidation.

14 JOINT AND SEVERAL LIABILITY

FA2003 - Section 18 introduces a targeted anti-fraud measure that imposes a joint and several liability for the payment of VAT and took effect from 10 April 2003. This applies to both the supplier and recipient of certain commodities strictly specified in the legislation. Businesses are expected to take additional safeguards to ensure that they are not unwittingly caught by this measure. However, new subsection 77A (6) says that a business paying less than the lowest open market value of less than a price previously paid by any of the previous suppliers in the chain, will fall within the definition of "having reasonable grounds to suspect" that VAT would not be paid. Therefore, businesses are very concerned about how they will ensure that they can demonstrate that they are not caught by this measure. There has been a short consultation period which ran until 10th June.

New subsection 77A(1) restricts the application of section 77A to specified goods. Initially these goods are telephones, parts and accessories, and computer equipment, parts, accessories and software.

Following the above consultation period, HMRC has issued new statements of practice concerning the right to recover input tax without a VAT invoice and the joint and several liability for VAT in specific sectors. The statement of practice in respect of joint and several liability takes the form of a new VAT notice.

The statements seek to offer guidance to businesses affected by the anti-fraud measures. Businesses will need to undertake strict checks in respect of suppliers and maintain adequate records. HMRC has set up a team which can verify whether particular VAT registration details are correct and current.

In R (oao Federation of Technological Industries and others) v C & E Comrs the issue concerns the new provisions introduced by FA 2003, which require a taxable person to provide security for VAT due from his supplier and the person to whom he makes supplies. The taxable person is also jointly and severally liable with them in the case of supplies of telephones and computers.

The claimants in this case were traders in mobile phones and computer processing units. They sought permission to apply for judicial review. The first issue related to the approach for permission to apply for judicial review and a reference to the

European Court of Justice. The second issue was whether the change in UK law was consistent with EEC law.

The High Court has referred the matter to ECJ. Their decision is eagerly awaited!

15 DIRECTORS' ACCOMMODATION

VAT is not recoverable on costs, such as repairs, incurred on accommodation provided by companies for their directors or the latter's families.

16 COMPANY GROUPS AND DIVISIONS OF BUSINESS

For the purpose of VAT a company group may be registered as a single business so that transactions between group member companies will not be liable to tax; alternatively each company in the group may register separately. The group may include overseas companies to the extent that they operate in the UK.

Trading divisions of a company may be registered separately, even though they are not incorporated. However separate registration of divisions is not allowable where the split into divisions or branches is made for the purpose of evading VAT, i.e., when such a division is below the exemption limit.

The Chancellor (Budget 2004) announced the following specific VAT avoidance measures on the restriction of ability to register corporate bodies as a VAT group. From 1 August 2004, two additional tests will have to be met before a body corporate can be included in a VAT group. The new rules will however only apply where the following conditions are met -

• the corporate body is either jointly owned with a third party or is run by a third party; and

• that corporate body will make supplies that are to be taxed at the standard or reduced rate to a member of the VAT group; and

• the VAT group would be unable to recover the VAT on such supplies in full.

The term corporate body includes limited liability partnerships, which will therefore also be affected by the measures. Limited partnerships will also be subjected to these tests where the general partner is a corporate body.

The two additional tests will deny VAT grouping where -
* the majority of economic benefits from the jointly owned or managed corporate body accrue primarily to a third party; or

* the jointly owned or managed corporate body is not (or would not be) included in the group accounts under generally accepted accounting practice (GAAP).

A company that ceases to be eligible to be a member of a VAT group as a result of the application of these measures may be removed from a VAT group from whatever date it ceased to be eligible.

The existing powers to remove a company from a VAT group for the protection of revenue will be retained.

17 PROPERTY TRANSACTIONS

17.1 Input tax recovery
A business can obtain the consent of the local HMRC VAT to tax previously exempt property supplies.

17.2 Self supply rules
Self supply rules apply to exempt or partially exempt businesses having a building constructed for their own use or making an exempt supply of the building. For this purpose the business must charge itself output tax on the cost of the land plus standard rated goods and services supplied; this applying to new buildings and civil engineering works valued above £100,000. From 1 January 1992 the rule was applied to extensions and reconstructions of buildings but only where the developer had no interest in at least 75% of the land over the last 10 years. Landlords of leases to developers are required to charge VAT on rents when the self supply provisions arise.

17.3 Options to acquire interests in land
On and from 1 January 1992 an option to acquire an interest in land is no longer exempt but if the purchase of the land or buildings was subject to VAT so would be the option.

18 ABOLITION OF EU FISCAL FRONTIERS

The rules may be summarised as follows:

18.1 Dispatches (exports) from the UK

Zero rating, where applicable, continues to apply in the UK to registered businesses selling to EC countries. Exporters must show on their invoices not only their own UK registration number but also the EC VAT registration number of the importer. If the importer is not VAT registered, that is a private individual not in business and the supplies do not fall within special schemes (see the following), VAT is chargeable by the exporter on the sale under the 'original principle'. The latter system applies to sales up to various limits imposed by member states and VAT on sales above these limits is payable in the importing member state. The limits at present imposed are: between - €35,000 and up to €100,000 Euros. As a result exporters may need to appoint tax representatives (or 'fiscal agents') in the member state of the importer, and these representatives will be responsible for paying VAT in the customer's state.

18.2 Acquisitions (imports) into the UK

Tax is charged on an acquisition in the UK from an EC member state when it is a taxable acquisition. A taxable acquisition is one where the goods acquired are not exempt; it is made in the furtherance of business, or not in the way of business by any body corporate, club, association, organisation or other unincorporated body; the supplier is acting in the course of business and is taxable in a member state of the EC from which the goods are removed. Imports from non-member states are taxable as for a customs duty.

The taxable value of an acquisition is the consideration in money paid for it, subject to a discount if applicable and if not payable by instalments; if not payable in money the consideration is the monetary equivalent. The open market value may be substituted by the authorities where the buyer and seller are connected persons. Currency is converted at the market rate at the time of acquisition. A person not liable to be registered can apply for registration.

18.3 Imports of a means of transport

VAT applies on acquisition under the destination system to new means of transport above the following limits:

motorised land vehicles	above 48cc or 7.2 kilowatts if electrical;
boats	above 7.5 metres in length;
aircraft	above 1550 kilograms take-off weight.

To be classified as new, land vehicles must not have travelled more than 3,000 kilometres; boats not have sailed for more than 100 hours and aircraft not have flown more than 40 hours. Means of transport more than 3 months old is not new. If the foregoing conditions do not apply VAT will be charged under the 'origin principle'.

18.4 Freight and transport charges
VAT on transport costs will be charged under the 'destination principle' either by the supplier of the customer, known as the 'reverse charge' basis, for transactions between EC states. Where carrier belongs to the same state as the customer VAT will be charged under the law of that state. For customers not registered for VAT the tax will be charged in the country from which the goods were sent or for loading and handling generally in the state where the services are provided.

18.5 Intermediate supplier
Where an intermediate supplier exports to the UK goods originally obtained from another member state the intermediate supplier and not the original supplier is responsible for VAT. In such circumstances a UK supplier can normally zero rate the supply.

18.6 Returns
Quarterly returns will continue to be required and these will provide details of both imports and exports. In addition what are known as Intrastat forms are required on each calendar month showing transactions with EC member states.

19 TREATMENT FOR INCOME TAX AND CORPORATION TAX

Where persons (including companies) are liable for VAT, income and expenditure is to be brought into the tax computation exclusive of VAT thereon. For exempt persons the expenditure to be brought into the computation for income tax or corporation tax includes the VAT charged thereon.

PART ELEVEN

CAPITAL GAINS TAX

BUDGET MARCH 2011

1) Entrepreneurs Relief

The rate of CGT for gains qualifying for entrepreneurs' relief remains at an effective rate of 10% and the lifetime limit on gains qualifying for entrepreneurs' relief is increased from £5 million to £10 million from 6 April 2011.

The pre 23 June 2010 system of a 4/9th's reduction in the gain which is then taxed at 18% is abolished in favour of an actual 10% rate so that the annual exemption will now save tax at 10% rather than at 18% as previously.

2) Annual exempt amount

The annual exempt amount for 2011-2012 is changed at £10,600.

1 INTRODUCTION

General

Capital gains are essentially the profits made on the disposal of a wide range of assets during the owner's lifetime. The profits are the excess of the amounts received on the disposal of the assets over the cost. Companies still benefit from an indexation uplift. Disposal is usually on the sale of the asset, but may include other forms of disposal, such as by transfer, demolition or gift. Capital losses may be deducted from capital gains. There are many exemptions, particularly for individuals, and certain assets are not chargeable.

Individuals (unless Entrepreneur's Relief is available) pay tax at a rate of 18% and/or 28%. The gain is added to other income and 28% is paid on any part of the gain that falls in the higher rate band of income tax after deducting capital losses and an annual individual exemption of £10,600 in 2011/2012 (£10,100 in 2010/2011). Companies, who do not receive an annual exemption, include the gains, less losses, as part of their profits chargeable to Corporation Tax.

2011/2012
Examples demonstrating the effects of the 18% and 28% rates of CGT.

a) In this example there is no effect of the June 2010 Budget.
Jazzy has net capital gains (assuming Entrepreneurs' Relief is not applicable) for 2011/2012 of £17,700, her other taxable income is £10,000.

	£
capital gains	17,700
Less: annual exemption	10,600
Taxable to Capital Gains Tax	7,100
Tax payable at flat rate of 18%	1,278
(due to be paid by 31 January 2013)	

Note: The total of Jazzy's income £10,000 and gains £7,100 is less than the maximum of the basic rate band £35,000.

b) Jazzy has the same net capital gains of £17,700 but now her other taxable income is £30,000.

Capital gains and other income are combined to evaluate if any part of her gains fall within the basic rate band and fall to be taxed at 18%, any excess that falls within the upper rate band is taxable at 28%.

	£	£
Taxable income (after personal allowance)		30,000
Capital gains	17,700	
Less Annual Exemption	10,600	
	7,100	
		£37,100

Tax thereon:	£	£
30,000 @ 20%		6,000
5,000 @ 18%		900
35,000		
2,100 @ 28%		588
£37,100		£7,488

This liability is arrived between taxable income and taxable gains as follows:

Taxable gains		
5,000 @18%	900	
2,100 @28%	588	
7,100		1,488

Taxable income		
30,000 @ 20%		6,000
Total tax as above		£7,488

Definition of Basic Rate Band

The basic rate band is defined by s 10(5)-(7), Income Tax Act 2007 (ITA 2007). The unused part of the individual's basic rate band is the amount by which it exceeds his or her taxable income. The individual's taxable income is calculated by going through the first three steps of the s 23, ITA 2007 income tax calculation. Broadly, it is the aggregate of the various components of his or her income after deducting:

• any personal allowance, including any age-related element, and blind person's allowance where appropriate; and

• any reliefs, such as trading losses, attaching to specific components of the taxable income (s 24, ITA 2007).

In calculating whether there is unused basic rate band, any Entrepreneurs Relief (ER) gains in the tax year must be taken into account and treated as forming the lowest part of the gains on which the individual is chargeable to CGT. Accordingly, where a valid ER claim is made for a qualifying gain chargeable in the tax year, any non-ER gains chargeable in that tax year, including those which would qualify for ER but for the taxpayer having utilised his or her lifetime allowance, are likely to be taxed at 28%.

Companies benefit from an indexation uplift. Disposal is usually on the sale of the asset, but may include other forms of disposal, such as by transfer, demolition or gift. There are many exemptions, particularly for individuals but also for associations such as charities: and certain assets are not chargeable. Companies include the gains, less losses, as part of their profits chargeable to corporation tax.

Capital losses may be deducted from capital gains.

A targeted anti-avoidance rule (TAAR) was introduced in FA2007 (Clause 27) to counter schemes to create and use artificial capital losses to avoid tax. The measure ensured that allowable capital losses are restricted to those arising from genuine commercial transactions.

2 WHO IS CHARGEABLE?

2.1 Individuals and residence
2.1.1 The system in general
Individuals are liable for capital gains tax on their chargeable gains less losses in a year of assessment. The liability applies to individuals who are resident in any part of the tax year or in which the taxpayer was ordinarily resident in the U.K. (TCGA 1992 s 2 (1)). Subject to the following qualifications, total capital losses are deducted from total capital gains in a year of assessment. From the balance of gains, if any, the individual is allowed an annual exemption of £10,600 in 2011/2012 (£10,100 in 2010/2011).

2.1.2 Dealing with losses
A targeted anti-avoidance rule (TAAR) was introduced in FA2007 (Clause 27) to counter schemes to create and use artificial capital losses to avoid tax. The measure will ensure that allowable capital losses are restricted to those arising from genuine commercial transactions.

Capital losses suffered in a year of assessment are deducted from the capital gains made in that year to give the taxable amount (TCGA 1992 s 2 (2) and s 3 (5)). There will be no charge to capital gains tax where that amount is no more than the individual exemption for the year (TCGA 1992 s 3) If the loss exceeds the capital gains the balance may be carried forward indefinitely until it can be set off against future gains.

Losses cannot be carried back except for a maximum of three years losses in the assessment year when a taxpayer dies (TCGA 1992 s 62 (3)).

Where the amount of chargeable gains less losses for any year of assessment is below the individual exemption no deduction is made for losses brought forward, or carried back from a year subsequent to that in which the taxpayer dies. Where the amount of chargeable gains less losses for the year of assessment is above the exemption limit losses brought forward (or carried back in the case of a deceased individual) may be deducted to the extent of the gains. No return of chargeable gains need normally be made for a year when the gains are covered by the individual exemption. This is provided that a statement is made to the effect that the consideration for all disposals does not exceed the exemption amount, but the Inspector of Taxes may require a detailed return of all chargeable gains in the year.

Trading losses may be set off against general income under TA 1988 s 380. To the extent that this procedure leaves a balance of unrelieved trading losses this balance can be set off against capital gains under FA 1991 s 72.

Not a real loss
In *Howard Peter Schofield v HMRC* TC00498 the Tribunal has held that a capital loss arising from a transaction involving no commercial purpose and did not risk the appellant's own resources was not a real loss and therefore not allowable to set off against gains under the Ramsay doctrine.

The Tribunal held that the appellant's loss was not a real loss. The sole purpose of the transaction was to avoid tax. There was no commercial purpose. The size of any financial reward or risk to Mr Schofield had not commercial sense and, moreover, was contrived.

The appellant's only other financial risk were the fees paid to PwC and the bank and all other funds flowed in a circle.

Time Shares
Some people have entered into contracts to buy time-shares in properties outside the UK, only to find that what they thought they had purchased did not exist. At first sight, it might appear that there is no possibility of claiming a capital loss on a non-existent asset because nothing has been acquired. But provided there is some kind of contractual documentation, however unenforceable, this will constitute a 'chose in action'. If the contact itself becomes worthless, then the loss may be claimed on the 'chose in action' quite independently of the object of the contract (i.e., the time-share).

Assets of negligible value

Where an asset has become of negligible value, the owner may claim to be treated as if the asset had been sold and immediately reacquired under s 24(2), TCGA 1992, giving rise to a capital loss. The deemed sale and reacquisition are to be treated strictly as occurring at the date of the claim. In practice, HMRC will accept a claim for the deemed sale and reacquisition to take place at a particular date provided the claim is made not later than two years after the end of the tax year/accounting period in which the date falls. The asset must, however, be of negligible value both at the date of claim and the earlier date.

Shares of negligible value

Shares allotted and issued to the appellant, Mr Harper (*David Harper v HMRC TC00317*), by a company in serious financial difficulties, were of negligible value when acquired and therefore a negligible value claim was not possible under section 24 TCGA 1992. In addition, Mr Harper's claim to set off the loss against income under, what is now, section 131-151 ITA 2007 was not allowed.

2.2 Companies liable to corporation tax

For these bodies, which include certain trading associations, capital gains are not charged by means of a separate tax, but form part of the profits subject to corporation tax and, where applicable, this may be at the small profits rate. The company is chargeable on gains wherever arising if it is resident and ordinarily resident in the U.K. The capital gains chargeable are those arising in the accounting period of the company and at the corporation tax rate applicable to the financial year. Deductions may be made for capital losses in that period and for those brought forward from previous periods.

2.3 Charities

Charities are exempt if the gains are used for charitable purposes (TCGA 1992 s 9).

2.4 Approved occupational pension and retirement annuity schemes

Schemes approved under TA 1988 are exempt on gains arising from investments which form part of the fund.

2.5 Housing corporations, registered housing associations and unregistered self-build societies

Disposals of land between these bodies are on a no gain, no loss, basis (TA 1988 s 488).

2.6 Approved self-build societies

These societies may claim exemption (within two years of the period of disposal) from tax on chargeable gains on a disposal of land to a member provided that none of its land is occupied by a non-member (TA 1988 s 489).

2.7 Husband and wife (applies equally to civil partners)
Transfers of assets between husband and wife are treated on a no loss or gain basis. They are therefore exempt from capital gains tax. Each party obtains the annual exemption and each is liable for tax on their chargeable gains as independent taxpayers.

This is a useful way of avoiding the 'bed and breakfasting' rules. One spouse sells the shares, the other buys them back the following day.

Civil partners can follow the same tax free transfer of assets as outlined above.

Transfer or sale within year of separation or divorce
Section 58, TCGA 1992 provides that transfers between husband and wife or partners within any year of assessment while they are living together are treated as taking place at no loss-no gain.

Where the divorce or separation takes place and one partner leaves the family home all within the same year of assessment, then s 58 is extended to cases where the transfer takes place after separation but within the same year of assessment.

Similarly, if both partners vacate the property and the sale takes place within the tax year when separation or divorce take place, then the CGT PRR will continue to apply. Apart from other considerations, the exemption for the final 36 months would be in point.

The situation outlined in the previous section is most unlikely, as transactions following divorce and separation take time. Where a partner who owns part of the family home leaves possibly acquiring another family home, any transfer of value regarding the former family home to the former spouse or partner is likely to take place during a year throughout which the individuals were permanently separated or had divorced.

In such circumstances the deemed consideration is either market value or, in some instances, actual consideration (see ss 17(1)(a) and 18 TCGA 1992).

CG22410 explains the date of transfer as follows:

* If the property was transferred by order of the courts, the date of the court order.

* If the property was not transferred by order of the courts, the date of the contract under which the asset was transferred.

* Where there is no formal written contract, the date of disposal, or (if earlier) the date on which there was a binding agreement between the parties to transfer

the property.

Matters become more complicated where the property is transferred under a consent order before the decree absolute or dissolution order is made final. CG22423 suggests that HMRC may accept the date of transfer agreed by the parties where little or no tax is at stake.

2.8 Partnerships
For capital gains tax purposes any partnership dealings are treated as dealings by the partners and not by the firm as such and the question of residence follows income tax rules. Likewise capital gains tax on the disposal of partnership assets is assessed and charged on the partners separately. These rules apply to partnerships carrying on a trade or business. (TCGA 1992 s 59).

2.9 Assets of deceased persons
The assets of a deceased person are deemed to be acquired by the personal representatives at the market value, e.g., probate value, at the date of death. However no disposal of the assets is assumed to have occurred by reason of the death so that no capital gains tax is payable on that occurrence. However, the personal representatives will be liable to pay capital gains tax on disposals made by the deceased before the death, and liability will arise on disposals by the trustees after the death (see following para.). No liability arises on a donatio mortis causa, a gift made in contemplation of approaching death, as the recipient is treated as acquiring a legacy at the date of death. (TCGA 1992 ss 62-65). (See 26 Death of taxpayer, p.490).

2.10 Trustees
Trustees of settlements are liable for capital gains tax at 28% on disposal of the trust assets, subject to an annual exemption of £5,300 in 2011/2012 (and £5,050 in 2010/2011). Gains are taxed at 28% for discretionary and accumulation trusts. (See Settled Property, p.485, for details of the somewhat complex rules relating to trusts).

3 WHAT IS CHARGEABLE?

The assets chargeable are all forms of property whether situated in the UK or not, including

*   options, debts and incorporeal property generally, and
*   any currency other than sterling,
*   and any form of property created by the person disposing of it, or otherwise coming to be owned without being acquired' (TCGA 1992 s 21).

A gain can arise on an asset which is non-assignable, such as a contract of employment, so that consideration received for releasing an employee from his contract of service is chargeable (*O'Brien v Benson's Hosiery (Holdings) Ltd* HL 1979).

There is a disposal even if no asset is acquired by the person paying the capital sum (TCGA 1992s 22) and in particular the following capital sums received are chargeable:

* compensation for damage or injury to, loss, destruction, dissipation, or depreciation (or the risk of it) of, assets, including sums received under an insurance policy;

* receipts in respect of forfeiture or surrender of rights, or refraining from exercising rights;

* consideration for the use or exploitation of assets.

It has been held that this provision applies only where no asset is acquired by the person from whom the capital sum is derived (*Montgomery v CIR* Ch D 1974; *Marren v Ingles* HL 1980).

4 WHAT IS NOT CHARGEABLE?

4.1 Agricultural grants, compensation for disturbance
Grants receivable by an individual from a scheme under s 27 of the Agricultural Act 1976 for relinquishing occupation of uncommercial agricultural units (TCGA 1992 s 249).

Compensation payable to a tenant for disturbance under s 34(2) of the Agricultural Holdings Act 1948 (*Davis v Powell* Ch D 1976), but compensation payable under s 9 of the Agricultural Holdings (Miscellaneous Provisions) Act 1968 is chargeable.

4.2 Betting winnings
These include football pools, Premium Bonds, the National Lottery and games with prizes (TCGA 1992 s 51).

4.3 Chattels
Chattels (i.e. tangible moveable property) are not chargeable if sold for £6,000 or less (TCGA 1992 s 262).

Two or more articles forming part of a set of articles sold to the same or connected persons, whether on the same or different occasions, are treated as one transaction.

If the sale proceeds exceed £6,000, marginal relief is given by reducing the gain to 5/3 of the excess of the sale price over £6,000. Maximum proceeds for marginal relief are £15,000.

	£
Carpet bought for £1,300, sold for £6,900. The marginal relief calculation is:	
Sale price	6,900
Original cost	1,300
Chargeable Gain	5,600
Gain is limited to £(6,900 - 6,000) x 5/3 =	1,500

The marginal relief does not apply to the calculation of a loss, but in that case the amount of the consideration, if less than £6,000 shall be deemed to be £6,000.

If there is a sale only of a right or interest in the property, the part retained must be treated as a sale (at market price) in making the above calculation, but the gain chargeable is only the proportion equivalent to the part sold.

Sales of commodities dealt with on a terminal market, or sales of foreign currency, do not come within this exemption.

Chattels which are wasting assets are wholly exempt unless capital allowances were claimable wholly or partly. Capital allowances from 6 April 1965 are to be deducted from the cost or notional acquisition at 6 April 1965 (TCGA 1992 ss 44-47).

4.4 Compensation
Compensation for wrong or injury suffered by an individual in his or her person or profession or vocation is not chargeable (TCGA 1992 s 51).

4.5 Corporate bonds
Various changes in the Finance (No.2) Act 2010 relate to the increased capital gains tax rates for gains accruing on or after 23 June 2010, have an adverse impact in relation to the exchange of shares for qualifying corporate bonds (QCBs). These impacts were not announced in the Budget press releases.

A situation arises with exchanges of entrepreneurs' relief qualifying shares for qualifying corporate bonds (QCBs). Taxpayers now have to choose whether to claim entrepreneur's relief and pay 10% tax now or defer the gain into QCBs in which case the gain may end up being taxed at 28%. There is no ability to claim entrepreneurs' relief but not pay the tax until the note is cashed in.

An individual who realises a gain on or after 23 June 2010 which would qualify for entrepreneurs' relief will have to choose whether:

- to bank the 10% rate and claim entrepreneurs' relief in respect of the gain; or

- to claim deferral relief and pay tax at the prevailing rate when a chargeable event occurs in respect of the deferred gain, causing it to fall back into charge to capital gains tax.

Previously where a gain qualified for entrepreneurs' relief, the taxpayer could claim deferral relief and then claim the entrepreneurs' relief at the time and deferred gain fell back into charge to capital gains tax, giving an effective rate of capital gains tax of 10%.

The exemption will apply regardless of the length of time the bond is held as well as to any option or contract to acquire or dispose of such bonds (TCGA 1992 ss 115-117).

A qualifying corporate bond (QCB) is any bond debenture, debenture stock or loan stock whether secured or unsecured issued by a company or UK or foreign public or local authority which meets the following conditions:

- it is a normal commercial loan as defined by TA 1988 Sch 18 para 1(5);

- the amount of the stock is expressed in sterling and is not subject to fluctuations of the value of sterling against any other currency or asset;

- the stock is not convertible into a foreign currency stock or is not redeemable in a foreign currency other than at the rate of exchange prevailing at the date of redemption;

- if the corporate bond was disposed of on or after 19 March 1991, the bond could have been convertible into other corporate bonds but not if it is convertible into shares or other kinds of securities.

In some takeovers and reconstructions of companies corporate bonds are issued in exchange for existing shares or securities. In such cases the exemption from capital gains tax on disposal of the corporate bonds does not apply and they are deemed to have been acquired at the same time and cost as those shares or securities which they have replaced (TCGA 1992 s 116). The same treatment applies to debentures which are not corporate bonds and which are received in a take-over or reconstruction in exchange for existing shares or securities (FA 1993 s 84).

4.6 Debts
A debt other than a debt on a security disposed of by the original creditor or his or her personal representative or legatee. The exemption does not apply to a debt which is owed by a bank and is in foreign currency unless it is for the taxpayer's (or a dependant's) personal expenditure overseas (TCGA 1992 ss 251 and 252).

4.7 Decoration for valour, unless purchased
(TCGA 1992 s 268).

4.8 Foreign currency
Foreign currency for personal use (including the provision or maintenance of a residence) of the taxpayer, or dependants, outside the UK (TCGA 1992 s 269).

4.9 Gains chargeable to income or corporation tax
Gains chargeable to income or corporation tax as income are not chargeable, except balancing charges and the capitalized value of certain income receipts (TCGA 1992 37)s.

4.10 Gilt-edged securities
The disposal of gilt-edged securities, and options or contracts to acquire or dispose of them, does not give rise to a charge to capital gains tax.

Securities, acquired in exchange for shares taken into public ownership, are to be taxed on gains accrued up to the date of exchange (with corresponding relief for losses) but the charge will not arise until the disposal of the new securities.

4.11 Land: small part disposals
In the case of part disposals by an individual not exceeding £20,000 in total in any year of assessment, and small in value compared with the whole before disposal, the proceeds are treated as reducing the cost (TCGA 1992 s 242). This exemption excludes disposals under compulsory purchase orders, and does not apply to any estate or interest in land which is a wasting asset.

A **small part disposal** is defined as 20% of the value of the holding on the date of disposal (FA 1986 s 60). Previously there was no statutory definition for small, and HMRC interpreted small as being less than 5% of the value of the holding on the date of disposal.

4.12 Life assurance and deferred annuity
Proceeds received by the original beneficial owner (TCGA 1992 s 237). Other types of policy are similarly exempt assets, **but** not so as to prevent sums received directly or indirectly thereunder being regarded as chargeable proceeds of a disposal of the asset to which they relate (TCGA 1992 s 204). Please see 5.9 Life Policy - Partial Disposal, p.147.

4.13 Endowment policy

The proceeds of endowment policies are tax-free to policyholders at the maturity of the policy, or if they are surrendered after 10 years' premiums have been paid (or three-quarters of the original term if less).

Actually, "tax-free" is a bit of a misnomer: the equivalent of basic-rate tax is paid by the life company on the income and gains of the underlying investments. if policies are surrendered earlier than this, then basic-rate taxpayers have no further liability, but higher-rate taxpayers may have a chargeable gain on which they must pay the difference between basic and higher-rate tax.

4.14 Motor vehicles

Vehicles commonly used and not unsuitable for the carriage of private passengers are not chargeable (TCGA 1992 s 263).

4.15 Principal Private Residence (PPR) - (defined as - 'main residence')

Principal Private Residence and grounds up to 0.5 hectare are not chargeable (TCGA 1992 ss 222-226). The grounds must be occupied at the time of disposal, so that a sale of part of them, following a sale of the house and the remaining grounds, will not be exempt (*Varty v Lynes* Ch D 1976). Strictly, a sale of a house after cessation of occupation would entail loss of exemption for the grounds, but, in practice, this will be so only where the grounds have development value (ICAEW Technical Release 233 para. 37). The gain on sale of a caravan and the plot of land on which it stands has been held to be exempt, because the caravan was used as the only residence of the taxpayer during his ownership of the land (*Makins v Elson* Ch D 1976).

In *Jason Terrence Moore v HMRC* TC00710, Mr Moore and his future wife Miss Archer purchased a property in Bishop's Rise, Loughton in December 1999 with the intention that this would become their home after renovation. At the time of purchase Miss Archer owned another property where they lived together.

Immediately after completion the couple became concerned about their neighbours and Miss Archer refused to go ahead with the plan to move there. The property was later transferred into Mr Moore's sole name in March 2001 and he sold the property in 2004/2005. He claimed that the property was his residence between December 1999 and February 2000 when he moved back to Hereward Green.

The First-tier Tribunal dismissed the taxpayer's claim for private residence relief on the grounds that the appellant (on whom the burden of proof rested) had not established that the Bishop's Rise property was his residence at all, let alone his only or main residence. Mr Moore lived at the Hereward Green property before 10 December 1999 and again from February 2000 and kept clothes there throughout. The Tribunal also noted that the appellant's evidence on crucial issues was 'unreliable, vague and sometimes inconsistent'.

The Tribunal cited *Goodwin v Curtis* 70 TC 478, in which the Court of Appeal said that 'there must be some assumption of permanence, some degree of continuity, some expectation of continuity to turn mere occupation into residence'. Mr Moore's occupation of the Bishop's Rise property did not have the quality that turned mere occupation of it into its being his residence. In establishing this, the Tribunal explained:

'We take into account the undesirable neighbourhood problems, Miss Archer's refusal to live in the Bishop's Rise Property, the fact that the Appellant has not proved that he registered as a resident of the Bishop's Rise Property for council tax purposes, water rates purposes, or DVLA's purposes, and that he could not produce insurance bills or telephone bills that would be some evidence of residence there.'

There are two learning points here:

(a)   There must be good evidence to substantiate a disputed period of residence, eg registration for council tax, phone, DVLA etc, bearing in mind that the claimed period of occupation may substantially predate the disposal.

(b)   The quality of the period of occupation is fundamentally important, as indicated in the Court of Appeal ruling in Goodwin v Curtis cited above.

The case of *Anthony Metcalfe v HMRC* TC00753 also turned on the quality of occupation and on the quality of the evidence. Mr Metcalfe owned three properties in 2003 - Everleigh, Landalewood and Westgate.

The issue for the Tribunal was whether or not Westgate was to be treated as the appellant's residence for capital gains tax purposes and consequently whether private residence relief was available upon its sale.

The Tribunal found as a fact that the appellant's written and oral evidence fell short of establishing that he had in fact ever resided at the apartment. The Tribunal found the electricity bill was improbably small for the winter months and did not accept the appellant's explanation as credible. Even if the Tribunal was satisfied that the appellant had, for a time, occupied the apartment at Westgate as his dwelling house, the question for determination was whether such occupation amounted to residence.

The Tribunal did not accept that the appellant had provided any evidence to show that the occupation of Westgate had any degree of permanence. It found that the evidence pointed to the contrary, in particular the facts that the appellant had not notified his change of address to either his bank or the Council and within either days or weeks of acquiring the property the appellant had obtained a valuation with a view to selling.

On those facts the Tribunal found that there was no degree of permanence and no expectation of continuity. At best, the appellant had temporary occupation of Westgate, which was insufficient to amount to residence. In conclusion, taking into account all of the evidence, both written and oral, the Tribunal found that the nature, quality, length and circumstances of the appellant's occupation of the Westgate apartment was such that it did not amount to residence. The appeal was dismissed.

In *Longson v Baker* the question was the extent to which the gain attributable to 7.56 hectares should attract the main residence relief for garden or grounds as falling within the 'permitted area'.

In 1979 L bought a property (the farm). The farm extended to 7.56 hectares and included *inter alia* a farmhouse, stables and an outhouse. L then put up a further building, which was used as a riding school.

On 15.12.95, following the failure of his marriage, L sold his beneficial interest in the farm to his wife. He appealed against a CGT assessment for 1995-96, contending that for purposes of s222(1)(b) TCGA 1992 the 'permitted area' of garden or grounds which attracted the relief was the whole of the area disposed of insofar as 'required for the reasonable employment of the dwelling-house as a residence'. It was agreed that for purposes of the appeal the dwelling-house included not only the farmhouse but also the stables and outhouse.

L's appeal was dismissed by the Special Commissioner: while it might have been desirable, it was not necessary to the reasonable enjoyment of the dwelling-house as a residence, having regard to its size and character, that the land should have a total area of 7.56 hectares. L appealed.

It was clear from the statutory words 'required for the reasonable enjoyment' that the test as to what any larger permitted area could consist of beyond the 1/2 hectare allowed was an objective test. Here, it was not obviously required (i.e. necessary) to keep horses at a house in order to enjoy it as a residence. Further, if the taxpayer's contention were valid, the permitted area might vary in accordance with the interests of the taxpayer family occupying the dwelling-house at the time of disposal. The appeal was therefore dismissed. (Longson v Baker 16.12.00 (2001) STI issue 2).

It must be the only, or main, residence throughout the period of ownership or throughout the period of ownership except for all or any part of the last three years. The period prior to 31 March 1982 is ignored and breaks within that period of up to three years are treated as residence, as are breaks of any length due to employment being outside the UK and breaks of up to four years where conditions of employment prevent residence. It is a condition that residence be resumed after such an absence but, in practice, this is not insisted on if the employment requires the employee to work elsewhere (ESC D4).

Lettings relief
If the property was at some point the PPR there is a 'lettings relief' available to each
spouse of a maximum of £40,000 covering the let period.

Example:
Take the case of Mr and Mrs Dunn, who purchased their residence for £250,000 on
7 April 2002. The couple occupied the property as their principal private residence
for three years until 6 April 2005. The property is then let for six years until it is sold
for £750,000 on 6 April 2011. Ignoring the costs of purchase and sale the CGT
computation might look something like this: Other taxable income, for each of them,
is £50,000 in 2011/2012.

		£
Sale price		750,000
Cost		250,000
basic gain		£500,000
Total period of ownership		9 years
Exempt periods:		
- Actual occupation		3 years
- Final 36 months		3 years
Exempt gain 6/9 x £500,000 =		£333,333
Taxable gain		166,667
Less: lettings relief		80,000
Chargeable gain		86,667
Annual exemptions (assumed)		20,200
Taxable		£66,467
Tax due at 28%		£18,611

The tax due might still seem high, but in fact it represents only 3.7 per cent on a gain
of £500,000. It is infinitely better than the tax payable if the property had not been the
principal private residence for any period, when the figures would be:

	£
Chargeable gain	500,000
Annual exemptions (2 x £10,100)	20,200
Taxable gain	£479,800
Tax due at 28%	£134,344

There are two things that should be said about the 'lettings' relief under s 223(4). The first is that the relief given cannot exceed the gain for the let period. This condition is met in the above example. The other issue is that HMRC Capital Gains Manual at CG 64716 and 64738 suggests that the granting of the '£80,000' lettings exemption may be subject to HMRC enquiry where the potential tax is significant. This would apply to the above example.

Apportionments are made where these conditions are not wholly fulfilled. A reasonable period of time in building, altering or redecorating, or in selling the old residence, is in practice allowed as a period of occupation.

A dwelling (or part) qualifies in respect of any period after 31 July 1978 when the owner lived in job-related accommodation, provided he or she intends in due course to occupy the dwelling.

When husband and wife (and civil partners) are living together and the residence requirement is satisfied as regards the one who is not the owner of the residence, it is regarded as satisfied as regards the owner (ESC D3). After separation the former matrimonial home may be regarded as continuing to be exempt up to the time of the financial settlement (on divorce or otherwise) between the spouses, provided one spouse continues to reside there and the claimant makes no claim in respect of any other residence for the same period (ESC D6).

This exemption does not apply if the residence was purchased with the object, wholly or partly, of selling it at a profit, nor to expenditure after purchase incurred with the same object, but it need not have been purchased with the intention to reside in it.

Only one residence ranks for this relief but the taxpayer may elect (in default of which the Inspector may decide subject to appeal) which of two or more residences shall be the main residence. The election would be effective for any period beginning within two years from the notice. (s222 (5) (a) TCGA 1992). Strictly speaking a claim could be made on one day, giving 2 years relief and changed back 7 days later. The only effect would be the loss of 7 days PPR on the original property.

Page CG64512 of HMRC manual deals with a scenario where someone has owned two homes, one a holiday home, for many years. By changing the 'main residence' nomination between the two, just for a week, the holiday home can get up to three years' worth of relief. The main home loses 1 week's worth of relief.

See Transfer or sale within year of separation or divorce above, p.429.

The exemption applies to the residence of a beneficiary entitled to occupy it under a settlement. 'Entitlement to occupy' covers any case where a beneficiary in fact occupied the residence by permission of the trustees, including under a trust for sale, will or intestacy trust and even a discretionary trust (*Sansom v Peay* Ch D 1976). By concession (ESC D5), relief is given where personal representatives dispose of a house which before and after the deceased's death has been used as their only or main residence by successors entitled to substantially the whole of the proceeds of sale for life or absolutely.

Where any part of the residence is used 'exclusively' for trade or other business purposes (*Jamaica CIR v Hanover Agencies* PC 1969; *Lewis v Wildcrest* Ch D 1978; *American Leaf Blending Co v Director General of Inland Revenue* PC 1978), or there is a change in the nature of use, appropriate reductions in the exemption are made. **Business** purposes may include lettings or working from home and each case is dealt with on an individual basis. A letting which is regarded as 'business' may qualify for relief. A letting to a lodger living as part of a family sharing the living accommodation and taking meals with them is not regarded as being for business (SP 14/80). The key word is 'exclusively' to avoid losing the exemption make sure that there is some personal or non-business use of the room or part of the house used mainly for business purposes.

Example:
A property is acquired on 1 January 2003. It is sold on 1 May 2011 with a gain of £300,000. The property has been used throughout as a main residence, apart from exclusive use of two rooms, which equates to an agreed business use of the property of (say) 25 per cent.

	£
25% of taxable gain of £300,000	75,000
Chargeable gain	£75,000

A residence provided before 6 April 1988 for a dependent relative rent-free and without any other consideration is exempt. Only one house at any one time ranks for the relief, and the conditions above apply. A dependent relative is defined as a relative incapacitated by old age or infirmity from maintaining himself or herself, or a mother widowed, separated or no longer married.

CGT relief for carers' private residences
The 2009 PBR contained the welcome announcement that, with effect from 9 December 2009, adult placement (AP) carers would no longer be restricted in the amount of private residence relief (PRR) they can claim on selling their home in which they have been caring for vulnerable adults.

Hitherto, AP carers had not been able to claim PRR on any part of their home that had been used exclusively for the purposes of their caring activity, because HMRC regards such activity as a 'business' for the purposes of s 224, Taxation of Chargeable Gains Act 1992.

HMRC had taken the view that letting relief could not apply to properties that qualified for exemption as being occupied by dependent relatives. This was set out at paragraph CG64718 of the Capital Gains Tax Manual.

HMRC changed its view and announced on 1 August 2007 that:

"CG64718 will be amended to reflect HMRC's change of view that lettings relief may be due (where a private residence is occupied by a dependent relative before 6 April 1988 and the residence has also been let as residential accommodation). HMRC will also withdraw CG65562 which says that lettings relief is not due where private residence relief is due on a residence occupied by a dependent relative."

4.16 Works of art, objects, etc. for public benefit
A gift of assets does not give rise to a chargeable gain if it qualifies for relief from inheritance tax by virtue of being a disposal to a body for national purposes (museums, etc.) or is in satisfaction of inheritance tax or estate duty (TCGA 1992 s 258). The disposal is deemed to have been made for a consideration giving rise to a no gain/no loss position. If the inheritance tax undertaking is not complied with or ceases to be eligible for relief, the gain will be charged by reference to the market value at the date of disposal.

If the asset was held at 31 March 1982, it is the value on this date that now applies.

5 ROLL-OVER RELIEF

5.1 Replacement of business assets

Where a person uses the whole proceeds of a sale of a business asset in purchasing another business asset, the gain which would be chargeable to tax may be deducted from the cost of the new assets instead of being charged to capital gains tax (TCGA 1992 ss 152-162).

Balloon Promotions Ltd. v Wilson (HMIT) (Sp C 524) was an important case before the commissioners concerning the valuation of goodwill in a franchised pizza restaurant.

A company (B) owned part of two franchised restaurant businesses. The franchisor Pizza Express (P) wished to purchase the businesses and operate them itself. B agreed to sell its interests to P. It attributed most of the consideration to goodwill, on which it claimed rollover relief. The Revenue rejected the claim on the basis that the goodwill already belonged to P, and that most of the consideration represented compensation for the early termination of the franchise agreements. B appealed.

The Special Commissioner reviewed the evidence in detail and allowed the appeal in principle, holding that the goodwill had belonged to B, and that the consideration for the goodwill qualified for relief. The Commissioner observed that 'goodwill distinguishes an established business from a new business and is built up by years of honest work and investment in the business'.

The Commissioner held that 'the ownership of goodwill between franchisor and franchisee is primarily a question of fact'. On the evidence, P was not 'a well-known brand' at the time B acquired the business, and B had 'established the reputation of their restaurants, which was based principally on the service they provided to their customers'. The appeal was allowed.

Although the facts of this case are somewhat unique and may not be directly applicable to other situations the principles should nonetheless not though be overlooked in terms of valuation of goodwill in other types of business and should be essential reading for those who have been involved in business incorporations in recent years.

If only part of the sale proceeds are so used, only that part of the total gain which is used in buying the further assets can be deducted.

Machinery cost £4,000, sold for £5,000. New machinery purchased to replace it costing £4,700. The gain is £1,000, but only £700 of this has been spent on the new machine. The remaining £300 is chargeable and the cost of the new machine is treated as £4,000 (£4,700 - £700).

The purchase of the new assets must be made within 12 months before or three years after the sale of the old assets. In *Watton v Tippett* (CA 1997 STI 696) having purchased a single property, part of it was sold. The taxpayer tried to roll over the gain against the original purchase. It was held that he couldn't as it had been a 'single' purchase. It therefore follows that if he had purchased the original assets in separate bits it would have been allowable. An unconditional contract ranks as a purchase, and the Board may extend the time limit. Where land has been compulsorily acquired but the owner is allowed to continue using it for his or her business, the three year period will normally run from the date he or she ceases to use it.

The new assets must be purchased with the object of using them in the trade and not wholly or partly to make a gain on their disposal. A site intended for use in the business which is never in fact so used, or even developed, is not eligible for relief (*Temperley v Visibell Ltd* Ch D 1973). However, it is thought that where part of the factory site, intended to be developed as an extension to the existing factory, is sold without being developed, relief can be claimed (*Newcastle City Council v Royal Newcastle Hospital* PC 1959, a rating case on 'use' which supports the proposition that actual use is not necessary in all circumstances). A plot of land over which an option to buy was granted before completion by the grantor of his contract to purchase the plot, has been held to have been acquired with a view to realization for gain (*More v Elders* Ch D 1971).

The assets acquired must be within one of the following classes:
*   Land, buildings, structures and fixed plant and machinery. HMRC accepts that the sale of a building and the land on which it is built can be treated as two separate assets for roll-over relief purposes. This would be beneficial where the taxpayer had failed to fully reinvest the proceeds for the sale of old business premises.

For example:

	£
Gain on entire premises	30,000
Proceeds of sale of old asset	200,000
Proceeds reinvested in new asset	150,000

No roll-over relief is due because the amount not reinvested exceeds the gain. But taking the land on its own, assuming the proceeds and gain are £130,000 and £20,000 respectively:

	£
Gain on land	20,000
Proceeds on sale of land	130,000
Proceeds reinvested in new asset	150,000

Roll-over relief of £20,000 is due as the proceeds have been fully reinvested.

Two or more replacement assets Taxpayers may take advantage of s 153, TCGA 1992, which deals with roll over relief where the proceeds are not wholly reinvested. For example, a trader sells asset A in 1990 for £1m and realises a gain of £350,000. In 1991, he buys asset B for £500,000, claiming that this is the partial reinvestment of the proceeds of asset A. In 1992, he sells asset B for £530,000 and buys asset C for £550,000.

The trader can claim roll-over relief by virtue of the aggregate expenditure on assets B and C of £1,050,000. It also appears that he can claim that the gain on asset A can be rolled over wholly against the cost of asset C.

This would result in only a modest gain arising on the sale of asset B.

- ships;
- aircraft;
- goodwill;
- hovercraft;
- satellites, space stations and spacecraft (including launch vehicles);
- milk quotas, potato quotas, quotas for ewes and suckler cows.

Where the business use of a building is partial, or where any asset was not used for business purposes for the whole period of ownership, an appropriate apportionment is made.

Land and buildings occupied for their business by land developers or dealers (and not treated as a trading asset) rank for relief.

Where the asset purchased is a wasting asset, the gain will be chargeable when it is disposed of or ceases to be used for the trade, or ten years after its acquisition if this is sooner, but, in certain circumstances, the gain can be transferred and deducted from a non-wasting asset instead of a wasting one.

The general commissioners' conclusion that two trades were carried on successively where there was a gap of nine years was a finding that could not be supported. So held Chancery Division in *Steibelt v Paling* (1999) STI 864.

On 22 October 1986, the taxpayer sold for £130,416 the inn from which he had carried on this trade of publican for a number of years, realising a chargeable gain of £52,219. On 10 February 1988, he paid £20,000 for a barge he intended to use as a wine bar and restaurant. Between December 1989 and November 1994 he carried out substantial improvements to the barge, costing £160,441. On 27 February 1995, the taxpayer submitted a claim for rollover relief, which the inspector rejected. The taxpayer appealed. On 15 August 1995, the barge was opened and business commenced.

The general commissioners allowed the taxpayer's claim for rollover relief on the basis that the time limit of three years specified in s 152(3), TCGA 1992 should be extended to six years.

HMRC appealed and it was found that the conclusion "that the trades were carried on successively" was not one that the commissioners could reasonably have come to.

Assets owned outside a family company
Such assets owned by an individual qualify for relief, if the company is the family company at the time of the disposal and acquisition.

Partnerships
Each partner's relief is calculated according to his or her share in the old and new assets. In practice a partner who lets an asset to the partnership is eligible for relief on disposal of that asset (SP D11).

Two trades
If a person carries on two trades in different localities which are concerned with goods or services of the same kind, they may be treated as one.

For the purposes of this relief all the trades carried on by members of a group are treated as if they were carried on by a single person. The effect is that, provided the company making the disposal is a member of a group at the time of disposal, its gain may be rolled over against acquisitions of any other company which is a member of that group at acquisition. It follows that there need not be a time when the disposer company and the acquiring company were both members of the same group (SP D19).

The relief applies to trades, professions, offices or employments, commercial woodlands and to the discharge of the functions of a public authority. Non profit-making trade protection associations and professional bodies are eligible to claim relief, as are non-profit making bodies generally in relation to acquisitions provided that such a body's buildings must be used and occupied, and its other assets must be used, by the body concerned.

A lessor of tied premises is treated as occupying the premises for trade.

Death of taxpayer (for an example see Death of Taxpayer, p.490)
When an asset ceases to be used for trading purposes because of the death of a
claimant to roll-over relief, it will not give rise to capital gains tax (ESC 16.12.93).

5.2 Gifts and sales of business assets or interests in family companies
A claim may be made to roll over any capital gain arising on a disposal by gift or at
an undervalue of:

• an asset (or interest therein) used for the purposes of a business carried on by
  the transferor or his or her family company; or

• shares or securities of the transferor's family trading company.

The claim must be made jointly by the transferor and transferee and the transferee
must be resident or ordinarily resident in the UK.

From 16 March 1993 roll-over relief applies when shares are sold in qualified
unquoted trading companies and the proceeds re-invested in other qualifying
unquoted trading companies. The conditions are that the claimant must have been a
full-time working director or employee engaged in a managerial or technical capacity
in the company of which the shares are sold; have owned for at least a year more
than 5% of the shares in that company; and hold at least 5% of the shares of the
company in which the re-investment is made within one year before and three years
after the sale of the original shares. For these purposes a qualifying unquoted
trading company includes one engaged in retailing or manufacturing but not one with
more than 50% of its assets in land or carrying on financial, leasing or land dealing
activities, or one letting on assured tenancies. Investors not exposed to any real risk
will not qualify for the relief. Capital gains tax will be chargeable when the new
shares are disposed of, when the claimant emigrates and if, within three years of the
re-investment the company ceases to be qualified.

If the disposal is wholly exempted under the retirement relief provisions, no claim is
needed or permitted.

Business includes any trade, profession or vocation and also any agricultural
property, not used for the purposes of a trade, but eligible for inheritance tax on the
transfer.

Trustees may also claim the relief in respect of the deemed disposal on a person
becoming absolutely entitled or termination of an interest in possession, for any trust
asset being either:

• a business carried on by the trustee or a beneficiary who had a life interest in possession before the deemed disposal, or

- Shares or securities in a trading company in which 25% of the voting power is exercisable by the trustee at the time of the deemed disposal (TCGA 1992 ss 165-169).

5.3 Gifts

Roll-over relief may be claimed where the asset transferred is a chargeable transfer for inheritance tax purposes or the transfers involved heritage property or political parties. Where the gift was made prior to 14 March 1989, there were no restrictions on the eligibility of the transfer for roll-over relief and the relief was granted on any transfer from an individual to another individual or to a trust. Where the transfer is between individuals, the claim must be made by both parties, but where the transferee is a trust the claim may only be made by the transferor (TCGA 1992 s 260).

5.4 Gifts of land to housing associations

Gifts of land to a registered housing association made on or after 14 March 1989 may be treated as a no gain/no loss situation if an election is made by the transferor and the association. The association is treated as acquiring the land when the donor did and at the same price (TCGA 1992 s 259).

5.5 Settled property

A claim for roll-over relief may be made where assets are transferred by one body of trustees to another body (TCGA 1992 s 90). The claim for the relief may be made by the transferor trustee.

5.6 Compulsory purchase

A claim for roll-over relief may be made where land is disposed of to an authority exercising or having compulsory powers and the proceeds from the disposal are used to acquire other land excepting a private residence. No relief will, however, be available if the transferor had advertised or indicated otherwise that the land was for sale. Where only part of the proceeds are re-invested partial relief only will be available (TCGA 1992 s 247).

5.7 Employee share ownership trusts

Roll-over relief may be claimed by a person who transfers after 19 March 1990, ordinary, fully-paid, non-redeemable shares in the founding company to the trustees of employee share ownership trusts (FA 1990 ss 31-35). There should be no special restrictions on the shares and the Trustees must be beneficially entitled to not less than 10% of the ordinary share capital of the founding company.

The roll-over relief will be granted where the transfer utilizes the consideration for the transfer in acquiring chargeable assets other than shares or securities of the same company and group. Where the whole amount of the consideration is applied the transfer will give rise to a nil gain/nil loss position. Where only part of the consideration is applied the amount of the gain chargeable is restricted to the amount of the consideration not applied and roll-over relief granted on the amount applied in re-investments.

5.8 Effect
The claim to roll over the gain takes effect by the rolled-over gain being deducted from the gain which would have been chargeable on the disposal and from the transferee's acquisition cost of the assets in question. Thus, the rolled-over gain will be taxed when the transferee disposes of the asset. The rolled-over gain is that which arises before retirement relief (where the gain exceeds the relief available). (See 5.9 following, Reductions in rolled-over gain).

5.9 Reductions in rolled-over gain
If an asset is disposed of at an undervalue and the consideration given to the transferor exceeds the allowable costs of the asset to him the rolled-over gain is reduced by the excess of that consideration over those costs.

If the asset had been used for business purposes for only part of its period of ownership, the rolled-over gain is proportionately reduced. Similarly, in the case of a building or structure which was used only for part of the period of ownership (or a substantial part of it), the rolled-over gain is reduced on a just and reasonable basis.

In the case of a disposal of shares in a company holding non-business assets, the rolled-over gain is reduced to the proportion which the market value of chargeable business assets bears to the market value of total chargeable assets.

If the gain is partly exempted by retirement relief, the rolled-over gain is reduced by the exemption (TCGA 1992 s 165).

5.10 Fish quota
A press release of 2 March 1999 stated the following.

(a)   A sale of a fishing vessel can involve a number of items (and it is possible, in certain circumstances, for one or more of these to be disposed of separately).

These items are:
- the vessel itself;

- the waiver of a fishing vessel licence entitlement;

- a track record (this is the amount of particular stocks of fish caught in previous years, including, from 1 January 1999, "fixed quota allocation units");

- fish quota (this is proportion of the total quotas for certain fish stocks allocated to the United Kingdom by the European Union, and issued annually according to rules prescribed by the Fisheries Departments).

(b)   Fishing vessel licences (and any associated track record and quota), are issued at the discretion of Ministers responsible for the Fisheries Departments. Like fishing vessels, these licences (and the items associated with them) are chargeable assets for capital gains tax purposes.

(c)   Roll-over relief is currently available for the vessel and the licence (the latter being treated as goodwill of the business as announced in an IR PR of 29 October 1987). It is now accepted that a track record which is associated with a particular licence may also be treated, on a similar basis, as goodwill. Fish quota, however, is not goodwill and has never been treated as such.

(d)   Regulations ("The Finance Act 1993, Section 86(2), (Fish Quota) Order 1999") have added fish quota to the list of qualifying assets.

6 HOW THE CHARGE IS COMPUTED

6.0 The actual date of disposal

The date of disposal of an asset is the time when the contract is made, and not when the asset is conveyed or transferred. Therefore in a property transaction it is the exchange of contracts rather than completion.

6.1 Disposals

The gain or loss is the difference between the amount realised on disposal and the actual cost, including allowable expenses of purchase and sale. For assets held at the 31 March 1982 the cost is assumed to be the value at that date and for later acquisitions the actual cost applies. Indexation no longer applies to assets held by individuals at 5 April 1998.

As indicated this means that the cost of all assets held at the 31 March 1982 is assumed to be the value at that date. This applies to all assets held at that date, there is no longer an option to use the original cost if purchased prior to that date.

An ESC issued on 16 March 1993 applies on an optional basis to the valuation of shares acquired on a no gain/no loss basis, such as from a husband or wife or by one member of a company group from another group member. Assuming the shares were held by the transferor at 31 March 1982 they are added to the transferee's holding of similar shares at that date for the purpose of rebasing and indexation. This option would be valuable where the larger holding would produce a greater value per share than a smaller holding, as is often the case.

6.2 The consideration

(a)   The consideration (or proceeds on disposal) excludes amounts chargeable to income tax or corporation tax (TCGA 1992 s 537).

(b)   The consideration for a gift is its value at the date when given.

(c)   The consideration embraces money received for the surrender of a right, such as for agreeing not to exercise an option to renew a lease.

(d)   The amount received from a part withdrawal of a life policy paid for by the taxpayer is treated as a consideration.

(e)   The fact that consideration stated in dollars was received in instalments did not entitle the taxpayer to an adjustment to a capital gain computation under s 40(2), CGTA 1979, on the basis that the sterling/dollar exchange rate at the date the instalments were received was different from that at the time the contract was made. So held Chancery Division in *Loffland Bros. North Sea Inc. v Goodbrand* (1997) STI 30.

6.3 Allowable costs

These Include:

(a)   Incidental costs of acquisition or sale, such as professional fees, duties, commission and VAT, including the costs of valuing assets (such as for a rebasing at 31.3.82).

(b)   Costs of enhancing the value of the asset and of preserving a right over the asset.

(c)   Advertising for a seller of an asset to be acquired or for a buyer of an asset to be sold (TCGA 1992 s 38).

(d)   In the case of a company interest charged to capital on borrowings to acquire an asset which is a building, structure or works (TCGA 1992 s 40).

(e)   No deductions are eligible for expenditure allowed for income tax or corporation tax purposes in a trade, profession or/vocation (TCGA 1992 s 39).

(f)   In certain circumstances cost can include otherwise eligible assets on which capital allowances or renewals allowances have been made, but in such cases the allowances will restrict the cost on disposal of the assets. (TCGA 1992 s 41).

(g)   The expenses incurred in appealing against a valuation for capital gains tax purposes were not allowable expenses in computing the capital gain on the disposal. So held the Court of Appeal in Administrators of the Estate of *Caton (deceased) v Couch* (1997) STI 770, confirming the High Court's decision.

7 INDEXATION ALLOWANCE

7.1 Individuals

For disposals post 6 April 2008 any chargeable asset disposed of on or after 6 April 2008, indexation is no longer allowed and 'taper relief' is also not available.

Where the asset was held prior to 31 March 1982 the taxpayer may no longer (from 6 April 2008) make an election whether to claim the market value at that date rather than on the expenditure incurred prior to that date. All assets held on that date their value on 31 March 1982 is now the base cost for CGT purposes.

Where there are two or more items of expenditure separate calculations have to be made for each item of expenditure.

Identification of securities: general rules

Prior to the enactment of the Finance Act 1982, shares and securities of the same class and issued by a single company were pooled by virtue of CGTA 1979 ss 65 and 66. However, FA 1982 s 88 introduced new rules for the identification of acquisition expenditure in respect of disposals of shares or securities held on 5 April 1982 (1 April in the case of companies); and a new form of pooling was introduced by FA 1985 s 68 and Sch 19 Pt III, in respect of the shares held on 6 April 1985 (1 April 1985 in the case of companies). Disposals are to be considered in chronological order with the earliest disposal being taken first. On each disposal, shares will be identified on a last in first out basis: i.e. they will be identified first with shares in the new pool, then with shares in a 1982 pool and finally with shares acquired with any unpooled holdings.

Where there is an acquisition and disposal within a period of ten days, the shares are matched for the purposes of calculating the indexation allowance and identification.

Identification of securities: special rules (FA 1982 s 89)

Shares transferred between spouses living together or between members of a group of companies are normally treated as having been transferred for a consideration which results in a nil gain/nil loss position. However, where such transfers are made in conjunction with transfers to a third party no allowance would apply.

7.2 Companies - (N.B. indexation continues - see Table 6. Capital Gains Tax - Indexation Allowance - RPI back to 1982, p.625)

A company may make an election for parallel pooling of qualifying securities held for twelve months or more and disposed of after 31 March 1982. The election must be made within two years of the end of the accounting period in which the first disposal of any securities is made and is irrevocable. The election must apply to all securities and they will be identified on a first in-first out basis for disposals made within twelve months of acquisition and thereafter any disposals will be from the pooled holding. The election will not apply to any gilt edged securities nor to securities held on 6 April 1965, where no election was made for the original costs to be used for the purpose of computation of capital gains. The amendment to the 1994 Finance Act relating to indexation, increasing or creating a loss does not relate to companies.

Identification of securities

The pooled holding will consist of all securities held for at least 12 months and will grow as more shares are added when the company has held them for 12 months and will reduce when disposals of qualifying shares are made. When shares are added to the pool, the cost of all shares in the pool will be averaged, and part disposals will be on the normal part disposal rules.

Pool expenditure

Each pool will have an unindexed and an indexed pool of expenditure as follows.

The unindexed pool expenditure is the aggregate cost of the acquisition of the shares plus the enhancement expenditure if any. If any expenditure such as consideration for rights issue, is incurred these cannot be added to the pool until twelve months after the expenditure was incurred and the shares do not form part of the pool until after that period. Similarly, where any reduction from the pool has to be made, e.g. small capital distributions or considerations for the sale of rights issues the reduction will not be made until after twelve months of the receipt or the event giving rise to the reduction.

The indexed pool expenditure is the aggregate cost (including enhancement costs) of the shares plus any indexation allowance in respect of options which would have applied to a disposal of the whole of the holding. When any adjustment is made to the unindexed pool a similar adjustment is made to the indexed pool, but before such an adjustment is made, the value of the pool has to be recalculated by reference to the indexed rise since the last adjustment.

The indexed rise is the sum produced by multiplying the value of the pool by the formula:

$$\frac{RE - RL}{RL}$$

where RE is the retail prices index for the month in which the event giving rise to the adjustment occurred and RL is the retail prices index for the month in which the last operative event occurred or the pool came into being whichever was the later. If RE is less than RL the indexed rise is nil.

Calculation of allowance

When a disposal is made the gains are computed by reference to the costs/value of the disposals in both pools and:

- If there is a gain on both basis, the allowance will be the difference between the two amounts.

- If there is a gain on the unindexed basis, but a loss on the indexed basis, the indexation allowance will be restricted to the amount of the unindexed gain.

- If there is a loss on both basis, no allowance will be due.

Share pooling

Shares of the same class held in the same capacity are pooled together and treated as a single asset. Separate pools are set up for shares held on 5 April 1982 (31 March 1982 for companies) and those acquired after those dates. As they form separate pools the basis of determining the pool expenditure are different and are as follows. Where the shares disposed of were held on 5 April 1982 (31 March 1982 for companies), the pool expenditure of the holding will be the total of the remaining expenditure of the shares after the deduction of the apportioned expenditure of any shares disposed of previously plus the remaining expenditure of the holdings added to it and this total expenditure will qualify for indexation.

Shares acquired after 5 April 1982 (31 March 1982 for companies) which are still held on 6 April 1985 (1 April 1985 for companies) are pooled together and treated as a single asset. This pool is referred to as the 'new holding' and the pool expenditure is the total of:

- the acquisition cost of all shares which were acquired after 5 April 1982 (31 March 1982 for companies) together with any subsequent allowable expenditure: and

- the indexation allowance (for companies only) is calculated by reference to the expenditure incurred between 1 April 1982 and 31 March 1985 and based on the assumption that the shares were disposed of immediately prior to 1 April 1985 and ignoring the twelve month waiting period.

If all of the shares were acquired after 31 March 1985 the indexed pool comes into being as soon as the qualifying expenditure is incurred.

8 ENTREPRENEURS' RELIEF

8.1 Small businesses
To compensate for the withdrawal of the '10%' band of taper relief (from 6 April 2008), proposals were enacted to the then flat rate of 18%.

Put simply, the relief works by allowing gains made on qualifying business disposals in a taxpayer's lifetime to be charged to CGT at an effective rate of 10% (being 5/9ths of the 18% rate).

*   'Entrepreneurs' Relief' provides an effective 10% tax rate on capital gains of up to a cumulative lifetime limit of £10 million from 6 April 2011(from 23 June 2010 - £5 million).

Tax Year	Entrepreneurs Lifetime Limit	
	Limit £	Effective Rate
2011/2012	10,000,000	10%
2010/2011 (from 23.06.2010)	5,000,000	10%
2010/2011 (to 22.06.2010)	2,000,000	10%
2009/2010 to 2008/2009	1,000,000	10%

The pre 23 June 2010 system of a 4/9th's reduction in the gain which is then taxed at 18% is abolished in favour of an actual 10% rate so that the annual exemption will now save tax at 10% rather than at 18% as previously.

	Pre 23 June 2010 £	Post 23 June 2010 £
Gains before adjustment	180,000	180,000
Adjustment	80,000	-
Gains £180,000 x 5/9 =	100,000	180,000
Less Annual Exemption	10,100	10,100
	£89,900	£169,900
Tax @ 18% / 10%	£16,182	£16,990

To qualify for Entrepreneurs' Relief the disposal must relate to:

- The whole or part of a qualifying business (excluding investment business) owned by the individual throughout the period of one year ending with the date of disposal, or;

- A business is defined as anything which is a trade, profession, or vocation and is conducted on a commercial basis and with a view to the realisation of profits.

8.2 Material disposal of business assets

There are three occasions for a material disposal of a business asset:

(a)   The disposal of the whole or part of a business
- meaning an individual disposing of a business carried on alone or in partnership which the individual has owned throughout the 12 months ending with the date of disposal.

(b)   The disposal of (or interests in) one or more assets in use, at the time at which a business ceases to be carried on, for the purposes of the business
- meaning an individual disposing of assets of a business in (a) above within three years of the cessation of that business.

(c)   The disposal of one or more assets consisting of (or interests in) shares in or securities of a company
- meaning that throughout the year ending with the date of disposal:

- the company is the individual's personal company - in other words, the seller owns at least 5% of the ordinary shares giving him at least 5% of the voting rights, and

- the company is a trading company or the holding company of a trading group - defined in the same terms as for taper relief, and

- the individual is an officer or employee of the company or one or more of the companies that are members of the group.

This is called 'Condition A' in the legislation.

Example:
Ricky has owned his business since April 2000. He sold the business as a going concern in May 2008 and made a gain of £500,000. As he has owned the business for over a year and sold the whole business the disposal would qualify for entrepreneurs' relief.

Where part of a business is being sold the old retirement relief case of *McGreggor v Adcock* should be referred to for the courts likely views. That case concerned the disposal of a 5 acre field out of 20 or so acres and was ineligible for retirement relief.

8.3 Post cessation relief
The legislation provides a very generous relief for post cessation disposals compared to the predecessor taper relief.

The disposal will also be material ('Condition B') where the company has, within the **three years immediately** preceding the disposal, ceased to be either a trading company or a member of a trading group but satisfied 'Condition A' throughout the year preceding cessation.

Example:
Walter has owned all of the shares in Yarn Limited since 1995. The company ceased trading as a result of Walter's ill health in June 2008. In December 2008 company was liquidated resulting in a capital gain of £1.2 million. As the disposal is within 3 years of the cessation of the trade which was carried on for at least one year immediately prior to cessation the first £1 million gain would qualify for entrepreneurs' relief.

8.4 Disposals of trust business assets
Disposal of 'trust business assets' by the trustees of a settlement may also be in a position to claim entrepreneurs' relief. Business assets mean either shares or securities in a company or assets used or previously used for the purposes of a business which are part of the settled property.

8.5 Associated disposals
Entrepreneurs' relief may also be available for disposals associated with relevant material disposals.

Three conditions must be met:

- The material disposal is either the disposal of the whole or part of the individual's interest in the assets of a partnership or the disposal of shares in or securities of a company.

- The individual concerned is making the disposal as part of his 'withdrawal from participation' in the business carried on by the partnership or by the company.

- Throughout the year ending with the earlier of the disposal and the cessation of the business, the assets disposed of are in use for the purposes of the business.

The relief may therefore be available in the situation where an individual disposes of a property that is used by the business from which he is withdrawing his participation in.

Example:
Kate is the controlling shareholder and director of her own fashion retail company. She has been renting premises that she owns personally to her company at full market rent throughout the 5 year period of ownership. The disposal of the premises at the same time of the shares would not qualify as an associated disposal.

Contrast this with the rules for taper relief where business asset taper was unaffected by the charging of rent.

However, relief is restricted (new section 169P) to a 'just and reasonable' amount taking into account:

• the relative lengths of periods of business and non-business use,

• the part of the asset used for business purposes

• the length of period that the individual was involved in carrying on of the business, and

• if the asset is property on which the individual receives rent, the extent to which the rent paid is less than the full market rent for the assets.

Where in the above example kate stopped charging rent to her company for the last year of ownership, one fifth of the gain would now be eligible for entrepreneurs' relief.

8.6 EIS and VCT shares - transitional rules
Gains can be rolled into an investment in EIS or VCT shares and will crystallise when the shares are sold. A transitional rule allows entrepreneurs' relief to be claimed when a deferred gain that was rolled over before 6 April 2008 comes into charge on or after that date. The relief is only available had the conditions for relief been met at the time of the actual disposal that gave rise to the deferred gain.

Various changes in the Finance (No.2) Act 2010 relate to the increased capital gains tax rates for gains accruing on or after 23 June 2010, have an adverse impact in relation to the enterprise investment scheme (EIS). These impacts were not announced in the Budget press releases.

EIS
Under the proposed amendments, and subject to any changes introduced in the committee stage debates, an individual who realises a gain on or after 23 June 2010 which would qualify for entrepreneurs' relief will have to choose whether:

- to bank the 10% rate and claim entrepreneurs' relief in respect of the gain; or

- to claim deferral relief and pay tax at the prevailing rate when a chargeable event occurs in respect of the deferred gain, causing it to fall back into charge to capital gains tax.

Previously where a gain qualified for entrepreneurs' relief, the taxpayer could claim deferral relief and then claim the entrepreneurs' relief at the time the deferred gain fell back into charge to capital gains tax, giving an effective rate of capital gains tax of 10%.

This seems to be an unfortunate change, because it seems unlikely an individual will opt for the second approach, and therefore is likely to discourage reinvestment of the proceeds into companies qualifying under the EIS.

8.7 Shares acquired under EMI share option scheme
One of the main attractions of the Enterprise Management Incentives (EMI) share option scheme has been the accrual of business asset taper from the date the options are granted to the date that the shares subject to the option are sold. Thus, since 6 April 2002 full 75% business asset taper would have accrued 2 years after granting. Many employees exercising EMI options have tended to sell their shares shortly after, often the same day if the business is being sold, and would qualify for full 75% business taper as the relief accrued from granting. In many cases the employees would pay an effective rate of 10% on the sale of their shares.

8.8 Claims for entrepreneurs' relief
The relief must be claimed, and the claim must be made on or before the first anniversary of the 31 January following the tax year in which the disposal is made.

8.9 Amount of relief
Post 23 June 2010 the relief is given by applying a rate of 10% on gains.
The lifetime maximum is £10 million from 6 April 2011 (post 23 June 2010 £5 million).

'Relevant gains' means gains on the disposal of a qualifying business disposal of shares or securities of a company and gains on the disposal of any 'relevant business assets' comprised in any other qualifying business disposal. 'Relevant losses' has a similar meaning with regard to respective losses. 'Relevant business assets' is defined as, broadly speaking, the assets used for the purpose of the business other than shares, securities and assets held as investments.

8.10 Directors beware!
One of the many peculiarities of entrepreneurs' relief (ER) if the different treatment afforded to businessmen simply as a result of the choice of trading vehicle.

For example, contrast the position of a sole trader ceasing to trade with that of a company director. A sole trader who has been in business for at least 12 months is allowed to claim ER in a situation where he has disposed of his business (or the assets used by the business) after the date he ceased to trade - provided such disposals take place no more than 36 months after the cessation date. The same rule applies to a partnership situation. If the conditions of the relief are met for at least 12 months before a partnership bust-up resulting in an individual ceasing to be a partner, the outgoing partner has up to three years to do a deal with his former partner(s) to extricate himself and conclude the necessary financial settlement.

However, now look at a similar situation but this time where the trading vehicle used is a company. Let's assume that Jim, who has owned 30% of the company (and been a director thereof) for several years, falls out with his two fellow director/shareholders. He immediately resigns as a director and walks out of the office demanding his fellow shareholders pay him £500,000 for his shares. He never sets foot in the company's premises again and eventually he sells his shares to the company for £200,000 realising a capital gain. Jim's capital gain cannot be reduced by ER because, as at the date of disposal of the shares in question, he will be neither an officer or employee of the company (as required by s 1691(6), TCGA 1992). Those who resign in haste overlook this measure!

9 TAPERING OF CAPITAL GAINS - abolished post 6 April 2008

For full details please see previous editions of this work.

10 ANNUAL EXEMPTIONS

10.1 Individuals
The annual exemption for 2011/2012 is £10,600 (2010/2011 was £10,100).

This exemption also applies to` personal representatives for the year of death and the following two years.

10.2 Bed and breakfasting
Up to 16 March 1998 an individual, near the end of a tax year could, in order to utilise the annual exemption, sell some shares to crystallize the gain and then repurchase them the next day.

From 17 March 1998, disposals and acquisitions by individuals or trustees of shares of the same class in the same company within a 30-day period are to be matched for capital gains purposes, so that no gain or loss is realised. Very often having to wait 30 days will involve unacceptable commercial risk. The new rule applies to shares, securities and other fungible assets. Companies are unaffected since they already have special identification rules. For a possible way to avoid this. Please see Husband and Wife, p.461.

10.3 Trusts for mentally disabled persons
A trust set up to secure benefits for the lifetime of a mentally disabled person or a person in receipt of attendance allowance or disability allowance is entitled to the same annual exemption as for individuals (TCGA 1992 s 3 and Sch 1) if:

- not less than half of the property which is applied, is applied for the benefit of that person, and

- that person is entitled to not less than half of the income arising from the property, or no such income may be applied for the benefit of any other person.

If a settlor makes more than one qualifying trust the annual exemption available to each group member is the greater of 1/10 of the exempt amount or the result obtained from dividing the exempt amount by the number of settlements in the group.

10.4 Other trusts
Trusts other than those described above are entitled to one half of the exempt amount available to individuals (TCGA Sch 1 (2)(2). Where the trust is one of a group, relief is available to each group member in an amount which is the greater of one tenth of the exempt amount or the result obtained from dividing the exempt amount by the number of settlements in the group.

The settlements excluded from obtaining annual exemption relief are:
- any settlement the trustees of which are not for the whole or any part of the year of assessment as resident or ordinarily resident in the UK;

- any settlement in which the property is held for charitable purposes only and cannot be applied for any other purpose;

- any settlement in which the property is held for the purpose of retirement schemes and funds set out in TCGA 1992 Sch 1 (7) and (8).

Effect on losses
Losses carried forward (or backward from the year of death) need not be deducted from net gains. So, if gains less losses of a year of assessment are less than the annual exempt amount, losses from a prior year can be carried through to the next

year. Where net gains in any year exceed the annual exempt amount, only the excess need be set against losses forward (or backward from the year of death).

Trading loss allocated against capital gain
Section 72 FA 1991 provides that any trading loss that is potentially allowable against total income under the terms of ITA 2007, s 64 (formerly ICTA 1988, s 380) can be offset against a capital gain where the loss exceeds the taxpayer's total income for the year. It is necessary, however, for the trading loss first to exhaust the income; thus, personal allowances are wasted and this is a tax planning point for consideration.

The maximum amount of trading loss that may be relieved against capital gains is restricted to the total net capital gains for the year. This is a notional amount comprised of the current year gains after deduction of current year losses, less capital losses brought forward from earlier years. This may result in the annual exempt amount for capital gains tax being wasted.

10.5 Husband and wife (includes civil partners)
Each spouse is entitled to his or her own annual exemption and this is not transferable. The chargeable gains are taxed separately and allowable losses can only be set off against gains made by that spouse either in the year in which the losses arose or carried forward to the next year and subsequent years.

To avoid the anti bed and breakfasting rules (Please see Bed and Breakfasting, p.459). One spouse can sell shares which are immediately repurchased by the other.

11 EXPENSES ALLOWED

11.1 General
These comprise (TCGA 1992 s 38):
*   the costs or value glven wholly and exclusively for the acquisition of the asset;
*   expenditure incurred wholly and exclusively in enhancing the value of the asset;
*   incidental costs of acquisition and disposal e.g professional fees, commission, duties and VAT, transfer costs and cost of advertising to find a buyer or seller);
*   expenditure in establishing, preserving or defending the title to the asset;
*   reasonable costs of making any necessary valuation or apportionment;
*   in practice, the cost of initial repairs undertaken to put a property into a fit state for letting (provided they have not been allowed in computing rental income).

11.2 Sale by personal representative

A scale of fees has been agreed to cover the cost of obtaining probate, allowable on a sale by personal representatives, as follows:

Gross value of estate	Allowable expenditure
A. £40,000 or less	1.75% of probate value of assets sold
B. £40,001 to £70,000	£700 apportioned to individual assets sold on the basis of probate value
C. £70,001 to £300,000	1% of probate value of assets sold
D. £300,001 to £400,000	£3,000 apportioned as in B
E. £400,001 to £750,000	0.75% of probate value assets sold
F. £750,001 or above	On the facts of the case by negotiation

On a sale of quoted securities by personal representatives, a flat rate deduction (not exceeding £5) for each transaction will be allowed as representing legal fees allowable as incidental costs of disposal (1975, BTR 913-4).

11.3 Discharge of liability

Where the discharge of a liability (e.g. under a guarantee) results in the acquisition of an asset (e.g. a right of subrogation), the settlement of the liability has been held not to be consideration given wholly and exclusively for the acquisition of a valueless asset on which a loss could be claimed (*Cleveleys Investment Trust Co v CIR* (No 2) CS 1975). Consideration, paid under a tax avoidance scheme each stage of which was from the outset bound (as a matter of contract) to take place, could not be regarded as wholly and exclusively paid for an asset bought and sold in the course of the scheme (*Eilbeck v Rawling* HL 1981). An insurance premium paid under a 'trust-breaking scheme' has been held to be consideration for the purchase of certain beneficiaries' contingent interests and not consideration for the acquisition of investments received in consequence. On a sale of the investments the premium was not deductible (*Allison v Murray* Ch D 1975).

12 EXPENSES NOT ALLOWED

Expenditure allowed (except as capital allowances) in computing profits of income tax or corporation tax and expenditure which would be so allowed if the assets concerned formed part of a taxable activity (TCGA 1992 s 39) is not deductible for capital gains tax. Rent paid to preserve a lease from forfeiture, in order that the lease could be realized by a company in liquidation and not trading at the time, is not deductible (*Emmerson v Computer Time International Ltd.* CA 1977); nor is such rent enhancement expenditure or expenditure on preservation of title.

Insurance premiums are not allowable (TCGA 1992 s 205); nor is expenditure met directly or indirectly by the Crown or any government or public or local authority, in the UK or elsewhere (TCGA 1992 s 50).

13 APPORTIONMENTS OF CONSIDERATION OR EXPENDITURE

These are made by the Inspector of Taxes with the right of appeal to the Commissioners. On a sale of shares on condition that the vendor waived certain loans, part of the consideration was directed to be apportioned to the waiver of the loans thereby reducing the consideration for the shares (*Aberdeen Construction Group Ltd. v CIR* HL 1978).

14 COMPANY REORGANIZATION

Where reorganization takes place time apportionment applies only up to the date of reorganization at which date a valuation is made. The whole gain (or loss) after the date of valuation is brought in, on disposal of the new holding. This does not apply to reorganizations concerning shares of the same class only.

The FA 2002 sought to bring the rules on reconstructions and share exchanges into line with the treatment previously operated under SP5/85. This follows the case of *Fallon & Kersley v Fellow* 2001 which highlighted a defect in the rules which was exploited by the taxpayers in that case. The position will now revert to the previous understanding.

15 PART DISPOSALS

Cost and expenses are apportioned according to the sale price of the part sold and market value of the part retained, but expenditure attributable to one part only need not be apportioned (TCGA s 42). Compensation and insurance money, relatively small capital distributions and small part sales of land under compulsory purchase orders can be treated as reducing the cost of the original asset (TCGA s 243). Compensation for compulsory acquisition is apportioned between constituent elements (land, loss of profits, etc.) in accordance with the facts. A payment for severance is deemed to be a part disposal (TCG s 245). The effect is that compensation for temporary loss of profits may be segregated and taxed as income (*Stoke-on-Trent City Council v Wood Mitchell & Co. Ltd.* CA 1978).

The apportionments are to be made in priority to provisions whereby no gain or loss is deemed to arise (e.g. company group transactions) (TCGA 1992 s 42).

16 PAYMENT DUE AFTER SALE

If the consideration for disposal of an asset is payable by instalments over at least 18 months beginning after the disposal date, the Board has discretion, if undue hardship would otherwise result, to allow payment by instalments over a period not exceeding eight years and ending not later than the date of the last instalment (TCGA 1992 s 280). Otherwise the full amount of the consideration is taken into account, whether paid or not in full at the due date, but if it is subsequently shown to be irrecoverable the tax will be adjusted (TCGA 1992 s 48). A sale, followed by the loan by the vendor of part of the proceeds to the purchaser on a mortgage repayable by instalments does not qualify (*Coren v Keighley* Ch D 1972). A right to a future instalment of sale consideration (which was unquantifiable at the time of the sale) is a chargeable asset which also gives rise to disposal on ascertainment and payment (*Marren v Ingles* HL 1980).

17 CONTINGENT LIABILITY

An appropriate allowance is made if a contingent liability of the following kinds becomes enforceable and is in fact being enforced (TCGA 1992 s 49):

- default re liabilities assumed by the assignee of a lease;
- quiet enjoyment or other obligation assumed as vendor or lessor of land;
- warranty or representation in respect of assets other than land.

It has been held that any contingent liability can be valued and taken into account as a deduction from the proceeds of disposal (*Randall v Plumb* Ch D 1974).

18 WASTING ASSETS: LEASES

18.1 Wasting assets

These are defined as assets with a predictable useful life, having regard to the purpose for which they were acquired, not exceeding 50 years. Freehold land and immature animals are excluded. The term includes a life interest in settled property if the predictable period of the life interest is 50 years or less. All plant and machinery, whatever the predictable life, is included (TCGA 1979 ss 44-47).

The asset, except one qualifying for capital allowances, is regarded as depreciating on a simple time basis down to scrap value over its predictable life. If the sale price exceeds the depreciated value at the date of sale, a charge will arise. Apportionments are made where there is part use, or use for part of a period.

Racehorses are dealt with according to special rules agreed with the racing authorities. Very broadly they are regarded as wasting assets over their mature life which is roughly (and with exceptions) from approximately five years to 16 years. All expenditure up to maturity, less a sum for maintenance, is allowable and in certain circumstances some expenditure after maturity is also allowed.

18.2 Leases of land (TCGA 1992 s 240 and Sch. 8)

18.2.1 General

A lease of land is not regarded as a wasting asset until the point of time arrives when its duration is 50 years or less. Accordingly, if the lease is say, 99 years, the first 49 years is ignored and no depreciation is deducted for that period.

Asset bought for £2,000. Predictable life 10 years. Predictable scrap value £400. Sold for £800 8 years later. The net cost is £2,000 - £800 = £1,200.

The actual period of ownership is less than the predicted 10 years. Accordingly, the depreciation to be deducted is 8/10 years x (£2,000 - £400 i.e. £1,600) = £1,280.

The liability is then:	£
Cost	2,000
Less depreciation	1,280
	720
Sale price	800
Chargeable profit	£80

The depreciation is not regarded as occurring evenly on a time basis as is the case with other wasting assets, but according to percentages laid down. These show a decreasing rate of depreciation as the period lengthens.

Apart from this different method of calculating the depreciation, the computation is the same as for other wasting assets.

If a lease is acquired subject to a sub-lease not at a rack-rent and the cost of the lease is less than its value at the time the sublease expires, it is not regarded as a wasting asset until the expiry of the sub-lease.

18.2.2 Premiums for leases
These include payments in lieu of rent or for the right to surrender the lease or variation or waiver of any of its terms (TCGA 1992 Sch 8). The premium is regarded as a partial disposal and an apportionment is made, the right to receive any future rent being valued and treated as an undisposed part of the property. Any amount charged to income tax is deducted from the consideration (See (c) following, Premiums for sub-lease out of short lease) in order to avoid double taxation.

Where the consideration for the variation or waiver is not the real value, the difference between this and an arm's length transaction is treated as a premium. The part of a premium which, for income tax purposes, is allowed as additional rent is not deductible as a cost, but not so as to create or increase again.

18.2.3 Premiums for sub-lease out of short lease
There are special provisions for computing the charge. They provide for deducting from the premium the amount of depreciation of the head lease occurring during the period of the sub-lease. If the premium is less than it would have been had the sub-lease rent been the same as the head lease rent, then only a corresponding proportion is allowed. The amount charged to income tax is deducted from the gain (not from the consideration), but not so as to create or augment a loss.

18.2.4 Terminable leases
The length of the lease is reckoned by taking the earliest date on which it can be determined by the landlord. If it is unlikely that it will continue beyond a date prior to that, this earlier date is adopted. Unlikelihood of continuation includes provisions for increase in rent or tenant's obligations after a certain date on which the tenant has power to determine.

If the duration of a lease has to be ascertained after the lease had terminated, then the actual date of termination is adopted. If the duration has to be ascertained whilst it is still running, the above rule must be applied according to the circumstances known or ascertainable at the time it is acquired or created.

Where the tenant has a right to extend the lease, the term lasts until the latest date to which the extension could be applied by the tenant (subject to the landlord's right to determine).

18.3 Lease of property other than land

Subject to any necessary modifications these are treated in the same way as land, except that the 50-year rule does not apply. The lease of a wasting asset which is moveable property is assumed to terminate not later than the end of its life (TCGA 1992 Sch 8 (9)).

Any charge to income tax is deductible, but not so as to convert a gain into a loss, or to increase any loss.

19 DEBTS AND LOANS

19.1 Debts

No liability arises on the sale of collection of a debt by the original creditor or his successor (TCGA 1992 s 251) unless it is a bank credit in foreign currency not for personal expenditure (TCGA 1992 s 252). An assignee of a debt is chargeable on any gain (and any loss is allowable) on the collection or further assignment of a debt. Any debt on a security is chargeable on the original creditor, his successor or assignee. **Debt on a security** is one (whether secured or unsecured) 'evidenced in a document as a security and may include an unsecured debenture'. It refers to those securities which are or can be subject to conversion (*Cleveley's Investment Trust Ltd v CIR* (No1) CS 1971). A loan may be converted into a debt on a security by the issue of debentures (*Aberdeen Construction Group Ltd v CIR* HL 1978). A statutory declaration evidencing acceptance of a loan has been held to be a security, but a loan to a company not evidenced by such a document cannot be a debt on a security (*W. T. Ramsay v CIR* HL 1981). A loss arising from a debt purchased from a connected person is not allowable.

19.2 Loans and guarantees for trading purposes

The relevant legislation is TCGA 1992 ss 254 and 255.

19.2.1 Qualifying loans

are those made for use wholly for the purposes of a trade, profession or vocation (except money lending) carried on (or about to be set up) by a UK resident. A loan to one member of a group qualifies if used for trading purposes of another member of the group. The loan must not be a debt on a security (which is, of course, a chargeable asset eligible for relief in any case). Outstanding purchase consideration (e.g. for the business) may not qualify, since, strictly, it is not a loan.

A qualifying loan includes a loan which is borrowed by a company and denominated in sterling and is to be treated under FA 1984 s 64(2) as a qualifying corporate bond. A claim for a capital loss as at the time of the claim may be made on satisfying the Inspector that:

- some or all of the principal has become irrecoverable from the borrower; and
- the right of recovery has not been assigned by the claimant; and
- the loan was not between spouses living together or members of a group at the time it was made or subsequently.

An allowable loss may be claimed for loans made, or guarantees given, if the loan subsequently becomes irrecoverable, or the guarantee enforceable.

19.2.2 Guarantee of a qualifying loan
creates a loss at the time any payment is made under the guarantee, equal to the amount of the payment less any recovery from a co-guarantor, provided the Inspector is satisfied that:

- some or all of the principle or interest has become irrecoverable from the borrower; and

- the claimant has paid the lender or co-guarantor in respect thereof; and

- no right of recovery accruing in consequence of the payment has been assigned by the claimant; and

- (a) when the loan was made or subsequently, the lender and the borrower were not married to and living with each other nor the companies in the same group; and (b) when the guarantee was given or subsequently, the claimant and the borrower were not spouses nor were the claimant and the lender members of the same group.

A guarantee of a loan which is a debt on a security is eligible for this relief.

Recovery after a claim is treated as giving rise to a chargeable gain equal to the proportion of the allowable loss which the amount recovered bears to the original loss or payment. Satisfaction (in money's worth) of a right of recovery of the assignment (other than at arm's length) of such right is deemed to constitute a recovery of that amount or of the market value of the right, as the case may be.

Irrecoverable amounts exclude amounts becoming irrecoverable in consequence of:

- the terms of the loan; or
- any arrangements of which the loan forms part; or
- any act or omission by the lender or guarantor (as the case may be).

19.2.3 Avoidance of double relief or taxation

Amounts taken into account for the purposes of tax on income are not eligible here also. A guarantor is not eligible for relief, or taxable on capital gains, in respect of rights acquired in consequence of payments made except as provided above.

If property is acquired from the debtor in satisfaction of the debt, it must not be treated as disposed of for more than its market value at the time of the acquisition. If a gain is ultimately made on the disposal of the property, the charge on the creditor is restricted to the amount which would have been chargeable had the market value on acquisition been equal to the amount of the debt.

19.2.4 Hire purchase

The asset is regarded as being disposed of at the commencement of the agreement, but adjustment is made if the hirer's possession of the asset ceases before the property legally passes to him (i.e. at the end of the agreement) (TCGA 1992 s 27).

20 OPTIONS (TCGA 1992 s 27)

The grant of an option is regarded as the disposal of an asset and the consideration for the option is part of the sale price of the transaction resulting from the exercise of the option (or deduction from cost in the case of an option binding the grantor to buy). If an option to buy or sell quoted securities is transferred, it is regarded as a wasting asset ending when the right to exercise the option ends or the option becomes valueless, whichever is the earlier. An option both to sell and to buy is treated as two separate options, the consideration being divided equally. The grant of an option over land is a part disposal of the land, which takes effect when the option is exercised (*Randall v Plumb* Ch D 1974).

Only options which can be regarded as property are within the scope of the tax (e.g. an option to acquire property but not an option to acquire a right to benefit which is not property) (*O'Brien v Benson's Hosiery (Holdings) Ltd* HL 1979).

A forfeited deposit of purchase money is treated as consideration for an option.

Where an option to subscribe for shares or to acquire assets for use in a trade is disposed of or abandoned:

•   the abandonment is regarded as the disposal of an asset (the option), and
•   the option is not treated as a wasting asset.

The option must be quoted on a recognized stock exchange or on the London International Financial Futures Exchange and dealt with in the same way as shares.

If it is dealt in within three months of reorganization, etc. (the time limit may be extended) it is regarded as being the same as the shares acquired by exercising it. See TCGA 1992 s 144, and FA 1994 s 96.

21 COMPENSATION AND INSURANCE PROCEEDS

The following kinds of capital sums are chargeable (TCGA 1992 s 23):

(a)   compensation for damage, loss or depreciation of assets, including insurance monies;
(b)   for surrender of rights or refraining from exercising rights;
(c)   for use or exploitation of assets.

But if the asset is not lost or destroyed and the monies are wholly applied in restoring it (except for any relatively small part which is not reasonably required for restoration), or if the capital sum received is small compared with the value of the asset, the receipt may be deducted from the cost of the new expenditure instead of being charged as a capital gain. This also applies to a part of a capital sum falling under para. (a), but not if it falls under para.'s (b) or (c).

If the asset is lost or destroyed and compensation under para. (a) is used within one year (the Inspector may allow a longer period) in replacing it, the taxpayer may claim that no gain shall accrue and that the otherwise chargeable gain shall be deducted from the cost of the new asset. A part of the receipt, up to the amount of the total gain, need not be spent. The chargeable gain is then reduced in proportion to the unspent part, and the balance is deducted from the cost of the new asset.

Cost of asset £1,000. Insured £1,200. Completely destroyed. £1,050 spent in replacing it. The charge would normally be £200 (£1,200 - £1,000). £150 of the receipt has not been spent. The chargeable gain is accordingly reduced to £150.

The cost of the new asset is then £1,000 (£1,050 - £50).

22 TWO OR MORE TRANSACTIONS: WHOLE WORTH MORE THAN ALL THE PARTS

Where a person acquires by way of two or more transactions made before 20 March 1985 from one or more persons with whom he is connected, assets where the separate values do not amount to the value of the total of them taken together, then the total value is apportioned rateably between the separate transactions.

Where the transactions are made after 19 March 1985, the charge to capital gains tax will arise when the person splits an asset or collection of assets by two or more transactions to connected persons and those transactions occur within six years of each other. A transaction made before 20 March 1985 would not normally form part of a series of transactions for this purpose unless a further transaction is made after 19 March 1985 and within two years of the transaction made before 20 March 1985 and it may then be included with the later transaction as part of the series to which the new provisions apply but only if the former provisions would have applied to the complete series if all the transactions had occurred before 20 March 1985 and the new provisions would have applied to the complete series if all the transactions had occurred after 19 March 1985.

23 TRANSACTIONS NOT AT ARM'S LENGTH

23.1 Gifts

The asset passing is treated as having been acquired or disposed of at market value (*Turner v Follet* CA 1973). A transaction is not to be treated as not at arm's length merely because the market value of the asset exceeds the negotiated price by the time the contract is made (*Clark v Follet* Ch D 1973). A transaction carried out by two members of a group of companies with the aim of securing the best financial consequences for the group as a whole has been said not to be at arm's length (*Harrison v Nairn Williamson Ltd* CA 1977):

- Person controlling company exercising that control so that the value passes out of shares or rights owned by that person or a connected person into other shares in or rights over the company; but not so as to create a loss, (TCGA 1992 s 29). 'Person' should be read as including the plural, so that the provision applies even where no single individual has control. Moreover, there need not be any positive act to constitute an 'exercise'. To fail to take up a rights issue may be such (*Floor v Davis* HL 1979).

- Acquisition of a lease and subsequent adjustments of rights and liabilities under the lease in favour of the lessee.

- Cancellation of any right or restriction to which an asset is subject.

If the tax is not paid within 12 months of the date it becomes payable the donee may be assessed (within two years of the payable date). (TCGA 1992 s 282).

23.2 Transactions between connected persons

Where the disposer and acquirer of an asset are connected persons, the transaction is treated as being not at arm's length, and accordingly market value is adopted. A loss is not allowed (except on a gift in settlement for educational, cultural or recreational purposes), but may be set against a gain on any transaction made when the same persons were connected. A loss on an option is not allowed except on disposal of the option to a person not connected with the disposer. Rights or restrictions enforceable by the disposer are valued at their market value and deducted from the full market value of the asset, except in certain specified circumstances where they are to be ignored (CGTA 1979 s 62).

A person is connected with an individual if that person is the individual's husband or wife, or is a relative, or the husband or wife of a relative, of the individual or of the individual's husband or wife.

A trustee is connected with the settlement if the settlor is a connected person, and is also connected with any person connected with such a settlor, and with any body corporate connected with the settlement. A 'settlement', in this context, connotes an element of bounty, so where full consideration was received by the settlor, the trustees are not connected with him.

A partner (and a spouse or relative) is connected with any other partner except as regards partnership assets bought or sold under bona fide commercial arrangements.

A company is connected with another company if there is common control. Common control is carefully defined and brings in the above connected persons.

A company is connected with a person who controls it, either alone or with connected persons.

Two persons acting together to secure or exercise control of a company are connected persons in relation to that company and with any person acting on their directions to secure or exercise control.

23.3 Disposals to charities, etc.

A gift (or disposal at not more than allowable costs) to a charity or certain specified bodies is treated as giving rise to neither gain nor loss, so that no tax is charged and the transferee acquires at the transferor's base cost. This also applies on chargeable events relating to settled property in which a charity is interested, provided no consideration is given (TCGA 1992 s 257).

23.4 Disposal on trust for the benefit of employees

Where a close company or an individual disposes of an asset to trustees in circumstances such that the relief from inheritance tax applies, the disposal is treated on a no gain, no loss basis, provided it is by way of a gift or for a consideration not exceeding the allowable costs (TCGA 1992 s 239). The trustees are then deemed to have acquired it when the company or individual did so. The relief applies also to a disposal to trustees by a company other than a close company and otherwise than under a bargain made at arm's length. In such a case the person for whose benefit (other than as income) the trusts permit the property to be applied must include all or most of the persons employed by or holding office with the company or group and must include all or most of the persons employed by or holding office with the company or group and must exclude:

(a) any person who is a participator of the company and who would be entitled to at least 5% or more of any class in issue;

(b) any person who is such a participator in any other company that has made an exempted disposal on the same trusts;

(c) any person who has been such a participator in a company within para. (a) or at any time after or during the ten years before, the company's disposal;

(d) any person who is connected with a person in para.'s (a), (b) or (c).

Persons within para.'s (a) to (d) may benefit if the trust is an approved profit sharing scheme.

23.5 Stock taken or supplied by proprietor
If the proprietor supplies stock he is deemed to have sold it to his business at market price and the profit is chargeable, but he may instead elect to charge the business at cost price (TCGA 1992 s 161).

If he takes goods from the business, the value credited to the business accounts is his acquisition cost.

23.6 Assets derived from other assets
Where assets have been merged or divided or have changed their nature, or rights or interest in them have been created or extinguished, an appropriate proportion of the cost of the old assets is taken into account in computing a gain on both the old and the new asset. The time apportionment rule is modified in such a case and the period of ownership of a derivative or merged asset includes that of the components (TCGA 1992 s 43).

23.7 Value shifting
In order to counter avoidance, power is given to the Inspector (subject to appeal to the Commissioners) to increase the consideration on certain disposals (TCGA 1992 ss 29 and 30). It applies to any disposal (other than to legatees, between spouses or within a group of companies) preceded or followed by a scheme or arrangement

which materially reduces the value of the asset disposed of and confers a tax-free benefit on any of the following persons:

- the person making the disposal;
- any person with whom the person making the disposal is connected;
- where it cannot be shown that avoidance of tax was not the main purpose or one of the main purposes of the scheme or arrangement, any other person.

A reduction in value is not caught if it is attributable to an intragroup dividend or transfer of asset.

In the case of a bear transaction (sale before acquisition), a disposal is also caught if the scheme or arrangement materially increases the value of the asset disposed of but subsequently acquired.

Tax-free benefit means money or money's worth, an increase in value of any asset in which the person in question has an interest, or a reduction in any liability to which the person is subject and which is not chargeable to income tax, corporation tax, or capital gains tax. The consideration is increased by such amount as is just and reasonable, having regard to the scheme or arrangement and tax-free benefit in question. Where the tax-free benefit is an increase in value of another asset, an allowance is made on the first subsequent disposal of that other asset. The consideration for its disposal is reduced by such amount as appears to the Inspector (or, on appeal, to the Commissioners) to be just and reasonable, having regard to the scheme or arrangement and to the increase made on disposal of the first asset.

24 COMPANY TRANSACTIONS

24.1 Close company transferring assets at under value
If a close company transfers an asset otherwise than by a bargain made at arm's length, and at less than market value, the under value is apportioned between the shares and deducted from the allowable expenditure in computing the liability on the disposal of them. This does not apply to certain kinds of transfer within a group of companies (CTGA 1979 s 125).

24.2 Close company having assets transferred to it
(TCGA 1992 Sch 2(21)). As regards assets held at 6 April 1965, if any of the persons who control (or are connected with the controller of) a company, transfer assets to it, any person controlling the company (or having a substantial holding of its shares or securities) may be chargeable on the 'time' basis. In this case the profit, so far as attributable to the assets transferred, is assumed to have grown uniformly from the date the assets were transferred to the company. This does not apply if a loss is incurred.

This only applies to assets where the computation is on a 'time' basis, i.e. not quoted securities and land, which must be computed on the 'valuation' basis.

24.3 Capital distributions by companies

A chargeable distribution is the disposal of an interest and the gain is chargeable. If the Inspector is satisfied that the distribution is relatively small it can, instead of being charged, be deducted from the cost when the gain on the ultimate disposal of the shares is computed (TCGA 1992 s 122). A capital distribution is one in money or money's worth which is not income for income tax purposes in the hands of the recipient and is taken at the market value of the receipt. There is a part disposal on the receipt or entitlement to receipt, of each such sum, but, in practice, on a winding-up assessments can be delayed until completion and time apportionment applies to each distribution as if it were made when the first distribution was made (SP D3).

24.4 Company reorganizations, take-overs, amalgamations and reconstructions (TCGA 1992 ss 136-242)

Reorganization includes a reduction of share capital (other than repayment of redeemable shares) and also includes:

- bonus and rights issues, i.e. allotment of shares or debentures in respect of, and in proportion to, holdings of shares in a company (or any class thereof);

- alteration of rights attaching to shares. Where more than one class is in existence.

- from 1 April 2000 the rules that all the companies must be UK resident are relaxed for as long as the assets transferred remain within the scope of corporation tax.

No disposal rule

Such a reorganization does not involve any disposal, and the new holding is treated as acquired as and when the original holding was acquired (i.e. for the same cost and at the same time) (TCGA 1992 s 127). Any consideration (not derived from the company's resources or capital) given for the new holding is treated as part of the cost of the original holding (CTGA 1992 s 128). However, the taxable amount (before grossing-up) of any stock dividend may be treated as such consideration, even though derived from the company's resources or capital (TCGA 1992 s 141). On the other hand, where the recipient is a trustee for a person or persons absolutely entitled (or so entitled but for a disability), receipt of a stock dividend is not regarded as a reorganization at all but the taxable amount (before grossing-up) is treated as consideration for the acquisition by the beneficiary of the new share capital (TCGA 1992 s 142). Accordingly, it seems that vesting one's shares in a nominee before a stock dividend will alter the incidence of, for example, the time apportionment rules from what but for the vesting it would be.

Part disposal rule
Receipt (actual, or deemed, e.g. on a bargain not at arm's length) of, or entitlement to, any consideration other than the new holding (e.g. a capital distribution or consideration from other shareholders) constitutes a part disposal of the original holding. The undisposed part then represents the new holding (TCGA 1992 s 128).

On disposal of a provisional allotment of shares or debentures, there is deemed to be a receipt of a capital distribution from the original shares. If the valuation rule for securities held on 6 April 1965, applies, it applies also to 'rights' held at the same time.

Apportionment on part disposal of new holding shares, debentures and units quoted within three months of reorganizations
The cost of the new holding is first to be apportioned among the separate classes of shares, etc. by reference to their market values on the first day (before or after reorganization) on which they were quoted. That market value is adjusted for any liability to provide new consideration which is reflected in the cost of the new holding (TCGA 1992 s 129). Thereafter, the ordinary part disposal rule applies.

Other new holdings
Any apportionment of costs between a part disposal and the remainder is made by reference to their respective market values (adjusted for liability attaching) on the date of disposal.

Conversions of securities
These are, *mutatis mutandis*, treated as on a reorganisation (TCGA 1992 ss 132-134). Securities includes any loan stock or similar security (whether secured or unsecured).

Conversion of securities includes:
- conversion of company securities into shares;
- conversion at the holder's option as an alternative to redemption;
- any exchange effected by a statutory compulsory acquisition of shares or securities.

Special provision is made for the conversion of the former exempt-range securities (TCGA 1992 s 134).

Take-overs
The rules for reorganization apply, as if only one company is involved, where shares or debentures are issued by one company in exchange for (*CIR v Littlewood's Mail Order Stores* HL 1963) shares or debentures of another company, provided that either
- the issuing company holds, or will in consequence of the share exchange hold,

more than 25% of the ordinary share capital of the other; or

• the issue is the result of a general offer to the members of the other company (or any class of them) conditional in the first instance on the bidder obtaining control (TCGA 1992 s 135).

Schemes of reconstruction or amalgamation

These are put on the same footing as take-overs, but the conditions specified there do not apply in such cases (CGTA 1979 s 86). A partition of a company, into two or more separate businesses and their transfer to separate companies with only some of the members of the old company becoming members of each of the new companies, would in practice, be regarded as a reconstruction, provided the partition was for bona fide commercial reasons. Further, it should be noted that the original shares and debentures must be either retained by the original holder (even if with altered rights as a result of reduction, consolidation, division or otherwise) or cancelled. Provided the transferor receives no consideration, and both companies are UK-resident, no liability will arise on the transfer of assets as part of the scheme (TCGA 1992 ss 137 and 138).

Schemes designed for tax avoidance

No liability arises on the issue of shares (or transfer of assets) made under a reconstruction or amalgamation scheme if:

• the scheme was effected for bona fide commercial reasons; and

• it was not effected with the main purpose (or one of the main purposes) of avoiding capital gains tax or corporation tax.

These conditions do not apply to;
• any person to whom shares or debentures are issued but who together with persons connected with him does not hold more than 5% of the shares in or debentures of the other company (or any class thereof; or

• any scheme for which advance clearance has been obtained from the Board.

A procedure is specified whereby application for advance clearance may be made and must be given or refused by the Board within 30 days (subject to allowance for the Board to obtain further and better particulars). If the Board fails or refuses to give clearance within 30 days, application may be made within a further 30 days to the Special Commissioners who may give or refuse a clearance (TCGA 1992 s 138).

A clearance is invalidated if full and accurate disclosure of material facts and considerations is not made. Tax due may be recovered from a member of a group to whom the securities have been transferred, if not paid within six months. Recovery is by assessment within two years of the due date and a right of indemnity is given. On a reconstruction or amalgamation tax due on assets transferred may be recovered from the transferee company or any member of the transferee's group to which the assets have been transferred.

Indexation allowance will not be granted where a company carries out the following transactions after 14 March 1988:

- disposes of, or receives payment in respect of, a debt on a security owed by a linked company;

- disposes of redeemable preference shares in a linked company;

- disposes of other shares in a linked company where the finance for the original purchase was provided from within the group for the sole or main purpose of obtaining an indexation allowance.

Companies are regarded as linked if they are in the same group or one controls the other or both are under common control (FA 1988 s 114 and Sch 11).

Compulsory acquisition in exchange for gilt-edged securities
The previous rules do not apply to takeovers under Acts of Parliament (e.g. by the National Enterprise Board) where the compensation consists of specified gilt-edged securities. The exchange is treated as not involving a disposal of the shares or securities compulsorily acquired, but the gain or loss on them up to the time of issue of the gilts, or of the grant of a right to receive them if earlier, is to be calculated by reference to the value of those assets as determined for the exchange. This gain or loss is charged or allowed only on a subsequent disposal of the gilts (or of the rights to them) by the person to whom they were issued, or by a person who acquired them as legatee, spouse, or member of a group without an intervening chargeable disposal or devolution on death. On a part disposal, a corresponding part of the gain or loss is charged or allowed. A disposal which is not chargeable because it is to a legatee, spouse or member of a group does not cause the held over gain or loss to be charged or allowed.

The gilts (or rights) received in exchange are treated as acquired on the date of issue (or grant), at the value of the assets taken over, and the gain or loss on their disposal is computed by reference to that value. Only this gain or loss qualifies for the exemption on disposals of gilts.

Identification rules provide that disposals of the gilts are deemed to be those acquired on the exchange, only after identification with any acquired otherwise but within the twelve months preceding disposal. First in first out applies to disposals identified with gilts acquired on exchange at different dates (TCGA 1992 s 134).

The FA2002 sought to bring the rules on reconstructions and share exchanges into line with the treatment previously operated under SP5/85. This follows the case of *Fallon & Kersley v Fellows* last year which highlighted a defect in the rules which was exploited by the taxpayers in that case. The position will now revert to the previous understanding.

24.5 Beneficial employee share arrangements

The gain on exercising a right to acquire the shares may be chargeable to income tax as may be the benefit of a stop-loss arrangement. Where this happens the amount so charged is added to the cost of the shares in computing any capital gains (TA 1988 Sch 29).

Employee share acquisitions

Another minor simplification in FA2002 allows employees acquiring shares under different employee share schemes on the same day to elect that the shares with the smaller gain are disposed of in priority to those with a higher gain. In the past the disposal would have been apportioned on a pro rata basis.

24.6 Transfer of business to a company (Incorporation Relief)

For transfers after 6 April 2002 there is the opportunity to elect for this treatment (holdover of gain) not to apply. This will allow sole proprietors or partners to take the benefit of taper relief rather than having the gain held over.

The election has to be made within two years of 31 January following the year of assessment.

This is a minor simplification but where an election is made it will be an all or nothing situation so capital gains tax will become payable on the part of the gain not covered by taper relief and the annual exemption. It will however in certain circumstances allow the proprietor to make use of the taper relief available rather than holding over the gain. This for example will assist if the shares in the company are to be disposed of in less than two years after the incorporation.

There are no changes to S165 TCGA 1992 gift relief which is commonly used as an alternative to the more restrictive relief available under S162.

Prior to 6 April 2002 this exemption only applied to transfers by individuals, and the transfer of the whole of a partnership business (TCGA 1992 s 162). A taxable gain arose only on the part of the consideration not taken in shares. The method was to compute the total gain on transfer of assets to the company. From this is to be deducted the proportion of the gain which the value received in shares bears to the total consideration. The balance was charged to tax and the deduction reduced the cost of the shares received in exchange on any subsequent disposal of them. There were provisions for apportionment where there are different classes of shares. The formula was modified where development value is realised on the transfer of the business.

Where liabilities are taken over it is the Board's practice not to treat them as consideration. Relief is not precluded by the fact that some or all of the liabilities are not taken over (ESC D32).

24.7 Transfer of assets to non-resident company

The company acquires the assets at their market value for the purposes of any future disposal by it.

Where the foreign trade and assets of a company resident in the UK are transferred to a non-resident company wholly or partly for shares and loan stock, so that the UK company holds at least one quarter of the foreign company's ordinary share capital, the net chargeable gains (or the proportion thereof referable to scrip consideration) are not charged until:

•   disposal of the securities received on the transfer (part being charged on a part disposal); or

•   disposal within six years after the transfer of any of the chargeable assets transferred (part being charged on a part disposal).

Intra-group disposals are ignored, but a disposal by a group transferee may trigger the deferred charge (TCGA 1992 s 140).

From 1 April 2000 non-resident companies can be members of the group or as the parent company of the group for as long as the assets remain within the scope for corporation tax.

24.8 Non-resident company holding assets in the UK

A non-resident company which carries out its operations in the UK through a branch or agency is liable to capital gains on the disposal of its assets on or after 14 March 1989. No liability arises on disposals prior to 14 March 1989 and all assets held at that date are deemed to have been acquired at market value immediately before that date (TCGA 1992 s 10).

Where the non-resident company ceases to use the assets either by ceasing to trade in the UK or removing the assets from the UK, this is to be treated as a deemed disposal at market value giving rise to a chargeable event.

Where the assets are transferred to a UK-registered company in accordance with a scheme for the transfer of the branch or agency's trade, and both the non-resident and UK companies are members of the same group, the transfers will be deemed to have been made for a consolidation giving rise to a nil gain/nil loss position.

Roll-over relief will only be granted on disposals on or after 14 March 1989 if both the new asset and old asset are situated in the UK-Disposals prior to that date were eligible for roll-over relief regardless of the location of the new asset (TCGA 1992 ss 159 and 160).

24.9 Authorised unit trusts and investment trusts

An authorised unit trust or investment trust is not chargeable to capital gains tax in respect of disposals (TCGA 1992 ss 99-101).

24.10 Company leaving group

There is provision for assessing the gain on assets taken by a company leaving a group. It applies to assets acquired from the group on or after 6 April 1965, and within six years before the company left the group (TCGA 1992 ss 178-181). A scheme for avoiding this provision by use of a sub-subsidiary which leaves the group in consequence of the winding up of its parent has been upheld (*Burman v Hedges & Butler Ltd* Ch D 1978). (If the valuation basis is adopted the Board's practice is to extend the 2 year time limit appropriately (SP D21)).

Exemption from capital gains tax is given where, as part of a merger, a company ceases to be a member of a group. (TCGA 1992 s 181).

24.11 Loss on disposal of shares; depreciatory transaction in a group (TCGA 1992 ss 176 and 177)

•   Where shares or securities of a subsidiary which later ceases to be a member of the group (unless because it or another member is wound up) are disposed of by a member of a group at a value which has been materially reduced by a disposal of assets within a group at less than market value, any loss arising is reduced by the amount which appears to the Inspector concerned, or on appeal the Commissioners, to be just and reasonable. In arriving at their decision they must take into account any other transaction on or after 6 April 1965, which has enhanced the value of the company's assets and depreciated the value of the assets of any other member of the group.

Where a disposal of shares or securities of another company which was a party to the depreciatory transaction occurs within six years of that transaction, and a gain arises from such disposal, a reduction will be made from that gain as is just and reasonable, having regard to the effect of the depreciatory transaction on the value of the shares at the date of disposal. Any adjustments required to give effect to these provisions may be made at any time.

A **depreciatory transaction** includes any other transaction where:
•   the company whose shares or securities as the subject of the ultimate disposal, or any 75% subsidiary of that company, was a party to the transaction, and

- the parties to the transaction were or included two or more companies which were members of the same group when the transaction occurred.

A transaction shall not be treated as a depreciatory transaction if it is a payment which is required to be or has been brought into account in computing a chargeable gain or allowable loss of the company making the ultimate disposal. This exemption also applies to a cancellation of any shares or securities under s 66 of the Companies Act 1948 which satisfies this condition, and would otherwise be treated as a depreciatory transaction.

24.12 Disposals of shares and securities within prescribed period
In order to prevent a claim for loss relief on shares or securities which, on account of a reacquisition within a short period, are retained, identification rules have been laid down for companies and groups (F(No2)A 1975 s 58). Such transactions had been popularly known as 'bed and breakfast' arrangements. It is not a prerequisite that a loss arise, but it is necessary that a company or a fellow member of the group held at any time during the prescribed period before the disposal, shares or securities amounting to not less than 2% of the number of that kind in issue. The shares or securities must have been held before and after the disposal in the same capacity, and not as trading stock. These provisions do not apply to specified gilt edged securities.

The **prescribed period** is one month for a disposal through a stock exchange or a body called Automated Real-Time Investments Ltd, and six months in any other case.

Where, within the prescribed period before or after a disposal of shares or securities, shares or securities of the same kind have been, or are, acquired (other than as a trading stock or on an intra-group transfer) by the same company or group ('available shares') then the shares disposed of are, so far as possible, to be identified with available shares (TCGA 1992 ss 105 and 106).

24.13 Groups: pre-entry loss
Capital losses accrued by a company before it joined a group (after 31 March 1987) are available only for set off against gains on assets held by that company on its entry into the group. This provision will apply to disposals on or after 16 March 1993 (FA 1993 s 88). The pre-entry proportion of the loss may, at the company's election, be either (a) on the basis of the market value of the asset when the company joined the group, or (b) on a time apportionment of the loss before the company joined the group. See also FA 1994 s 94.

25 FOREIGN TRANSACTIONS

25.1 Non-resident companies

A shareholder (but not a loan creditor as such) of a non-resident company, who is resident or ordinarily resident in the UK (and, if an individual, is domiciled in the UK) is chargeable on the proportion of any chargeable gain made by the company (TCGA 1992 s 13). The company must be one which would be a close company if it were resident in the UK. If the proportion of the gain to which he or she would be entitled on a winding-up is less than 1/20th, the individual is exempt.

It does not apply to any chargeable gain:
* which is distributed within two years, or

* arising on the disposal of tangible assets, or a lease of these, used for a business carried on wholly abroad, or the disposal of a foreign bank deposit for the purpose of trade outside the UK, or

* where the company is chargeable to tax, or

* gains on disposals of foreign bank deposits being money in use for foreign trade, are exempt from tax.

The tax paid, if not reimbursed by the company, can be added to the cost on subsequent disposal of the shares. If the company pays the tax the shareholder will not be assessed to income tax, capital gains tax or corporation tax on the benefit thus received.

25.2 Non-resident trusts (TCGA 1992 ss 80-98 and FA 1994 s 97)

A beneficiary of a non-resident trust is liable to capital gains tax if:

* the trustees are not resident and not ordinarily resident in the UK, and

* the settlor, or one of them, is domiciled in the UK, and resident or ordinarily resident in the UK, either when he made the settlement or when the gain occurred, and

* the beneficiary is domiciled in the UK, at any time in the year of assessment when the gain occurred, and

* there are trust gains for the year, and

* a capital payment must be received by the beneficiary.

In addition to formally constituted trusts, any disposition, agreement or arrangements made after 1984/85 will be treated as a trust. A person may be regarded as a settlor if he or she made the settlement indirectly such as in the case of a settlement arising under a will or intestacy or by undertaking to provide the funds or by making reciprocal arrangements with another person for that person to make the settlement (FA 1984 s 71).

The trust gains for the year are the aggregate of the gains for that year which would be chargeable had the trustees been resident in the UK and similar gains brought forward from earlier years. A capital payment is a payment receivable by a beneficiary attributable to chargeable gains accruing after 6 April 1981. Where the beneficiary is resident and ordinarily resident in the UK, the payment must be a payment in respect of which he or she is not chargeable to income tax, and may be made in money, property or specie or any other benefit including a loan on beneficial terms. The payment need not be made directly to the beneficiary and may be used to pay off debts, paid or applied for his or her benefit, or paid to a third party. Where the beneficiary is not resident or ordinarily resident in the UK, a capital payment is a payment which is received otherwise than as income.

The amount of any capital payment which is an outright payment of money is the sum actually paid. In any other case, it is taken as the value of the benefit conferred by it. If the payment takes the form of a loan on beneficial terms, the amount of payment is not the face value of the loan, but the value of the terms which makes it more favourable than those regarded as normal for such a loan.

The liability on the beneficiary arises on the proportion of the trust gains equivalent to his or her proportion of the total net capital payments for all beneficiaries, restricted to the actual amount of net capital payments made to him or her.

In the case of a settlement made before 6 April 1965, a beneficiary who cannot obtain any part of the capital is exempt. Collection of tax charged in respect of a reversionary interest is postponed until the title becomes absolute or the capital benefit is obtained. There is no corresponding allowance of a loss incurred by the trustees.

Where there is a liability to capital gains tax on a capital payment made to a beneficiary and the payment is made on or after 6 April 1992, there will be a further supplementary charge of 10% of the tax for each year up to a maximum of six years based on the period between the capital gains realized by the trust and the distributions being made to the beneficiary (FA 1991 s 90 and Sch 17).

Where the trustees of a settlement cease to be resident in the UK on or after 19 March 1991, a charge to capital gains tax will arise on the deemed disposal of the assets. The trustees would be deemed to have disposed of the assets and immediately re-acquired them at the market value before the relevant time or the time of ceasing to be resident in the UK. Special rules apply where the residential status of trustees is changed because of the death of a trustee to grant relief from the capital gains tax charge. The charge to capital gains tax will also arise where the trustees remain resident in the UK, but acquire residential status in another country (i.e. they become dual-resident trustees), but by virtue of a double taxation agreement the assets of the trust are exempt from UK capital gains tax.

Where a settlement is created on or after 19 March 1991 or any funds are added to an existing trust on or after 19 March 1991 and the trusts are non-resident trusts in which the settlor has retained an interest, any capital gains made by the trustees will be treated as accruing to the settlor and taxed accordingly.

25.3 Double taxation relief
This is given in the same way as for income tax where there is a foreign tax similar to the capital gains tax (TCGA 1992 s 277).

25.4 Location of assets
Rules are laid down (TCGA 1992 s 275) to determine the location of assets (rights over property, shares, ships, goodwill, patents, judgement debts, etc.).

25.5 Delayed remittances
If a person is unable to transfer to the UK gains made abroad because of laws or actions of the foreign government, or the impossibility of obtaining foreign currency, and reasonable endeavours had been made to remit the gains, he or she is not charged on the gains until it can be remitted. A claim must be made within six years after the year of assessment in which the gain arises (TCGA 1992 s 279).

25.6 Foreign currency
Foreign currency (i.e. currency in foreign banks) for personal expenditure outside the UK (including maintenance of residence) of the taxpayer or dependents is exempted from tax (TCGA 1992 s 252).

26 SETTLED PROPERTY (TCGA 1992 ss 65 and 68-98)

26.1 Meaning
A transfer into a settlement is a disposal, even if it is revocable and the transferor is a beneficiary or a trustee (TCGA 1992 s 70). Where full consideration is given for the interest disposed of, there is a disposal of that interest (*Berry v Warnett* HL 1982). It is equally important to establish that a settlement is created, for, if the donor remained absolutely entitled to the property as against the trustees, there would be no settlement. **Settled property** is any property held in trust other than that held by a person as a nominee, or as a trustee for another absolutely entitled as against him

or for one who would be so entitled but for being an infant or other person under disability (or for two or more persons who are or would be jointly so entitled). (TCGA 1992 s 60).

Absolutely entitled means having the exclusive right, subject only to trustees' lien, charge or other right to resort to the asset for payment of taxes, costs or other outgoings, to direct how that asset shall be dealt with (TCGA 1992 s 60). Neither the life tenant nor the remainderman have exclusive power to direct the trustee, nor do they jointly have such power, for jointly means currently (not consecutively) or as tenants in common (*Kidson v Macdonald* Ch D 1973). Accordingly, property settled in trust for A, for life, remainder to B, is settled property, but property given to A and B as joint tenants in common absolutely is not settled property. However, in the case of a trust for sale of land where only some of the interests are absolutely and indefeasibly vested in possession, no one is 'absolutely entitled' until the land is sold, because until then no one can direct the trustees as to how to deal with the property (*Crowe v Appleby* Ch D 1975).

Joint beneficial owners are absolutely entitled if (a) their interests are concurrent and (b) their interests are the same. Shares held by trustees subject to a shareholders agreement, therefore, are not settled property (*Booth v Ellard* CA 1978).

Trustees' lien, charge or other right of resort does not include a beneficial interest (e.g. an annuity) under the settlement. Property subject to an annuity is settled property. The contingent interest of an infant under a trust whereby he or she will attain an absolute, vested interest at the age of 18 years, arises out of settled property. The infant is not a person who would be absolutely entitled for being an infant, because the status of infancy is not the only bar to title, he or she also has to live to the age of 18 years (*Tomlinson v Glyn's Exor. & Trustee Co Ltd* CA 1969).

A residuary legatee of a Scottish estate is not absolutely entitled during the course of the administration (*Cochrane's Exors. v CIR* CS 1974). The position would be the same for an English estate.

26.2 Settlor-interested trusts

(a)   On 10 December 2003 the Chancellor announced the end to holdover relief under Ss165 and 260 TCGA 1992 in connection with the transfer of assets to settlor-interested trusts.

(b)   A trust in which the settlor of any of the settled property (or his spouse) has an interest is treated for this purpose as a settlor-interested trust. References to the settlor's spouse do not include:

(i)   a spouse from whom the settlor is separated (whether under a court order, under a separation agreement or in circumstances such that the separation is likely to be permanent); or

    (ii)   a widow or widower of the settlor.

(c)   The provisions deny holdover relief for disposals made to settlor-interested trusts on or after 10 December 2003. In addition to a straightforward transfer, two rather more convoluted arrangements have been anticipated and stopped by S169B TCGA 1992:

    (i)   it is not possible for individual A to have an arrangement under which he transfers assets to a trust in which individual B has an interest, in return for B transferring assets to a trust in which he (A) has an interest; and

    (ii)   a settlor cannot sidestep the holdover restriction by the use of a chain of transfers which interposes one or more intermediate trusts or individuals between the settlor and the trust of which he is a beneficiary.

(d)   The Finance 2004 also claws back relief in relation to disposals made on or after 10 December 2003 to trusts which were not at the time settlor-interested but which later became so within a specified period. This period begins with the disposal and ends immediately before the sixth anniversary of the start of the tax year following that in which the disposal was made - see the example below of the timescale.

A gift of a business asset by Jenny to a non-settlor interested trust on 12 May 2004 will be caught by the clawback charge if the trust becomes one in which Jenny has an interest prior to 6 April 2011.

When holdover relief is clawed back by virtue of S169C TCGA 1992, a chargeable gain equal to the amount of the held over gain accrues to the settlor in the tax year in which the trust becomes settlor-interested. It should be noted that, since the sum charged is the amount of the held over gain, no taper relief is available in these circumstances.

26.3 The trustees
They are treated as one body (despite changes in composition, which do not create a disposal). That body is resident and ordinarily resident in the UK, unless the general administration of the trust is carried on abroad and the trustees (or a majority of them) are not resident or not ordinarily resident in the UK. However, a person, whose business includes management of trusts and who acts in the course of that business, is not resident in the UK in relation to a trust if the property is derived from property provided by a person not domiciled, resident or ordinarily resident in the UK at the time of provision, or on death for a will or intestacy trust. In such a case, if the majority of trustees are treated as resident abroad, the general administration is regarded as carried on abroad (TCGA 1992 s 69).

The same persons may be trustees under distinct settlements of the same property. Thus where property is appointed or advanced from one settlement to be held on different trusts, but by the same trustees, the property has left the first settlement and become part of the second settlement (*Hoare Trustees v Gardner* Ch D 1977). The exercise of a special power of appointment as opposed to the irrevocable exercise of a power of advancement or general power of appointment is not regarded as creating a change, because the property is regarded as remaining subject to the same settlement as before the exercise. Trustees are liable to tax at 34% in 1997/98 and 1996/97 (35% previously), except where a person is (or would but for disability be) alone or jointly absolutely entitled to the property. In such a case the trustees' dealings are treated as made by the beneficiary (TCGA 1992 s 78).

26.4 On becoming absolutely entitled
There is a disposal by the trustees when a beneficiary becomes absolutely entitled to any part of the settled property. The disposal is at the market value of the assets comprised in that part. For this purpose absolute entitlement need not be beneficial, so that trustees may become absolutely entitled to property appointed or advanced to them out of a distinct settlement (*Hoare Trustees v Gardner* Ch D 1977).

The trustees are deemed to reacquire those assets at market value as nominee for the person concerned (TCGA 1992 s 71).

Such a beneficiary can be called upon to pay the tax, within two years of the tax becoming payable, if the trustees fail to pay within six months of the due date and to the extent that the beneficiary has received the assets or their proceeds (TCGA 1992 s 69). Unrelieved losses of the trustees relating to, or to property represented by, the property to which a person becomes absolutely entitled, can be passed on to the beneficiary. They are treated as a loss accruing to the beneficiary at the time he becomes absolutely entitled, to the extent that they exceed gains of the trustee in that year but before that time (TCGA 1992 s 71). The trustees' gains or losses, on the beneficiary's becoming absolutely entitled to the property, are to be treated as the beneficiary's gains or losses. Otherwise, the trustees could be taxed on gains on the beneficiary's becoming absolutely entitled, whilst available losses could only be passed on to the beneficiary for carrying forward.

The beneficiary need not become absolutely entitled solely by virtue of the trust instrument. Where a UK resident beneficiary under a foreign discretionary settlement is appointed a contingent interest in the trust assets, and which he or she assigns to a non-resident company, but, before the interest vests absolutely, he or she contracts to acquire those assets from the assignee, the latter becomes absolutely entitled by virtue of the appointment, assignment and contract when the contingent interest becomes absolute (*Chinn v Collins* HL 1980).

26.5 Termination of a life interest in possession
Life interest includes a right to the income of, or the use or occupation of, settled

property for the life of a person other than the one entitled to the right, or for lives (TCGA 1992 ss 72 and 73). It does not include any right contingent on the exercise of a discretion by any person, nor any annuity unless

- some or all of the settled property is appropriated by the trustees as a fund out of which the annuity is payable, and

- there is no right of recourse to settled property not so appropriated, or to the income thereof;

in which case that fund is treated as a separate settlement.

A life interest in part of the settled property is treated as an interest in a separate settlement. Likewise, if it is an interest in income without recourse to the remainder of the settled property, or to the income thereof. A life interest in a fraction of a trust fund is a life interest in a part of the settled property.

The charge
The termination of a life interest otherwise than on the death of a life tenant will not give rise to a deemed disposal and re-acquisition by the trustees. If however, the termination results in a beneficiary becoming absolutely entitled to the settled property a disposal is deemed to have been made.

Exemptions from the charge on death
No tax is charged when the person entitled to the life interest dies, even if a person then becomes absolutely entitled to the settled property (TCGA 1992 s 72). This applies equally on the death of a life tenant *per autre vie*. Nevertheless, there is a deemed disposal and reacquisition at market value, and this also applies to an interest for the life of another. Moreover, where an annuitant, whose interest is not a life interest, dies, there is a deemed disposal and reacquisition at market value on the death, but no tax is charged (TCGA 1992 s 75). This also applies on the death of an *autre vie*, if on death inheritance tax becomes payable because he or she had an interest in possession within the last seven years. If part only of the property is so liable to inheritance tax, the complementary part is charged to CGT on the deemed disposal and reacquisition.

If on the death of a life tenant in possession, the settled property reverts to the disponor, no chargeable gain accrues and the disponor is deemed to have acquired the property as and when the trustees acquired it (TCGA 1992 s 93).

27 DEATH OF TAXPAYER

Broadly, to the extent that inheritance tax is chargeable, the value of the asset is not subjected to Capital Gains Tax as well. Death is usually hard to predict. A double charge to both Capital Gains Tax, and Inheritance Tax will be payable on the net proceeds, if chargeable assets are sold prior to death.

Example:
Simon is seriously and terminally ill. He wishes to tidy up his affairs, and after making a will, sells all his shares realising a taxable gain of £100,000. Lets say that the Capital Gains Tax on this gain is £28,000.

He dies two weeks later. The cash of £100,000 falls into his estate of £500,000 and the Capital Gains Tax bill of £28,000 is a charge on his estate. Inheritance Tax of £28,800 (40% x £72,000 (£100,000 - £28,000)) is also due on the net proceeds of the shares.

If Simon had not sold the shares prior to his death Inheritance Tax of £40,000 (40%) would have been payable on the £100,000. Thus saving his estate tax on this sale of £16,800. ((Shares sold pre death. Tax payable = CGT £28,000 + IHT £28,800) less (Shares sold on death = IHT £40,000)).

But Simon is probably past caring!

27.1 Assets passing on death
On the death of a person the personal representative or executor acquires without any charge to tax on the deceased's estate the following assets:

(a)   assets of which the deceased was competent to dispose of by will (other than under a power of appointment), assuming him or her to have been of full age and, if not domiciled in the UK to be domiciled in England, and assuming the assets to be situate in the UK; and

(b)   the severable share in any assets to which the deceased was beneficially entitled as joint tenant;

(c)   gifts in contemplation of death (donatio mortis causa);

(d)   variations or disclaimers of the deceased's dispositions of assets within (a), by instrument in writing made within two years of death. Written election is necessary (in the case of a variation) within six months of the instrument (unless the Board allows a longer time). For variations or disclaimers there must be no consideration other than another variation or disclaimer affecting the same estate.

The assets are deemed to be acquired by the personal representative (i.e. executor or administrator) at the market value at the date of death, but the death does not represent a disposal of the assets.

Market value means the value for inheritance tax, where it has been ascertained for the charge on death (TCGA 1992 ss 62 and 63 and s 274).

27.2 Gifts *inter vivos*
If the asset is at the time of death owned by the donee or comprised, or deemed to be comprised, in the settlement made by the donor, the chargeable gain which accrued on the gift is unaffected, but the asset (or the proportion of it) which the value charged to inheritance tax bears to the market value is deemed to be disposed of and reacquired at 'market value' at the time of death; but not so as to give rise to a chargeable gain (TCGA 1992 s.260).

27.3 Carry-back of losses
Allowable losses sustained by the individual in the tax year of death may, so far as they exceed gains of that year, be set off against chargeable gains in the three preceding years of assessment (taking later years before earlier ones) (TCGA 1992 s 62(2).

27.4 Dealings by personal representatives
The personal representatives are treated as a single and continuing body having the deceased's residence, ordinary residence and domicile at death (TCGA 1992 s 62 (3)). Accordingly if the deceased was then resident or ordinarily resident in the UK, the representatives will be chargeable to capital gains tax on any disposals made by them. The gain (or loss) will be the difference between the proceeds and the 'market value' on death. Excess losses cannot be passed to legatees.

27.5 Transfers to legatees
No chargeable gain accrues on transfer and the legatee is deemed to acquire the assets at the value and time of the personal representatives acquisition (i.e. 'market value' on death) (TCGA 1992 s 62(1)). **Legatee** includes a recipient of a *donatio mortis causa,* trustees of any settlement created by any testamentary disposition or on intestacy, the remainderman who takes an interest on extinction of a prior interest during administration of the estate and a pecuniary legatee to whom assets are appropriated under a power. A pecuniary legatee who takes an appropriation by consent may, together with the personal representative, elect to be treated as a legatee.

The incidental costs of transfer of a legatee who becomes absolutely entitled, and those incurred by the personal representatives, are allowed to the legatee on a disposal of the asset acquired.

28 MISCELLANEOUS

28.1 Market value
No deduction is to be made by considering the effect of placing all the assets on the market at the same time.

Quoted shares are to be valued at the lower of
- one quarter up on the lower stock exchange price, or

- the middle price of bargains (other than bargains at special prices) unless there are special circumstances causing the quoted prices not to be a proper measure of market value. 'Special circumstances' do not include information known to directors which was not available to the market (e.g. take-over negotiations) for that is not exceptional, abnormal or unusual. A 'stale quotation' or the placing of a parcel which would not in practice be put through the market might be special circumstances (TCGA 1992 ss 272-274).

Unit trust units are valued at the lower quoted price.

A valuation at 6 April 1982 made in order to compute a gain is to be at the higher of the middle stock exchange price, or the middle price of bargains (other than bargains at special prices) unless there are special circumstances.

Otherwise, market value is the price which the assets might reasonably be expected to fetch on a sale in the open market. In ascertaining market value for unquoted shares and securities it is to be assumed that there is available to a prospective purchaser all the information which a prudent purchaser might reasonably require if proposing to purchase the asset from a willing vendor by private treaty and, at arm's length TCGA 1992 s 273).

The High Court held in *Couch v Administrators of the Estate of Caton* (deceased) (1996) STI 26 that the costs of appeal against a valuation of shares was not an allowable expense in computing the capital gain on the disposal of those shares.

28.2 Marketable securities and commodities
Shares (including securities) of a company of the same class held by one person in one capacity are regarded as indistinguishable parts of a single asset. The shares issued to an employee on terms which restrict his or her right to dispose of them, are treated as a separate class (TCGA 1992 Sch 2(4)).

28.3 Time of acquisition and disposal
If there is a contract, it is the time the contract is made (and not, if different, the time of conveyance or transfer), but, if the contract is conditional or subject to the

exercise of an option, it is the time when the condition is satisfied (TCGA 1992 s 28). A **conditional contract** is one subject to a condition precedent the non-fulfilment of which prevents the contract from taking effect (*Eastham v Leigh London & Provincial Properties* CA 1971).

In the case of a compulsory acquisition, it is the time at which the compensation is agreed or otherwise determined at first instance, or, if earlier, the time when the authority lawfully enters on the land (TCGA 1992 s 264).

In the case of other compensation receipts, the time of disposal is the time of receipt of the sum (TCGA 1992 s 22).

A sale on hire purchase is deemed to take place at the beginning of the period of hire (TCGA 1992 s 27).

28.4 Disposal of annuities and interests in settlements
No chargeable gain arises on the disposal of an allowance, annuity or capital sum payable out of a superannuation fund, or an annuity (other than a deferred annuity) from a company carrying on an annuity business, or an annual payment under a covenant not secured on any property (TCGA 1992 ss 76 and 234) **Annual payment**, for this purpose, has been held to include patent royalties, so that the distribution in specie by a company to its shareholders of its rights to certain royalties was held to be a chargeable disposal of those rights (*Rank Xerox Ltd v Lane* HL 1979). Similarly, no chargeable gain arises on the disposal of an annuity or other interest under a settlement by the beneficiary, or another person if it has not been purchased for consideration other than another interest under the settlement.

28.5 Husband and wife (and civil partners)
If the husband and wife are living together, transactions between them are treated as if the disposal price were such that no gain or loss arises (i.e. at base cost). This does not apply to trading stock, or if the disposal is on the occasion of the death of the disposer when market value will apply. After the breakdown of marriage and separation, transfers of assets will be liable to capital gains tax. However, if the matrimonial home is occupied by one spouse to whom it is subsequently transferred as part of the divorce settlement, no gain will be chargeable unless an election has been made for some other house to be the main residence of the transferring spouse (ESC D6).

Each spouse is entitled to the basic annual exemption and chargeable to tax on his or her own gains at the appropriate rate of tax. Transactions between spouses are treated on a no gain no loss basis under (TCGA 1992 s 58).

Please note that the proposed Gay Partnership agreements will extend these rules to same sex partnerships.

28.6 Woodlands

The sale of trees and underwood by an occupier is not chargeable, nor are insurance proceeds in respect of destruction or damage to such trees by fire or other hazard. In computing any charge on the woodland (i.e. the land itself as distinct from the trees), the part of the cost or sale proceeds attributable to the trees growing on it is excluded (TCGA 1992 s 250).

28.7 Underwriters

The trustees are assessed on the full amount of any capital gains arising from the investments of a premium trust fund, special reserve fund or any other required or authorised trust fund. The member must then claim repayment in respect of any losses or reductions due, as he or she is regarded as the owner of the investments (TCGA 1992 ss 206-209).

As from 1988/89 the tax chargeable on the trustees will be at the basic rate of income tax, and any higher rate tax chargeable will be assessed on the underwriting member and credit being given for the tax assessed on the trustees.

28.8 Mineral royalties

One half is charged to income tax (or corporation tax) the other half being subject to capital gains tax (TCGA 1992 s 201). Expenses of management are not deductible in computing capital gains tax. An allowable loss which accrues on the expiry, termination or disposal of lease may be carried back and set against gains accruing during the fifteen years ending with the date of the event. An election for this set-off must be made within six years of the date of the event (TCGA 1992 s 202).

28.9 Partnerships

The partners are separately assessed and charged to tax, and partnership dealings treated as dealings by the partners individually (TCGA 1992 s 59).

HMRC issued a SP (D12) which set out a number of general points agreed with professional bodies relating to the capital gains tax treatment of partnerships. The main points are set out below.

Each partner will be regarded as owning a fractional share of the partnership assets and no discount will be made, on valuation, on account of his owning a share in, and not the whole of, the asset.

Disposals and part disposals of partnership assets to outside parties will be treated accordingly. The fractional share will be determined by reference to the agreed share in surplus assets, failing which, by reference to the actual division in the accounts, failing which, by reference to profit-sharing ratios.

On a distribution *in specie* to some of the partners, only that part of the gain not attributable to the recipients will be charged. The recipients will be deemed to have acquired the assets at market value less the gains not charged.

On a change in shares in surplus assets, there will be a disposal by a partner whose share decreases, and an acquisition by one whose share increases, at the current balance sheet value of all the assets concerned, provided no payment of consideration is involved.

On a revaluation of a partnership asset there will be a disposal at the revaluation figure, if and when a partner's surplus-asset ratio is reduced, with a corresponding acquisition for one whose share increases.

On a payment between partners outside the partnership accounts the recipient makes a disposal, and the payer an acquisition, for that consideration in addition to any taken into account as above. The recipient may offset any costs reflected in the accounts (not claimed as above) or representing similar payments made by him or her, where appropriate valuation as at 6 April 1965, can, of course, be claimed. The payer will have a loss only when leaving the partnership, or reducing his or her share, and receiving no, or less, consideration. Where no payment is made through or outside the accounts on a change in partnership ratios, a tax charge will arise only if the transaction is not at arm's length or between connected persons.

Market value may be substituted (as if it were a payment) if the parties are connected or not at arm's length by virtue of family relationship, unless no greater than actual consideration would have passed between parties not so related.

Annual payments to a retired partner (but not a lump sum or the cost of a purchased life annuity) will not be treated as consideration for a disposal and corresponding acquisition, unless it is more than reasonable recognition of past service, when the capitalised value can be treated as consideration.

The following will be regarded as 'reasonable recognition':

Complete years in partnership (or predecessor on merger)	Fraction of share of partnership profits (before capital allowances or charges)
1-5	01/60ths each year
6	08/60ths each year
7	16/60ths each year
8	24/60ths each year
9	32/60ths each year
10	40/60ths each year

If a lump sum is also received, one-ninth is added to the annuity in order to determine whether or not the annuity is over the exempt limit (SP1/79).

28.10 Mortgages and charges

The creation or redemption of a mortgage or charge by way of security is not a disposal (TCGA 1992 s 26). However, the creation of a legal charge, followed by the release of the charge in consideration for the conveyance of the fee simple (i.e. freehold) is 'in substance a sale, even though it was carried out by two separate documents' (*Thompson v Salah* Ch D 1971). Dealings with the security by the mortgagee or chargee are treated as dealings by the mortgagor or charger. Encumbrances are not to be taken as reducing the consideration for, or value of, an asset on its disposal or acquisition.

When a third party is claimed to be merely a financier of a deal, but the land is in fact conveyed to him by the vendor and only conveyed to the purchaser when the finance is repaid, that is not a transfer by way of security unless the taxpayer can adduce sufficient evidence that the intent (security) was different from the form (sale and re-sale) (*Beattie v Jenkinson* Ch D 1971).

28.11 Insolvents' assets

The trustee in bankruptcy or under a deed of arrangement is the nominee of the debtor as regards dealings with assets. The tax on disposals by the trustee is payable by priority to other debts (*Re McMeekin* QB(NI) 1973).

Assets of a deceased debtor are deemed to be held, after death, on behalf of personal representatives and to be assets of which he or she was competent to dispose at death, if they are held by, or vest in, a trustee in bankruptcy or under a deed of arrangement and are not 'settled property' (TCGA 1992 s 66).

28.12 Mutual Society takeovers or conversions

Where shares are issued to building society and mutual insurance company members in these circumstances legislation provides that no capital gains liability arises on receipt of the shares. For the purpose of computing any gain on a subsequent sales of the shares they are treated as acquired for the amount paid for them, if nothing is paid for the shares the acquisition cost will be nil.

Share account holders are liable to CGT on the cash payments they receive in respect of their share accounts.

28.13 Accident Insurance

From 3 July 1992 the proceeds of accident insurance policies are not chargeable if paid for on disability or death.

PART TWELVE

INHERITANCE TAX

BUDGET 2011

1) Nil Rate Band

The nil rate band will remain frozen, at £325,000, until 5 April 2015 (2014/2015). Thereafter it will rise by the CPI.

2) 2012/2013 Reduced Rate

The 2011 Budget announced that a reduced rate of Inheritance Tax (IHT) will apply where 10 per cent or more of a deceased's net estate (after deducting IHT exemptions, reliefs and the nil rate band) is left to charity. In those cases the current 40 per cent rate will be reduced to 36 per cent. The new rate will apply where death occurs on or after 6 April 2012. There will be consultation on the detailed implementation of this measure, which ends 31 August 2011.

IHT Charity relief example

Arthur, a bachelor, dies 6 April 2012 (2012/2013)

	£
Estate (net) before zero rate band	625,000
Nil rate band	325,000
Net estate chargeable to IHT	300,000
Bequest to charity £50,000 (greater than 10% of net estate = £30,000)	50,000
Revised chargeable estate	250,000
Tax charged @ 36% (40% less 10% reduction)	£90,000

If Arthur had died on 5 April 2012 (2011/2012)

Tax payable @ 40% (£250,000 @ 40%)	£100,000
Tax saved by dying one day later	£10,000

---

1 THE GENERAL SCHEME OF INHERITANCE TAX

1.0 Transfer of unused nil-rate band

From 8 October 2007 the unused element of the nil-rate band, at that time £300,000 per individual, became transferable to a surviving spouse (or civil partner). This applies on the death of a surviving spouse or partner after 8 October 2007, regardless of when the first death occurred.

The amount of the nil-rate band available for transfer is based on the proportion of the nil-rate band that was unused when the first spouse or partner died. The unused proportion will be applied to the amount of the nil-rate band in force at the date of the surviving spouse or partner's death.

For example, Mr A died 10 October 2007 leaving his children £100,000 (i.e. one-third of the 2007/2008 nil-rate band) with the rest of his estate passing to his wife. On Mrs A's subsequent death, her nil-rate band will then be increased by two-thirds.

So if the nil-rate band at the time of Mrs A's death is £360,000 she will be able to leave £600,000 free of inheritance tax, i.e. £360,000 plus £240,000 (two-thirds of £360,000).

If a person marries more than once, the nil-rate band of the survivor can only be increased by a maximum of 100%.

HMRC have published nil-rate band tables for all years from August 1914, www.hmrc.gov.uk/rates/inheritance.htm.

Currently the nil rate band is frozen @ £325,000 until 2014/2015.

1.1 The essentials

Inheritance tax is charged on the value of the estate passing on the death of an individual and on certain gifts and transfers made within seven years before death. The tax applies to the total value of the estate plus the chargeable gifts which exceeds £325,000 from 6 April 2011 (£325,000 from 6 April 2010) and the rate of tax is 40%. Where the deceased was domiciled or deemed domiciled in the UK at the date of death the tax applies to all assets, wherever situated. For individuals not domiciled in the UK the tax is charged only on the assets situated in the UK, although in that case double taxation relief may apply. Certain expenses may be deducted from the gross value of the estate, some assets are excluded and there are a number of exemptions and reliefs. About 6% of estates fall within the IHT 40% band (1997 2%). It is expected that 16,000 estates will pay IHT in 2010/2011 - House of Commons Library (18.5.2011).

1.2 Estate, excluded property and liabilities

1.2.1 Meaning of estate

The total of all property including rights and interests of any description to which a person is beneficially entitled is his estate (IHTA 1984 s 5). Beneficial ownership has been said to entail 'the right at least to some extent to deal with the property (or interest) as your own' (*Wood Preservation Ltd v Prior* CA 1968). A person's estate includes that part of any settled property in which he or she is beneficially entitled to an interest in possession (IHTA 1984 s 49). A beneficiary of a discretionary trust has no interest in the settled property, until the trustees exercise their discretion in his or her favour (*Gartside v CIR* H L 1967). A residuary legatee under an English will or intestacy has no beneficial interest in the residuary estate during the course of its administration (*Comm. Stamp Duties (Queensland) v Livingstone* PC 1964). However, he or she will be deemed to have an interest in possession as from the date of death, if so entitled as from the completion of the administration. A shareholder of a company in the course of winding up is not beneficially entitled to a share in the company's assets (*Ayerst v C & K Ltd* H L 1975). The shareholder's interest is still in shares, and whatever distributions they produce must be valued.

A person is beneficially entitled to property or money (not being settled property but including an interest in an approved pension fund) if he or she has a general power. A **general power** means a power or authority enabling the person by whom it is exercisable to appoint or dispose of property as he or she thinks fit (IHTA 1984 s 5(2)).

A reversionary interest expectant (whether in possession or not) in settled property which is acquired by the person entitled to the latter interest, is not part of that person's estate (IHTA 1984 s 48).

Sums promised without consideration but not paid before the relevant date are not part of the estate at that date. An apparent exception may be the compensation payable by the Criminal Injuries Board which, although it is ex gratia, has been held to be recoverable by a deceased victim's estate provided its amount has been determined before death (*R v CICB Ex parte Tong* C of A 1976).

1.2.2 Excluded Property

A person's estate does not include 'excluded property' and its transfer will not have a transfer value (IHTA 1984 s 48). The types of excluded property are listed below.

- Property situated outside the UK if the person beneficially entitled to it is an individual and is domiciled outside the UK.

- A reversionary interest unless:
  (a)   it has at any time been acquired for consideration in money or money's worth; or

(b)   it is one to which either the settlor or spouse is beneficially entitled; by a settlement made after 15 April 1976 or reversionary interest acquired after 9 March 1981; or

(c)   it is the interest expectant upon the determination of a lease treated as a settlement.

but, if the property comprised in the settlement is situated outside the UK a reversionary interest in it is excluded property if the person beneficially entitled to it is domiciled outside the UK.

- Property situated outside the UK and comprised in a settlement, unless the settlor was domiciled in the UK at the time the settlement was made. In relation to a settlement made before 10 December, 1974, general domicile only is considered.

- Government securities specifically exempted from UK tax so long as they were:
  (a)   in the beneficial ownership of a person neither domiciled nor ordinarily resident in the UK; or

  (b)   comprised in a settlement under which such a person is beneficially entitled to an interest in possession in them (participators in a close company which has an interest in possession in settled government securities may be treated as having themselves an appropriate part of that interest in order to satisfy this condition);

  (c)   comprised in a settlement under which all known persons who are or might become entitled to the securities or an interest in them are persons not domiciled nor ordinarily resident.

- Emoluments and certain chattels of a member of the Visiting Forces and Staff of allied headquarters of designated countries, provided the person is not a British subject (IHTA 1984 s 155).

- Persons domiciled in the Channel Islands or the Isle of Man following migration from the UK are treated as domiciled in the UK in respect of chargeable events occurring before 15 March 1983. However, the following were excluded property during the deemed domicile:

  (a)   Savings: War Savings Certificates; National Savings Certificates (including Ulster Savings Certificates); Premium Bonds; deposits with the National Savings Bank or with a Trustee Savings Bank; deposits with a savings bank with respect to which a certificate of the Treasury under TA 1970 s 414 is in force; any certified contractual savings scheme within the meaning of TA 1970 s 415.

(b)   Property derived from emoluments or business. Property transferred after 28 July 1977, by a person domiciled in the Islands (ignoring the deemed UK domicile) derived either directly or indirectly from:

(i)   emoluments from an employment or office in the Islands other than under or with a connected person in a business as mentioned below;

(ii)   profits from a business carried on in the Islands by the transferor or a company controlled by him except a business consisting wholly or mainly of dealing in securities, stocks, or shares, or in land or buildings situated outside the Islands; and/or making or holding investments other than in land or buildings situated within the Islands.

(c)   Settled property: property situated outside the UK at the time of the settlement and derived from personal endeavour as in para. (b).

1.2.3 Liabilities
In arriving at the value of the estate liabilities are deductible but, except when imposed by law (e.g. taxes) only to the extent that they are incurred for consideration. Discount is to be made, if necessary, to allow for the liabilities not immediately due. If there is a right to reimbursement including a right of recovery of Inheritance Tax from a person other than transferor's spouse the liability is to be reduced by it, except to the extent that reimbursement cannot reasonably be expected to be obtained (IHTA 1984 s 162).

An incumbrance on any property is to be taken as reducing the value of that property, so that, for example, excluded property which is mortgaged will, in effect, be exempt only as regards the net value of the equity of redemption. Expenses of transfer are not liabilities for the above purposes, but reduce the value transferred if borne by a person benefiting from the transfer.

1.3 Valuation of the estate
The relevant legislation is IHTA 1984 ss 160 - 170. The value of any property, right or interest is the price which it might be expected to fetch if it were sold in the open market, no reduction being made on the ground that the whole is to be placed on the market at one time (IHTA 1984 s 160).

The general principles of valuation for taxation purposes apply and the valuation of particular property is shown below.

Date of Gift
Curnock v IRC SpC 365
A cheque drawn on the account of the deceased on the day preceding his death did not clear until after the death.

The HMRC argued that the amount of the cheque comprised part of the Estate as the gift had failed due to the payment not clearing. The Special Commissioners supported the HMRC's view based on earlier case law that a gift is not complete until the cheque has cleared. NB This also applies to gifts to couples getting married. They are given in 'consideration of marriage' and therefore should be cleared in advance (see p.553).

1.3.1 Agricultural property relief (APR)
See IHTA 1984 ss 115-124, s 169.

Extension of APR and woodlands relief to land in the EEA
Section 122, FA 2009 extends the IHT reliefs for agricultural property (APR) and woodlands (WR) to property in the European Economic Area (EEA). This is in response to the European Commission's opinion that the previous territorial restrictions contravened European law.

The change applies to transfers of value where the IHT would have been due on or after 22 April 2009, or was paid or due on or after 22 April 2003. In order to qualify for relief the property must meet the usual conditions for APR or WR, as appropriate, and must be located in an EEA state at the time of the event chargeable to IHT. All claims for relief must have been made by 21 April 2010.

Valuation
Agricultural value is the value of the agricultural property if it were subject to a perpetual covenant which prohibits the use of the property otherwise than as agricultural property. Farm cottages which are occupied by persons solely for agricultural purposes are to be valued without taking into account their suitability for non-agricultural purposes (IHTA 1984 s 115(3); s 169).

Conditions for relief
Relief from inheritance tax is available on the transfer of agricultural property as follows (IHTA 1984 ss 116, 117 and 118). The agricultural property must have been:

*   occupied by the transferor for the purposes of agriculture throughout the period of two years ending with the date of transfer, or

*   owned by the transferor for the period of seven years ended with the date of transfer and have been occupied by the transferor (or another person) for the purposes of agriculture.

Relief

The relief available from 10 March 1992 is 100%, of the agricultural value of the property calculated before tax and deduction of annual and other exemptions, but after deduction of any mortgage or secured liability if either

- the transferor has vacant possession of the agricultural property (or the right to obtain it within the next twelve months) immediately before the transfer; or

- the transferor also has been beneficially entitled to the property since before 10 March 1981, and the following conditions are satisfied:

- for a transfer immediately before 10 March 1981 agricultural relief applied to the extent that the relief would not have been excluded by the £250,000 or 1000 acres restriction, and between the 10 March 1981, and the date of transfer the transferor was not entitled to vacant possession (or the right to obtain it within the next twelve months) and lack of entitlement thereto was not due to any act or deliberate omission during that period.

- Agricultural land let on tenancy starting after 31 August 1995.

In all other cases the relief is 50% (from 10 March 1992).

A partner in a farming partnership is treated as occupying the land to the extent of any interest in the land (even where the partnership farms under a tenancy from one or more of the partners).

Recent cases concerning APR & farmhouses

Recent cases have concerned the availability of APR for farmhouses.

In the case of *Atkinson and another (executors of Atkinson deceased) v HMRC* TC00420 it was emphasised that to qualify for agricultural property relief (APR) the agricultural property (in this case a farmhouse) has to be used for an agricultural purpose for seven years, but the use does not have to be continuous.

A farmhouse qualifies as agricultural property (s 115, IHTA 1984) subject to being 'of a character appropriate' and provided it meets the occupation test of s 117, IHTA 1984. Section 117(b), relevant in this case, requires the transferor to own the property for seven years and for it to be occupied throughout that period by him or another for the purposes of agriculture.

Mr Atkinson, who owned the farmhouse (actually a bungalow), died in 2006. In the four years prior to that he lived in a care home but he did visit the bungalow which still contained his belongings. The bungalow plus other farm property and land owned by Mr Atkinson was let to the family farming partnership. He was still involved in farming decisions as the senior partner.

His executors claimed APR but HMRC refused the claim on the grounds that the bungalow had not been occupied by Mr Atkinson throughout the previous seven years and had not been used for agricultural purposes while he was in the care home. The tribunal decided for the executors, on the grounds that the bungalow was occupied by the farming partnership and, in relation to the 'purposes of agriculture' test, it was used to accommodate the diminishing needs of the senior partner.

This case gives guidance to those elderly farmers in a similar situation, and perhaps the action plan of the relatives is not to rush out and let the farmhouse the day after the farming partner moves into a care home! This could be quite difficult for some farming partnerships which would need the rental income to pay for the care home. Equally the property should be kept available for use by the elderly partner and not emptied of his possessions.

In the Antrobus case, *Lloyds TSB (PR of Antrobus dec'd v IRC* (SpC 336)), it was held that the property was occupied as a farmhouse and that the farm had been run from the property which had also been used as a farm canteen. The property therefore qualified for APR.

The Revenue then came back by claiming that the farmhouse had a value in excess of its agricultural value. Section 116(1) of IHTA 1984 limits relief to the agricultural value of the property and s 115(3) defines that value as:

"the value which would be the value of the property if the property were subject to a perpetual covenant prohibiting its use otherwise than as agricultural property".

At Miss Antrobus's death, the farmhouse was valued at £608,475 and the Capital Taxes Office claimed 30 per cent of this was attributable to non-agricultural value.

The Tribunal agreed with the Revenue that 30 per cent of the value of the house was non-agricultural value - the difference between its open market value and the value it would have had, had occupation been limited to a working farmer. However, the non-agricultural value will always depend on the facts of the particular case and the 30 per cent attribution in Antrobus should not be taken as a rule of thumb.

However, in the Higginson case, *Higginson's Exec v IRC* (SpC 337), the decision was that the property was not a farmhouse. In this case, the property had formerly been a hunting lodge and although it had been occupied by the land owner whilst part of the land had been used as a farm, it was held that the property did not have the nature of a farmhouse. To be a farmhouse, the land must predominate with the buildings being ancillary to the farm. In this case, there was a house with some farm land; it was not a farm house.

The conflicting results in these cases show that it is essential to examine the nature and the use of the property concerned. This may be of concern to clients with houses which had originally been the hub of a large farm but where parcels of land have been sold off, or where the activities undertaken stray from farming into other areas.

In *Rosser v IRC* SpC 368 the deceased occupied a house which had previously been the farmhouse for a 41 acre farm. The majority of the land (39 acres) was gifted to the son, with the deceased and her spouse continuing to live in the house. A barn was on the retained 2 acres.

Certain services were provided from the house, including the provision of meal for farm workers. The barn also continued to be used for agricultural purposes.
Although it was accepted that the 2 acres was agricultural land, it was not accepted that the house continued to satisfy the definition of farmhouse in relation to those 2 acres, thus failing the "Character appropriate" test. Therefore APR was not available in respect of the house but was available in respect of the barn.

In *Farnander and others (Executors of McKenna Deceased) v HMRC [2006] SpC 565* the Special Commissioners ruled on Agricultural Property Relief and Farmhouses.

"Agricultural property", in terms of the relief (s 115(2) IHT 1984), means agricultural land or pasture and also includes such cottages, farm buildings and farmhouses, together with the land occupied with them, as are of a character appropriate to the property.

Determining whether a country house is of "a character appropriate to the property" is not always an easy decision (see above). The Antrobus case established the "elephant test" - you would know a farmhouse if you saw one. Both of these cases featured large houses with small amounts of agricultural land.

In the McKenna case, the property was described in sale particulars as "an historic and substantial Manor House, Listed Grade II" and also as "an outstanding manor house and private estate". Rosteague House sat in six acres of gardens surrounded by 110 acres of farmland, and 52 acres of coastal land. Farming was done on a contract basis. There had been various farming contractors over the years, and there were a range of buildings on the estate, of mixed farming and domestic uses. Agricultural Property relief was claimed on the house, some buildings and the farmland. The Mckennas were never what you would term "hands on farmers", but the estate had been farmed historically.

The commissioner decided that, if Rosteague House was a farmhouse, then it was not "of a character appropriate to the property" within the meaning of section 115(2). she also determined that it had not been occupied for the purposes of agriculture throughout the period of two years ending with the relevant dates of death within the meaning of section 117(a).

The key factor in this case, which is important for those hoping to buy a farm and make substantial inheritance savings, is that Mr McKenna was not actively involved in running his farm and could not really be described as a farmer. Even his obituary failed to mention any interest in farming.

Grazing

The Special Commissioner held that a meadow used solely for grazing horses, where the horses were kept neither as livestock nor as part of a stud farm business, was not 'occupied for the purposes of agriculture'. The land was thus not eligible for agricultural property relief for inheritance tax purposes. The deceased had owned the land for seven years prior to his death, during which time it had been subject to a grazing agreement between the deceased and G. The meadow had been used solely for feeding horses that were neither kept for stud nor draught animals (*Wheatley and Another (Executors of Wheatley, deceased) v IRC*, SpC 149 (1998) STI 559).

Christmas tree farms

HMRC has said that the growing of Christmas trees can fall within the definition of a nursery, as the trees are not grown to maturity and are harvested for sale (see the Inheritance Tax Manual at IHTM24103).

Therefore, the land is occupied for the purposes of agriculture for Agricultural Property Relief (APR), because the definition (from the Agricultural Holdings Act 1986) includes market gardens and nursery grounds. HMRC also took into account the fact that Christmas tree farms are defined as nurseries for income tax and VAT.

Accordingly, APR is available under s 115, IHTA 1984.

The reported case involved a protected agricultural tenancy, so APR was available at 50%. However, it follows that 100% APR should be available where the relevant conditions are met.

Successions

Where the transfer occurred after 9 March 1981, and the property was inherited on a death, the transferor is deemed to have owned it (and if he subsequently occupied it, to have occupied it) from the date of death. If the deceased person was the transferor's spouse, the period of ownership (or occupancy) is extended to include any period of ownership (or occupancy) by the spouse (IHTA 1984 s 120).

Where the conditions described above are not satisfied, relief may still be claimed if all of the following conditions are satisfied:

*   where the whole or part of the value transferred by an earlier transfer was

eligible for relief after 9 March 1981, or would have been if such relief could have been claimable, and

- where the whole or part of that property became the transferor's or spouse's because of the earlier transfer, and at the time of the later transfer was occupied for agricultural purposes by that person or the personal representatives of the first transferor.

- that property or part of the property directly or indirectly replacing it would have qualified for relief except for the conditions above, in relation to the subsequent transfer of value.

- either of the transfers was a transfer on death (IHTA 1984 s 121).

1.3.2 Business property relief
See IHTA 1984 ss 103-114.

Definition
Relevant business property (see IHTA 1984 s 105) means:
(a)   a business (including the exercise of the profession or vocation) carried on for gain, or interest in such a business; or *

(b)   shares in or securities of a company which are quoted and which immediately before the transfer gave the transferor control of the company; or

(c)   unquoted shares which either by themselves or together with other shares owned by the transferor give 25% or more of the votes capable of being exercised in a company. The transferor must have held votes giving more than the 25% voting rights for at least two years before the transfer (IHTA 1984 s 105; FA 1987 s 58 and Sch 8.);

(d)   any land or building, machinery or plant which, immediately before the transfer, was used wholly or mainly for the purposes of a business carried on by a company of which the transferor then had control, or by a partnership of which he or she was then a partner;

(e)   BPR on holiday lettings - HMRC had previously allowed claims for Business Property Relief on holiday letters of furnished property and caravan sites where:

    - the lettings were short term and;

    - The owner himself, or through an agent such as a relative, was substantially involved with the holidaymakers in terms of their activities on and from the premises.

Further to advice from the Solicitor's Office, HMRC have announced at IHTM25278 that they have reconsidered their approach in cases where BPR claims are made in this situation, and will be looking more closely at the level and type of services provided (rather than who has provided them). Until further notice, claims are being referred to the Technical Team (Litigation) for early consideration;

but excludes a business which, or shares or securities of a company the business of which, consists wholly or mainly of:

• dealing in securities, stocks or shares (except by a UK jobber (TA 1970 s 477) or discount house);

• dealing in land or buildings;

• making or holding investments (except by a holding company whose business consists of holding shares in companies not excluded by para.'s (a) to (c)). It was held in *Powell v IRC* (1997) STI 657 that a business of a caravan park which hired out pitches both on long and short term lets was categorised as holding investments.

• The Special Commissioner found, as a question of fact, that the company, in which the deceased owned 50% of the shares, did not 'require' £300,000 of its cash reserves. This cash was thus an <u>excepted asset</u> for the purposes of calculating business property relief on the value of the shares in her estate on her death in November 1990 (see *Barclays Bank Trust Co Ltd v IRC* SpC 158 (1998) STI 738).

Also excluded is any relevant business property for which a binding contract of sale has been entered into at the time of transfer (unless the transaction is either the sale of a business or interest in a business to a company which is to carry it on and is made in consideration wholly or mainly of shares or securities in that company; or is the sale of shares or securities for the purpose of reconstruction or amalgamation). Shares in and securities of a company in winding up otherwise than for reconstruction or amalgamation are excluded from relevant business property.

* Cases show how this relief works.
(a)   The deceased worked in partnership with her daughter and retained an interest in the business after retirement by way of sums owed to her by the business. The partnership had no written agreement but profits were shared equally. Over £100,000 was still outstanding on her capital account at death.

It was contended that the deceased had an interest in the business qualifying as relevant business property. However, the Special Commissioner held that the deceased's interest changed on her retirement. On her retirement her rights, in the absence of any agreements to contrary, were simply those of a creditor of the business. *Beckham v IRC* Spc 226 2000 SWTI 162.

(b) Caravan park qualifies for BPR. The special commissioner found, on the particular facts of the case, that the deceased's two-thirds interest in a partnership that ran a caravan park was eligible for business property relief, because it did not consist simply of 'holding and managing investments'. For inheritance tax purposes, it was irrelevant that the caravan park's income was assessed as trading income. Looking at the business carried on at the park, the net profit that caravan sales generated during the years 1993 to 1996 exceeded that from renting caravan pitches. In addition, the deceased's son and partner and three employees undertook a considerable amount of maintenance work as well as looking after the park's residents' welfare. The business could not therefore be said to consist wholly or mainly of holding investments (see *Furness v IRC* Spc202 (1999) STI 1316).

(c) But in another case the number of sales of caravans was small, and the company's accounts showed that: pitch fees exceeded the proceeds from caravan sales in four out of the six years. Where the commissioner concluded that the pitch fees were not ancillary to the income from caravan sales, rather the reverse, and that the company's business consisted mainly of holding and making investments. The HMRC's notice of determination denying business property relief was accordingly upheld (see *Weston (executor of Weston, deceased) v IRC* SpC 222 (1999) STI 1890).

(d) This is yet another case (*IRC v George and Another* (2003)) concerning business property relief and the status of caravan site operations. The Court of Appeal allowed the taxpayers' appeal this long running saga over the availability of business property relief for caravan sites. The appellants were the executors of the will of the deceased, who held 85 per cent of the shares in a company which owned land on which it ran, and provided services to, caravan sites. Those services included caravan storage, warehousing the a shop, and fields licensed to farmers for grazing animals. They appealed against a High Court decision denying business property relief.

The Court of Appeal held that the holding of property as an investment was only one component of the business. The Special Commissioner had found that it was not the main component. Also, it was difficult to see why such an active family business should be excluded from business property relief, merely because a necessary component of its profit-making activity was the use of land.

(e) On the particular facts of the case, the special commissioner allowed the appeal of a farming estate's executors against the inspector's refusal of business property relief. The deceased, who died in 1997, carried on the business of farming and letting surplus properties on the farm. For most of the eight years preceding his death, the farming turnover exceeded the rents received, but the net profit form the lettings exceeded the net profit from the farm. The probate value of the farmhouse, farm buildings and farm land exceeded that of the let properties. The HMRC determined that the business consisted mainly of making and holding investments and was thus ineligible for business property relief under s 104, IHTA. The commissioner considered that the overall context of the business, the capital employed, the time spent by the employees and the levels of turnover, supported the conclusion that the business consisted mainly of farming, while the profit figures supported the opposing view. The commissioner concluded that, when the whole business was considered in the round and predominance was not given to any one factor, the business consisted mainly of farming and not making or holding investments. Accordingly, the executors' appeal was allowed (see *Farmer and another (executors of Farmer deceased) v IRC* SpC 216 (1999) STI 1684).

Valuation

The valuation of relevant business property (IHTA 1984 ss 110-112) is based on the net value, that is, the value of the assets used in the business (including goodwill) less the liabilities incurred for the purposes of the business (IHTA 1984 s 110). The value of a member of a group is ascertained as if any company with an excluded business, was not a member of a group. For this purpose, a company is not regarded as having an excluded business if its business consists wholly or mainly of holding properties wholly or mainly occupied by members of the group whose businesses are not excluded (IHTA 1984 s 111). The value of individual assets is not eligible for relief if they were not used wholly or mainly for the business throughout the whole or the last two years of ownership prior to the transfer of value or are not, at the time of the transfer, required for future use for the business (IHTA 1984 s 112). For this purpose, the business of members of a group which are not to be left out of account under the rule stated above are in effect treated as one business. An asset for which the minimum period requirement need not be fulfilled because of a death, need be so used only between the two transfers. Apportionment may be made where part of any land or building is not used exclusively for business purposes, i.e is used for personal benefits, and the relief would not otherwise accrue (IHTA 1984 s 112).

Minimum period of ownership

A transfer of value is to be reduced by a percentage of the value of any relevant business property which has been held for a minimum period of two years immediately preceding the transfer (IHTA 1984 s 106) or replaced other property which qualified, and the two or more properties were owned by the transferor for at least two years out of the last five years. (IHTA 1984 s 107).

Minority shareholdings do not qualify as replacement property, but changes due to reorganization of share capital, a conversion or amalgamation or reconstruction during the two year period are related back to the original acquisition if they would be so treated for the purposes of capital gains tax (IHTA 1984 s 107).

If the property was not held for the minimum period as defined above, but the property was acquired by the transferor or spouse by a transfer on which relief was or would have been due, and either the earlier or later transfer took place on death, relief would still be due (IHTA 1984 s 109).

Relief

The relief (IHTA 1984 s 104) is given by a percentage reduction of the value transferred before tax appropriate to the class of property as follows:

	Percentage reduction in value transferred
Business property relief	%
• Interest in a business	100
• farm tenancy held personally	100
• Listed shares giving control	50
• Unlisted shares (including companies quoted on AIM)	100
• Fixed assets used by a company which the transferor controls or by a partnership in which the transferor is a partner	50
• Trust property used by a life tenant in own business	50

Relief cannot be obtained if relief for agricultural property (above) has been claimed on the value of the same assets. The relief for woodlands is to be deducted before calculating the value of trees or underwood eligible for business relief (IHTA 1984 s 114).

Business relief is available to members of the London Stock Exchange and the London International Futures and Options Exchange.

1.3.3 Amounts receivable

Debts and other rights to receive a sum due under any obligation are to be assumed to be good, except to the extent that recovery is impossible or not reasonably practicable, unless due to the act or omission of the person to whom the sum is due (IHTA 1984 s 166).

Using a little-known concession, IHT relief can be claimed for accountants' fees incurred in obtaining an income tax repayment, where the repayment falls into the estate. The concession is published only in the Capital Taxes General Examination Manual (para 17.11). Maximum relief is to equal 10% of the repayment.

1.3.4 Land sold within three years of death

If an interest in land comprised in the deceased's estate is sold within this period for less than 95% of its value on death or for at least £1,000 less than its value on death, its value may be reduced to the 'sale value', on a claim made by any person liable for the inheritance tax on it. A disposal outside this period under a compulsory purchase in pursuance of a notice to treat served before death or within three years after death also qualifies (IHTA 1984 ss 190-198).

A sale is excluded from the relief if it is either:
- a sale by a personal representative or trustee to:

  (a) one who has been beneficially entitled to, or to an interest in possession in, the interest sold; or

  (b) the spouse, child or remoter descendant of a person within para. (a); or

  (c) trustees of a settlement under which a person within para.'s (a) or (b) has an interest in possession in the interest sold;

- a sale which does not exclude the vendor or anyone within para.'s (a) to (c) above from acquiring any interest in the land in question.

Sale value means the price for which it is sold or, if greater, the best consideration that could reasonably have been obtained for it at the time of sale, ignoring in each case any incidental expenses, but adjusted for certain intervening transactions, namely:

- a change, in the nature of incidents of the interest or in the state, or incidents of the land in which it subsists, which reduces or increases the value (IHTA 1984 s 193);

- depreciation of a lease for less than fifty years is added back (IHTA 1984 s 194 and TCGA 1992 Sch 8);

- the reduction in the price obtained because the interest was sold separately from any interest held within it at death is added back (IHTA 1984 s 195);

- the profit on any other sale of interest in land (including 'excluded' sales) and on any exchange of land within the three year period is offset (IHTA 1984 s 196);

  purchase of any interest in land between the death and four months after the last relevant sale, excluding a compulsory sale completed outside the three years relief is withdrawn to the extent that purchases match sales in value

(IHTA 1984 s 192).

The time of sale or purchase is when the contract is entered into, subject to special provision for compulsory acquisitions (FA 1975 Sch. 10 para 40).

Appeals against determinations of the value of land made by the HMRC are to be directed to the Lands Tribunal, not the Special Commissioners after the Royal Assent to the 1993 Finance Act.

1.3.5 Leases
Reversions on leases treated as settlements are valued at the full value of the property concerned multiplied by the consideration actually received on grant and divided by the value of the full consideration at the time of the grant (IHTA 1984 s 170).

1.3.6 Life assurance policies and annuities
Life policies and contracts for annuities commencing on death are to be valued at not less than the aggregate of all premiums or other sums paid thereunder, less the aggregate of any receipts therefrom, except when the transfer of value arises on death or does not result in the policy ceasing to be part of the transferor's estate and in the case of certain term assurances (IHTA 1984 s 167).

In other words, surrender value (assuming that to be open market value) is taken only when it exceeds net aggregate premiums, etc., paid. However, in the case of unit-linked policies, the value of the units allocated, if less than net aggregate premiums, is taken.

1.3.7 Related property
Assets of the transferor's spouse, and of any settlement made before 27 March 1974, by the transferor or his spouse in which no interest in possession subsists, are regarded as part of the transferor's holding in respect of transfers of value before 10 March 1981 (IHTA 1984 s 161). Related property also includes any property which has been transferred under an exempt transfer made after 15 April 1976, to a charity or other body by the transferor or spouse, even if the property is no longer owned by that body but was so owned within the preceding five years (FA 1976 s 103; applies to transfers of value after 15 April 1976). The value of the estate property and the related property transferred is apportioned in the proportion that the value of the estate property bears to the aggregate values. In the case of the shares, debentures and units of any other type of property, the apportionment is based on the number of shares, etc; and not the values.

Valuation of half share of farm
In *Arkwright and another (personal representatives of Williams, decd) v IRC* SpC 392 Mr and Mrs W owned Ash Land Farm as tenants in common in equal shares which they occupied together until the death of Mr W.

Under the terms of his will Mr W gave to Mrs W a life interest in Mr W's 50% share of the tenancy in common of Ash Lane Farm, with the remainder to his daughters.

In January 2002, Mrs W and the daughters amended the will by Deed of Variation so that Mr W's interest in Ash Lane vested in his daughters.

The open market value of Ash Lane Farm immediately before the death of Mr W was £550,000. The HMRC were of the view that inheritance tax was due on one-half of that value, namely £275,000. HMRC took the position that Mr W's interest was a mathematical one-half of the vacant possession value by applying the related property rules.

The personal representatives appealed claiming that the value of Mr W's interest was less than a mathematical one-half of the vacant possession value of Ash Lane Farm because immediately before his death Mrs W had the right to occupy the house and not have it sold without her consent. Under such circumstances a discount of 15% is commonly applied.

The Special Commissioner decided that the value of the father's share should be discounted to take into account the right of occupation of the spouse.

Next the Commissioner addressed what effect the related property rule had, if any, on Mr W's interest. Mrs W's interest as tenant in common of Ash Lane Farm fell within the meaning of related property and thus special valuation rules applied. These special rules required one to first determine the value of the aggregate; then the value of each share separately and establish a ratio; then the ratio had to be applied to the aggregate; and, if the value of the deceased's share of the aggregate was greater than the value of his separate share, the value of his share was taken to be his part of the aggregate.

Where one had units of property like shares the ratio of the related property value was the ratio of the smaller number to the greater number. HMRC had argued that the shares of Mr and Mrs W were "units of any other description of property" from which it followed that the ratio was one-half.

The personal representatives claimed that this rule did not apply because incorporeal shares in land were not "units of property" because a percentage of half share could not be a unit but was rather a fraction of a unit. The Commissioner agreed with the personal representatives' interpretation that this rule did not apply to Mr and Mrs W's interests.

Therefore, the decrease in value of Mr W's interest in Ash Lane Farm, which occurred by reason of his death, had to be taken into account when determining the value of his interest immediately before his death.

N.B. It should be remembered that when gifts of shares of property are made, this principle may have implications regarding the size of the PET. These are always calculated using the diminution of the estate concept. Accordingly, let us assume that a father gifts half his house to his daughter (tenants in common) as she also lives there. This should take them into the exemption from the GWR rules contained in Section 102B(4) IHTA 1984 (as a result of the FA 1999 changes). Say that the property were worth £500,000. The value of the PET would not be £250,000 (50% of the whole) but £287,500 (£500,000 - (£250,000 X 85%)). Clearly the PET exceeds the nil band which could lead to the daughter paying tax if the PET fails. Obviously a reduced value asset is then retained in Father's estate.

1.3.8 Related property sold within three years after death
Where the estate of a deceased person includes related property, or other property valued in conjunction with property comprised in the estate but not vested in the vendors of the former property at any time since death a claim may be made for relief by reduction of the valuation on death if the property is sold within three years after death (IHTA 1984 s 176). The reduction is the amount by which the value of the sold property was increased on death because it was valued in conjunction with related or such other property as above.

The relief is available only where the sale price, adjusted for intervening changes in circumstances, is less than the valuation on death allowing for any difference in circumstances between the times of death and the sale.

The sale must satisfy the following conditions:
- the vendors are the personal representatives or other person (e.g. a surviving joint tenant) in whom the property vested on death; and

- the sale is at arm's length for a price freely negotiated at the time of the sale and not made in conjunction with a sale of the related or other property in question; and

- no person interested in the sale, nor any connected person, must have an interest in the purchase; and

- it must be an outright sale of the interests of vendors.

In the case of shares or securities in a close company there must have been no intervening reduction (of more than 5%) in their value on account of an alteration of extinguishment of rights in the capital of the company.

1.3.9 Restrictions on freedom to dispose
Restrictions on the right to dispose of an asset created by contract are to be taken into account in valuing that asset on the first chargeable transfer relating to that

asset, but only to the extent that consideration was given (IHTA 1984 s 163). This creates an exception to the rule which applied for estate duty, that a restriction on the transferability of property is to be ignored on the hypothetical sale assumed for valuation purposes but is to be assumed to apply thereafter (Please see Unquoted Shares and Securities, p.518) (*CIR v Crossman* H L 1936). It has been suggested, that a purely personal restriction intended to apply only to a particular owner which cannot be treated on the same footing as a general restriction which 'runs with' the asset (*Thorn v CIR* ChD 1976, a stamp duty case).

1.3.10 Shares and securities
Quoted shares and securities
The established rule applied in practice is that the value of quoted shares and securities is the lesser of:

*   the lower of the two prices quoted in the Stock Exchange Daily Official List for the relevant date, plus a quarter of the difference between the two prices; and

*   the average of the highest and lowest prices for normal bargains marked on that date.

If there is no trading on that date the prices to be used are the latest previous or earlier subsequent dates whichever gives the lower figure.

In the case of unit trusts, the value is the lower of the two prices published by the managers of the trust.

Where special circumstances exist and the quoted prices are not a true measure of the market value, the shares are valued on the same basis as unquoted shares to ascertain the open market value.

Quoted shares sold within 12 months after death
Where qualifying shares are sold within 12 months after death, a reduction is made in the value of the investments sold if the values at the date of death of the shares sold exceeds the sales proceeds of all sales. The reduction is the difference between the values at the date of death, and the sales proceeds (IHTA 1984 s 179).

The reduction is, however, further proportionately reduced to the extent that reinvestment in the share investment takes place by the claimant within the period from death to two months after the last sale concerned (IHTA 1984 s 180). The claim must be made by the person actually paying the tax attributable to the investments and personal representatives and trustees are to be treated as a single and continuing body of persons (IHTA 1984 s 178).

Where only a part of a holding of investments is comprised in an estate (e.g. the deceased is a joint tenant of a settled estate), the whole of the holding is included in the calculation and the reduction in the loss on sale is determined by the proportion which the value of the part holding bears to the value of the whole holding. Investments exchanged for other property, not necessarily quoted securities, when their value exceeds the value on death are to be treated as sold on that date at market value, unless the exchange is one which is not treated as a disposal for capital gains tax purposes (IHTA 1984 s 184). Any capital consideration (including the sale proceeds of rights) received at any time after death from investments sold within 12 months of death is to be added to the gross proceeds of sale or best consideration (IHTA 1984 s 181). Similarly, the value on death is to be increased by calls paid at any time on such investments but not so as to create a greater loss than if no additions were made (IHTA 1984 s 181). Exchanges and reorganisations of securities or units, not treated as disposals for capital gains tax are ignored. The new holding is treated as the same as the original holding, any new consideration given for the new holding being added to the value of the original holding on death, but not so as to create a greater loss than if no additions were made.

If any investments comprised in the new holding is sold, the value on death of these investments shall be determined by the formula:

$$\frac{Vs(H - S)}{(Vs + Vr)}$$

where Vs is the sale value of the investments; Vr is the market value at the time of the sale of any investments remaining in the holding after the sale; H is the value on death of the new holding; and S is the value on death of any investments which are originally comprised in the new holding but have been sold on a previous occasion or occasions (IHTA 1984 s 183).

If additions (other than on exchange or reorganisation) are made to a holding before the sale, the sale is deemed to comprise investments held at death in the same proportion as they bear to all the investments of that description held before the sale (IHTA 1984 s 185).

The relief is available if, although the quotation was suspended at death, it has been restored at the time of sale or exchange (IHTA 1984 s 178).

The time of sale or purchase is the date of entering into a contract or, where the transaction results from the exercise of an option, the date of its grant (IHTA 1984 s 189).

It will be necessary, for some purposes (e.g. capital gains tax on subsequent disposals) to know the value of specific investments as at the date of death but after allowing for a due proportion of the above loss relief (IHTA 1984 s 187). This is ascertained as follows.

The gross proceeds of sale (or best consideration), including capital amounts received, will become the base cost, so that the costs of sale will be a CGT loss. However, that value is to be reduced by calls paid or new consideration given on an exempt exchange, etc. for these will be allowable costs for CGT. Where there has been reinvestment, so as to cause total or partial loss of relief, the value of any specific investment is to be increased by a proportion of the difference between its value as above and its value on death, if the latter exceeds the former, and reduced by a proportion of that difference in the converse case. The proportion is that by which the relief is reduced on account of reinvestment

Relief for loss on quoted investments
There is an important post-mortem relief where there is a sale of quoted investments within the period of 12 months immediately following the date of death. This will be an important case, *Leigh and Another (Executors of Leigh Deceased) v IRC* (2002) SpC 349, for those dealing with probate and the valuation of estates during a time of falling stock market prices.

The deceased died on 20 November 2000 and at the time of his death held an investment in an equity income fund. His executors made enquiries of the fund's provider in December 2000 but were told there were no investments held by the deceased. However, after making further enquiries the executors discovered the deceased's investment in February 2002 by which time the investment was lower than at the date of death. The executors' appealed against a notice of determination dated 30 August 2002 stating that as the investment had not been sold within 12 months of the deceased's death no relief for sales at a loss within that period was available.

The Special Commission dismissed the appeal and confirmed the notice of determination. Although he was sympathetic to the executors' difficulties he stated that Parliament had not provided for the case where through no fault of the executors' assets were discovered more than 12 months after death by which time they had gone down in value.

This case reminds us of the importance of making prompt enquiries as to the investments held by a deceased person. If relief is required those assets must be sold within 12 months of the date of death in order to substitute the realisation proceeds instead of the probate value.

Unquoted shares and securities
The general principles stated previously apply but, in addition, such assets are to be valued on the assumption that there is available to the purchaser all the information which a prudent prospective purchaser might reasonably require on a purchase by private treaty at arm's length, whether or not it may be expected to be obtained (IHTA 1984 s 168).

If shares of more than one class will fetch more if sold together, such a sale is to be assumed (*A. G. Ceylon v Mackie* PC 1952). A dormant company has been valued at approximately two-thirds of what would be realized on winding up (*Re Courthope* KBB 1928). On the other hand, it has been said of a property company, that even though a purchaser could not force a winding-up, it may be assumed that the other shareholders would concur in realizing the company's assets to the best advantage (*M'Connel's Trustees v CIR* C SS 1927). As a rule of thumb, for equity shares carrying less than a controlling interest (less than 50%), dividend yield is of prime importance. For holdings of 10-24.9% account must be taken of the influence wielded in a general meeting, assuming other interests to be smaller. Over 25% holdings can block a special resolution. More than 50% of the equity enables distribution policy and the constitution of the Board to be controlled, so that earnings assume more importance. Over 75% interest in the equity enables special resolutions to be passed, so that assets assume some importance. However, only in exceptional circumstances should a going concern be valued on a break-up basis.

Investments cancelled
Where qualifying investments are cancelled within 12 months following death, without being replaced by other shares or securities, they are treated as having been sold for a nominal consideration of one pound (FA 1993 s 198).

Dealings suspended
Where dealings for investments on a recognised stock exchange or the Unlisted Securities Market are suspended at the end of 12 months after death they are valued as at the latter date, assuming that value exceeds the value at death (FA 1993 s 198).

Jointly owned property
In *Barrett v HMRC* the tax case concerned the valuation of half a house on the death of one of the owners.

Mr Barrett (B) was joint owner of a semi-detached house built in the 1930s. When he died in 2002 the Revenue determined the value of his interest in the property as £144,500. His personal representative (who was the joint-owner) appealed, contending that the house should be valued at £288,000 and that with a 15% discount for the joint ownership, the value of B's interest should be taken as £122,400.

The Lands Tribunal (23.11.05) reviewed the evidence in detail and held that the house should be valued at £315,000. Using a 15% discount for joint ownership, the value of B's interest was therefore £133,875.

The Revenue's valuation was based on the following approach:

*   To arrive at an unadjusted value for the subject-property by reference to four

comparable properties;

* To make a deduction for the particular condition of the property compared to the comparables and for two specific matters; and

* Finally to reduce the value by an agreed figure of 15% for joint ownership and by 50% to arrive at the half-share owned by B at the date of the hypothetical disposal on 19.7.02.

The two specific matters affecting the valuation were firstly a shared driveway which represented a serious disadvantage in comparison with the other properties and merited a discount. Secondly, the existence of a long-running dispute over the shared driveway would not be given as much weight by a hypothetical purchaser as it was by the hypothetical vendor (the PR) in reaching her discount.

The most significant aspect of this case is the confirmation that a 15% discount should be applied in the case of jointly owned property.

1.4 Returns
Revenue & Customs has an initiative to ensure that the inheritance tax returns of dead people match the earnings that they declared during their lifetime.

The Special Compliance Office, HMRC's investigative arm, compare inheritance tax returns with returns completed during the deceased's lifetime.

If there is evidence that the deceased underpaid tax, they will then seek to determine how much was owed at death. Beneficiaries must wait until the end of the inquiry to see how much of the deceased's estate is left for them.

Accounts (i.e. returns) by persons liable for tax are dealt with in IHTA 1984 ss 216-218). The 1999 Finance Act strengthened and updated the voluntary compliance of the administration and collection of Inheritance Tax.

In relation to potentially exempt transfers the recipient is required to deliver to the Board an account specifying, to the best of his or her knowledge and belief, all property to the value of which tax is (or would if chargeable be) attributable and its value. For deaths occurring on or after 9 March 1999, personal representatives are, in addition, required to include in their account details of any chargeable transfers made by the deceased within the seven years before his/her death. This information is also relevant in determining the amount of any tax chargeable on the death estate. If a full account has already been made by some other person, other than by a co-trustee, no further account need be delivered. The time limit for submission of the accounts is 12 months from the end of the month in which the death occurs.

Personal representatives are to specify all property which formed part of the deceased's estate immediately before his or her death and its value. However, a provisional estimate of the value (to be followed by a further account when ascertained) may be submitted if the exact value is not ascertainable after reasonable enquiries.

The time limit for submission of the accounts is 12 months from death or, if later, three months from the date the representatives first act as such.

Persons liable on assets of national interest which fail to satisfy the conditions of exemption, or on disposal of woodlands, must render an account within six months of the end of the month of the chargeable event.

Persons (except barristers) concerned professionally in the making of a settlement are required to notify the Board of the names and addresses of the settlors and trustees within three months of making the settlement, if they know or have reason to believe:

- that the settlor was domiciled in the UK; and
- that the trustees are not (or will not be) resident in the UK

A return is not necessary for a will trust nor if one has been made by any other person (IHTA 1984 s 218).

Defective accounts must be corrected within six months of the person's discovery of any material defect or omission (IHTA 1984 s 217).

Other information may be required from any persons for the purposes of inheritance tax and must be given within 30 days of written notice by the Board. Such a notice may be combined with one relating to income tax but may not (with minor exceptions) invade the professional privilege of barristers and solicitors.

Accounts and other documents are to be in the form prescribed by the Board and may be required to be supported by books, papers and other documents and to be verified on oath or otherwise (IHTA 1984 s 257).

Where an estate is straightforward and qualifies as an <u>excepted estate</u>, the personal representatives are not required to submit a return to HMRC. An excepted estate is one which satisfies all of the following conditions.

These are estates where there can be no liability to tax because the gross value of the estate does not exceed the IHT nil-rate band.

The conditions for these estates are that

- the deceased died on or after 6 April 2004, domiciled in the United Kingdom, and

- the gross value of the estate, including

  (a) the deceased's share of any jointly owned assets
  (b) any specified transfers
  (c) any 'specified exempt transfers'

does not exceed the nil-rate band, where (for deaths on or after 1 September 2006)

  (a) if the estate includes any assets held in trust, they are held in a single trust and the gross value does not exceed £150,000,

  (b) if the estate includes foreign assets, their gross value does not exceed £100,000,

  (c) if there are any 'specified transfers' (IHTM06018) their chargeable value does not exceed £150,000,

  (d) the deceased had not made a gift with reservation of benefit, and

  (e) a charge does not arise under IHTA1984/S.151A-C (IHT charge on an alternatively secured pension fund).

For these purposes, the IHT nil-rate band means the amount above which IHT is payable that applied at the date of death. The one exception to this rule is where

- the deceased died after 5 April but before 6 August in any one year, and
- a grant of representation is applied for before the 6 August.

Where this is the case, it is the IHT nil-rate band from the tax year before that in which the deceased died that applies.

Examples:
Joan Brown died on 9 May 2007 and the grant was taken out on 21 July 2007. The correct threshold to use was £285,000.

David Smith died on 7 June 2007 and the grant was taken out on 21 August 2007. The correct threshold to use was £300,000.

- the deceased was domiciled in the United Kingdom;

- none of the assets of the estate pass under the terms of a trust or involves a "gift with reservation";

- the value of the estate outside the United Kingdom totals not more than

£75,000; and

- any taxable lifetime gifts within seven years of death were only cash, quoted shares or quoted securities, totalling in value not more than £100,000.

Deceased Estates - procedures for Income Tax and CGT (Tax Bulletin 66)
New Practice (for deaths after 5 April 2003)
For estates where the date of death was on or after 6 April 2003, HMRC will normally accept a simple computation of the estate's Self Assessment liability if:

- the estate is not regarded as complex (see below), and
- the tax arising during the whole of the administration period is less than £10,000.

In these cases, HMRC will provide the personal representative with a payslip to allow them to pay the tax due. In all cases where the tax liability for the whole of the administration period is £10,000 or more, or where the estate is one we regard as complex, HMRC will still require Self Assessment returns. (HMRC Trusts offices will normally issue these, not local service offices.)

HMRC regard an estate as complex where:
- there is a very high probate/confirmation value, generally over **£2.5 million**, or

- the administration of the estate is continuing and has entered the third income tax year from the date of death, or

- the personal representatives have disposed of a chargeable capital asset, and the proceeds of sale exceed **£250,000**.

1.5 Notice of determination
Notice of determination (i.e. assessments) may be given by notice in writing to any person who appears to be a claimant of relief or to be liable for any of the tax chargeable on any transfer of value or capital distribution (IHTA 1984 s 221). The notice of determination may specify any matters relevant to the charge and collection or repayment of inheritance tax and shall be in accordance with accounts or returns made, if the Board are satisfied therewith, or shall be made to the best of the Board's judgement in any other case.

The time limit for, and manner of, appealing against any determination must be stated in the notice of determination.

Unless varied by agreement in writing or on appeal, a notice is conclusive against the person on whom served.

Determinations made on the basis of a view of the law generally received or adopted in practice, but subsequently shown to be wrong, cannot be revised once payment has been made and accepted in satisfaction thereof (IHTA 1984 s 255).

A notice of determination which has become conclusive, i.e. no longer varied or quashed on appeal, is sufficient evidence of all matters therein.

1.6 Appeals

An appeal against any determination may be made in writing within 30 days of the service of the notice of determination, specifying the grounds of appeal. The appeal will be heard by the Special Commissioners (or, in the case of land and buildings valuations, the Lands Tribunal) unless the appellant and the Board agree to go directly to the High Court. In the absence of such an agreement, the High Court, on application by the appellant, may give leave for an appeal directly to it, if satisfied that the substance of the appeal relates to matters of law. The Lands Tribunal has exclusive jurisdiction to determine the value of land in the UK (IHTA 1984 s 222).

Appeals may be made out of time with the consent of the Board or, if it refuses, of the Special Commissioners (IHTA 1984 s 223).

Appeal from the Special Commissioners or the Lands Tribunal on a point of law lies to the High Court by way of case stated, if a written request (accompanied by a fee of £25) is made to the Special Commissioners within 30 days of their determination. The case stated must be transmitted to the High Court within 30 days of its receipt and a copy of it must be sent to every other party at or before the time of transmission. The High Court may affirm, reserve or amend the Special Commissioners determination, may remit the case stated for amendment, or make such other order as it thinks fit (IHTA 1984 s 225).

Representation may be by a barrister, solicitor, or any accountant of an incorporated society of accountants, or, with leave, by any other person. There is power to require production of books, etc. and witnesses may be summoned and may be examined on oath. They may allow amendment of the grounds of appeal (IHTA 1984 s 224).

The Board may require a person, having custody or possession of property to be valued, to allow reasonable access, on pain of a fine, on summary conviction, of up to £20 for one who wilfully delays or obstructs the Board's agent (IHTA 1984 s 220).

1.7 Payment of tax

1.7.1 Payment of IHT - change from 5 November 2007

HMRC announced a change from 5 November 2007 to the process for making the initial payment of inheritance tax on delivery of form IHT200. Where payment is sent by cheque, it will have to be accompanied by a bank-approved payslip carrying an IHT reference. This means that executors or their advisers need to contact HMRC to obtain an IHT reference and the payslip before submitted form IHT200. HMRC says that this should be done - as a minimum - three weeks before you expect to be delivering form IHT200.

This new process should also be used to obtain a reference number before paying under the Direct Payment Scheme or with funds with National Savings.

Applications for a reference number must be made, in writing, for any case where there is tax to pay on delivery of form IHT200. There will be two ways to do this:

- online through the HMRC website. This options will be available from 22 October; or

- by post, using form D21, which can be downloaded from the HMRC website or a paper copy obtained from the Forms Orderline on 0845 30 20 900.

HMRC will allocate a reference to the estate and send details of the reference together with a payslip and a pre-addressed envelope by post. it will aim to reply within five working days for online requests and within 15 working days for postal requests.

When paying the tax, the completed payslip and the cheque (but nothing else) should be put in the pre-addressed envelope and sent to the HMRC Cashiers at Nottingham. The form IHT200 and supporting papers should be sent to HMRC Capital Taxes at either Nottingham or Edinburgh (as appropriate).

1.7.2 General rule
Inheritance tax is normally due six months after the end of the month in which death occurs. Additional tax on a potentially exempt transfer, chargeable on account of the transferor's death within seven years, is due six months from the end of the month of the death (IHTA 1984 s 226).

Personal representatives must pay the whole amount of tax on delivery of their account (or return) and may then pay any other tax which they have been asked to discharge by the persons liable (IHTA 1984 ss 227-228).

An election may be made by notice in writing for the tax payable on any potentially exempt transfer arising on death to be paid by 10 equal yearly instalments commencing six months after the transfer so far as it is attributable to the value of:

(a) land and buildings wherever situated;

(b) shares or securities of a company controlled by the deceased;

(c) unquoted shares or securities not within para. (b) provided that not less than 20% of the total tax chargeable is attributable thereto or to other assets in respect of which postponement is possible, or the Board are satisfied that the tax attributable to the value of the shares or securities cannot be paid in one sum without undue hardship; or

(d)   unquoted shares (not within para. (b)) of a value in excess of £20,000 and representing 10% of the nominal value of all shares in the company at death or being ordinary shares (FA 1975 Sch 4 para 3), 10% of all shares of that class at the time of death; or

(e)   a business (including a profession or vocation) carried on for gain or an interest in such a business.

A business within para. (e) is to be taken at the net value of the assets (including goodwill) of the business, less all liabilities incurred for the purposes of the business, and an interest in a business is to be valued without regard to non-business assets or liabilities.

1.7.3 Interest on instalments
Interest at the prescribed rate is added to each instalment where applicable and payable accordingly (IHTA 1984 s 234; FA 1975 Sch. 4 para 19(1); SI 1982 No. 1585).

The whole amount of the tax outstanding and interest accrued thereon may be paid at any time, and the tax and interest thereon must be paid if and when any of the assets concerned are:

•   sold, or

•   otherwise disposed of (except on another death) if the original transfer was not made on death, or

•   cease to be settled property if the original transfer was the termination of an interest in possession in settled property. The payment, under any partnership agreement or otherwise, of any sum in satisfaction of the whole or any part of an interest in a business otherwise than on a sale, is to be treated as a sale.

1.7.4 Interest on unpaid tax and overpayments of tax
Interest is chargeable on any unpaid tax from the due date to the date of payment at the prescribed rates.

Where HMRC accepts works of art, historic buildings, etc., after 16 March 1987 in satisfaction of tax the interest may be calculated up to the date of the offer and not the date of acceptance. The choice of the valuation will be the taxpayer's (FA 1987 s 60).

The additional tax chargeable on a potentially exempt transfer arising on account of the death of the transferor within seven years is regarded as arising from a transfer on the death as are also gifts to charities or political parties where liabilities arise because of the transferor's death within one year of the making of the gift.

Where a transfer has been reported late, the amount on which interest is payable is not to be increased in respect of any time before the expiry of six months from the date of discovery.

Interest is payable to the taxpayer on any repayment of tax or interest and the interest will be at the prescribed rates from the date of payment to the date of repayment.

Interest paid or received is not taken into account for income tax or corporation tax purposes.

1.7.5 Adjustments for underpayments or overpayments

Underpayments of tax and interest (IHTA 1984 ss 240-241) may be recovered, even though the liability was settled in accordance with a notice of determination, unless either:

- a certificate of discharge has been granted (IHTA 1984 s 239); or

- the limitation period has expired after the submission of an account and the making of a payment in accordance therewith, which is accepted by the Board in full satisfaction of the tax due.

On the expiry of the limitation period, any HMRC charge for the tax is also extinguished.

The **limitation period** is six years from the later of:
- the date of payment (or last payment of an instalment) of tax which was accepted; and

- the due date of that tax (or last instalment of tax), except that in the case of fraud, wilful default or negligence, time begins to run only from the time when the defect comes to the knowledge of the Board.

Overpayments of inheritance tax or interest proved to the satisfaction of the Board must be made on a claim within six years from the payment (or last payment of instalments).

1.7.6 Surrender of property in discharge of tax

The Board may, with the agreement of the Secretary of State, accept property as stated below, in whole or part payment of tax (IHTA 1984 ss 230-231). The acceptable properties are:

- any land as may be agreed between the Board and the person liable to tax;

- objects which are or have been kept in buildings surrendered for tax or estate duty, or in certain buildings of national importance, if the Treasury thinks it is desirable for the objects to remain associated with the building; certain articles of national, historic, scientific or artistic interest;

- any property liable to be sold in order to raise money for the payment of tax.

1.8 Recovery of tax
1.8.1 HMRC charge for unpaid tax and interest
An HMRC charge may be imposed on any property to the value of which any unpaid tax or interest is attributable and on any property comprised in a settlement where the chargeable transfer is the making of the settlement or any subsequent chargeable event (IHTA 1984 ss 237-238). The charge is postponed to any incumbrance allowable in valuing the property for inheritance tax. However, it takes priority over any disposition of the property, unless the purchaser had no notice of the facts giving rise to the charge, or a certificate of discharge had been given by the Board and the purchaser had no notice of any fact invalidating the certificate. Notice includes constructive notice. A 'purchaser' means a purchaser in good faith, for consideration in money or money's worth which is not nominal, and includes a lessee, mortgagee or other person who for such consideration acquires an interest in the property.

If property is disposed of to a purchaser, and at the time of the disposition:
- in the case of land in England and Wales, the charge was not registered as a land charge, or in the case of registered land, was not protected by notice on the register;

- in the case of land in Northern Ireland the title to which is registered under the Local Registration of Title (Ireland) Act 1891, the charge was not entered as a burden on the appropriate register maintained under that Act or was not protected by a caution or inhibition under that Act or, in the case of other land, the purchaser had no notice of the facts giving rise to the charge;

the property will cease to be the subject of HMRC charge, but the property representing it will be the subject of HMRC charge. When an HMRC charge remains in effect after a disposition (e.g. by registration or actual notice), it will cease to have effect six years after the later of:

- the due date of the tax; and

- the date on which a full and proper account (or return) of the property was first submitted.

Up to 9 March 1999, on a chargeable transfer on death, an HMRC charge did not attach to property vesting in personal representatives, if it was personal or moveable property (including leaseholds, joint tenancies and tenancies in common) situated in the UK, which was beneficially owned by the deceased (other than by virtue of owning an interest in possession) immediately before death.

This anomaly has been removed by extending HMRC protective charge to cover

• leasehold interests, for deaths occurring on or after 9 March 1999;

• tax charged on or after that date in respect of assets previously given heritage tax reliefs.

1.8.2 Legal proceedings for recovery of inheritance tax or interest
Agreement in writing, or determination by notice, of the amount due is a prerequisite to recovery proceedings but, where appeal is made against a notice of determination, only an amount agreed or determined not to be in dispute may be recovered, pending the outcome of the appeal at first instance. If a further appeal is made the amount determined at first instance may be recovered (IHTA 1984 ss 242-244).

Unpaid tax on interest may be recovered out of any property to which it is attributable and which is being administered by a court.

1.8.3 Certificate of discharge
There are two types of certificates of discharge (IHTA 1984 s 239).

Property
The Board must on application, and on being satisfied that the tax has been or will be paid, may give a certificate to that effect.

Persons
These must be given by the Board if:
• application is made more than two years (or at the Board's discretion, any shorter period) after the death of a person who is or might be liable for any inheritance tax; and

• the applicant submits a full account (or return) of all property concerned in the transfer of value or capital distribution; and

• the tax (if any) determined to be due thereon has been paid.

No certificate is valid in a case of fraud or failure to disclose material facts and does not protect against recovery of additional inheritance tax which becomes due on discovery of property omitted from an account of a deceased person's estate or arising from a variation or disclaimer after death.

The property certificate above remains valid in favour of a purchaser without notice of any facts invalidating the certificate.

Property means any property directly or indirectly representing it.

1.9 Penalties
Proceedings for recovery of penalties (IHTA 1984 ss 245-253) by the Board may be taken before the Special Commissioners (by summary proceedings) or in the High Court (as a civil proceeding by the Crown). Appeal lies to the first Tier Tax Tribunal either party, on a question of law, or by the defendant, on the amount of the penalty. In the latter case, it should be noticed that the penalty may be increased, reduced or confirmed (IHTA 1984 s 249). The Board has discretion to mitigate or remit penalties (IHTA 1984 s 253).

1.9.1 Time limit for recovery proceedings
Proceedings must be brought within three years of the date on which the Inheritance Tax properly due, in respect of the chargeable transfer concerned, was notified to any of the persons liable for any of it. The death of any person who has incurred a penalty does not affect the time limit or the right to recover it from his estate (IHTA 1984 s 250).

1.9.2 Awards of penalties
Non-compliance, fraud, delay etc. attract stricter penalties.

1.9.3 Constructive negligence
A person who renders an account, etc. is deemed to be negligent if it comes to his notice that it was incorrect in a material respect and he unreasonably delays in remedying the error (IHTA 1984 s 248). A person (who did not render the account, etc.) who discovers an error whereby inheritance tax, for which he is liable, has been or might be underpaid has a duty to inform the Board and is deemed to be negligent if he unreasonably delays in doing so.

1.10 Management
Management of Inheritance Tax is with the Board of HMRC (IHTA 1984 s 215). The department dealing with the tax is the Capital Taxes Office in London.

Only one copy of accounts need to be submitted, unless a copy of the account as amended by the office is required, when two should be submitted. In the case of inheritance tax payable by instalments, the account should include those due up to the delivery of the account.

2 THE CHARGE ON THE ESTATE AT DEATH

2.1 The charge

On the death of any person there is deemed to have been a transfer of value immediately before death, equal to the value of the person's estate (IHTA 1984 s 4(1)). This makes it clear that property or interests which change in character on death are to be included in (or excluded from) the estate and valued, according to their nature before death. An interest in a settlement which ceases on death will be taken and valued as an interest in a subsisting settlement. If the interest is an interest in possession, the settled property in which it subsists will be deemed to be part of the deceased's estate. If the deceased is a partner in a partnership which ceases on death and a lease of the deceased's property terminates simultaneously, the deceased's estate will be taken to include an interest in a partnership and the reversion on the lease not vacant possession. The commencement of an annuity payable under the partnership agreement would not be chargeable, the charge being on the share in the partnership forming part of the estate. A *donatio mortis causa* (a gift in contemplation of death) will be part of the deceased's estate.

A change in the value of the estate by reason of the death shall be taken into account as if occurring before the death except:

- the termination on the death of a life interest; or

- the passing of an interest by survivorship; or

- any decrease in the value of assets caused by an alteration of a close company's unquoted shares or loan capital or any rights attached thereto (IHTA 1984 s 98 and s 171).

A prime example would be an insurance which became payable to the deceased's personal representatives, and the proceeds of which will be treated as part of the deceased's estate. Any tax liability, not in fact paid after death, which was originally deducted from the estate deemed to be transferred as above, is added back into the value of the estate.

2.2 The estate

Subject to the general comments made previously the estate of a deceased person is deemed not to include certain specific items of property, as follows.

- Excluded property (IHTA 1984 s 5).

- Settled property in which the deceased was entitled to an interest in possession, but which on death reverted to either, the settlor (if then living); or the settlor's spouse (if then domiciled in the UK) unless either the settlor or spouse had acquired a reversionary interest in the property for consideration. 'Spouse' here includes the settlor's widow or widower where the settlor died less than two years before the deceased or the deceased died before 1 April 1977.

- An interest in an exempt superannuation fund, which consists of a right to a pension or annuity only.

- An option under an approved retirement annuity contract to have a sum (e.g. return of premiums) paid to the deceased's personal representatives (IHTA 1984 s 152).

- Certain pensions, gratuities and other sums in respect of foreign government service (generally in former colonies) (IHTA 1984 s 153).

- Generally the benefits under an ordinary approved scheme will not be chargeable unless the personal representatives have a legally enforceable claim to benefits accruing on death or the deceased held a general power of nomination or appointment (PR IR 7 May 1976).

- An interest in possession in settled property is left out of the estate to the extent that it is no more than a reasonable amount of remuneration for the deceased's services as trustee of the settlement (IHTA 1984 s 90).

The estate is deemed to include any amount recoverable under a court order made under Inheritance (Provision for Family and Dependants) Act 1975, s 10 and any inheritance tax (and interest) repaid in consequence (IHTA 1984 s 146).

2.3 Special deductions from the estate on death
Allowance is to be made for:
- reasonable funeral expenses (IHTA 1984 s 172), including a reasonable amount for mourning for the family and servants (ESC, F1);

- expenses (up to 5% of the value of the property) incurred in administration or realization of property situated outside the UK, which are attributable to the situation of the property (to be deducted from that property, (IHTA 1984 s 173); transfers of value by instalments (non-chargeable portion) (IHTA 1984 s 175 and s 262).

2.4 Commorientes rule
When it cannot be known who is the survivor of two or more persons, they shall be assumed to have died at the same instant (IHTA 1984 s 4(2)).

2.5 Provision for family and dependants

2.5.1 General

Such provisions ordered by a court under s 2 of the 1975 Act (that is, an order varying the effect of the deceased's will or of the intestacy rules) is deemed to take effect on death. Interest on any consequent payment or repayment of inheritance tax will not run for any period prior to the making of the order (IHTA 1984 s 146).

2.5.2 Statutory legacy in intestacy

This is not an IHT point but relates to deceased estates. The Ministry of Justice announced an increase in the levels of Statutory Legacy from 1 February 2009. This is the level that surviving spouses or civil partners are allowed to inherit if their spouse or civil partner dies without leaving a valid will.

From 1 February 2009 the statutory legacy increased to:

- £250,000 (from £125,000) where there is a surviving spouse or civil partner and children;

- £450,000 (from £200,000) where there is a surviving spouse or civil partner and parents or siblings, but no children.

The statutory limits only apply in certain circumstances. In some situations, the surviving spouse or civil partner, or the children, can inherit without any limit. The full rules on inheritance in intestacy are as follows:

(a)   If there is a husband, wife or civil partner, and children:

- The spouse/partner gets the personal chattels, the first £125,000 and a life interest in half of what is left.

- The children of the deceased, including illegitimate and adopted children share between them half what is left straight away, if they are 18 or over; and the other half when the surviving parent dies.

(b)   If there is a husband, wife or civil partner, and relatives but no children:

- the husband or wife gets the personal chattels, the first £200,000 and half what is left.

- The parents of the dead person, or if they have died, the brothers and sisters or their descendants, share the other half of what is left.

(c)   If there is a surviving husband, wife or civil partner, but no other relatives:

- The surviving spouse/partner gets everything.

PART 12 - INHERITANCE TAX

(d)   If there are children, but no living husband, wife or civil partner:

- The children share everything equally.

(e)   If there is no husband, wife, civil partner or children:

- Everything will pass to the next available group of relatives.

(f)   If there are no available relatives:

- Everything goes to the State.

2.6 Exemptions and reliefs
2.6.1 General and partial exemptions

The exemption which apply on a deemed transfer on death and also allowable on a potentially exempt transfer are as follows.

Basic limit (IHTA 1984 s 7 and Sch 1). No tax is payable on the first £325,000 of a chargeable transfer made on or after 6 April 2009. It will remain at this level until 2014/2015 and thereafter rise by CPI. The zero amounts prior to that date can be found in Table 13. Inheritance Tax - Nil Rate Band - 2011/2012 back to 1997/1998, p.638.

Transfers between spouses (& civil partners) are exempt where both spouses are of UK domicile. Where the transferee spouse is not domiciled in the UK immediately before the transfer, exemption for the assets transferred is limited to £55,000 (IHTA 1984 s 18).

Gifts to charities, national bodies, employee trusts and to registered housing associations in relation to transfers after 13 March 1989. The exemption applies to transfers on death as for potentially exempt transfers.

Gifts to qualifying political parties are exempt if made on or within one year of death. A qualifying party is one where at the last general election preceding the transfer:

- two members of that party were elected to the House of Commons;

- one member of that party was elected to the House of Commons and not less than 150,000 votes were given to candidates who were members of that party.

Death on active service (IHTA 1984 s 154). No inheritance tax is paid on the death of a member of the armed forces killed from a wound, accident or disease contracted whilst on active service or from aggravation during that time of a previously contacted disease (*Barty-King v Ministry of Defence* QBD 1978). This exemption also applied to estates of members of the Royal Ulster Constabulary who died from injuries caused in Northern Ireland by terrorist activity (ESC, F5).

Abatement of exemptions
Where a death occurs on or after 26 July 1989 and the exempt beneficiary settles a claim against the estate from assets not derived from the estate, the exemption is abated by the amount settled and this amount is to be treated as a chargeable specific gift by the estate (IHTA 1984 s 29A; FA1989 s 172).

Partial exemptions
Where only part of the estate is exempt, special provisions apply to allocate the tax chargeable and the benefit of the exemption. These provisions are contained in IHTA 1984 ss 36-42.

2.6.2 Quick succession relief (Tax credit on successive charges)
Where there is a second transfer of any property and this occurred within five years of an earlier transfer and increased the transferor's estate a credit against the inheritance tax payable on the second transfer is allowed (IHTA 1984 s 141) if:

- the second transfer arises on death; or
- it is of settled property and:
- the transferor is entitled to an interest in the possession of the property and
- the first transfer was of the same property
- the property became, or it was already, settled property on the first transfer.

The credit allowable is dependent on the time span between the transfers and the tax payable on the second transfer is reduced by the following percentages:

Percentage of tax on first transfer	Period between transfers:
One year or less	100%
Between one and two years	80%
Between two and three years	60%
Between three and four years	40%
Between four and five years	20%

If the tax charge on the second transfer is less than the credit allowable any excess credit may be given on later transfers in chronological order until the full amount of credit has been utilized.

2.6.3 Relief by reduction of valuations
Relief is granted by a reduction in the valuation of the assets equivalent to the difference between the sales proceeds and the valuation on death of assets as follows:

- quoted shares sold within 12 months of death (IHTA 1984 s 179);
- land sold within four years of death (FA '93);
- related property sold within four years of death (FA '93).

Relief by a reduction in the valuation is also granted in respect of agricultural property (IHTA 1984 s 116) and business property (IHTA 1984 s 104).

2.6.4 Relief for woodlands
Extension of APR and woodlands relief to land in the EEA
Section 122, FA 2009 extends the IHT reliefs for agricultural property (APR) and woodlands (WR) to property in the European Economic Area (EEA). This is in response to the European Commission's opinion that the previous territorial restrictions contravened European law.

The change applies to transfers of value where the IHT would have been due on or after 22 April 2009, or was paid or due on or after 22 April 2003. In order to qualify for relief the property must meet the usual conditions for APR or WR, as appropriate, and must be located in an EEA state at the time of the event chargeable to IHT. All claims for relief must have been made by 21 April 2010.

On the deemed transfer of value on death, the value of growing trees or underwood may be excluded from the estate if election is made in writing within two years of the death or such longer time as the Board may allow (IHTA 1984 ss 125-130). In order to prevent 'deathbed purchases', the deceased must have been beneficially entitled to the land throughout the immediately preceding five years (unless acquired by inheritance or gift).

When the trees or underwood (or any part) are subsequently disposed of (alone or with the land), before another death on which no election is made, inheritance tax becomes chargeable on the net proceeds of sale or, if it was not a sale for full consideration, on the net value at the time of disposal, of the trees or underwood. The rate(s) of tax are fixed by reference to marginal rate(s) (according to the current rate table) of the last estate on which an election was made. If there is more than one such disposal the charge is cumulative.

If the woodlands are ancillary to agricultural land or pasture, agricultural property relief would be granted instead of the relief above.

Any further disposal of the same trees or underwood is not charged again in relation to the same death. The charge does not crystallize on an inter-spouse disposal. Only the person entitled to the proceeds of sale or to the value if the transaction was not a sale is liable for the tax. If the disposal is itself a transfer of value (e.g. a gift) the tax chargeable as above reduces the value transferred by that disposal.

2.7 Calculation of the tax

2.7.1 Abatement

It might happen that the testator's assets are insufficient to meet all gifts. If so, the gifts are to be abated before considering questions of exemption (IHTA 1984 s 37). On the other hand, the grossing-up required under the provisions about to be considered might cause the gifts for tax purposes to exceed the value transferred. If so, once again abatement is required and the terms of the will or of any applicable rule of law apply to abate the gifts as on a distribution of assets.

2.7.2 Attribution of value to gifts

In order to calculate the inheritance tax payable some value has to be attributed to gifts for tax purposes, and different values are appropriate for different kinds of gifts. Exempt gifts are taken at probate value (IHTA 1984 s 38), since the burden of inheritance tax is not to fall on them even if the will provides otherwise (IHTA 1984 s 41). However, to the extent that a specific gift, i.e. as any gift other than of residue gift, is not exempt and does not bear its own tax grossing-up is appropriate. Specific gifts bearing their own tax (e.g. devises of realty) are taken at probate value. If more than one specific gift is relevant to the question whether an exemption limit has been exceeded, the excess is first attributed to gifts not bearing their own tax, then to gifts bearing their own tax, and allocated proportionately within either class to individual gifts. In so far as value is not attributed to specific gifts it must, of course, be attributed to residue (IHTA 1984 s 39). The rules are to be separately applied to gifts taking effect separately out of separate funds (FA 1975 Sch 6 para 21).

2.7.3 Grossing-up chargeable specific gifts

The grossing-up of chargeable specific gifts not bearing their own tax differs according to whether or not they are the only chargeable gifts (IHTA 1984 s 38). In the former case, those gifts are grossed-up at the rates applicable on the assumption that they are the only value chargeable. In the latter case, those gifts are grossed-up at an assumed rate of tax. This assumed rate is found by first calculating the amount of tax which would be payable if chargeable specific gifts not bearing their own tax were grossed-up on the assumption that they were the only value chargeable and that other specific gifts and residue were ascertained accordingly. Having calculated that amount, it is divided by the aggregate chargeable gifts (of all kinds) thus giving the assumed rate. Grossing-up the chargeable specific gifts not bearing their own tax at this assumed rate gives their value for the purpose of calculating the actual tax payable, the other specific gifts being taken at probate value and the exempt and chargeable residue being taken as the balance.

There are special pro rata apportionment rules for cases where the aggregate value of a number of gifts is less than the value transferred.

3 THE CHARGE ON LIFETIME TRANSFERS BY INDIVIDUALS (GIFTS)

3.1 General

Inheritance tax is charged by reference to **transfers of value** which are widely defined to cover gifts and transactions with a gratuitous element which might not ordinarily be regarded as gifts. *Exempt transfers* are not chargeable and, if a transfer is exempt only to a limited extent, it is a chargeable transfer only insofar as it exceeds that limit (IHTA 1984 s 2). The rate of tax chargeable on lifetime transfers is half of the death rate and tapering relief is allowable for potentially exempt transfers.

The liability to inheritance tax on lifetime gifts was substantially changed in respect of gifts made on or after 18 March 1986 and which are only liable to tax if they become chargeable transfers on the death of the transferor within seven years of making the gift. Gifts made prior to 18 March 1986 were liable to inheritance tax when the gift was made.

3.2 Lifetime Gifts

The conditions governing the liability on lifetime gifts are as follows.

3.2.1 Transfer of value

Any disposition which results in a reduction in value of the estate of the person making the disposition is a transfer of value (IHTA 1984 s 3). That reduction is referred to as the **value transferred** and that person as the **transferor**. However, a disposition is not a transfer of value if it is shown that it was not intended, and was not made in a transaction (or series of transactions or any associated operations) intended to confer any gratuitous benefit on any person and either:

- that it was made in a transaction, series of transactions or any associated operations at arm's length between persons not connected with each other; or

- that it was such as might be expected to be made at arm's length between persons not connected with each other (IHTA 1984 s 10).

There are, however, two types of transaction which are treated as transfers of value despite the lack of donative intention:

- disposition by which a reversionary interest is acquired; or

- sale of unquoted shares or debentures unless it is shown that the sale was at a price freely negotiated at the time of or at a price such as might be expected to have been freely negotiated at that time.

Excluded property which ceased to form part of a person's estate in consequence of a disposition is not a transfer of value.

3.2.2 Disposition
The action on behalf of the taxpayer which activates the charge to inheritance tax is the making of a disposition.

However, a 'disposition' is not defined and has a very wide meaning (*Ward v CIR* PC 1956). Its meaning is expressly extended to include the omission to exercise a right, which diminishes an estate and enhances either another's estate or settled property in which there is no interest in possession unless it is shown that the omission was not deliberate (IHTA 1984 s 3). But it does not appear to include the extinction of a right, since it has been held that 'the primary meaning of disposition, at any rate in relation to property, is to deal with the property in any one of a number of ways, the property remaining in existence' (*Re Leven (Earl)* Ch D 1954). A dividend waiver executed within 12 months before any right of the dividend has accrued, is not a transfer of value (IHTA 1984 s 15).

If it is intended that a gift should be effective as from a particular date, the donor must then have done all within his power to vest the beneficial ownership in the donee. In the case of shares, the transfer must be executed and delivered, but need not have been registered (*Re Rose* Ch D 1952). A written direction to the company is sufficient to renounce a right to the allotment of shares (*Letts v CIR* Ch D 1956). If Treasury consent to the transfer is required, this must be obtained (*Re Fry* Ch D 1946). It has been held that a cheque is not effective, until paid by the drawee bank (*Re Owen* Ch D 1949). The intention to effect an equitable assignment of a right such as the right to the proceeds of a life policy on maturity must be made quite clear (*Dalton v CIR* Ch D 1958), and the necessity for written evidence of a disposal of an equitable or trust interest should not be overlooked (Law of Property Act 1925 s 53(1); *Grey v CIR* HL 1960; *Oughtred v CIR* H L 1960; *Vandervell v CIR* H L 1967).

3.2.3 Associated operations
A 'disposition' includes one affected by associated operations (IHTA 1984 s 268), i.e. any two or more operations (including omissions) of any kind being:

- operations which affect the same property, or one of which affects some property and the other or others affect property which represents directly or indirectly that property or income or accumulations of income from it; or

- any two operations of which one is effected with reference to the other, or with a view to enabling or facilitating the other being effected, and any further operation having a like relation to any of those two, and so on.

It does not matter that the operations may have been effected by different persons or at different times. However, the granting of a lease for full consideration is not associated with any operation effected more than three years after the grant.

Any transfer of value is to be treated as made at the time of the last associated operation. Relief is to be given for value transferred by the same transferor under earlier operations, except to the extent that the earlier operations are entitled to the exemption for spouses.

A sale by instalments followed by a release of the instalments as they fall due would be regarded as associated operations, so that the value of the asset at the date of the last release could be looked at by the HMRC. Gifts of cash to cover inheritance tax payable by instalments are not, however, associated with the transaction which gives rise to the liability.

3.2.4 Value transferred
The value transferred is the reduction in the value of the transferor's estate and is reduced by:

- the amount of any liability to capital gains tax arising as a result of the transfer, if that tax is borne by the donee or beneficiary (IHTA 1984 s 165);

- expenses incurred by the transferor in making a transfer, which are borne by a person benefiting from the transfer (IHTA 1984 s 164);

- inheritance tax on the transfer agreed to be paid by the transferor (FA 1975 Sch 10 1(2));

- any relief granted under FA 1976 s 99 in respect of transfers made within three years before death.

3.2.5 Transfers of value by instalments
A disposition made for consideration under which the transferor is required to make payments (or transfer assets) more than one year after the disposition is made, is treated as if each instalment were a separate transfer of value, equal to $(A \times B)$ times the amount of the instalment where A is the whole value transferred by the disposition and B is the aggregate of all instalments made or to be made under it (IHTA 1984 s 262).

If the transferor dies before the last instalment is made, the liability deductible from his or her estate in respect thereof is the nonchargeable portion only of each outstanding instalment (IHTA 1984 s 175).

3.2.6 'Back-to-back' insurance arrangements
A transaction whereby a life policy is made, varied, or substituted for an earlier one (the benefit thereof being vested in a person other than the insured) and an annuity is purchased at any time on the life of the insured, is treated as a transfer of value by the purchaser of the annuity. Such a transfer of value is deemed to be made at the

time that the benefit of the policy became vested in that other person unless it is shown that the purchase of the annuity, and the making, etc. of the life policy were not associated operations (IHTA 1984 s 263).

The value transferred is the lesser of:

(a)   the aggregate of the consideration given for the annuity and any premium paid under the policy on or before the transfer; or

(b)   the value of the greatest benefit capable of being conferred at any time by the policy.

It should be noted that, quite apart from this provision, a back-to-back arrangement may be a transfer of value on account of the vesting or of the purchase and the vesting, being associated operations.

3.2.7 Chargeable transfers affecting more than one property
Tax chargeable on value transferred is to be attributed to properties in proportion to their respective values, but subject to any provision affecting a particular property (e.g. agricultural property) (IHTA 1984 s 265).

Where the value transferred depends on the order of making transfers, they are to be deemed to be made in the order which results in the lowest value chargeable. Nevertheless, the rate of tax attributable to any chargeable transfers on the same day is to be the average rate for all those transfers taken together (IHTA 1984 s 266). Chargeable transfers out of the same settlement are treated as made by the same person. However, neither rule affects the deemed transfer on death.

3.2.8 Joint property
The beneficial interests, in real property in particular, often do not correspond with the legal title, even in the absence of express stipulation by the parties concerned. This is because the law, in the interests of equity, often implies the existence of a beneficial interest in some person other than the legal owner. Most often, but not invariably, this will concern spouses and, whilst they remain married and both are domiciled in the UK, there will be no inheritance tax problem, on account of the exemption for inter-spousal transfers.

In the absence of written stipulation, the beneficial interests in a property depend on the parties' intentions, to be inferred from evidence as to their words and conduct at the time of purchase (Law of Property Act 1925 s 53(1) does not apply to such trusts; see *Pettitt v Pettitt* H L 1969). In the absence of evidence it is presumed that a contributor towards a purchase is intended to have a proportionate beneficial interest (*Gissing v Gissing* H L 1970). A person may become entitled to a beneficial interest in improvements to a property, if he or she contributes in money or money's worth to those improvements (Matrimonial Proceedings and Property Act 1970 s 37;

Kawalczuk v Kawalczuk CA 1973). The position is, generally, the same between persons who are not spouses (e.g. engaged couples and unmarried persons cohabiting) (*Cooke v Head* CA 1972). The law on this topic is in a state of flux and consultation of a leading and up-to-date work on real property or trusts is advised in cases of doubt.

In the absence of contrary agreement, savings from house-keeping money are regarded as owned in equal share (Married Women's Property Act 1964, s 1).

The main problem arises where unmarried persons deal with the property, particularly on a separation, in a manner which is inconsistent with the beneficial interests which the law imputes to each. In such cases there may be a transfer of value, bearing in mind that the onus of disproving donative intent is squarely on the taxpayer. Moreover, on the death of any person the estate may be greater or less than at first sight might appear.

3.2.9 Partnership property
Provided that there is no intention to confer any gratuitous benefit on anyone, it seems that the 'Boden-type' partnership arrangement remains effective as a bona fide sale and cannot be regarded as a transfer of value. Briefly, the arrangement is one whereby the senior partners give up rights to partnership assets in return for the junior partners' assuming a progressively greater part of the actual conduct of the business and, on death of any senior partner, the estate does not include the partnership assets thereby transferred (*A-G v Boden* KBD 1912). Further, if annuities are provided for on retirement there will be no chargeable transfer in the case of a bona fide commercial agreement.

Partnership life assurance schemes involving trusts for the surviving partners, and entered into before 15 September 1976, and not varied after that date, will not be treated as settlements. The scheme must not involve any element of gift, but rather must be a normal business arrangement.

3.2.10 Pension schemes
Contributions to an approved scheme may be chargeable transfers and should be notified to HMRC. Likewise an irrecoverable nomination or the disposal of benefits by a member of any scheme in his or her lifetime (other than in favour of the spouse) may be chargeable (PR IR 7 May 1976).

3.2.11 Pools syndicate (& also presumably 'Lotto' syndicates)
A share in winnings of such a syndicate is not chargeable on the person in whose name the claim is made on behalf of the syndicate, provided the agreement to share winnings was in existence before the win (PR IR 16 September 1977).

3.2.12 Gifts with reservations
Please see Gifts with Reservation of Benefit (GWR), p.561

3.3 Reliefs and exemptions

The methods of relief available for lifetime transactions are as follows:

3.3.1 Excluded property

Excluded property is not treated as part of the estate either before or after the transfer and its transfer cannot therefore give rise to a transfer of value.

3.3.2 Relief for dispositions which are not transfers of value
Dispositions for maintenance of the transferor's family

The following dispositions (whether in settlement or not) are not transfers of value (IHTA 1984 s 11):

- by one party to a marriage (or former marriage if made on annulment or divorce, or in variation of a disposition so made) in favour of the other party or of a child, step-child or adopted child of either party: (a) for the maintenance of the other party; or (b) for the maintenance, education or training of the child for a period ending not later than 5 April after his or her 18th birthday, or after ceasing to undergo full-time education of training (if later);

- by any person for the maintenance, education or training of a child not in the care of a parent, for a period ending not later than 5 April following his or her 18th birthday, or if later, after ceasing to undergo full-time education or training provided the child has been in the care of the disponor for substantial periods before his or her 18th birthday;

- by any person for the maintenance, education or training of his or her illegitimate child for a period ending not later than 5 April following his or her 18th birthday or, if later, after ceasing to undergo full-time education or training;

- by any person in favour of a dependent relative as a reasonable provision for the care and maintenance of the dependent relative. A dependent relative is a relative of the disponser or spouse who is incapacitated by old age or infirmity from maintaining himself or herself or the widowed, separated or divorced mother or mother-in-law;

- by a child in favour of his or her unmarried mother for her care and maintenance if she is genuinely financially dependent on that child (ESC, F12).

A disposal of an interest in possession in settled property for the above purposes will not give rise to a charge on that property and a disposition can be severed so that the part which qualifies as above is not charged.

Any order by the court under the Matrimonial Causes Act 1973, ss 22 and 23 will be regarded as maintenance, even in the case of a lump sum provision or of a transfer of property in satisfaction thereof. An order under s 24 (Property Adjustment Order) will be regarded merely as giving effect to the equitable rights of the parties and not as involving any disposition for inheritance tax, on the assumption that it cannot be shown to be 'for maintenance.'

If a voluntary re-arrangement of property rights is made after divorce or annulment, and it cannot be shown to be 'for maintenance', there will be a transfer of value unless donative intention can be negatived and the transaction is on arm's length terms.

In the case of transfers to children, the transfer may be for education or training, in which case there will be no transfer of value.

Deeds of family arrangement, disclaimer, commutation of surviving spouse's life interest

Any variation or disclaimer of the dispositions (by will or intestacy or otherwise) of a deceased person is not a transfer of value, if made:

- by written instrument; and
- by all or any of the beneficiaries; and
- within two years of the deceased's death; and
- other than for consideration in money or moneys worth (except another variation or disclaimer).

The variation or disclaimer takes effect as if made by the deceased, no matter in whose favour it is made, and must be made in writing to the Board within six months (or such longer time as the Board may allow) after the date of the instrument.

In the case of a variation it is necessary to have a joint election signed by the persons making the instrument and, if additional tax becomes payable by them, by the personal representatives who can refuse to join in the election only if they have insufficient assets to pay the tax.

Variations causing property to be held in trust for not more than two years from death are ignored (except as to actual dispositions and applications in that period) and the disposition taking effect at the end of that period is related back to death.

A legacy bequeathed subject to a precatory gift (a request) which is carried into effect within two years after the testator's death, is not a transfer of value by the legatee, and the property transferred is regarded as having been bequeathed by will (IHTA 1984 s 17 and s 143).

Family provision by Court order out of a deceased person's estate (Inheritance (Provision for Family and Dependants) Act 1975, s 2) is deemed to have effect as if the property had devolved on death (IHTA 1984 s 146).

An election by a surviving spouse to take a lump sum in place of a life interest is not a transfer of value and the spouse is to be treated as having been entitled to that sum from death.

An interest in settled property disclaimed gratuitously is deemed never to have existed, so that there will be no transfer of value and, for example, no termination of an interest in possession.

In the case of *Lau v HMRC SpC 740*, the children of Lau deceased disclaimed their inheritance from the estate of their father in favour of the widow, Mrs Lau. However, the advice letters released by the family's solicitor clearly demonstrated that the legacies would be disclaimed in return for large cash gifts from Mrs Lau to each of the children once the estate was finalised. HMRC successfully argued that the gifts to the children were consideration for the deed of variation, and hence the deed of variation failed for IHT purposes.

It appears that the solicitors advising the Lau family had not fully appreciated the need to keep any subsequent gifts completely separate from the arrangements to make the deed of variation.

Business and other expenses and pension provision for employees
Dispositions made by any person and allowable in computing profits or losses for income tax or corporation tax (assuming them to be so chargeable) are not transfers of value covered by this relief, whether or not connected with a business in the strict sense (IHTA 1984 s 12). For example, contributions to an approved retirement benefits scheme, or provision made for unconnected persons for equivalent unapproved benefits, transfers of value. A right of occupancy of a dwelling at less than an arm's length rent is to be treated as an unapproved pension at a rate equal to the difference. Excessive expense or provision is treated as made under a separate disposition which may be a transfer of value. This provision will normally operate to exempt payments made by an employer under an accident insurance policy (PR IR 6 January 1976).

Waiver of dividend
A waiver of dividend is not a transfer of value provided the waiver is made within 12 months before any right to the dividend has accrued (IHTA 1984 s 15).

Waiver of remuneration or repayment
A waiver of remuneration or repayment is not a transfer of value if apart from the waiver or repayment, (i) it would have been assessable as earned income, and (ii) it would have been an allowable deduction of the payer for income tax or corporation tax but by reason of the waiver or repayment it is not so allowed or, if allowed, is brought back into charge (IHTA 1984 s 14).

Trusts for the benefit of employees
Trusts for the benefit of employees, to which property is transferred by a disposition, either by a close company or by an individual beneficially entitled to shares in a company, receive the property free of inheritance tax if certain conditions are satisfied (IHTA 1984 s 13).

Disposition, by close companies to trustees on trusts for the benefit of working individuals, qualify if the trusts permit the property to be applied for the benefit of persons who include all or most of the employees or officers of the company or group. The persons who may benefit (ignoring applications of income) at any time must, except where the trust is an approved profit sharing scheme, exclude:

(a)   any person who is a participator in the company concerned and who would be entitled to at least 5% of its assets on winding up or who is beneficially entitled to shares (or rights to acquire shares) amounting to 5% or more of any class in issue;

(b)   any other person who is such a participator in any close company that has made a disposal (eligible for this relief) or the same trusts;

(c)   any other person who has been such a participator in any company within para.'s (a) or (b) at any time after, or during the 10 years before, the disposition in question;

(d)   any person who is connected with a person in para.'s (a), (b) or (c).

3.3.3 Exempt transfers
To the extent that value transferred is within the limit or one of the following exemptions, that transfer is an exempt transfer and is not chargeable to inheritance tax (IHTA 1984 s 2).

Potentially exempt transfers
Please see Potentially Exempt Transfer, p.558

Transfers between spouses (& civil partners)
Transfers between spouses (IHTA 1984 s 18) are exempt to the extent that the value transferred is attributable to property which becomes comprised in the estate of the transferor's spouse or to the extent that the estate is increased where property does not become so comprised, unless the disposition is postponed to another interest or, except in the case of a survivorship clause, for a specified period, or the disposition is subject to a condition not satisfied within 12 months of the transfer. The termination of an interest in possession is not exempt if the spouse acquired the reversion for consideration. A gratuitous or partly-gratuitous loan of property to a spouse qualifies as if the borrower's estate were increased thereby.

If the transferee spouse is not domiciled in the UK, but the transferor is, the transfer is exempt to the extent that the value transferred (ignoring inheritance tax thereon) does not exceed £55,000 less any amount previously taken into account for the purpose of the exemption

(a)   T gives a half share in the matrimonial home to his wife to take effect immediately but provided she survives him by 30 days. If the gift takes effect, it is exempt.

(b)   He settles shares on trust for his aged mother for life, remainder to his wife. The gift is not exempt on account of the mother's prior interest.

(c)   He gives his country cottage worth £10,000 to his wife and daughter as tenants in common in equal shares, the value of each being £5,500. The transfer is exempt to the extent of £5,000 (being one-half of the 'value transferred').

(d)   transferor who is domiciled in the UK, transfers £100,000 to his or her spouse who is, immediately before the transfer, domiciled abroad only £55,000 of the value transferred is exempt, less any amounts previously transferred to the spouse.

Annual allowance
Gifts up to a total of £3,000 in any fiscal year are exempt from inheritance tax (IHTA 1984 s 19). If the total of the gifts made during the year is less than £3,000, the shortfall may be carried forward to next year only and added to the allowance for that year. Any excess over £3,000 is apportioned to a later transfer rather than an earlier one and to transfers on the same day according to their respective values. The value of gifts is calculated without the tax and life insurance premiums paid net of tax are treated as net values for inheritance tax purposes (PR IR 17 January 1979). Each spouse is entitled to this annual allowance.

Small gifts to the same person
Outright gifts of £250 to the same person in any fiscal year are exempt from inheritance tax. Gifts above £250 are set off against the annual allowance of £3,000. Each spouse is entitled to this exemption (IHTA 1984 s 20).

Normal expenditure out of income
A transfer of value is exempt if it is shown that it was made as part of the normal expenditure of the transferor taking one year with another, provided he was left with sufficient income to maintain his usual standard of living (IHTA 1984 s 21). A payment of an insurance premium under a back-to-back arrangement on the transferor's life, under which an annuity was purchased, or a gift intended to cover the premium, is not part of normal expenditure, unless it can be shown that the

policy and annuity were not associated operations.

It is thought that 'normal expenditure' means expenditure of a type (not amount) (*A-G v Heron* CA (N.I.) 1959) which is habitual for the transferor concerned. Presumably, the first of a kind will be allowed if it could be shown to be likely to be part of the future pattern. The practice is to take 'income', on accountancy principles net of tax (see 1976 BTR 872 for practice statement). A chargeable loan of property may be exempted if such a 'loan' is normal for the transferor.

Gifts in consideration of marriage (& civil partnership ceremony)

Gifts in consideration of marriage (IHTA 1984 s 22) are exempt to the extent that they do not exceed in respect of any one marriage the following: It should be remembered that if the gift is by cheque it should be cleared through the banking system no later than the day of the marriage. (See p.501 re Curnock v IRC SpC 365).

• £5,000 by a parent of either party to the marriage;

• £2,500 by one party of the marriage to the other party, or by a grandparent or remoter ancestor.

• £1,000 in any other case.

The values transferred are calculated as values on which no tax is payable and any excess over the limits is attributed in proportion to the values transferred.

Gifts must be outright gifts to a party to the marriage or in the case of settled gifts must be for the benefit of:

(a)   the parties to the marriage, issue of the marriage, or a wife or husband of any such issue;

(b)   a subsequent wife or husband of a party to a marriage, or any issue, or the wife or husband of any issue, of a subsequent marriage of either party;

(c)   as respects a reasonable amount of remuneration, the trustees of the settlement.

The exemption would still apply if some benefit may be obtained by some person other than a party specified in para.'s (a) to (c), only in the event of any issue to the marriage dying without attaining a specified age or the operation of a protective trust.

Child includes an illegitimate child, an adopted child and a step-child, and parent, descendant and ancestor shall be construed accordingly.

Issue includes any person legitimated by a marriage or adopted by the husband and wife jointly.

Charities

Gifts to charities, political parties, for national purposes for public benefit and for maintenance of historic buildings are exempt on certain conditions (IHTA 1984 ss 23-25 and Schs 3 and 4). The whole amount of the value transferred (i.e. of the reduction in the transferor's estate) is exempt (subject to the limits that follow), even if the benefit to the recipient body is lower (PR IR 15 April 1976).

The disposition by which it is given must not:

- take effect on the termination, after the transfer of value, of any interest or period (i.e. must not be postponed); or

- be subject to a condition not satisfied within 12 months after the transfer; or

- be defeasible, unless in fact it was not defeated within 12 months after the transfer and is thereafter not defeasible; or

- be less than the donor's full interest in the property or be given for a limited period; or

- allow the possibility of the property (or any part of it) becoming applicable for purposes other than those of a body eligible for the relief; or

- (if the subject matter is an interest in possession) operate otherwise than to terminate the settlement so far as the subject matter is concerned; or

- (if the subject matter is land or a building) be subject to an interest reserved or created by the donor, entitling that donor or spouse or a connected person to possession or occupation of any of that property at less than a full rent; or

- (in the case of any other kind of property) be subject to an interest reserved or created by the donor, unless for full consideration or such that it does not substantially affect the donee's enjoyment of the property.

Where the body acquires a reversionary interest in settled property for consideration, the termination of the interest on which it is expectant is not to be exempted. Where any exempt body has, acquired an interest in settled property for consideration and other than from another exempt body, any settled property which subsequently becomes the property of any exempt body is not exempted on its transfer.

National Heritage property

Exemption was granted on transfers made of designated property to specified national and public bodies subject to certain conditions (IHTA 1984 s 26). This exemption applies to 'conditionally exempt transfers' as follows (IHTA 1984 s 30):

- the transfer must be of property designated by the Board under IHTA 1984 s 31 to be of national, scientific, historic, artistic, architectural or outstanding scenic interest; and

- (a) the transferor and/or spouse must have been beneficially entitled to the property throughout the six years ending with the transfer; or (b) the transferor acquired the property on a death and the acquisition was a conditionally exempt transfer.

The types of property which may be **designated** by the Board (IHTA 1984 s 31; FA 1985, s 94; Sch 26) are:

(a)   pictures, prints, books, manuscripts, works of art, scientific collections or other things not yielding income which appear to the Board to be of national, scientific, historic or artistic interest. A computerized register of conditionally exempt works of art is obtainable from the Capital Taxes Office on payment of a fee;

(b)   land which in the opinion of the Board is of outstanding scenic, historic or scientific interest;

(c)   any building for the preservation of which special steps should in the opinion of the Board be taken by reason of its outstanding historic or architectural interest;

(d)   land which adjoins any building as mentioned in para. (c) and which in the opinion of the Board is essential for the protection of the character and amenities of the building. Where the transfer occurs after 18 March 1985 the restriction for the land to be adjoining to the building is removed and the exemption will be granted on amenity land, i.e. any area of land which the Board considers essential for the protection of the character and amenities of the building;

(e)   any object which in the opinion of the Board is historically associated with such a building as mentioned in para. (c).

Where property has been designated by the Board as being eligible for conditional exemption, they require **undertakings** to be given by such a person as they consider to be appropriate to the circumstances until that person dies or the property is disposed of (IHTA 1984 s 31; FA 1985 Sch 26 para 2). The undertakings require in all cases that the public must have reasonable access to the property and:

- in the case of property in under para. (a), the property will be kept permanently in the UK and will not leave it temporarily without the approval of the Board; and

- in the case of land under para. (b), reasonable steps will be taken for its maintenance and preservation of its character; and

- in the case of any property under para.'s (c) - (e), reasonable steps will be taken for its maintenance, repair and preservation and, in the case of an object under para. (e), for keeping it associated with the building concerned.

Where any transfers are made, an additional undertaking (referred to as **specified steps**) has to be given for the maintenance, repair and preservation of the property and for securing reasonable access to the public. The 1998 Finance Act increased the opportunities which the public must have access. The specified steps means such steps as are agreed by the Board and the person giving the undertaking and are to be specified in the undertaking.

In the case of amenity land being transferred, it will also be necessary for the person beneficially entitled to the land to give a further undertaking to maintain, repair and preserve it and to provide reasonable access to it until the death of the owner of:

- the building of outstanding historical or architectural interest; or

- any other areas of amenity land lying between the building and the amenity land subject to the undertaking or in the opinion of the Board physically closely connected with the land or building. Separate undertakings have to be given by each person beneficially entitled to any amenity land or other property referred to under para. (a) or (b) and it is the responsibility of the person seeking the exemption to ensure that any necessary undertakings by third parties are obtained.

Where there has been a material breach of an undertaking above or on a transfer caused by death, inheritance tax becomes payable on the first occurrence of such a **chargeable event** (IHTA 1984 s 32; FA 1985 s 26 Sch 4). The tax is chargeable on the person beneficially entitled to the property if the chargeable event arises on death or on a breach of the undertaking, and in the case of a disposal by sale or gift or otherwise the tax is chargeable on the person by whom or for whose benefit the property is disposed of.

There is no chargeable event if:

- the property is given or sold by private treaty to a national body or is accepted by the Board in satisfaction of tax. If the transfer occurred on death, the disposal must be within three years of death;

- the transfer is on death or by gift and is itself a conditionally exempt transfer, or the undertaking previously given is replaced by a corresponding undertaking.

Where there is a chargeable event because of a breach of an undertaking it is also a chargeable event of all the associated property. However, the Board may direct that the event relates only to the item concerned if they are satisfied that it does not materially affect the associated property.

The tax is **charged** on the value of the property at the time of the event and where the event was a bona fide arm's length sale, the value is to be taken as the sale proceeds (proportionately reduced where conditional exemption applied only to part of the property), less any capital gains tax chargeable (IHTA 1984 ss 33, 34).

The rate of tax on the transfer is the rate applicable to the property if it was added to the cumulative total of the transfers made at the date of the chargeable transfer by the 'relevant person'.

The **relevant person** is:
- the person who made the only conditionally exempt transfer of the property since the last chargeable event or disposal not treated as a chargeable event (if any); or

- where there are two or more such transfers; either (a) the person who made the last of them, if not more than one of them occurred in the preceding 30 years; or (b) the person selected by the Board, if more than one of them occurred within that period.

There is provision to prevent a double charge where the chargeable event is, or has been preceded by, a chargeable transfer of the property. A deduction from the value is allowed for any CGT chargeable on the same occasion.

In order to prevent any advantage to the person who made the last conditionally exempt transfer, by its being left out of that person's cumulative total of chargeable transfers, the total is increased by the value charged. This has the effect of increasing the tax rate on any subsequent chargeable transfer or, in the case of the death of the transferor, on any subsequent chargeable event in relation to conditionally exempt property. If the asset is settled property at the time of the event or within the preceding five years, the settlor's cumulative total is increased if the settlement was made within the preceding 30 years and a conditionally exempt transfer of the property was made within those 30 years and the 'relevant person' did not make the last conditionally exempt transfer of the property before the chargeable event (IHTA 1984 s 34).

The previous provisions apply, with appropriate modifications, to a conditionally exempt distribution payment or deemed capital distributions.

Maintenance funds for buildings of historic or architectural interest

Transfers (made after 2 May 1976, and before 8 March 1982) are exempt if the property to which the value transferred is attributable becomes comprised in a settlement which precludes its application other than for the maintenance, repair or preservation of, or making provision for public access to, such a building (IHTA 1984 s 27 and Sch 4). If there is surplus income, that must accrue to a body for national purposes or to a charity which exists wholly or mainly for the preservation of items of national heritage and on termination of the settlement the property must devolve to such a body or charity. The Treasury must direct that exemption be given, if they are satisfied that these requirements are complied with and that the property is appropriate in character and amount, and if the trustees are approved by them. The building itself must have been the subject of, or be such that had there been a transfer of it would have been eligible for, a conditional exemption, and no event must have since occurred which causes, or would (if conditional exemption had been claimed) cause, tax to be charged on.

Mutual transfers: exemption for donee's gift

A transfer of value by a donee is exempted to the extent that it is matched by a previous chargeable transfer to him by a donor within the period of seven years after March 1986 beginning with the date of the donor's transfer previously 10 years (IHTA 1984 s 148 and FA 1986 s 10).

The donee's transfer must:
* be made in the donor's lift-time and increase the estate of the donor, or spouse domiciled in the UK at the time of the donee's transfer; or

* be made within two years after the donor's death and increase the estate of the donor's widow or widower so domiciled at the donor's death.

If the donee makes more than one such transfer, their aggregate value is exempt to the extent that it does not exceed the amount by which the donee's estate was increased by the donor's transfer. If neither donor nor spouse or widow are domiciled in the UK at the relevant time, the provision does not apply.

The donor's and donee's transfers must be by way of a disposition and any deemed disposal (other than an omission) is excluded.

The relief for the donor's gift is granted by the charge being retrospectively cancelled.

Trusts for benefit of employees

A transfer of value made by an individual giving shares in a company to trusts for the benefit of employees is exempt from inheritance Tax provided (IHTA 1984 s 28):

- the value transferred (or part of it) is attributable to shares in or securities of the company; and

- the persons for whose benefit the trust permit the property to be applied include all or most of the employees or officers of the company; and

- at, or within one year after, the transfer the trustees hold more than half the ordinary shares and a majority of the voting power and this cannot be altered without the trustees' consent;

- the trust does not permit any of the settled property to be applied at any time (except payments which are income of the recipient for income tax purposes) for the benefit of:

  (a) any person who is a participator in the company and who owns, or is entitled to acquire, 5% of more of any class of shares in issue or who would be entitled to 5% or more of the assets on winding up;

  (b) any other person who is such a participator in any close company that has made a disposition eligible for relief under;

  (c) any other person who has been such a participator in any company within para.'s (a) or (b) at any time after, or during the ten years before, the transfer of value in question;

  (d) any person connected with the persons in para.'s (a) to (c).

3.3.4 Relief by cancellation of chargeable transfers
Mutual transfers: relief for donor's gift
In the case of a mutual transfer where exemption is available to the donee, the donor may, within six years after the donee's transfer back to him or her, claim to have the inheritance tax position adjusted as follows (IHTA 1984 s 149):

- the value transferred on the donor's chargeable transfer is to be cancelled to the extent specified below (the 'cancelled value');

- the donor's cumulative total of chargeable transfers, for any chargeable transfer after the claim, is to be reduced by the 'cancelled value';

- the tax (including interest) on the cancelled value is to be repaid (with interest from the date of the claim) or discharged.

The **cancelled value** is the grossed-up equivalent of so much of the value transferred by the donee's transfer as does not exceed:

- (a) the amount by which the donee's estate was increased by the donor's transfer; less (b) any part of that amount taken into account on an earlier donee's transfer; less (c) 4% of (a), or (a) less (b) as the case may be, for every 12 months that have elapsed between the donor's and the donee's transfer; or

- if smaller, the amount by which the donor's estate was increased by the donee's transfer; or

- if there was a previous donee's transfer, so much of the amount applying as above which was not taken into account as the value cancelled by that transfer.

The grossing-up is at the donor's actual rate if the rates have changed.

Where the cancelled value is only part of the value transferred by the donor's transfer, it is treated as the highest part of that amount. A later donor's transfer is to be cancelled before an earlier one to the same donee and the same value transferred by a donor's transfer is not to be relieved more than once.

If the donor has died a claim may be made by the widow or widower, if the donee's transfer is one made within two years of that death, or by the donor's personal representatives in any other case. The 4% reduction does not apply, for the purpose only of charging additional tax on account of the donor's death within three years of the transfer, to the extent of any donee's transfer before death. Where a donee's transfer increases the estate of the donor's spouse, widow or widower, any chargeable transfers by the latter, which have increased the donee's estate will preclude cancellation of the donor's transfers to the donee (whether or not a claim is made by the spouse, widow or widower).

Voidable transfers
Where, on a claim made for the purpose, it is shown that the whole or any part of a chargeable transfer has, by virtue of any enactment or rule of law, been set aside as voidable or otherwise defeasible (e.g. on bankruptcy), adjustments shall be made for inheritance tax purposes, as follows (IHTA 1984 s 150):

- Inheritance tax (including interest) shall be repaid (with interest from the date of the claim) to, or discharged for, the claimant, if that tax (and interest) would not have been payable (whether on the voidable transfer or any other chargeable transfer) if the voidable transfer (or part) had not been made.

- Inheritance tax, on any chargeable transfer made after the claim by the person who made the voidable transfer, is to be charged as if that transfer (or part) had not been made.

Where the chargeable transfer was a disposition, by a person since deceased, which is wholly or partly set aside by court order because it was intended to defeat claims for financial provision out of the deceased's estate (Inheritance (Provision for Family and Dependants) Act 1975, s 10), the deemed transfer of value on death is taxed as if that disposition (or the part of it set aside) had not been made, but as if the deceased's estate included the amount ordered to be repaid and the tax (and interest) repayable under this provision.

3.3.5 Relief by reduction of valuation

Where a transferor dies within three years after making a chargeable transfer and the property transferred is still owned by the transferee or spouse or has been sold as a qualifying sale by the transferee or spouse, the inheritance tax payable on the transfer is recomputed by reference to the rates applicable on the death of the transferor. This charge does not apply, however, to property which is tangible movable property that is a wasting asset (IHTA 1984 ss 131 and 132).

A **wasting asset** is property which, immediately before the transfer had a predictable useful life not exceeding 50 years, having regard to the purpose for which it was held by the transferor, and plant and machinery shall always be regarded as having a predictable useful life of less than 50 years (IHTA 1984 s 132(2)).

A **qualifying sale** is a sale at arm's length for a price freely negotiated at the time of the sale between unconnected persons and there must be no provision for the vendor to acquire any part of the property sold or the interest therein (IHTA 1984 s 131(3)).

Where the market value at the date of death or qualifying sale is less than that at the time of the transfer, a claim may be made by the person liable to pay the tax for the lesser value to be used in computing the additional inheritance tax payable (IHTA 1984 s 131(2)).

Where the chargeable transfer was made before 26 March 1980, and a person dies after a reduction in the rates applicable on death and within three years of making a chargeable transfer before the reduction, the additional tax is chargeable as if the new rates of tax applicable at death had applied to the transfer.

In computing any charge above, the market value of the property is the price which the property might reasonably be expected to fetch if sold on the open market, but that price shall not be assumed to be reduced on the ground that the whole property is on the market at one and the same time. The market value of quoted shares and securities is computed in accordance with FA 1975 Sch 10 para 13 (IHTA 1984 s 140(2)).

Where there are intervening transactions between the date of the chargeable transfer and the date of death or qualifying sale, adjustments are made to the valuation of specified property as follows:

Shares: capital receipts
The value is to be increased by any capital receipts (including the proceeds from the sale of rights issues) from the shares (IHTA 1984 s 133).

Payment of calls
The value is to be reduced by any payment of calls made by the transferee or spouse (IHTA 1984 s 134).

Reorganization of share capital
A new holding received by the transferee or spouse is treated as the same property transferred, but where any consideration is given for the new holding the market value is reduced accordingly (IHTA 1984 s 135).

Transfers of value by close companies
An adjustment up or down is to be made where a transfer of value, or an alteration in the rights of unquoted securities is made by a close company and that transaction has reduced or increased the value of the shares (IHTA 1984 s 136).

Interests in land
An adjustment up or down is to be made where there has been a change in the nature or interests in the land to reflect the difference in the market value of the land at the date of the transfer and what would have been the market value at that date if the change had prevailed at that date (IHTA 1984 s 137). Any statutory compensation received is added to the market value at the date of death or qualifying sale.

Leases
Where the lease is for a period of less than 50 years, the market value is increased by an amount equal to the fraction (as shown below) of the market value (IHTA 1984 s 138). The fraction is:

$$\frac{P1 - P2}{P1}$$

where P1 is the percentage as shown in Table 6. Capital Gains Tax - Indexation Allowance - RPI back to 1982, p.625 for the duration of the lease at the time of the transfer, and P2 is the percentage for the duration of the lease at the date of death.

Other property
Where the property at the date of death or qualifying sale is not the same as the property transferred an adjustment up or down is made to reflect the difference in the market value of the property at the date of the transfer and what would have been

the market value at that date if the change in the property had prevailed at that date (IHTA 1984 s 138).

4 GIFTS

4.1 Potentially exempt transfer (PET)

A transfer of value made on or after 18 March 1986 by an individual is a **potentially exempt transfer** if it is made as a gift to an individual or as a gift into an accumulation and maintenance trust or a disabled person's trust. It is exempt from inheritance tax unless the donor dies within seven years of making the gift in which case it is brought into charge in ascertaining the inheritance tax payable. The value which has to be brought into charge is the value at the date of transfer and not the value at the date of death. Where the donor survives seven years after making the gift, the transfer is an exempt transfer, and where the donor dies within seven years of making the gift it becomes a chargeable transfer (IHTA 1984 s 3A; FA 1986 s 101 and Sch 19).

Rates of tax

Where a potentially exempt transfer made after 14 March 1988 became a chargeable transfer, inheritance tax is chargeable at the rate of tax applicable to the aggregate of all chargeable transfers made in the previous seven years at the current rates at death.

However, tapering relief is allowed where the transfer was made more than three years before death and the tax chargeable will be as follows:

Years before transfer and death	Rate %
3-4	32
4-5	24
5-6	16
6-7	8

Annual exemption

An annual exemption of £3,000 is allowable and in the event of a potentially exempt transfer becoming chargeable, it is to be assumed that it was made after utilizing the annual exemption (IHTA 1984 s 19, FA 1986, Sch 19).

For example,
let us suppose that Lucy gives her son £250,000 in October 1998. No tax is payable because it is a PET. She gives £250,000 to her daughter in September 2001. No tax

is payable on this either as it is a PET. Her daughter had got married three months earlier. Lucy gives £55,000 each to her two grandchildren in November 2006. No tax is payable at this time because the gifts are PETs. She dies in August 2009, when her estate is £350,000.

The gift to her son is completely exempt because it was made more than 7 years before her death. The gift to her daughter is also exempt because it was made more than 7 years before her death. The gifts to the grandchildren are chargeable because they were made in the 7 years before her death. The tax payable will be determined by adding these gifts to the gift to the daughter which was made in the previous 7 years (the gift to her son was made more than 7 years before the gift to the grandchildren). To determine the IHT payable on the estate at the date of death it will be necessary to add its value to that of the gifts to the grandchildren but not the two earlier gifts which are outside the chargeable period.

How much tax will Lucy pay?

(i) IHT payable by Lucy's grandchildren on their gifts

	£	£
Amount of gifts (Nov 2006)	110,000	
Less yearly gift allowance 05/06 and 06/07	(6,000)	
Chargeable		104,000
Added to:		
Value of gift to daughter (Sep 01)	250,000	
Less yearly gift allowance 01/02 and 00/01 (unused and brought forward)	(6,000)	
Chargeable		244,000
Total chargeable		348,000
Less limit for 2009/10		(325,000)
Net chargeable		£23,000
Net tax payable by grandchildren at 40%		£9,200

Each grandchild will now have to find £4,600 within 6 months of Lucy's death (i.e. by 28 February 2010). The gifts were made within three years of Lucy's death, so there is no tapering relief. If they had been given the money a year earlier, in November 2002, tapering relief would have operated, and the total tax payable would have been £7,360 (£9,200 x 80%).

(ii) IHT payable on Lucy's estate

	£	£
Estate at death		350,000
Added to: value of gifts to		
grandchildren (Nov 2006)	110,000	
Less yearly gift allowance 05/06 and 06/07	(6,000)	
		104,000
Chargeable		454,000
Less limit for 2009/10		(325,000)
Net chargeable		£129,000
Net tax payable by executors of estate at 40%		£51,600

So Lucy doesn't leave £350,000; her beneficiaries will receive only £298,400. By using the annual reliefs every year, and the £5,000 exemption available when her daughter got married (the gift was after the marriage and not in 'anticipation') she could have reduced the tax payable on the November 2006 gift and on her death. Note that an insurance policy could also have been taken out at the time of the gifts to cover the potential tax liability both to Lucy's grandchildren and to her estate.

Transfers of property for national heritage purposes
Transfers of property such as works of art, etc. for national heritage purposes are exempt if the transferor survives seven years after making the transfer (IHTA 1984 526A; FA 1986, Sch 19 paras 6-12). However, where the transferor does not survive seven years, a claim for conditional exemption could be made for the property to be designated under s 31 IHTA 1984 as being of national, scientific, historic or artistic interest.

Where there is a breach of the undertaking thereby resulting in a 'chargeable event,' tax is charged at the half rates appropriate to lifetime chargeable transfers.

Business property relief
Business property relief is available on potentially exempt transfers where the property is relevant business property as defined in s 105 IHTA 1984 and the business property or replacement business property was owned by the transferee until the transferor's death (or the transferee's death, if earlier). Replacement property is property which has been bought within 3 years after 30.11.93 (previously

12 months) of the sale of some or all of the original property and the sale and the purchase are made at arm's length transactions (IHTA 1984, ss 113A and 113B; FA 1986, Sch 19 para 21, and FA 1994 s 247).

Agricultural property relief
Agricultural property relief is available on potentially exempt transfer on a similar basis to business property relief explained before (IHTA 1984, ss 124A and 124B; FA 1986, Sch 19 para 22, and FA 1994 s 247).

4.2 Gifts with reservation of benefit (GWR)
(1)   There is a free-standing income tax charge which applies from 6 April 2005 on the benefit an individual receives from having a free or low cost enjoyment of assets which they formerly owned.

The charge broadly follows the benefit in kind rules and be subject to a de minimis threshold of £2,500 of benefit. A range of exemptions apply, including an exemption for all gifts made before 18 March 1986 (the starting date for inheritance tax). Transitional relief allows those caught by the new rules to elect by 31 January 2007* that the property falling within the income tax charge will instead be regarded as part of their estate for inheritance tax purposes. Where the first tax year of the new tax charge is later than 2005/2006 the election deadline is 31 January* in the next tax year.

* However the FA2007 allows HMRC to accept late elections.

(a)   Pre-owned assets - the new proposals (FA 2004 Cl 84 and Sch 15)
(i)   Where a father has given an asset to, say, a son or daughter and he continues to enjoy the use of that asset, either free of charge or at below market rent, it is proposed that income tax will be charged, from 2005/06 onwards, on the benefit of using the asset which the donor formerly owned.

(ii)   In effect, the father is treated in much the same way as an employee who enjoys the use of an asset owned by his employer and who pays tax on the resulting benefit in kind.

(b)   Pre-owned assets - the main details
(i)   The new provisions will bite where an individual occupies or enjoys land or chattels and either:

- the disposal condition; or
- the contribution condition is met.

(ii)   Disposal condition (FA 2004 Paras 3(2) and 6(2) Sch 15)
The disposal condition is satisfied where the individual who

owned the land or chattels has disposed of all or part of his interest in the relevant asset on or after 18 March 1986 (the starting date for IHT and the GWR rules) other than by means of an excluded transaction.

(iii) Contribution condition Paras 3(3) and 6(3) Sch 15)
The contribution condition is satisfied where the individual has funded the acquisition of the land or chattels by someone else other than by means of an excluded transaction.

(iv) Excluded transactions (Para 10 Sch 15)
The term excluded transaction covers the following arrangements:

*   the individual disposed of the asset in an arm's length bargain to an unconnected person (the Press Release dated 17 March 2004 states that the consideration must have been paid in cash, but this does not appear to be a statutory stipulation);

*   the individual disposed of the asset to a connected person, but still on an arm's length basis;

*   the asset was transferred to a spouse or to a former spouse under a court order - this includes the case where the transfer was to an interest in possession trust of which the spouse or former spouse is a beneficiary (however, the exemption comes to an end if the trust interest is terminated); and

*   the asset was transferred to an interest in possession trust of which the settlor is the beneficiary (in this case, the asset is anyway still the settlor's for IHT purposes).

(v) Taxable values (Paras 4 and 7 Sch 15)
On the assumption that the individual has satisfied either the disposal condition or the contribution condition, the taxable value of his benefit will be:

*   in the case of real property, the market rent; and

*   in the case of other assets such as art or antiques, interest at a prescribed rate on the asset's capital value (probably the official rate used for measuring the taxable value of cheap or interest free loans - currently 5%).

(vi)   If the entire asset has not been disposed of (or if the financing contribution was not for the whole of the asset), the taxable value will be scaled down proportionately. And the amount charged to income tax will be subject to a set-off for any rent actually paid by the disponor for his continued use of the asset.

(vii)   De minimis let-out (Para 13 Sch 15)
No income tax charge is due under these provisions unless the aggregate amounts otherwise chargeable exceed £2,500. If the taxable value exceeds £2,500, the full amount is caught. It should be noted that, for this purpose, no account is taken of any rent paid by the disponor.

(viii)   Some further exceptions (Para 11 Sch 15)
There are a number of further exceptions which deal with situations where an income tax charge would be inappropriate, i.e:

- where the former owner is enjoying the asset in circumstances in which he is anyway caught by the existing GWR legislation so that, on his death, the asset in question would still be included in his taxable estate;

- where a parent gives a half-share in the family home to, say, a son or daughter who lives with them; or

- Where an individual gives a property to, say, a son or daughter and, at a later stage, he goes to live with the son or daughter because he is unable to look after himself through old age or illness - the detailed rules for this relief are set out in Para 6(1)(b) Sch 20 FA 1986.

(ix)   Scope of the charge (Para 12 Sch 15)
The territorial scope of the charge is as follows:

- the charge will not apply in any tax year when the individual in question is not resident in the UK;

- when an individual is resident in the UK but domiciled elsewhere (for IHT purposes), the charge only will apply to UK-situated assets; and

- when an individual is domiciled in the UK having previously been domiciled elsewhere, the charge will not apply to assets which were disposed of prior to the acquisition of his UK domicile.

(2)   A gift subject to a reservation (FA 1986, s 102 and Sch 20) is a disposal of any property made on or after 18 March 1986 by an individual and either:

•   possession and enjoyment of the property is not bona fide assumed by the donee at or before the beginning of the relevant period; or

•   at any time in the relevant period the property is not enjoyed to the entire exclusion or virtually to the entire exclusion of the donor and of any benefit to him or her by contract or otherwise. Virtually means where the benefit retained by the donor is insignificant. The HMRC interprets 'virtually to the entire exclusion' as permitting limited benefit to the donor from the gifted property without bringing the gift with reservation provisions into play. A number of examples are given to illustrate the HMRC's approach. For instance, a house that becomes the donee's, but where the donor subsequently resides with the donee for less than one month a year or, without the donee, for not more than two weeks a year, would not be regarded as a reservation of benefit. Similarly, social visits to an extent no greater than would have been made to the donee in the absence of the gift, temporary stays for convalescence or while the donor's house is being redecorated, or visits for domestic reasons such as baby-sitting, will not amount to a reservation of benefit. Other cases cited are a car that the donee uses to give occasional lifts to the donor (less than three a month), land used by the donor for walking his dog or riding and a library that the donor visits less than five times a year to borrow a book. Conversely, the use by the donor of such gifts in excess of that suggested in the illustrations would be regarded as a reservation of benefit.

The relevant period is the period ending on the date of the donor's death and beginning seven years before that date or the date of the gift, if it is later. An insurance policy written on the life of the donor or spouse is to be treated as property subject to a reservation where the benefits to the donee vary according to the benefits received by the donor. But transfers made by way of gift and treated as exempt transfers as shown below are not property subject to reservation. The exempt transfers are:

•   transfer between spouses;
•   small gifts;
•   gifts in consideration of marriage;
•   gifts to charities;
•   gifts to political parties;
•   gifts for national purposes;

- gifts for public benefit;
- maintenance funds for historic buildings;
- employee trusts;
- gift of land made to a registered housing association after 13 March 1989.

Where a gift subject to a reservation includes business property or agricultural property in respect of which relief may be available depending on ownership or occupation, the 'donee' is substituted for the donor where the donor dies or the reservation ceases during his or her life.

A gift subject to a reservation is to be treated as property held by the donor at the date of his or her death if it is not excluded property as defined in s 6 IHTA 1984. However, the property will cease to be a gift subject to a reservation if the donor makes a disposition which is a potentially exempt transfer and the normal rules for a potentially exempt transfer will apply from the date of that disposition.

The HMRC have reversed the House of Lords decision in the *Lady Ingram* case 1999 STC 37; 1999 2 WLR 90).

Subject to the exceptions explained next, the new provisions will apply to gifts of interests in land where the gift is made on or after 9 March 1999 and:

- there is some interest, right or arrangement which enables or entitles the donor to occupy the land to a significant degree or enjoy a significant right in relation to the land without paying full consideration;

- the gift is made within seven years after the interest, right or arrangement concerned is granted, acquired or entered into.

The new provisions 'restore the position to what it was understood to be' before the Ingram decision, i.e. the previous situation will still be treated as reservation of benefit, in contrast to what the House of Lords found.

The new provisions will apply to gifts whether the donor or his/her spouse is the person with a significant right or interest, or is a party to an arrangement, relating to the land.

The extended provisions will not apply where:
- as with the existing rules

  - the gift is itself covered by the main exemptions from inheritance tax, including transfers between spouses;
  - the retained right or interest is negligible so that the donor is virtually entirely excluded from any enjoyment of the land;
  - the donor pays full consideration for his/her occupation of the land; or

- the occupation of the land is effectively forced on the donor by some unforeseen downturn in his/her financial circumstances;

- the gift is made more than seven years after the right, interest or arrangement concerned is created or entered into;

- the donor may occupy the land or enjoy some right in relation to it only on the determination of the interest that he/she has given away; for example, the donor gives away a leasehold interest and retains the freehold reversion which entitles him/her to re-occupy the land when the lease expires; or

- the gift is of a share in land, which the donor then occupies jointly with the other owner (the donee) providing the donor receives no other benefit at the donee's expense in connection with the gift.

These exceptions might be hard to demonstrate. For example, a home-owner who gifts a part interest to his (adult) daughter and then occupies the house jointly may well receive many benefits from her. Who is to say which of them are 'in connection with the gift'?

There will, it seems, be innocent arrangements which could be caught by the new provisions. A farmer who gifts the freehold of two farms respectively to his two sons will not be caught if his partnership with one of those sons is the tenant on the first farm. If the other son is not jointly occupying the other farm, then the anti-avoidance provisions apply.

Brief details of the Ingram case are that on 29.3.87 Lady Ingram transferred her house outright to her solicitor. Later that day the solicitor declared that he held the property as nominee for Lady Ingram and agreed to deal with it as she might direct. The following day at Lady Ingram's direction the solicitor granted to her two leases which together extended to the whole of the property for a 20 year term from 30.3.87 rent-free. On 31.3.87 again at Lady Ingram's direction the solicitor transferred the property subject to the leases to her two sons and her grandson (the trustees). Also on that day the trustees acting on Lady Ingram's direction executed two declarations of trust to the effect that the trustees held the property subject to the leases for the benefit of certain beneficiaries from which Lady Ingram was irrevocably excluded.

The following consequences were envisaged:
- There would be an effective settlement, with no liability to ad valorem stamp duty;

- Lady Ingram's interest under the leases would be created before the gift to the beneficiaries under the trust;

- The transfer in favour of the beneficiaries would be a PET;

- The gift of the reversion would be a chargeable transfer if Lady Ingram died within seven years and in terms of valuation would benefit from the leases continuing in favour of Lady Ingram's estate.

Lady Ingram died on 3.2.89 within two years of the settlement. However, the HMRC refused to accept the previous consequences and issued a notice of determination on the basis that the property attracted IHT at the death rate as property subject to a reservation within s102(2) FA 1986. The executors appealed.

Following hearings in the high court and court of appeal, the case finally reached the House of Lords who in 1998 found in favour of Lady Ingram (*Ingram & Another v IRC* (1998) STI 1739).

In the 'Eversden' case (*IRC v Eversden* (2003) EWCA Civ 668 and (2003) STC 822) only brief details will be given as a late insertion of a clause S102(5A) on 20 June 2003 into the Finance Bill 2003 has now blocked the following loophole.

Both the High Court and Appeal Court decided that the exception in the current Gift with Reservation charge for gifts to a spouse applies in the case of settled property even after an initial interest in possession for the donor's spouse comes to an end. This effectively opened the way for schemes structured around a short-lived interest for the donor's spouse to escape the normal charge. They could, for example, allow a husband and wife to remove the family home, or a portfolio of financial assets, from IHT on both their deaths, but to continue living in the home, or enjoying the financial assets, throughout their lifetimes.

(3) Pre-owned assets regulations (issued 07.03.2005)
    The main points on the regulations are as follows:

- The valuation date for a tax year will be 6 April in the year or, if later, the beginning of the 'taxable period' for which the asset in question first becomes chargeable.

- The 'prescribed rate' (for values of chattels and intangible assets) will be equal to the 'official rate' of interest (currently 5.0%).

- Land and chattels will be valued in the first tax year in which the asset first becomes chargeable and then every five years. That valuation will be used in any of the four succeeding years in which a charge arises. If a charge arises in the fifth year, a fresh valuation will be made which will apply in the next four succeeding years and so on.

- The Regulations will exempt from charge bona-fide equity release schemes with arm's length providers. The existing exemption will be extended following concerns that many intra-family part-disposals would be caught. the Paymaster's statement says: "Bringing together these different considerations, the regulations will extend the existing exemption (described above) to all sales done at arm's length where they involve the whole or a part of the vendor's interest in their asset. They will extend this exemption to any part sale, even if not a arm's length, so long as it was made before today and on arm's length terms. And this will also apply to future disposals if they are made for a consideration other than money or readily realisable assets."

5 THE CHARGE RELATED TO SETTLEMENTS AND CLOSE COMPANIES

5.1 Introduction

Settlements and close companies have been the most effective vehicles for mitigation and avoidance of taxation liabilities and legislation has been introduced to counteract such schemes. Before considering the implications of settlements and close companies in relation to inheritance tax it is necessary to define the terms and objects of such schemes.

5.1.1 Settlements

A settlement (IHTA 1984 s 43(2)) is a disposition of property (however effected) whereby property is, for the time being:

• held in trust for persons in succession or for any person subject to a contingency; or

• held on trust for accumulation of income, or for payments at the discretion of any person out of income (with or without power to accumulate surplus income); or charged or burdened (other than for full consideration to the person making the disposition) with any annuity or other periodical payment payable for a life or any other limited or terminable period.

5.1.2 Lease of property

A lease of property is a settlement, if it is for a life or lives, or for a period ascertainable only by reference to a death, and unless it was granted for full consideration (IHTA 1984 s 43(3)). A lease is terminable at the time the rent can, under the terms of the lease, be increased, if it was not granted at a rack rent. The lessee's interest is to be taken as the complement of the fraction which the value of the lessor's interest bears to the value of the property (IHTA 1984 s 50(6)).

5.1.3 Settlor

The settlor (IHTA 1984 s 44) is the person who directly or indirectly made, or provided the funds (including under reciprocal arrangements) for the purpose of, or in connection with the settlement. Where there is more than one settlor in relation to any settlement, the property is to be regarded as comprised in separate settlements.

5.1.4 Trustee

The trustee is (if otherwise there would be no trustee) the person in whom the settled property or its management is vested (IHTA 1984 s 45). Apart from this it must bear its ordinary meaning.

5.1.5 Reversionary interest

Reversionary interest (IHTA 1984 s 47) means a future interest under a settlement, whether it is vested or contingent, (including an interest expectant on the termination of an interest in possession). It therefore includes the interest of a remainderman, as well as the interest of a settlor on reversion. Also included is the contingent, or vested but defeasible, interest of, for example, an infant under an accumulation trust (i.e. where income is directed to be accumulated) where the accumulations may not accrue to the person in question.

5.1.6 Interest in possession

Interest in possession is not defined in the legislation. However, only the interest in possession to which an individual is beneficially entitled is covered, except that a company's interest counts if:

- its business consists wholly, or mainly in the acquisition of such interests; and
- it acquired the interest concerned for full consideration from an individual beneficially entitled to it.

Moreover, the participators in a close company are to be regarded as beneficially entitled to a close company's interest in possession, according to their respective rights and interests (including winding up and other rights) in the company (IHTA 1984 s 101).

A person who has merely what is called a spes (a hope of some benefit), but no claim recognised in law or equity, has no 'interest' in settled property, at least so long as there are two or more members of the class of possible objects (*Gartside v CIR* H L 1967). That the interest must be 'in possession must mean that your interest enables you to claim now whatever may be the subject of the interest'. It therefore excludes all 'reversionary interests', as defined above. However, this does not exclude property which is currently producing no income or other benefit. It is sufficient that, if there were income, the person in question could claim it, so there can be a beneficial interest in possession in a settled policy of life assurance (*Westminster Bank Limited v CIR* H L 1958). Moreover, an interest in income (if any) which is vested but defeasible (e.g. on exercise of a power of appointment or revocation or on the birth of new members of the class) is nonetheless an interest in possession and not a future interest (*Kilpatrick's Policy Trusts C A 1966*). The above interpretation accords with a statement by HMRC (PR IR 12 February 1976). The trustees' right to claim expenses or other outgoings properly chargeable to income does not affect an interest in possession (e.g. if they need the income). A discretion or power to withhold income (including a power of appointment or of accumulation) does not negate an interest in possession, provided the beneficiary has a vested interest in whatever income is not taken from him or her in exercise of such discretion or power (*Pearson v CIR* C A 1979).

Examples of interests which are 'interests in possession' would be:

- a **life interest in possession:** For example, property is settled on T for life, remainder to X for life, remainder to Y absolutely. T has an interest in possession and X and Y reversionary interests. When T's interest ends, X will have an interest in possession and Y a reversionary interest.

- an **annuity:** For example, property is settled for B absolutely, subject to an annuity to A for life. A has an interest in possession for the amount of his annuity, and B has an interest in possession and also a reversionary interest expectant on A's death.

- **other vested interests in income:** For example, property is settled on C until he or she attains the age of 25 years, the income to be accumulated in the meantime. During C's Minority there is no interest in possession, but, when he or she attains 18 years of age, s 31(1)(ii) Trustees Act 1925 confers a vested interest in income on him or her (unless excluded by the trust deed) and he or she then has an interest in possession until he or she attains an absolute interest or dies. The settlor has a reversionary interest expectant on C's death.

A person entitled to part only of the income is treated as beneficially entitled to a proportionate part of the property comprised in the settlement (IHTA 1984 s 50). The Treasury has power to prescribe a notional rate of income, presumably to deal with the case where settled property temporarily produces a low income yield and the person's share is a specified amount (e.g. an annuity) (IHTA 1984 s 50 (3)). The rate of the gross yield is computed by reference to the FT Actuaries Share Indices for British Government Stocks ('Irredeemable').

An annual value is to be attributed to the use enjoyed by tenants in common or joint tenants who have no right to income as such between them according to their respective annual values (IHTA 1984 s 50 (6)).

5.1.7 Residence occupied by beneficiary
The existence of a power to permit a beneficiary to occupy a dwelling house on such terms as the trustees think fit is not regarded as excluding any interest in possession. Whether or not an interest in possession already exists in the property, the exercise of such a power will not be regarded as creating an interest in possession if the occupation is non-exclusive or under a contractual tenancy for full

consideration. Creation of a lease for a term or a periodic tenancy for less than full consideration does not create an interest in possession. However, the exercise of the power so as to create an exclusive or joint right of residence (even if revocable), for a definite or indefinite period, with the intention of providing a permanent home for a beneficiary will be regarded as creating an interest in possession (SP 10/79).

5.1.8 Limited interests in residue

Limited interests in residue of a deceased person's estate do not confer any beneficial interest until the administration is completed. Accordingly, the fact that the administration of the estate is not for the time being completed will not prevent an interest in possession being deemed to exist (IHTA 1984 s 91), and the legatee will be regarded as interested in the underlying assets.

General legatees are not entitled to income until the end of the 'executor's year', so that the legatee with a limited interest will have no interest in possession during that period (*Re Harrison* ChD 1918). However, there are exceptional cases, particularly that of children of the testator, when an interest in possession may accrue as from the date of the death.

5.1.9 Survivorship clauses

If the property is held for any person on condition that such person survives another for a specified period of not more than six months, the disposition taking effect at the end of that period or on earlier death, is deemed to have taken effect at the beginning (IHTA 1984 s 92). An election not to apply the above provision may be made within 12 months (or longer if the Board allows), if the person with the conditional interest is the spouse of the other person and dies within the survivorship period and before 1 January 1977. The election must be made by the personal representatives of each spouse and the trustees of every settlement in which either of them had an interest in possession immediately before their death. The election will be advantageous where the first spouse to die has a lower aggregate of chargeable transfers than the second spouse would have if the latter's estate included the bequest from the first to die.

A widower acquired an interest in possession under the terms of his wife's will, which left her interest as tenant-in-common in the matrimonial home to her daughter, subject to her husband's having a right of sole and secure occupancy of the property until his death. Accordingly, on his death his interest in the property should be valued as the entire freehold interest and not merely the half-share he held prior to his wife's demise as tenant-in-common. Chancery Division so held in *IRC v Lloyds Private Banking Ltd* (1998) STI 578.

5.2 The charge on making a settlement

When a person makes a settlement other than for full consideration, there will be a chargeable transfer subject to any exemption or relief, being available against the liability arising thereon. In certain circumstances, charges may also arise during the life and the termination of the settlement. Whether or not the creation of a settlement is in fact a transfer of value will depend on whether or not there is a beneficial interest in possession in the settlement and to whom that interest belongs. If there is such an interest and it belongs to the settlor, there will be no transfer of value, as the person beneficially entitled to an interest in possession in a settlement is regarded as beneficially entitled to the property comprised in the settlement (IHTA 1984 s 49). The property continues, despite the settlement, to be regarded as part of the settlor's estate and there is no reduction in the value of the estate. If the settlor's spouse is domiciled in the UK and entitled to the interest in possession in the settlement, there would be a transfer of value, but it would be an exempt transfer. The same would apply where a person or body other than the spouse became entitled to the interest in possession, but that person or body conferred exemption on the transfer. A settlement of 'excluded property' would not create any transfer of value; nor could there be any subsequent occasions of charge in relation to such property (IHTA 1984 s 53). A settlement created by a disposition which is deemed not to give rise to a transfer of value would not impose any liability on the settlor.

In the case of any other settlement, there will be a chargeable transfer of value when it is made and when any property is added. There is no chargeable transfer on the creation of a settlement in which no interest in possession subsists, if the settlor is a mentally disabled person or in receipt of attendance allowance, and the settled property is applicable wholly or mainly for his or her benefit during his or her life (IHTA 1984 s 89).

A charge on settlements will arise where no interest in possession is created or where such an interest arises, but the transfer is neither relieved, nor exempted.

There is provision to forestall the avoidance of inheritance tax by procuring a superannuation fund to make a settlement of a lump sum benefit on behalf of the settlor.

5.3 The charge related to interests in possession
5.3.1 The charge
The disposal of an interest (or part) is not of itself a transfer of value, but is treated as a termination of the interest (or part) by reference to which inheritance tax is chargeable (IHTA 1984 s 51). It is necessary to consider what constitutes a 'disposal', for, in the absence of any definition, it may be taken to have its ordinary meaning. As such it is to be expected that any dealing which reduces the beneficial enjoyment of the interest will be a disposal.

Accordingly, not only a sale or gift, but also the charging or mortgaging of, and the grant of an option (if exercise would be specifically enforceable) over the interest in possession may be a disposal of at least part of the interest. Likewise, the surrender of a right will be a disposal, but not the gratuitous disclaimer of an interest. A variation of a trust, involving the surrender of an interest in possession and the creation of a discretionary trust, has been held to 'operate as a voluntary disposition' of the interest in possession (*Thorn v CIR* ChD 1976, a stamp duty case).

Any consideration (other than a reversionary interest under the same settlement) received for the interest (or part) disposed of reduces the value transferred (IHTA 1984 s 52(2)).

The termination of an interest (or part) during the lifetime of the person beneficially entitled is treated as a transfer of value by that person at the value of the property (or part) in which the interest (or part) subsisted (IHTA 1984 s 52(1)). However, there is no such charge where, if estate duty had continued in force, the interest would have been eligible for 'surviving spouse exemption' on the assumption that the transferor (i.e. the surviving spouse) died immediately before the (*inter vivos*) termination of the interest. If the person whose interest terminates immediately becomes beneficially entitled to the property, or to another interest in possession in the property, inheritance tax will not be charged except to the extent that the value of the new interest is less than that of the terminated interest.

Certain transactions reducing the value of settled property (e.g. an interest-free loan) are regarded as terminations of interests in possession and termination is deemed to occur *pro tanto* when the value of the property in which an interest in possession subsists is reduced by virtue of a transaction made between the trustees and a person who either:

(a)   is beneficially entitled to the interest in possession concerned, or

(b)   is beneficially entitled to any other interest in that property, or to any other property comprised in the settlement, or

(c)   may have any of the settled property applied for his benefit, or

(d)   is connected with a person within para.'s (a), (b) or (c).

However, this applies only where the transaction would be a transfer of value if carried out by an individual (IHTA 1984 s 52(3)).

Where a person acquires an **interest in possession** in settled property as a result of a disposition for a consideration in money or money's worth, the decision as to whether or not such a purchase is a transfer of value is determined by the actuarial value of the interest acquired, and not the value of the underlying assets supporting the interest (IHTA 1984 s 49(2)).

5.3.2 Reliefs
The reliefs available for settlements with interests in possession are as follows:

Inheritance (Provision for Family and Dependants) Act 1975

The provision for family and dependants of a deceased person made by a court order under the Inheritance (Provision for Family and Dependants) Act 1975 where the death occurred after 6 April 1976, does not give rise to a charge to inheritance tax as the property is treated as having devolved on death (IHTA 1984 s 146(6)).

Reversion to settlor or spouse (or civil partner)

On termination of an interest (during life or on death) and a reversion to the settlor during the latter's life, inheritance tax is not chargeable, unless the settlor or spouse acquired the reversion for money or money's worth (IHTA 1984 s 53(5)). Similarly, inheritance tax is not charged if the settlor's spouse (or where the settlor died less than two years previously, a widow or widower of the settlor) becomes beneficially entitled to the settled property, provided that he or she is then domiciled in the UK and neither of them had acquired any reversionary interest in the property for consideration (IHTA 1984 s 53(4)).

Successive charges relief

Where a person's estate is increased by a chargeable transfer made within five year's preceding death, the tax chargeable on death is reduced by a percentage of the tax paid in respect of the first transfer (IHTA 1984 s 141). The percentages are:

*   100% if within one year;
*   80% if outside one year but within two years;
*   60% if outside two years but within three years;
*   40% if outside three years but within four years;
*   20% if outside four years but within five years;

The relief is only available in relation to settlements if:

*   the first transfer was (or included) the making of the settlement or was made after the making of the settlement, and
*   the value transferred by the later transfer relates to the value of settled property in which the transferor had an interest in possession, and
*   the value transferred by the first transfer related to the value of that property.

If full relief cannot be granted because the tax charge on the second transfer is insufficient, credit may be given against tax chargeable on the next subsequent transfer and so on in strict chronological order until relief has been allowed for the whole of the tax paid on the first transfer.

Trustees' annuities

The termination or disposal of an interest in possession does not give rise to a charge to inheritance tax to the extent that the interest is no more than reasonable remuneration for services as trustee of the settlement (IHTA 1984 s 90).

Potentially exempt transfers

Where transfers or other events as listed next occur on or after 17 March 1987, they are treated as potentially exempt transfers, i.e. there will be no charge to inheritance tax if the event occurred more than seven years before the death of the transferor (IHTA 1984 s 3A; F(No.2)A 1987 s 96). The events treated as potentially exempt are:

- an individual settling property in his or her absolute ownership or trust for the benefit of another individual with an interest in possession;

- the termination of an interest in possession by an individual during his or her lifetime followed by the property being vested to another individual or becoming the subject of an accumulation and maintenance trust or a disabled trust;

- the termination of an interest in possession by an individual during his or her lifetime followed by the property becoming subject to another trust in which another individual has an interest in possession;

- the purchase of a reversionary interest by the beneficiary entitled to the interest in possession.

5.4 The charge when no interest in possession subsists

In order to determine the inheritance tax liability on discretionary trusts it is necessary to define the settled property which is referred to as 'relevant property' (IHTA 1984 s 58).

5.4.1 Relevant property

Relevant property means settled property with no qualifying interest in possession other than:

Changes to the way trusts are treated for IHT were announced on 22 March 2006 (Budget day). Some were effective immediately. A few changes were made prior to royal assent of the Finance Act.

The trusts affected are Accumulation & Maintenance trusts (A&M) and Income in Possession trusts (IIP).

With limited exceptions A&M and IIP trusts established after 22 March 2006 will be regarded as 'relevant property' trusts.

Existing A&M trusts

Pre 22 March 2006 A&M trust become 'relevant property' from 6 April 2008 and the periodic and exit charges will apply. The first periodic charge after that date will arise by reference to the ten-yearly anniversaries from the original date of the settlement.

However, the first periodic charge will be adjusted to reflect the fact that the property has not been 'relevant property' for the whole of the ten year period. None of this will apply where the terms of the trust are modified before 6 April 2008 so that the assets go to a beneficiary absolutely at the age of 18 (increased to 25 during passage of the Bill).

Existing IIP trusts

The pre-existing rules continue to apply for IIP trusts until the interest in the trust property at 22 March 2006 comes to an end. If someone then becomes absolutely entitled to the property by transfer on death the normal IHT rules will apply. Similarly if the transferor is still alive the transfer will be a PET (potentially exempt transfer).

- property held for a limited time or otherwise for charitable purposes only;
- property held on accumulation and maintenance trusts;
- property held for maintenance of historic buildings;
- property held by trustees of superannuation funds;
- property held by trustees for employees, etc., and newspaper trusts;
- property held on protective trusts;
- property held on trusts for disabled people;
- property comprised in a trade or professional compensation fund;
- excluded property;

5.4.2 Occasions of charge to inheritance tax

The legislation imposes three kinds of charge on relevant property: an entry charge, a periodic charge and an exit charge.

An immediate "entry" IHT charge of 20% will apply on lifetime transfers into the trusts that exceed the IHT threshold;

A "periodic" IHT charge of 6% will apply on the value of trust assets over the IHT threshold once every ten years; and

An "exit" IHT charge, proportionate to the periodic charge, will apply when funds are taken out of a trust between ten-year anniversaries.

However, no charge will arise under the following conditions:

- if the event occurs within three months of the day on which the settlement commenced or a ten-year anniversary; or

- on a payment of costs or expenses; or

- on a payment which is income in the hands of the recipient; or

- on property which ceases to be relevant property on becoming held indefinitely for charitable purposes, held on employee trusts, comprised in a maintenance fund or excluded property.

The charge to inheritance tax is on the amount of the reduction in the relevant property and if the tax is paid out of relevant property then the charge is on the grossed-up amount.

Discretionary payments out of residue
From 16 March 1993 such payments are treated as the income of the recipient and as gross amounts after deduction of tax at the basic rate. The imputed tax may be recovered by exempt bodies, such as charities, and by individuals not liable to tax, but the grossed up income may be liable to higher rate tax.

Trustees are liable for the additional rate on the income and for imputed tax at 20% on dividends received by the trust.

5.5 The charge on reversionary interests
5.5.1 Acquisition of a reversionary interest
Where a person entitled to an interest (whether in possession or not) in any settled property acquires a reversionary interest expectant (whether immediately or not) on that interest, the reversionary interest is not part of the estate (IHTA 1984 s 55).

5.5.2 Disposition of a reversionary interest
A reversionary interest is excluded property (IHTA s 48), unless

- it has at any time been acquired for consideration; or

- it is one (under a settlement made after 15 April, 1976) to which either he settlor or his or her spouse is beneficially entitled; or

- it is the reversion to a lease treated as a settlement (FA 1975 s 24(3)).

Excluded property does not, however, include a reversionary interest in settled property situated outside the UK, unless the person beneficially entitled to it is an individual domiciled outside the UK (IHTA 1984 s 48).

The disposition of a reversionary interest prior to 17 March 1987 is not a potentially exempt transfer, but if the event occurs after 16 March 1987 it is a potentially exempt transfer (IHTA 1984 s 55; F(No.2)A 1987s 96).

5.6 The charge on apportionment of transfers of value by close companies
5.6.1 The charge on individuals
Where a close company makes a transfer of value, inheritance tax is charged on such transfers at the rates which would have applied had a due proportion of the transfer of value been made by each of the participators in the company (other than

persons who are participators by reason only of being loan creditors).

The value transferred by the company is to be apportioned among the participators according to their rights and interests in the company (including rights to distributions in the event of winding up or in any other circumstances) but ignoring preference shares where the effect of a transfer of value on them is comparatively small immediately before the transfer.

In ascertaining the rights and interests of participators in a subsidiary company which had transferred an asset at an undervalue to a member of a 75% group free of tax on chargeable gains the rights and interests of minority participators in the company are to be ignored provided the transfer has only a small effect on the value of their rights and interests compared with its effect on the other rights and interests. Accordingly, none of the transfer of value will be apportioned to the minority participators. Minority participators are those who are not participators in the ultimate parent company or in any of its participators and who are not connected with any such participators (IHTA 1984 s 97).

The following are exempt and not apportioned:

- any value attributable to any payment or transfer of assets to any person which is taken into account in computing the transferee's profits, or gains or losses for the purposes of income tax or corporation tax;

- dividends and other distributions not chargeable to corporation tax under TA 1988 s 208;

- a surrender of a surplus of advance corporation tax or losses within a group under TA 1988 s 402 and FA 1988 s 240;

- any amount attributable to the value of property outside the UK which is apportionable to an individual domiciled outside the UK.

Amounts apportioned to a close company are sub-apportioned among its participators, until none is apportioned to a close company.

Inheritance tax is charged at the rate appropriate to the difference between:

- the grossed up equivalent of each individual participator's apportioned amount, and

- the increase, by reason of the company's transfer, in the value of the participator's estate (excluding any rights or interests in the company), or in the value of the part of the estate of another company attributable to the participator's direct or indirect interests in that other company (IHTA 1984 s 94).

Transfers of value, chargeable to income tax or corporation tax on the recipient, or attributable to the value of property situate outside the UK and apportionable to an individual domiciled thereout, are not to be apportioned.

In determining the rate at which inheritance tax is to be chargeable, the participator can set the annual exemption of £3,000 against any amounts apportioned on that person, but not the exemptions for small gifts, normal expenditure gifts or gifts in consideration of marriage (IHTA 1984 s 94).

5.6.2 The charge on trustees of settlements

Where a person is a participator in the capacity as trustee of a settlement any amount apportioned to that person less any increase in the value of the settled property not attributable to the apportionment is charged as follows.

- If there is a qualifying interest in possession in the property, the charge is made as bringing to an end the appropriate part of the settled property.

- If there is no qualifying interest in possession in the property, the charge is made as if it had been a capital distribution (IHTA 1984 s 99).

5.6.3 Liability for tax

The company is primarily liable for tax on amounts apportioned to the participators, but if it is not paid by the due date for payment the liability for the payment will fall on the participators and any individuals benefiting from the transfer subject to the following limitations.

- A person to whom not more than 5% of the value transferred is apportioned is not liable for any such tax.

- Each of the other persons to whom only part of the value transferred has been apportioned is liable only for the tax corresponding to that part apportioned to him.

- A person benefiting from the transfer by an increase in the value of his or her estate is liable only to the extent of that increase.

A person not liable under the 5% exception is not regarded for future transfers by him or her as having made any transfer of value by virtue of the apportionment (IHTA 1984 s 94(4)).

An apportioned amount will be regarded as a 'relevant transfer' in relation to settled property even though it is not more than 5% of the whole (IHTA 1984 s 99).

5.7 Foreign aspects of inheritance tax and transitional provisions
5.7.1 Territorial limitations of inheritance tax

There are two primary connecting factors which limit the scope of inheritance tax. These are domicile of the transferor, settlor or deceased and the situation of the property.

5.7.2 Free estate

A person domiciled in any part of the UK is chargeable on dispositions of property or, on death, property comprised in his or her estate, no matter where that property is situated. On the other hand, a person not so domiciled is not chargeable on dispositions of property situated outside the UK, nor does his or her estate on death include such property for it is 'excluded property.'

Certain exemptions are dependent on domicile. Thus, the exemption on inter-spousal dispositions is restricted to £90,000 if the transferee is not domiciled in the UK. On the other hand, the exemptions for National Savings and certain exempt Government securities are dependent on domicile in the Channel Islands or Isle of Man. Exceptionally, the relief for members of visiting forces is dependent on any member not being a citizen of the UK and colonies. Moreover, presence here as a member of a visiting force will not count as residence in the UK (e.g. for the extended meaning of 'domicile' see 5.7.4 Domicile, p.581) nor constitute a change of residence or domicile (IHTA 1984 s 155).

5.7.3 Settled Property

The first problem is to ascertain whether or not a foreign disposition constitutes a 'settlement'. There is a settlement, if either:

- there would be a settlement if the disposition were regulated by the law of any part of the UK; or

- the effect of the foreign law governing the administration of the property is equivalent to that which would apply if it were a settlement (IHTA 1984 s 43).

Whether or not a foreign law governs the administration of property is a matter of international law. For example, the law where the property is situated governs immovables (e.g. land).

Having ascertained that there is a settlement, the next question will be whether or not there is an 'interest in possession'. The legislation is silent on which law is to govern here. Presumably, there will be an interest in possession if the effect of the disposition, or of the property's administration, is that a person has rights equivalent in effect to a person with an interest in possession in an English settlement.

If the property comprised in the settlement is situated outside the UK, it is excluded property unless the settlor was domiciled in the UK when the settlement was made.

Accordingly, dealings with an interest in possession will not be charged, nor will the property representing it be included in a deceased person's estate. On the other hand, a reversionary interest in such property is excluded property only if the person beneficially entitled to it is an individual domiciled outside the UK. The annual charge on non-resident settlements with no interest in possession is limited to property situated in the UK., unless the settlor was domiciled in the UK.

5.7.4 Domicile

The domicile of a person under general law is extended for the purposes of inheritance tax (IHTA 1984 s 267) by treating a person not domiciled in the UK as so domiciled if:

*   he or she was domiciled in the UK after 9 December 1974, and within (not throughout) the three years immediately preceding the relevant time; or

*   he or she was resident in the UK after 9 December 1974, in not less than 17 of the 20 years of assessment ending with the year then current (residence has the same meaning as for income tax, except that any dwelling house available for use in the UK is disregarded).

This extended meaning of domicile in any part of the UK is referred to as the 'extended domicile'. It is to be noted that, for some inheritance tax purposes, the 'general domicile' applies (e.g. certain excluded property) and this has been indicated in the text above. Unless so indicated, domicile in the above text has the extended meaning although by virtue of double taxation treaties the extended meaning may be excluded.

Domicile of choice

Civil Engineer v IRC - SpC 299 case concerns the acquisition of domicile of choice for inheritance tax. Mr C was born in England and he had an English domicile of origin. He started working as a consulting civil engineer in London in 1949 and in 1960 he took up a permanent pensionable post in Hong Kong. In 1966 he set up his own consulting practice in Hong Kong in 1966, later setting up offices in four other countries. In 1967 he also became a partner in a London firm of consulting engineers. Throughout his stay in Hong Kong he had lived in rented accommodation and he finally left Hong Kong in 1989. Mr C had owned a property in the UK between 1960 and 1976, which had been occupied for his parents for part of the time.

In 1976 he closed his London office and disposed of his UK property and his UK visits varied between nil and 36 days a tax year between 1980/81 and 1988/89. A letter from Mr C's accountants to the inspector of taxes stated that he had severed his business, social and personal connections with Hong Kong as of November 1990. He notified the UK HMRC that he had arrived in the UK in June 1990 but had been resident in Jersey between January and April 1990. During his brief stay in Jersey he set up two offshore trusts with nominal amounts of capital, one of which had charitable objects.

On the day of his arrival in the UK in April 1990 Mr C transferred £375,000 to one of the settlements and £75,000 to the other. On the same day he completed the purchase of a UK house for himself and his wife to live in as their main residence.

HMRC subsequently served Mr C with a determination to inheritance tax in respect of the two transfers made in April 1990, being chargeable lifetime transfers. Mr C appealed contending inter alia that he was not domiciled in the UK at the time of the transfers.

The Special Commissioner agreed with HMRC's contention that Mr C had never acquired a domicile of choice in Hong Kong. The key issue when it comes to determining domicile is the taxpayer's intention, particularly for the future. There had been a clear indication of intention when Mr C had disposed of his UK property and closed his London office in 1976 as a result of tax changes in Finance Act 1974 with the introduction of Capital Transfer Tax and this was further supported by his refusal on several occasions to buy UK property when his wife wanted him to do so. The Special Commissioner agreed with HMRC that this was indicative of his intention to cease to be resident in the UK but was not relevant to domicile. It was common knowledge that many British people worked in Hong Kong during the British lease intending to retire to England and thus retained their English domicile of origin. Leaving Hong Kong in 1989 with the intention of not returning would result in the immediate revival of his English domicile of origin even if he had acquired a domicile of choice in Hong Kong.

The Special Commissioner dismissed the appeal and confirmed the determination to inheritance tax in respect of the two chargeable transfers.

5.7.5 Double Tax Relief

Provision is made for allowing credit for foreign taxes of a similar character, or chargeable by reference to death or gifts *inter vivos*, and for fixing the situation of any property (IHTA 1984 ss 158, 159). Unilaterally, credit relief is to be given for foreign tax of a similar character (including any tax on, or by reference to, death or gifts *inter vivos*) which is chargeable by reason of the same disposition or other event and which is attributable to the value of property in a foreign territory. Provision is made for cases where property is regarded as situated in both the UK and abroad (e.g. on account of conflicts of law) and where property is taxed in more than one foreign country.

PART THIRTEEN
FOREIGN MATTERS AND
MISCELLANEOUS ITEMS

BUDGET 2011

In the March 2011 Budget the Government announced that they will reform the taxation of non-domiciled individuals by:

- increasing the existing £30,000 annual charge to £50,000 for non-domiciled individuals who have been UK residents for twelve or more years and who wish to retain access to the remittance basis of taxation. The £30,000 charge will be retained for those who have been resident for a least seven years but less than twelve years;

- removing the tax charge when non-domiciled individuals remit foreign income or capital gains to the UK for the purpose of commercial investment in UK businesses; and

- making technical simplifications to some aspects of the current rules to remove undue administrative burdens for non-domiciled individuals.

The Government will consult on the detail in June ahead of legislating in Finance Bill 2012.

The current rules that determine tax residence for individuals are unclear and complex. the Government will consult in June on the introduction of a statutory definition of residence to provide greater certainty for taxpayers.

The Government intends to implement the reforms to non-domicile taxation and the statutory definition of residence from April 2012. There will be no other substantive changes to these rules for the remainder of this Parliament.

1 THE £30,000 ANNUAL CHARGE AND OTHER CHANGES

1.1 Residence and domicile
There is an annual £30,000 charge on non-UK domiciled individuals resident in the UK for at least seven out of the previous nine tax years who wish to claim the remittance basis for 2008/2009 onwards. The Chancellor announced that the rules will not be substantially revisited for the rest of this Parliament and the next one. There are however a number of changes to the original proposals.

1.1.1 The residence test
Any day in which an individual is present in the UK at midnight will count as a day's presence. Days spent in transit, even involving changes between methods of transport, will not count as a day's residence, unless the individual carries out activities that are substantially unrelated to the transit process (e.g. a business meeting).

1.1.2 Non-domiciliaries' income, losses and mortgage interest
Non-domiciled individuals who claim the remittance basis of taxation are called 'remittance basis users' (RBUs). RBUs with unremitted foreign income and gains of less than £2,000 a year will be exempt from the £30,000 charge and will not lose their entitlement to certain allowances and reliefs. Those who do claim the remittance basis are not then entitled to UK personal allowances (Income Tax) and CGT annual exemption. The £30,000 charge will only apply to adults. Non-domiciled individuals who are not RBUs in any given tax year will get relief for their foreign capital losses. Untaxed foreign income that is used to fund interest payments on existing offshore mortgages secured on UK property will not be treated as a taxable remittance. This applies to all payments from 6 April 2008 until the end of the mortgage or 2028 if sooner.

1.1.3 The £30,000 charge
Individuals who pay the £30,000 charge will have RBU status for that year. They may then choose what foreign unremitted income or gains the charge relates to. Then any earmarked income or gain will not be taxed again if it is remitted to the UK. However, untaxed unremitted foreign income and gains are taxed as if they are remitted first before the income and gains on which the £30,000 charge has been paid. It should be possible to credit the £30,000 charge against foreign tax. If the £30,000 is paid directly to HMRC from an offshore source, the payment will not itself be taxed as a remittance.

2 FOREIGN INCOME AND PERSONS ABROAD

2.1 Introductory
The taxation system in this country currently reaches out beyond its shores in three ways:

- It taxes all income of persons who reside in this country, no matter from what part of the world it comes.

- It taxes all income which arises in this country, even though it belongs to persons resident abroad.

- It taxes all income derived from the territorial seas surrounding the UK and certain income from UK zones of the continental shelf, even though it belongs to persons not resident in the UK.

As other countries generally also tax all income arising within their own borders, or belonging to their own residents or, in some cases, nationals, it follows that two countries will often tax the same income. This hardship has become widely recognized, and in order to ensure that tax is not thus borne twice and that each country concerned obtains a reasonable proportion, arrangements known as **double taxation relief agreements** have been made between a large number of countries.

The law concerning foreign income and persons abroad is complex, and is best considered by dealing separately with the two main subjects referred to above:

- persons in the UK with foreign income.
- foreign persons with income in the UK.

Before doing so it is necessary to understand clearly the meanings of the terms **domicile, residence** and **ordinary residence**, as they are connecting factors which determine chargeability and the extent of liability.

2.2 Domicile
In general domicile is the country and State which a person considers to be his or her permanent home. This simple statement is qualified by the fact that a person may have a domicile of origin, choice or dependency.

A domicile of origin is his or her domicile at birth. This will normally be the father's domicile at that time, but in the case of an illegitimate child or one born after the father's death the child's domicile will be that of the mother. A person's domicile of origin can be abandoned by choosing another place of domicile and taking up permanent residence there. If the new domicile of choice is abandoned the domicile of origin is re-established until another domicile is chosen.

A domicile of dependency applies to infants (e.g., under age 16) and persons of unsound mind. An infant's domicile is normally the current domicile of the father; or that of the mother of an illegitimate child, or a child living with a mother separated from her husband, or if the father is dead.

A company is domiciled in its place of incorporation.

The long running residency case of *Robert Gaines-Cooper (2010) EWCA Civ 83* went to the Court of Appeal. Where it confirmed that for those who do not satisfy the rules around taking up full-time employment abroad, there is a need to provide evidence of the severing of connections with the UK to show that the individual has indeed 'left' the UK and become non-resident. This decision was a co-joined judicial review where the taxpayer argued that he had complied with HM Revenue & Customs' then guidance (IR20) in relation to his residency position. HMRC argued it was not bound by its own leaflet and it gave rise to no legitimate expectation. It then accepted that it was indeed bound by the terms of IR20 but that Mr Gaines-Cooper had not adhered to all the terms of that guidance as he did not make a distinct break from the UK. The court agreed. Mr Gaines-Cooper is expected to fight on to the Supreme Court.

2.3 Residence
2.3.1 General meaning
The meaning of residence is not defined in the Taxing Acts and depends on HMRC practice and decisions in the Courts. For some tax purposes it is necessary to distinguish 'ordinary residence' from mere residence.

In general a person is resident in the UK if he or she has a place of abode in this country and lives here for however short a period in the year of assessment.

A tax case on residence was *Shepherd v Revenue Commissioners (2005 SpC 484)*. Captain Shepherd was an airline pilot, splitting his time between Cyprus and the UK. The commissioner found that Captain Shepherd's time in Cyprus constituted temporary absences from the UK and that his presence in the UK was not casual or temporary but substantial and continuous. It was decided that there was not distinct break in the pattern of his life and the most that could be said was that he resided in both the UK and Cyprus. The commissioner took into consideration all the evidence, including Captain Shepherd's past and present habits of life, the regularity and length of his visits, and his ties with the UK. He concluded that Captain Shepherd continued to be resident in the UK, although he seemed to spend only about 80 days a year here. Captain Shepherd appealed to the High Court but it fully supported the commissioner's decision on the facts.

In *Gaines-Cooper v HMRC 2007 EWHC 2617 (Ch)*, Mr Gaines-Cooper failed to establish that he had changed his domicile to the Seychelles, and this case serves to emphasise how tricky the concept of domicile can be. As of August 2010 he has been granted the right to appeal to the Supreme Court, having failed at the Court of Appeal in February 2010.

Tax residence has come up twice. Mr. Grace, a British Airways pilot, was born in South Africa and lived both there and in the UK. From 1997, he regarded his main home as South Africa but retained a house in the UK for use when flying here. Despite the abolition some years ago of the rule that available accommodation could automatically cause somebody to be a tax resident here, HM Revenue & Customs (HMRC) used the fact that Mr. Grace had a house in the UK, plus his regular visits (albeit well under the classic 90 days per year), to argue that he was a UK tax resident. The Special Commissioner allowed the taxpayer's appeal (*Grace v HMRC SpC 663*), pointing out that all relevant facts had to be considered which included the nature of his presence and connection with the UK. After 1997 he was really resident in South Africa; his presence in the UK was for temporary and occasional purposes, with no intention of it being his residence.

If Mr. Grace was successful, Mr. Barrett was less so. He contended that he had left the UK on 5 April 1998 for a whole tax year and so was not resident when he received a significant pay bonus.

The problem was there was no conclusive evidence of where he actually was during the year, demonstrating again that facts are crucial in tax cases (*Barrett v HMRC SpC 639*).

Ordinary residence means continuous residence in the UK as a settled way of life.

The status of resident is not affected by occasional visits abroad for short periods and a person who stays abroad for less than a complete tax year remains a resident in the UK. A stay abroad for more than a tax year to carry on a trade or profession, or for employment, loses residential status from the date of departure, although UK tax allowances remain available for the tax year of departure. These allowances resume on the day before return. ESC A11 provides for the splitting of the tax year in relation to residence. This splitting of the tax year also applies to an accompanying spouse, but that spouse is treated is treated as a resident for any year or part year in which a visit is made to this country (amendment to ESC A11 dated 4 December 1991).

Where a person goes abroad for any other reason than to carry on a trade or profession or for employment, residential status in the UK is retained until the habit of life indicates otherwise. The retention of a place of abode in the UK and visits to the UK for three months in a year are evidence that UK residential status has been retained.

For PAYE purposes an individual coming to the UK is treated as resident in the UK if he or she:

(a) Comes to live permanently in the UK or intends to stay in the UK for at least 3 years; or
(b) is in the UK for more than 183 days in a tax year; or
(c) visits the UK regularly for an average of 91 days per tax year over a 4 year period.

Crucial to this is what exactly is a 'day' in the UK Is it any day you so much as step foot here or is it something different? As a result of a series of tax cases, dating back many years, Revenue & Customs has developed a working practice in this area which ignores days entering and days leaving the UK in determining those dates which count for residency purposes. This is enshrined in Revenue leaflet IR 20. This leaflet was last updated in 1999 and is heavily relied on by tax practitioners.

However from 6 April 2008, the above definition of days has changed to where the person is at midnight (see 1.1.1 The residence test above, p.584).

The Revenue view on its own guidance has been called into question by the special commissioners' decision in *Gaines-Coopers SpC 568*. In this case an individual was seeking to argue he was not resident in the UK. Although he did spend a considerable amount of time here, by excluding days of arrival and departure into the UK he kept within the 91-day rule. Apparently arguing against its own practice, the Revenue contended in Gaines-Cooper that visits where only one night was spent in the UK should count as one day. The taxpayer lost his case and other individuals were left in some confusion as to how to work out their residency position. This is currently under appeal to the Supreme Court.

The Revenue has now issued a Briefing Note in this area (01/07). This states that in the Revenue's view, the 91-day test is only applicable to individuals who have left the UK in judging whether an individual has either left the UK or visits the UK regularly in the Revenue's view the commissioners in Gaines-Cooper had to establish the taxpayer's pattern of residency in the UK, and to disregard his days of departure and arrival would be misleading. The 91-day test was irrelevant in this case as the taxpayer did not 'leave' the UK. Therefore the Revenue is contending its IR 20 guidance is still sufficient.

See also under 2.3.4 Ordinarily resident, p.589.

2.3.2 The place of abode

A place of abode is ignored in determining residence. Duties which are independent of the overseas duties are not regarded as incidental, even if they only amount to one-twentieth of the activities, as in the case of an airline pilot who made occasional flights to the UK, the test being qualitative, not quantitative (*Robson v Dixon* ChD 1972).

A person is regarded as resident here if:

* he or she is in this country for six months (*Wilkie v CIR* ChD 1951) or more in any tax year to 5 April (*Lysaght v CIR* HL 1928); or

* he or she visits this country for three months or more each year for five successive years. In these circumstances the person is regarded as resident here for the fifth year. If, however, the intention from the outset was to make substantial and regular visits, residence in the UK is established from the first year. (Note: This has no statutory force. It is the interpretation by HMRC and has been generally accepted for many years.)

2.3.3 Temporary visits to the UK

Where an individual is on a temporary visit to the UK, and this visit has to be extended because of exceptional circumstances beyond his or her control such as illness or hostilities in the country to which he or she should have returned, any days spent in the UK because of the exceptional circumstances will be excluded from any calculation in determining the time spent in the United Kingdom (SP 2/91).

Political unrest in North Africa and the UK residence rules

Affects of the 'exceptional circumstances' arising from the political unrest in Egypt, Tunisia and Libya and the UK residence rules. Extra days spent in the UK purely as a result of evacuations from these countries will constitute 'exceptional circumstances' and so be disregarded in considering whether an individual is resident in the UK.

HMRC has confirmed that the Foreign and Commonwealth Office (FCO) has advised individuals to leave as soon as it is safe to do so.

'Exceptional circumstances' will only apply for the period individuals were advised by the FCO to leave the countries affected and the week thereafter.

2.3.4 Ordinarily resident

This phrase has puzzled the lawyers, some holding that it means precisely the same as 'resident'. The general view, however, is that it is narrower in its application and means residence as part of a settled way of life, as distinct from occasional or casual residence (*Miesegeas v CIR* ChD 1957). A person who had a place of abode in the UK where he or she stayed for at least two complete tax years would be regarded as ordinarily resident in the UK. In case of limited companies, the attempt to distinguish 'resident' and 'ordinarily resident' has been abandoned (*Egyptian Delta Land and Investment Co. Ltd v Todd* HL 1929).

For PAYE purposes an individual coming to the UK would be regarded as 'ordinarily resident' where:

(a)   He or she intends to stay for at least 3 years, or
(b)   visits the UK regularly and the visits average 91 days or more in a tax year over 4 years.

2.3.5 Change of residence

When a person takes up permanent residence abroad, or comes from abroad to take up permanent residence in the UK, to stay for three years, or to take employment which is expected to last for at least two years, by concession (ESC No. A11) the assessment for the year of change is limited to the period of actual residence in the UK instead of the whole year. But the individual must not have been ordinarily resident in the UK prior to arrival or on departure, and the concession would not apply, for example, where a person ordinarily resident in the UK left for intended permanent residence abroad but returned to reside here before the end of the tax year following the year of departure. The concession has only limited application to changes of permanent residence between the UK and Eire and to income arising in Eire.

2.3.6 Bodies corporate

On and after 17 March 1993, and with certain special exemptions for companies which had migrated from the UK, all companies incorporated after that date in the UK are treated as resident in the UK.

The term 'ordinarily resident' has the same meaning as 'resident' when applied to a company.

2.3.7 Dual residence

Individuals may be resident in more than one territory by the respective local laws and thus could be doubly taxed. Where a double taxation agreement exists between the UK and the other territory, there is usually provision for resolving the conflict and regarding the individual as resident in only one of the territories for the purpose of the benefits under the agreement. The criteria usually are:

*   permanent home, but if one in each territory
*   centre of vital interests, but if it cannot be determined
*   habitual abode, failing which
*   nationality, failing which
*   mutual agreement of the HMRC Authorities

Thus, in the last resort a sole residence will be chosen.

Companies also may have more than one residence but a double taxation agreement will often provide that the company is to be deemed resident where its place of effective management is situated. Unfortunately, in the absence of mutual agreement, it appears that a company may be regarded as having two places of residence, notwithstanding such a provision.

2.3.8 Appeals
Appeals on questions of residence, ordinary residence, or domicile are made only to the Special Commissioners (TA 1988 s 207).

2.4 UK residents employed abroad
Income Tax (Earnings and Pensions) Act 2003
The most prominent term that has been replaced is 'Schedule E', which now has the three successor categories 'employment income', 'pension income' and 'social security income'. Three further terms that have disappeared are 'Case I', 'Case II' and 'Case III' as set out in ICTA 1988, s. 19(1) para. 1. These terms do not have direct successors the different implications of the three cases for income tax purposes have been set out in ITEPA - and in particular in Pt. 2, Ch. 5, which refers to overseas matters. For ease of understanding by the reader I have kept the same structure as the old Cases I, II and III of Schedule E.

2.4.1 Assessments
UK residents are assessed under:

(a)   Applies to persons who are resident and ordinarily resident in the UK. The whole remuneration is assessable subject to a deduction where the duties are performed wholly or partly outside the UK, and an exception for a person who is domiciled abroad and whose employer is resident abroad; or

(b)   Applies to persons who are not resident in the UK, or not ordinarily resident. It taxes remuneration for duties performed in the UK, subject to the same exception as in (a) above.

(c)   Applies to all other remuneration of UK residents. The remittances basis is adopted here. Capital allowances for machinery and plant are not given, but the usually admissible expenses are allowable so long as a double allowance is not given. Payments under a retirement benefits scheme are not regarded as income of the employee if he or she is a (c) subject or within (a) or (b) only in respect of foreign emoluments.

2.4.2 Foreign emoluments
Foreign emoluments are those of a person domiciled abroad and whose employer is resident abroad and outside the Republic of Ireland. Amounts assessable under (a) or (b) but for one of the deductions that follow, will not be taxed under (c) if remitted.

2.4.3 Payment when absent
Emoluments for periods of absence from duties are treated as emoluments for duties in the UK unless it can be shown that, but for the absence, they would have been emoluments for duties outside the UK.

2.4.4 Incidental duties in the UK

These are disregarded where the duties are in substance performed abroad in the year of assessment, in deciding whether a person is resident, and whether or not the duties are performed wholly outside the UK.

2.4.5 UK duties

These include:

*   Crown employments of a public nature, if the emoluments are payable out of public revenue of the UK or Northern Ireland. In practice UK tax is not charged on locally engaged (as distinct from UK based), unestablished staff working abroad in certain circumstances (see ESC A25 - now obsolete - enacted in the Section 28 ITEPA 2003).

*   Duties on UK coastal vessels, or by a UK resident on a vessel or aircraft in the UK for part of its journey.

2.4.6 Artificial inflated overseas earnings

With effect from 17 March 1998 the 100% deduction is abolished.

2.5 Exceptions for non UK-domiciled individuals

2.5.1 General

Duties performed wholly outside the UK by a person domiciled outside the UK for an employer not resident in the UK are exempted from charge. Such an office or employment is not within (b) which applies to duties in the UK.

If the duties of such a person for a non-resident employer are performed wholly or partly in the UK liability will arise. Reimbursement of travelling expenses between the UK and the home country will not be assessed, if the employee retains a place of abode in his or her home country.

2.5.2 Amount of emoluments eligible for any reduction

The emoluments are to be reduced by capital allowances and pension contributions, or their equivalent under a foreign law if the Board allows (TA 1988 s 192 (3) (5)).

2.6 Employees coming from abroad

The following are liable to tax to the extent that their remuneration is attributable to work performed in the UK: employees who come from abroad and are not resident (or are resident but not ordinarily resident) in the UK. They are also taxable in the UK for work performed overseas if the remuneration is received in the UK and provided they are resident (but not ordinarily resident) in the UK. Where UK employers of such persons pay an employee a single salary covering work performed in the UK as well as abroad such employers are obliged to deduct tax under PAYE from the total remuneration (PR IR32 30.11.93).

2.7 Pensions for foreign or colonial service under the Crown
Such pensions, which are payable in the UK but not out of its public revenue, are chargeable on a UK-resident recipient on 90% of the amount arising.

2.8 Expenses of foreign offices or employments
From the emoluments of an office or employment, the duties of which are performed wholly outside the UK, a deduction may be claimed by the taxpayer for the following expenses (TA 1988 ss 193/5):

- Travelling expenses from any place in the UK to take up the employment and returning to any place in the UK on the termination of the employment;

- Travelling expenses reimbursed or paid to the employer in connection with the costs of family visits by the employee or members of his or her family provided:

  (a)   the employee is absent from the UK for continuous periods of 60 days or more to perform the duties of the employment;

  (b)   not more than two visits will be allowed for the family, i.e. a spouse or any child (including step-child) of the employee in any year of assessment;

  (c)   an unlimited number of visits by the employee to the UK provided each visit is made after carrying out duties that can only be performed outside the UK and if followed by an outward journey to resume such duties.

- Board and lodging expenses outside the UK incurred by the employee and reimbursed by the employer or where the expenses are borne by the employer and therefore assessable as benefits in kind.

Where the duties are performed wholly or partly outside the UK the travelling expenses between the two places of employment will be allowable.

2.9 UK residents with investments or property abroad
The liability is divided into: **securities** and **possessions**. Possessions include:

- (a) income immediately derived from any trade, profession or vocation, either solely or in partnership; (b) income from any pension;

- other foreign income.

The liability is on the income arising (whether or not remitted) for British residents and for foreigners having a residence in Great Britain and domiciled here.

Foreign pensions are assessed on 90% of the amount arising (except for persons of foreign domicile, or of British or Irish nationality and not ordinarily resident in the UK). Pensions payable by the German Federal Republic or Austrian Governments to victims of Nazi persecution are exempt from tax.

Income is assessable on a current year basis. British subjects not ordinarily resident here, and foreigners not domiciled although resident here, are assessable on all classes of income on remittances only.

In arriving at a liability no deduction can be made for foreign tax on profits on realisation of foreign securities (*Scottish American Loan Investment Co Ltd v CIR* CS 1938).

No relief is given to UK shareholders of a foreign company in respect of the UK tax borne by the company. A limited form of relief is given to UK companies receiving dividends from foreign companies (TA 1988 s 790).

A premium on repayment of a loan made to a foreign company at a low rate of, or free of, interest is assessable as other income (*CIR v Nelson & Sons Ltd* CS 1938).

Where notes are issued at a discount, and repaid at par, the difference, together with any premium payable, is not assessable (*Lomax v Peter Dixon & Son Ltd* CA 1943). A stock dividend (i.e. bonus shares) received under a foreign will has been held to be a capital receipt, not income, as there was no element of recurrence. It was not therefore assessable as income from foreign possessions (*Lawson v Rolfe* ChD 1969). Similarly, a distribution received from an Italian company paid out of its share premium reserve is a return of capital, not income (*Courtaulds Investments Ltd v Fleming* ChD 1969). The position under the foreign company law when the income emerges from its source, determines the nature of the receipt (*Rae v Lazard Investment Co.* HL 1963). A person domiciled abroad is assessable for the first year of residence in the United Kingdom on remittances, although not resident here during that year (*Carter v Sharon* KBD 1936).

Foreign income is treated as reduced by foreign tax payable on it, except when the remittances basis applies, or double taxation relief is given, or in computing the personal reliefs due to a non-resident (TA 1988 s 811).

2.10 The remittance basis
(please see section at beginning of this part for changes effective now and proposed, p.584)
Reference has been made in the previous section to assessment on the basis of amounts remitted to the UK. This is an unusual but advantageous method of assessment, but special problems arise out of it, which are dealt with briefly as follows. Note, however, that under some double tax treaties (e.g. those with USA and Canada) the reliefs granted do not apply to income not taxed in the UK by virtue

of not being remitted.

At the outset, where the remittances basis applies, it should be clearly understood that apart from the fact that they come from the same source, there is no connection whatsoever between the amount earned and the amount assessed for any particular year. Earnings may be accumulated over several years and then remitted in one large sum to the UK. The result of this will be that no assessments will be raised for many years, and then there will be one very large assessment in a single year based on the single large remittance. There is no right to have this spread back over the years in which it was earned.

For a year in which a source of income ceases, the remittances of the whole income tax year are assessable, not merely those from 5 April to the date the source ceased (*Joffe v Thain* ChD 1955).

Not all remittances are assessable, but only those made out of the kind of income which is being assessed. A person may have other kinds of non-taxable monies abroad (e.g. gifts, investments sold), and if these are remitted to the UK, no UK tax is payable. Sometimes a remittance will be a mixture of such monies and taxable items, in which case an apportionment should be agreed with HMRC. Apart from this it is often far from easy to decide whether a particular remittance is one of capital, and hence not taxable, or income of an assessable kind, and the precise facts of the case must be carefully considered (*Kneen v Martin* CA 1934). Loans received by a taxpayer from an overseas company controlled by 'men of straw' and derived, via a company controlled by the taxpayer, from the taxpayer's overseas earnings have been held to be a remittance of emoluments (*Harmel v Wright* ChD 1973).

Savings out of taxable income cannot be disguised by investing them abroad and then at some later date realising the investment and remitting the proceeds to the UK. The origin of the monies will be looked at, and this kind of remittance will be taxed (*Scottish Provident Institution v Farmer* CS 1912).

The settlement of a UK debt out of foreign monies is treated as a remittance.

A lump sum paid by a provident fund to an employee on retirement is not regarded as a taxable remittance.

No liability arises on remittances out of earnings from a person, who is resident and wholly employed abroad, to a spouse in this country, unless the remittances are based on a deed or other enforceable agreement.

Where remittances are unavoidably delayed, a claim may be made to have the income assessed at the time it arose instead of the time it was remitted (TA 1988 s 585).

The delay in transmitting the income must be due to the law of a foreign territory or executive action of its government, or the impossibility of obtaining foreign currency, and there must be no want of reasonable endeavour on the taxpayer's part.

A pension (or increase in pension) granted retrospectively may be related back to the years to which it relates.

The method of giving relief is to deduct and recharge the delayed remittances in the appropriate basis periods and recompute the liability. Where the basis period for the relief year is used for both the current and following years of assessment, relief is given for both years; but where the basis period in the charging year is used for two years of assessment, the charge is only made once - for the year in which the income arose.

The usual six-year time limit for making a claim and the usual rights of appeal apply.

2.11 UK residents with business abroad
If a business abroad is carried on by a person resident in the UK, the full profit arising is assessable, as trading income, in the same way as the profit of a business in the UK. When, however, the business abroad is owned by a person resident here, but not carried on by that person, the income is dealt with as income from a foreign possession. Where the taxpayer is absent from the UK and this absence is due wholly and exclusively to enable him or her to carry out his trade, profession or vocation, the following types of expenditure are allowable:

• travelling expenses from and return to any place in the UK;

• board and lodging expenses at the location where the trade, profession or vocation is being carried on;

• where the trade, profession or vocation is being carried on at two or more overseas locations, the expenses incurred in travelling between the locations;

• if the absence overseas is for a continuous period of 60 days or more, the cost of visits made by the taxpayer's family, i.e. spouse or child up to two such journeys by any individual in any year of assessment (TA 1988 ss 80(1)).

The profits of a resident UK partner from a foreign partnership are assessable to UK tax notwithstanding the decision of the High Court in *Padmore v CIR* (1987) STC 36.

2.12 Persons resident abroad with UK income
A person who resides abroad, whether a foreigner or a British subject, is taxable upon the whole of his income which arises in the UK except interest on certain Government securities. This applies to every type of income: rent, interest, profits, salary, pension etc. He is, however, exempt from UK tax on any dividends or interest

payable in the UK (FA 95 S128). The taxpayer has to make the choice of whether to claim his UK personal allowance, if he does the dividends and interest become taxable, any balance being offset against the other sources of income. There are also provisions under the various double taxation agreements with foreign countries for relief or exemption from UK tax on various sources specified, but, in the case of financial concerns, such exemption of interest or dividends is not permitted to create losses or set-off against general income (TA 1988 s 808).

No action is taken to obtain the tax on UK interest received in full (e.g. bank interest) but it may be deducted by a paying agent and will be recovered where there is a claim to relief.

Where a person visits this country for less than six months in any year of assessment and is not regarded as a resident in the UK, he or she is usually exempted from tax under the double taxation relief agreement with that country, upon profits and remuneration (taxable in the foreign country) for personal services performed for a person resident there. The profits or remuneration of stage artists and similar persons are not, however, usually given this relief.

Exemption from UK tax is given in respect of certain India, Pakistan, Burma and Colonial pensions (and relevant UK pension fund), pensions under the Overseas Service Act 1958, and the Overseas Pensions Act 1973, or paid out of the Central African or Overseas Service Pension Funds, and in respect of certain pension funds for overseas employees (TA 1988 ss 614-617). Exemption is also given to a member of a visiting force who is not a citizen of the UK or its colonies. This also applies to certain employments connected with NATO (TA 1988 s 323).

Foreign sportsmen in the UK
Since April 2010, foreign sports stars competing in Britain are liable for a top rate of income tax of 50 per cent, the tax is charged not just on the money they earn in Britain but on a proportion of their worldwide sponsorship income.

Under the old rules, athletes' tax bills were based on how many days they competed in Britain, so if they competed in the country for one week, they would be charged one 52nd of their endorsement earnings.

Now, HMRC bases its charge on what proportion of an athlete's competitions take place in Britain. An athlete competing in 10 events globally with one of them held in Britain could be charged one 10th of his worldwide earnings at a top rate of 50 per cent.

2.13 Persons coming to reside in the UK
The general principles explained above apply when a person comes to take up a permanent residence in the UK but some concessionary treatment is given. It may be helpful to summarize the liability of such a person, as follows:

- Salary earned abroad and other foreign income to which the remittances basis applies: If the employment or source ceased before UK residence began there is no liability to tax. If it continued after UK residence began, then liability arises on the remittances basis. This is modified where employment or source ceases in the year UK residence commences, or the following year, so that the total assessments do not exceed the actual income arising from the date of arrival in the UK until the employment of source ceased.

- A foreign pension is similarly assessed on the remittances basis.

- Foreign income assessable on the 'arising' basis: The liability is first computed on the normal basis for the whole year, but only a proportion from the date UK residence commenced is assessed.

- Income from the specially exempted British Government securities is taxable from the date of arrival in the UK.

- Personal reliefs are given for the whole tax year in which UK residence commences; they are never apportioned.

- Lump sums received from a foreign provident fund on termination of the foreign employment are not assessed to UK tax (ESC No A10).

2.14 Allowances

The personal allowances can be claimed by any individual who is resident in Great Britain and Northern Ireland. They may also be claimed (TA 1988 s 278) by a person resident abroad who is:

- a British subject, a Commonwealth citizen (withdrawn for non residents from 6 April 2010), or a citizen of the Republic of Ireland;

- a resident in the Isle of Man or the Channel Islands;

- a person who is, or has been, employed in the service of the Crown, or a missionary society, or of a territory under the protection of Her Majesty;

- a person previously resident in the UK and now residing abroad on account of his health or that of some member of his family living with him;

- a widow whose late husband, or (in 1990/91) a widower whose late wife was a UK resident and was in the service of the Crown (TA 1988 s 278 and FA 1988 s 31).

In the case of a person resident abroad but entitled to claim under one of the previous headings, the tax payable is that proportion which his or her British income bears to his or her total income, of the tax which his or her total income would have borne if he or she were a British resident.

In computing the amount of repayment due all income from investment abroad must be included in the statement of total income. Income ranking for double taxation relief must be included as foreign income but the relief is ignored; and in computing the income tax payable, tax which ranks for double taxation relief is also ignored. Relief given under this section is then ignored when computing the double taxation relief. Foreign tax is not to be deducted from the foreign income in calculating the proportion of personal reliefs allowable. Interest on exempt UK Government securities is treated as foreign income.

Any person who is dissatisfied with the decision of the HMRC on claim for allowances as a resident, or on the amount of the allowances due to him, may appeal to the Special Commissioners.

2.15 Double taxation relief

The UK unilaterally gives relief to its residents for foreign taxes suffered on foreign income and, in addition, agreements for relief from double taxation may apply (TA 1988 ss 788-816). The UK has concluded many bilateral double taxation relief treaties many of which, particularly those with European countries, reflect the main provisions of the Organization for Economic Co-operation and Development (OECD)'s model treaty. It must be emphasized that, as many of the treaties differ in important respects, the relevant treaty should be consulted where practical advice is required. The main features of the relief are as follows:

Relief is given for **foreign income tax** paid on the foreign income against UK taxes chargeable in respect of that income. The direct foreign income tax only is allowable by credit, but individuals may exceptionally be entitled to relief for indirect (or underlying) foreign income tax by virtue of an agreement and companies are entitled to relief for underlying taxes on income from which dividends are derived, unilaterally where 10% (in some circumstances, less than 10%) of voting power is directly or indirectly controlled, or by agreement where, usually, at least 10% of voting power is directly owned (TA 1988 s 790).

The **underlying foreign tax** includes any UK or foreign tax paid on the company's profits and (subject to certain conditions) any underlying tax on a dividend received from a third company, or by a third company from a fourth company, and so on. The companies must be related, i.e. there must be directly or indirectly at least 10% voting held by one in the other (TA 1988 s 801; ESC C1).

The relief applies only to **residents in the UK** in respect of foreign source income. By concession, royalties and 'know-how' payments received from abroad may, in certain circumstances, be regarded as foreign income for double taxation relief purposes, even though the source of income is the UK. For a person other than a company the **credit for foreign tax** is not to exceed income tax at the marginal rate on the foreign income. The method is to compute UK income tax firstly by including the foreign income at the gross figure before deduction of the foreign tax (usually the direct tax) to which the relief applies; and then re-compute excluding the income on which relief is claimed. The relief for foreign tax must not exceed the difference between these two figures. Where there are several sources ranking for relief this method is applied successively, excluding each time from both computations sources previously dealt with (TA 1988 s 796).

For corporation tax the credit must not exceed the corporation tax attributable to the income (TA 1988 s 797), and reliefs and set offs may be taken first against UK income of that, or in groups, another member company.

The **total relief for foreign tax** must not exceed the total UK income tax paid and borne by the taxpayer for any year of assessment.

Where the income tax assessment is based on **remittances** the UK assessment is increased by the amount of the foreign tax (including where applicable underlying tax on dividends). In other cases (i.e. where the 'arising' basis applies) no deduction is allowable on foreign tax relieved by credit in computing the UK liability, and the income is increased by any underlying tax which ranks for relief (TA 1988 s 795).

In the case of **portfolio investment**, the income is received through a UK paying agent who deducts UK income tax at basic rate before passing on the income to the owner. In so doing credit is given for taxes directly charged on the dividend and, where there is an agreement, this will normally be a withholding tax of 5% to 25%, so that full relief can be given. In some cases (e.g. Switzerland) the withholding tax is greater than that creditable and the difference must be reclaimed from the local authorities.

The underlying tax attributable to a **dividend** is the amount of tax on the profits out of which the dividend was paid, less any such tax imputed to the dividend by way of tax credit for charging foreign tax, multiplied by the dividend (before withholding tax) and divided by the profits available for distribution (per the accounts, not as for tax computations) (*Bowater Paper v Murgatroyd* HL 1969). Rules are laid down for identifying the profits out of which the dividend is regarded as paid (TA 1988 s 799).

Unilateral relief for tax paid in those Islands is due to persons resident in the Isle of Man and the Channel Islands as well as to residents in the UK.

In some cases double taxation relief may be restricted as a result of the reduction of UK assessments by **capital allowances**. Where this occurs, a claim may be made to defer such capital allowances, wholly or partly, and carry them forward to the following year. The following provisions (TA 1988 s 810) apply in such cases:

• the foreign tax laws must give allowances corresponding to the UK capital allowances;

• the basis of foreign capital allowances compared with the UK allowances must reduce the foreign income in the year of claim, but increase it in subsequent years.

2.16 Securities held by non-residents exempted from tax
2.16.1 British Government securities
Persons not ordinarily resident in Great Britain and Northern Ireland may reclaim any tax deducted from the interest on certain British Government securities held by them in beneficial ownership including 3½% War Stock 1952 or after; 4% Funding Stock 1960-90; 5½% Treasury Bonds 2008-12. This exemption, subject to certain restrictions (TA 1988 ss 474-475), includes a bank, assurance or investment company, carrying on business but not ordinarily resident in the UK.

A person who comes to the UK from abroad and is in a mental home for several years is not entitled to this exemption (*Mackenzie v A.G.* KBD 1941).

Where the resident executor of a non-resident life tenant receives interest from untaxed Government securities, the whole of the interest received is assessable (*Wood v Owen* KBD 1940).

An annuity payable out of a fund consisting of taxed investment income and interest on exempt securities, in the absence of specific appropriation, had to be regarded as paid rateably out of the constituent parts of the fund (*CIR v Crawshay* CA 1968).

2.16.2 Inter-American Development Bank securities
These are exempt from tax in the hands of a non-resident even though the securities or income are issued, made payable or paid in the United Kingdom or in sterling, and even though the Bank maintains an office or other place of business in the UK (TA 1988 s 583).

2.17 Miscellaneous points
2.17.1 Territorial extension of the UK
Primarily to ensure that a proper proportion of profits from natural resources in UK coastal waters is received in tax revenue, the boundaries of the UK have been extended for tax purposes (TA 1988 s 830).

For all income tax, corporation tax and capital gains tax purposes the territorial sea of the UK is deemed to be part of the UK.

Profits or gains from exploration or exploration activities, or from rights granted in connection therewith in designated areas of the Continental Shelf, are to be regarded as derived from property or activities in the UK, or from disposals of assets within the UK, for income tax, corporation tax, capital gains tax. In the case of a non-resident the like profits are deemed to accrue from a UK branch for corporation tax and capital gains tax. Emoluments of an office or employment performed in such an area in connection with such activities are to be treated as in respect of duties performed in the UK.

2.17.2 Unremittable overseas profits
Where overseas income cannot be remitted to the UK by reason of:

• the laws of, or executive action in, the overseas territory, or

• the impossibility of obtaining foreign currency in that territory and such income has not been realized elsewhere for sterling or other remittable currency, notice may be given before an assessment becomes final that such income be omitted from assessment (TA 1988 s 584).

The value of the unremittable income is determined by the generally recognized value in the UK (if any), or, in the absence of any such value, according to the official rate of exchange of the territory in which the income arises.

When the income ceases to be unremittable it is assessable at its value at that date and additional assessments may be made within six years after that date.

2.17.3 Promotion of foreign developments
UK companies who obtain relief from foreign tax because they are promoting development abroad, may treat the foreign tax as if it had been paid and obtain double taxation relief, where an agreement so provides (TA 1988 s 788).

2.17.4 Foreign employee's superannuation fund
The fund is given exemption for UK tax as if it were not resident or domiciled in the UK (TA 1988 s 614). Where the annuity is paid to a person who is not resident in the UK, tax is not deductible, and does not have to be accounted for by the trustee under s 349 TA 1988.

2.17.5 Patent rights, capital sums received
A person not resident in the UK is liable in respect of capital sums received for patent rights.

A non-resident who sells a UK patent may elect to spread the capital sum over six years beginning with the year in which it was received. Notice must be given within two years after the end of the year of assessment in which the capital sum is received. The purchaser must deduct tax at basic rate when making the payment, whether or not this election is made (TA 1988 s 524).

2.17.6 Returns of persons treated as employees

A person working for at least 30 days in the UK under a contract with a non-resident employer, but for the benefit of a resident business, is to be regarded as an employee of the latter who may be required to include the 'employee' in his PAYE returns. The 'employee' may also be required to make a return of income (whether or not chargeable).

2.17.7 Compensation for National Socialist persecution

Annuities payable under the law of the Federal German Republic (or any part of it) and specifically exempted from German tax, are exempted from UK tax (TA 1988 s 330).

2.17.8 Controlled foreign companies (CFCs)

FA 1988 s 750 provided that additional tax is payable by UK companies which control foreign companies resident in low tax areas. The additional tax is the excess of the tax which would be payable on the foreign company's profits if these profits were subject to UK tax, over the foreign tax payable. Up to 15 March 1993 the additional tax is payable where the foreign tax is less than half of what would be payable if UK tax applied. On and after 16 March 1993 a company will be considered in a low tax area if its foreign tax is less than three-quarters of the UK tax which would be payable. (FA 1993 s 119). A number of countries are excluded, or with qualified exclusion, from these provisions.

A list of excluded countries was published by the HMRC on 5 October 1993 by a Press Release of that date.

In the case of a non-trading CFC the additional charge is removed if that company distributes in the UK at least 90% of taxable profits less capital gains. The further deduction of foreign tax was included on 30.11.93. The required standard distribution is 50% of profits less capital gains for a trading company. No charge is made where the foreign company's profits do not exceed £20,000. See also FA 1994 s 134.

A press release following the July 1997 budget stated "the UK's CFC legislation is unusual in not requiring companies to include in their tax returns amounts taxable under the CFC rules. Instead, HMRC must first identify that a UK company has a CFC before any tax assessment can be made. This is not a secure basis for ensuring that all CFC tax that is potentially due is in fact charged, nor is it fair to those taxpayers who do not make use of CFCs for avoidance.

In requiring companies to include in their tax returns amounts chargeable under the CFC rules, the Government wants to keep the administrative cost to business of complying with the new rules to the minimum necessary" Clauses concerning the above were included in the 1998 Finance Act.

The Vodafone 2 decision

The Vodafone 2 case was decided in favour of HMRC in the Court of Appeal, which reverses the High Court decision in favour of the company *(Vodafone 2 v HMRC (2009) EWCA 446)*. As there are several billion pounds 'riding' on the decision, Vodafone is certain to apply for leave to appeal.

The Court of Appeal decision is that in the light of the judgment of the ECJ in the Cadbury Schweppes case, the UK controlled foreign company (CFC) legislation can be considered to be compliant with the EC Treaty. This is on the grounds that it is permissible to 'read across' into the existing CFC domestic legislation an additional rule to the effect that the CFC legislation will not apply if a CFC 'is actually established in another member state of the EEA and carries on genuine economic activities there'.

HMRC argued that the interest income of the Luxembourg subsidiary should be treated as if it had been received by the UK parent company under the then CFC legislation.

In settlement Vodafone agreed to pay £1.25 billion.

3 AVOIDANCE SCHEMES

The principal ways in which it has been sought to avoid or minimise liability to the higher rates of income tax, and the legal bars which have been set up to prevent such avoidance, are as follows.

3.1 Life assurance

No allowance is made for life assurance premiums in charging excess liability. Interest on money borrowed directly or indirectly for the purpose of paying assurance premiums is disallowed except as follows (TA 1988 s 554) for interest at rate not exceeding 10% on:

(a)   money borrowed on the security of a property other than an insurance policy and the premium is payable under a policy which provides against failure of a contingent interest or is the first premium, not exceeding 10% of the sum assured, under a policy taken out solely to provide for the repayment of the loan;

(b)   money borrowed to pay premiums under a policy which assures throughout the period a capital sum payable on death provided the annual premium (including the first premium) does not exceed one-eighth of the capital sum assured and the borrowing was exceptional and no similar borrowing was made in the three preceding years;

(c)   money borrowed to pay premiums under a policy which is a qualifying policy under S 266 (3) TA 1988 or each premium is one of a series of equal premiums payable at equal intervals of not more than one year and the premiums are not such as those specified in para.'s (a), (b) and (e). The interest allowable must not exceed £100;

(d)   money borrowed to pay premiums under a policy taken out before 15 April 1930 which assures a fixed capital sum payable on death or at the end of a period not less than ten years after the commencement of the policy;

(e)   money borrowed from an insurance company before 6 April 1929 and the premium was payable under a policy which secured the repayment of the loan;

(f)   money borrowed before 20 March 1968 and the policy falls within para. (a) of s 539(2) of TA 1988 re mortgage repayment scheme, and is not in respect of premiums as specified in para. (c), nor does it relate to borrowing which was exceptional and no similar borrowing was made in the three previous years.

Premiums on life insurance policies paid out of an annuity due to the taxpayer form part of his income for excess liability (*CIR v Forster* KBD 1935).

3.2 Restrictive covenants
Where a director or employee entered into an agreement not to carry on business in a certain period, or otherwise to restrict his future conduct or activities, in return for which he received a substantial payment from his employers, this payment used to be exempt from tax (*Beak v Robson* HL 1942), but is now assessable to excess liability (TA 1988 s 313).

A payment of £40,000 to a barrister as an inducement to give up his practice and become an employee of a company was not taxable as a consideration for a restrictive covenant. (*Vaughan Neil v CIR* Ch D 1979).

3.3 Transfer of income to persons abroad
If a taxpayer transfers assets so that the income therefrom becomes payable to persons domiciled or resident out of the UK, while he himself has forthwith or in the future power to enjoy that income, then such income is deemed to be his for income tax purposes (*Latilla v CIR* HL 1936; *Corbett's Exors. v CIR* CA 1943; *Congreve & Congreve v CIR* HL 1948; *Ramsden v CIR* Ch D 1957; TA 1988 ss 739-742).

If an individual receives, in consequence of such a transfer, any loan, repayment of loans, or other capital sums which are not paid for full consideration in money of money's worth the income of the person resident or domiciled abroad (including a company (*Gasque v CIR* KBD 1940) or other corporate body incorporated abroad whether resident there or not) shall be deemed to be the income of that individual. This applies even if the person abroad receives the income indirectly under a will (*Bambridge v CIR* HL 1955). Income is to be taken in the UK income tax sense so that management expenses of a foreign resident investment company cannot be deducted from investment income (*Lord Chetwode v CIR* HL 1976).

These provisions, however, do not apply if the individual can show that the transfer was not made wholly or partly for the purpose of avoiding liability to taxation or that it was a bona fide commercial transaction and not designed for the purpose of avoiding liability to taxation (TA 1988 s 741; *Herdman v CIR* HL 1969). There is a heavy onus of proof on the taxpayer and the 'sins' of the father may be visited upon his son (*Philippi v CIR* CA 1971).

The HMRC has power to obtain full particulars of such transactions from any person acting on behalf of others. This does not apply to a solicitor who has given professional advice regarding such transactions. In other cases a solicitor is only required, unless his client consents, to disclose the names and addresses of the persons concerned in the operation. A banker also is not required to disclose any ordinary banking transactions between the bank and the customer unless the bank has acted for the customer in connection with the formation or management of a company or trust abroad (TA 1988 s 745; *Clinch v CIR* QBD 1973).

4 FOREIGN EXCHANGE GAINS AND LOSSES (FOREX)

The legislation broadly provides that company exchange gains or losses on monetary assets are calculated as they accrue, following the normal accounting treatment (PR IR43 30.11.93). An election can be made for the basic profits and losses to be made in the local currency concerned, subject to translation into sterling for the tax computation (PR IR 24.1.94). Special rules apply to insurance companies. Very detailed rules for the calculation of FOREX gains and losses, and the relevant draft regulations are set out in press releases dated 14.2.94, 23.2.94 and 17.3.94. See FA 1994 s 162.

5 PERSONS ENTITLED TO RECLAIM TAX

Subject in some cases to certain limitations, claims of repayment of part or whole of the tax deducted from interest, rents or other income received, may be made by the following persons or bodies.

Various traders, societies, etc.	**Exempt from:**
Unregistered friendly societies whose income does not exceed £160 (TA 1988 s 459).	Income tax and corporation tax.
Registered friendly societies which do not write assurance policies under which the total premiums payable in any period of 12 months exceed £200, or grant annuities not exceeding £156 (TA 1988 ss 466 and 467).	Income tax and corporation tax, so far as derived from life or endowment business (subject to certain exceptions)
Registered trade unions or police federations which do not insure for more than £4,000 or grant annuities of more than £825 p.a. (TA 1988 s 467)	Income tax and corporation tax, so far as such income is applied to provident benefit, i.e. sickness, out of work, superannuation, accident and funeral benefits, etc., including legal assistance payments (*R v Special Commissioners (ex parte NUR)* QBD 1966: SP6/78).
Savings Banks certified under Act of 1863 (TA 1988 s 484).	Tax on interest on money invested with National Debt Commissioners. Tax so far as such interest is used in paying interest to depositors. But the depositor must himself pay tax on the interest just as on any other income, and the bank must make returns of all sums over £21 paid in interest or dividends arising from investments with National Debt Commissioners.
National Insurance Fund (TA 1988 s 614).	Tax on interest (including investment with building societies) and on any other funds or credits.
Hospitals; public schools; almshouses. Charities generally (TA 1988 s 505).	Tax on rents, etc., received; Business Tax if the business is carried on mainly by the labour of the recipients of the charity or in the course of carrying on the charity and the profits are applied solely to charitable purposes.

Approved superannuation (TA 1988 s 590), overseas pension funds (TA 1988 s 614-615), retirement annuity funds (TA 1988 s 620).	Tax on invested funds (including investments with building societies). Tax on annuities paid under deduction of tax at basic rate and assessable on the recipient as earned income, may be set against tax borne on non-exempt income (ESC A16).
State Bank of India or Pakistan Issue Departments (TA 1988 s 517)	Tax on profits or income.

6 THE COUNCIL TAX

6.1 General nature of the tax
The council tax is payable by the owner, lessee or licensee of all kinds of dwellings, including houses, flats, mobile homes and houseboats, subject to the exemptions and reliefs noted as follows.

6.2 The bands of property values
Each dwelling was revalued at its open market price on 1 April 1991, plus the value of improvements up to 1 April 1993, and allocated to one of the eight bands of values as shown as follows. The valuation was made by the Valuation Office of HMRC. Band D comprised property of average value and a standard amount of tax (depending on the expenditure of each council) was charged for dwellings falling within that band. Different proportions of the standard charge are levied on properties falling within the other bands. Properties in Wales were re-set on 1 April 2005 based upon 2003 valuations.

Appeals may be made against the banding of a particular property. Extensions to a dwelling after valuation may justify an upward rebanding when the property is sold, and a change for the worse in the local environment may cause a lower banding of all the properties involved. General changes in house prices since valuation are ignored, but it seems that the sale of a dwelling at a price above its band may justify it being placed in a higher band.

6.3 Liability for payment of the tax
(a)   Generally, as previously indicated, the liability for payment of the tax falls on the resident, whether freeholder, leaseholder, assured tenant, statutory tenant or licensee.

(b)   The owner of the property will be liable where: the resident is under 18 years of age; the dwelling is empty or a holiday home; hostels and houses divided into bed sitting rooms with common washing and cooking facilities; care homes and nursing homes; dwellings occupied by ministers of religion but not owned by them; domestic servants etc., not living in homes of their own.

(c) There is joint and several liability for the tax by joint owners, husbands and wives and unmarried couples living together.

6.4 Exempt properties

These include properties occupied exclusively by: individuals under 18 years of age; students and trainees, including student nurses and apprentices; those who are severely mentally impaired. Also exempt are empty unfurnished dwellings up to 6 months; those which have undergone major alterations or repair up to 6 months after completion of the work and are empty; those left empty by individuals who have gone into hospital, nursing home or a residential care home, and also for an indefinite period applies to a property if it was the occupier's sole residence immediately prior to his move to another place (not being a hospital, residential care home, nursing home or hostel) for the purpose of receiving personal care required because of his old age, disablement, illness, past or present drug dependence or past or present mental disorder.

6.5 Reliefs and rebates

(a) A discount off the tax may apply if there are no residents in a dwelling. The discount is 25% where only one person is resident in a dwelling. For this purpose the following are not treated as residents: persons under 18 years of age; students and trainees; and the severely mentally impaired.

(b) Where a resident, whether an adult or child, is disabled and the property has to be specially adapted for that reason, it will be allocated to the next lower band, except where originally placed in band A.

(c) Exemption of 100% of the tax is available for individuals receiving income support. Other persons on low income may receive benefit depending on their financial and personal circumstances. A 'second adult rebate' may be claimed by liable persons for someone (not a spouse, partner or lodger) living with them who is on income support or who has a low income.

6.6 Payment of council tax by employer

Where under the terms of the employment an employee's council tax is paid by the employer such payment will be treated as remuneration on which the employee is normally liable for income tax. The payment will normally be treated as deductible in computing the employer's profits. National insurance contributions on the amount of the council tax concerned will be payable by both employer and employee.

6.7 Free accommodation

In some cases the employer will pay the council tax for property in which the employee is required to live to carry out his or her duties. The value of this free accommodation is not normally chargeable to income tax on the employee nor is the council tax paid by the employer.

6.8 Employees required to work at home

Where employees are required to work at their homes for the purpose of their employment they can normally obtain relief of income tax for the cost - such as lighting, heating and cleaning - of accommodation set aside for the work. This relief extends to the appropriate proportion of the council tax related to the home.

7 AIR PASSENGER DUTY (APD)

New rates of APD for travel that begins on or after 1 November 2010 have been introduced. Irrespective of when the ticket was booked or purchased.

The new bands and the rates of duty from 1 November 2009 & 2010 are as follows:

Band, and approximate distance in miles from	In the lowest class of travel (Reduced rate)		In other than the lowest class of travel* (Standard rate)	
	01.11.09	01.11.10	01.11.09	01.11.10
Band A (0 - 2000)	£11	£12	£22	£24
Band B (2001 - 4000)	£45	£60	£90	£120
Band C (4001 - 6000)	£50	£75	£100	£150
Band D (over 6000)	£55	£85	£110	£170

* However if only one class of travel is available and that class provides for seating in excess of 40" then the standard (rather than the reduced) rate of APD applies.

The March 2011 Budget announced a deferral of the April 2011 increase until April 2012, when both will be implemented.

Distances are based on the distance between London and the capital city of the destination country/territory.

This is an excise duty payable in respect of aircraft passengers. No duty applies to passengers (a) in aircraft of below 10 tonnes authorised takeoff weight, or (b) aircraft with 20 or less authorised seating places. The duty is payable to HMRC by the aircraft operator or, where the latter's place of business is outside the UK, by an appointed 'fiscal representative'; otherwise by a 'handling agent'. No doubt, however, the duty will be ultimately borne by the passenger. FA 1994 ss 28-44.

8 INSURANCE PREMIUM TAX

This applies to general insurance at the rate of 6%. The tax is payable to HMRC by the insurer, who must be registered. A tax representative must be appointed and registered by an insurer who does not have a business establishment in the UK. Where the tax cannot be obtained from the insurer or tax representative, a 'liability note' can be issued by HMRC to the insured, who will be responsible for paying the tax, subject to a claim for reimbursement from the insurer. A notional premium as under open market conditions may be substituted by HMRC if the actual premium is below such notional premium.

A higher rate of 20% was introduced, as an anti avoidance measure. This higher rate of IPT applies to insurance sold by suppliers of specified goods and services e.g. mechanical breakdown insurance, travel insurance and insurance when sold with TV and car hire. The higher rate of 20% is payable on all sales through travel agents and tour operators. Selective higher rates of insurance premium tax (20%) do not apply to ordinary motor insurance sold by car dealers or to home contents insurance sold by retailers.

These reliefs are provided for by ESC rather than by legislation, and such insurance will be liable to the lower 6% rate of IPT. This is not the same thing, however, as insurance-backed maintenance deals provided by car dealers or motorcycle dealers, which will continue to be caught by the higher rate.

The following insurances are not subject to the tax (subject to conditions):

(a)   Reinsurance.

(b)   Long-term insurance under the Insurance Companies Act 1992, Sch 1. A measure was laid before Parliament on 2 July 1997 effective 1 October 1997. To close a loophole where medical insurance written under a long-term contract was avoiding IPT when a short-term contract did not. Other long-term health insurance, such as permanent health, critical illness and long-term care policies are unaffected by this change.

(c)   On commercial ships of less than 15 tonnes.

(d)   On lifeboats.

(e)   On commercial aircraft of less than 8,000 kilograms.

(f)   On commercial aircraft.

(g)   On motor vehicles hired to disabled persons.

(h)   On risks outside the UK and export credit insurance.

FA 1994 ss 48-74.

9 LAND FILL TAX

A land fill tax was introduced from 1 October 1996 to encourage business and consumers to produce less waste and to promote recycling rather than disposal of waste. Where inert waste is used for restoration of land fill sites it is exempted from the tax entirely. The tax on a tonne of active waste is:

2011/2012	£56
2010/2011	£48
2009/2010	£40
2008/2009	£32
2007/2008	£24
2006/2007	£21
2005/2006	£18

It is intended that the standard rate will increase by £8 per tonne p.a., and by at least that amount in years thereafter, until at least 01.04.2015.

10 SCOTTISH TAX

The Scotland Bill was laid before Parliament on 30 November 2010. It provides for revenue raising powers to be given to the Scottish Parliament.

The aim is to have the new powers in place by 2015 and for them to be introduced from 2016.

The proposals on income tax are for the UK parliament to reduce the 20% basic rate, the 40% higher rate and the 50% additional rate of income tax that apply to all

UK income taxpayers, to 10%, 30% and 40% respectively for Scottish taxpayers. At the same time there would be a corresponding reduction in the block grant, plus provisions to allow the Scottish Parliament to levy new rates of income tax on Scottish taxpayers. If the Scottish Parliament decided to levy income tax at 10% then Scottish taxpayers would end up paying the same overall amount of income tax as at present.

The new tax provisions for Scotland would replace the Scottish Parliament's existing powers to vary the rate of income tax paid by Scottish taxpayers by up to 3 pence (the Scottish Variable Rate).

The Scotland Bill will also provide for the devolution of stamp duty land tax and landfill tax by firstly ceasing the application in Scotland of these UK wide taxes and then giving the Scottish Parliament the competence to create an equivalent land tax and landfill tax of its own.

Previously under the proposals contained within the Scotland Act, a person who is resident in the UK and spends as many days in Scotland as he spends elsewhere in the UK, is defined as a Scottish taxpayer. For example, where a taxpayer is UK resident but spends 130 days in Scotland, 130 days in England and 105 days in the US, he will be liable to pay Scottish tax because he is UK resident and spends an equal amount of time in Scotland and England. It is the location of the taxpayer at midnight which will be the deciding factor. The number of days spent outside of Scotland is irrelevant under the proposed rules.

The tax varying powers of the Scottish Parliament allows the basic rate of tax set by the UK Parliament to be varied by up to 3p, i.e. the Scottish basic rate could be 25%.

However, it should be noted that Scottish taxpayers will remain UK taxpayers for such purposes as double tax treaties.

TABLES

**Our Tax Facts E-Book is also available. This currently has
91 tables of key current and historical data.**

visit our website at:

www.smithstaxation.co.uk

1. Capital Allowances - New Rates 2012/2013 back to 2008/2009

Allowance	From	End Date	Rate	Type of Business Effected
Annual Investment Allowance (AIA) †	01.04.08 *	31.03.10 *	100%	All, up to £50,000 p.a.
	01.04.10 *	31.03.12 *	100%	All, up to £100,000 p.a.
	01.04.12 *	No limit	100%	All, up to £25,000 p.a.
Excess over AIA + Pools b/f	01.04.08 *	31.03.09	20% WDA	All
Excess over AIA **	01.04.09	31.03.12	40% FYA	All
Pools b/f	01.04.09	31.03.12	20% WDA	All
	01.04.12	No limit	18% WDA	All
Integral Plant (fixtures & fittings)	01.04.08 *	31.03.12	10% WDA	All
	01.04.12	No limit	8% WDA	All
Energy Efficient Equipment	01.11.00	No limit	100%	All - companies only
Enterprise Zones	16.03.93	31.03.11	100%	All
Flat Conversion Allowance	11.05.01	No limit	100%	All
Business Premises Renovation	11.04.07	No limit	100%	All
Capital R & D	01.04.00	No limit	100%	Small & Medium #
Low Emission Cars - ≤110gm/km CO_2	01.04.08	31.03.13	100%	All
Cars - ≤ 160gm/km CO_2	01.04.09	31.03.12	20% WDA	All
	01.04.12	No limit	18% WDA	All
Cars - ≥ 161gm/km CO_2	01.04.09	31.03.12	10% WDA	All
	01.04.12	No limit	8% WDA	All
Vans - Electric	01.04.10	No limit	100%	All
Energy Efficient & Water Saving	11.08.08	No limit	100%	All
Long Life Assets	01.04.08 *	31.03.12	10%	All
	01.04.12	No limit	8%	All
IBA & ABA	01.04.10 *	31.03.11 *	1%	All
	01.04.11	-	0%	All

* For unincorporated businesses the effective dates are the 05.04 or 06.04 as appropriate rather than 01.04 or 31.03 for incorporated businesses

** Excludes special rate items (charged at 10%) and motor cars.

† See Table 2 - AIA pro rated for accounting periods spanning 1 April 2012.

\# Small or medium defined: These are that the business is under on two of the following conditions:

Size of Business	Turnover	Balance Sheet Total	No. of Employees
Small	£5.6m	£2.8m	50
Medium	£22.8m	£11.4m	250

2. Capital Allowances - Annual Investment Allowance (AIA) 2012 Calculator

Decreased to £25,000 from 1 April 2012 (Corporation Tax) & 6 April 2012 (Income Tax)

Accounting Period:

Start date	End date	Days pre 1 April 2012	AIA for period pre 1 April 2012	Days post 1 April 2012	AIA for period post 1 April 2012	Total Days
Corporation tax						
01/04/2011	31/03/2012	366	100,000	0	0	366
01/05/2011	30/04/2012	336	91,803	30	2,049	366
01/06/2011	31/05/2012	305	83,333	61	4,167	366
01/07/2011	30/06/2012	275	75,137	91	6,216	366
01/08/2011	31/07/2012	244	66,667	122	8,333	366
01/09/2011	31/08/2012	213	58,197	153	10,451	366
01/10/2011	30/09/2012	183	50,000	183	12,500	366
01/11/2011	31/10/2012	152	41,530	214	14,617	366
01/12/2011	30/11/2012	122	33,333	244	16,667	366
01/01/2012	31/12/2012	91	24,863	275	18,784	366
01/02/2012	31/01/2013	60	16,393	306	20,902	366
01/03/2012	28/02/2013	31	8,493	334	22,877	365
01/04/2012	31/03/2013	0	0	365	25,000	365

Note: Unlike in 2010 the AIA for the two periods are not aggregated. The pre & post amounts are distinct limits.

Start date	End date	Days pre 6 April 2012	AIA for period pre 6 April 2012	Days post 6 April 2012	AIA for period post 6 April 2012	Total Days
Income Tax						
06/04/2011	05/04/2012	366	100,000	0	0	366
01/05/2011	30/04/2012	341	93,169	25	1,708	366
01/06/2011	31/05/2012	310	84,699	56	3,825	366
01/07/2011	30/06/2012	280	76,503	86	5,874	366
01/08/2011	31/07/2012	249	68,033	117	7,992	366
01/09/2011	31/08/2012	218	59,563	148	10,109	366
01/10/2011	30/09/2012	188	51,366	178	12,158	366
01/11/2011	31/10/2012	157	42,896	209	14,276	366
01/12/2011	30/11/2012	127	34,699	239	16,325	366
01/01/2012	31/12/2012	96	26,230	270	18,443	366
01/02/2012	31/01/2013	65	17,760	301	20,560	366
01/03/2012	28/02/2013	36	9,863	329	22,534	365
01/04/2012	31/03/2013	5	1,370	360	24,658	365
06/04/2012	05/04/2013	0	0	365	25,000	365

Note: Unlike in 2010 the AIA for the two periods are not aggregated. The pre & post amounts are distinct limits.

3.   Capital Allowances - Cars - 100% FYA

The following table lists, as at 20 June 2011, the top 20 Petrol, Diesel & Petrol Hybrid cars that qualify for 100% FYAs
source: http://carfueldata.direct.gov.uk.

The best PETROL vehicles:

Ranking	Make	Model	Engine Capacity cc	Transmission	CO_2 (g/km)
1	FIAT	500 and 500C 2010 onwards, TwinAir Dualogic	875	SAT5	92
2	FIAT	500 and 500C 2010 onwards, TwinAir	875	M5	95
3	SMART	fortwo coupé Model Year 2011, fortwo coupé 71 bhp mhd with Softip & 15" rear wheels	999	5 AMT	97
4	SMART	fortwo coupé Model Year 2011, fortwo coupé 71 bhp mhd with Softouch & 15" rear wheels	999	5 AMT	98
5	SMART	fortwo cabrio, Model Year 2011, fortwo cabrio 71 bhp mhd with Softip & 15" rear wheels	999	5 AMT	99
6	TOYOTA	iQ Model Year 2011, 1.0 VVT-i 5 speed Manual	998	M5	99
7	TOYOTA	iQ Model Year 2010, 1.0 VVT-i 5-speed manual	998	M5	99
8	HYUNDAI	i10, 1.0I SOHC	998	M5	99
9	SMART	fortwo cabrio Model Year 2011, fortwo cabrio 71 bhp mhd with Softouch & 15" rear wheels	999	5 AMT	100
10	SUZUKI	Alto, 1.0 SZ-L from VIN MA3GFC31S00223865	996	5MT	103
11	SUZUKI	Alto, 1.0 SZ2 from VIN MA3GFC31S0106451	996	5MT	103
12	SUZUKI	Alto, 1.0 SZ4 from MA3GFC31S0010676	996	5MT	103
13	SUZUKI	Alto, 1.0 SZ3 from VIN MA3GFC31S0010209	996	5MT	103
14	NISSAN	Pixo, 1.0	996	M5	103
15	CITROEN	C1, 1.0i 5 door PNCFB4	998	M5	103
16	CITROEN	C1, 1.0i 3 door PMCFB4	998	M5	103
17	PEUGEOT	107 Facelift, 1.0 (68 bhp)	998	M5	103
18	CITROEN	C1, 1.0i 5 door PNCFB0	998	M5	105
19	CITROEN	C1, 1.0i 3 door PMCFB0	998	M5	105
20	TOYOTA	Aygo, 1.0 VVT-i 5 speed Manual	998	M5	105

The best DIESEL vehicles:

Ranking	Make	Model	Engine Capacity cc	Transmission	CO_2 (g/km)
1	SMART	fortwo cabrio Model Year 2011, fortwo cabrio 54 bhp cdi with Softip & 15" rear wheels	799	5 AMT	86
2	SMART	fortwo coupé Model Year 2011, fortwo coupé 54 bhp cdi with Softip & 15" rear wheels	799	5 AMT	86
3	SMART	fortwo coupé Model Year 2011, fortwo coupé 54 bhp cdi with Softouch & 15" rear wheels	799	5 AMT	87
4	SMART	fortwo cabrio Model Year 2011, fortwo cabrio 54 bhp cdi with Softouch & 15" rear wheels	799	5 AMT	87
5	SKODA	New Fabia Hatch 2010, 1.2 CR TDI 75PS GreenLine II	1199	M5	89
6	SKODA	New Fabia Estate 2010, 1.2 CR TDI 75PS GreenLine II	1199	M5	89
7	VOLKSWAGEN	New Polo, 1.2 TDI 75PS BlueMotion	1199	M5	91
8	SEAT	Ibiza ST, 1.2 CR TDI 75PS Ecomotive	1198	M5	92
9	SEAT	Ibiza 5 door, 1.2 CR TDI 75PS Stop-Start Ecomotive	1198	M5	92
10	SEAT	Ibiza Coupé, 1.2 CR TDI 75PS Stop-Start Ecomotive	1198	M5	92
11	VAUXHALL	Corsa 3 Door Hatchback Model Year 2011, 1.3CDTi (95PS)	1248	M5	94
12	ALFA ROMEO	MiTo, 2011 onwards, 1.3 JTDm-2 85 bhp	1248	M5	95
13	FIAT	Punto Evo From January 2010, 1.3 16v MultiJet 85 ECO	1248	M5	95
14	RENAULT	Clio, dCi 86 90G	1461	M5	98
15	FORD	Fiesta Model Year Pre 2010¼, 1.6 Duratorq TDCi (90PS)(+DPF) (ECO)	1560	M5	98
16	FORD	Fiesta Model Year Post 2010¼, 1.6 Duratorq TDCi (90PS)(+DPF) (ECO)	1560	M5	98
17	FORD	Fiesta Model Year Post 2010¼, 1.6 Duratorq (95PS)(+DPF)(ECO)	1560	M5	98
18	VAUXHALL	Corsa 3 Door Hatchback, Model Year 2010 ½, 1.3CDTi 16v 95PS	1248	M5	98
19	PEUGEOT	207, From August 2009 onwards, 1.6 HDi FAP (92 bhp) Oxygo	1560	M5	98
20	PEUGEOT	207, From August 2009 onwards, 1.6 HDi (90 bhp) 99g ECONOMIQUE	1560	M5	99

The best PETROL HYBRID FUEL vehicles:

Ranking	Make	Model	Engine Capacity cc	Transmission	CO$_2$ (g/km)
1	TOYOTA	Prius, Model Year 2009 T3 1.8VVT-i hybrid E-CVT	1798	E-CVT	89
2	TOYOTA	Prius, Model Year 2009 T Spirit with Solar Roof 1.8VVT-i hybrid E-CVT	1798	E-CVT	89
3	TOYOTA	Auris Hybrid, Model Year 2010 T4 89g 1.8 VVT-i hybrid E-CVT	1798	E-CVT	89
4	TOYOTA	Prius 10 Anniversary Special Edition 1.8VVT-i	1798	E-CVT	92
5	TOYOTA	Prius, Model Year 2009 T Spirit 1.8 VVT-i hybrid E-CVT	1798	E-CVT	92
6	TOYOTA	Prius, Model Year 2009 T4 1.8 VVT-i hybrid E-CVT	1798	E-CVT	92
7	TOYOTA	Auris Hybrid, Model Year 2010 T4 1.8 VVT-i hybrid E-CVT	1798	E-CVT	93
8	TOYOTA	Auris Hybrid, Model Year 2010 T Spirit 1.8 VVT-i hybrid E-CVT	1798	E-CVT	93
9	LEXUS	CT, MY2011 CT200h	1798	E-CVT	94
10	HONDA	Insight, Model Year 2010 1.3 IMA S 5 door	1339	CVT	101
11	HONDA	Insight, Model Year 2010 1.3 IMA SE 5 door	1339	CVT	101
12	HONDA	Insight, Model Year 2011 1.3 IMA SE, SE-T	1339	CVT	101
13	HONDA	Jazz, Model Year 2012 1.3 IMA	1339	CVT	104
14	HONDA	Insight, Model Year 2011 1.3 IMA ES, ES-T, EX	1339	CVT	105
15	HONDA	Insight, Model Year 2010 1.3 IMA ES 5 door	1339	CVT	105
16	HONDA	Insight, Model Year 2010 1.3 IMA ES-T 5 door	1339	CVT	105
17	HONDA	Civic Hybrid, Model Year 2010 1.4 IMA ES Saloon	1339	CVT	109
18	HONDA	Civic Hybrid, Model Year 2010 1.4 IMA EX Saloon	1339	CVT	109
19	HONDA	Civic Hybrid, Model Year 2010 1.4 IMA ES Leather Saloon	1339	CVT	109

4. Capital Allowances - 2012 Hybrid Rates of WDA (20% down to 18%)

Corporation Tax (12 months accounting period) ending:	Hybrid rate
31 March 2012	20.00%
30 April 2012	19.84%
31 May 2012	19.67%
30 June 2012	19.50%
31 July 2012	19.33%
31 August 2012	19.16%
30 September 2012	19.00%
31 October 2012	18.83%
30 November 2012	18.67%
31 December 2012	18.50%
31 January 2013	18.33%
28 February 2013	18.17%
31 March 2013	18.00%

Income Tax (12 months accounting period) ending:	Hybrid rate
31 May 2012	19.69%
30 June 2012	19.53%
31 July 2012	19.36%
31 August 2012	19.19%
30 September 2012	19.03%
31 October 2012	18.86%
30 November 2012	18.69%
31 December 2012	18.52%
31 January 2013	18.36%
28 February 2013	18.20%
31 March 2013	18.03%
5 April 2013	18.00%

5. Capital Allowances - 2012 Hybrid Rates of WDA (10% down to 8%)

Corporation Tax (12 months accounting period) ending:	Hybrid rate
31 March 2012	10.00%
30 April 2012	9.84%
31 May 2012	9.67%
30 June 2012	9.50%
31 July 2012	9.33%
31 August 2012	9.16%
30 September 2012	9.00%
31 October 2012	8.83%
30 November 2012	8.67%
31 December 2012	8.50%
31 January 2013	8.33%
28 February 2013	8.17%
31 March 2013	8.00%

Income Tax (12 months accounting period) ending:	Hybrid rate
5 April 2012	10.00%
30 April 2012	9.86%
31 May 2012	9.69%
30 June 2012	9.53%
31 July 2012	9.36%
31 August 2012	9.19%
30 September 2012	9.03%
31 October 2012	8.86%
30 November 2012	8.69%
31 December 2012	8.52%
31 January 2013	8.36%
28 February 2013	8.20%
31 March 2013	8.03%
5 April 2013	8.00%

6. Capital Gains Tax - Indexation Allowance - RPI back to 1982

The gains arising on the disposal of an asset may be reduced by an indexation allowance which is calculated by reference to increases in the Retail Prices Index published by the Department of Employment. The allowance is available from 6 April 1981 (1 April 1981 for companies). The Index was published until January 1987 using an average of 100 for January 1974 as a basis and after January 1987 using an average of 100 for January 1987 as a basis. The Retail Price Index figures published are:

Indexation for disposals post 5 April 2008 ceased for individuals, but there was no change for taxpayers liable to Corporation Tax.

Prices at January 1987 = 100:

Year	Jan.	Feb.	Mar.	Apr.	May	June	July	Aug.	Sept.	Oct.	Nov.	Dec.
2011	229.0	231.3	232.5	234.4	235.2	235.2	223.6	224.5	225.3	225.8	226.8	228.4
2010	217.9	219.2	220.7	222.8	223.6	224.1	213.4	214.4	215.3	216.0	216.6	218.0
2009	210.1	211.4	211.3	211.5	212.8	213.4	216.5	217.2	218.4	217.7	216.0	212.9
2008	209.8	211.4	212.1	214.0	215.1	216.8	216.5	217.2	208.0	208.9	209.7	210.9
2007	201.6	203.1	204.4	205.4	206.2	207.3	206.1	207.3	208.0	200.4	201.1	202.7
2006	193.4	194.2	195.0	196.5	197.7	198.5	198.5	199.2	200.1	200.4	201.1	202.7
2005	188.9	189.6	190.5	191.6	192.0	192.2	192.2	192.6	193.1	193.3	193.6	194.1
2004	183.1	183.8	184.6	185.7	186.5	186.8	186.8	187.4	188.1	188.6	189.0	189.9
2003	178.4	179.3	179.9	181.2	181.5	181.3	181.3	181.6	182.5	182.6	182.7	183.5
2002	173.3	173.8	174.5	175.7	176.2	176.2	175.9	176.4	177.6	177.9	178.2	178.5
2001	171.1	172.0	172.2	173.1	174.2	174.4	173.3	174.0	174.6	174.3	173.6	173.4
2000	166.6	167.5	168.4	170.1	170.7	171.1	170.5	170.5	171.7	171.6	172.1	172.2
1999	163.4	163.7	164.1	165.2	165.6	165.6	165.1	165.5	166.2	166.5	166.7	167.3
1998	159.5	160.3	160.8	162.6|	163.5	163.4	163.0	163.7	164.4	164.5	164.4	164.4
1997	154.4	155.0	155.4	156.3	156.9	157.5	157.5	158.5	159.3	159.5	159.6	160.0

Year	Jan	Feb	Mar	Apr	May	Jun	Jul	Aug	Sep	Oct	Nov	Dec
1996	150.2	150.9	151.5	152.6	152.9	153.0	152.4	153.1	153.8	153.8	153.9	154.4
1995	146.0	146.9	147.5	149.0	149.6	149.8	149.1	149.9	150.6	149.8	149.8	150.7
1994	141.3	142.1	142.5	144.2	144.7	144.7	144.0	144.7	145.0	145.2	145.3	146.0
1993	137.9	138.8	139.3	140.6	141.1	141.0	140.7	141.3	141.9	141.8	141.6	141.9
1992	135.6	136.3	136.7	138.8	139.3	139.3	138.8	138.9	139.4	139.9	139.7	139.2
1991	130.2	130.9	131.4	133.1	133.5	134.1	133.8	134.1	134.6	135.1	135.6	135.7
1990	119.5	120.2	121.4	125.1	126.2	126.7	126.8	128.1	129.3	130.3	130.0	129.9
1989	111.0	111.8	112.3	114.3	115.0	115.4	115.5	115.8	116.6	117.5	118.3	118.8
1988	103.3	103.7	104.1	105.8	106.2	106.6	106.7	107.9	108.4	109.5	110.0	110.3
1987	100.0	100.4	100.6	101.8	101.9	101.9	101.8	102.1	102.4	102.9	103.4	103.3
1986	96.25	96.60	96.73	97.67	97.85	97.79	97.52	97.82	98.30	98.45	99.29	99.62
1985	91.20	91.94	92.80	94.78	95.21	95.41	95.23	95.49	95.44	95.59	95.92	96.05
1984	86.84	87.20	87.48	88.64	88.97	89.20	89.10	89.94	90.11	90.67	90.95	90.87
1983	82.61	82.97	83.12	84.28	84.64	84.84	85.30	85.68	86.06	86.36	86.67	86.89
1982			79.44	81.04	81.62	81.85	81.88	81.90	81.85	82.26	82.66	82.51

Using RI as the Retail Price Index for March 1982 if the asset was acquired prior to April 1981, or the month in which the asset was acquired or expenditure incurred, and RD is the Retail Price Index for the month in which the disposal was made (or April 1998 if later and an individual), the indexation allowance is calculated by the formula:

$$\frac{RD - RI}{RI}$$

rounded to the nearest third decimal place.

7. Corporation Tax - Rates - 2014 back to 1994

Financial year i.e. year beginning 1 April	Full rate %	Small Profits Rate %	Small Profits Rate Profit limit £	Upper profit limit £	Marginal relief Fraction
2014	23	T.B.A.	T.B.A.	T.B.A.	T.B.A.
2013	24	T.B.A.	T.B.A.	T.B.A.	T.B.A.
2012	25	T.B.A.	T.B.A.	T.B.A.	T.B.A.
2011	26	20	300,000	1,500,000	3/200
2010	28	21	300,000	1,500,000	7/400
2009	28	21	300,000	1,500,000	7/400
2008	28	21	300,000	1,500,000	7/400
2007	30	20	300,000	1,500,000	1/40
2006	30	19	300,000	1,500,000	11/400
2005 *	30	19	300,000	1,500,000	11/400
2004 *	30	19	300,000	1,500,000	11/400
2003 *	30	19	300,000	1,500,000	11/400
2002 *	30	19	300,000	1,500,000	11/400
2001	30	20	300,000	1,500,000	1/40
2000	30	20	300,000	1,500,000	1/40
1999	30	20	300,000	1,500,000	1/40
1998	31	21	300,000	1,500,000	1/40
1997	31	21	300,000	1,500,000	1/40
1996	33	24	300,000	1,500,000	9/400
1995	33	25	300,000	1,500,000	1/50
1994	33	25	300,000	1,500,000	1/50

* From 1 April 2002 there was a starting rate of 0% for the first £10,000, thereafter a rate of 23.75% applied to £50,000 where the 19% rate applies to all profits up to £300,000. From 1 April 2004 there was also a restriction on the 0% band if dividends are paid to non-corporate shareholders. From 1 April 2006 the £10,000 0% band and dividend restriction was withdrawn.

8.   HMRC - Assessment Time Limits

The new time limits need a transitional period and so will become fully operative on and after 1 April 2010.

(a)   New Time Limits

Tax	Mistake	Discovery	Failure to take reasonable care	Deliberate understatement or Failure to notify liability
VAT	4 years	N/A	4 years	20 years
IT & CGT	N/A	4 years	6 years	20 years
CT	N/A	4 years	6 years	20 years
PAYE	4 years	N/A	6 years	20 years

Time limits for taxpayers' claims will also be aligned, at 4 years.

(b)   Old Time Limits

The previous time limits for changing the amount of tax due by assessment, varied across the taxes. The old time limits are set out below:

Tax	Mistake	Failure to take reasonable care	Deliberate understatement
VAT section 77 VATA 1994	3 years	3 years	20 years
IT and CGT sections 34 & 36 TMA 1970	5 years 10 months	20 years 10 months	20 years 10 months
CT Para 46 Schedule FA 1998	6 years	21 years	21 years
PAYE sections 34 & 36 TMA 1970	5 years 10 months	20 years 10 months	20 years 10 months

9. Income Tax - Benefits - Cars - Emission Percentages (2011/2012 & 2010/2011)

The tax charge is based on a percentage of the car's list price, graduated according to the level of the car's carbon dioxide emissions.

A table giving details of how the taxable benefit is calculated is given below:

2011/2012		2010/2011	
CO_2 Emissions in grams Per Kilometre	% of cars price taxed	CO_2 Emissions in grams Per Kilometre	% of cars price taxed
0	0	0	0
1 - 75	5 *	1 - 120	10*
76 - 120	10 *	121 - 129	15 *
121 - 129	15 *	130	15 *
130	16 *	135	16 *
135	17 *	140	17 *
140	18 *	145	18 *
145	19 *	150	19 *
150	20 *	155	20 *
155	21 *	160	21 *
160	22 *	165	22 *
165	23 *	170	23 *
170	24 *	175	24 *
175	25 *	180	25 *
180	26 *	185	26 *
185	27 *	190	27 *
190	28 *	195	28 *
195	29 *	200	29 *
200	30 *	205	30 *
205	31 *	210	31 *

210	32 *	215	32 *
215	33 **	220	33 **
220	34 ***	225	34 ***
225	35 ****	230	35 ****
230	35 ****		

If the CO_2 figure doesn't end in a 5 or 0 round down to the nearest 5 grams per kilometre

Diesel Supplements - if car runs solely on diesel add the following

* add 3 per cent / ** add 2 per cent / *** add 1 per cent / **** maximum charge so no diesel supplement

As a rule of thumb automatics are high in emissions, and diesels low.
Check individual models of each car they vary greatly!
DVLA Website - www.vcacarfueldata.org.uk.

Due to the lack of reliable sources of data for CO_2 emissions prior to January 1998, cars registered before that date will be taxed according to their engine size as follows:

Engine Size (cc)	Percentage of car's price charged to tax
0 - 1,400	15 per cent
1,401 - 2,000	22 per cent
2,001 and more	32 per cent

Electric Cars - From April 2010 the appropriate percentage for company car tax is reduced from 9% to 0% for 5 years. This reduces the employee car benefit charge to £NIL and removes the Class 1A charge on employers.

10. Income Tax - Flat Rate Deductions by Trade 2008/2009 onwards (previous)

Industry	Occupation		£
Agriculture	All workers		100 (70)
Airlines	Uniformed pilots and co-pilots and other uniformed flight deck crew working in UK (excludes cabin staff). Effective 2006/2007		
		- basic	850 (850)
		- specified activities	100 (100)
Aluminium	(a)	Continual casting operators, process operators, de-dimplers, driers, drill punchers, dross unloaders, firemen *, furnace operators and their helpers, leaders, mouldmen, pourers, remelt department labourers, roll flatteners	140 (130)
	(b)	Cable hands, case makers, labourers, mates, truck drivers and measurers, storekeepers	80 (60)
	(c)	Apprentices	60 (45)
	(d)	All other workers	120 (100)
Banks & Building Societies	Uniformed doormen and messengers		60 (45)
Brass and copper	All workers		120 (100)
Building	(a)	Joiners and carpenters	140 (105)
	(b)	Cement workers and roofing (asphalt) labourers	80 (55)
	(c)	Labourers and navvies	60 (45)
	(d)	All other workers	120 (85)
Building materials	(a)	Stone-masons	120 (85)
	(b)	Tilemakers and labourers	60 (45)
	(c)	All other workers	80 (55)

* See notes at end of table

Industry	Occupation		£
Clothing	(a)	Lacemakers, hosiery bleachers, dyers, courers and knitters, knitwear bleachers and dyers	60 (45)
	(b)	All other workers	60 (45)
Constructional engineering *	(a)	Blacksmiths and their strikers, burners, caulkers, chippers, drillers, erectors, fitters, holders up, markers off, platers, riveters, rivetheaters, scaffolders sheeters, template workers, turners, welders	140 (115)
	(b)	Banksmen labourers, shop-helpers, slewers, straighteners	80 (60)
	(c)	Apprentices and storekeepers	60 (45)
	(d)	All other workers	100 (75)
Electrical and electricity supply	(a)	Those workers incurring laundry costs only	60 (45)
	(b)	All other workers	120 (90)
Engineering (trades ancillary to)	(a)	Pattern makers	140 (120)
	(b)	Labourers, supervisory and unskilled workers	80 (60)
	(c)	Apprentices and storekeepers	60 (45)
	(d)	Motor mechanics in garage repair shops	120 (100)
	(e)	All other workers	120 (100)
Particular engineering *	(a)	Pattern makers	140 (120)
	(b)	All chainmakers; cleaners, galvanisers, tinners and wire drawers in the wire drawing industry, tool makers in the lock-making industry	120 (100)
	(c)	Apprentices and storekeepers	60 (45)
	(d)	All other workers	80 (60)
Fire Service		Uniformed Fire Fighters and Fire Officers	80 (60)
Food		All workers	60 (45)
Forestry		All workers	100 (70)
Glass		All workers	80 (60)

* See notes at end of table

Industry	Occupation		£
Healthcare (from 1998/99)	(a)	Ambulance staff on active service, (i.e. excluding staff who take telephone calls or provide clerical support.)	140 (110)
	(b)	Nurses and Midwives, Chiropodists, Dental Nurses, Occupational, Speech and other therapists, Orthoptists, Phlebotomists, Physiotherapists, Radiographers. Shoes & stockings/tights. Where the wearing of a prescribed style/colour is obligatory in the hospital allow £12 & £6 p.a. respectively.	100 (70)
	(c)	Plaster Room Orderlies, Hospital Porters, Ward Clerks, Sterile supply workers, Hospital domestics, Hospital catering staff	100 (60)
	(d)	Laboratory staff, Pharmacists and Pharmacy Assistants	60 (45)
	(e)	Uniformed ancillary staff - maintenance workers, grounds staff, drivers, parking attendants and security guards, receptionists and other uniformed staff	60 (45)
Heating	(a)	Pipe fitters and plumbers	120 (100)
	(b)	Coverers, laggers, domestic glaziers, heating engineers and their mates	120 (90)
	(c)	All gas workers, all other workers	100 (70)
Iron and steel	(a)	Day labourers, general labourers, stockmen, time keepers, warehouse staff and weighmen	80 (60)
	(b)	Apprentices	60 (45)
	(c)	All other workers	140 (120)
Iron Mining	(a)	Fillers, miners and underground workers	120 (100)
	(b)	All other workers	100 (75)
Leather	(a)	Curriers (wet workers), fellmongeringworkers, tanning operatives (wet)	80 (55)
	(b)	All other workers	60 (45)
Police force	(a)	Uniformed police officers (ranks up to and including Chief Inspector) (Includes Police Community Support Officers)	140 (110 - 2007/08 only) (55 - 2004/05 - 2006/07)
	(b)	Community support officers	140 (0)
	(c)	Other uniformed police employees	60 (0)
Precious metals		All workers	100 (70)

Industry	Occupation		£
Printing	(a)	Letterpress Section:	
	(b)	Electrical engineers (rotary presses), electrotypers, ink and roller makers, machine minders (rotary), maintenance engineers (rotary presses) and stereotypers	140 (105)
	(c)	Bench hands (P & B), compositors (Lp), readers (Lp), T & E section wire room operators, warehousemen (Ppr box)	60 (45)
	(d)	All other workers	100 (70)
Prisons		Uniformed prison officers	80 (55)
Public service	_Dock and inland waterways_		
	(a)	Dockers, dredger drivers, hopper steerers	80 (55)
	(b)	All other workers	60 (45)
	Public transport		
	(a)	Garage hands (including cleaners and mechanics)	80 (55)
	(b)	Conductors and drivers	60 (45)
Quarrying		All workers	100 (70)
Railways	(a)	(See the appropriate industry code lists for craftsmen, e.g. engineers, vehicle builders, etc)	100 (70)
	(b)	All other workers	
Seamen	(a)	Carpenters (seamen) Passenger liners	165 (165)
	(b)	Carpenters (seamen) Cargo vessels tankers, coasters and ferries	140 (130)
	(c)	Other seamen - Passenger liners	nil (nil)
	(d)	Other seamen - Cargo vessels, tankers, coasters and ferries	nil (nil)
Shipyards	(a)	Blacksmiths and their strikers, boilermakers, burners, carpenters caulkers, drillers, furnacemen (platers), holders up, fitters, platers, plumbers, riveters, sheet iron workers, shipwrights, tubers, welders	140 (115)
	(b)	Labourers	80 (60)
	(c)	Apprentices and storekeepers	60 (45)
	(d)	All other workers	100 (75)

Industry	Occupation		£
Textiles & Textile Printing	(a)	Carders, carding engineers, overlookers (all), technicians in spinning mills	120 (85)
	(b)	All other workers	80 (60)
Vehicles	(a)	Builders, railway wagons, etc., repairers and railways wagon lifters	140 (105)
	(b)	Railway vehicle painters and letterers, railway wagon, etc., builders and repairers assistants	80 (60)
	(c)	All other workers	60 (45)
Wood and furniture	(a)	Carpenters, cabinet makers, joiners, wood carvers and woodcutting machinists	140 (115)
	(b)	Artificial limb makers (other than in wood), organ builders and packing case makers	120 (90)
	(c)	Coopers not providing own tools, labourers, polishers and upholsterers	60 (45)
	(d)	All other workers	100 (75)

* Notes:

In the entry relating to aluminium, "firemen" means persons engaged to light and maintain furnaces;

"Constructional engineering" means engineering undertaken on a construction site, including buildings, shipyards, bridges, roads and other similar operations; and

"Particular engineering" means engineering undertaken on a commercial basis in a factory or workshop for the purposes of producing components such as wire, springs, nails and locks.

11. Income Tax - Personal Allowances - 2011/2012 back to 2006/2007

	2011/2012 £	2010/2011 £	2009/2010 £	2008/2009 £	2007/2008 £	2006/2007 £
Personal						
Single	7,475 #	6,475 #	6,475	6,035	5,225	5,035
Age: Taxpayer or wife over 65 years						
Single	9,940	9,490	9,490	9,030	7,550	7,280
Married couple's allowance *	n/a	n/a	6,865	6,535	6,285	6,065
Income limit †	24,000	22,900	22,900	21,800	20,900	20,100
Higher age: Taxpayer or wife over 75 yrs.						
Single	9,940	9,640	9,640	9,180	7,690	7,420
Married couple's allowance *	7,295	6,965	6,965	6,625	6,365	6,135
Income limit †	24,000	22,900	22,900	21,800	20,900	20,100
Married couple's allowance * - Minimum amount	2,800	2,670	2,670	2,540	2,440	2,350
Blind person's allowance	1,980	1,890	1,890	1,800	1,730	1,660

From 2010/2011 this allowance is restricted, to £NIL, by £1 for every £2 over £100,000.
* Allowances reduced by £1 for each £2 by which the claimant's total income exceeds the limit.
† Allowance restricted to 10%, one spouse needs to have been born before 6 April 1935.

12. Income Tax - Rates - 2011/2012 back to 2006/2007

2011/2012		2010/2011		2009/2010		2008/2009		2007/2008		2006/2007	
Taxable income £	Rate %	Taxable income £	Rate %	Taxable income £	Rate %	Taxable income £	Rate %	Taxable income £	Rate %	Taxable income £	Rate %
								First 2,230	10	First 2,150	10
First 35,000	20 *	First 37,400	20 *	First 37,400	20 *	First 34,800	20 *	Next 32,370	22	Next 31,150	22
35,001 - 150,000	40	37,401 - 150,000	40	Over 37,400	40 *	Over 34,800	40 *	Over 34,600	40	Over 33,300	40
Over 150,000	50	Over 150,000	50								

* The 10% starting rate is for savings income only, with a limit of £2,560 for 2011/2012 and £2,440 for 2010/2011. If an individual's taxable non-savings income is above this limit then the 10% savings rate will not be applicable. There are no changes to the 10% dividend ordinary rate or the 32.5% dividend upper rate for 40% taxpayers or 42.5% for 50% taxpayers.

13.   Inheritance Tax - Nil Rate Band - 2011/2012 back to 1997/1998

Transfers on death (between these dates)	Nil Band £	Rate on excess %
06.04.2011 - 05.04.2012	325,000 *	40
06.04.2010 - 05.04.2011	325,000 *	40
06.04.2009 - 05.04.2010	325,000	40
06.04.2008 - 05.04.2009	312,000	40
06.04.2007 - 05.04.2008	300,000	40
06.04.2006 - 05.04.2007	285,000	40
06.04.2005 - 05.04.2006	275,000	40
06.04.2004 - 05.04.2005	263,000	40
06.04.2003 - 05.04.2004	255,000	40
06.04.2002 - 05.04.2003	250,000	40
06.04.2001 - 05.04.2002	242,000	40
06.04.2000 - 05.04.2001	234,000	40
06.04.1999 - 05.04.2000	231,000	40
06.04.1998 - 05.04.1999	223,000	40
06.04.1997 - 05.04.1998	215,000	40

From 9 October 2007 the 'proportion' of unused IHT nil band on the death of a spouse or civil partner can be used by the second spouse or civil partner. The proportion is used on the second death and applies to the IHT nil band effective in the year of the second death. Claims may be made retrospectively for any surviving spouse or civil partner alive on 9 October 2007. For civil partnerships the first death must have occurred on or after 5 December 2005, the date the Civil Partnership Act became law in the United Kingdom.

* The 2010 March Budget announced this rate to be frozen until 2014/2015.

14. Landfill Tax - Rates - 1 April 2012 back to 1 October 1996

Date of change	Standard Rate £ per tonne	Lower Rate (c) £ per tonne
01.04.2012	64	2.50
01.04.2011	56	2.50
01.04.2010	48	2.50
01.04.2009	40	2.50
01.04.2008	32	2.50
01.04.2007	24	2
01.04.2006	21	2
01.04.2005	18	2
01.04.2004	15	2
01.04.2003	14	2
01.04.2002	13	2
01.04.2001	12	2
01.04.2000	11	2
01.04.1999	10	2
01.10.1996	7	2

Notes:
(a) Landfill tax was introduced on 01.10.1996. It applies to most waste disposed of at registrable sites.
(b) Exempt waste includes dredgings, disposals from mines and quarries, and waste from the clearance of contaminated land.
(c) The lower rate of tax applies to listed inactive wastes.
(d) The 2009 Budget stated that the standard rate would increase by £8.00 per tonne from 01.04.2010 and by that amount in years thereafter, until at least 01.04.2015.
(e) The 2010 March Budget announced that, in future, the standard rate would not fall below £80 per tonne.

15. National Insurance - Weekly Rates - 2011/2012 & 2010/2011 Class 1 - Class 4

	2011/2012			2010/2011		
	Income £	Employee* %	Employer† %	Income £	Employee %	Employer %
Class 1:	First 102.00 (LEL)	0	0	First 97.00 (LEL)	NIL	NIL
Contracted in	102.01 - 136.00 (ST)	0	0	97.01 - 110.00 (PT/ST)	0	NIL
	136.01 - 139.00 (PT)	0	13.8	110.01 - 844.00 (UEL)	11.0	12.8
	139.01 - 817.00 (UEL)	12.0	13.8			
	Excess over 817.00	2.0	13.8	Excess over 844.00	1.0	12.8
Married Women's Election	136.01 - 139.00	0	13.8	110.01 - 844.00	4.85	12.8
	139.01 - 817.00	5.85	13.8	Excess over 844.00	1.0	12.8
	Excess over 817.00	2.0	13.8			
Class 1:	First 136.00	0	0	First 110.00	NIL	NIL
	136.01 - 139.00	0	10.1			
Contracted out	139.01 - 817.00	10.4	10.1	110.01 - 844.00	9.4	9.1
COSR Scheme	Excess over 817.00	2.0	13.8	Excess over 844.00	1.0	12.8

N.B.
Lower Earnings Limit (LEL)
Primary Threshold (PT)
Secondary Threshold (ST)
Upper Earnings Limit (UEL)

The March 2011 Budget announced that bands will be uplifted as follows from April 2012.
* By CPI
† By RPI

Class 1:	2011/2012			2010/2011		
	First 136.00	0	0	First 110.00	NIL	NIL
	136.01 - 139.00	0	12.4			
Contracted out	139.01 - 817.00	10.4	12.4	110.01 - 844.00	9.4	11.4
COMP Scheme	Excess over 817.00	2.0	13.8	Excess over 844.00	1.0	12.8

C.O.S.R. = Contracted Out Salary Related scheme
C.O.M.P. = Contracted Out Money Purchase scheme

		2011/2012	2010/2011
Class 2	Self employed	£2.50 p.w.	£2.40 p.w.
	Small earnings exemption	£5,315 p.a.	£5,075 p.a.
	Special rate for share fishermen	£3.15 p.w.	£3.05 p.w.
	Special rate for volunteer development workers	£5.10 p.w.	£4.85 p.w.
Class 3	Voluntary	£12.60 p.w.	£12.05 p.w.
Class 4	Self employed		
	Assessable profits	£7,225 - £42,475 p.a.	£5,715 - £43,875 p.a.
	Rate	9%	8%
	Excess over £42,475	2%	
	Excess over £43,875		1%

16.   National Minimum Wage - 1 October 2010 back to 1 April 1999

Effective from	Adult 21+ * £ / hr	Development 18 - 20 † £ / hr	Younger 16 - 17 £ / hr
01.10.2011	6.08	4.98	3.68
01.10.2010	5.93	4.92	3.64
01.10.2009	5.80	4.83	3.57
01.10.2008	5.73	4.77	3.53
01.10.2007	5.52	4.60	3.40
01.10.2006	5.35	4.45	3.30
01.10.2005	5.05	4.25	3.00
01.10.2004	4.85	4.10	3.00
01.10.2003	4.50	3.80	0
01.10.2002	4.20	3.60	0
01.10.2001	4.10	3.50	0
01.10.2000	3.70	3.20	0
01.06.2000	3.60	3.20	0
01.04.1999	3.60	3.00	0

*   Prior to 1 October 2010 effective age was 22
†   Prior to 1 October 2010 effective upper age was 21

17. Pension Contributions & Retirement - Pension Contributions & Limits

(a) Lifetime allowance & contributions Limit

There is a maximum lifetime allowance of pension savings and this limit increases annually as shown in the following table.

Tax Year	Maximum Lifetime Allowance £	Annual Contribution Limit * £
2012/2013	1,500,000	50,000
2011/2012	1,800,000	50,000
2010/2011	1,800,000	255,000
2009/2010	1,750,000	245,000
2008/2009	1,650,000	235,000
2007/2008	1,600,000	225,000
2006/2007	1,500,000	215,000

* Annual contributions are still restricted to the higher of £3,600 or 100% or net relevant earnings.

(b) Retirement Annuity - Maximum annual allowable premiums for pension schemes approved after 3 January 1988 and up to 1988/1989 (% of net relevant earnings)

	%
Under 50 years of age	17.5
51 - 55 years	20.0
56 - 60 years	22.5
61 years or more	27.5

(c)   **Personal Pensions - Maximum annual allowable premiums from 1989/1990**

	%
Under 36 years or less	17.5
36 - 45 years	20.0
46 - 50 years	25.0
51 - 55 years	30.0
56 - 60 years	35.0
61 and over	40.0

(d)   **The maximum amount of net relevant earnings (and notional) to which the percentages in (c) above could be applied were:**

	£
2011/2012	129,600 (notional)
2010/2011	123,600 (notional)
2009/2010	123,600 (notional)
2008/2009	117,600 (notional)
2007/2008	112,800 (notional)
2006/2007	108,600 (notional)
2005/2006	105,600
2004/2005	102,000
2003/2004	99,000
2002/2003	97,200
2001/2002	95,400
2000/2001	91,800
1999/2000	90,600
1998/1999	87,600
1997/1998	84,000
1996/1997	82,200

18. Social Security Benefits - 2011/2012 & 2010/2011

Main taxable benefits from	2011/2012		2010/2011	
	Weekly £	Total £	Weekly £	Total £
Retirement pension				
Single (contributor)	102.15	5,312	97.65	5,078
Wife not a contributor	61.20	3,182	58.50	3,042
Additional Pension for persons over				
80 years:	00.25	13	00.25	13
Widow's Benefit:				
Pension (maximum) †	102.15	5,312	97.65	5,078
Widowed mother's allowance (basic)	102.15	5,312	97.65	5,078
Attendance Allowance - lower rate	49.30	2,564	47.80	2,486
- higher rate	73.60	3,827	71.40	3,713
Statutory sick pay:				
Standard rate	81.60	4,243	79.15	4,116
Earnings threshold	102.00	5,304	97.00	5,044

† The rate is variable and dependant on the husband's contributions and the age of the widow.

For a full list of benefits visit: www.dwp.gov.uk

19. VAT - Car Fuel Scale add back rates from 1 May 2011

VAT fuel scale charges for 12 month periods

CO₂ band, g/km	VAT fuel scale charge, 12 month period, £	VAT on 12 month charge, £	VAT exclusive 12 month charge, £
120 or less	630.00	105.00	525.00
125	945.00	157.50	787.50
130	1,010.00	168.33	841.67
135	1,070.00	178.33	891.67
140	1,135.00	189.17	945.83
145	1,200.00	200.00	1,000.00
150	1,260.00	210.00	1,050.00
155	1,325.00	220.83	1,104.17
160	1,385.00	230.83	1,154.17
165	1,450.00	241.67	1,208.33
170	1,515.00	252.50	1,262.50
175	1,575.00	262.50	1,312.50
180	1,640.00	273.33	1,366.67
185	1,705.00	284.17	1,420.83
190	1,765.00	294.17	1,470.83
195	1,830.00	305.00	1,525.00
200	1,890.00	315.00	1,575.00
205	1,955.00	325.83	1,629.17
210	2,020.00	336.67	1,683.33
215	2,080.00	346.67	1,733.33
220	2,145.00	357.50	1,787.50
225 or more	2,205.00	367.50	1,837.50

VAT fuel scale charges for 3 month periods

CO₂ band, g/km	VAT fuel scale charge, 3 month period, £	VAT on 3 month charge, £	VAT exclusive 3 month charge, £
120 or less	157.00	26.17	130.83
125	236.00	39.33	196.67
130	252.00	42.00	210.00
135	268.00	44.67	223.33
140	283.00	47.17	235.83
145	299.00	49.83	249.17
150	315.00	52.50	262.50
155	331.00	55.17	275.83
160	346.00	57.67	288.33
165	362.00	60.33	301.67
170	378.00	63.00	315.00
175	394.00	65.67	328.33
180	409.00	68.17	340.83
185	425.00	70.83	354.17
190	441.00	73.50	367.50
195	457.00	76.17	380.83
200	472.00	78.67	393.33
205	488.00	81.33	406.67
210	504.00	84.00	420.00
215	520.00	86.67	433.33
220	536.00	89.33	446.67
225 or more	551.00	91.83	459.17

VAT fuel scale charges for 1 month return periods

CO_2 band, g/km	VAT fuel scale charge, 1 month period, £	VAT on 1 month charge, £	VAT exclusive 1 month charge, £
120 or less	52.00	8.67	43.33
125	78.00	13.00	65.00
130	84.00	14.00	70.00
135	89.00	14.83	74.17
140	94.00	15.67	78.33
145	99.00	16.50	82.50
150	105.00	17.50	87.50
155	110.00	18.33	91.67
160	115.00	19.17	95.83
165	120.00	20.00	100.00
170	126.00	21.00	105.00
175	131.00	21.83	109.17
180	136.00	22.67	113.33
185	141.00	23.50	117.50
190	147.00	24.50	122.50
195	152.00	25.33	126.67
200	157.00	26.17	130.83
205	162.00	27.00	135.00
210	168.00	28.00	140.00
215	173.00	28.83	144.17
220	178.00	29.67	148.33
225 or more	183.00	30.50	152.50

Where the CO_2 emission figure is not a multiple of 5, the figure is rounded down to the next multiple of 5 to determine the level of the charge. For a bi-fuel vehicle which has two CO_2 emissions figures, the lower of the two figures should be used. For cars which are too old to have a CO_2 emissions figure, you should identify the CO_2 band based on engine size, as follows:

If its cylinder capacity is 1,400cc or less, use CO_2 band 140;

If its cylinder capacity exceeds 1,400cc but does not exceed 2,000cc, use CO_2 band 175;

If its cylinder capacity exceeds 2,000cc, use CO_2 band 225 or above.

20. VAT - Flat Rate Percentages - by Trade Sectors - from 4 January 2011 (20%)

Category of business	Appropriate percentage %
Accountancy or book-keeping	14.5
Advertising	11
Agricultural services	11
Any other activity not listed elsewhere	12
Architect, civil and structural engineer or surveyor	14.5
Boarding or care of animals	12
Business services that are not listed elsewhere	12
Catering services including restaurants and takeaways	12.5
Computer and IT consultancy or data processing	14.5
Computer repair services	10.5
Dealing in waste or scrap	10.5
Entertainment or journalism	12.5
Estate agency or property management services	12
Farming or agriculture that is not listed elsewhere	6.5
Film, radio, television or video production	13
Financial services	13.5
Forestry or fishing	10.5
General building or construction services *	9.5
Hairdressing or other beauty treatment services	13
Hiring or renting goods	9.5
Hotel or accommodation	10.5
Investigation or security	12
Labour-only building or construction services *	14.5
Laundry or dry-cleaning services	12
Lawyer or legal services	14.5
Library, archive, museum or other cultural activity	9.5
Management consultancy	14

Manufacturing fabricated metal products	10.5
Manufacturing food	9
Manufacturing that is not listed elsewhere	9.5
Manufacturing yarn, textiles or clothing	9
Membership organisation	8
Mining or quarrying	10
Packaging	9
Photography	11
Post offices	5
Printing	8.5
Publishing	11
Pubs	6.5
Real estate activity not listed elsewhere	14
Repairing personal or household goods	10
Repairing vehicles	8.5
Retailing food, confectionary, tobacco, newspapers or children's clothing	4
Retailing pharmaceuticals, medical good, cosmetics or toiletries	8
Retailing that is not listed elsewhere	7.5
Retailing vehicles or fuel	6.5
Secretarial services	13
Social work	11
Sport or recreation	8.5
Transport or storage, including couriers, freight, removals and taxi	10
Travel agency	10.5
Veterinary medicine	11
Wholesaling agricultural products	8
Wholesaling food	7.5
Wholesaling that is not listed elsewhere	8.5

* "'Labour-only building or construction services" means building or construction services where the value of materials supplied is less that 10 per cent of relevant turnover from such services; any other building or construction services are "general building or construction services".

21. VAT - Registration and Deregistration Limits - 1 April 2011 back to 27 November 1996

Effective Date	Registration Annual Turnover £	Deregistration Annual Turnover £
01.04.2011	73,000	71,000
01.04.2010	70,000	68,000
01.05.2009	68,000	66,000
01.04.2008	67,000	65,000
01.04.2007	64,000	62,000
01.04.2006	61,000	59,000
01.04.2005	60,000	58,000
01.04.2004	58,000	56,000
10.04.2003	56,000	54,000
25.04.2002	55,000	53,000
01.04.2001	54,000	52,000
01.04.2000	52,000	50,000
01.04.1999	51,000	49,000
01.04.1998	50,000	48,000
01.12.1997	49,000	47,000
27.11.1996	48,000	46,000

TABLE OF CASES

Note: A case may often be found under the name of the other party, as the names were often reversed on appeal to a higher court.

INDEX

A

B

C

FEEDBACK/COMMENTS
FORM

Without feedback we cannot improve our service or give you
what you want.

Please use this form to pass on your coments.
You may send, fax or e-mail it.
(Please complete the following 'optional' contact details)

Name & Position. . . . .

Company Name . . . .

Address . . . .

. . . .

Telephone Number. . . . .

e-mail address . . . .

Your feedback/comments (please quote page numbers if appropriate):

. . . .

. . . .

. . . .

. . . .

. . . .

Then forward it to: -
Clive Steward - Editor
Smith's Taxation
7 Spoonbill Road
Bridgwater
Somerset   TA6 5QZ
Tel/Fax: 01278 427006
e-mail: editor@smithstaxation.co.uk

Please Photocopy